T0181093

Lecture Notes in Computer Science   11196

Commenced Publication in 1973
Founding and Former Series Editors:
Gerhard Goos, Juris Hartmanis, and Jan van Leeuwen

More information about this series at http://www.springer.com/series/7409

Marinos Ioannides · Eleanor Fink
Raffaella Brumana · Petros Patias
Anastasios Doulamis · João Martins
Manolis Wallace (Eds.)

Digital Heritage

Progress in Cultural Heritage: Documentation, Preservation, and Protection

7th International Conference, EuroMed 2018
Nicosia, Cyprus, October 29 – November 3, 2018
Proceedings, Part I

Springer

Editors
Marinos Ioannides
Cyprus University of Technology
Limassol, Cyprus

Eleanor Fink
American Art Collaborative Linked Open
Data Initiative
Arlington, VA, USA

Raffaella Brumana (iD)
Politecnico di Milano
Milan, Italy

Petros Patias
The Aristotle University
Thessaloniki, Greece

Anastasios Doulamis
National Technical University of Athens
Athens, Greece

João Martins (iD)
CTS-UNINOVA
Caparica, Portugal

Manolis Wallace (iD)
University of the Peloponnese
Tripoli, Greece

ISSN 0302-9743   ISSN 1611-3349 (electronic)
Lecture Notes in Computer Science
ISBN 978-3-030-01761-3   ISBN 978-3-030-01762-0 (eBook)
https://doi.org/10.1007/978-3-030-01762-0

Library of Congress Control Number: 2018956722

LNCS Sublibrary: SL3 – Information Systems and Applications, incl. Internet/Web, and HCI

Cover illustration: Wall painting (end of 15th century) of the Last Judgement from the north wall of the Church of the Monastery of Christos Antifonitis, Kalograia after it had been forcefully removed, following the 1974 Turkish invasion and occupation. With permission of the Ministry of Transport, Communications and Works, Department of Antiquities, Lefkosia, Cyprus.

This Springer imprint is published by the registered company Springer Nature Switzerland AG
The registered company address is: Gewerbestrasse 11, 6330 Cham, Switzerland

Preface

EuroMed 2018, the traditional biennial scientific event, was held in the capital city of Cyprus, the island which has always been a bridge to three continents going back to the origins of civilization. It is a place where the fingerprints of several ancient cultures and civilizations can be found, with a wealth of historical sites recognized and protected by UNESCO.

Several organizations and current EU projects (such as the H2020 Marie Skłodowska Curie RISE Fellowship project TERPSICHORE, the H2020 Marie Skłodowska Curie ITN CHANGES, the H2020 R&I Reflective 7 – INCEPTION, the H2020 COOP 8 CSA Virtual Multimodal Museum, the H2020 Reflective 6 CrossCult, the H2020 REACH, the Research Infrastructure DARIAH-EU ERIC and DARIAH-CY, the COST Action Innovation in Intelligent Management of Heritage Buildings [i2MHB], the H2020 Teaming Excelsior, H2020 Teaming Medstach, H2020 Twinning Athena and H2020 ERA Chair Mnemosyne) decided to join EuroMed 2018 and continue cooperation in order to create an optimal environment for the discussion and explanation of new technologies, exchange of modern innovative ideas, and in general to allow for the transfer of knowledge between a large number of professionals and academics during one common event and time period.

The main goal of the event is to illustrate the programs underway, whether organized by public bodies (e.g., UNESCO, European Union, national states, etc.) or by private foundations (e.g., Getty Foundation, World Heritage Foundation, etc.) in order to promote a common approach to the tasks of recording, documenting, protecting, and managing world cultural heritage. The 7th European-Mediterranean Conference (EuroMed 2018) was definitely a forum for sharing views and experiences, discussing proposals for the optimal attitude as well as the best practice and the ideal technical tools to preserve, document, manage, present/visualize, and disseminate the rich and diverse cultural heritage of mankind.

This conference was held during the second half of the EU Framework Programme, Horizon 2020, which is the largest in the world in terms of financial support on research, innovation, technological development, and demonstration activities. The awareness of the value and importance of heritage assets have been reflected in the financing of projects since the first Framework Programme for Research and Technological Development (FP1, 1984–1987) and continues into the current HORIZON 2020 that follows FP7 (2007–2013). In the past 35 years, a large community of researchers, experts, and specialists have had the chance to learn and develop the transferable knowledge and skills needed to inform stakeholders, scholars, and students. Europe has become a leader in heritage documentation, preservation, and protection science, with COST Actions adding value to projects financed within the FP and EUREKA program and transferring knowledge to practice and support the development of SMEs.

The EuroMed 2018 agenda focused on enhancing and strengthening international and regional cooperation and promoting awareness and tools for future innovative research, development, and applications to protect, preserve, and document the European and world cultural heritage. Our ambition was to host an exceptional conference by mobilizing also policy-makers from different EU countries, institutions (European Commission, European Parliament, Council of Europe, UNESCO, International Committee for Monuments and Sites ICOMOS, the International Committee for Documentation of Cultural Heritage CIPA, the International Society for Photogrammetry and Remote Sensing ISPRS, the International Centre for the study of the Preservation and Restoration of Cultural Property ICCROM, and the International Committee for Museums ICOM), professionals, as well as participants from all over the world and from different scientific areas of cultural heritage.

Protecting, preserving, and presenting our cultural heritage are actions that are frequently interpreted as change management and/or change in the behavior of society. Joint European and international research yields a scientific background and support for such a change. We are living in a period characterized by rapid and remarkable changes in the environment, in society, and in technology. Natural changes, war conflicts, and man-made interventions and changes, including climate change, as well as technological and societal changes, form an ever-moving and colorful stage and pose a challenge for society. Close cooperation between professionals, policy-makers, and authorities internationally is necessary for research, development, and technology in the field of cultural heritage.

Scientific projects in the area of cultural heritage have received national, European Union, or UNESCO funding for more than 30 years. Through financial support and cooperation, major results have been achieved and published in peer-reviewed journals and conference proceedings with the support of professionals from many countries. The European Conferences on Cultural Heritage research and development and in particular the biennial EuroMed conference have become regular milestones on the never-ending journey of discovery in the search for new knowledge of our common history and its protection and preservation for the generations to come. EuroMed also provides a unique opportunity to present and review results as well as to draw new inspiration.

To reach this ambitious goal, the topics covered include experiences in the use of innovative technologies and methods as well as how to take the best advantage to integrate the results obtained so as to build up new tools and/or experiences as well as to improve methodologies for documenting, managing, preserving, and communicating cultural heritage.

We present here 97 papers, selected from 537 submissions, which focus on interdisciplinary and multidisciplinary research concerning cutting-edge cultural heritage informatics, physics, chemistry, and engineering and the use of technology for the representation, documentation, archiving, protection, preservation, and communication of cultural heritage knowledge.

Our keynote speakers, Dr. Ronald de Bruin, Director of the COST Association, Dr. Robert Sanderson (Getty Foundation), Prof. Craig Knoblock, USC Information Sciences Institute, Mrs. Diane Zorich, Director of the Smithsonian's Digitization Program Office (DPO), Dr. Charalambos Chaitas, Executive Director for Arts, Heritage, and Education for the Public Investment Fund, Saudi Arabia, Mr. Joan Cobb, Principal IT Project Manager at J. Paul Getty Trust, Mr. Harry Verwayen, Executive Director of EU Digital Library Europeana, Prof. Koen van Balen, KUL, UNESCO Chair on Preventive Conservation, Monitoring, and Maintenance of Monuments and Sites, and UNESCO CHAIR Disaster Mitigation for Urban Cultural Heritage, Japan, Mr. Brigadier General Fabrizio Parrulli, Carabinieri for the Protection of Cultural Heritage Commander, Mrs. Nada R. Hosking, Director, Programs and Partnerships, Global Heritage Fund, and Mrs. France Desmarais are not only experts in their fields, but also visionaries for the future of cultural heritage protection and preservation. They promote the e-documentation and protection of the past in such a way that it is preserved for the generations to come.

We extend our thanks to all authors, speakers, and those persons whose labor, financial support, and encouragement made the EuroMed 2018 event possible. The international Program Committee, whose members represent a cross-section of archaeology, physics, chemistry, civil engineering, computer science, graphics and design, library, archive, and information science, architecture, surveying, history, and museology, worked tenaciously and finished their work on time. The staff of the IT department at the Cyprus University of Technology helped with their local ICT and audiovisual support, especially Mr. Filippos Filippou, Mr. Lefteris Michael, and Mr. Stephanos Mallouris. We would also like to express our gratitude to all the organizations supporting this event and our co-organizers, the European Commission scientific and policy officers of the DG Connect Mr. Albert Gauthier, Mrs. Adelina-Cornelia Dinu, the COST director Dr. Ronald de Bruin, the officers Mrs. Federica Ortelli, Mrs. Estelle Emeriau, the director general of Europeana Mr. Harry Verwayen, the Getty Conservation Institute and World Monuments Fund, the Cyprus University of Technology, the Ministry of Energy, Commerce, Industry and Tourism especially the permanent secretary and digital champion Dr. Stelios Himonas and Mr. Constantinos Karageorgis, the Ministry of Education and Culture and particularly the minister Mr. Kostas Champiaouris, the director of the Cultural Services Mr. Pavlos Paraskevas, the director of the Cypriot National Library Mr. Demetris Nicolaou, the Department of Antiquities in Cyprus, all the members of the Cypriot National Committee for E-documentation and E-preservation in Cultural Heritage, and finally our corporate sponsors, CableNet Ltd, the Cyprus Tourism Organization, the Cyprus Postal Services, and Dr. Kyriakos Themistokleous from the Cyprus Remote Sensing Society who provided services and gifts of kind that made the conference possible.

We express our thanks and appreciation to the board of the ICOMOS Cyprus Section for their enthusiasm, commitment, and support for the success of this event. Most of all we would like to thank the organizations UNESCO, European Commission, CIPA, and ICOMOS that entrusted us with the task of organizing and undertaking this unique event and wish all participants an interesting and fruitful experience.

September 2018

Marinos Ioannides
Eleanor Fink
Raffaella Brumana
Petros Patias
Anastasios Doulamis
João Martins
Manolis Wallace

Acknowledgments and Disclaimer

The EuroMed 2018 Conference was partly supported by the Republic of Cyprus, by the Cyprus University of Technology, by the Cyprus Tourism Organization, by CIPA (http://cipa.icomos.org/), ICOMOS Cyprus, the aforementioned EU projects, the DARIAH-EU ERIC and DARIAH-CY, the H2020 INCEPTION, and H2020-ViMM projects.

However, the content of this publication reflects the authors' views only, and the European Commission, the Republic of Cyprus, CIPA, ICOMOS, ICOMOS-Cyprus, Getty, Cyprus University of Technology, and the EU projects H2020 Marie Skłodowska Curie RISE Fellowship project TERPSICHORE, the H2020 Marie Skłodowska Curie ITN CHANGES, the H2020 R&I Reflective 7 – INCEPTION, the H2020 COOP 8 CSA Virtual Multimodal Museum, the H2020 Reflective 6 CrossCult, the H2020 REACH, the Research Infrastructure DARIAH-EU ERIC and DARIAH-CY, the COST Action Innovation in Intelligent Management of Heritage Buildings (i2MHB), the H2020 Teaming Excelsior, H2020 Teaming Medstach, H2020 Twinning Athena, the UNESCO Chair on Digital Cultural Heritage at Cyprus University of Technology, and the EU H2020 ERA Chair Mnemosyne are not liable for any use that may be made of the information contained herein.

Organization

Conference Chairs

Marinos Ioannides
Eleanor Fink
Raffaella Brumana
Petros Patias
Anastasios Doulamis
João Martins
Manolis Wallace

Local Organizing Committee

Vasilis Athanasiou
Robert Davies
Simos Georgiou
Theodoros Gkanetsos
George Hadjidemetriou
Maria Katiri

Charalambos Leventis
Elias Nobilakis
Chrisanthos Pissarides
Christiana Polycarpou
Konstantinos Skriapas
Kyriakos Themistokleous

International Scientific Committee

Fabrizio Banfi, Italy
Luigi Barazzetti, Italy
George Bebis, USA
Marco Bertini, Italy
Matthaios Bimpas, Greece
Frank Boochs, Germany
Gumersindo Bueno, Spain
Lorenzo Cantini, Italy
George Caridakis, Greece
Ying-Mei Cheng, Taiwan
Jiri Chmelik, Czech Republic
Paola Condoleo, Italy
Jorbi Conzalez, Spain
Stefano Della Torre, Italy
Iason Diakoumakos, Greece
Nikolaos Doulamis, Greece
Charalambos Georgiadis, Greece
George Giannoulis, Spain

Angelo Giuseppe Landi, Italy
Andrina Granić, Croatia
Alberto Grimoldi, Italy
Sang-sun Jo, South Korea
Dimitrios Kaimaris, Greece
Nikos Karanikolas, Greece
Norman Kerle, The Netherlands
Dimitrios Kosmopoulos, Greece
Chiao-Ling Kuo, Taiwan
Fotis Liarokapis, Czech Republic
George Livanos, Greece
Federica Maietti, Italy
Konstantinos Makantasis, Cyprus
Maria Merchan, Spain
Pilar Merchan, Spain
Luisa Migliori, Italy
Daniela Oreni, Italy
Pedro Pereira, Portugal

Contents – Part I

3D Digitization, Reconstruction, Modelling and HBIM

Digital Cultural Heritage – Smart Technologies

The New Era of Museums and Exhibitions

Non Destructive Techniques in Cultural Heritage Conservation

E-Humanities

Contents – Part II

Digital Applications for Materials Preservation in Cultural Heritage

Digital Cultural Heritage Learning and Experiences

3D Digitalisation, Reconstruction, Modelling and HBIM

Visualization of the Past-to-Recent Changes in Cultural Heritage Based on 3D Digitization

Naoki Mori[1], Tokihisa Higo[1], Kaoru Suemori[2], Hiroshi Suita[1], and Yoshihiro Yasumuro[1(✉)]

[1] Kansai University, Suita, Osaka 564-8680, Japan
yasumuro@kansai-u.ac.jp
[2] National Museum of Ethnology, Suita, Osaka 565-8511, Japan
kaorudoco@hotmail.com

Abstract. 3D digitization techniques, such as laser scanning and/or SfM (Structure from Motion), are often used for recording and documenting the archaeological heritages at many sites recently. As-is situations can be easily captured by those techniques for archiving the present geometrical information. Since excavation, different research teams might have conducted investigations and/or restoration work in different periods to date. Throughout the repeated re-excavation and backfill, there may be the places where some aspect dramatically changes. The photo records taken in the past investigations sometimes look very different from the present appearance and the differences are also difficult to describe and to record objectively. This paper proposes a methodology to support the collation of past photo data and current presence by image-processing. Estimating the 3D position and the orientation of the camera which took the photo in the past, by using correspondences between the pixels on the past photo and the reconstructed 3D shape of the current scene. By making corresponding pairs of the identical feature points between the past photo and the current 3D scene, solving PnP problem gives a good estimate of the camera viewpoint in the past. By rendering CG of the current 3D scene from the estimated viewpoint of the past camera, the CG and the past photo image can be aligned and overlaid precisely on the same view. This overlaid image allows to check the temporal changes of the object with pixel-unit precision and to help the maintenance work for inspection and repair. This paper applies to the actual site of Barbar temple at the Kingdom of Bahrain and shows the quantitative evaluation capability.

Keywords: Investigation history · Structure from motion (SfM)
PnP problem · Photos taken in the past

1 Introduction

Since 2015, the Centre for the Global Study of Cultural Heritage and Culture (CHC) at Kansai University has been carrying out investigations in relation to the preservation of Barbar Temple archaeological site in Kingdom of Bahrain. The Barbar Temple is located in the village of Barbar near the northern coast of Kingdom of Bahrain. This temple is the largest and the oldest temple in the country built in 3000 BC and is

© Springer Nature Switzerland AG 2018
M. Ioannides et al. (Eds.): EuroMed 2018, LNCS 11196, pp. 3–14, 2018.
https://doi.org/10.1007/978-3-030-01762-0_1

thought to have been dedicated to the water god Enki. P. V Glob discovered in 1954, and an excavation study by the Danish team was conducted until 1962 [1]. Additional excavations were also made by the Bahrain authorities afterward. Later, a report on the excavation survey was published, and among them, many recorded pictures at the time of the survey were included.

Temple of Barbar is currently used as a tourist resource. It is also registered in the provisional list of UNESCO World Heritage sites. In the temple, there are existing structures showing the aspect of the time, such as an article holder, a water storage facility, and an enclosure for victims. The maintenance of the temple after the excavation survey is done by the Bahrain authorities. However, after excavation, they performed backfilling for conservation and reinforcement of collapsible structures as tourist facilities, so the situation has changed considerably from the state described in the report. Figure 1 shows photographs taken in 1959 (left column) and 2017 (right column). As you can see the differences in the staircases and stone arrangements, obvious conditional changes in about 60 years are observed in every part of the temple.

It is necessary to grasp the change or difference between at the time of the excavation and the present for future conservation restoration, maintenance and maintenance of World Heritage aimed at Bahrain authorities. However, in comparison between pictures, we can only judge this difference qualitatively. Also, if the difference in appearance is severe, the verification work itself becomes difficult. In order to solve such problems, this paper proposes a systematic support of the visual verification work by using three-dimensional shape data based on photogrammetry technique.

Fig. 1. Photographs taken in 1959 (left column) and 2017 (right column) at Barbar temple site

2   Related Work

The data recorded by three-dimensional (3D) measurement is widely used not only for preservation but also for academic, educational and tourism. CyArk [2], for example, a nonprofit organization in the United States, publishes a digital archive on the website that associates 3D data acquired by a laser scanner and photogrammetry and related academic information. A walkthrough system that allows free movement and viewpoint change within the created 3D space is implemented so that the user does not need to visit the actual place and can observe the object from a place that cannot actually enter. In recent years, As the performance of UAV improves and the price drops, 3D modeling over cultural property structures and wide area is spreading for management of the site and post disaster assessment [4–7]. Yasumuro et al. [8] focused on the fact that joint activities and information sharing by many experts are necessary for academic research in the preservation, restoration and utilization methods of cultural properties. Therefore, they constructed a database that can store and share information associated with arbitrary places in the virtual space that reproduced the site based on the 3D measurement and constructed a database that supports AR (Augmented Reality) was implemented. These systems utilizing 3D data are intended for reporting the results and disclosing the information, and there are many examples. In addition to 3D, time axis is added to information modeling used for managing the cultural site by accumulating the 3D data captured in different years [9, 10]. However, since every 3D data is supposed to be prepared by simply using the recent technologies of laser scanning and photogrammetry, the recorded history span is so short and limited to recent years. There are few studies on information technologies that continuously support the maintenance and management of cultural properties in cultural assets under decades of investigation history. The main reason is that due to the decades of separation, it is not possible to collect enough amount of past photos, applying photogrammetry only with photos of those days is difficult. The purpose of this paper is to make full use of limited past photographs and to develop precise collation methods with the current situation.

3   Method

3.1   Overview

In order to grasp the difference between the current and the past conditions of the site, it is necessary to geometrically connect the current 3D data with the past record data. Therefore, in this research, we will reproduce the photographing position of the recorded photograph in the current 3D space coordinate. Observing the scenery from the same viewpoint enables to confirm and examine the differences over the time. Figure 2 shows the process flow of the proposed method. First, current 3D shape data is prepared by photogrammetry and laser scanning. Next, we use the geometrical relationship between the real photograph and the camera to estimate the photographing position. Using these two data, we render current 3D scene from the viewpoint of photography at camera position of the past and superimpose the recorded picture on it.

By superimposing and observing the past and the current situation from the same viewpoint, you can visually grasp the differences between them precisely.

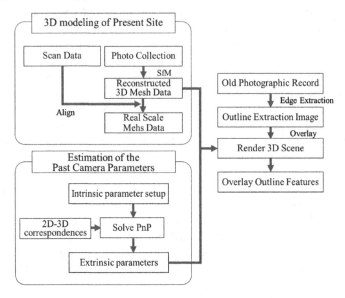

Fig. 2. Process chain of the proposed method

3.2 Preparing 3D Data

3D shape data is created using structure from motion (SfM) [10]. This technique is to simultaneously restore the 3D shape of the scene captured in the image from the multi-viewpoint image group and the shooting position of each image. In this research, we use multiple photos taken with a UAV. The 3D data created by SfM cannot restore the actual size of the object in principle. As a method of giving a real dimension, there is a marker that can understand the scale and GCPs (ground control points) such as watermarks and related survey points. By including a plurality of images reflecting these points, it is possible to give an actual size and geodetic coordinate system. Since GCP and markers were not arranged at the time of aerial photographing this time, scaling and positioning are performed on the laser-scanning data which measured the same place, so that the actual size is given to the 3D shape data.

3.3 Estimation of the Camera Parameters Used in the Past Survey

A point of view that passes one point on the photographing line from the focal point of the camera draws a straight line in 3D space and reaches a corresponding point on the subject. If it is constrained that this relationship holds at a plurality of points captured in one image, the photographing position and direction of the camera can be obtained. This problem is called PnP (Perspective-n-Points) problem [11] and is an important way to implement Augmented Reality (AR). In fact, we estimate the shooting position and direction (extrinsic camera parameters) of the photograph from the correspondence between the internal parameters which are characteristic of the camera and the three-dimensional coordinates of the object and the 2D coordinates (pixel coordinates) of the image. In recent years, natural features in images such as SIFT (Scale-Invariant Feature Transform), SURF (Speed-Up Robust Features), ORB (Oriented FAST and Rotated BREIF) [12–14] are effectively used for finding corresponding points between images. However, it is extremely difficult to associate with pictures each other separated by decades even in the same place. Figure 3 shows the result of detecting and associating natural features with ORB for two photos with the same shooting location and different era. As shown in the figure, automatic correspondences between photographs cannot be found correctly, and it is difficult to use them for estimating the position of the camera automatically. Therefore, in this research, we manually find the correspondences between past photo and a rendered current 3D scene as shown Fig. 4.

Fig. 3. Example results of automatically finding correspondences between a past photo and a rendered current 3D scene by natural feature points (ORG)

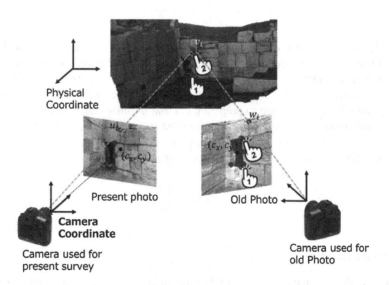

Fig. 4. A figure caption is always placed below the illustration. Short captions are centered, while long ones are justified. The macro button chooses the correct format automatically.

3.4 Intrinsic Camera Parameters

In order to obtain the external parameters of the camera, parameters specific to the individual camera (internal parameters) such as the focal length of the photographed camera and the image center are required. Camera calibration is a method of estimating internal parameters of the camera. This is generally known as a method [9] of estimating internal parameters from the correspondence between images obtained by photographing a checkerboard for calibration from multiple viewpoints and actual images.

To estimate the external parameters of the recorded photograph, the internal parameters of the camera used at that time must be used. However, information on the camera is unknown. Therefore, it is impossible to acquire internal parameters by calibration. Therefore, in this research, pay attention to the aspect ratio of recorded pictures being close to 1, and prepare the initial internal parameters. Generally, the camera matrix is expressed as follows.

$$A = \begin{bmatrix} f_x & 0 & c_x \\ 0 & f_y & c_y \\ 0 & 0 & 1 \end{bmatrix} = \begin{bmatrix} \frac{fw}{w_p} & 0 & \frac{w}{2} \\ 0 & \frac{fh}{w_p} & \frac{h}{2} \\ 0 & 0 & 1 \end{bmatrix}, \tag{1}$$

where, f_x and f_y are focal length in pixels for x and y direction, (c_x, c_y) is the center position in the image plane, respectively. The parameter f is the focal length in mm, and w, h are the height and the width in the actual dimension of the image sensor plane. The parameters w_p, h_p are originally the size of width and height of the single image sensor for the single pixel and can be derived as follows.

$$w_p = \frac{w}{I_w}, h_p = \frac{h}{I_h}, \tag{2}$$

where, I_w and I_h. are the width and the height size of the image in pixels, that is scanned image size from the printed photo taken in 1960. We assume that the camera used for the documentation in 1960 was medium format in still photography. Referring to the 6×6 frame size in *120* film format, whose one side of the nominal size of the file is 56 mm. Using this value to prepare the initial intrinsic camera parameters. After solving PnP problem and applying the estimated camera parameter to align the past phot and the current scenery, slight changes are added to the focal length in intrinsic parameter and we select the best fit in alignment result.

$$\text{fovy} = 2\tan^{-1}\left(\frac{I_h}{2f}\right) \tag{2}$$

3.5 Photo Overlay

By applying the external parameters to the camera in the 3D space, the screen in which the current state is observed is rendered from the past photographing viewpoint. By transparently superimposing the recorded pictures on this screen, we can visually grasp the difference between then and the present. When superimposing, in the original image, the 3D data behind and the color mix with each other, making it difficult to recognize the difference. Therefore, only the outline portion of the subject is extracted from the photograph, and the color tone is changed and highlighted. Alpha blending is used for blending during overlapping. In this process, a parameter representing transparency called an alpha value is required. Therefore, a channel for storing the alpha value is newly created in the image from which the outline is extracted. Then, only the outline portion is made opaque from the color information in the pixel. As a result, only the information of the image to be displayed is rendered on three dimensions.

4   Implementation

4.1   3D Digitization

In the existing remains, we restored the water storage facility, which is considered to be related to the water god in the temple, by SfM processing in three dimensions. 3D shape of the site was reconstructed by using about 150 photo images taken with Phantom 4 (DJI Inc.) on the UAV and SfM processing software PhotoScan (Agisoft).

Next, in order to give the actual size to the SfM data, scanning the same place with the laser scanner Focus 3D (FARO) was conducted. By using a free software CloudCompare, scan data was used as reference data to perform regisatration. This process is for acquiring necessary movement, rotation, and scaling parameters in order to match the SfM data to the scan data. As a result, the current 3-dimensional shape data with actual size was created (Fig. 5.)

Fig. 5. A figure caption is always placed below the illustration. Short captions are centered, while long ones are justified. The macro button chooses the correct format automatically.

Fig. 6. Prepared corresponding points between a past photo (left) and a rendered current scenery (right). (Color figure online)

4.2   Case Study (North Wall in the Water Storage)

Camera Pose Estimation. Here, we aligned the photo taken of the north wall of the water storage facility, which was a pivotal facility of the temple with a sacred spring used for worship of Sumerian water god Enki. It was expected that the piled-up blocks of the stone construction surrounding the spring has caused strains on itself and changed its appearance. Figure 6 (left) shows the photo used for our study. The size is 931 pixels width and 877 pixels height. Using the formula in 3.3, we selected the focal length of the camera from among the manually changed values of the focal length, the one with the least error in position of the viewpoint as the internal parameter.

In pairs of 2D coordinates and 3D coordinates, twenty invariant feature points were selected by pixel selection while confirming the 3D shape. Also, 3D coordinates were acquired by mouse picking as shown in numbered red points in Fig. 6. Past shooting position and direction were obtained using the set internal parameter and association pair. For implementation, we use a function in OpenCV for solving PnP problems with RANSAC (RANdom SAmpling Consensus) algorithm that suppresses the influence of outliers, considering that noise included in image data [15].

Image Feature Extraction. The Canny function implemented in OpenCV was used to detect the image features of edges and contours of stone blocks from recorded pictures (Fig. 7(1)). The Canny edge filter [16] is a contour detector suitable for extracting a single line. Upon contour detection, the image was smoothed by using a Gaussian filter to reduce noise. According to the response levels of the ridgelines of the stones and other parts in the photo, we elaborately tuned the parameters of the Gaussian filter kernel size and the threshold value in the Canny function manually until the stone edge line appears to be usable as landmarks, as shown in Fig. 7(2).

In order to display only the colored part of the created image, a 4-channel matrix was created by adding for alpha value. For the last one channel, a threshold value is set for the RGB value, and if it is smaller, the transparency of the pixel is set to 0. We set alpha blending and superimposed images with transparency on top of 3D data (Fig. 7(3)) as viewed from the past shooting viewpoint. (Figure 7(4)) The angle of view of the camera at this time was manually adjusted so that the photograph and the three dimensions overlap. As a result, we were able to visually grasp the minute difference between the excavation and the present situation, such as sediment deposition condition and stone defect.

4.3 Case Study (North Wall in the Water Storage)

Similar processing was carried out using another photograph. We targeted the south wall and of the water storage facility (Fig. 8(1)). The width and height of this image are 700 pixels and 661 pixels, respectively. It is thought that this place was used as a well which pours out the necessary water for the festival. As shown in Fig. 8(1), there is a water intake in which rounded characteristic stones are arranged, and now most of them are backfilled as shown in the reconstructed 3D mode in Fig. 8(3). By the same procedure as in Sect. 4.2, the ridgelines and edges are extract from Figs. 8(1) and 8(2) was generated. In addition, 27 corresponding points are selected to estimate the viewpoits of Fig. 8(1). The results of superimposing Fig. 8(2) on (3) is shown in Fig. 8(4).

Looking at this result, we can confirm the location of the stones hidden in the backfilling sand and the ridgelines of the stones are displaced. This is considered to be due to the earth pressures by backfilling. So the local site managers need to consider the influence on such artifacts due to the construction for maintenance. By superimposing in this manner, it is possible to confirm the small differences and to use this visual information as a reference for restoration of the correct arrangement of the stones.

Fig. 7. Result of the proposed method.

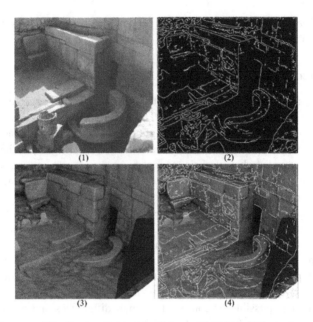

Fig. 8. Another result of the proposed method.

5   Discussion and Conclusions

5.1   Quantitative Inspection

Since the 3D data contains the real dimensions, by placing a ruler of physical scale in the 3D space at an arbitrary place, the difference caused by the elapsed years can be measured quantitatively. In Fig. 9, the displacement in the central enclosure was measured by placing a virtual ruler along the wall. We could confirm that there is a displacement of about 3 cm for the current one. This seems to have been caused by the stone being shifted due to the influence of the iron fence which is thought to be inserted for reinforcement in the present enclosure. In this way, by giving past records to the present, it can be used not only for collation work but also for past records and review.

Fig. 9. Overlaid virtual ruler

5.2 Concluding Remarks

In this research, we looked back on the history of survey records of cultural properties and noted that there is a need to check and review the difference from that time. Therefore, we proposed a system that visualizes this difference by superimposing recorded pictures on three-dimensional data created using SfM and a laser scanner. In addition, by making actual dimensions of 3D data, we tried quantitatively measuring this difference experimentally. In the future, we plan to increase application examples and visualization methods that are easy for users to understand.

References

1. Helmuth Andersen, H., Hojlund, F.: The Barbar Temples. Jutland Archaeological Society Publications, Aarhus University Press, Aarhus (2003)
2. CyArk. http://www.cyark.org/. Accessed 21 May 2018
3. Themistocleous, K., Ioannides, M., Agapiou, A., Hadjimitsis, D.: The methodology of documenting cultural heritage sites using photogrammetry, UAV and 3D printing techniques: the case study of Asinou Church in Cyprus. In: Proceedings of SPIE - The International Society for Optical Engineering, vol. 9535, pp. 953510-1-7 (2015)
4. Lo Brutto, M., Garraffa, A., Meli, P.: UAV platforms for cultural heritage survey: first results. ISPRS Ann. Photogramm. Remote. Sens. Spat. Inf. Sci. II-5, 227–234 (2014)
5. Themistocleous, K., Agapiou, A., King, H.M., King, N., Hadjimitsis, D.G.: More than a flight: the extensive contributions of UAV flights to archaeological research – the case study of curium site in cyprus. In: Ioannides, M., Magnenat-Thalmann, N., Fink, E., Žarnić, R., Yen, A.-Y., Quak, E. (eds.) EuroMed 2014. LNCS, vol. 8740, pp. 396–409. Springer, Cham (2014). https://doi.org/10.1007/978-3-319-13695-0_38
6. Meyer, D., Hess, M., Lo, E., Wittich, C.E., Hutchinson, T.C., Kuester, F.: UAV-based post disaster assessment of cultural heritage sites following the 2014 South Napa earthquake. In: Proceeding of Digital Heritage 2015, pp. 421–424 (2015)
7. Themistocleous, K., Agapiou, A., Hadjimitsis, D.G.: 3D documentation and BIM modeling of cultural heritage structures using UAVs: the case of the Foinikaria Church. In: The International Archives of the Photogrammetry, Remote Sensing and Spatial Information Sciences, vol. XLII-2/W2, pp. 45–49 (2016)
8. Yasumro, Y., Matsushita, R., Higo,T., Suita, H.: On-site AR interface based on web-based 3D database for cultural heritage in Egypt. In: GCH 2016 – Eurographics Workshop on Graphics and Cultural Heritage, pp. 183–186 (2016)
9. Glowienka, E., Michalowska, K., Opalinski, P., Hejmanowska, B., Mikrut, S., Kramarczyk, P.: Use of LIDAR data in the 3D/4D analyses of the Krakow Fortress objects. In: Materials Science and Engineering Conference Series, vol. 245, pp. 042080, October 2017
10. Hartley, R., Zisserman, A.: Multiple View Geometry in Computer Vision. Cambridge University Press, Cambridge (2004)
11. Tomasi, C., Kanabe, T.: Shape and motion from image streams under orthography: a factorization method. Int. J. Comput. Vis. 9(2), 137–154 (1992)
12. Lowe, D.G.: Object recognition from local scale invariant features. In: Proceedings of IEEE International Conference on Computer Vision (ICCV), pp. 1150–1157 (1999)
13. Bay, H., Tuytelaars, T., Van Gool, L.: SURF: speeded up robust features. Comput. Vis. Image Underst. 110(3), 346–359 (2008)

14. Rublee, E., Rabaud, V., Konolige, K., Bradski, G.: ORB: an efficient alternative to SIFT or SURF. In: International Conference on Computer Vision (2011)
15. Fischler, A.M., Bolles, C.: Random sample consensus: a paradigm for model fitting with applications to image analysis and automated cartography. Commun. ACM **24**(6), 381–395 (1981)
16. Canny, J.: A computational approach to edge detection. IEEE Trans. Pattern Anal. Mach. Intell. (PAMI) **6**, 679–698 (1986)

Treatise of Digital Reconstruction and Restauration of Lace Porcelain

Lien Acke[1], Kristel De Vis[1(✉)], Tim De Kock[2], Erik Indekeu[3],
Johan Van Goethem[4], Seth Van Akeleyen[5], Mathieu Cornelis[6],
Jouke Verlinden[5], and Stijn Verwulgen[5]

[1] Conservation-Restoration, Antwerp University, Antwerp, Belgium
lien.acke@student.uantwerpen.be,
kristel.devis@uantwerpen.be
[2] PProGRess/UGCT, Department Geology, Ghent University, Ghent, Belgium
tim.dekock@ugent.be
[3] Juwellery Design, Gold and Silversmithing, University College Antwerp,
Antwerp, Belgium
erik.indekeu@ap.be
[4] Radiology, Antwerp University Hospital, Edegem, Belgium
johan.vangoethem@uantwerpen.be
[5] Product Development, Antwerp University, Antwerp, Belgium
{seth.vanakeleyen, stijn.verwulgen}@uantwerpen.be
[6] Materialise, Leuven, Belgium
mathieu.cornelis@materialise.be

Abstract. Lace porcelain is a fragile type of ceramics that is used to be in fashion in 19th century Dresden artworks. It is known to break easily while manual repair is nearly impossible. Instead, we considered digital scanning, reconstruction, and 3D printing of the damaged areas towards new digital restauration methodologies. One reference case was used throughout testing the enabling technologies, and the combination of micro CT and polyjet 3D printing proved to be most useful. However, defining a proper workflow are specifically digital modeling of porcelain lace requires complex modelling strategies, especially to make it fit for 3D printing.

Keywords: Porcelain lace · Ceramics restoration · Digital modeling
3D printing

1 Introduction

Lace porcelain is made by dipping real lace into a porcelain sludge and then draping it onto the molded basic form of the figurine. This technique gained popularity in 19th century Dresden artworks. When baking at high temperature, the original fabric burns away and the porcelain structure remains. Every object with draped lace is therefore unique, although several identical basic shapes have been produced and similar figurines exist [1]. The lace porcelain structures are often complex because of the folds and the perforations of the lace while the non-trivial folded and perforated surface is relatively thin, about 0.4 mm. All these aspects make a conventional manual restoration practically impossible without further damage (Fig. 1, right).

© Springer Nature Switzerland AG 2018
M. Ioannides et al. (Eds.): EuroMed 2018, LNCS 11196, pp. 15–26, 2018.
https://doi.org/10.1007/978-3-030-01762-0_2

Fig. 1. Reference case (290 × 228 × 202 mm), right: the damage in the porcelain lace under investigation.

Digital 3D technology has proven to be useful for digital inventory or representation through virtual reality or 3D printing [3, 4]. Examples of restoration of ceramics include the filling of a broken tuition of a Delft tulip vase [5], the restoration of a heavily damaged terracotta image [6], the supplementing a ceramic lion from the Nuzi temple in Iraq [7] and a fruit plate with tracery [8]. This is therefore mainly about larger or more massive objects. 3D technology already has numerous applications in the medical world. The non-invasive character of a computer tomography allows applications in the heritage field, particularly in documentation, identification and analysis of archaeological finds [9, 10].

The first phase of applying 3D technology is 3D scanning. The challenge lies primarily in accurately imaging the damage and its fracture edge. The subsequent phase, 3D modeling via CAD software (Computer Aided Design), builds on this by using the scan as a basis to model the repaired piece. A difficulty here is that there is no reference shape with geometric identical properties to fit the gap. In the final step, it is important to print the repair parts as accurately as possible to obtain an appropriate result.

This article discusses in succession the three aforementioned phases, in which the advantages and limitations of each method are discussed with regard to the case object under investigation. After this, possibilities for further research will be highlighted and a conclusion will be drawn on whether the method used is useful for effective restoration of lace porcelain.

2   Method

The case object is a damaged porcelain figurine of a musical ensemble (Fig. 1). This statue was produced between 1940 and 1990 in Schwarzburger Werkstatten fur Porzellankunst, Unterweissbach, Schwarzburg-Rudolstadt, Germany [2]. There are one large void and a smaller hole in the lace porcelain dress of the woman.

The treatise includes the workflow of scanning, reconstructing, and reproducing the damaged part of the lace porcelain. An additional challenge is that there is only one reference object on which various methods should be testen non-destructively. Generic steps of imaging (scanning, post-processing and reconstruction), simulation (digital modeling) and materialization (3D printing) were performed on the case object.

3 Imaging

The 3D model, obtained from the scan, must be of the highest possible resolution and must have the highest possible degree of detail detailing in order to have a good basis for reconstruction. In the case of lace porcelain, the consideration needs to be given to capture the edges of damaged gaps and the lace pattern/resolution. The most commonly used 3D scanners work on the basis of structured light because of their ease of use and low cost. A disadvantage of optical based scanning is potential occlusions in complex folded surfaces and also artifacts due to reflection. With the application of computed tomography, a more advanced imaging technique was therefore opted and compared with structured optical light scanning.

3.1 Structured Light Optical Scanning

With structured light optical scanning (SLS), the scanning device casts geometric light patterns onto the object while either the scanner moves around the object or the object rotates around its axis. One or more cameras in the scanning device analyze these patterns and their distortions by triangulation, so that a 3D image is constructed. In order to visualize next to the geometry the texture of the three-dimensional object to be scanned, a photogrammetry scan can be performed simultaneously or separately.

A first limitation in this scanning technique is the smooth surface of the porcelain. When this is the case, such as porcelain, majolica, faience, glass and metal, for example, a scattered light will produce a lot of scattering of the light so that no correct image is formed by the scanner. Moreover, the porcelain has a certain degree of translucency through the transparent glaze layer and the light porcelain structure. This partially absorbs the light from the scanner. To remove the gloss on the image, a powder coating is usually applied. Due to the fragile condition of the lace dress, however, this induces too much risk for further damage. Reflective and translucent surfaces in the 3D model give rise to uneven, pit-like surfaces, unscanned parts and loss of detail.

A second limitation has to do with the complex structure of the pleat. The many folds and undercuts, including the rupture edges, stop the light so that the underlying parts are not scanned (shadowing). With SLS, only an image is formed of the scanned surface and the result will therefore be an incomplete 3D model. By means of automatic or manually controlled software this can be completed afterwards, but the question then is whether it is still an exact scan, especially when the surface has non-trivial curvature, folding and a unique shape, i.e. no shape models are available for prior knowledge and or training reconstruction algorithms.

The third limitation is in the maximum achievable resolution of the scanner. Because of the high detail and fineness of the lace structure, 0.4 mm thick with perforations, a high-resolution scan is required of at least 100 μm. The available structured light scanners (Artec-Eva) with a resolution of 150–500 μm did not meet this requirement. As a result, the perforations were not registered and the fracture seam was not displayed finely enough.

3.2   Computer Tomography Scanning

pXRF Analysis
In order to detect the possible presence of disturbing elements, a portable X-Ray Fluorescence (pXRF) analysis was performed prior to computer tomography (CT) scanning.
The pXRF measurements were carried out with an Olympus-InnovX Delta Professional with rhodium anode with a maximum current of 200 μA. The voltage was 40 kV to detect the L lines of the heavier elements and 10 keV to detect the lighter elements. The live time for each spectrum was 15 s. In total, 7 spot measurements were carried out on the object.

The largest share of the pXRF measurements are light elements, mainly the raw materials Si and Al, which do not constitute a limitation when performing a CT. The measured amounts of heavy metals, indicated in Fig. 2, in combination with other properties of the figurine, such as the thickness and the density of the porcelain and glaze, can lead to noise. Only relative quantification of the amount of heavy metals present is possible, as a result of which its exact influence remains difficult to determine.

Fig. 2. Detected elements at the 7 spots during pXRF measurements.

CT Scanning
The following computer tomographs were performed:
<u>Medical CT - Lightspeed VCT:</u>
In the University Hospital Antwerp (UZA) a scan was carried out with the Lightspeed VCT device developed for scanning patients. The scan was carried out with

a tube voltage of 100 kV and an amperage of 600 mA. The resulting spatial resolution is 512 μm in the X and Y directions and 625 μm in the Z direction, resulting in a voxel size of 512 × 512 × 625 μm3. A total of 512 radiographs were taken, but due to a cone beam effect (unsharp image at the edges) the first and last detected radiographs are of poor quality. This leaves 498 usable radiographs suitable for tomographic reconstruction.

Micro-CT - Hector

The figurine was also scanned with micro-CT scanner Hector, developed by Ghent University in collaboration with XRE Bvba. This non-destructive "High-Energy CT system" allows scanning large and heavy objects up to 1 m and 80 kg with maximal field of view (FOV) 40 × 40 cm. The highest possible resolution is 4 μm.

The distance from the source to the object (SOD: 307.489 mm) and from the source to the detector (SDD: 1100.080 mm) was optimized to obtain the highest possible resolution and minimize noise. For this, the region of interest (ROI) was confined to the dress with the gaps. The ROI rotated around its axis during the measurement while the static radiation source irradiated the figurine for 45 min and detected 1 image per second. For the source a 0.5 mm Al-filter was placed to filter out low-energy x-rays, improving the signal to noise ratio. The scan was carried out with a tube voltage of 120 kVp and 291.66 μA. The spatial resolution is 55 μm in both the X, Y and Z directions, so the voxel size is 55 × 55 × 55 μm^3. From the number of voxels, 2002 × 2002 × 2002, translated in 2002 shadow images, a total of 1667 .tiff files (Tagged Image File Format) was used for the tomographic reconstruction.

Reconstruction

The structured light scans are visualized almost immediately. The 3D image obtained from the 2D radiographs, on the other hand, required converting software to perform a tomographic reconstruction. The reconstructed images were optimized and then converted to a 3D polygonal mesh.

The post-processing of the medical CT was done with Vesalius 3.1 for compatibility with medical imaging file format (DICOM). The micro-CT was post-processed with Octopus Analysis (© XRE bvba). To segment the porcelain of the air and to minimize noise, various algorithms were applied to the .tiff files. For example, a threshold value in the gray value histogram was visually determined and binary operations were applied to further eliminate isolated pixels such that no details are lost (Fig. 3).

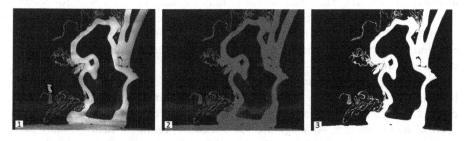

Fig. 3. Post-processing, vertical cut; 1. Raw image including noise, 2. Cut-off value applied, 3. Binary operation.

After post-processing segments, the .tiff files were loaded into VGStudio Max 3.0 (© Volume Graphics) for converting the pile of 2D images into a 3D view. Two ROIs were selected from the 3D view; the small hole and the substantial void (Fig. 4). These ROIs were converted to two CAD compatible polygonal meshes (stl). A balance was sought between reducing the number of polygons, which implies a loss of detail, and the workability. The small hole allowed retaining the smallest polygons (super precise mesh).

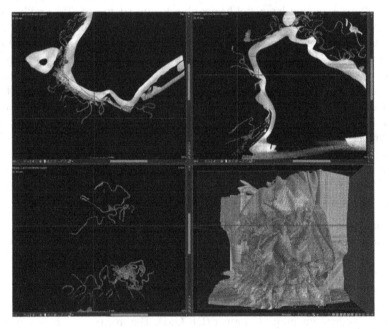

Fig. 4. ROIs and corresponding meshes of the small and large void.

4   Simulation

Since there is no reference for the missing folds, that part required re-modeling, either manually or in CAD. The small hole was fully digitally modeled with Rhinoceros 5.0®, allowing to work with both meshes and NURBS, complemented with a T-splines plugin (© Autodesk) for accurate deformation of the models. For the substantial void, containing more complex missing fold of various curvature, both manual and digital simulations were tested.

Despite the high detail micro-CT, the fracture edges could not be defined unambiguously or mathematically. As a result, no straight fracture surface, nor normals could be defined for further reference. Polylines in Rhinoceros 5.0 were used to draw a curve along the fracture. Although not 100% accurate, result are easily visually evaluated (seen in Fig. 5(1) for the small hole and Fig. 7(4) for the substantial hole).

4.1   Modeling the Small Hole

The mesh model was simulated with a wavy NURBS surface (patch via drape points). The fracture line was projected, with an offset of 0.1 or 0.2 mm inwards for the (slightly smaller) supplement to fit into the gap. A thickness of 0.4 mm was given to the wavy surface. Different sizes of perforations (0.4 - 0.6 - 0.7 - 0.8 mm) were tried out, with different spacing rings, projected via flow along surface. In addition, several scales (85 - 90 - 95 - 100%) of the model were tested for the supplement to fit the gap (Fig. 5).

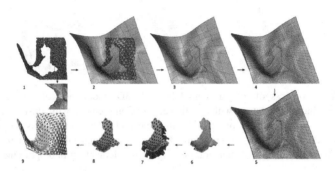

Fig. 5. Workflow small gap in Rhinoceros 5.0; 1. Mesh from VGStudio MAX 3.0 and break line via polyline on mesh, 2. Patch surface via drape points, 3. Break line projected on the surface and cut out with an offset curve of 0.1 mm inwards, 4. Surface with thickness 0, 4 mm, 5. Projection of the perforations, 6. Cut out basic shape, 7. Addition after extrusion and cutting of the perforations, 8. Final digital addition, 9. Digitally rendered result.

4.2   Modeling the Substantial Void

For computational reasons, the number of polygons at the substantial void were reduced to 75%. For example, a file of 330 Mb was transferred to a workable file of 32 Mb. This model is only used for modeling. A low-cost Fused Deposition Modeling (FDM) 3D print was made from the medical CT for having a test dummy that can be manipulated manually. From this test model, several manual and digital options were considered to convey the supplement (Fig. 6).

The following non-exhaustive list of methods have been tested

Method 1 (Fig. 6(2) and (4a + b)): A cut-out piece of perforated fabric was attached to the FDM print with glue, on the inside of the fracture edges. The substance filling was fixed with a coating of 10% Parallel B-72 in 80/20 acetone/ethanol, applied via airbrush. The correct color and gloss can be obtained by applying acrylic brushes and varnishes with airbrush, in accordance with conventional retouching methods for ceramic restoration. After drying the coatings, the supplement could be cut loose along the fracture edges.

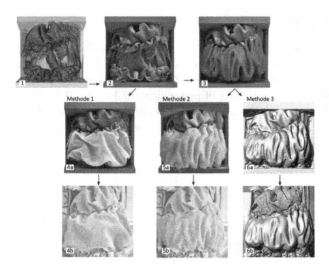

Fig. 6. Modeling process of the substantial hole; 1. 3D-model medical CT, 2. FDM-print medical CT, 3. Supplementation with plasticine, 4a. Complement with dust, 4b. Photoshop simulation of the fixed and cut out fabric supplement (1), 5a. Double dust supplement on plasticine, 5b. Photoshop simulation of the fixed and cut out fabric supplement (2), 6a. Photogrammetry of plasticine supplement, 6b. Digital supplement on photogrammetry.

Method 2 (Fig. 6(3) and (5a + b)): On the FDM-print, a plastic imitation was sculpted with plasticine, starting from the folds of similar figurines. A double layer of dust, perforated fabric sewn onto a neutral layer of dust, was manually placed on the molded supplement and pushed. A double layer of dust is necessary to avoid contaminating the perforated fabric with plasticine. The substance was then fixed, retouched and cut out like method 1.

Method 3 (Figs. 6(3), (6a + b) and 7): The modeled supplement was also scanned by means of a quick and accessible but less accurate method: possibilities are a handheld scan (Artec Eva) or proprietary photogrammetry via an online 3D service. This 3D scan was placed as accurately as possible in the model of the micro-CT in order to digitally model the supplement more easily. The original defined fracture line (polyline on mesh) was projected onto the 3D scan of the modeled supplement. The superfluous faces were removed so that only the supplement remained within the fracture edge. Because of the ease of use and time saving in this test phase, the number of meshes was greatly reduced. Through using Rhinoceros 5.0 plugin T-splines, the scanned supplement was adapted to the original fracture line. To make the supplement printable, a thickness of 0.4 mm (offset mesh) was given to the mesh.

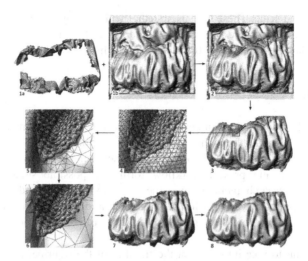

Fig. 7. Digital modeling process major gap; 1a + b. Micro-CT of the gap + Photogrammetry of the plasticine supplement, 2. Photogrammetry in the micro-CT, 3. Removal of superfluous faces, 4. Blue fracture seam micro-CT and projected green fault line on the photogrammetry, 5. Removal of faces outside the projected fracture line and mesh reduction, 6. Further reduction and use of T-Splines to pull the curves from the green break edge to the blue polyline, 7. Digital end result to print, 8. Application weld vertices for a smoother effect on the digital model. (Color figure online)

5   Materialization

The most decisive aspect in the selection of 3D printing techniques were layer resolution and wall thickness. To types of prints were found eligible to that end: PolyJet and SLA.

5.1   PolyJet

The errors (non-manifold edges, naked edges, non-oriented surfaces, open surfaces) after exporting the model to an stl file were repaired in Rhinoceros 5.0 and Autodesk Netfabb. The test prints were carried out with Stratasys Objet Eden 260 V. A wall thickness of 0.4 mm was achieved, in accordance with the thickness of the modeled 3D supplement. The printing material, a UV-curing photopolymer, can lose strength over time and can yellow. It is not suitable as a durable restorative material. Also cleaning the support material under high pressure or polishing the print to remove the matt effect is impossible due to the fragility of the fine print. The test prints were cleaned in cold water with a toothbrush, in combination with a toothpick and a needle to remove the support material as well as possible.

5.2   Stereolithography

The simulated addition of the small hole was printed several times with the PolyJet technique and subsequently adapted to a few prototypes varying in offset distance, size of perforations and scale. These models, together with the digital model of the big gap, were printed by Materialize via stereolithography technique Taurus, a UV-curing epoxy, with a layer thickness of 50 μm and a wall thickness of 400 μm.

6 Discussion

Scanning, simulation/modeling and printing are research fields with many applications. 3D technology is constantly evolving, inducing new opportunities due to technological advances, more support hard- and software with increasing accessibility.

The techniques and present workflow form one possible strategy for use in restoration. This research included only the steps up to and including the physical design of the supplement. The further steps in restoration, retouching and confirming the supplement are not covered in this study and still have to be researched and elaborated.

It is important to take into account the fragility of the figurine, but also the compatibility and reversibility of the adhesives and possible attachments in order to promote the life or durability of the restoration and the object itself. This can be done from the known restoration materials and methods, but here too innovative ideas can offer a way out.

To overcome the limitations of SLS with reflective, smooth objects and to scan the full volume of fine structures, micro CT is an excellent method. Specific knowledge and computing resources are required for imaging. If an extreme level of detail (<100 μm) is not necessary for the further workflow, SLS can be sufficient with the greatest advantages accessibility and the 3D image immediately visible and available in a polygonal mesh that is editable in various CAD software.

Further routes with regard to scanning could be sought at the medical branch of the dental restoration. Here too, radiographs and computer tomography are used for imaging. The dental cone beam CT may produce good results, since dental restoration is also about small objects. The spatial resolution achieved here is between 90 and 400 μm, coupled with a cost price that is only one fifth of a CT scanner.

In the modeling phase, Rhinoceros 5.0 offered a sufficient, but not complete, solution for reconstructing the gaps. Within this software there is a big difference in processing and modeling possibilities between meshes on the one hand and NURBS surfaces on the other. These shortcomings can be bridged by using other software such as 3DS Max, Blender, ZBrush and Sculptris. Furthermore, the limitations are mainly in the hardware of the computer and the extent to which the user is familiar with the various CAD software. CAD modeling and more specifically the design of the substantial void (and its perforations) could also be outsourced. Digital drawing is a discipline in itself and good management of CAD software can take years. The complete digital modeling can, without an FDM aid print, therefore depend on the modeling skills of the implementer. In this case, for reasons of workability, the medical CT could serve as a basis and the supplement can then be imported into the micro-CT model for fine-tuning, whether or not reduced.

In order to lean closer to the restoration conventions of porcelain during modeling, further experiments with zellaan can be carried out. The acrylate in powder form, diluted with water to a porcelain cut, can serve to fix the perforated fabric or edge. This technique was briefly tested during this research, but needs to be further investigated to produce satisfactory results. The main complication found is that the plaster clogs the perforations of the substance. Zellaan can also serve as casting compound in a silicone or alginate mold of a 3D print. The perforations are also a problem here, but this can be solved making a relief pattern in the 3D model instead of perforations. An additional limitation is that zellaan, although very hard, is still quite fragile. This supplement, therefore, like the lace porcelain, would be rather fragile.

3D model of the large supplement did not yet qualitatively serve as a final print model. This was mainly due to the visible polygons and the lack of perforations. After the printing phase, it can also be decided for the small addition that no print is required to be used immediately for the restoration of the small gap. However, with corrections to the 3D model, it could be possible to use (new) 3D prints during the restoration of the figurine.

In accordance with conventional ceramic restoration materials, water-based acrylic paints and a necessary UV-resistant coating can be applied to slow the aging process of the photopolymer. In addition, the (minimum) visible layer thickness of the SLA print can play a role. By applying layers of paint the layer thicknesses can remain visible or even be enlarged. Both the matt and the smooth side of the PolyJet print may be good substrates for a paint and varnish layer.

When the processes and materials used in dental restoration are taken into consideration, Selective Laser Sintering of porcelain or stereolithography with zirconia would also be an option for the restoration of porcelain, but also depending on the possible layer and wall thickness.

7 Conclusion

The aim of this research was to describe a possible method for restoring a small hole and a substantial void in fragile lace porcelain, using as little as possible the figurine itself to prevent further damage. Three phases were completed: 3D scanning, 3D modeling and 3D printing, in which an attempt was made to achieve as accurate and detailed as possible, taking into account the limitations and difficulties at each step.

In this investigation, two 3D scans based on structured light and computer tomography were tested and compared. Here the medical and micro CT were the most useful options, but also with their own limitations. The medical CT had too low a resolution to serve as an accurate basis. The micro-CT required strong hardware, the post-processing is intensive and digital handling time-consuming. However, both scans can be used and were used as a basis in the next phase.

The 3D modeling was done with CAD software Rhinoceros 5.0. The small hole was fully digitally modeled. With respect to the large gap, manual methods were necessary due to the complexity of the fold. Of these digital additions, test prints were systematically carried out with a PolyJet printer, chosen because of the high resolution and wall thickness. However, the resulting printed plastic is not suitable as a restoration material and requires further research.

The results of scanning, modeling and printing show that, with some adjustments proposed in this study, a 3D-printed supplement may be useful in the restoration of lace porcelain. Yet it is not self-evident to use only digital methods and a manual (interim) step can offer a solution. Depending on the case and the necessity, availability of tools and materials, individual skills and creativity in solution-oriented thinking, such a compromise can also be achieved when restoring other complex heritage objects.

This research and previous successful restorations reveal the enormous potential of using 3D technology. Considering the rapid technological progress, it can be expected that such techniques will play an increasingly important role in the implementation of restorations in the future.

References

1. Art Kaleidoscope: Lace Porcelain Art, visited 7 April 2018. http://vsemart.com/lace-porcelain-art/
2. Antique China Porcelain & Collectibles: Unterweissbach Porcelain History, Geraadpleegd 7 April 2018, http://antique-china-porcelain-collectibles.com/unterweissbach-porcelain-history.html
3. Gherardelli, M., Adembri, G., Balleri, R., Di Tondo, S.: Methods and tools for the classification and cataloging of antique mould from the collection of the Richard-Ginori factory. J. Cult. Herit. **15**, 479–489 (2014)
4. Scopigno, R., et al.: Using optically scanned 3D data in the restoration of Michelangelo's David, pp. 1–10. ISTI-CNR, Moruzzi (2003)
5. Hawotte, S.: L'impression 3D au service du traitement de conservation restauration d'une tulipière en faïence de Delft. Bulletin **04**, 15–19 (2014)
6. Arbace, L., et al.: Innovative uses of 3D digital technologies to assist the restoration of a fragmented terracotta statue. J. Cult. Herit. **14**, 332–345 (2013)
7. Powell, A.: An ancient statue, re-created: through technology, museum augments shards of ceramic lion. The Harvard Gazette, 4 December 2012, Geraadpleegd op 7 April 2018. https://news.harvard.edu/gazette/story/2012/12/an-ancient-statue-re-created/
8. Antlej, J., Celec, K., Sinani, M., Mirtic, E., Ljubi, D.: Restoration of a Stemmed Fruit Bowl Using 3D Technologies, Преглед НЦД 21, no. 29, pp. 141–146 (2012)
9. Karl, S, Kazimierski, K.S., Hauzenberger, C.A.: An interdisciplinary approach to studying archaeological vase paintings using computed tomography combined with mineralogical and geochemical methods. A Corinthian alabastron by the Erlenmeyer Painter revisited. J. Cult. Herit. (2017). https://doi.org/10.1016/j.culher.2017.10.012
10. Appelbaum, N., Appelbaum, Y.: The use of medical computed tomography (CT) imaging in the study of ceramic and clay archaeological artifacts from the ancient near east. In: Uda, M., Demortier, G., Nakai, I. (eds.) X-rays for Archaeology. Springer, Dordrecht (2005)

HBIM Feeding Open Access Vault Inventory Through GeoDB HUB

Raffaella Brumana[1](✉) , Paola Condoleo[2] , Alberto Grimoldi[3] ,
Angelo Giuseppe Landi[3] , Dario Attico[1], Anna Turrina[1],
Fabrizio Banfi[1] , and Mattia Previtali[1]

[1] DABC - Department of Architecture, Built Environment and Construction
Engineering, Politecnico di Milano, Via Ponzio 31, 20133 Milan, Italy
{raffaella.brumana, fabrizio.banfi,
mattia.previtali}@polimi.it,
AtticoDario@msn.com, annaturrina@gmail.com
[2] DICA - Department of Civil and Environmental Engineering,
Politecnico di Milano, Milan, Italy
paola.condoleo@polimi.it
[3] DASTU - Department of Architecture and Urban Studies,
Politecnico di Milano, Milan, Italy
{alberto.grimoldi, angelogiuseppe.landi}@polimi.it

Abstract. This paper describes a methodological workflow starting from a punctual informative Historical Building Information Models (HBIM) - derived from the geometric analysis of the construction technology of vaulted systems - used to feed an open access Geospatial Data Base based on a Virtual Hub technology. Vaulted systems, which are characterized by a variety of solutions developed across time and space, and whose knowledge is obtained during the analysis and diagnostic phases planned for preservation purposes, are mostly unknown to the public and collected information risks to be missed. This way, the chain of knowledge transfer is interrupted both for more informed future sustainable interventions and touristic purposes. The potentials offered by the adoption of a Pan European Virtual Hub to manage open data with semantic, spatial and temporal sub-setting allows to reconstruct a new framework of the construction techniques widespread across the world, permanencies and muta-tions to the common typologies with the contribution of skilled workers moving during the centuries across Europe. The case study of Palazzo Magio in Cre-mona with a rich abacus of vaults apparently belonging to a simple 'cloister' typology is described from the HBIM generation to data publication in the GeoDB HUB. Different Level of Detail, Geometry and Information, acquired in other Cremona Palaces, are feeding the DB and its vocabulary in a bottom-up process. The result is a contribution to the construction of an open access updatable inventory model inheriting the tradition of historical repertoires.

Keywords: HBIM · Open access · GeoDB · Virtual Hub · Vault
Stereotomy · Terrestrial laser scanning · Photogrammetry · Modelling
Thermography

© Springer Nature Switzerland AG 2018
M. Ioannides et al. (Eds.): EuroMed 2018, LNCS 11196, pp. 27–38, 2018.
https://doi.org/10.1007/978-3-030-01762-0_3

1 Introduction. A Short Overview of an European Perspective

After an eclipse of almost one hundred years, vaults have returned to the center of architectural heritage studies and radically renewed the perspectives of architectural history between the fourteenth and eighteenth centuries, from the late Gothic to the Baroque. In France, thanks to the policy set up by Jean Marie Pérouse de Montclos, the revival of the inventory in 1964 led to a census in the significant realizations of stereotomy and the re-evaluation of the wide and learned writing treatises on the subject from the 16th to the 19th centuries, as in the case of the treaties made by 'Philibert De l'Orme architecte du roi 1514-1570' [1]. In Spain, available studies are less systematic and more recent, but they have renewed substantially the history of architecture focusing on the quality of stereotomic construction in the late Gothic and in Renaissance construction period [2]. In England, as in France, stating from the first quarter of the 19th century [3] the classification of vaulted systems represented an essential moment in the re-evaluation of medieval construction, but the scarce diffusion of real vaults in the construction of the Modern Age has circumscribed the theme to its most monumental and ancient heritage, which is relatively scarce. In Germany, on the other hand, from the Middle Ages to the Baroque period and throughout the 19th century, stone vaults, and moreover brick vaults, were very common and the technical literature and drawings increased steadily right up to the Modern Age [4]. Italian treatises – with the significant exception of the Guarini's one – are often elementary and repetitive. From mid 17th century, direct reference is made to the French texts [5]. Contemporary studies therefore lack of an overview work to be used as a reference leading inevitably to an involuntary localism – see the "Manuali del recupero" which are generally focused on a specific city. Even if some more extensive works exist they seem focusing on specific time-space perimeter and "geographical" skills of the authors. Within such a rich framework, it is difficult to reconstruct regional specifics. Piedmont stands out for the quantity of complex examples and for their success in historiography [6]. The result of this scenario is an extremely fragmented and heterogeneous picture where the level of knowledge is function of the methodological way the analysis is carried out, with a discontinuity in term of Level of Detail acquired and of space and time extension of the analysis.

2 Inventory Model: Search for the Limits

Starting from the previously described scenario, a general classification of vaults turns out to be a system with infinite variables, which would bring difficulties even in the choice of the main parameters to be considered. For this reason, it is very hard to define the limits, according to which a classification must be undertaken. The problem is simpler if we consider a specific territory, restricted to a certain historical period. Indeed, the knowledge on local expertise and materials facilitates the formation of a recognizable way to build, which is defined by specific characteristics. However, we do not have to forget that constructive experimentation and exchange of people and experiences also existed and these two elements lead to exceptions. The boundary between exception and rule also becomes uncertain. In addition, a merely geographical delimitation might be distorting, because a certain expertise formed in a specific area is often exported. Indeed, mobility was a significant aspect in the medieval and modern Europe especially at the highest level of technical skills. Obviously, mobility was even larger at the highest level, between architects and engineers. Taking into account this wide variability, the approach developed in the past to study this problem was based on an elementary classification: it is what the stereotomists followed by Guarini have called "maîtresses voûtes", within a different linguistic framework.

The punctual analysis of the geometry and characteristics of the each vault represents the starting point, within a bottom up process. Indeed, natural or institutional boundaries can univocally delimit even an area, and in the same way, a temporal horizon can be identified as a reference period comparing the related information. A classification can only be an open scheme enriched by semantics, with different point of views enclosed into a not-finite knowledge frame, continuously updatable.

3 Bottom-Up Methodology: HBIM of the Vault Systems Feeding a GeoDB HUB

For the previously listed reasons, the definition of a database (DB) of the vault systems - as well as for the architectural and cultural heritage DB domain in general - cannot be but an open system based on different variables coming from the punctual analysis, on the context frame of research. The proposed methodology reverses the process toward a bottom-up inventory model progressively fed up by the granular analysis carried out within the HBIM generation (Fig. 1). In the last years many efforts have been invested in the cultural heritage digitization. Surveying, modelling, diagnostic analysis and historic data collection of architectural heritage have been acquired particularly during the analysis phases addressed to the preservation and restoration process. The number of informative models testifying the multifaceted richness of the unicity of the architectural heritage and its components as in the case of the vaulted systems is progressively increasing. Unfortunately, once concluded the research or the construction site, they are mostly left abandoned in the drawers or in the local memory of the computers, in a latent status destined to the oblivion, when not totally missed. Just few of them are saved in a server or in the cloud for the duration of the restoration, but without any connection with the maintenance process of historic architectures or dissemination and knowledge transfer purposes. Loss of data means loss of the ring among past, present and future; loss of memory and loss of knowledge.

HBIM informative models, in the meaning of systems connecting models to information, give us the opportunity to join many information of the vaulted system derived from the surveying, modeling and historical analysis. Among the most important information we have: vault typology, conceptual geometry, construction technology of the components, the arrangement, the texturing of the brick block elements, their dimensions, the structural elements and components, the materials, the dates of construction, archive documents, ancient maps, and other historical documentations.

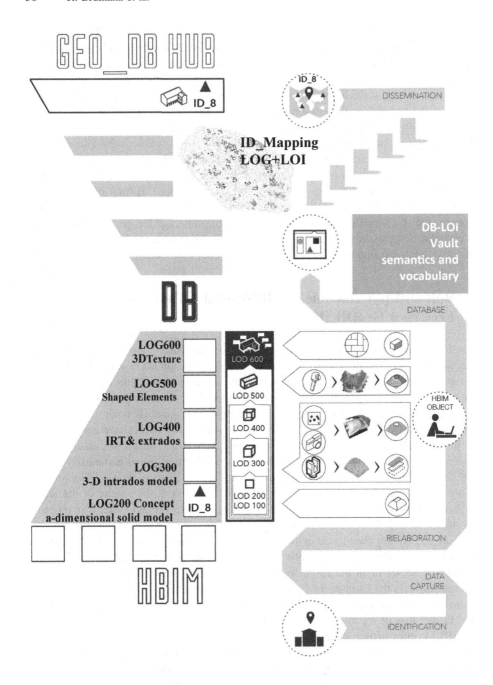

Fig. 1. The bottom-up methodologic workflow: from the vault HBIM (model and information) with different LOG-LOI data collection across the territory, to the GeoDB HUB population and Web Map Data Visualisation based on semantics.

Each HBIM represents a 'case dense of knowledge', a precious drop in the ocean represented by the monuments and vaulted systems in the world, with scarce accessibility to a large public, and without cross relation to other similar libraries. HBIM can feed the DB within a spatial temporal framework. From the last decade, the HBIM informative models can be accessed as HBIM libraries, as in the case of the product catalogue in the construction industry, or as Open Access formats according to OpenBIM on developing, or simplified common formats. In this paper, it was analysed the possibility to create an inventory model made by the built HBIMs coming from the different case studies, and using them to feed a geographic data base (GeoDB). A GeoDB HUB has been conceived in order to publish and access the gained information within a geographic domain where to meet the different data sources and perform different searches. This open approach will reveal unexpected correlations in the world, as well as it will highlight in a common framework exchanges of expertise. For example, this is in the case of the cloister vaults realized with the contribution of skilled workers coming from the north of Italy toward North and Central Europe, and vice versa. Another famous example is the Magistri Comacini family from the Lake of Como toward Europe in the middle age. The construction of an abacus of constructive elements [7] collecting the different solutions adopted during the on-site construction by the workers in the past can contribute to the knowledge growing, awareness rising among professionals and larger public. The aim is to obtain an open updatable system, with information on different areas and different epochs that can track common typologies of vaulted systems across space and time nowadays unknown in historic manuals.

3.1 The Case of the HBIM Vault-Abacus of Palazzo Magio

Here it is summarized the case of the abacus of the HBIM vaulted system in the Magio Palace in Cremona. Starting from data acquisition (laser scanning, photogrammetric survey, IRT thermal analysis), the processing and data modeling phase, managed within HBIM environment, gave back an High Resolution Level of Detail, Geometry and Information model evidencing different geometry related to the apparently similar typology of the 'cloister vault' [8]. As demonstrated from many researches, included this case study, the construction technologies influences the simplified conceptual shape coming from the vault typology classification (barrel vault, cloister vault, sail-dome), generating typologies turned toward mixed typologies [7]. Laser scanning and photogrammetry data were acquired at the intrados to get the 3D model and orthophoto and to generate the "vault" BIM Object parametrizing the complex NURBS based generative modeling managed within modeller tools. IRT thermal images at intrados have been addressed to the indirect detection of the texture arrangement. In addition, the survey at the extrados - where viewable or reachable – was aimed to reconstruct the texture of the BIM components. The survey integration evidenced the different arrangements and components highlighting three different shape of vaults apparently belonging to similar cloister vaults (Fig. 2): (i) the Manfredini Hall, facing on the court, with the typical rectangular slices, coming from the intersection of two conceptual cylindrical solids (Fig. 2 - centre); (ii) the Manfredini Hall on the road tuned to trompe (Figs. 2 top and 3); (iii) the Stair Hall a dome turned to a cloister (Fig. 2 - bottom).

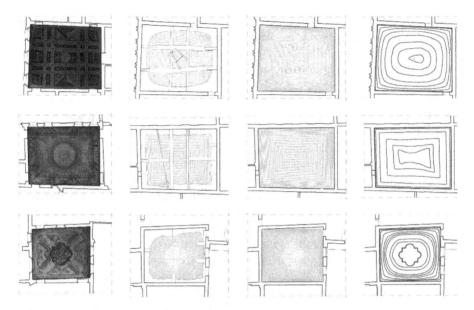

Fig. 2. The surveying of the 3 different vaults apparently belonging to the 'cloister' typology: the orthophotos (intrados), the extrados arrangements coming from the orthophotos at the extrados or intrados-IRT (details), and the different horizontal profiles from the clouds. The cloister vault (Manfredini Hall on the court, centre), the one tuned toward 'trompe' corners (Manfredini Hall on the road, top) and the one tuned to trompe-dome solution (Stair Hall, bottom), due to the constructive technology adopted to speed the execution limiting the centring costs.

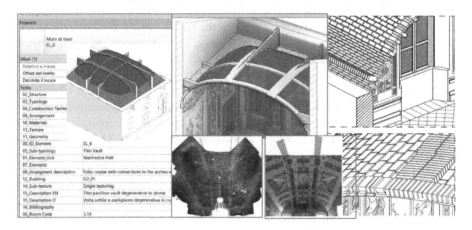

Fig. 3. The HBIM reconstruction of the Manfredini Hall on the road (a cloister tuned toward a trompe corner) with the mixed structure made by arches and the vault components: the portion of cloister at the spring line (red) as evidenced by the IRT; the arches with brick block soldier laid (red) springing from the cloister portion (red), the trompe-vault with 'in folio' tiles (green), 3÷4 cm height, the 'frenelli' (sand) and extrados tie roads. The properties of each component (i.e., ID_building, sub-typology of each component, arrangement, dimensions, description) are inserted in the HBIM DB (LOI) and related to a LOG600 (3D texture of the arrangements). (Color figure online)

In particular, at a first glance the intrados the Stair Hall seems a common cloister vault, but analysing shape and arrangements it resulted a dome turned to a cloister shape through the 'trompe' shape at the four corners (Fig. 4).

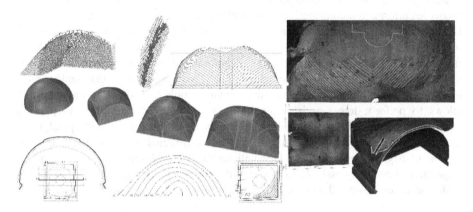

Fig. 4. The Stair Hall. The arrangement (upper), the conceptual analysis of the spherical dome (centre) tuned to a cloister rectangular vault through the 'trompe' at the corners, and the geometric profiles extracted to recognize the shape, vertical and diagonal (bottom).

4 Pan-European Virtual Hub for DH: Toward a Common Space to Share Spatial DB Model of Vaulted Systems

4.1 Pau-European Virtual Hub and Gazetteers

The growing availability of Big data in the form of Open Data (including Geographic Open Data), is progressively demanding new paradigm and new tools supporting open data search with innovative solution capable to empower knowledge transfer and data sharing. Virtual Hubs were introduced in the field of Earth Observation to facilitate multi-temporal, spatial sub-setting and semantic search of data, as well as their access, as in the case of GEO-DAB (Discovery and Access Brokering System) implemented by the CNR-IIA for the Group of Earth Observation (GEOSS) [9]. Within this framework a Pan-European Virtual Hub was implemented within the EU project 'European Network Re-distributing of Geographic Open Data' (ENERGIC-OD) introducing the concept of DAB, and its functionalities in the world of Open Data (OD). On the top of this Virtual Hub systems a set of innovative application were developed. Among them GeoPAN APP was developed in order to manage multi-temporal maps, including historical map archive series [10] supporting most of the current OD format (i.e. JSON, SHP, WMS, WFS, GEOTIFF, among the others). The Virtual Hub system supports a multi-lingual vocabulary gazetteer (the GEMET vocabulary) in order to facilitate search functionalities and content sharing among different languages. Gazetteer is defined as a geographical dictionary (as at the back of an atlas) or directory used in conjunction with a map or atlas. Nowadays vocabularies are growing in many fields. As in the case of the Getty Thesaurus of Art & Architecture [11]: even if very rich, they can't be exhaustive of the richness of the granularity that characterized the construction systems all over the world and, thus, of the terminology coming from deeper punctual investigation, as previously shown. For example, searching within that vocabulary, the noun Cloister Vault is missed with all the properties information contributing to the multiplicity of their variety. Examples of this large variety are the case of degenerative cloister vaults turning toward sail-dome or other shapes with double curvature as in the case of the 'trompe' corner of the Manfredini Hall. Also the term 'frenelli' (the wall component contributing with the tie roads to the structural stability) is not contained. The possibility to meet geographic information and expanding the query by using semantic tools like SPARQL endpoint will allows to perform free search across space and time. The possibility to perform semantic searches across time and space can be implemented by conceptual icons facilitating the comprehension and will support multilingual searches. Thus, the generation of a growing live vocabulary will be further analysed. This activity, to be implemented and progressively extended, will require the formalization of definitions with researchers from different countries while feeding the GeoDB with their data.

4.2 Spatial DB Model of Vaulted System

Spatial humanities constitute a rapidly developing research field. In particular [12] defines spatial humanities (or GeoHumanities) as the 'rapidly growing zone of creative interaction between geography and the humanities'. This (re)introduction of the geographic concept of space into humanities has the potential to create a step-change in the ways in which the humanities interact each other, thus allowing new definition of analysis and researches. For fruitful integration between geographic and humanities disciplines a fundamental step is the design and the creation of the required humanities datasets. Beyond this, there is the need to define appropriate research queries and to enrich the DB with parameters and words capable to transmit the findings coming from the detailed HBIM informative models, both of which can involve prolonged discussion and debate. As it is the ongoing discussion on the best terminology to be adopted in case of dome tuned to cloister: which is the main typology and which the subtypology? Another example is the cloister degenerative vault tuned to the corner trompe with double curvature. The discussion on the vocabulary is only at the beginning ant it will be for sure enhanced by information sharing. This section present an application of those concepts in the case of vault typology distribution. All the properties detected by the surveying and HBIM analysis have been managed into a common Data Base (DB). The main steps for the creation of a spatial database model were:

1. characterization of the data and aim of the analysis;
2. set-up of the database model;
3. connection with a Geographic server;
4. online publishing.

The first step of the implemented procedure aimed at characterizing the datasets to be analyzed (geographic and humanities datasets, their content, structure and typology of information). In particular, the vault datasets exploited three different sources: (i) historical data, (ii) geometrical data and models of the construction elements (i.e. vaults, walls) and (iii) construction technology data. Nine main entities were identified one of which had spatial attributes and could thus be geo-referenced. The conceptual model of the database is provided in the form of an Entity Relationship Diagram (ERD). Lastly, the logical model of the vault database (Fig. 5) was designed, which defines the attribute data for each entity in the DB. The primary characteristic of the database model is the centrality of the entity "Constructive element"; in fact, it is related to most entities in the database, and of the entity "Building" since it is the one with geographical attributes. Other geometrical information (e.g., 3D model, ortho-photo, HBIM) are linked with external web-link. Along with the DB, a data dictionary was developed to store information on the attributes defined for each entity (Fig. 6): a data entry mask illustrates the architecture of the DB granular information.

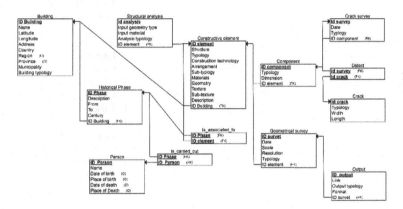

Fig. 5. Logical model of the vault database.

4.3 Populating the Open GeoDB and Vocabulary from HBIM: 3D Linked Model and Related Information

The DB is connected with a geographic server. In particular, the server-side software used is GeoServer a powerful Open Source platform for publishing spatial data and interactive mapping applications on the web and standard GIS software (both commercial software, such as ESRI ArcGIS, and Open Source software, such as QGIS). In particular, GeoServer allows the visualization of produced data by using OGC standards like WMS, WMTS, WFS and WCS that are compatible with different solutions allowing datasets to be published on the Pan-European Virtual Hub [13]. Currently the link between the GeoDB and other 3D data is represented by an external link. Indeed, among the different attributes in the GeoDB there is the "External_3d_link" that is a web link to a web published resource. The published formats include: proprietary BIM (e.g.,.rfa,.rte REVIT Autodesk ©), OpenBIM, web link (e.g., A360 Autodesk© Platform), Object Library and 3D mesh models supporting texture (e.g., OBJ, X3D). For a simple consultation of the data a web application was also designed (Fig. 7) allowing data query and analysis using the Common Query Language (CQL), created by the Open Geospatial consortium (OGC), and an extended version of this language ECQL allowing for ID filters and having a higher similarity with Standard Query Language (SQL). Let's assume for example to perform a query aimed at extracting only barrel vaults from the GeoDB HUB. The query can be formulated simply as:

VAULT_TYPOLOGY = 'Barrel'

In the case we want to filter the results into a specific area, we can specify the query as follows

VAULT_TYPOLOGY = 'Barrel' AND BBOX (the_geom, TLX, TLY, BRX, BRY)

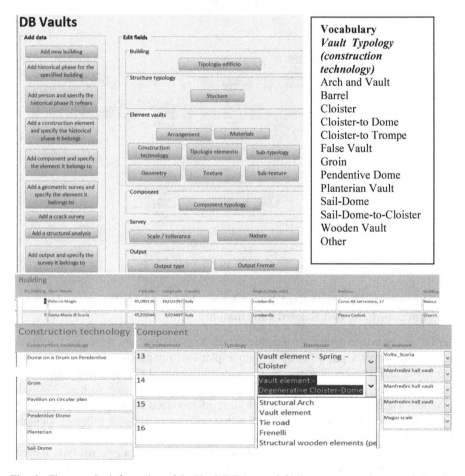

Fig. 6. The granular information of the Vault DB (upper left); here are some data populating the DB coming from different case studies alimenting the ongoing vocabulary, as the Vault Typology (on the right), the ID_building with the geographic position, Vault element sub-typology of each component of the vault, i.e. Degenerative Cloister-Dome and the ID_room (bottom).

Where TLX and TLY are the top left coordinates of the bounding box of area we are interested in while BRX and BRY are the bottom right coordinates of the bounding box. Similar queries can be formulated also for temporal constraints. In the future, the system might be implemented as an updatable crowdsourced system.

Fig. 7. The GeoPAN APP (GeoDB Hub): the vault inventory of the Cremona Palaces entered in the Data Model and the vault DB queried for a specific building, ID_08, Palazzo Magio, Cremona (Italy), with a linked 3DHBIM model, and its DB contents.

5   Conclusions

The DB architecture developed can be tested and adapted on the base of the richness of documented vault systems or other construction elements and techniques. Being the methodology followed to its definition a bottom-up process, the database implements the elements for the main typologies of vault elements, including components, arrangements, properties and a new provisional taxonomy detailing the construction technologies and their related effects on the geometry. The GeoPAN APP allows to inherit the richness coming from the HBIM high level of detail connecting the different DB information across time and space with possibility of semantic queries giving back unexpected relationship among different vaults with regional widespread, thus contributing to increasing knowledge and rising awareness on the vault construction across Europe.

Acknowledgements. The research leading to the results of this paper is partially funded under the ICT Policy Support Programme (ICT PSP) as part of the Competitiveness and Innovation Framework Programme by the European Community (CIP) GA n°620400.

References

1. Pérouse de Montclos, J.M.: Philibert De l'Orme architecte du roi, pp. 1514–1570, Paris, Mengès (2000)
2. Palacios Gonzalo, J.C.: Trazas y cortes de cantería en el Renacimiento español. Ministerio de cultura, Instituto de conservacion y restauracion de bienes culturales, Madrid (1990)
3. Willis, R.: On the construction of the vaults of the middle ages. In: Transactions of the Royal Institute of British Architects, vol. 1, part 2, pp. 1–61. Longman, Brown, Green and Longmans, London (1842)
4. Wendland, D.: Lassaulx und der Gewölbebau mit Selbsttragenden Mauerschichten: Neumittelalterliche Architektur um 1825–1848. Imhof, Petersberg (2008)
5. Forni, M.: La cultura architettonica nella prima metà del Settecento: considerazioni ed ipotesi sulle relazioni con il quadro europeo. Ph.D. thesis, Politecnico di Milano (1993)
6. Piccoli, E.: Le strutture voltate nell'architettura civile a Torino, 1660–1720. In: Dardanello, G. (ed.) Sperimentare l'architettura. Guarini, Juvarra, Alfieri, Borra e Vittone, pp. 38–96. Fondazione CRT, Torino (2001)
7. Oreni, D., Brumana, R., Georgopoulos, A., Cuca, B.: HBIM for conservation and management of built heritage: towards a library of vaults and wooden beam floors. In: Grussenmeyer, P. (ed.) ISPRS Annals of Photogrammetry, Remote Sensing and Spatial Information Sciences, vol. II-5/W1, pp. 215–221. Copernicus Publications (2013)
8. Brumana, R., Condoleo, P., Grimoldi, A., Banfi, F., Landi, A.G., Previtali, M.: HR LOD based HBIM to detect influences on geometry and shape by stereotomic construction techniques of brick vaults. Appl. Geomat (2018). https://doi.org/10.1007/s12518-018-0209-3
9. Dear, M., Ketchum, J., Luria, S., Richardson, D.: Introducing the geohumanities. In: GeoHumanities, pp. 21–22. Routledge (2011)
10. Mazzetti, P., Latre, M.Á., Ernst, J., Brumana, R., Brauman, S., Nativi, S.: Virtual hubs for facilitating access to open data. In: EGU General Assembly Conference, vol. 17 (2015)
11. Previtali, M.: Geopan atl@s: a brokering based gateway to georeferenced historical maps for risk analysis. In: International Archives of the Photogrammetry, Remote Sensing and Spatial Information Sciences, vol. 42, no. 2W5, pp. 583–589 (2017)
12. Thesaurus of Geographic Names®: http://www.getty.edu/research/tools/vocabulary/tgn/ Getty, http://www.getty.edu/research/tools/vocabularies/aat/index.html. Accessed 7 Aug 2018
13. Dear, M., Ketchum, J., Luria, S., Richardson, D.: Introducing the geohumanities. In: GeoHumanities, pp. 21–22. Routledge (2011)
14. http://www.vh.energic-od.eu/. Accessed 7 Aug 2018

SCAN to HBIM-Post Earthquake Preservation: Informative Model as Sentinel at the Crossroads of Present, Past, and Future

Raffaella Brumana$^{(\boxtimes)}$ ⓘ, Stefano Della Torre ⓘ, Daniela Oreni ⓘ,
Lorenzo Cantini ⓘ, Mattia Previtali ⓘ, Luigi Barazzetti ⓘ,
and Fabrizio Banfi ⓘ

Department of Architecture, Built Environment and Construction Engineering,
Politecnico di Milano, Via Ponzio 31, 20133 Milan, Italy
{raffaella.brumana,stefano.dellatorre,daniela.oreni,
lorenzo.cantini,mattia.previtali,luigi.barazzetti,
fabrizio.banfi}@polimi.it

Abstract. In the last years it has been progressively invested many efforts in the cultural heritage digitization: surveying, modeling activities, diagnostic analysis and historic data collection of architectural heritage. Such actions have been mainly acquired for the preservation process, during the restoration and construction site. Unfortunately, many of them are left abandoned in a latent status without any connection with the long life cycle of the historic architectures or connection to the dissemination. The paper presents the case of an informative model for the Basilica di Collemaggio generated on high resolution surveying (laser scanning, photogrammetric point clouds and IRT Infrared Thermography) to manage the knowledge acquired on the geometry and the collected information on materials, construction technology and decay analysis for the design and conservation after the earthquake occurred at L'Aquila. The paper illustrates the HBIM (Heritage Building Information Model) achieved to support the restoration process funded by EniServizi within the project 'Restart from Collemaggio'. It is described the generative modelling process implemented to embody the complexity and specificity of the morphology related to the collected information on the state of the art, the sum of the current damages and transformations during the centuries, for the preservation plan of the monument. Many damaged structures as in the case of the north wall with the Holy Door and of the arched naves with the ancient pillars have been restored preserving the maximum level of authenticity of the materials and construction techniques. The HBIM of the Basilica, re-opened to the public on December 2017, is ready to a sentinel role among past present and future.

Keywords: HBIM · Informative models · Preservation · Generative modelling
Authenticity · Conservation plan · Materials · Open access · NURBS
DB · LOD · LOG · LOA · LOI

© Springer Nature Switzerland AG 2018
M. Ioannides et al. (Eds.): EuroMed 2018, LNCS 11196, pp. 39–51, 2018.
https://doi.org/10.1007/978-3-030-01762-0_4

1   Introduction

EniServizi (the Italian multi-national energy agency operating in many countries), after the earthquake that occurred at L'Aquila in April 2009, in December 2012 funded - with around 14 million euro - the project 'Ricominciare da Collemaggio' ('Restart from Collemaggio') to restore the Basilica di Collemaggio. On April 6th, 2009 at 3:32 a.m. an Earthquake (Richter Magnitude 5.9) struck L'Aquila (Central Italy). More than 10 billion euro of estimated damage, about 100 churches uninhabitable for the major collapses, along with thousands of historic buildings in the old town and surrounding hamlets. Among them, the Basilica di Collemaggio was significantly stricken (Fig. 1): the dome, the transept and triumphal arches collapsed with their pillars, and great damage occurred to the apses, to the pillars of the arched walls of the nave, and to the longitudinal north front with the 'Holy Door' [1]. EniServizi required an advanced HBIM based on "SCANtoBIM" process to address decision-making processes among the different actors involved in the preservation process, conscious of the potential role in the complex building and infrastructure.

The Basilica di Collemaggio is a famous medieval Romanesque masterpiece characterized by a dense history dating back on 1275-87 with many stratified interventions across the centuries. The project 'Restarting from Collemaggio'[1] has been undertaken and funded by EniServizi with the aim of giving new hope to the L'Aquila community: the project of restoration and preservation has been carried out together with the Superintendence Office of L'Aquila and a large scientific team of universities. The HBIM [2] has been carried on by integrating the laser scanning[2] [3] with the hands-on survey of the pillar ashlar[3] [4] and the support of the historical research[4]. The diagnostic phase with the material, construction technology and decay analysis has been carried on by the Conservation Plan[5]. The Basilica of Collemaggio has been re-opened to the public on December 2017 after the restoration undertaken between 2015-2017.

---

[1] The Superintendence Office carried on the restoration project with the scientific support of the Università degli Studi de L'Aquila, the Università La Sapienza di Roma, under the coordination of the Politecnico di Milano (Scientific Responsible Prof. Stefano Della Torre).

[2] The geometric surveying, HBIM and LOG/GOG contribution has been carried out by the Politecnico di Milano (Prof. R. Brumana) - Geomatics surveying research team (L. Barazzetti, F. Roncoroni, M. Previtali, B. Cuca), HBIM (F. Banfi) - ABClab GIcarus http://www.gicarus.polimi.it.

[3] The pillar ashlars surveying, interpretation and HBIM data integration, plan and section interpretation, has been carried out by Daniela Oreni (Politecnico di Milano), feeding the LOG F and G proposal.

[4] The historical research by the team of the Università La Sapienza Roma (Prof. G. Carbonara). The structural analysis under Polimi and the Università degli Studi de L'Aquila.

[5] The analysis of materials, decay and construction technologies for the Conservation Plan have been carried on by Lorenzo Cantini (Polimi) feeding the HBIM LOI, LOG F&G.

Fig. 1. The area stricken by the earthquake at L'Aquila and the Basilica di Collemaggio.

2   HBIM from Surveying: Geometries as Sentinels of the Past Transformation and Current Assets After the Earthquake

The surveys of the Basilica, started on February 2013, have been addressed to document the geometric and morphologic state of the art of the whole complex and its components (external walls, internal arched walls and the pillars, vaulted systems, trusses, wooden secondary order of the roof), as a result of the earthquake damages and transformation occurred across the centuries, enlargements, restorations, including the ones carried out after the past earthquakes. The objective of the survey was: (i) to support informed decision making devoted to guarantee the maximum level of material preservation, the structural functionality of the single elements and of the dynamic relations among themselves; (ii) to support a cooperative multi-disciplinary interaction through reliable geometric information, punctually surveyed, and geospatially correlated, with an high Level of Accuracy (LOA) comparable to a 1:20 scale. The geodetic network allowed to obtain a robust co-registration of the laser scanning point clouds integrated by the photogrammetric image blocks acquired along the surfaces, including the UAV RGB & IRT flight. The result is a rigorous reading of the out of plumbs starting from the external and internal sections, the different thickness of the vertical walls (Fig. 2).

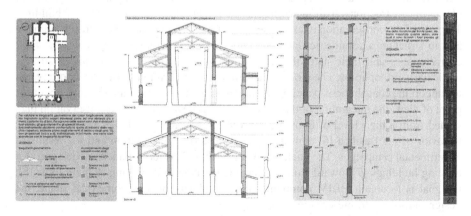

Fig. 2. The vertical sections of the Basilica highlighting the complex geometry of the damaged walls, punctually represented with the different out of plumbs and thickness ranges.

This approach represented the 'guide line' followed in the restitution phases, with a rich description of the anomalies and irregularities detecting the shapes of each object, the superimposition of the plans at the different levels evidencing the fragile structures standing on empty zones of the crypt in corresponding of the cracked apses. The surveying geometries can be considered as sentinels of the past transformation and current assets after the earthquake, of the history enriched by precious physical traces that can be at the disposal of the different actors to improve the comprehension for the present and future intervention and uses.

3 Conservation Plan: The Classification of the Traces of Masonry Structures and Construction Technologies

Given the main aim, which was to preserve the maximum level of material authenticity, functional behavior and construction techniques, HBIM generation of the Basilica needed to take into account the whole complex monument with all the structural components relating one to the others. The Conservation Plan has been developed to answer to the following issues: (i) an architectural design project supporting a decision-making process devoted to preservation aims, (ii) the management of critical issues regarding the preservation of authenticity of materials and construction techniques, and (iii) to guarantee safety in case of other earthquakes more severe with respect to the last occurred, at least equal to it. The classification of the traces of masonry structures, construction technologies, and the related decay analysis, are crucial for the design proposal [5]. The Basilica conserved several interventions characterizing its masonry structures, realized with a technological system based on roughly shaped stone blocks, revealing both minor and also profound changing during the long history of the building. All the traces of the repairing techniques applied to the damaged walls, performed on occasion of the frequent seismic events occurred to the church, are visible on its lateral elevations. The north façade shows different masonry textures, presenting a palimpsest of the main phases of construction, repair interventions and integrations experienced by the building. The role of the conservation plan was set for studying and classify these traces, with the aim to structure a parametric database, collecting information on the materials, their characteristics and their state of conservation, integrated with the advanced survey, particularly orthophotos. The model obtained by the application of BIM technology had to support the contributions developed through the conservation plan. From an operative point of view, the integration of the various analysis developed by the conservation plan started from a high level of knowledge produced by previous studies on the dynamic behavior of the Basilica [6] considering both historical information and the results of experimental campaigns. The challenge was to adapt BIM tools, which are designed for existing buildings [7] toward Built Heritage Conservation deploying shaping tools [8]: the goal is to obtain HBIM combining the complexity of the geometrical shape, the design purposes and preservation aims.

3.1 The Holy Door and the North Wall: The Database and the Materials Analysis Integrated to the HBIM

The damaged north wall with the Holy Door represents an important symbol to be preserved for the future. The analysis and the intervention aimed to guarantee its preservation. The Basilica attracts about 30,000 people for the Forgiveness Feast Day (Festa della Perdonanza) on 28-29th August (Fig. 3) established every year by the Pope Celestino V (before the Jubilee - 'Giubileum' - set up by Pope Bonifacio VIII nowadays recurring in the world every 25 years). The Feast is celebrated with the procession ceremony transferring the original Bull from the Municipality to the Holy Door of the Basilica. The result is an extraordinary mix of tangible and intangible values; the design and the intervention intended to preserve and transfer them to the future.

Fig. 3. The opening of the Holy Door during the Forgiveness Feast procession: the provisional structure to put in safety people during the restoration (August 2017).

The metric surveying highlighted the geometry of external walls and arched internal wall. The punctual out of plumbs and profiles have been extracted from the scans. The detailed categorization of each masonry texture constituted the base for recognizing the values collected on this part of the church. The stratifications of different masonry textures, visible on the north wall, testify the changings and the new additions occurred to the building during the time. If the traces of closed large windows are clearly recognizable, a precise representation of the various masonry typologies was realized on the 3D orthophotos thanks to the level of details (pixel resolution 1 mm) with the materials analysis, decays mapping and the intervention subdivided into specific actions (cleaning, sealing and protection phases). To this aim a database containing all the masonry textures classified, with an ID code, a short description, their dating, the material components, dimensions and main proportions, the surface finishing, the picture documentation and the masonry layout was structured (Fig. 4). The geometrical mapping of the Basilica has been integrated together with the DB within the HBIM (Fig. 5). The material decays and the analysis of the crack pattern of the north façade supported the further research on the correct interventions. The advanced survey provided important results for peculiar aspects, like the analysis of the out of plumb of the masonry walls, which are considered another important index of the vulnerability in seismic conditions.

The positive response offered by the masonry structures to the seismic actions indicated that the modifications occurred to the church during the time, after other earthquakes, gave origin to a reliable structural system, able to face the dynamic deformations imposed by the ground acceleration. According to this statement, supported by further evaluations of the dynamic behaviour of the building realized by integrating the 3D model with qualitative and quantitative results obtained by various analysis, the conservative intervention for the north façade and the Holy door was organized. The lack of connection between the decorative elements and the load bearing walls was reinforced by limited interventions (like the introduction of metal connectors) and the vulnerability between some parts repaired in the past was corrected by implementing the monolithic behaviour of the entire walls through local injections and metal bars strengthening.

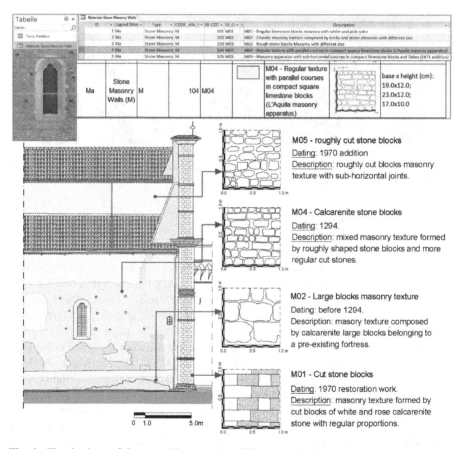

Fig. 4. The database of the materials: a portion of the north façade, with the material mapping drawing obtained on the 3D orthophoto, and the detailed description of some masonry textures according to the historical analysis of the building.

4 HBIM Generative Modelling: LOD (LOG + LOI) for Preservation Purposes

It is nowadays recognized by different researches carried out in the last years that BIM can take a rule in a holistic organization of models and information, needing to define a framework for the HBIM, considering the 'specific' case of documentation of architectural heritage [9] and its preservation [4]. BIM adoption required to be turned to the preservation aims, with a deeper level of knowledge since the starting phase of the design [8], restoration and management process, developing a coherent level of accuracy model matching the complexity [2] of the architectural heritage. The concept of the Level of Development (LOD) has been applied to the BIM management in the case of new construction, thus based on a linear process progressively enriching both the model and the information across the different phases (AIA, AEC, NBS): LOD100 (conceptual a-dimensional model), LOD 300 (three-dimensional model in the design phases), LOD350-400 (the model implemented for the construction site), LOD500 (the as-built updating, thus oriented to manage all the information useful for the maintenance process of the building in the time, including the layers stratigraphy). Such linear approach cannot be automatically applied to the restoration-preservation-management process: it risks to delay the knowledge of the geometry, the state of the art and behavior of the structures with high cost increasing during the process due to unexpected framework; also, lack of information limits the possibility to undertaking design solutions coherent with the state of the art, and the preservation actions.

The Level of Geometry (LOG) and the Level of Information (LOI) – part of the LOD concept (UNI 11337-4/2016)- have been further defined in the HBIM specification criteria in order to match the preservation aims. The research undertaken developed a mixed and reverse LOD approach [10], based on the accurate 3D surveys [3] feeding the HBIM since the first architectural design phases (Fig. 5). In particular, a high resolution Level of Geometry model was generated and enriched by 3D arrangement texturing and by the information on the stratigraphic layers (materials, decay, chronological phasing). The concept of GOGs (Grade of Generation) [10] protocols have been introduced to describe different modelling requirements (Level of Geometry), in function of the geometry detected by the scans. Mainly, for the damaged walls, pillars and vaults, a NURBS based GOG 9 (edge border detection and internal dense slicing from the cloud) and GOG 10 (edge border and point clouds) has been generated for each element, gaining a morphological accuracy of the model (Level of Accuracy - LOA of the model) coherent with the surveying LOA. Hereafter a summary of the HBIM phases (Fig. 5) in the generative modeling workflow:

- Phase 1: Geometric primitives determination.
- Phase 2: Level of Geometry (LOG) – GOG 1-8 vs. GOG 9-10. The analysis of the geometrical irregularities detected by the survey lead to the selection of the proper GOG. For example, vertical walls with a standard deviation respect to the planarity check ≥ 25 mm (the tolerance of the survey), or out of plumb ≥ 25 mm; and pillars, vault elements or others component with a standard deviation respect to the generative conceptual solids ≥ 20 mm, needs GOG 9-10 and NURBS based

objects modelling. GOG 1-8 have been adopted for a standard deviation of the clouds respect to the conceptual solids $< 2.0 \div 2.5$ cm.

- Phase 3: Automatic Verification System (AVS). The verification of the accuracy of the modelled object concerning the point cloud. With NURBS modelling a final standard deviation concerning the cloud points ≤ 2 mm was achieved
- Phase 4: BIM parameterization of the NURBS model and Database (DB) generation integrating the LOI gained by the material and decay analysis.

The HBIM obtained is the sum of each element (Fig. 5) modelled in function of its geometry. It is interoperable with the construction site management (CO.SI.M), with the finite element analysis (BIM-to-FEA) [11], Design Tools, and Conservation Plan purposes, thus contributing lowering the impact cost of the HBIM generation (Fig. 6).

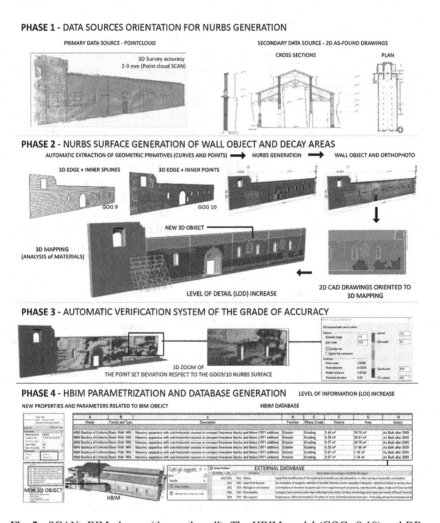

Fig. 5. SCANtoBIM phases: (the north wall). The HBIM model (GOGs 9-10) and DB.

5   The Preservation of the Damaged Pillars of the Arched Nave

The main damages observed on the building were concentrated on the pillars of the naves and the walls of the apses. The transept, completely collapsed, conserved only a portion of the lateral walls with their Baroque style altars. The philosophy of the intervention was based on this main assumption: conservation could be applied to the survived damaged structures, whereas the no-more existing transept had to be integrated by the realization of the missing volumes of the building. The juxtaposition of new architectural bodies to existing ones is always a controverted issue, involving discussion on the preservation of the authenticity of a historic building and its safety response.

The introduction of an integration for connecting the naves body of the Basilica with the apse was used here as a strategic design for providing a new resistant element, able to reinforce the global dynamic behavior of the building to seismic actions. This sort of strong backdrop is realized by a contemporary reinforced concrete technology and shaped according to the geometrical information collected by the historical analysis. The analysis applied to the pillars consisted in a first classification of the materials, distinguished in structural blocks and integrations added during the last restoration designed by Mario Moretti in the second half of the previous century. The analysis of

WALL	INTERNAL SPACE VOLUME	WALL VOLUME	GROSS FLOOR AREA	TIME REQUIRED BIM GENERATION BY GOG 2013 (GOG 9-GOI 1-2) & 2017 (GOG 10-GOI 1-2)	TIME REQUIRED BIM GENERATION BY TRADITIONAL PROCESS (GOG 9)	LEVEL OF DETAIL (LOD)	REF. HBIM OBJECTS
	m³	m³	m²	(Hours - h)	(Hours- h)		
MAIN FACADE	/	1274	/	30h, 2013 & 15h, 2017	35-40	300	
TOWER	929	190	LEV.01+02=140	6h, 2013 & 2h,2017	10-12	300	
NORTH WALL	/	1141	/	20h, 2013 & 3h,2017	30-35	500	
SOUTH WALL	/	941	/	8h, 2013 & 3h,2017	12-15	500	
INTERNAL NORTH WALL ARCHES	/	537	/	20h, 2013 & 3h,2017	12-15	500	
INTERNAL SOUTH WALL ARCHES	/	460	/	15h, 2013 & 6h,2017	20-25	500	
BELL TOWER	437	180	LEV.01+02=25	20h, 2013 & 15h,2017	25-30	400	
APSE WALLS	11491	1790	LEV.01=823	60h, 2013 & 25h,2017	70-80	500	
APSE VAULTS	/	160-190	/	50h, 2013 & 20h,2017	60-70	500	
CRYPT	977	250	LEV.00=336 LEV.01=280	60h, 2013 & 20h,2017	50-60	400	
ROOF	36987	7244	LEV.01=2194	120h, 2013 & 50h,2017	130-140	500	
TOT.	51 000~	14 000~	3798~	409h~, 2013 162h~,2017	522~		

Fig. 6. The HBIM NURBS based model objects (volumes and hours effort). On the right, the case of restored north wall with the BIM to FEA (Finite Element Analysis).

the diffused crack pattern characterizing the pillars received fundamental support by the detailed analysis of the out of plumb of each structure, combined with the manual measurements of each stone component that allows recognizing the masonry section characteristics. This approach drove to an in-depth knowledge of the real extension of the damage of each pillar and drove to the final decision: conservation with local repairing interventions for almost all the pillars and reconstruction limited to two pillars, due to their damage condition. Unfortunately, it was not possible to analyze the inner core of the pillars directly, due to the reduced safety of the structure. The ultrasonic investigation had been performed in a first phase, but these tests did not give a significant response on the nature of the inner core, because of the diffused cracks influencing the velocity of the signals and its distribution maps in the plane sections. Thanks to an hands-on survey of all the pillar ashlars it was hypothesized an average of 35% of damaged ashlars (yellow) to be necessarily substituted during the intervention, in the consciousness that this percentage would undoubtedly increase during the works (Fig. 7). The analysis of the compressive strengths required a careful choice of the new stones. The hypothesis was to substitute damaged ashlars with new ones, with the same external shape and dimensions but prolonged to replace all the angle of the central core, there-fore strengthening the section anyway. The HBIM LOD500 obtained embodies out of plumbs, geometry with the 3D ashlars elements (Fig. 7). The careful survey aimed at enabling the control of local repair works, avoiding or minimizing the total dismantle of pillars. In the design step the decision, based on the lack of confidence on the quality of the inner core, was to disassemble only the most damaged pillars, also exposed to the highest actions in case of an earthquake.

AS-DESIGNED BIM FOR THE RESTORATION OF THE DAMAGED PILLARS

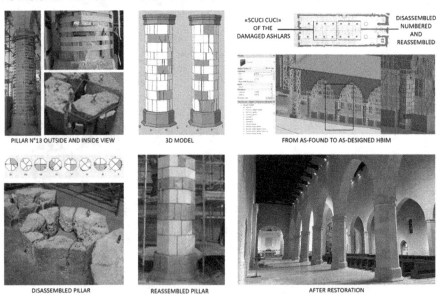

Fig. 7. The hypothesized HBIM design and the restoration of the most damaged pillars. (Color figure online)

6 HBIM for ALL: AS-FOUND to aS-BUILT, and Beyond

The detailed surveying of the plan of the Basilica highlighted different alignments within the Basilica (Fig. 8), particularly among the portion represented by the apse and the crashed domes with the first pillars and the part of the naves with the 12 pillars. The historical research report carried out [12] together with the geometric analysis contributed to reconstruct the different transformation occurred in the different chronological phases. Such analysis have been taken into account in the various design solutions for the HBIM design simulation (Fig. 8):

1. a solution with the reconstruction of the crashed dome (built in the seventies by Moretti during the restoration);
2. a solutions with the rebuilding of a dome on pendentives and a groined vault;
3. a solution with the wooden trusses and coverage of the naves and transept. The final decision of the wooden coverage solution remembers the first implant of the Basilica dating back to the 'Angevin' period.

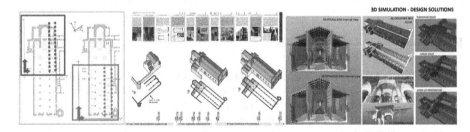

Fig. 8. The AS-FOUND BIM with the different geometric alignments of two portions highlighting the transformations occurred (left): the historical research (G. Carbonara ©) with concept model and timeline (centre); the AS-DESIGNED BIM coverage solutions (right).

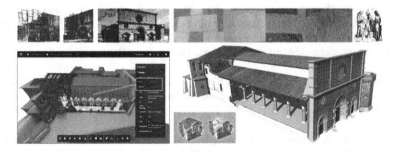

Fig. 9. BIM OUT for ALL: MR enriched by BIM open access information

7 Conclusions

On the lesson learnt, the current Codification criteria (UNI11337-2009) has been updated with the UNI11337-4-2016: for HBIM adoption a draft proposal is on course of definition with the new LOG-LOI F&G levels (UNI11337-3-2017) on the restoration and maintenance domain, requiring morphologic complexity in the HBIM models (besides the conceptual structural models), as-built updating, and the monitoring during the times. Transferring the HBIM richness into the Life Cycle Management process will contribute to lower the initial HBIM model costs spreading its usability after the restoration process, taking in account the knowledge and information gained. An Open Access HBIM can represent a bridge toward Mixed Reality (Fig. 9): historical transformations, DBs, documents, the different materials and masonry texture in the past intervention and recent restorations (i.e. the façade after the earthquake of 1915). Memory of the past through the present toward the future.

The HBIM delivered is now at the crossroads of entering into the phase of forgetfulness, or it can play the critical role of a precious witness into the future being, transferring the richness of such virtual informed model to the people, tourists, citizens and future actors involved in the maintenance management. HBIM Open access is ready to be tested and to be harvested within Europeana networks in order to enhance the portability of the information gained and to share them with other case studies within a space-temporal framework: this will allow the comparison of masonry texture, history of material finishing and skilled workers across space and time.

References

1. Gattulli, V., Antonacci, E., Vestroni, F.: Field Observations and Failure Analysis of the Basilica S. Maria di Collemaggio after the 2009 L'Aquila Earthquake, Engineering Failure Analysis (2013). http://dx.doi.org/10.1016/j.engfailanal.2013.01.020
2. Brumana, R., Della Torre, S., Oreni, D., Previtali, M., Cantini, L., Barazzetti, L., Franchi, A., Banfi, F.: HBIM challenge among the paradigm of complexity, tools and preservation: the Basilica di Collemaggio 8 years after the earthquake. Int. Arch. Photogramm. Remote. Sens. Spat. Inf. Sci. – ISPRS Arch. 42, 97–104 (2017). https://doi.org/10.5194/isprs-archives-XLII-2-W5-97-2017
3. Barazzetti, L., Banfi, F., Brumana, R., Previtali, M.: Creation of parametric BIM objects from point clouds using. Photogramm. Rec. 30(152), 339–362 (2015)
4. Oreni, D., Brumana, R., Della Torre, S., Banfi, F., Barazzetti, L., Previtali, M.: Survey turned into HBIM: the restoration and the work involved concerning the Basilica di Collemaggio after the earthquake (L'Aquila). ISPRS Ann. Photogramm. Remote. Sens. Spat. Inf. Sci. 2 (5), 267–273 (2014)
5. Cantini, L., De Ponti, R., Massari, G., Binda, L.: Effect of misuse and lack of maintenance on a historical building. In: proceedings of the 4th International Conference on Structural Defects and Repair (CINPAR 2008), 25–28 June 2008, Aveiro (2008). ISBN 978-989-95695-3-9
6. Antonacci, E., Beolchini, G., Di Fabio, F., Gattulli, V.: The dynamic behaviour of the Basilica S. Maria of Collemaggio. In: 2001 2nd International Congress on Studies in Ancient Structures (2001)
7. Volk, R., Stengel, J., Schultmann, F.: Building information modeling (BIM) for existing buildings. Autom. Constr. 38, 109–127 (2014)
8. Della Torre, S.: Shaping tools for Built Heritage Conservation: from architectural design to program and management. Learning from Distretti culturali. Van Balen, K., et al., Community Involvement in Heritage, pp. 93–102 (2015)

9. Fai, S., Sydor, M.: Building information modeling and the documentation of architectural heritage: between the 'typical' and the 'Specific'. In: Allison, G., et al. (eds.) Digital Heritage, vol. 1, pp. 731–734. IEEE (2013). CFP1308 W-USBISBN: 978-1-4799-3169-9

10. Banfi, F.: BIM orientation: grades of generation and information for different type of analysis and management process. Int. Arch. Photogramm. Remote. Sens. Spat. Inf. Sci. **42** (2/W5), 57–64 (2017). https://doi.org/10.5194/isprs-archives-XLII-2-W5-57-2017

11. Barazzetti, L., Banfi, F., Brumana, R., Gusmeroli, G., Previtali, M., Schiantarelli, G.: Cloud-to-BIM-to-FEM: structural simulation with accurate historic BIM from laser scans. Simul. Model. Pract. Theory **57**, 71–87 (2015). https://doi.org/10.1016/j.simpat.2015.06.004

12. Carbonara, G., Vivio, B.A., Mancini, R.: L'Aquila: Santa Maria di Collemaggio. Storia e restauri. Aracne Editrice, in c.d.s (on course of publication) (2017)

Towards the Definition of Workflows for Automation in HBIM Generation

Mattia Previtali[(⊠)] and Fabrizio Banfi

Department of Architecture, Built Environment and Construction Engineering,
Politecnico di Milano, Via Ponzio 31, 20133 Milan, Italy
{mattia.previtali, fabrizio.banfi}@polimi.it

Abstract. In the last years creation of as-built Building Information Modelling (BIM), and Historic Building Information Modelling (HBIM) in particular, has become a widely researched topic. In particular, the so-called "Scan.-to-BIM" procedure has received a lot of attention. This is mainly given by the fact that nowadays, terrestrial laser scanning (TLS), either static and mobile, and 3D photogrammetry are quite popular techniques to acquire building geometry raw data. However, turning a set of scans into a BIM model is still a labor-intensive and manual work. This paper presents two workflows for increasing the automation in HBIM generation. The presented approaches differ in the level of automation achieved and in the level of maturity. Indeed, while the first one presents a higher level of automation it is designed only to work in the case straight geometrical features are dominant in the scene (i.e., Manhattan world assumption holds). In addition, it is currently implemented in Matlab. On the other hand, the second one is closer to semi-automated modelling since some manual operations are still needed. However, it is implemented as a Revit Plug-in and for this reason it is more user-friendly.

Keywords: HBIM · Automation · Segmentation · Point cloud
Add-in

1 Introduction

In the last years creation of as-built Building Information Modelling (BIM), and Historic Building Information Modelling (HBIM) in particular, has become a widely researched topic. For historical buildings, as-found information concerning building geometry is often sparse, not accurate/updated or even missing. For this reason, the availability of a solid geometrical model is fundamental for other analysis like the definition of a conservation plan, restoration works planning, etc. In particular, the so-called "Scan.-to-BIM" procedure has received a lot of attention. This is mainly given by the fact that nowadays, terrestrial laser scanning (TLS), either static and mobile, and 3D photogrammetry are quite popular techniques to acquire raw data of a building geometry. This achievement was boosted by significant advances both in scanning technology and automated processing of images. Many issues, which were underlined in the past as critical in laser scanning, like effortful data acquisition and registration, nowadays are no more a problem due to an increase in automation of such phases. The

© Springer Nature Switzerland AG 2018
M. Ioannides et al. (Eds.): EuroMed 2018, LNCS 11196, pp. 52–63, 2018.
https://doi.org/10.1007/978-3-030-01762-0_5

reduction of instrumental cost also boosted static laser scanning in new fields. Mobile and handheld laser scanning systems (MLS) were also developed to speed up the acquisition phase using Simultaneous Localization and Mapping (SLAM) technology. Even if the accuracy of MLS is generally worst with respect to the one of TLS their higher productivity is an important advantage that allowed such platform to gain popularity. Finally, the availability of commercial software packages with a high level of automation both in the image orientation and in dense matching steps determined a new youth to photogrammetry. Even if TLS or MLS may provide reliable as-found information with a few hours (or days) of surveying operations, they are providing just raw data (point clouds) that are generally not suitable for any real application. For this purpose, a time-consuming work in needed to derive a consistent 3D model of the buildings starting from them. This procedure is still mainly manual and skilled operators are requested to turn raw point cloud into a ready-to-use BIM product. To reduce the time needed for the production of "as-found" BIM, the topic of increasing the automation of the building reconstruction pipeline starting from point clouds has been paid a lot of attention in the literature in the last years [1, 2]. However, point clouds acquired from real-world commonly feature several properties that may pose severe challenges for any algorithm designed to extract information from the raw data. The different approaches developed generally subdivide the "Scan-to-BIM" problem into four specific steps: scan preprocessing, segmentation of the point cloud, classification of detected objects and final reconstruction of the BIM model. The aim of scan preprocessing is to re-organize data to increase computational efficiency, like organizing point cloud into a k-dimensional tree (k-d tree). The preprocessed point cloud is then segmented into a set of primitives (using specific criteria); next step is the classification of detected segments by using frameworks exploiting local and contextual information. Finally, labelled segments are used to combine parameters (both geometry and semantic) for the reconstruction of the BIM model using specific reconstruction algorithms. Another important bottleneck of the "Scan-to-BIM" procedure is connected to the fact that BIM modelling tools were initially designed for the design and maintenance of new constructions and not for historical building. The adaptation BIM software and tools to this latter category of buildings pose some important challenges, e.g., the lack of free-form modelling instruments in commercial BIM software packages; the low level of usability of existing tools in the case of historical constructions, etc. All those aspects boosted the research to find solutions and workaround with commercial software. In particular, several procedures and protocols were defined in order to combine modelling tools with parametric software [3, 4]. However, still lacks the definition of a systematic workflow for semi-automated and guided "Scan-to-BIM" modelling capitalizing the previously listed research. In this paper, we are presenting two workflows for increasing the automation in HBIM generation. The first one (Sect. 3) presents a higher level of automation but it is designed only to work in the case straight geometrical features are dominant (i.e., Manhattan world assumption). On the other hand, the second workflow (Sect. 4) is based on a semi-automated modelling. Main contributions presented in this paper are:

- implementation of segmentation methodology for point clouds acquired in historical buildings;

- definition of a hierarchical semantic object classification technique based on first-order logic sentences;
- development of a Revit Plug.in whose aim is to implement a semi-automated procedure for HBIM production.

2 Related Work

As previously anticipated point clouds are nowadays widely diffused as the starting point for as-built BIM reconstruction. This procedure is referred to as "Scan-to-BIM" and it is currently mainly labour-intensive and manual. For this reason, several works in literature are currently focusing on this subject [5, 6]. Presented approaches are generally based on a multi-step architecture. The main phases are: (i) segmentation of the unstructured point cloud; (ii) semantic classification of detected elements, (iii) feature detection and clustering, (iv) creation of the model combining geometry and semantic information. In some cases the order of this phase can vary between different approaches or some steps can be performed simultaneously. This paper is mainly addressing the first two topics. Point cloud segmentation is generally defined as the process aimed at grouping similar points. The similarity between points can be related both to geometrical aspect and/or other related attributes like intensity or colour. The segmentation procedure can be designed to introduce some level of organization to data [7], or as a first step in object recognition and model fitting [8]. In the past decades, various techniques have been designed to extract surfaces from point clouds. They can be mainly grouped as [9]: (i) region growing, (ii) model-based methods, (iii) edge-based detection, (iv) and machine learning. In region growing methods [10, 11] it is assumed that neighbouring points presents (present similar characteristics (either geometrical or radiometric). Generally, region growing methods are a combination of two steps. Firstly, a "seed" is identified as a starting point for the following "growing" phase. Model-based methods [12, 13] assumes that man-made objects can be decomposed into geometric primitives. Starting from this, points conforming to a defined primitive are grouped as belonging to the same cluster. Identification of geometric primitives is generally performed by using robust estimators like RANSAC, MLESAC, MSAC, PROSAC, etc. As described by [14], edge-based segmentation algorithms [15] can be seen as the combination of two different steps. In the first one, the border of each surface is identified while in the second one points inside the detected boundaries are grouped into different regions. In machine learning applications, a trainer takes advantages of some examples to infer the underlying probability distribution of the characteristics of interests (features). Staring from this the trained operator can be used to take decisions for point cloud classification. Definition of features play an important role in these problems and their definition is one of the main bottlenecks Semantic classification is generally the second step of automated "Scan-to-BIM" procedure. Each extracted cluster or segment derived by the first step is processed to compute its class labels (e.g., wall, floor, ceiling, etc.). Classification is generally performed by taking into consideration a set of features (e.g., geometrical, radiometric, etc.) and contextual information (e.g., neighbouring relationship) [16].

Classification can be performed either using heuristics or machine learning approaches. Heuristic methods [17] are taking into consideration some knowledge about the characteristics of the building objects to derive classification rules. Heuristics do not require intensive learning or large data sets in order to compute the class of an observation. However, heuristics may be biased and are often case specific. Machine learning approaches methods relies on training phase to set up a discriminant criteria among object classes. A second possibility for speeding up the modelling pipeline is the development is the development of specific add-ins clustering set of commands available in commercial software. In recent years, the diffusion of Add-ins has allowed the implementation of specific commands for modelling software such as Autodesk Revit and Mc Neel Rhinoceros with the aim to extend specific internal functionality. In particular, the development of the software's internal functions has made it possible to improve the modelling and the generation of BIM-based energy/structural analyses and the related production of schedules, databases and material computing. Most of the time, the diffusion of these additional modules for modelling applications takes place through the main web service platforms such as *Autodesk App Store* [18] and *Food4Rhino* [19]. The main apps downloaded for Autodesk Revit are mainly oriented to three categories such as (1) *Reality capture/animation/rendering* like, Lumion® LiveSync® by Act-3D [20] and BIMobject by BIMobject® Corporation [21]; (2) *Interoperability* in which it is possible to download Import/Export contents to other software like Excel by Virtual construction and technology BIM One Inc [22], IFC 2017 and on by Autodesk, Inc [23] and 3DWarehouse-For-Revit ™ by AMC Bridge; (3) *Structural Simulation & Analysis* like Structural Analysis Toolkit 2018 and Advance Steel 2018 Extension and on by Autodesk, Inc [24]. On the other hand, the most downloaded add-ins in Food4Rhino are Kangaroo Physics [25], Lunchbox [26], and Grasshopper ® [27]. The latter is a graphical algorithm editor tightly integrated with Rhino's 3D modelling tools and allow the creation of complex shapes using generative algorithms. Unlike RhinoScript, Grasshopper requires no knowledge of programming or scripting, but still allows designers to build form generators from the simple to the awe-inspiring. In order to automating repetitive tasks in Autodesk Revit, Dynamo add-in has been developed to create scripts that can explore complex design problems and simplify BIM work modelling flows [28]. In particular, thanks to an extremely flexible open source visual programming environment, Dynamo allows the composition of customized algorithms (procedures or formulas to solve problems) to process data and create geometries through a block graphical interface (nodes). However, based on a series of generative tests, both solutions have been discarded because they are not able to create BIM object with the direct management of laser scanning scans. For this reason, the second part of this study (development of a semi-automatic SCAN to BIM add-in) avoided the implementation of the generative process of simple/complex models through the integration of Grasshopper® and Dynamo into Autodesk Revit. The most suitable solution was the application of the grades of generation (GOG) described in a previous study applied to the generation of H-BIM [29]. The choice of the method was mainly based on three factors: (1) grades of generation GOG 9 and 10 allow better levels of automation in the generation of SCAN to BIM, (2) the grade of accuracy (GOA) reached is about 1/2 mm (deviation value between

BIM object and point cloud), (3) Revit API libraries permit the integrations of the GOGs into Autodesk Revit's add-in and improve the modeling of complex objects.

3   Data-Driven Automated Classification

The data-driven approach is aimed at detecting building features (e.g., walls, roof, ceilings, etc.) from TLS data. In a first stage, planar entities are detected in the row point cloud by means of a hybrid segmentation strategy and the geometric modelling of the building is accomplished. In particular, in this step detected elements are turned into simple geometric entities like lines and polygons. In a second stage, detected elements are classified into building objects.

3.1   Point Cloud Segmentation

As previously anticipated one of the most important steps in an automated "Scan-to-BIM" pipeline is the segmentation problem. One of the main problems connected to this task is the presence of noise and clutter in the data. For the segmentation step was can define as "noise" not only the instrumental noise but also all objects that are not of interest to the definition of the building geometry like furniture and moving people.

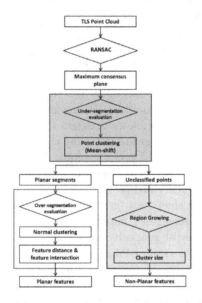

Fig. 1. Workflow of the segmentation process for historical building indoors.

The approach presented in this paper is an adaptation to historical buildings of the model-based method developed for façade segmentation that has been presented in a previous paper [30], see workflow in Fig. 1. The choice of a model based method is supported by a set of reasons: (i) model-based methods are less influenced by noise with respect to region growing, (ii) parameter governing the output are directly connected to geometrical characteristics of the building and (iii) in contrast to machine learning no training is requested. Traditional approaches using model-based assumption general face some bad-segmentation problem, either over-segmentation or under-segmentation. This is motivated by at least two fundamental aspects: (i) model based methods generally do not take into consideration topological information and (ii) model based algorithms only measures the consensus with respect to a geometrical model and do not take into consideration architectural priors. In order to partially cope with those problems, a modified RANSAC-based algorithm was developed to adapt model-based segmentation to face real-world problems. In particular, the developed segmentation approach is a hybrid approach that combining the robustness of RANSAC and the spatial (topological) information that is generally associated with region growing methods. Indeed, the developed approach firstly identifies the maximum consensus by using RANSAC and in a second stage classifies and groups the points by using a bottom-up clustering strategy in order to prevent under-segmentation problems. Even if an unstructured points clouds there is not a topological relationship between points we can assume that in a real-world scene points belonging to the same object should be sufficiently close to one another while points belonging to different objects should be separated by a spatial gap. For this reason, a mean shift clustering approach is adopted to cluster the different group of points. Results obtained in this way generally present a slight over-segmentation. To reduce this problem once all features are detected a grouping of the clusters is carried out to group together similar features. Object clustering is performed by evaluating three parameters: (i) similarity of normal vectors; (ii) perpendicular distance between planes; and (iii) intersection between clusters. In particular, two steps are carried out: (i) the whole group of detected segments are clustered by using the mean shift clustering algorithm using similarity of normal vectors; (ii) the perpendicular distance between features classified as different object is evaluated and if this distance is lower than the user-defined RANSAC threshold and the convex hulls of the point clusters intersects, they are recognized as a single object and merged together. In particular, the developed RANSAC strategy is used to identify planar objects (e.g. walls, floors, sidewalls, etc.) the remaining points are classified using a region growing method and grouped into objects using a strategy similar to the one previously described to cluster objects and prevent under-segmentation. Only objects whose dimension is larger than a user-defined threshold are kept as a real object while the remaining clusters are rejected and classified as "noise".

3.2 Hierarchical Semantic Object Classification

One of the main aspects of BIM model is their semantic characterization. For this reason, the classification and the annotation with their identity labels (e.g., 'wall') of features detected at the previous step is one of the main important points to boost the automation in the "Scan-to-BIM" pipeline. To perform such a classification a hierarchic object classification was designed starting from the consideration that each building feature has a number of attributes, which are similar within the same feature type and different with respect to other features. Similarly, also spatial relations between different features can be used in the classification. The main features addressed in this paper are summarized in Table 1.

Table 1. Parameters used in data processing.

Features		Spatial relationship	
Class	Parameter(s)	Class	Parameter(s)
Size	- Length - With - Area - Volume	Intersection	- Intersection of the bounding box
Orientation	- Normal direction of the fitting plane	Angle	- Parallelism and orthogonality between normal direction of the fitting plane
Position	- Height with respect to the lowest element	Inside	- Intersection of the bounding box

All these information about feature attributes can be formulated in terms of first-order logic to define the initial rules of the knowledge base classification. For example, a wall (f_1) can be defined as a large vertical element above the floor (f_2) and perpendicular to it:

$$\forall f_1 IsType(f, Wall)$$
$$\Rightarrow IsLarge\ (f) \land IsVertical(f) \land \exists f_2\ IsAbove(f_1, f_2) \land IsPerpendicular(f_1, f_2) \land IsType(f_2, Floor)$$

Similarly an window 'window' (f_1) is an intrusion of the wall (f_2) parallel to the wall and contained into the wall itself:

$$\forall f_1 IsType(f_1, Window)$$
$$\Rightarrow \exists f_2 \neg IsOut\ (f_1, f_2) \land IsParallel(f_1, f_2)\ ) \land IsInsideO(f_1, f_2) \land IsType(f_2, WallFacade)$$

In particular, for indoors the classification starts with evaluating both area and position of any detected objects. First, floor and ceiling are detected because both of them are horizontal (or pseudo horizontal) object. The first is characterized by lower height while the latter at the highest level. Walls are vertical objects that are in between ceiling and floor. Finally, windows and doors are detected. Indeed, while doors are classified in correspondence of gaps into walls that are connected to the floor, windows are characterized by gaps into walls that are not connected to the floor.

3.3 Examples

The presented segmentation and classification procedure was tested on a couple of data sets named 'Salone' and 'Volta ad ombrello'. The two datasets consist of approximately 36 million points for 'Volta ad ombrello' and approximately 42 million points for 'Salone'. Those data sets were acquired with a static terrestrial laser scanner namely Faro Focus 3D.

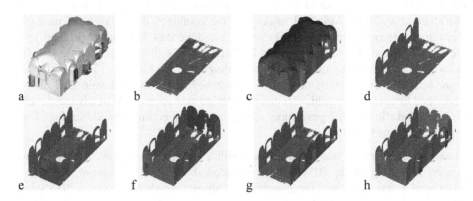

Fig. 2. 'Salone' data set. Original data (a) and results of the classification: floor (b), ceiling (c), walls (d–g) and windows (h).

The parameters used for the segmentation are summarized in Table 2 while results are shown in Figs. 2 and 3 for the two data sets.

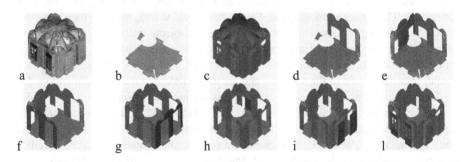

Fig. 3. 'Volta ad ombrello' data set. Original data (a) and results of the classification: floor (b), ceiling (c), walls (d–g) and doors (h–l).

Table 2. Parameters used in data processing.

Parameter	Value
RANSAC plane threshold (ε)	1 cm
RANSAC normal threshold (α)	30°
Mean shift clustering threshold (β)	1 cm

4 Revit Add-in for Semi-automated Modelling

The developed add-in structure is composed of four families able to interact with each other. Each family consists of (i) internal functions present in Revit, (ii) functions implemented by Revit APIs and finally (iii) the combined development of multiple Revit tools. Internal Revit functions, tools and functions have been recalled and hierarchized to simply the generation of as-found and as-built models. Autodesk Revit is known for the difficulty of activating modelling tools and functions. The first reason is the lack of a user-friendly interface for advanced functions. The main goal of the developed Plug-in was to achieve a more simplified activation mode of advanced tools such as automatic database generation, schedules and computing. The add-in (Fig. 4) is divided into four families.

Scan Management. It was intended to facilitate the import of point clouds and to support its setting of the BIM project in Autodesk Revit. As is known, Revit has introduced a few years ago the possibility of displaying point clouds in 3D digital space. Once the point clouds have been imported, it is not possible to apply GOG 9-10 directly. To bridge this gap, the key idea was to combine multiple functions that make point clouds more manageable. In particular, the main one was designed to help the user to the correct inserting point clouds in Revit without losing the correct geo-referencing of laser scanning scans, facilitating BIM project setup operations.

Modelling (GOGs). This section integrates the GOGs, (from 1 to 10) in the software structure through the direct activation of the main BIM objects such as wall, roof, floor and ceiling. The choice to include these types of objects was dictated by their great use in SCAN to BIM projects. The other categories of objects such as a door, window, scale and supplies have not been inserted in order to manage only the 3D wall generation in the modelling section. The functions associated with them can be retrieved from the main interface of the software and are easily linked to the objects developed in the developed add-in. The main objective of this section was to support the user with a user-friendly guide oriented to the creation of SCAN to BIM models. In particular, for this section, it was found that the APIs for the development of modelling tools were not made available by Autodesk, thus preventing the implementation of the modelling limitations available in the Revit default interface. To bridge this gap, the writing of SCAN to BIM protocols has permitted the integration of a process based on interoperability and use of software able to generate NURBS models such as MC Neel Rhinoceros and Autodesk Autocad in the Revit's logic.

Database Generation. The main features included in this section are the automatic generation of databases and computing able to extract the numeric value such as volume, area, material and descriptive information. The main feature of a BIM is that it can extract automatic computing and information from the previously generated model. The development of the add-in has followed the SCAN to BIM process outlined in recent years thanks to the direct application of historical case studies and on existing industrial and residential buildings.

Interoperability Levels. GOGs are based on the BIM-based import/export requirements such as the correct export of the model, to create two-dimensional drawings from the model to proper export schedules and databases in MS Access, Excell and IFC. The final objective of this section was to improve the interaction with the BIM project, external information and other types of BIM-based analysis. Mainly the new BIM utility paradigm has been supported thanks to the definition of interoperability schemes for the appropriate transfer of the SCAN to BIM model for finite element analysis and virtual reality via SAT, ACIS, DWG formats and energy analysis via IFC and GBxlm formats.

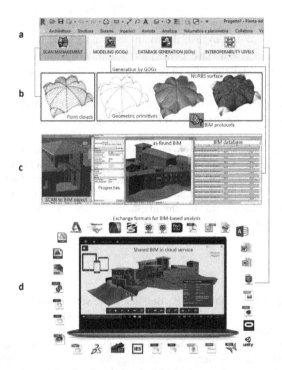

Fig. 4. The four section of the developed Revit Add-in for semi-automated modelling (a). The first section 'Scan management' (b) the second section 'Modelling GOGs' (c) implemented functions for automatic 'Database generation' and (d) Interoperability levels

5 Conclusions

Today, HBIM is a new paradigm in the world of built cultural heritage for the management of buildings since they are the source of geometric and semantic information. However, the generation of this models is still a labour-intensive and manual work. This research tried to contribute to increase the automation in the "Scan-to-BIM" process. In particular, two procedures were presented. The first methodology combines bottom-up modelling and top-down propagation of knowledge for segmentation and semantic classification of the acquired point cloud. Although the developed procedure showed a good flexibility against data quality and data density, some priors have to be associated with the top-down propagation of knowledge. In particular, it is assumed that the Manhattan world assumption holds. In the highly irregular environment the presented procedure will probably fail. Currently, the presented methodology is focusing on segmentation of the unstructured point cloud and semantic classification of detected elements. However, feature detection and clustering as well as the creation of the final model combining geometry and semantic information, which represent two crucial step in "Scan-to-BIM" process, were not tackled. This will be the subject of further works. The second methodology presented is focusing on a different approach. Indeed, it tries to speed up the BIM modelling pipeline by developing specific Add-in to commercial software packages. In this Add- in a clustering of most useful commands is performed in order to accomplish the main tasks associated to a BIM process (scan management, modelling; database generation and interoperate with other software). The developed Add-in developed a semi-automated and guided workflows for HBIM production in commercial software packages. Even if some workaround were found to reduce bottlenecks connected with commercial software some major barriers remains when facing constraints imposed by API availability.

Acknowledgements. Research leading to this results is partially funded by Regione Lombardia - Bando "Smart Living: integrazione fra produzione servizi e tecnologia nella filiera costruzioni-legno-arredo-casa" approvato con d.d.u.o. n.11672 dell'15 novembre 2016 nell'ambito del progetto "HOMeBIM liveAPP: Sviluppo di una Live APP multi-utente della realtà virtuale abitativa 4D per il miglioramento di comfort-efficienza-costi, da una piattaforma cloud che controlla nel tempo il flusso BIM-sensori – ID 379270".

References

1. Volk, R., Stengel, J., Schultmann, F.: Building information modeling (BIM) for existing buildings—literature review and future needs. Autom. Constr. **38**, 109–127 (2014)
2. Meschini, S., Iturralde, K., Linner, T., Bock, T.: Novel applications offered by integration of robotic tools in BIM-based design workflow for automation in construction processes. In: Advanced Construction and Building Technology for Society, p. 59 (2016)
3. Banfi, F.: Building information modelling – a novel parametric modeling approach based on 3D surveys of historic architecture. In: Ioannides, M., et al. (eds.) EuroMed 2016. LNCS, vol. 10058, pp. 116–127. Springer, Cham (2016). https://doi.org/10.1007/978-3-319-48496-9_10
4. Chiabrando, F., Donato, V., Lo Turco, M., Santagati, C.: Cultural heritage documentation, analysis and management using building information modelling: state of the art and perspectives. In: Ottaviano, E., Pelliccio, A., Gattulli, V. (eds.) Mechatronics for Cultural Heritage and Civil Engineering. ISCASE, vol. 92, pp. 181–202. Springer, Cham (2018). https://doi.org/10.1007/978-3-319-68646-2_8
5. Macher, H., Landes, T., Grussenmeyer, P.: From point clouds to building information models: 3D semi-automatic reconstruction of indoors of existing buildings. Appl. Sci. **7**(10), 1030 (2017)
6. Bassier, M., Van Genechten, B., Vergauwen, M.: Classification of sensor independent point cloud data of building objects using random forests. J. Build. Eng. (2018)

7. Filin, S., Pfeifer, N.: Segmentation of airborne laser scanning data using a slope adaptive neighborhood. ISPRS J. Photogramm. Remote. Sens. **60**(2), 71–80 (2006)
8. Rabbani, T.: Automatic reconstruction of industrial installations using point clouds and images. Publications on Geodesy, vol. 62 (2006)
9. Grilli, E., Menna, F., Remondino, F.: A review of point clouds segmentation and classification algorithms. Int. Arch. Photogramm. Remote Sens. Spat. Inf. Sci. **42**(2), W3 (2017)
10. Xiao, J., Zhang, J., Adler, B., Zhang, H., Zhang, J.: Three-dimensional point cloud plane segmentation in both structured and unstructured environments. Robot. Auton. Syst. **61**(12), 1641–1652 (2013)
11. Vo, A.V., Truong-Hong, L., Laefer, D.F., Bertolotto, M.: Octree-based region growing for point cloud segmentation. ISPRS J. Photogramm. Remote Sens. **104**, 88–100 (2015)
12. Chen, D., Zhang, L., Mathiopoulos, P.T., Huang, X.: A methodology for automated segmentation and reconstruction of urban 3-D buildings from ALS point clouds. IEEE J. Sel. Top. Appl. Earth Obs. Remote Sens. **7**(10), 4199–4217 (2014)
13. Poux, F., Hallot, P., Neuville, R., Billen, R.: Smart point cloud: definition and remaining challenges. ISPRS Ann. Photogramm. Remote Sens. Spat. Inf. Sci. **4**, 119 (2016)
14. Rabbani, T., Van Den Heuvel, F., Vosselmann, G.: Segmentation of point clouds using smoothness constraint. Int. Arch. Photogramm. Remote Sens. Spat. Inf. Sci. **36**(5), 248–253 (2006)
15. Castillo, E., Liang, J., Zhao, H.: Point cloud segmentation and denoising via constrained nonlinear least squares normal estimates. In: Breuß, M., Bruckstein, A., Maragos, P. (eds.) Innovations for Shape Analysis, pp. 283–299. Springer, Heidelberg (2013). https://doi.org/10.1007/978-3-642-34141-0_13
16. Weinmann, M., Jutzi, B., Hinz, S., Mallet, C.: Semantic point cloud interpretation based on optimal neighborhoods, relevant features and efficient classifiers. ISPRS J. Photogramm. Remote Sens. **105**, 286–304 (2015)
17. Wang, C., Cho, Y.K., Kim, C.: Automatic BIM component extraction from point clouds of existing buildings for sustainability applications. Autom. Constr. **56**, 1–13 (2015)
18. Autodesk App Store Homepage. https://apps.autodesk.com/it Accessed 17 May 2018
19. Food for Rhino Homepage. http://www.food4rhino.com/. Accessed 17 May 2018
20. Lumion® LiveSync® by Act-3D download webpage in Autodesk App Store
21. BIMobject® by BIMobject download webpage in Autodesk App Store
22. Import/Export Excel by Virtual construction and technology BIM One Inc, download webpage in Autodesk App Store
23. IFC 2018 by Autodesk, Inc. download webpage in Autodesk App Store
24. Advance Steel 2018 Extension Autodesk, Inc. download webpage, in Autodesk App Store
25. Kangaroo Physics by Daniel Piker download webpage, in Food for Rhino
26. Lunchbox by Nathan Miller download webpage, in Food for Rhino
27. Grasshopper Home page. http://www.grasshopper3d.com/. Accessed 17 May 2018
28. Dynamo Home page. http://dynamobim.org/. Accessed 17 May 2018
29. Banfi, F.: BIM orientation: grades of generation and information for different type of analysis and management process. Int. Arch. Photogramm. Remote. Sens. Spat. Inf. Sci. **42** (2/W5), 57–64 (2017)
30. Previtali, M., et al.: Automatic façade segmentation for thermal retrofit. Int. Arch. Photogramm. Remote Sens. Spat. Inf. Sci. **40**, 197–204 (2013)

Direct Numerical Analysis of Historical Structures Represented by Point Clouds

László Kudela[1]([⊠]), Umut Almac[2], Stefan Kollmannsberger[1], and Ernst Rank[1,3]

[1] Chair for Computation in Engineering, Technical University of Munich, Arcisstr. 21, 80333 Munich, Germany
laszlo.kudela@tum.de
[2] Faculty of Architecture, Istanbul Technical University, Istanbul, Turkey
[3] Institute for Advanced Study, Technical University of Munich, Munich, Germany

Abstract. An important field in cultural heritage preservation is the study of the mechanical behavior of historical structures. As there are no computer models available for these objects, the corresponding simulation models are usually derived from point clouds that are recorded by means of digital shape measurement techniques. This contribution demonstrates a method that allows for the direct numerical analysis of structures represented by point clouds. In contrast to standard measurement-to-analysis techniques, the method does not require the recovery of a geometric model or the generation of a boundary conforming finite element mesh. This allows for significant simplifications in the complete analysis procedure. We demonstrate by a numerical example how the method can be used to compute mechanical stresses in a historical building.

1 Introduction

In the past decade, there has been a growing attention towards three-dimensional shape measurement techniques in the context of cultural heritage (CH) preservation. The low cost of equipments and the increasing efficiency and accuracy of the related software have made it possible to create highly detailed 3D, or even 5D digital content of objects both in small and large scales. These digital models are employed in a wide variety of CH related fields, such as documentation, digital restoration, visualization or structural analysis [1–3]. The latter is particularly important in order to prevent structural failure and to aid the planning of restoration works of damaged structures. In these cases, precise knowledge is needed about the mechanical stresses present in the object.

The most popular technology in engineering for analyzing the stress state of mechanical parts is the Finite Element Method (FEM). It can handle almost arbitrarily complex geometries and topologies which makes the method especially well-suited for the analysis of objects known in the CH context. In standard engineering applications, the FEM model of an object is derived directly from

© Springer Nature Switzerland AG 2018
M. Ioannides et al. (Eds.): EuroMed 2018, LNCS 11196, pp. 64–75, 2018.
https://doi.org/10.1007/978-3-030-01762-0_6

digital plans, e.g. CAD models. However, for many historical structures, there are no digital models available. Moreover, even if there are schematic drawings, the shape of the object may differ from them, especially when the structure is exposed to damaging effects, such as erosion, floods, earthquakes or wars. To overcome this issue, a bridge between shape measurement techniques and the FEM is needed.

Past years' research efforts towards establishing the above link brought forth numerous approaches. Generally, the main steps of such measurement-to-analysis pipelines can be characterized as follows:

1. *Data acquisition*
   A 3D shape measurement technique is employed to capture the shape of the domain of interest. This step usually provides a discrete sampling of the surface of the structure, consisting of a large set of points, usually referred to as *point clouds*.
2. *Geometry recovery*
   A geometric model is derived from the point cloud information using geometric segmentation and surface fitting methods. The resulting geometric model is stored using standardized geometric representation techniques, such as STL, STEP or IGES files.
3. *Mesh generation*
   The CAD model from the previous step is discretized into a set of finite elements, commonly referred to as *mesh*.
4. *Finite Element Analysis*
   The mesh is handed over to a finite element solver together with the corresponding material properties and structural constraints.

There are numerous applications that implement the above steps in the context of the structural analysis of CH objects, such as statues [4,5], masonry arches [6], and historical buildings [7,8].

An extensive overview of *data acquisition* techniques for CH applications can be found in [9]. The most popular methods are based either on laser scanning, such as in the famous *digital Michelangelo project* [10], or photogrammetric methods, as in [11,12]. There are applications that aim at combining the advantages of laser scanning and photogrammetry, e.g. the approach in [4].

As for the second step, most approaches convert the point clouds into a surface triangulation by using surface recovery techniques, such as [13,14]. Because triangulations lack the approximation power to reproduce smooth and curved surfaces efficiently, many applications transform the model further into a more advanced geometric representation format, usually based on non-uniform rational B-splines (NURBS) [15]. These cloud-to-mesh algorithms are implemented in open source tools [16,17] as well as commercial products, such as Polyworks or Geomagic Studio.

Although there are many open source and commercial meshing solutions available for the third step, it still poses a severe bottleneck in the complete analysis process. Even in standard engineering practice, where geometric models are readily available, the process of mesh generation requires a great amount of human interaction, and may take up to 80% of the total labor time of an engineer [18].

Clearly, the steps of the measurement-to-analysis pipeline are difficult to automate, as a solution which is tailored to a specific class of geometries may not be directly applicable on other types of objects. Furthermore, as the steps require the interplay of methods ranging from point cloud processing to finite element mesh generation, the analyst performing the structural analysis needs to be experienced with a wide variety of softwares and be aware of their respective pitfalls.

In recent years, there has been an increasing interest in the computational mechanics community towards methods that ease the transition from a geometric representation to a finite element model. These research efforts have brought forth many promising approaches, such as the Finite Cell Method (FCM), introduced in [19]. The FCM relies on the combination of approaches well-known in computational mechanics: immersed boundary methods [20] and high order finite elements [21]. It promises very accurate results for geometrically complex objects with almost no meshing costs.

In its simplest implementation, the only information that FCM needs from a geometric model is inside-outside state: given a point in space, does this point lie in the structure of interest or not? A wide variety of geometric representations is able to provide such *point membership tests* and have been shown to work well in combination with the FCM.

The aim of this contribution is to show that the measurement-to-analysis pipeline can be drastically simplified by applying the FCM directly on geometries represented by oriented point clouds. It will be shown that these clouds provide the necessary information for point membership tests, rendering the second and third step of the pipeline unnecessary. The proposed method can be conveniently applied for the structural analysis of CH objects, which will be demonstrated on a real example of a historical structure.

2   Structural Analysis on Point Clouds Using FCM

In the following, the basic ideas of the FEM and the FCM are summarized. The aim of the discussion is to recall the basic concepts only and avoid complex mathematical expressions and derivations. For a thorough analysis, refer to [22] and [23].

2.1   The Finite Element Method

The FEM is a numerical tool which aids engineers and scientists in gaining insight into physical processes that are governed by Partial Differential Equations (PDEs). These equations provide the mathematical basis to describe e.g. how heat propagates in the walls of a building, sound waves travel in halls, or how structures deform when subjected to external forces. While PDEs can be often solved analytically for simple geometries (planar walls, box-like rooms, rectangular plates), it is often impossible to solve them directly for complex shapes. The FEM seeks to overcome this issue by following a bottom-up approach: it breaks down the problem into elementary pieces that behave according to the governing PDE-s in an *approximate* sense (Fig. 1).

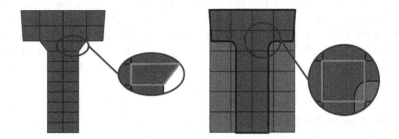

Fig. 1. Schematics of the Finite Element (left) and Finite Cell (right) methods. In the FEM, the geometry of interest (gray-colored region) is discretized into a set of boundary-conforming elements. In the FCM, the domain is immersed into a bounding box that contains an extremely soft material, marked with light blue color. The bounding box is subdivided into a regular mesh of quadrilaterals. In contrast to the FEM, finite cell boundaries (dark blue color on the detailed views) do not necessarily conform with the domain boundaries. (Color figure online)

When, for example, an elementary piece – element – is subjected to a mechanical load, its original shape will undergo a deformation, resulting in a deformed shape. If elementary pieces are carefully assembled together into an interconnected network – mesh –, the individual element deformations together become able to represent the changing shape of the large, more complex-shaped original system.

In the standard, linear version of the FEM, only simple deformations of elements are possible. For example, a side that is straight in the undeformed setting remains straight also in the deformed configuration, even if the underlying physical laws would dictate otherwise. Due to this restriction, the deformation of the complete structure computed by the FEM is only an approximation of the exact deformation that happens in reality. This *discretizaton error* can be reduced in various ways, for example by *refining* the mesh into smaller elements. It can be shown that as the size of the elements in a mesh decreases, the displacements (and the associated stresses) computed by the FEM get close – converge – to the true values. The tradeoff is that increasing the number of elements leads to longer computational times.

Another popular strategy for reducing the discretization error is to extend the possible deformation modes of the individual elements, which is, for example the approach taken by high-order finite elements (p-FEM) [21]. In p-FEM applications, straight element edges may deform into non-straight, higher order shapes. This strategy also comes at the expense of a higher computational effort.

However, for smooth problems, the results offered by p-FEM are subject to much smaller errors than mesh refinement. On the other hand, mesh refinement is a good choice for non-smooth problems, where rapid variations in the displacement field are expected. These phenomena appear typically in the neighborhood of concave corners or material interfaces.

Obviously, the elements in the mesh need to resolve the boundary of the original object as precise as possible. However, they are only allowed to possess simple geometries like triangles, quadrilaterals, tetrahedra, hexahedra etc. Further, they need to satisfy a set of criteria concerning their shape and connectivity properties. These make finite element mesh generation a difficult and time consuming procedure, even if numerous automatic mesh generation softwares are available.

2.2 The Finite Cell Method

One solution to the problem of mesh generation is offered by the Finite Cell Method. The idea of the FCM is to submerge the physical geometry of interest into a virtual box that is filled with an infinitely soft material, referred to as the *fictitious domain*. As the box has a simple geometry, it can be meshed easily, as depicted in Fig. 1. Instead of computing on a mesh that resolves the boundaries of the original, *physical domain*, FCM uses a mesh that resolves the boundaries of the box. In this setting, there are *cut elements* that contain parts from the original domain and the fictitious domain as well. Because the fictitious material is infinitely soft, it does not influence the deformation of the physical domain in these elements. However, the deformation may be too complex to be resolved by a coarse mesh of linear elements. Therefore, FCM employs elements from p-FEM, which provide accurate results with moderate computational costs compared to the standard FEM.

In its simplest implementation, the only information that the FCM requires from a geometric model is the inside-outside state: which parts of a given element belong to the fictitious material and which parts to the physical material? Many geometric representations are able to answer such inside-outside queries and have been successfully applied in combination with the FCM. Examples include voxel models from CT-scans [24], constructive solid geometries [25], boundary representations [26] and STL descriptions [27].

2.3 Point Membership Tests on Oriented Point Clouds

As explained in the introduction, many CH applications that follow the measurement-to-analysis pipeline start from point clouds that represent the structure of interest. Often, the points $\mathbf{p}_i$ in the cloud are equipped with normal vectors $\mathbf{n}_i$, which determine how the local tangent plane of the underlying surface is oriented. The idea is depicted in Fig. 2.

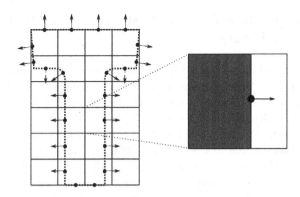

Fig. 2. Point membership classification on oriented point clouds. The points and the associated normal vectors represent the local tangent planes of the geometry of interest. They separate the space into physical (gray) and fictitious (white) parts.

This implies a very simple approach for point membership classification:

1. Given a query point $\mathbf{q}$, find the point $\mathbf{p}$ and its associated normal $\mathbf{n}$ in the cloud that lies the closest to $\mathbf{q}$. The two values $\mathbf{p}$ and $\mathbf{n}$ define the local tangent plane of the geometry.
2. Determine the side of the tangent plane on which $\mathbf{q}$ lies, by evaluating the following the scalar product:

$$(\mathbf{p} - \mathbf{q}) \cdot \mathbf{n} \tag{1}$$

3. If the value in Eq. 1 is greater than 0, the query point $\mathbf{q}$ lies in the domain. Otherwise, it lies outside.

The above steps provide the necessary point membership classification needed by the FCM: for any point in any element, it can be decided whether it lies in the physical or the fictitious part of the geometry.

The clouds generated by most scanning procedures are usually not completely clean. They may contain outliers and carry a certain amount of measurement noise, causing the above point membership test to deliver false positives. These effects can be attenuated by performing the test in the k-neighbourhood of the query point. In this process, instead of checking against a single closest point, the k nearest points of $\mathbf{q}$ are found and the point membership with respect to each of them is computed. If $\mathbf{q}$ lies inside with respect to the majority of the points in the k neighborhood, its membership is determined as *inside*, otherwise *outside*. Alternatively, when a greater amount of outliers and noise is present in the cloud, their influence can be reduced by applying cleaning procedures e.g. as in [28].

3   Numerical Example: The Cistern of the Hagia Thekla Basilica in Turkey

The archaeological site at Hagia Thekla (Meryemlik) was a major pilgrimage site in late antiquity [29]. It was intimately tied to the life of Thekla and her post-mortem miracles. There are numerous structures of different types in the site, which can be identified above ground by sight.

The cistern of the Thekla Basilica is part of the water storage and distribution system of the main church of the site and its sacred area enclosed by walls. It has a rectangular plan measuring approximately 12×14.6 m in the interior. The interior space is divided into three aisles by two rows of columns (Figs. 3 and 4). The columns in each row are connected by arches. Three barrel vaults cover the interior running in the north-south direction.

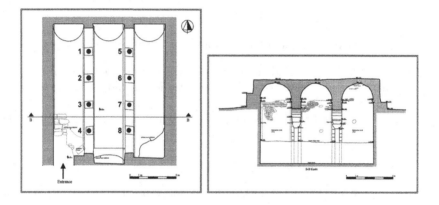

Fig. 3. The cistern of Hagia Thekla Basilica, plan and cross section.

Fig. 4. A view from the interior of the cistern

The columns supporting the upper structure originally had a diameter of approximately 45 cm. They are made of a pink calcareous stone. The columns have double capitals made of limestone. It is not possible to make observations about the condition of the column bases and the floor, due to the thick layer of earth accumulated inside the cistern over centuries. The outer walls are built with a multi-leaf masonry construction system. The outer facing of the walls are made of big limestone blocks, while the inner faces are constructed with brick and mortar. As seen in Fig. 4, the cross-sections of the columns have decreased remarkably. The exterior surfaces are flaking due to physicochemical effects; the erosion continues. In addition to surface erosion with a non-uniform pattern, there are deep cavities on the columns. One of the columns (Column 3) has already collapsed and was replaced by a concrete column in the 1960's.

The shape of the decayed column surfaces and cavities are difficult to record using traditional (hand) recording techniques. Therefore, a high definition surveying scanner was employed to document these elements. During the field campaign, the instrument was set up at a number of positions around each column at a distance of a few meters. Thus, overlapping and maximum point density of approx. 5 mm was ensured to represent the highly decayed columns. More details on the measurement process can be found in [7].

3.1 Numerical Results Computed by the FCM

To examine the stresses throughout the structure under its self weight, a numerical analysis using the FCM was employed. In order to reduce the required computational effort, only one quarter of the structure was investigated. This symmetry reduction is possible because the overall shape of the cystern is symmetric. The point cloud containing columns 5, 6, the voussoir and the supporting wall was immersed in a mesh of 6336 finite cells, as shown in Fig. 5.

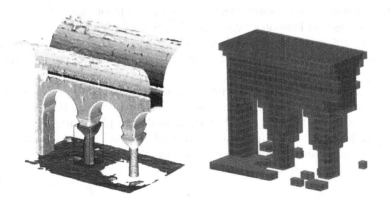

Fig. 5. Point cloud representation of the structure of interest and the corresponding mesh of finite cells. Cells that lie completely in the fictitious domain are not plotted. (Color figure online)

The most vulnerable elements of the structure are the columns. As stress concentrations are expected at the cavities on the surfaces of the columns, a reduction of the discretization error by mesh refinement is needed. For reasons of efficiency, it is important to refine the mesh only around the columns, where the stress field is expected to change rapidly. For the FEM and the FCM, such *local refinement* techniques have been well-studied recently. In our applications, we employ the *multi-level hp-adaptivity* technique of [30]. In the refinement procedure, those cells that are intersected by the points representing column 5 (the blue points on Fig. 5) are recursively subdivided into eight equal subcells, until a subdivision depth of 5 is reached. A cross sectional view of the refined mesh is depicted in Fig. 6.

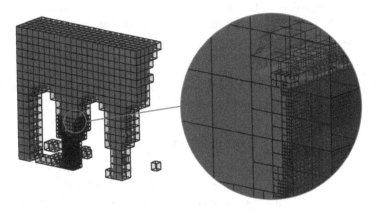

Fig. 6. Locally refined finite cell mesh. The cells around the column of interest are recursively subdivided towards the geometric boundary.

The material properties were defined to be linear elastic and isotropic, with an elastic modulus and Poisson's ratio of $E = 2 \cdot 10^4$MPa and $\nu = 0.2$, respectively. The specific gravity of the material was set to 27kN/m^3. In the fictitious domain, the material was given a stiffness of 2MPa. The foundation of the structure was rigidly fixed to the ground.

The maximum principal stress distribution computed by the FCM is depicted in Fig. 7. As expected, the highest compressive stresses occur in the columns. The stress values are in the range of 2..4 MPa, while the peak value occurs at the connection between the column and the capital. This is in good agreement with the values computed in [7], following the traditional measurement-to-analysis procedure.

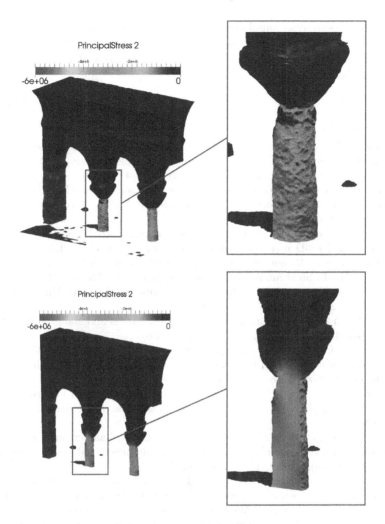

Fig. 7. Maximum principal stress distribution computed by the FCM, with a detailed view over column no. 6. Top: the stress field on the surface. Bottom: internal stresses along a cross-section. The values are in Pa.

4   Conclusions

This contribution presented a technique that aims at the direct structural analysis of CH structures represented by oriented point clouds. The approach is based on the Finite Cell Method, which, in its simplest implementation, only requires inside-outside information from the geometric model of interest. It was shown that oriented point clouds are able to provide such point membership tests. In contrast to standard approaches, the proposed technique does not need the recovery of a geometric model or the generation of a boundary conforming finite element mesh. This allows for significant simplifications in the measurement-to-analysis pipeline, establishing a seamless connection between shape measurement techniques and numerical simulations. A numerical example demonstrated that the method can be conveniently applied for the structural analysis of historical structures.

References

1. Bruno, F., Bruno, S., De Sensi, G., Luchi, M.-L., Mancuso, S., Muzzupappa, M.: From 3D reconstruction to virtual reality: a complete methodology for digital archaeological exhibition. J. Cult. Herit. **11**(1), 42–49 (2010)

2. Stanco, F., Battiato, S., Gallo, G.: Digital Imaging for Cultural Heritage Preservation: Analysis, Restoration, and Reconstruction of Ancient Artworks. CRC Press, Boca Raton (2011)

3. Doulamis, A., et al.: 5D modelling: an efficient approach for creating spatiotemporal predictive 3D maps of large-scale cultural resources. In: ISPRS Annals of Photogrammetry, Remote Sensing & Spatial Information Sciences (2015)

4. Kalisperakis, I., Stentoumis, C., Grammatikopoulos, L., Dasiou, M.E., Psycharis, I.N.: Precise 3D recording for finite element analysis. In: 2015 Digital Heritage, vol. 2, pp. 121–124. IEEE (2015)

5. Borri, A., Grazini, A.: Diagnostic analysis of the lesions and stability of Michelangelo's David. J. Cult. Herit. **7**(4), 273–285 (2006)

6. Riveiro, B., Caamaño, J.C., Arias, P., Sanz, E.: Photogrammetric 3D modelling and mechanical analysis of masonry arches: an approach based on a discontinuous model of voussoirs. Autom. Constr. **20**(4), 380–388 (2011)

7. Almac, U., Pekmezci, I.P., Ahunbay, M.: Numerical analysis of historic structural elements using 3D point cloud data. Open Constr. Build. Technol. J. **10**(1), 233–245 (2016)

8. Castellazzi, G., D'Altri, A.M., Bitelli, G., Selvaggi, I., Lambertini, A.: From laser scanning to finite element analysis of complex buildings by using a semi-automatic procedure. Sensors **15**(8), 18360–18380 (2015)

9. Pavlidis, G., Koutsoudis, A., Arnaoutoglou, F., Tsioukas, V., Chamzas, C.: Methods for 3D digitization of cultural heritage. J. Cult. Herit. **8**(1), 93–98 (2007)

10. Levoy, M., et al.: The digital Michelangelo project: 3D scanning of large statues. In: Proceedings of the 27th Annual Conference on Computer Graphics and Interactive Techniques, pp. 131–144. ACM Press/Addison-Wesley Publishing Co. (2000)

11. Agarwal, S., et al.: Building Rome in a day. Commun. ACM **54**(10), 105–112 (2011)

12. Muzzupappa, M., Gallo, A., Spadafora, F., Manfredi, F., Bruno, F., Lamarca, A.: 3D reconstruction of an outdoor archaeological site through a multi-view stereo technique. In: 2013 Digital Heritage International Congress (DigitalHeritage), vol. 1, pp. 169–176. IEEE (2013)

13. Kazhdan, M., Hoppe, H.: Screened poisson surface reconstruction. ACM Trans. Graph. (ToG) **32**(3), 29 (2013)

14. Calakli, F., Taubin, G.: SSD: smooth signed distance surface reconstruction. In: Computer Graphics Forum, vol. 30, pp. 1993–2002. Wiley Online Library (2011)

15. Piegl, L., Tiller, W.: The NURBS Book. Springer, Heidelberg (2012). https://doi.org/10.1007/978-3-642-59223-2

16. Cignoni, P., Callieri, M., Corsini, M., Dellepiane, M., Ganovelli, F., Ranzuglia, G.: MeshLab: an open-source mesh processing tool. In: Eurographics Italian Chapter Conference, vol. 2008, pp. 129–136 (2008)

17. Rusu, R.B., Cousins, S.: 3D is here: point cloud library (PCL). In: IEEE International Conference on Robotics and Automation (ICRA), Shanghai, China, 9–13 May 2011
18. Cottrell, J.A., Hughes, T.J.R., Bazilevs, Y.: Isogeometric Analysis: Toward Integration of CAD and FEA. Wiley, Hoboken (2009)
19. Parvizian, J., Düster, A., Rank, E.: Finite cell method. Comput. Mech. **41**(1), 121–133 (2007)
20. Peskin, C.S.: The immersed boundary method. Acta Numer. **11**, 479–517 (2002)
21. Szabó, B., Düster, A., Rank, E.: The p-version of the finite element method. In: Encyclopedia of Computational Mechanics (2004)
22. Zienkiewicz, O.C., Taylor, R.L., Zienkiewicz, O.C., Taylor, R.L.: The Finite Element Method, vol. 3. McGraw-hill, London (1977)
23. Düster, A., Rank, E., Szabó, B.: The p-version of the finite element and finite cell methods. In: Encyclopedia of Computational Mechanics, 2nd edn. (2017)
24. Ruess, M., Tal, D., Trabelsi, N., Yosibash, Z., Rank, E.: The finite cell method for bone simulations: verification and validation. Biomech. Model. Mechanobiol. **11**(3–4), 425–437 (2012)
25. Wassermann, B., Kollmannsberger, S., Bog, T., Rank, E.: From geometric design to numerical analysis: a direct approach using the Finite Cell Method on Constructive Solid Geometry. Comput. Math. Appl. **74**(7), 1703–1726 (2017)
26. Kudela, L., Zander, N., Kollmannsberger, S., Rank, E.: Smart octrees: accurately integrating discontinuous functions in 3D. Comput. Methods Appl. Mech. Eng. **306**, 406–426 (2016)
27. Elhaddad, M., Zander, N., Kollmannsberger, S., Shadavakhsh, A., Nübel, V., Rank, E.: Finite cell method: high-order structural dynamics for complex geometries. Int. J. Struct. Stab. Dyn. **15**, 1540018 (2015)
28. Schall, O., Belyaev, A., Seidel, H.-P.: Robust filtering of noisy scattered point data. In: 2005 Eurographics/IEEE VGTC Symposium Proceedings Point-Based Graphics, pp. 71–144. IEEE (2005)
29. Hill, S.: The Early Byzantine Churches of Cilicia and Isauria. Variorum, Aldershot (1996)
30. Zander, N., Bog, T., Kollmannsberger, S., Schillinger, D., Rank, E.: Multi-level hp-adaptivity: high-order mesh adaptivity without the difficulties of constraining hanging nodes. Comput. Mech. **55**(3), 499–517 (2015)

Innovative Technologies in Digital Cultural Heritage

The Use of CT Scans and 3D Modeling as a Powerful Tool to Assist Fossil Vertebrate Taxonomy

George Theodorou[1]([✉]), Yiannis Bassiakos[2], Evangelos Tsakalos[2],
Evyenia Yiannouli[3], and Petros Maniatis[4]

[1] National Kapodistrian Univeristy of Athens, 15784 Athens, Greece
gtheodor@geol.uoa.gr
[2] Insitute of Nanoscience and Nanotechnology, NCSR, Demokritos,
15310 Athens, Greece
y.bassiakos@inn.demokritos.gr, Tsakalos.e@gmail.com
[3] Maritime Archaeology Laboratory, University of the Peloponnese,
Kalamata, Greece
eyiannouli@gmail.com
[4] CT and Interventional Department, Konstantopouleio Hospital,
Athens, Greece
peatman@otenet.gr

Abstract. 3D scans and 3D modeling are used to assist the taxonomy of a new unique fossil specimen of an elephant maxilla with molars heavily eroded by coastal sea waves, encrusted in extremely hard sediment, making the preparation and measurements with classical digital calipers impossible. The elephant fossil has been collected north of Poros on the coast at SE Kephallenia in consolidated fan- conglomerates and sands. The elephant maxilla is the first significant elephant fossil from Kephallenia and all the Ionian Islands. According to its dimensions and characteristics it is attributed to a new endemic island species, *Elephas cephallonicus* that lived isolated from the mainland 104.2 ± 18.5 ka ago. The existence of an island endemic specimen at this period in Kephallenia is in full accordance with the palaeogeographic evolution of the Ionian Islands, which is strongly indicated by the natural climatic changes during the last hundred thousand years. The *Elephas cephallonicus* became extinct possibly during the last ice age.

Keywords: CT scans and 3D modeling · Kephallenia · Greece
Elephas cephallonicus n. sp

1 Introduction

In the last centuries, palaeontologists have documented occurrences of Upper Pleistocene Proboscideans all over Greece in more than a hundred localities [2]. These finds can be divided in three general categories.

- Continental forms of mainland Greece.
- Island endemic forms on numerous Greek islands and Cyprus (and other Mediterranean Islands, Sicily, Malta, Sardinia etc.).

© Springer Nature Switzerland AG 2018
M. Ioannides et al. (Eds.): EuroMed 2018, LNCS 11196, pp. 79–89, 2018.
https://doi.org/10.1007/978-3-030-01762-0_7

- Island finds not easily attributed to mainland or island forms. These forms are in reality new endemic species that represent the first stages of dwarfism. Up to now the best Greek example is the *Elephas (Palaeoloxodon) chaniensis* [2, 14].

Typical island endemics are quite small and clearly shorter than their mainland relatives. They belong to isolated populations that migrated to the island by swimming during periods of low sea level. It is documented that even on islands with endemic forms the first arrivals belong to mainland forms. The study of these forms is quite demanding since they represent types in transition from mainland to insular forms. Some authors accept that mainland types are encountered on Crete, but so far the documentation of undisputable mainland forms in Crete is still unsatisfactory. The study of the largest elephants of Crete revealed a population with members smaller than the mainland forms. This population was attributed to *Elephas (Palaeoloxodon) chaniensis* from finds collected in the submerged cave at the area of Vamos near Chania. The fact that Cyrpus, Tilos, Rhodos, Naxos [1, 13, 16, 19, 27] for example, were never connected to the mainland during the Upper Pleistocene, even at periods of very low sea level, is reasonably cogent with the occurrence of small endemic forms on the respective islands.

2 The Kephallenia Fossil Vertebrates

In the case of the Ionian Islands, Zante and Kephallenia, we need to consider first the palaeogeography. These islands were located close to the mainland and it is conceivable that at periods of low sea level elephants and hippos and possibly deer could have easily migrated there, in more than one migration events, even if these islands were never connected to the mainland by a land bridge. The available fauna composition cannot help, because it is hardly evidenced. It is known that there are no mainland Pleistocene Carnivora, Bovidae and Suidae, documented for these islands up to now, while it is difficult to infer the existence of land bridges at least for the last 120.000 years [3].

Up to now there is a serious lack of adequate palaeontological studies on this island to elucidate its Pleistocene fauna. In the recent past, we had the opportunity to discuss an elephant molar fragment from the sea bed near Minies, the coastal stretch close to the airport of Kephallenia. In addition, on the Island of Zante, trace footprints in aeolianites can be attributed to elephants [9].

Up to this day, an old paper [11] mentions the occurrence of mainland hippopotamus on Kephallenia near Mantzavinata. New hippopotamus material is not yet available and the old specimen has to be studied again systematically for the sake of updating our assessment regarding its taxonomic status. Our own research during the last decade did not provide any information on elephant remains on Kephallenia or other Ionian islands. One exception is to be found on the island of Zante. In both cases, on Zante and on Kephallenia, field survey failed to yield satisfactory and adequate specimens to assist a good taxonomical determination (Fig. 1).

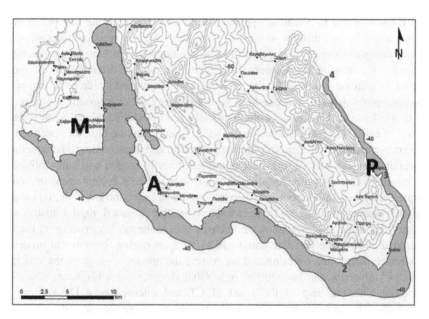

Fig. 1. The Kephallenia elephant and hippopotamus sites. Actual fossils of Elephants were located in the coast of greater Poros (this paper) and all on the sea bed of Minies, close to the Kephallenia airport [9]. The existence of 3 interesting vertebrate localities in Kephallenia (from left to right, Mantzavinata, Airport beach at Minies and the coast of Poros) together with the footprint locality on Zante opens up new horizons for the study of Quaternary fossil vertebrates in the Ionian Islands, unpublished project report [26], the *A.Sho.Re.* Study area stretching along *nos* 1–4).

3 The Material

A unique fossil elephant specimen (Stored at, Athens Museum of Palaeontology and Geology, Code AMPG 900) was collected during summer 2015 from Quaternary coastal river conglomerate deposits in the area of Poros, SE Kephallenia. The specimen was at first glance quite large to be a typical endemic dwarf form, but also rather small to represent a typical mainland type. Did it belong to an undisputable mainland form or to an endemic large form? The specimen, being heavily eroded by sea water, proved impossible to measure with sufficient accuracy by means of digital calipers for classical measurements. Consequently, we decided to use the new powerful tool of CT scanning and modeling to find the correct answers by taking the correct and adequate measurements directly on the computer screen. The fossil elephant maxilla fragment, is the only fossil vertebrate yielded by the Archaeological Shoreline Research Project (*A.Sho.Re.*) conducted along the SE coastline of Kephallenia, the largest of the Ionian Sea island complex. *A.Sho.Re.* Introduces a geoarchaeological platform of investigation aiming at the understanding of geological and historical evolution of coasts in the long term through the systematic and extensive documentation of the available evidence [25, 26].

E. Bassiakos and E. Yiannouli provided G. Theodorou with the first photo of the find *in situ* and invited him for further collaboration. Direct inspection ascertained that the find, encrusted in very hard consolidated conglomerate of coastal river deposits, belonged to the maxilla of a Quaternary elephant. Significant fragments of the molars survived on both sides of the Maxilla. G. Theodorou organized its removal with power tools, after protecting the find carefully with a plaster case of gypsum. It was impossible to use hand tools to remove the extremely hard consolidated sediment or apply methods of extraction using ordinary hand tools. Being a unique find, the specimen had to be removed *ad hoc* to secure its efficient protection and preservation. The lamellae of the available molars were to our disappointment heavily eroded and substantial parts were missing. This fact arrested all efforts to complete any typical measurement or accurate description on the spot, and also later in the lab, with the aid of digital calipers. Only the enamel width could be measured by the standard digital instruments. Extremely bad state pf preservation could easily lead to the total destruction of the find. The eroded and broken lamellae could easily fall apart during the removal process of the extremely hard crust covering and supporting the molars. The specimen was taken to Athens University and later to the Agia Olga Hospital for a CT scan, which was carried out with the help of the Head of CT and interventional Department, Dr. P. Maniatis. The maxilla revealed easily its internal morphological details on the computer screen. That is the number of molars available on each side, the angle among the long axis of the M^2 sin and M^2 dext. the lamellar frequency, the enamel thickness and the maximum height, etc. Only after having these measurements and data in hand, did it become possible to retrieve the correct answers. We thence had to compare available data with published data from mainland or island endemic types of Quaternary elephants. This very powerful technology was used by us *for the first time in order to assist the taxonomical study* of a Greek fossil, where all other methods failed.

In the past, we had the opportunity to describe *Elephas (Palaeoloxodon) tiliensis* [10] based on scans made by hospital CT equipment. In that case, the analysis of the available CT scans proved inadequate to yield all the detailed internal micro morphology of the bone.

Theodorou et al. [17] worked further on skeletal proportions and morphology based on CT and Laser scans and, shortly afterwards, Theodorou *et al.* [18] proposed the comparison of overlapping 3D scans for comparative studies of morphological data of 3D models of fossils (Thalis project MIS 380135). In the following years, Liakopoulou [5] and Liakopoulou *et al.* [6, 7] used Micro CT scan for the *Elephas (Palaeoloxodon) tiliensis* petrosum and *Phanourios minor* petrosum As far as the members of the NKUA excavation team are concerned, this is the first time to use CT scanning for pure taxonomic purposes, where external measurements with calipers could not be easily applied. This new powerful tool is now available to vertebrate.

4 Methodology

High resolution computed tomography was used to observe the sample. The method of predilection was chosen, owing to its non-invasive/non-destructive nature. Also, due to the fact that during the last years it proved to be the most appropriate to study a large number of palaeontological specimens. The extensive use of CT scanning provides high-resolution images that are treated with advanced imaging software (e.g. Avizo 8.1, Mimics). The CT data are processed to provide the digital reconstructions of the sample, allowing for an internal view of the samples and exposing internal structures for further analysis. Consequently, this approach supports all digital measurements, volumetric and linear ones, as 3D models will be the key for exploring the differences in the proboscidean dentition, as with the Kephallenia case. More specifically, access was gained to a Philips CT 64-slice tomographer, located in the Konstantopouleio General Hospital "Agia Olga". The calibrations of the machines for optimal imaging were carried out and a series of 906 slices was acquired with an interslice spacing of 1 mm.

The digital reconstruction of the sample was made using Avizo 8.1 imaging software. The slices produced by the CT-scanning were loaded and the contrast was fixed for better depiction of the lamellae of the molars. Since the fossil is characterized by a poor preservation state, higher contrast was needed. Once satisfactory contrast was achieved, the 3D models were rotated in such position so that the molars were in a perpendicular view to the observing plane in order to be measured.

The linear and angular measurements include the Basic Elephant molar measurements for taxonomic purposes that follow:

- **Molar Length** - It is usually the longest available measurement of the molar. **Molar Width**-The available measurement parallel to the occlusal surface.
- **Lammellar Frequency** - The number of Lamellae along an axis of 10 cm taken parallel to the masticating surface. This measurement varies with wear in all specimens.
- **Angle** of the longest axes of the molar series.
- **Lamellae height** - The largest available height of any lamellae. This measurement was applied at the highest available lamellae of M^2 sin.
- **Enamel width** - This measurement could be taken also by digital calipers.
- A usual question in studying molars of elephants has to do with the **number and status of the available molars**, eroded or not or just being ready to erupt from alveoli.

5   Results and Discussion

In the past, X-rays were used [14] for the study of an elephant lower mandible from Crete. It was our first attempt to look at the inner morphology of a fossil. In the present case of the Kephallenia specimen, it became easy to document a series of 3 molars on the left side. An erupting molar (M^3 sin) where only 3 lamellae were present, a complete M^2 sin made up by 11 lamellae and an eroded with heavy wear molar M^1 sin. On the right side of the maxilla are available part of the root of M^1 dext, M^2 dext and two lamellae from the erupting M^3. The 3 molars on the left side belong to M^1, M^2 and the erupting lamellae to M^3. It has so far been established that it is almost impossible to exclude the possibility that sin PM^4, M^1, M^2 are present as opposed to M^1, M^2 and M^3.

In either case, however, our final conclusions would be convergent, since all comparisons in both cases point to a large, but not a typically endemic form.

Table 1. Basic measurements of available molars from the Kephallenia specimen. On the right side only lamellae measurements. LF, and L width were available (Figs. 2 and 3).

M^2 sin length	20 cm - 11 Lamellae available
Molar width (sin)	70–72 mm near the occlusal surface
Enamel average width – (Sin. and dext.)	3.3 to 4.0 mm
Lamellar Frequency – (Sin. and dext.)	5.5 to 6.5
Angle of molars (M^2 sin. – M^2 dext.)	20–23°
Max Lamellar height of sin. M^2 sin.	155 mm

The critical question to be answered in studying molars of elephants relates to the number and status of the available molars, eroded or not, or just waiting to erupt from molar alveoli. On Kephallenia, all available data point to the existence of an elephant of

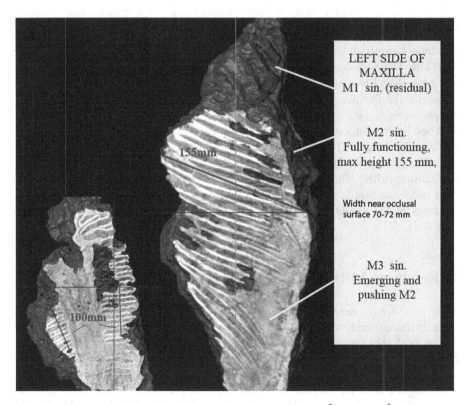

LEFT SIDE OF
MAXILLA
M1 sin. (residual)

M2 sin.
Fully functioning,
max height 155 mm,

Width near occlusal
surface 70-72 mm

M3 sin.
Emerging and
pushing M2

Fig. 2. Best possible section parallel to the occlusal surface of M^2 sin and M^2 dext. Arrows across the sin, and dext. M^2 have a length of 10 cm, allowing for a good Lamellar Frequency view. It is well known that LF is influenced by the curvature of the molar and the relative position of the lamellae and the wear. Width of M^2 near occlusal surface 70–72 mm.

medium size that is not typical for a small endemic elephant. Its lamellar frequency, varying from 5.5 to 6.5 and the maximum lamellar width 71–72 mm close to the occlusal surface, point to an elephant of intermediate size. Such value is very small for a typical mainland type [4, 12]. This value (Lamellae width) is, however, larger if taken away from the occlusal surface, being also influenced by the stage of wear and the shape of cross section of molars [21]. The size range of continental *P. antiquus* upper molars is statistically not known. And it has no meaning to use a mean value based on different North European localities.

The richest biometrical data collection for Greece relates to the endemic elephant *Elephas (Palaeoloxodon) tiliensis* [15, 19]. Comparison with Sicily or Cyprus cannot help, since *Elephas falconeri* and *E. Cypriotes* and *Elephas xylofagou* are smaller [1]. Tilos specimens are smaller to about 30% in relation to the Kephallenia new specimen [15]. The Kephallenia specimen has dimensions very close to *Elephas. creutzbugi* from Rethymno area or *Elephas mnaidrensis* from Malta [12, compare Table 1, p. 34]. In addition, quite large values of typical mainland *P. antiquus* exist for specimens of Grevena area [23] or for specimens of Megalopolis [8], and new finds to study by Theodorou, *pers. communication*,). Therefore, the evidence from the available comparanda impels us to accept that the Kephallenia specimen belongs to an *endemic island form of a middle size as large as E. creutzburgi from Crete* and smaller than a typical mainland *Elephas (Palaeoloxodon) antiquus* [8, 23, 24].

6 Biogeography and Absolute Dating

Understanding the palaeoenvironment, along with the coastal formation processes, is a basic concern of the *A.Sho.Re.* Project and a central issue of work. However, the significance of a unique find, such as the identification of a fossil vertebrate in SE Kephallenia and indeed the Ionian Sea, reasonably begs the question. Were Kephallenia elephants separated from the mainland for some period? If Kephallenia was connected to the mainland at the time of the deposition of the conglomerates, no endemic elephant could be present. To understand the palaeodistribution of *Elephas (Palaeoloxodon) antiquus* and its descendants on the Ionian Islands we need the absolute dating of the fossiliferous formation. That is, it is necessary to know if the Kephallenia elephants at the time of deposition were isolated from the mainland or not. Ferentinos *et al.* [3] document that Kephallenia was an island at about 110 and 35 ka BP.

During the *A.Sho.Re.* campaign sediment samples were selected for determining their absolute date. A sediment sample, belonging to the relevant fossiliferous layer, was dated at the Luminescence Dating Laboratory, of the National Centre for Scientific Research (NCSR) «Demokritos» . The Infrared Optically Stimulated Luminescence of feldspar (IRSL) [20, 22] was employed for dating the sediment sample containing the elephant maxilla. Using IRSL an age of 104.2 ± 18.5 ka was obtained. The Infrared Optically Stimulated Luminescence of feldspar (IRSL) [20, 22] was employed for dating the sediment with the elephant maxilla. This chronology proves that the Kephallenia elephant lived at a period of a high sea level that was followed by the last

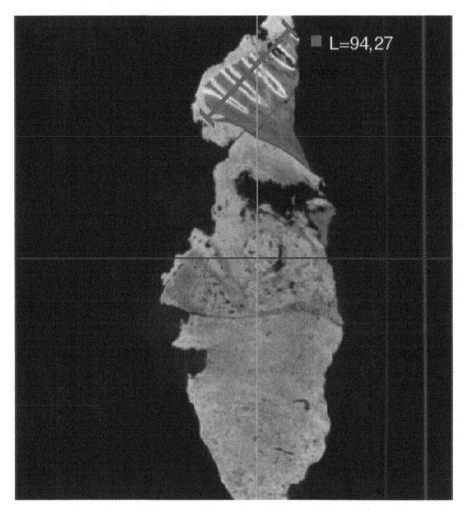

Fig. 3. Left side of maxilla. L of M^1 = 94, 27 (=94,3 Residual)

major ice period. During high sea level periods the possibility of isolation was significant and a corresponding reduction of size could have occurred quite fast. Since it is well documented that around 110 to 35 ka Kephallenia was insular [3], we cannot reject the hypothesis that the available data point to the existence of an endemic, isolated species with a first degree of endemism. The Kephallenia endemic elephants were smaller than mainland Quaternary elephants, but they were not as small as other endemic species as those of Tilos [15, 19], Cyprus [1] etc. whose high degree of endemism is due to an isolation for long periods. All these facts compel us to describe a new endemic species for Kephallenia.

SYSTEMATICS

Ordo –	**Proboscidea, Illiger, 1811**
Family-	Elephantidae, Gray, 1821
Genus-	*Elephas* Linnaeus, 1758
(Subgenus)	*(Palaeoloxodon Matsumoto, 1924)*
Species	*cephallonicus*
	Elephas (Palaeoloxodon) cephallonicus n. sp.
Holotype	*Fragment of Maxilla with heavily eroded molars on both sides. Code AMPG 900. Available are M^2 dext., M^1 sin, M^2 sin, M^3 sin (errupting).*
Basic Synonym catalog	*Elephas,* Milan *et all,* 2015
Etymology	*after the Ionian Island of Kephallenia*
Type locality	*Rocky, north coast of Poros, SE Kephallenia*
Stratigraphy	

Quaternary, fan- coastal conglomerates, overlying uncomormably the alpine basement. Fossiliferous layer along the coast overlies small costal shelters created after the deposition of the conglomerates. These shelters, possibly similar to the available small coastal caves, are correlated with a phase of coastal marine erosion.

Absolute date   104.2 ± 18.5 ka.

Diagnosis and differential diagnosis. A dwarf endemic middle size species of the Elephantidae Family. Molars are larger than those of *Elephas tiliensis* and close to those of *Elephas creutzburgi* and *Elephas mnaidriensis*. These two forms are smaller than *Elephas chaniensis,* whose fossils are larger generally larger than *Elephas creutzburgi* and smaller than *Elephas (Palaeoloxodon) antiquus.* The M^2 sin from Kephallonia has 11 lamellae (all in situ), maximum width (close to the occlusal surface) 71-72 mm. and total length about 21 cm. Lamellar Frequency 5.5- 6.5 and maximum Lamellar height about 15 cm. Angle between left and right M^2 is 20-22 degrees.

Geographic distribution: The Greek island of Kephallenia, the Ionian Sea.

Extinction time.   Not known with accuracy. During the last Ice Age

Possible Extinction cause.   Climatic changes and flora and fauna turn over during Quaternary. Human interaction cannot be excluded.

Taphonomic remarks on the site. The very hard conglomerate did not allow for any taphonomic study. It is obvious that other fossil elephant parts are still in situ, but they cannot be extracted in an appropriate way to facilitate taphonomic studies.

7   Conclusions

The new fossil elephant specimen from the coast of Poros, SE Kephallenia, belongs to a new island endemic species the *Elephas cephalonicus* n.sp, that lived isolated on the island in 104.2 ± 18.4 Ka. For the first time, the NKUA team employed CT scans and 3D modeling to assist the taxonomic study of a Greek vertebrate fossil. Its size is closer to *Elephas creutzburgi* from Rethymno, Crete. It became extinct during the last Ice

Age. Possible causes for its extinction is change of flora due to natural climatic changes and interaction with humans on the island during the last 100 Ka.

Acknowledgements. The authors would like to thank the University of the Peloponnese, The Institute for Field Research (UCLA), the National and Kapodistrian University of Athens and its Research Account and Evangelia Tsipra and Petros Moschuris of Kosntantopouleio Hospital, who helped us open new horizons for Vertebrate Palaeontology in Greece. Particular thanks are due to Dionysia Liakopoulou for work on the digital documentation of the find.

References

1. Athanassiou, A., et al.: Cranial evidence for the presence of a second endemic elephant species on Cyprus. Quatern. Int. **379**, 47–57 (2015)
2. Dikaioulia, E., Symeonidis, N., Theodorou, G.: Palaeontology, vol. III, 1st edn. NKUA, Athens (2003)
3. Ferentinos, G., Gkioni, M., Geraga, M., Papatheodorou, G.: Early seafaring activity in the southern Ionian Islands, mediterranean sea. J. Archaeol. Sci. **xxx**, 1–10 (2012)
4. Kevrekidis, C., Mol, D.: A new partial skeleton of *Elephas* (*Palaeoloxodon*) antiquus falconer and cautley, 1847 (*Proboscidea, Elephantidae*) from Amyntaio, Macedonia, Greece. Quat. Int. **406**, 35–56 (2016)
5. Liakopoulou, D.: Observations on the inner morphology of os petrosum of island endemics with the use of micro CT. Master thesis, Univeristy of Lille 1. Sciences and Technologies-UFR Earth Sciences, Grance (2016)
6. Liakopoulou, D., van Heteren, A.H., Georgitsis, M., Theodorou, G.: Observations of the inner morphology of os petrosum of *Phanourios minor* with the use of micro CT. In: 15th Congress of the R.C.M.N.S. Exploring a physical laboratory: the Mediterranean Basin, 3–6 September 2017, Athens, Greece, p. 114 (2017). Abstracts
7. Liakopoulou, D., van Heteren, A.H., Theodorou, G.: The inner morphology of petrosal bone of insular mammal: *Elephas tiliensis*, with the use of microCT. In: 15th Congress of the R.C. M.N.S. Exploring a physical laboratory: the Mediterranean Basin, 3–6 September 2017, Athens, Greece, Abstracts, p. 113 (2017). Abstracts
8. Melentis, I.: Studien über die fossile Vertebraten Griechenlands: Die Dentition der Pleistozänen proboscidial des Beckens von Megalopolis im Peloponnes: (Griechenland). Ann. Géol. Des Pays Hellèniques 12, 153–262, Athens (1961)
9. Milan, J., Theodorou, G., Loope, D., Panayides, I., Clemmensen, L., Gkioni, M.: Vertebrate tracks in Late Pleistocene-Early Holocene (?) Carbonate aeolianites, Paphos, Cyprus. Ann. Soc. Geol. Pol. **85**, 507–514 (2015)
10. Provatidis, Ch., Theodorou, E., Theodorou, G.: Computed tomography and CAD -CAE methods for the study of the Osseus Inner Ear Bone of Greek quaternary endemic Mammals. Mediterr. Archaeol. Arcaheometry **11**(2), 121–127 (2011)
11. Psarianos, P.: Über das Vorkommen von Hippopotamus auf Kefallinia (Griechenland). Prakt. Akadimias Athinon **28**, 408–412 (1953)
12. Sen, S., Barrier, E., Crété, X.: Late Pleistocene dwarf elephants from the Aegean islands of Kassos and Dilos, Greece. Ann. Zool. Fennici **51**, 27–42 (2014)
13. Symeonides, N.: Die Entdeckung von Zwergelefanten in der Höhle "Charkadio" auf der insel Tilos (Dodekanes, Griechenland). Ann. Geol. Pays Hell. **XXIV**, Taf. XV, 445–461 (1972)

14. Symeonides, N., Theodorou, G.: New fossil elephants on Crete Island. Ann. Geol. Pays Hellen. **31**, 113–129 (1982)
15. Theodorou, G.: The fossil dwarf elephants of Charkadio Cave at Insel Tilos. Ph.D. thesis. (Offset edition), Athens (1983)
16. Theodorou, G.: Environmental factors affecting the evolution of island endemic: the Tilos example from Greece. Mod. Geol. **13**, 183–188 (1988)
17. Theodorou, E., Mitsopoulou, V., Vasilopoulos, T., Provatidis C., Roussiakis, S.: Toward a better knowledge of *Elephas tiliensis* skeletal proportions and morphology. In: 14th Congress of Regional Committee on Mediterranean Neogene Stratigraphy, 8–13 September 2013, Istanbul, Turkey (2013)
18. Theodorou, G., et al.: A study case for a 3D skeletal reconstruction of *Elephas tiliensis* based on CT and Laser scans; morphology, population data and taphonomy. In: 10th North American Paleontological Convention, Abstract Book, The Paleontological Society Special Publications, vol. 13, p. 172 (2014)
19. Theodorou, G., Symeonidis, N., Stathopoulou, E.: *Elephas tiliensis* n. sp. from Tilos island (Dodecanese, Greece). Hell. J. Geosci. **42**, 19–32 (2007)
20. Thiel, C., et al.: Luminescence dating of the Stratzing loess profile (Austria)-testing the potential of an elevated temperature post-IR IRSL protocol. Quatern. Int. **234**(1–2), 23–31 (2011)
21. Todd, N.: New Phylogenetic Analysis of the Family *Elephantidae* Based on Cranial-Dental Morphology. Anat. Rec. **293**, 74–90 (2010)
22. Tsakalos, E., et al.: Luminescence geochronology and paleoenvironmental implications of coastal deposits of southeast Cyprus. J. Archaeol. Antropol. Sci. **10**(1), 41–60 (2016)
23. Tsoukala, E., Lister, A.: Remains of straight tusk elephant, *Elephas (Palaeoloxodon)* antiquus Falc & Caut. (1847). ESR dated to oxyden isotope Stage 6 from Grevena (W. Macedoniam Greece). Bolletino Della Soc. Palaeontol. Ital. **37**(1), 117–139 (1998)
24. Tsoukala, E., et al.: *Elephas antiquus* in Greece: new finds and a reappraisal of older material (Mammalia, Proboscidea, Elephantidae). Quatern. Int. **245**, 339–349 (2011)
25. Yiannouli, E.: A.Sho.Re. 2011–2015, SE Kephallenia in the Ionian Sea: Investigating the geoarchaeology of the coastal zone. In: Photos-Jones, E., et al. (eds.) Proceedings of the 6th Symposium of the Hellenic Society for Archaeometry, Athens 16–18 May 2013, The Acropolis Museum. British Archaeological Reports S2780. Oxford, Archaeopress, Chap. 26, pp. 179–185 (2016)
26. Yiannouli, E.: Arcaheological shoreline research (A.Sho.Re.) on the island of kephallenia: the university of the peloponnese interdisciplinary investigation of the Coastal Zone. In: Proceedings of the 10th International Panionion Conference, 30th April–4th May 2014, Corfu. Kerkyraika Chronika IA, pp. 327–340 (2017). (in Greek)
27. Van der Geer, A.L., Lyras, G., Van den Hoek Ostende, L., Vos, J., Drinia, H.: A dwarf elephant and a rock mouse on Naxos (Cyclades, Greece) with a revision of the palaeozoogeography of the Cycladic Islands (Greece) during the Pleistocene. Palaeogeogr., Palaeoclim., Palaeoecol. **404**, 133–144 (2018)

i-Wall: A Low-Cost Interactive Wall for Enhancing Visitor Experience and Promoting Industrial Heritage in Museums

Christina Gkiti[✉][iD], Eirini Varia[iD], Chrysi Zikoudi[iD],
Athina Kirmanidou[iD], Io Kyriakati[iD], Spyros Vosinakis[iD],
Damianos Gavalas[iD], Modestos Stavrakis[iD],
and Panayiotis Koutsabasis[iD]

Department of Product and Systems Design Engineering,
University of the Aegean, Syros, Greece
{c.gkiti, e.varia, c.zikoudi, a.kyrmanidou, i.kyriakati,
spyrosv, dgavalas, modestos, kgp}@syros.aegean.gr

Abstract. Interactive walls have been employed in many museums with the aim to enhance the visitor experience. These are usually large in size and expensive, while their typical use is to present generic content about the museum. As a result, they may not be easily set-up at multiple locations inside a museum and serve the purpose of presenting narratives about particular exhibits. This paper presents i-Wall, an affordable interactive wall system built from off-the-shelf components and technologies. i-Wall has been designed for the Syros Industrial Museum (Greece) and presents a narrative about a particular exhibit, the Enfield E8000, which is the first electric car that reached small-scale production (in 1973). i-Wall provides information to visitors about the concept, the design, the problems, the creators and the socio-political context related to the exhibit, in an interactive way. It also allows visitors to appreciate the interior of the car as well as its functions via augmented reality (AR) technology. The design of i-Wall combines interactive storytelling, animations, projection mapping, conductive paint, touchboard and AR.

Keywords: Industrial cultural heritage · Interactive wall · Augmented reality
Physical computing · Off-the-shelf components · Affordable technologies
Iterative design · Prototyping

1 Introduction

Industrial heritage tourism refers to "the development of touristic activities and industries on man-made sites, buildings and landscapes that originated with industrial processes of earlier periods" [1]. Industrial museums are the major hosts of industrial cultural heritage and are attractive environments for heritage tourism [2, 3]. These museums affect people by connecting them with each other, amplify social inclusion

M. Ioannides et al. (Eds.): EuroMed 2018, LNCS 11196, pp. 90–100, 2018.
https://doi.org/10.1007/978-3-030-01762-0_8

Fig. 1. Views of the interactive wall inside the industrial museum (on the left) and during use (on the right).

and diversity and engage visitors with new and potentially inspiring experiences that combine heritage and tourism [4] (Fig. 1).

In many traditional museums, the perception of information about exhibits is relatively passive [5]. Visitors are only able to look at the exhibits from a safe distance and often have no basic guidance or information to connect the exhibits with other narratives related to the museum's collections [6, 7].

Over the past two decades, several museums introduced interactive installations (such as interactive walls, tables, boards, monitors, video projections etc.) in order to attract more visitors, spark their interest [8] and engage them in a unique social experience [9, 10]. While in the past, static imagery was enough, nowadays visitors seek more interactive elements, participation in the action and social engagement with others [11]. Current trends indicate that cultural organizations invest in sustaining the engagement of people with museums and raising connectedness between museum practices and the everyday personal experiences of the visitors [12].

Most of these interactive installations are costly and large in size, like the Van Gogh Alive[1] exhibition or the Gallery One interactive wall [13]. Therefore, they are not affordable for many small-sized museums. In addition, large installations pose restrictions about their positioning inside the museum. Furthermore, sizeable installations typically present generic information about the museum rather than stories or narratives about important exhibits.

This research explores the potential of interactive content presentation of industrial cultural heritage content in museums with the design, implementation and evaluation of a cost-effective, customizable interactive wall system. In addition, through an iterative approach of design and evaluation it explores the design of touch interactions with the i-Wall and AR (augmented reality) app content.

i-Wall aims at engaging visitors of an industrial museum to a storytelling interactive experience. i-Wall is adaptable to various sizes and it can present customized, exhibit-specific cultural content in a museum. It comprises affordable components and technologies: wooden surface, conductive paint, commodity sensors, microcontrollers and video projection. The system is accompanied by a marker-based augmented reality

---

[1] http://www.vangoghaliveuae.com/.

(AR) application which allows visitors to interact with a 3D model of the exhibit. An initial prototype has been designed and implemented for the industrial museum of Hermoupolis, in the island of Syros, Greece. It presents the story of a specific museum exhibit, the first electric car that as been produced worldwide [14] (in small scale), the Enfield E8000, which has been on display at the museum for the past few years.

Enfield E8000 is unique piece of industrial cultural heritage that has references to historical facts, engineering practices, social practices and the economic and political status of the time. The island of Syros faces a transformation towards a mix of cultural and tourist activities, while its capital city Hermoupolis is known for its rich industrial heritage [15], since it has been the primary harbour and industrial area in Greece for a period of about 60 years (1830–1890). The i-Wall project has been developed in the context of a graduate course on interactive systems design (studio).

2   Related Work

Several research works have focused on how to avoid the formal aspects of experiencing cultural heritage content in museums and cultural contexts. The aim has been to involve the visitor more actively by engaging and motivating him to participate in an interactive interplay with tangible and intangible heritage.

In the past two decades a large number of interactive board technologies are used in museums and cultural heritage sites; multi-touch tables are the most popular among them, used to present interactive representations of the exhibits. Lately, large scale interactive walls and video projection technologies are also deployed for visualizing cultural content [16, 17]. In a parallel development, new methods are actively researched that combine different interaction techniques and styles in terms of visitor-exhibit interaction and social collaboration in the museum or public settings [18, 19].

Applications based on interactive walls in any form, either for the purpose of entertaining or informing, have been implemented in various museums and exhibitions, for the presentation of products, services or other exhibits.

The project "Living Walls" developed by the "High, Low technology" research group at MIT, is a series of interactive wallpapers able to record their environment, to reproduce sound, to control the lighting in the room and to send messages to a friend. Their purpose was strictly for display [20].

The interactive wall at the "100% Brisbane" exhibition, co-developed with Liquid Interactive [21] and the artist Sophie Blackhall-Cain, presents an interactive wall that explores data through touch, sight and sound within a collaborative environment where visitors co-experience information about the city in a playful and interactive way [22].

The Ferrari raising DNA Interactive touch Wall[2], developed by DigiMagic, has been created for Ferrari during the world championship Formula 1 in 2016 in Singapore. The "wall" served the purpose of informing users about the history of the Ferrari in an interactive way. This interactive wall uses conductive paint technology.

---

[2] https://www.youtube.com/watch?v=mpO0Q7u4Qg8.

Another example of interactive wall is that of the "Retail Design Expo" in London in 2015. It had the form of a 'open-square' shaped projected surface and has been constructed by the office of "Dalziel and Pow"[3]. This interactive kiosk represents a fine example of a creative mixture of various technologies aiming at connecting visitors and providing useful content about an important event.

With respect to AR, many systems have been implemented to provide cultural digital content to visitors, especially when the artefacts on display are not directly accessible [23, 24]. Touching the exhibits is normally forbidden in museums and therefore active interaction with (or examination of) any exhibited artefact is not possible. This can be resolved by using AR technology as it can present to the user additional interactive 2D or 3D content on top of markers or POIs (Points of Interest). The application of AR is widespread in the car industry.

McLaren has created an AR application[4] for the models of McLaren570S and McLarenP1. Users can install the apps on their phone or tablet and, by using a marker (available from the company's website) the car can be observed in a 3D form. The user can also see the car frame and receive information on the car's technology. AR technology is also widespread in museums, as in [25] which presents an AR app that allows users to change the colours of an artwork from the artist's palette.

3   Design and Prototyping

The i-Wall system has been developed following an iterative design process that involved incremental prototyping and technical testing of the main system components, i.e., the touch sensor, projection mapping, animation design, storytelling and AR application. This section outlines the design of the system components. The i-Wall setup is illustrated in Fig. 2.

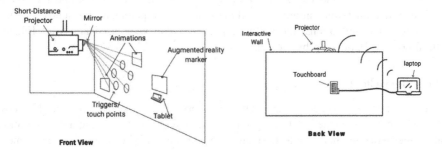

Fig. 2. The interactive wall setup. **On the left**: the front of the i-Wall consists of (a) The plywood surface, (a) Touchpoints drawn with conductive ink, (c) An AR marker placed onto the surface, (d) A projector and (e) Animations played upon the user touching the touchpoints. **On the right**: a touchboard (connected to a laptop) is mounted on the back of the i-Wall.

---

[3] https://www.youtube.com/watch?v=poA9bZ76iJk.

[4] http://cars.mclaren.com/apps.

3.1   Touch Sensor

The touch interaction was implemented with TouchBoard technology, by Bare Conductive, which is compatible with the Arduino Genuino software. This board can enhance any surface with touch interaction. It comes with sensors that may respond when they are connected (i.e. simply painted) with conductive paint. Each user touchpoint (trigger) is drawn onto a plywood surface in the form of an icon that relates to a story about the E-8000 electric car and is physically linked through the plywood via metallic nails to short wires onto the TouchBoard.

3.2   Projection Mapping

The layout of content projected on the interactive wall has been designed with the "Mad Mapper" software. Mad Mapper is installed on a laptop computer connected with the projector and the TouchBoard. Upon the user's touching a touchpoint/trigger, this event is identified by TouchBoard and, through MadMapper, it is matched to an animation/projection subsequently projected around/next to the touchpoint. The projections comprise short animations, edited in the context of this project.

3.3   Animation Design

On the i-Wall there are five triggers, each one corresponding to one part of the story:

1. The idea of the creation of the car.
2. The sociopolitical context in Syros during the production of the car.
3. The problems that arose during the production up to the closing of the factory.
4. The creator, John Goulandris.
5. The materials and the method of construction.

The style of the videos follows a simple line, the designs are flat and the colour pallete is neutral (white figures, light blue details, transparent background). For the creation of the animations, the software packages that were used are After Effects, Illustrator and Photoshop by Adobe.

3.4   Storytelling

Our main goal was to achieve an interactive storytelling experience via short videos. These have been designed with the minimum amount of text possible and their duration is around two and a half minutes. The touchpoints are placed in a circular arrangement on the surface of the wall so that the user is free to choose from which point they want to start the story of Enfield, and they are the master of the flow that unravels in front of them. However, we added some arrows connecting the touchpoints, indicating the "correct" line of selection, however without making it necessary that people had to follow this line of viewing. The AR app was also an aspect of the storytelling.

3.5   AR Application

The AR application was the most suitable means to help the user understand the interior of the electric car. We accompanied the AR interaction with explanatory text, since the interior of the car is not actually visible to the museum visitors. A tablet was constantly available next to the interactive wall and the user could pick it up to use the AR application. The AR application presents the information about the inside of the car in an interactive way, after the user has aimed the camera of the tablet on a marker that is onto the i-wall. Then the model of the car appears in a 3D form, on the screen of the tablet and the user can interact with it, by turning the model around, or selecting certain parts of it and reading the specific information.

For the creation of this application we used several software packages. The app was created using Unity, Vuforia and Android Studio. The model of the car was created with Cinema 4D by Maxon.

3.6   Prototype

Low Fidelity Prototype

A low fidelity prototype was developed in a canvas, with a long-distance projector mainly to check the lighting and the colour pallete of the animations, as well as the arrangement of the triggers and their connection to the TouchBoard.

High Fidelity Prototype

The high-fidelity prototype was created onto a light-coloured plywood (dimensions 1.20 m x 2.40 m) and a short-distance projector in order to avoid shadows during the use of the wall. The prototype was placed on a wall, half a meter high from the ground. The distance between the i-Wall and the projector was set to 1 m.

Throughout the development of the second prototype, we tested several trial setups of the various system elements. The prototyping process helped us reach to the basic characteristics of the i-wall system:

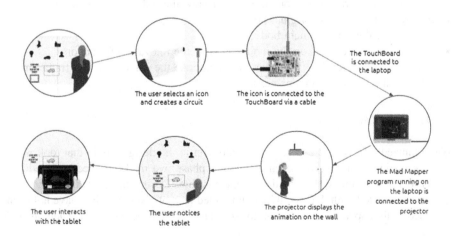

Fig. 3. The main workflow of the i-Wall triggered by user interactions.

- Simple and playful representation of the car's history
- Only touch operation
- Sound response from the system when someone touches a touchpoint
- Main use of white colour for the icons and animations
- Large projections with sufficient space between them
- Intuitive interaction through the AR app allowing the exploration of the car's interior.

4   Interaction Design

The interaction with the wall is deliberately kept simple, given the fact that it is part of a tour in an already rich in content museum. The aim was not to overload the visitor with intense visual stimuli. The function of the interactive wall starts from the touch of the user's hand on a touchpoint which triggers a series of actions. The basic steps are (see Fig. 3):

- Touch the desired video/trigger;
- Activate the touchboard via a circuit;
- Transfer the command to the laptop (which has projection mapping installed);
- Activate the video through the program;
- Project the video to a specific location (depending on the touchpoint).

System performance (i.e. the system's responsiveness to user actions) has been a key consideration, hence, we have ensured that the above procedure is executed in fractions of a second. In order for the user to realize that his touch is enough to activate the projections, the speed and sound have been adjusted to respond directly. By using one or even all the touchpoints at the same time the i-Wall can be controlled by one or more users simultaneously. Regarding the AR app, users may interact with a 3D model of the "Enfield E8000". Users can interact by:

- Applying basic transformations in order to view the different sides of the car;
- Reverting it back to its original position;
- Changing colour of the main body;
- Tapping on active areas on the model to view the relevant information;
- Exploring the different components that comprise the car model (car frame, main frame, wheels, electric engine etc.).

5   Evaluation

We organized a formative user-centred evaluation in the design studio that took place in three distinct phases. After each evaluation phase, we made the necessary adjustments to improve the system to the extent possible. During the evaluation, the participants interacted with the i-Wall in an unguided fashion. Namely, they have not been provided with a specific usage scenario, so that we could monitor their reactions and responses.

5.1 Phase One

The participants were eight users; these were the supervisors of our interaction design studio course, who were familiar and informed about the subject and the technologies. We chose this group specially to get important information about the overall design and interactions. The main conclusions of the first round of evaluation included:

- To attract the attention of the visitor and intensify his curiosity was achieved with the element of surprise. The explanation under the title encouraged visitors to come up and touch one of the icons, but without explaining what exactly will happen when they touch one of the touch points!
- To amplify this transition, we added sound effects to every touch point so that users would understand that the icon has been activated.
- We also added background music, giving an exhilarating atmosphere to the environment.
- The title of the installation became more prominent: from a static image it was redesigned to blink so as to draw the attention of visitors.
- We placed the AR marker on a location that was easier to observe.
- Regarding the AR implementation, we noticed that the interaction did not fully correspond the user's instructions (i.e. it was not fully functional and comprehensible). Therefore, the touchpoint icons were redesigned and the code was redesigned, for a better response to user moves.

5.2 Phase Two

The participants were fourteen students who were familiar with the project but not with the technology in the form implemented. The main conclusions of his round of evaluation were:

- Participants were quickly acquainted with the technology and entertained with the interaction and sounds at touchpoints.
- Most of them did not manage to watch the videos, and specifically the flow of information, as videos had longer durations than required for that concept.
- Most of them were unable to control the projections of the animations due to the lack of controls, such as pause and start. This resulted in relatively tedious interaction and gradually losing interest in the animations.
- The implementation of AR seemed to have a greater appeal; the users spent time interacting with the car model and understood the function of the controls.
- A small percentage of users expressed the desire to navigate and discover their own functions in the AR app. Thus, we added user instructions in the beginning.

For the transition from the second to the third phase, we focused on the concept's functionality, such as improving the start time of the projections, as it was causing interaction problems. Also, we noticed for the first time the need of users to know the location of projection on the wall, as the attendance of several visitors at the same time led to some confusion. An animated line has been chosen to address this issue: as soon as the user touched an icon, he listened to a sound, which was then followed by the animated line that framed the icon and continued its path until the video was viewed (illustrated in the video[5]).

5.3   Phase Three

The participants were a mix of our supervisors and students. The aim of the third round of evaluation was to optimise performance and experience issues. The main conclusion was that i-wall was fully functional and it had great appeal to users, however:

- Some users would prefer a narration.
- Some users pointed out the need to switch language (between English and Greek).
- Additional indications suggesting the chronological order of the animations.
- The duration of some projections remained long enough, so additional visual indication of the duration of the projected clips was proposed.
- Regarding the AR app, some users would appreciate more possibilities and inter-action affordances (Fig. 4).

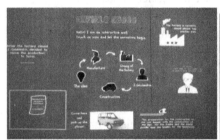

Fig. 4. On the left: the i-Wall with all animated content activated. On the right: a user interacting with the AR app.

6   Summary and Conclusions

This paper presented an interactive wall system (i-Wall) for engaging visitors of an industrial museum to a storytelling interactive experience. i-Wall comprises of affordable components and technologies: a wooden surface, conductive materials, wiring, touchboard and video projection. The AR application has proved a suitable tool to complement the main installation and offer a different perspective of the exhibit. The wall installation is adaptable to various sizes and it can present customized, exhibit-specific interpretive content in a museum. The i-Wall system has been developed for the industrial museum of Hermoupolis, in the island of Syros, Greece and it presents the story of a specific museum exhibit, the Enfield E8000, the first electric car manufactured worldwide.

---

[5] https://www.youtube.com/watch?v=YzJo9qQVy2s.

Throughout the process of research, design and evaluation, we have found that there is a need for a different and more participatory approach to the design of interactive systems for museums. In particular, we have found that the i-Wall for Enfield E8000 contributes to a more experiential and entertaining experience while also promoting the industrial history of Syros island. A significant feature of the system is the combination of navigation, the sense of touch, sound and observation of the narration as it unfolds. The flow of storytelling directs users, without binding them to make specific choices, as the element of surprise remains throughout the interaction with the exhibit. Finally, i-Wall is flexible, as it can incorporate different means of interaction, while it can also be adapted to any space, when designed appropriately.

References

1. Edwards, J.A., i Coit, J.C.L.: Mines and quarries industrial heritage tourism. Ann. Tour. Res. **23**(2), 341–363 (1996)
2. Goodall, B.: Industrial heritage and tourism. Built Environ. **19**(2), 93 (1993)
3. Xie, P.F.: Industrial Heritage Tourism. Channel View Publications, Bristol; Buffalo (2015)
4. Hospers, G.-J.: Industrial heritage tourism and regional restructuring in the European union. Eur. Plan. Stud. **10**(3), 397–404 (2002)
5. Goulding, C.: The museum environment and the visitor experience. Eur. J. Mark. **34**(3/4), 261–278 (2000)
6. Roberts, L.C.: From Knowledge to Narrative: Educators and the Changing Museum. Smithsonian Institution Press, Washington, D.C. (1997)
7. Packer, J., Ballantyne, R.: Motivational factors and the visitor experience: a comparison of three sites. Curator: Mus. J. **45**(3), 183–198 (2002)
8. vom Lehn, D., Heath, C.: Accounting for new technology in museum exhibitions. Int. J. Arts Manag. **7**(3), 11–21 (2005)
9. Vermeeren, A., Calvi, L., Sabiescu, A. (eds.): Museum Experience Design: Crowds, Ecosystems and Novel Technologies. SSCC. Springer, Cham (2018). https://doi.org/10.1007/978-3-319-58550-5
10. Vermeeren, A., Calvi, L., Sabiescu, A., Trocchianesi, R., Stuedahl, D., Giaccardi, E.: Involving the crowd in future museum experience design. In: Proceedings of the 2016 CHI Conference Extended Abstracts on Human Factors in Computing Systems, New York, NY, USA, pp. 3347–3354 (2016)
11. Fleck, M., Frid, M., Kindberg, T., O'Brien-Strain, E., Rajani, R., Spasojevic, M.: From informing to remembering: ubiquitous systems in interactive museums. IEEE Pervasive Comput. **1**(2), 13–21 (2002)
12. Iversen, O.S., Smith, R.C.: Connecting to everyday practices: experiences from the digital natives exhibition. In: Giaccardi, E. (ed.) Heritage and Social Media: Understanding Heritage in a Participatory Culture. Routledge, Taylor & Francis Group, London (2011)
13. Alexander, J.: Gallery one at the cleveland museum of art. Curator: Mus. J. **57**(3), 347–362 (2014)
14. Westbrook, M.H.: The Electric Car: Development and Future of Battery, Hybrid and Fuel-cell Cars. IET, Lucknow (2001)
15. Stratton, M., Trinder, B.: Hermoupolis: the archaeology of a mediterranean industrial city. Ind. Archaeol. Rev. **16**(2), 184–195 (1994)

16. Hakvoort, G.: The immersive museum. In: Proceedings of the 2013 ACM International Conference on Interactive Tabletops and Surfaces, New York, NY, USA, pp. 463–468 (2013)
17. Marton, F., Rodriguez, M.B., Bettio, F., Agus, M., Villanueva, A.J., Gobbetti, E.: IsoCam: interactive visual exploration of massive cultural heritage models on large projection setups. J. Comput. Cult. Herit. **7**(2), 12:1–12:24 (2014)
18. Price, S., Sakr, M., Jewitt, C.: Exploring whole-body interaction and design for museums. Interact. Comput. **28**(5), 569–583 (2016)
19. Caggianese, G., Gallo, L., Neroni, P.: Evaluation of spatial interaction techniques for virtual heritage applications: a case study of an interactive holographic projection. Future Gener. Comput. Syst. **81**, 516–527 (2018)
20. Living Wall: High-Low Tech, 12 November 2010
21. Data you can touch | Liquid Interactive. (2017). https://www.liquidinteractive.com.au/news-article/data-you-can-touch. Accessed 15 Jun 2018
22. 100% Brisbane Exhibition Tour – Museum of Brisbane. https://www.museumofbrisbane.com.au/education/100-brisbane-exhibition-tour/. Accessed 15 June 2018
23. Sylaiou, S., Liarokapis, F., Kotsakis, K., Patias, P.: Virtual museums, a survey and some issues for consideration. J. Cult. Herit. **10**(4), 520–528 (2009)
24. Galatis, P., Gavalas, D., Kasapakis, V., Pantziou, G., Zaroliagis, C.: Mobile augmented reality guides in cultural heritage. In: Proceedings of the 8th EAI International Conference on Mobile Computing, Applications and Services, pp. 11–19 (2016)
25. AR Museum: A Mobile Augmented Reality Application for Interactive Painting Recoloring - Disney Research. https://www.disneyresearch.com/publication/ar-museum/. Accessed 27 June 2018

Historical Buildings Affected by Failures. The Case of the Basilica di Collemaggio in L'Aquila

Lorenzo Cantini[(✉)] [iD]

Department of Architecture, Built Environment and Construction Engineering,
Politecnico di Milano, Via Ponzio 31, 20133 Milan, Italy
lorenzo.cantini@polimi.it

Abstract. Since the deep damages occurred to the European architectural heritage after the Second World War, the conservation theory had to face with a complex issue: the partial or totally missing cultural heritage. Among the application of different solutions, the use of reconstruction of destroyed buildings became a recurrent proposal, adopted in many occasions, from Warsaw Castle to Mostar Bridge. In addition, the buildings hit by earthquakes represent a limit conditions for the application of the common procedures coming from the conservation approach. The recent intervention on the Basilica di Collemaggio, a building deeply damaged after the 2009 L'Aquila earthquake, showed an interesting development of the design choices, based on a multidisciplinary approach to the preservation issue. This restoration work collects the difficulties belonging to the theoretical background met in previous experiences, like the discussion on the early 2000 reconstruction of the Frauenkirche in Dresden or the Cathedral of Noto. Moreover, respect to other cases here presented, the set of interventions characterizing Collemaggio were defined according to multi-criteria analyses supported by the different levels of details provided by the digital model of the religious complex.

Keywords: Basilica di Collemaggio · Earthquake · Conservation design

1 Introduction

By the recent inauguration of the restored Basilica di Collemaggio in L'Aquila, last 2017 December 20th, one of the most important religious building of the town was open to the public after the 6th April 2009 earthquake that hit Abruzzi Region. The consequences of that seismic event had a deep impact on a large territory and the historical center of L'Aquila suffered a large amount of damages. Observing the failures of the main important churches and palaces, the scenario could be compared to the damages inflicted by war events.

As shown by the recent 2016 Amatrice and Norcia earthquakes, the high vulnerability of the Italian cultural heritage to seismic events constitutes an open issue. Therefore, the interventions on deeply damaged buildings promote the discussion on the choices among different solutions, from conservation of the ruins to reintegration of the missing parts, recalling a debate developed after the war devastations and recently

© Springer Nature Switzerland AG 2018
M. Ioannides et al. (Eds.): EuroMed 2018, LNCS 11196, pp. 101–112, 2018.
https://doi.org/10.1007/978-3-030-01762-0_9

updated during the Balkans conflict and the iconoclastic destructions occurred to archaeological remains carried out by new religious radicalisms in the Middle East.

The aim of this paper is to offer an overview on the heated discussion around the criteria set for the repairing and conservation methods applied to the Basilica of Collemaggio. Among the different technical aspects of this multidisciplinary project, the work will focus on the analyses, the strengthening intervention and the conservation design for the damaged pillars of the Basilica. The risk assessment of these load-bearing elements drove to the final choices. This procedure recalls previous experiences, where the masonry structures induced a partial failure to historical buildings, due to some lacks in their realization. In these cases, the comprehension of the mechanical response of the building elements requires a multilevel analysis of the state of conservation of the architectural heritage and shared activities among several experts. The definition of the final intervention is an issue involving theoretical, methodological and strategical decisions, especially for very borderline conditions, in case of collapse of building portions.

Among the different methodologies followed in recent interventions on buildings deeply damaged by a limited response offered by their structural layout, the Noto Cathedral in Sicily and the St. Biagio Church in L'Aquila showed some common points with the Basilica di Collemaggio. Respect to the famous cases of the entire reconstruction of the Warsaw Castle [1], or the more recent reconstruction of the Mostar Bridge, the three cases here treated present some important theoretical differences. Warsaw Castle and Mostar Bridge followed the principle of the national identity redemption trough the re-proposition of a copy of the lost architecture. This approach has several similar witnesses, matured after war conflicts or natural disasters: an idea of removal of the tragic event by proposing a sort of tranquillizing theatrical backdrop. The idea of maintaining the social relationships between inhabitants and their town promoted this kind of reconstruction, but the copy-like effect confirms the common attitude of hiding the trauma, and the causes at its origin, in order to obliterate it.

2 Buildings Failures and Preservation Strategies

2.1 A Short Theoretical Background

The methodology for preserving historical buildings, based on the 1975 Declaration of Amsterdam [2], defined a process based on three main aspects: (i) the deep knowledge of the building materials and the constructive techniques; (ii) the decay phenomena afflicting them; (iii) the necessary measures to contrast worsening processes. When the unexpected scenario of deep failures appears, the high level of damages imposes special solutions. A sort of compromise hanging between the conservation issue and the will to replicate the lost historical buildings for recovering the war or the natural damages.

The conservation design is an articulated process, able to produce different insights concerning the history of the building and several technical aspects. Next to issues more related to architectonic style and surface finishing, also the technological solutions testified by the structural elements became a field of interest. To this purpose, networks of experts like The International Scientific Committee on the Analysis and Restoration of Structures of Architectural Heritage (ISCARSAH), founded in 1997, worked on shared documents promoting the preservation of historical structural elements [3]. Structures were commonly considered as an invisible support of the external skin of the buildings that could be subjected to deep alterations as implementing invasive strengthening interventions.

The attention for this sort of hidden component of the historical buildings drove to the development of the modern diagnostic techniques, a set of procedures able to detect the main properties of the buildings units. The development of the research on the constructive techniques used in different periods for various building typologies enriched the knowledge on the state of the art concerning the building technologies in different context. In seismic areas, like Greece, Spain and Italy, the expert in structural engineering and history of architecture observed very peculiar building systems set with the aim to face earthquake induced forces. The evaluation of the vulnerability of historical buildings required an important effort for recovering information about traditions in the art of building, avoiding the simplification and the trivialization of the technical knowledge into common given categories.

The example of the three religious buildings here presented shows the deep impact that some technological aspects, expression of a local building culture, influenced by geographical and cultural conditions, produced on the reliability of the constructive systems. The further decisions about the intervention strategy are a direct consequence of the development of this path to knowledge that characterizes the conservation process.

2.2   Building Vulnerability and Traditional Solutions

South European countries are periodically hit by telluric phenomena and the damages, in terms of victims and failure of ancient buildings is always relevant. Since past time, the organization of a specific legislation on the first measures for preventing the seismic risk can be attributed to the Spanish administration that had to face the problem of the reconstruction of entire towns after the earthquake that struck South-East Sicily in 1693 and the one occurred in South Italy in 1783. A codification of rules for reinforcing the masonry buildings were introduced during the reconstruction and specific treaties appeared for spreading the new rules for constructions.

Taking into account the work published by Vivenzio in 1788 [4], the methodology proposed for studying the effects of the seismic events presented significant common features with the actual one. For important monuments, the detailed survey of the crack pattern observed on the building was the first step for evaluating the damages to the load bearing elements. According to the interpretation of the damages level, the building could undergo to different interventions: repair by using the common building technologies, reinforcement of the masonry walls, and addition of new wooden or iron strings for improving the connections among different structural elements. In case of complete impairment of the structures, the solution was the realization of a similar one or a new one. As observed by Antonino Giuffrè, the development of this strengthening technology was finalized to achieve a structural layout presenting a sort of monolithic behavior [5]. The modern evaluation of the vulnerability of historical buildings to seismic risk is based on this principle. The more the building structures present a simple static layout based on a reliable linkage between the different load bearing elements, the more the high level of connections provides the necessary stiffness to the building for facing seismic actions.

In this scenario, the architectural heritage of south Europe countries, more subjected to seismic events, presents peculiar characteristics, locally developed for increasing the monolithic behaviour of the buildings. In Greece, for example, the use of timber elements into the masonry wall became a common feature for monuments and also poor buildings [6]. In Portugal, the Pombalina wall presents a timbering system reinforcing the vertical walls that has many similarities with the so-called "casa baraccata" diffused in South Italy, a vernacular construction belonging to the local building traditions of Calabria Region [7].

3 Recent Experiences: Failure and Success of Preventive Policies

The high number of collapsed buildings, observed after the 2009 L'Aquila earthquake, renovated the discussion around the lack of preventive measures on the historical buildings, except some important case. The St. Biagio church and the Basilica di Collemaggio presented similarities with the case of the failure occurred to the Cathedral of Noto. The three cases here mentioned presented these main problems:

- The Noto Cathedral, a Baroque style monument built in 1703, is a famous case where the intrinsic vulnerability of the load bearing structures produced a large failure of the building in 1998 (Fig. 1a);
- St. Biagio Church suffered a partial collapse of the façade during the 2009 L'Aquila earthquake (Fig. 1b), but the rest of the structural layout of the building was able to face positively the seismic event without losing other parts;
- The Basilica di Collemaggio, documented since 13th century, presented several damages after the 2009 L'Aquila earthquake and the complete collapse of the transept area (Fig. 1c).

Fig. 1. Three cases of partially collapsed buildings: (a) Noto Cathedral (Courtesy of prof. L. Binda); (b) St. Biagio Church (courtesy of prof. L. Binda); (c) Basilica di Collemaggio (courtesy of prof. R. Brumana)

3.1   Standards Addressing the Interventions

Several technical aspects concerning the design for buildings and their planned management are available in supranational acts, like the Eurocodes series in Europe and in national standards. In Italy, for example, the technical indications for interventions referred to historical buildings are contained in a specific chapter of the National Building Code named NTC2008 [8]. The code, as the further guidelines for protected buildings [9, 10], promotes controls and interventions for existing buildings, sited in seismic areas, subdivided in three categories: improvement interventions, seismic adaptation and local repairing.

These indications are addressed to a large sample of architectural heritage, constituted by several typologies: from archaeological ruins to religious buildings, from vernacular complexes to aristocratic palaces. The different actors involved in the preventive interventions and the conservation design should collaborate to a balanced process that will evaluate the strategy for the study of the historical buildings and the calibration of the further interventions.

3.2   Learning from Recent Experiences

According to the conservation principles applied to historical buildings contained in the Italian Code for Cultural Heritage [6], the protection of the original material integrity of the historical buildings imposes difficult choices when the level of the damage is not limited to the surfaces of the building or to some structural element. For this reason, a short article of the code introduces the possibility for the application of invasive interventions, like retrofitting, for those buildings, under protection, sited in seismic area. This assumption provides to the structural engineers a clear role when the interventions refers to the architectural heritage stricken by earthquakes. Therefore, the request for an immediate involvement since the first phase of the design became part of the actual discussion on the policies for the conservation of cultural heritage in seismic areas [11, 12].

On 2017 December 20th, the Basilica di Collemaggio in L'Aquila, founded in 1287, was open back to the public after 2 years for the completion of the works and 8 years from the earthquake that deeply damaged the entire historical center of the city. It was the conclusion of an articulated design process that involved public and private subjects, recognizing a precise hierarchy of competences.

The case of Collemaggio represents one of the first application, in Italy, of a cooperative arrangement between public and private institutions. The energy company ENI Servizi financed the entire costs of the intervention, providing also its technical expertise in real estate field. The superintendence officers of L'Aquila realized the design supported by an external group of experts composed by academic institutions.

The Church of St. Biagio, near the L'Aquila Cathedral, was the first religious building that opened back to the public on 2012 July 22. In this case, the church presented a partial collapse of the main façade and a diffused crack pattern on walls and pillars. The proposal for the final design, followed by a private studio, was supported by the advisor activity of Politecnico di Milano. In detail, the study of the state of conservation of the main load bearing structures leaded to the definition of the strengthening interventions. The same designers worked before on the reconstruction of the Noto Cathedral, after the collapse of the roof, the cupola and an entire row of the pillars of the main nave.

4   Setting the Intervention Through the Path to Knowledge

During 2001, when the first characterization on the masonry walls and pillars of the Noto Cathedral were ongoing, the idea of the designers was to maintain the north side of the pillars with the overlying original wall of the central nave that was not involved in the collapse (Fig. 2a). After examining the mechanical properties of the load bearing elements, through a combination of non-destructive and minor destructive tests [13], the pillars were indicated as totally compromised by the effects of the load into a long term behavior condition [13]. The pillars where rebuilt following the compatibility criteria, creating special supports for the pre-existing masonry arches and the over-laying wall. The previous organization of the masonry section, composed by a rubble nucleus confined into cut border blocks (Fig. 2b) was not replicated. The rebuilt pillars were arranged by a regular texture composed by well-shaped sandstone blocks (Fig. 2c) coming from local quarries and reinforced by a FRP vertical bars placed in the internal core [14]. By this solution, the mimetic integration of the building was realized (Fig. 2d), hiding the signs of the trauma caused by the failure of the dome and the roof and providing a safer building that should demonstrate a better response to future seismic events.

A mimetic reconstruction for the façade of St. Biagio Church was proposed also in L'Aquila. In this case, the large use of different investigation tests on the walls and the pillars drove to an extensive knowledge level of the structures [15]. With the intro-duction of the Building National Code (NTC2008), this knowledge path is requested for supporting the design choices on the building, in order to justify improvements or retrofitting interventions. The results obtained on the pillars of the main nave (Fig. 3) showed a non-uniform distribution of the damages, involving the bases of the pillars aligned along the west side. Thanks to this detailed level of knowledge, the integrity of the structure was respected and specific local interventions were arranged for rein-forcing the masonry elements characterized by a low connection [15]. The contained damages observed on the main structures were due to a positive application of the roles of art for the building developed in the constructive tradition of L'Aquila during previous seismic events.

Collemaggio Basilica showed a positive response for some reinforced structures and total failure for others. Among these examples, the state of damage of the pillars of the main nave constituted an issue that deserved the main attention. These octagonal columns supported the highest walls of the building and the large crack pattern required an interpretation together with their mechanical response.

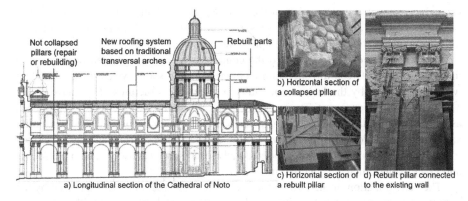

b) Horizontal section of a collapsed pillar

c) Horizontal section of a rebuilt pillar

d) Rebuilt pillar connected to the existing wall

a) Longitudinal section of the Cathedral of Noto

Not collapsed pillars (repair or rebuilding)

New roofing system based on traditional transversal arches

Rebuilt parts

Fig. 2. Noto Cathedral re-integration project: (a) Longitudinal section with the survived pillars (picture from [14] and graphically modified by the author); (b) Horizontal section showing a multiple leaf masonry of a pillar (courtesy of prof. A. Saisi); (c) The horizontal section of a rebuilt pillar and (d) the connection between a rebuilt pillar and the overlaying wall.

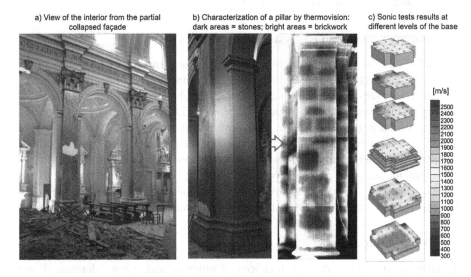

a) View of the interior from the partial collapsed façade

b) Characterization of a pillar by thermovision: dark areas = stones; bright areas = brickwork

c) Sonic tests results at different levels of the base

[m/s]

Fig. 3. St. Biagio church in L'Aquila: (a) View of the interior conditions; (b) Evaluation of the masonry texture by thermographic tests; (c) Evaluation of the damage distribution by velocity range distribution obtained through direct sonic tests (pictures and elaborations by the author).

5   The Intervention Methodology Proposed for the Basilica di Collemaggio

After the 2009 earthquake, the Basilica di Collemaggio was divided in three parts: the body with the main facade and the naves was separated from the apse by the collapsed transept. The proposed methodology for the intervention took into account the following issues: the conservation of the stratified material authenticity still present in the naves and the apse bodies; the conservation of the artistic testimonies hosted in different areas of the complex; the improvement of the structures.

The two survived parts presented the conditions to be strengthened by improving the connections between the structural elements, but the static system of the building was compromised by the lack of continuity between the structures of the naves body and the ones of the apse part. The reconstruction of the collapsed transept was proposed as necessary mending with the aim to restore the structural continuity of the entire architectural complex. For the survived volumes, the conservation plan was developed following the common procedures based on advanced survey activity, materials, decays and crack pattern analysis, and diagnostic investigations.

The categorization of the different aspects taken into account was supported by the geometrical survey, realized by using a laser scanner and integrated with high resolution digital picture rectifications. The refine 3D model of the damaged Basilica was adopted as digital documentation device: an instrument used for understanding the construction logic and interpreting, in detail, the structural response of the complex [16]. It allowed recording the results given by several analyses: from historical, structural and artistic point of view [17].

5.1 Materials and Masonry Textures

The analysis of the materials was used for connecting some contents reported in the historical research about the presence of the signs matured during previous earthquakes and still conserved along the vertical walls of the building. Up to eight different masonry textures were identified thanks to the direct inspections and by the available digital rectification of the prospects. Each texture was shortly described by a legend supporting the material mapping vector representations, forming the graphic body of the definitive conservation design, whilst more detailed reports described the characteristics of the analyzed masonry typology (Fig. 4). The changings applied to the building technology, indicating the evolution of the constructive methods in a territory characterized by seismic risk, are testified by deep differences reported in the surveys.

5.2 Decay Analysis

The analysis on the conservation conditions of structural and coating elements allows evaluating the causes of the alterations and deteriorations. By mapping the areas afflicted by specific degradation processes, the interventions are outlined and a final costs computation is available. This graphic analysis reports a synthetic legend associating the materials with the observed decays. More detailed data sets characterize the reports on the conservative interventions, where a brief description of the decays is supported by high resolution pictures. Two main sections compose the document providing generic information on the artistic work and a list of actions defined in operative manuals for the definition of the conservative procedure. Figure 4 provides an example of a material decay mapping with its short legend and the information for the intervention recorded in a database set for a future association to the geometrical advanced survey of the building. The improvement of different levels of the details, like

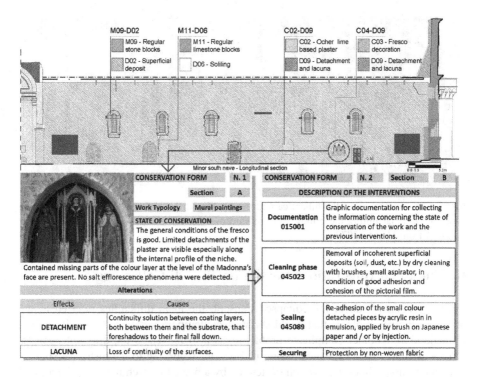

Fig. 4. Longitudinal section of the south minor nave with the materials and decay mapping with an example of the indications for the conservation design applied to a fresco decoration.

the pathological materials conditions and the structural deformations, associated with the interactive 3D digital model represents an innovative novelty supported by the interdisciplinary approach carried out by the research unit of Politecnico di Milano and presented in [17].

The comprehension of the structural properties of the pillars received a fundamental support by the historical analysis, underlying the deep changings occurred after the Baroque restyling of the naves and the further elimination of the decorations and stucco works belonging to that period (Fig. 5), according to the controversial 20th century restoration carried out by Moretti [18, 19].

Furthermore, a manual survey stone by stone restituted the exact geometry of each stone block of the pillars, very useful for interpreting the intrinsic vulnerability due to the stones displacement. Also the study of the out of plane profiles of the pillars supported the interpretation of their crack pattern and their mechanical response [20]. According to ISCARSAH document promoting the conservation of the structures in the built heritage, this study drove to the final proposal for the pillars, without the elimination of the stone elements. The pillars were mainly repaired by applying the "scuci-cuci" technique: selecting the broken stone elements and replacing them by using local stone cut as the substituted elements.

Fig. 5. The restoration of the pillars carried out by Moretti in 1960: (a) The nave in Baroque style; (b) A pillar during the removal of the stuccoworks; (c) The nave after the intervention (pictures from Moretti 1972)

6   The Final Integrations for the Basilica di Collemaggio

For the reconstruction of the collapsed transept, the main difficulties referred to the aspect of the new volume that could show its contemporary nature or hide it under a mimetic skin. Another complicate problem was also related to the different configurations assumed by the Basilica during its history. According to the historical sources [21], the transept, in origin, was characterized by a byzantine arch in its upper part that was further substituted by new structures, as the dome built after the 15th century earthquake and the last reinforced concrete and brick dome realized in the second half of the 20th century (Fig. 6a). The idea of the designers of the local superintendence office was to avoid the revival of the dome, a stylistic element that was not clearly defined in the historical sources about the real proportions and its realization. In addition, both experts in history of architecture and in structural engineering agreed on the necessity of limiting the vulnerability of the church by rebuilding an element that during each important seismic event revealed to be the weakest part of the complex (Fig. 6b) [22, 23]. The historical analysis showed that the pillars of the transept increased their dimension after each failure, with the aim to reinforce this part of the church.

The realization of a new structure, replacing the pillars of the transept and reconfiguring the upper crown by an arch shaped in byzantine style (Fig. 6c), was than assumed by the advisors for the structural reinforcement as the strategic condition for introducing a resistance filter between the two survived parts. This structure, intended as a "resistant backdrop", was designed in reinforced concrete for providing a dampen effect to the mass accelerations of the naves body and the apse body during seismic events. The surface treatment for this new element, among the different choices, was mimetic: the survived stones coming from the collapsed masonry pillars, previously arranged during the 20th century restoration, were recovered and re-used as second skin of the new reinforced concrete pillars.

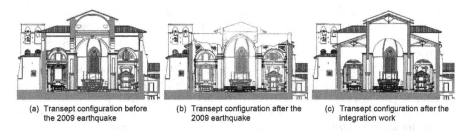

(a) Transept configuration before the 2009 earthquake (b) Transept configuration after the 2009 earthquake (c) Transept configuration after the integration work

Fig. 6. Layouts of three different configurations of Collemaggio transept (courtesy of Professor R. Brumana and modified by the author)

7 Conclusions

The described cases introduced the integration of the collapsed volumes as a mandatory condition for ensuring a reliable conservation of the original parts. The role of the diagnostic investigations showed that an adequate level of knowledge can have a deep impact on the intervention methodologies. The crack pattern analysis carried out on the pillars of the naves of three churches showed a high level of damage for the Noto Cathedral and the Basilica di Collemaggio, whilst the St. Biagio Church presented a diffused crack pattern concentrated at the bases of the pillars.

In Collemaggio, thanks to the detailed survey of the long and large cracks associated to the 3D digital model on the pillars, a study in depth of the damage level was carried out. The separations between the blocks revealed the difference between the existing elements and the parts substituted in the last restoration work promoted by Mario Moretti. This survey allowed differentiating the real structural damages from the superficial damages. The intervention on the pillars had the aim to preserve a significant quantity of the existing elements. The final proposal, through the "scuci-cuci" intervention, was realized for saving more than the 50% of the masonry pillars.

References

1. Majewski, P.: Ideologie und denkmalplege der wiederaufbau des warschauer konigsschlosses 1944–1980. In: Bingen, D., Hinz, H.M. (eds.) Zerstorung und Wiederaufbau historischer Bauten in Deutschland und Polen, pp. 107–116, Wiesbaden (2005)
2. ICOMOS: Amsterdam Declaration (1975). https://www.icomos.org/en/and/169-the-declaration-of-amsterdam. Accessed 25 May 2018
3. ISCARSAH, Icomos: Heritage Structures (2008). http://iscarsah.icomos.org/index.php?option=com_content&view=article&id=51&Itemid=613. Accessed 30 May 2018
4. Vivenzio, G.: Storia de' tremuoti avvenuti nella provincia della Calabria ulteriore e nella città de Messina nell' anno 1783: e di quanto nella Calabria fu fatto per lo suo risorgimento fino al 1787: preceduta da una teoria, ed istoria generale de' tremuoti, vol. 1 (1788)
5. Giuffrè, A.: Letture sulla meccanica delle murature storiche. Kappa ed., Turin ((1998)
6. D.L. 22 gennaio 2004, n. 42. Codice dei beni culturali e del paesaggio, ai sensi dell'articolo 10 della legge 6 luglio 2002, n. 137. Gazzetta Ufficiale n. 45 del 24-2-2004 - Suppl. Ordinario n. 28

7. Poletti, E., Vasconcelos, G., Lourenço, P.B.: Timber frames as an earthquake resisting system in Portugal. In: Correia, M.R., Lourenço, P.B.,Varum, H. (eds.) Seismic Retrofitting: Learning fromVernacular Architecture, pp. 161–166. Taylor & Francis Group, London (2015)

8. Ferrigni, F.: L'edificato storico in zona sismica: insieme vulnerabile o fonte di conoscenza? In: Scala, B. (ed.) Verso una cultura della prevenzione: le strategie di protezione sismica del territorio gardesano, pp. 141–170. Nardini, Bassano del Grappa (2017)

9. D.M. 14.01.2008, Nuove norme tecniche per le costruzioni, G.U 4.02.2008, n.29, Ministero delle Infrastrutture, dell'Interno e Dipartimento Protezione Civile, Roma

10. Circolare n.617, 2. 2009. Istruzioni per l'applicazione delle Nuove norme tecniche per le costruzioni. Ministero per i beni e le attività culturali, Roma: Gazzetta Ufficiale n.47 26-2-2009 - Supplemento n.27

11. Borri, A., et al.: Analisi dell'efficacia degli interventi realizzati su edifici del centro storico di Norcia colpiti dai sismi del 2016. In: XVII Convegno ANIDIS L'ingegneria Sismica in Italia, pp. 29–48. Pisa University Press (2017)

12. Della Torre, S.: Terremoto e prevenzione. ΑΝΑΓΚΗ 79, pp. 5–8. Altralinea Editrice, Firenze (2016)

13. Binda, L., Anzani, A., Saisi, A.: Failure due to long term behaviour of heavy structures: the pavia civic tower and the Noto Cathedral. In: 8th International Conference on STREMAH 2003, Structural Studies Repairs and Maintenance of Heritage Architecture, pp. 99–108 (2003)

14. Tringali, S., De Benedictis, R.: La Ricostruzione della Cattedrale di Noto. L.C.T. Edizioni, Noto (2000)

15. Cantini, L., Tedeschi, C., Binda, L., La Rosa, R., Tringali, S.: Non-destructive investigation as a tool for the diagnosis of masonry damaged by the earthquake and as a support for the right choice of repair techniques. In: Forde, M.C. (ed.) Structural Faults and Repair-2012. 14th International Conference, pp. 1–12 (2012)

16. Barazzetti, L., Banfi, F., Brumana, R., Previtali, M.: Creation of parametric BIM objects from point clouds using. Photogram. Rec. **30**(152), 339–362 (2015)

17. Brumana, R., et al.: Generative HBIM-modeling to embody complexity. Surveying, preservation, site intervention. The Basilica di Collemaggio (L'Aquila). Appl. Geomat. (2018). https://doi.org/10.1007/s12518-018-0233-3. Springer Berlin Heidelberg

18. Moretti, M.: Collemaggio. De Luca ed., Roma (1972)

19. Pane, R.: Il massacro di S. Maria di Collemaggio. Restauro **1**(3), 94–95 (1972)

20. Oreni, D., Brumana, R., Della Torre, S., Banfi, F., Barazzetti, L., Previtali, M.: Survey turned into HBIM: the restoration and the work involved concerning the Basilica di Collemaggio after the earthquake (L'Aquila). ISPRS Ann. Photogramm., Remote. Sens. Spat. Inf. Sci. **2**(5), 267–273 (2014)

21. Bartolomucci, C.: Santa Maria di Collemaggio: Interpretazione critica e problemi di conservazione. Palombi Editori, Rome (2004)

22. Cartapati, E.: Sistemi di controventamento e di dissipazione di sommità per pareti libere di grandi dimensioni: intervento sulla Basilica di S. Maria di Collemaggio a L'Aquila (1997–2001). In: Carbonara, G. (ed.), Atlante del Restauro, tomo II, sez. G7: Presidi antisismici, tavv. 23–25, pp. 648–650 (2004)

23. Antonacci, E., Gattulli, V., Martinelli, A., Vestroni, F.: La Basilica di S. Maria di Collemaggio in L'Aquila: prima e dopo il terremoto. In: Milano, L., Morisi, C., Calderini, C., Donatelli, A. (eds.) L'Università e la Ricerca per l'Abruzzo: il patrimonio culturale dopo il terremoto del 06 Aprile 2009, pp. 45–51. Textus Edizioni, Pescara (2012)

UGESCO - A Hybrid Platform for Geo-Temporal Enrichment of Digital Photo Collections Based on Computational and Crowdsourced Metadata Generation

Steven Verstockt[1]([⌗]), Samnang Nop[1], Florian Vandecasteele[1],
Tim Baert[2], Nico Van de Weghe[2], Hans Paulussen[3], Ettore Rizza[4],
and Mathieu Roeges[5]

[1] IDLab, Ghent University-Imec, Ghent, Belgium
steven.verstockt@ugent.be
[2] CartoGIS, Department of Geography, Ghent University, Ghent, Belgium
[3] KU Leuven and Imec, Kortrijk, Belgium
[4] Information and Communication Science Department,
Université libre de Bruxelles, Brussels, Belgium
[5] Direction opérationnelle CegeSoma/Archives de l'Etat DO4,
Brussels, Belgium

Abstract. The majority of digital photo collections at museums, archives and libraries are facing (meta) data problems that impact their interpretation, exploration and exploitation. In most cases, links between collection items are only supported at the highest level, which limits the item's searchability and makes it difficult to generate scientific added value out of it or to use the collections in new end-user focused applications. The geo-temporal metadata enrichment tools that are proposed in this paper tackle these issues by extending and linking the existing collection items and by facilitating their spatio-temporal mapping for interactive querying. To further optimize the quality of the temporal and spatial annotations that are retrieved by our automatic enrichment tools, we also propose some crowdsourced microtasks to validate and improve the generated metadata. This crowdsourced input on its turn can be used to further optimize (and retrain) the automatic enrichments. Finally, in order to facilitate the querying of the data, new geo-temporal mapping services are investigated. These services facilitate cross-collection studies in time and space and ease the scientific interpretation of the collection items in a broader sense.

Keywords: Digital heritage collections · Geo-temporal mapping
Metadata enrichment · Microtask crowdsourcing · Named entity recognition
Rephotography

1 Introduction

The current metadata scope of digital heritage collections (such as the historical photo archives shown in Fig. 1) is too narrow and too high-level to allow easy and adequate exploration of the collection data. Mostly, temporal and spatial annotations are missing,

© Springer Nature Switzerland AG 2018
M. Ioannides et al. (Eds.): EuroMed 2018, LNCS 11196, pp. 113–124, 2018.
https://doi.org/10.1007/978-3-030-01762-0_10

which makes it difficult to query the collections based on location or time periods, i.e., a user needs to analyze the picture labels to know when or where a picture was taken. Nonetheless, time and location entities can mostly be extracted automatically from the textual descriptions of the picture using named entity recognition (NER) or by using computer vision algorithms on the picture itself. In this paper, we combine both techniques and extend it with microtask crowdsourcing techniques to improve the quality (and quantity) of the collection metadata. We will mainly focus on photo collections, but the UGESCO methodology and tools can also be used for other types of cultural heritage data, such as video archives.

Fig. 1. Historical photo archives of CegeSoma – each collection item consists of an image (a), a Dutch/French picture label (b) and some general collection info/keywords (c).

The location and time features that are generated by the enrichment tools allow us to analyze where and when a picture was taken, and in combination with (semantic) scene/object tags clustering they can be fed into spatio-temporal mapping tools to perform in-depth studies of the data (such as clustering and collection linking). We have also undertaken first steps in the direction of the rephotography of the collection pictures, i.e., to be able to explore the pictures of the past in the StreetView of today (similar to the Museum of London StreetMuseum app[1]). This is also part of the demonstrator platform on which users can up-/or downvote location and metadata tags. Based on their input and voting behavior, the reliability of each of the user contributions is estimated. Finally, it is important to mention that, due to its generic architecture, other types of metadata (e.g. stories and audio recordings) can easily be added to the platform.

The remainder of this paper is organized as follows. Section 2 gives an overview of the UGESCO framework and discusses each of the building blocks of our generic architecture for automatic collection enrichment. Subsequently, Sect. 3 presents the UGESCO dashboard that is used for crowdsourced enrichment/validation. Within this

---

[1] https://www.museumoflondon.org.uk/Resources/app/Dickens_webpage/home.html.

dashboard, we also implemented a first version of the StreetView rephotography tool. Next, Sect. 4 proposes UGESCO's web tools to explore the enriched collections, i.e., a metadata filtering/clustering web service and a geographic information system (GIS) for spatio-temporal data exploration. Finally, Sect. 5 lists the conclusions and points out directions for future work.

2 UGESCO Framework

The general architecture of the UGESCO framework is shown in Fig. 2. First, collection (meta) data (i.e., images and their captions/labels) are fed to the NER and computer vision building blocks to detect the city level, street level or pinpoint location, scene/building type and time period of each item. Subsequently, the named entity disambiguation step further improves the detection results using the thesaurus keywords and Wikidata knowledge[2]. Furthermore, we also propose a StreetView scraping/matching methodology to verify pinpoint location data and to detect the field of view (FOV) of each picture of which we found the exact location metadata. Next, microtask crowdsourcing (focusing on validation/completion of the time, space and attribute aspects of the collection items) is used on the output of these automatic tools. The crowd are the collaborative brains that help in further improving the metadata quality. Finally, a spatio-temporal web-based GIS application allows users (e.g., researchers, local historians, and the public at large) to view and compare the data at different points in time n time and space, with case dependent mapping tools such as the triangular model[3] proposed in [1]. In this section, we will now further discuss each of the automatic enrichment tools.

2.1 Detection of Spatio-Temporal Named Entities

Natural language processing (NLP) tools are used to detect words and phrases expressing location and time. The NLP task used to detect these spatio-temporal expressions is called "named entity recognition" (NER). UGESCO's NER task differs in various aspects from previous NER projects, involving a number of challenges related to the nature and the type of texts used for picture descriptions and the types of enrichments required for geo-temporal named entity recognition.

Originally, NER was limited to the detection of proper nouns referring to names of persons, organizations and locations, but the categories were later on extended to other types, including numerical information (referring to time, date and different numbering systems). In UGESCO, we limit NER to two main categories: location and time. The location category is expanded from the general LOC type (referring to any type of location, including names of cities, regions or countries) to a set of subcategories,

---

[2] https://www.wikidata.org - free and open knowledge base that can be read and edited by both humans and machines.

[3] The Triangular Model (TM) constitutes an alternative to the limited linear model and facilitates the interpretation of complex time depending data.

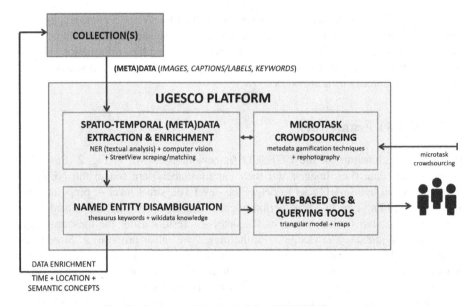

Fig. 2. General architecture of the UGESCO framework.

including POIs[4]. The following LOC subcategories are used: PLACE, STREET, ROAD, WATERWAY, BUILDING, SPACE and MONUMENT. In the case of timestamps, the TIMEX[5] categories are used. This subcategorization typology facilitates fine-grained selection of locations and time.

The main issue of NER processing in the UGESCO project is the brevity and the structure of the photo descriptions. Unlike ordinary running text, text samples describing pictures are usually short texts, lacking co-textual information, necessary to disambiguate the words. Moreover, description fields often have a reduced syntactic structure (e.g. subject missing, use of infinitives), so that specific training and/or adaptation of existing NLP tools is required.

Figure 3 gives a schematic overview of the different steps used in the NER processing. As an example, we use a French input text (ugc-001-fr.txt), but the same approach is used for texts in any other language. First of all, some pre-processing is required: the text is cleaned, tokenized and tagged. Tokenization involves the process of separating words from non-words (e.g. punctuation). Each token is then assigned a part-of-speech tag, indicating the word category, so that you can distinguish verbs from nouns or any other word category. After pre-processing the tokens, the NER process can start, using two extra inputs: the language model (LG) and a gazetteer. The LG model is the result of a supervised training process, based on previously annotated data and template based algorithm for NER detection. The gazetteer is principally a kind of location dictionary, containing a set of commonly used locations. On the basis of these extra resources, the NER process detects named entities in the text samples.

---

[4] Points-of-interests, such as names of specific buildings, roadways and important landmarks.

[5] http://www.timeml.org/.

The result of the NER process is stored in an output file (ugc-001-fr.ner), and in two extra files in a special format (output ending in yml and json), which enables further processing by other tools.

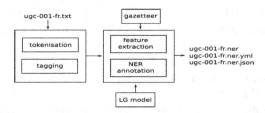

Fig. 3. NER processing of picture labels

2.2 Computer Vision-Based Place Recognition

In case NER is not able to detect the exact location of a particular image (or in case we want to validate the NER output) we can detect the location (or some of its features) by using one of the computer vision based geolocalization algorithms that have been proposed in literature [2]. Feature matching with georeferenced image datasets is by far the most useful/accurate geolocalization technique [3, 4]. Based on a feature point matching algorithm, such as the one proposed in [5], this algorithm searches the best match of the POI image within a dataset of georeferenced images that are taken in the POI neighborhood. However, such georeferenced dataset will not always be available or it will be computationally too hard to build it up for an entire region/city. For this reason, we introduce a place recognition filtering step based on semantic scene understanding. The generated semantic features facilitate the construction of a geo-referenced dataset. The approach that is most closely related to our setup is the hier-archical, multi-modal approach of Kelm et al. [6] for georeferencing Flickr videos. Both textual toponym identification in video metadata and visual features of the video key frames are used to identify similar content. Their approach, however, is still global and the accuracy is rather limited, i.e., only one third of the video dataset is correctly geotagged within a 1 km error margin, which is too limited for UGESCO's desired search relevance and querying efficiency and effectivity.

Semantic Scene Understanding for Place Recognition. Visual scene recognition is a trending topic since last few years. Previous studies heavily focused on feature engi-neering where features are generated based on statistical analysis, previous knowledge and feature performance evaluation. This requires expensive human labour and mostly relies on expert knowledge. A more recent trend is to use feature learning techniques where different positive and negative samples are shown to the system and, based on these examples, the parameters of the network are changed accordingly. As discussed in [7], feature learning mechanisms achieve outstanding results compared to hand-crafted features for different localization tasks, which is also the reason for using it in

UGESCO. A trained convolutional neural network (CNN) such as Places365-VGG[6] is able to give scene predictions and their corresponding prediction confidence [8]. In combination with a semantic vocabulary and appropriate semantic distance measures, this allows us to fine-tune and determine the context of the scene.

UGESCO's place recognition tool tags each image with a set of semantic descriptors using the MIT places model[7]. The Places model suggest the most likely place categories representing the image, using Places-CNN, and identifies if the image is an indoor or an outdoor place. The indoor/outdoor information is also used to select the correct mode (indoor/outdoor) in the Street View mapping and rephotography (which is further discussed in Sect. 4). The output of the places model can also be used for data filtering and picture grouping. In the CegeSoma collection, for example, we can easily filter out pictures that do not contain location clues or we can group pictures based on semantic concepts (such as building types like churches and castles). In order to improve the image categorization, we also analyze the co-occurrence of semantic concepts using a similar approach as discussed in [9]. Figure 4 shows the output of the place recognition on some pictures of the CegeSoma collection. This output can be further optimized by also taking into account semantic relationships between the suggested keywords.

Street View Scraping and Matching. Depending on the metadata output of the NER and computer vision modules, different strategies for Street View matching have been developed to find the exact location of an image if we only have its city or street name. If, for example, NER tells us the street and city name, we can request/extract an Open Street Map (OSM) street polygon, process the Street View (SV) panorama images of this region (to create a SV dataset), filter the SV dataset on semantic similarity (based on places output – or other CNNs) and match the query image to the SV dataset (as shown in Fig. 5). Of course, NER and computer vision output will not always be able to give such detailed location estimation. If, for example, we only know that it is a church in Ghent, we will first query DBpedia[8] for all churches in Ghent and use address geocoding to build up the SV datasets of all possible candidates. If we don't know the city, or we can't find a good match, we will try to get more detailed information from the named entity disambiguation step or collect crowdsourced contributions of the particular image.

2.3   Named Entity Disambiguation

The NER and computer vision phase result in a list of names of locations mentioned in the photo captions or found by the visual place recognition algorithm. However, as already discussed, this information will frequently be too vague to perform a good location estimation or will lead to conflicting NER and computer vision results. For example: "Gare du Nord" does not tell us much if we don't have additional location info. Which "Gare du Nord" is it? Is it in Brussels or Paris? And what does

---

[6] http://places.csail.mit.edu/.

[7] http://places2.csail.mit.edu/.

[8] https://wiki.dbpedia.org/.

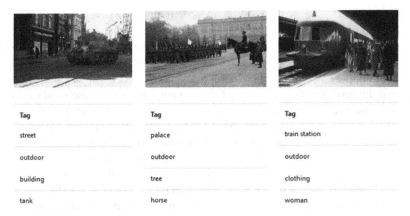

Tag	Tag	Tag
street	palace	train station
outdoor	outdoor	outdoor
building	tree	clothing
tank	horse	woman

Fig. 4. Place recognition results – pictures from CegeSoma collection.

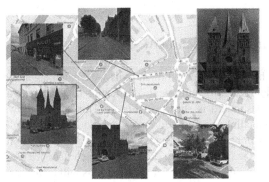

Metadata => Bij Sint-Jacobs, Ghent

1. request/extract OSM street polygon
2. request/process StreetView (SV) panorama images > SV dataset
3. filter SV dataset (semantic similarity)
4. match query image with SV dataset

Alternative approach

Metadata => church, Ghent

>> DBpedia query + address geocoding

Fig. 5. Streetview scraping – matching with georeferenced dataset.

"Cinquantenaire" mean, which has several pages in Wikipedia? To find the answer, we need to be able to link each of these locations to a standardized entry in a database, then choose the one that is most likely the place where the picture was taken. This process of trying to automatically link words in a document (e.g. place names) to an external database (e.g. Wikipedia) is called "Entity Linking", "Named Entity Disambiguation", "Reconciliation" or "Entity resolution". Although much progress has been made since the seminal works [10], the task is far from being solved. Its difficulty varies according to the quality and the length of the text. A tweet or a SMS, for example, can be ambiguous even for a human. The same goes for short photo captions. The temporal context is also important. When a picture taken in 1940s says that the scene took place in "Hamme, Belgium", we must not forget that, at the time, at least three Belgian municipalities had this name, in three different provinces.

The proposed method of disambiguation uses original clues from the photo database, i.e., the thesaurus keywords that archivists have applied to folders containing groups of photos related to the same theme. These keywords sometimes contain a place name, such as a city, a province, or a region. Using these terms, which we parsed out from the keywords, we will apply an algorithm that will query Wikidata[9] using SPARQL[10] queries and API calls. For each location previously extracted from the photo captions and the computer vision output, the algorithm will select the possible candidates and choose the most likely based on the available clues.

When multiple places are mentioned in the same picture, it will use the same clues to rule out the least likely. The results of the computer vision are also used to perform the disambiguation. In the case of "Cinquantenaire", which can refer to both a park, a museum or a bridge, the classes mentioned by the computer vision (e.g. "Bridge") will help to determine the most appropriate entry. When computer vision predictions seem to contradict each other (for example if the place can be a church, a synagogue or a palace at the same time), Wikidata's ontology is used to find the broader category that "subsume" these classes (in this case, the superclass "Building"). Finally, if the ambiguity is too strong, the system will not try to guess further and will simply indicate that this text or this photo must be verified by the crowd. The first results obtained from a sample of pictures are encouraging and must now be tested on a larger scale and later subjected to a human evaluation.

3   Crowdsourced Validation and Enrichment

To further improve the outcome of the automatic enrichment tools we created a generic dashboard for crowdsourced enrichment of multimedia collections. The general architecture of the Django[11]-based dashboard is shown in Fig. 6. This set-up allows users to vote for different types of datalinks and to add new datalinks. Each datalink consists of a data object (such as an image) and a metadata object (e.g., its location, time period, keyword). The votes and the quality of the datalinks of each user are used to generate a credibility score. Based on this score, his/her contributions will have more (or less) impact on the UGESCO metadata generation. The user interface of the dashboard is shown in Fig. 7 and can be evaluated at the UGESCO website[12]. The crowdsourced rephotography (which is discussed in the next section) is not yet fully supported, but will be integrated soon.

3.1   Crowdsourced Rephotography

Aligning a historical photograph in a modern rephotograph[13] (or vice versa) can serve as a remarkable visualization of the passage of time and can be used across a plethora of application domains (e.g., tourism, media and interactive museum applications). Crowdsourced and computational rephotography modules try to accurately map images of the past on the buildings and landscapes of today. As described in [5], estimation of

---

[9] https://www.wikidata.org - a kind of structured version of Wikipedia, readable both by humans and machines.

[10] https://www.w3.org/rdf-sparql-query.

[11] https://www.djangoproject.com/.

[12] http://tw06v074.ugent.be/.

[13] https://en.wikipedia.org/wiki/Richard_Prince.

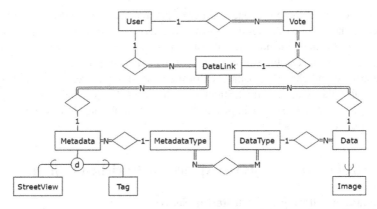

Fig. 6. General architecture of the UGESCO generic dashboard for crowdsourced enrichment of multimedia collections.

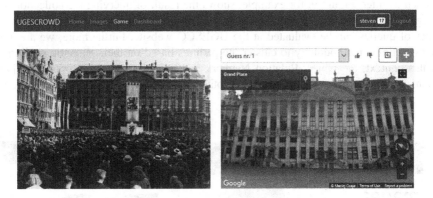

Fig. 7. UGESCO dashboard for crowdsourced enrichment – Street View localization task.

Fig. 8. Rephotography tool to align a historical photograph with its Street View location.

FOV can be found automatically by following a random sample consensus (RANSAC) homography matching. Another approach, focusing on outlier filtering and viewpoint clustering, is proposed by Makantasis et al. [11]. However, in order to optimize and validate the results of these approaches, a crowdsourced rephotography module will be integrated in the dashboard. Figure 8 shows an example of how this is currently done. It is important to mention, however, that the geometric alignment is still rather basic and requires more research/development. However, the tool already allows to zoom, navigate around and change transparency of the collection picture, which continuously is dynamically placed at its correct Street View location. These crowdsourced dynamic image overlays can be used to improve the computational algorithms, i.e., they can learn from the crowd's actions.

4   UGESCO's Web Tools to Explore the Enriched Collections

4.1   Metadata Filtering and Clustering Service

The first web-based tool that can be used to explore the enriched collections is a metadata filtering & clustering service. Several metadata types and values can be defined as filter. Figure 9, for example, shows the result of querying the collection for images that (a) contain a horse and a church, or (b) a tank and a man. These and other types of queries can be evaluated at the UGESCO website. Furthermore, we are also investigating a methodology to cluster the pictures based on their semantic similarity. In this context, the Object Relation Network and bag of semantics proposed in [12] seems interesting mechanisms. However, other approaches will also be evaluated.

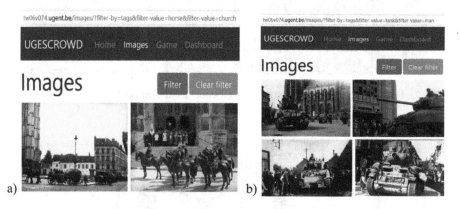

Fig. 9. Metadata filtering and clustering service.

4.2   WebGIS for Spatio-Temporal Data Exploration

The UGESCO WebGIS lets end users explore the enriched datasets using temporal and spatial mapping tools, and study how the data evolves in time and space. The time intervals are structured within the interactive Triangular Model (TM), where each point is a time interval with the center of the interval on the x-axis and the duration on the y-axis [1]. The WebGIS allows user to select specific objects based on different Allen relations and derivatives, and to combine them with the basis of set theory on the TM or the map. An example of the TM is shown in Fig. 10, which gives a spatio-temporal overview of all battles that happened before the battle of Moscow.

The WebGIS is implemented in Javascript and uses (i) the Leaflet[14] library for generating the interactive maps, (ii) plotly.js[15] as graphing library for the TM and (iii) turf.js[16] for the advanced geospatial analysis.

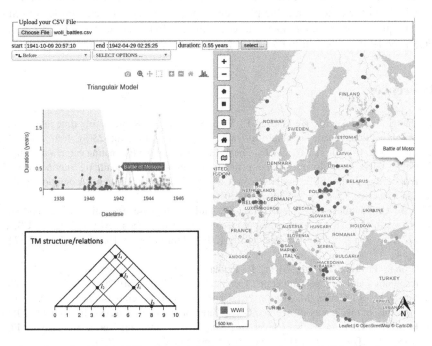

Fig. 10. Triangular Model (TM) of battles during WWII – selection of all battles that happened before the battle of Moscow. The inset shows the TM structure and relations between points in the model.

5   Conclusions and Future Work

This paper gives an overview of the UGESCO building blocks that can be used for computational and crowdsourced geo-temporal (meta) data extraction and enrichment of digital photo collections. The enriched collection items can be linked and analyzed in time and space using the discussed dashboard and web services. The strengths of the proposed methodology compared to state-of-the-art alternatives are its unique combination of NLP, computer vision and named entity disambiguation (for improved

---

[14] https://leafletjs.com/.

[15] https://plot.ly/javascript/.

[16] http://turfjs.org/.

location and time tagging), its semantics driven image filtering/matching (which leads to better geolocalization), and its WebGIS for generating spatio-temporal overviews.

In order to further improve the quality of the NER tool, we will mainly focus on how to improve language model training and how to handle gazetteer processing more efficiently, so that the learning algorithm can be improved as well. Furthermore, more research needs to be performed on automatic place recognition (e.g. architectural style detection) to create more valuable place descriptions, which on their turn lead to more relevant queries and facilitate location based linking. In this context, the Field-Of-View (FOV) model described in the work of Lu et al. [13] seems very interesting.

References

1. Qiang, Y., Valcke, M., De Maeyer, P., Van de Weghe, N.: Representing time intervals in a two-dimensional space: an empirical study. J. Vis. Lang. Comput. **25**(4), 466–480 (2014)
2. Cham, T.J., Ciptadi, A., Tan, W.C., Pham, M.T., Chia, L.T.: Estimating camera pose from a single urban ground-view omnidirectional image and a 2D building outline map. In: Proceedings of the IEEE Conference on Computer Vision and Pattern Recognition (CVPR), San Francisco, CA, US, pp. 366–373 (2010)
3. Arth, C., Reitmayr, G., Schmalstieg, D.: Full 6DOF pose estimation from geo-located images. In: Lee, K.M., Matsushita, Y., Rehg, J.M., Hu, Z. (eds.) ACCV 2012. LNCS, vol. 7726, pp. 705–717. Springer, Heidelberg (2013). https://doi.org/10.1007/978-3-642-37431-9_54
4. Gronat, P., Havlena, M., Sivic, J., Pajdla, T.: Building streetview datasets for place recognition and city reconstruction. Technical report, CTU-CMP-2011-16, pp. 1–13 (2011)
5. Verstockt, S., Gerke, M., Kerle, N.: Geolocalization of crowdsourced images for 3D modeling of city points of interest. Geosci. Remote Sens. Lett. **12**(8), 1670–1674 (2015)
6. Kelm, P., Schmiedeke, S., Cluver, K., Sikora, T.: Automatic geo-referencing of Flickr videos. In: eBook and USB Produced by Sigma Orionis, p. 32 (2011)
7. Zhou, B., Lapedriza, A., Khosla, A.: Places: a 10 million image database for scene recognition. IEEE Trans. Pattern Anal. Mach. Intell. **40**(6), 1452–1464 (2018)
8. Wang, L., Guo, S., Huang, W., Qiao, Y.: Places205-VGGNet models for scene recognition. arXiv:1508.01667 (2015)
9. Bengio, S., Dean, J., Erhan, D., Rabinovich, A., Shlens, J., Singer, Y.: Using web co-occurrence statistics for improving image categorization. arXiv:1312.5697v2 (2013)
10. Rao, D., McNamee, P., Dredze, M.: Entity linking: finding extracted entities in a knowledge base. In: Poibeau, T., Saggion, H., Piskorski, J., Yangarber, R. (eds.) Multi-source, Multilingual Information Extraction and Summarization, pp. 93–115. Springer, Heidelberg (2013). https://doi.org/10.1007/978-3-642-28569-1_5
11. Makantasis, K., Doulamis, A., Doulamis, N., Ioannides, M.: In the wild image retrieval and clustering for 3D cultural heritage landmarks reconstruction. Multimed. Tools Appl. **75**(7), 3593–3629 (2016)
12. Chen, N., Prasanna, V.K.: Semantic image clustering using object relation network. In: Hu, S.-M., Martin, R.R. (eds.) CVM 2012. LNCS, vol. 7633, pp. 59–66. Springer, Heidelberg (2012). https://doi.org/10.1007/978-3-642-34263-9_8
13. Lu, Y., et al.: GeoUGV: user-generated mobile video dataset with fine granularity spatial metadata. In: Proceedings of the 7th International Conference on Multimedia Systems, pp. 43–46, New York, USA (2016)

Using Biographical Texts as Linked Data for Prosopographical Research and Applications

Minna Tamper[1(✉)] [iD], Petri Leskinen[1] [iD], Kasper Apajalahti[1] [iD],
and Eero Hyvönen[1,2] [iD]

[1] Semantic Computing Research Group (SeCo), Aalto University, Helsinki, Finland
{minna.tamper,petri.leskinen,kasper.apajalahti,eero.hyvonen}@aalto.fi
[2] HELDIG – Helsinki Centre for Digital Humanities,
University of Helsinki, Helsinki, Finland
http://seco.cs.aalto.fi, http://heldig.fi

Abstract. This paper argues that representing texts as semantic Linked Data provides a useful basis for analyzing their contents in Digital Humanities research and for Cultural Heritage application development. The idea is to transform Cultural Heritage texts into a knowledge graph and a Linked Data service that can be used flexibly in different applications via a SPARQL endpoint. The argument is discussed and evaluated in the context of biographical and prosopographical research and a case study where over 13 000 life stories form biographical collections of Biographical Centre of the Finnish Literature Society were transformed into RDF, enriched by data linking, and published in a SPARQL endpoint. Tools for biography and prosopography, data clustering, network analysis, and linguistic analysis were created with promising first results.

1 From Text to Semantic Structures

Digital Humanities (DH) [3] is a major new research paradigm at the crossroads of computing, humanities, and social sciences. The main idea is to develop and use novel computational methods, such as data analysis, topic modeling, visualization, and network analysis, to solve research problems in Social Sciences and Humanities (SSH) based on big data that is becoming available as a result of digitalization of the society.

Much of the primary data of DH is available only in textual form, and there is an ever-growing need for structuring it for semantic analysis. The research hypothesis of this paper is that representing texts as semantic Linked Data (LD), based on standards, data models, and best practices of W3C[1], provides a useful basis [6] for analyzing their contents in DH research and for Cultural Heritage (CH) application [9] development: Firstly, the data can be published

---

[1] https://www.w3.org/standards/semanticweb/ accessed: 13 August 2018.

© Springer Nature Switzerland AG 2018
M. Ioannides et al. (Eds.): EuroMed 2018, LNCS 11196, pp. 125–137, 2018.
https://doi.org/10.1007/978-3-030-01762-0_11

in standard RDF formats in a data service on the Semantic Web that can be queried in flexible ways for extracting the data for different use cases. Secondly, the Linked Data paradigm facilitates data enrichment by data linking and fusion from related data repositories. Thirdly, the semantics of LD is defined in terms of logic, which facilitates data enrichment by reasoning [8].

This paper investigates and evaluates this hypothesis by four case studies. First (Sect. 2) a natural language (NL) pipeline for transforming texts into a knowledge graph to be published in a SPARQL endpoint service is presented. After this (Sect. 3), we investigate using the graph in four different use cases in order to test and demonstrate the versatility of the approach. As for the data, the National Biography of Finland, a collection of short textual biographies in addition to other peer-reviewed biographical collections from the Biographical Centre of the Finnish Literature Society totaling in 13 000 life stories, are used. In conclusion (Sect. 4), contributions of the paper and lessons learned are summarized, and related work discussed. The novelty of this paper regarding our earlier publications [13,17] about the Semantic National Biography of Finland (SNBF), is to present the underlying NL transformation pipeline in detail and to show how new tools for prosopography related to clustering, network analysis, and linguistic analysis, can be added on top of the LD service.

2   A Pipeline for Transforming Text into Linked Data

For transforming Finnish texts into knowledge graphs, we have created a general NL pipeline. The pipeline has two branches: (1) one for semi-structured text and (2) one for free text. This is because a part of the texts in focus in our use case, i.e., in biographies, are written in a concise, semi-formal way, explicating the major events, achievements, and other biographical data about the protagonist [28]. Here, for example, listings and abbreviations are widely used (for educational degrees, professions, honorary medals, etc.), and verbs are rarely used for brevity.[2] The main life story, on the other hand, is written in terms of normal full sentences.

The target data model in our study is Bio CRM, an extension of the CIDOC CRM ISO standard[3] for biographical data. The key idea of the model is to represent biographies as sequences of events that the protagonist participated in space and time and in different roles. The Bio CRM model is presented in more detail in [26].

Pattern-Based Knowledge Extraction. For the semi-structured part of the bios, extraction rules based of regular expressions were used. This part includes, for example, descriptions of family relations of the protagonist and lists of her/his

---

[2] In some use cases, e.g., in person registries [12], the whole registry entry may be written using this kind of semi-formal language.

[3] http://cidoc-crm.org accessed: 13 August 2018.

professional history. An example of such descriptions for the architect *Eliel Saarinen* is given below:

> Gottlieb Eliel Saarinen S 20.8.1873 Rantasalmi, K 1.7.1950 Bloomfield Hills, Michigan, Yhdysvallat. V rovasti Juho Saarinen ja Selma Maria Broms. P1 1898 - 1902 (ero) Mathilda Tony Charlotta Gylden (sittemmin Gesellius) S 1877, K 1921, P1 V agronomi Axel Gylden ja Antonia Sofia Hausen; P2 1904 - kuvanveistäjä Minna Carolina Louise (Loja) Gesellius S 1879, ...

The semi-formal expressions here have uniformity in structure that can be used effectively for pattern-based information extraction: First, the person's given and family names are mentioned and after that the fields of birth and death information are separated with *S* for birth, and *K* for death. These fields contain the time and place of the event. A field beginning with *V* contains the information about the person's parents with father followed by mother, their names, occupations, and possible places and times of birth and death. Likewise, fields beginning with *P*, or if several *P1*, *P2* etc., carry the information of possible spouses indicating the year of marriage, and the spouse's living time. The data field may also contain information about the parents of the spouse in *PV*, *PV1*, *PV2*, etc. fields. At the end of the description there is a list of children with their names, occupation, and times and places of birth and death. The process has running time complexity $O(n)$ in relation to the amount of text descriptions, and extracting all the 52 476 family relations from the dataset took 5.2 s.

The semi-structured text also includes the events of the person's career:

> URA. Käynyt kaksi luokkaa Viipurin suomalaista klassillista lyseota 1883 - 1887, kolme luokkaa Viipurin Alkeiskoulua 1887 - 1890; ylioppilas Tampereen reaalilyseosta 1893; arkkitehti Suomen Polyteknillisestä opistosta 1897; ...

Here Eliel Saarinen's career events, beginning with the word "URA", are separated into parts with semicolons. Each part contains text indicating, e.g., the person's education, employer, or other description, followed by years. Entities and their relations in the semi-structured texts were extracted with Python scripts using regular expressions. From this data altogether 102 004 life time Bio CRM events were generated. Extracting the events took 147.6 s and they used 330.0 Mb of disk space.

Knowledge Extraction from Free Text. For the free text part, more complex NL processing is needed. Like in NewsReader [24] and FRED [21], this pipeline branch was built using pre-existing NLP tools. The process consists of linguistic analyses (such as tokenization and morphological tagging) and converting the document structures and the linguistic data into RDF. The NLP Interchange Format (NIF)[4] [7] supplements the RDF representation with a Core Ontology that provides classes and properties to describe the relations between texts and documents. This provides flexibility and structure to divide a document into paragraphs, titles, sentences, and words that can be complemented with structural metadata supplied by NIF and linguistic information, such as lemmas and part-of-speech (POS) tags from NLP tools. In addition to the NIF

---

[4] http://persistence.uni-leipzig.org/nlp2rdf/specification/core.html accessed: 13 August 2018.

format, the commonly used CIDOC CRM ISO standard, Dublin Core Metadata[5], and custom namespace[6] are used to supply classes and properties for describing document metadata.

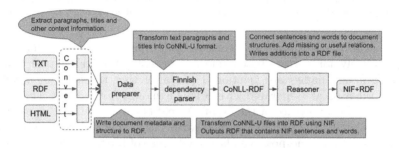

Fig. 1. Pipeline for text processing

The model for transforming text into RDF can be seen in Fig. 1. The pipeline supports RDF, HTML, and text input formats. Their processing starts by extracting paragraphs and titles from each document. The use of RDF input format requires that there is a pre-existing document structure in RDF that can be mapped to the NIF format by the converter. The HTML documents are split into paragraphs utilizing p tags whereas the text document is split to paragraphs based on the assumption that there is an empty line separating the paragraphs from one another. The titles are picked from HTML using the h tags for headers of different levels. From the text input, titles are picked using regular expressions with the assumption that a title is a paragraph that never ends with a dot. After the extraction and conversion phase, the Data preparer writes an RDF file that describes the document structures using CIDOC CRM class *crm:E31_Document* for documents, and NIF format classes *nif:Title* and *nif:Paragraph* for titles and paragraphs within the text document to record substrings using *nif:isString* property and to connect the substrings with *dct:isPartOf* to the document instance representing the full text. These structures are accompanied by properties to describe document sources (using *nbf:docRef* to store the identifier to the original document), substring order, and other structural data, such as HTML links included in the original text. The HTML links are currently added to the *nif:Paragraph* instances using *dct:references* and defined as instances of custom *nbf:Anchor* class that has *nif:isString* property for the anchor texts and *nbf:anchor_link* for the links. The Data preparer module does not structure text but outputs the substrings in separate text files for the following phases.

After the Data preparer phase, the pipeline proceeds to execute the Finnish dependency parser[7] [5] as shown in Fig. 1. Using the texts produced by the

---

[5] http://dublincore.org/documents/dcmi-terms/ accessed: 13 August 2018.

[6] Denoted with prefix nbf in the RDF examples.

[7] http://turkunlp.github.io/Finnish-dep-parser/ accessed: 13 August 2018.

data preparer, the parser transforms the texts into CoNNL-U[8] [22] format for each paragraph and title. For example, from the biography of the architect *Eliel Saarinen*, the title and paragraphs are analyzed and the application produces separately for each of them a file containing sentences and words, their positions, lemmas, POS tags, morphological features, dependencies, and other linguistic information. The results of the transformation of text to CoNLL-U format produces a file where each word or token of a sentence is represented on a separate line with original form, lemma, and linguistic information. The sentences are separated with empty lines. The Finnish dependency parser was selected for this task because it is an open source tool, easy to plug in, and reliable (estimated accuracy is 81% [5]) for Finnish language texts. However, if the tool's performance does not yield satisfactory results, it can be complimented[9] or replaced with other tools.

The transformation of text to CoNNL-U format is followed by conversion into RDF using the CoNLL-RDF tool [1] that transforms sentences and words into RDF using corresponding *nif:Sentence* and *nif:Word* classes. In addition, the CoNLL-RDF tool generates the identifiers for the instances of *nif:Sentence* and *nif:Word* classes and adds the CoNLL-U data as properties to provide linguistic information of the words. The tool writes the data into an RDF file. For example, the title of the biography of Eliel Saarinen is split to several tokens that form one sentence. The output of this tool can be shown in the Fig. 2 where the title of the protagonist's bio (*Saarinen, Eliel*) is presented in RDF format.

The results of the CoNLL-RDF transformation are next used in the Reasoner module (cf. Fig. 1) that uses RDF files of the previous phase to add missing relations between the sentences, words, and the general document structure (namely paragraphs, titles and biography documents). The results of the reasoner are shown in Fig. 3. The reasoner has added *dct:isPartOf* relation for the *nif:Sentence* instance to attach it to the *nif:Title* and *crm:E31_Document* instances. In addition, the sentence instance is complemented with an order number that has been deduced from the sentence identifier shown in Fig. 2. Similarly, the instances of the *nif:Word* have been supplied with *dct:isPartOf* and *nif:sentence* relations to connect it with the biography and the sentence correspondingly. Similarly to the sentence order property, the sentence identifier is deduced from the word instance's identifier. This enables, for example, the user to query words relating to a particular biography document, paragraph, or sentence (this is needed in linguistic analyses). In addition, by adding the order property for sentences, it is easy to query the sentences in correct order. Lastly, the Reasoner component writes an RDF file that contains all of these relations. Once the text is processed, the pipeline returns a set of RDF files or can upload them directly into a SPARQL endpoint. The process was executed for all life stories (total of 13 000 biographies). It runs in linear time[10], and with these life

---

[8] http://universaldependencies.org/format.html accessed: 13 August 2018.

[9] For example, the SeCo LAS [19] is a combination of several Finnish NLP tools.

[10] The running time complexity $O(mn)$, where n is the amount of files and m their size in bytes.

stories it takes on average 1.9 s for each file (totaling in 161 076 files containing titles and paragraphs using 7.4 GB of disk space).

```
@prefix nbf:    <http://ldf.fi/nbf/biography/> .
@prefix conll:  <http://ufal.mff.cuni.cz/conll2009-st/task-description.html#> .
@prefix nif:    <http://persistence.uni-leipzig.org/nlp2rdf/ontologies/nif-core#> .

nbf:t10539#s1.0 a       nif:Sentence .          # Sentence instance
nbf:t10539#s1.1 a       nif:Word ;              # Word instance of "Saarinen"
        nif:next        nbf:t10539#s1.2 ;
        conll:EDGE      "root" ;
        conll:FEAT      "Case=Nom|Number=Sing" ;
        conll:HEAD      nbf:t10539#s1.0 ;
        conll:ID        "1" ;
        conll:LEMMA     "Saarinen" ;
        conll:UPOS      "PROPN" ;
        conll:WORD      "Saarinen" .
nbf:t10539#s1.2 a       nif:Word ;              # Word instance of a comma
        nif:next        nbf:t10539#s1.3 ;
        conll:EDGE      "punct" ;
        conll:HEAD      nbf:t10539#s1.1 ;
        conll:ID        "2" ;
        conll:LEMMA     "," ;
        conll:UPOS      "PUNCT" ;
        conll:WORD      "," .
nbf:t10539#s1.3 a       nif:Word ;              # Word instance of "Eliel"
        conll:EDGE      "conj" ;
        conll:FEAT      "Case=Nom|Number=Sing" ;
        conll:HEAD      nbf:t10539#s1.1 ;
        conll:ID        "3" ;
        conll:LEMMA     "Eliel" ;
        conll:UPOS      "PROPN" ;
        conll:WORD      "Eliel" .
```

Fig. 2. Output of the CoNLL-RDF tool

3   Analyzing and Using Biographies as Knowledge Graphs

This section presents how the pipeline of Sect. 2 was used in four use cases, illustrating and evaluating the research hypotheses presented in Sect. 1.

```
nbf:t10539#s1.0 nbf:order       1 ;                     # Sentence
        dct:isPartOf            nbf:s10539 ;            # reference to instance of crm:E31_Document
                                nbf:t10539 .            # reference to instance of nif:Title
nbf:t10539#s1.1 nif:sentence    nbf:t10539#s1.0 ;       # Word
        dct:isPartOf            nbf:s10539 ;            # reference to instance of crm:E31_Document
                                nbf:t10539 .            # reference to instance of nif:Title
```

Fig. 3. Output of the reasoner

Case Study Setting and Data. The National Biography of Finland[11] (NBF), edited by the Finnish Literature Society, is a collection of biographies written by the experts in the fields of history, science, art, culture, and business. The collection consists of several datasets: National Biography core, Admirals and Generals of Finland, Finnish Clergy, and Business Leaders. There are altogether 13 000 biographies [13]. The data was available in CSV format that contains for each person a biographical description article, basic information, such person name and lifetime information, and article level metadata, such as the author and date of publishing. The article about the protagonists written in free text followed by semi-formal synopsis text, as presented above, In addition, the HTML versions of the biographies contain manually annotated internal links to other

---

[11] https://kansallisbiografia.fi/ accessed: 13 August 2018.

biographies. They have been constructed by the editors and include the person's name as an anchor text and a link to the person's biography.

The biographies were transformed into RDF by using the pipelines of Sect. 2, and were uploaded into a data service and SPARQL endpoint at the Linked Data Finland service[12] [14]. From there, the data can be easily accessed and used for biographical and prosopographical research and data analysis. For this purpose, a semantic portal was created. The portal and the underlying linked data service are called jointly "Semantic National Biography of Finland" (SNBF).

Use Case 1: Biography and Prosopography. NBF is the authoritative biography collection of notable Finns. It is used for studying individual life stories in biography research [23] by close reading. Based on transforming the bios into linked data and the data service, also prosopographical research based on distant reading [25] becomes possible. Prosopography [4,27] is a method that is used to study groups of people through their biographical data. The goal of prosopography is to find connections, trends, and patterns from these groups. However, it is slow and infeasible to go through thousands of biographies by hand and analyze them from different perspectives. SNBF helps here by supporting data analysis.

This use case from the end user's view point has been reported in more detail in [13,17], and we only summarize the results here. The RDF used was extracted from the semi-formal parts of the biographies. On the portal side, a faceted search tool was created and used to (1) search biographies of interest and (2) to filter out target groups for prosopographical research. The facets were based on biographical basic attributes, like time and place of birth and death, profession, name, or gender.

For biography research, "home pages" for the protagonists were created and the data was enriched by linking them to ten external data repositories and data services, such as Wikidata. The events extracted from the life stories were visualized on timelines and on maps for a spatiotemporal biographical perspective.

As for prosopography, visualizations, such as pie charts, histograms, and sankey diagrams were used for studying the properties of the target group filtered out by selections on the facets. For example, a statistic page of the group contains five column histograms illustrating people's life span, the age of marriage, the age of getting the first child, the amount of children, and the number of spouses.

The data service uses two SPARQL endpoints, the service for person ontologies at http://ldf.fi/nbf/sparql has 4 600 000 triples, and the service for linguistic data produced by the pipeline at http://ldf.fi/nbf-nlp/sparql has 120 000 000 triples (7.4 Gb of data). Our dataset includes 98 953 person entries of which 54 409 are relatives whose information was extracted from the structured textual descriptions (In addition to 13 000 protagonists there are 30 000 people mentioned in the table of contents, and 1000 mentioned as authors). In the CIDOC CRM based Bio CRM data model births and deaths are modeled as events linked to the actor. The family relations are modeled according to the Bio CRM model as relations with corresponding roles [26]. The network of family relatives was build using only simple, direct relations like Parent with

---

[12] http://www.ldf.fi accessed: 13 August 2018.

subclasses Mother and Father, Child with subclasses Daughter and Son, and Spouse. The inverse family relations were later inferred from the data using reasoning. The family relation descriptions were converted from source data into RDF using Python scripts which, e.g., extracted the time spans, and separated a person text field into his/her occupation, given, and family names by using regular expressions. Events of birth and death contain the time and the place name. The place names were linked to the place ontology of SNBF [17] using SPARQL ARPA tool[13]. The place ontology consists of Finnish places extracted from Hipla [11,15], and of Foreign places located with Google Maps API[14]. Altogether the process produced 54 409 people, 23 762 births, 15 952 deaths, and 88 356 family relations.

Use Case 2: Clustering Data for Recommending. The research problem addressed in this use case is: Given a person in the biography collection, are there other people with "similar" lives, and how could these people be found automatically? Finding out such clusters of similar people could give insight on what kind of groups there actually are in the biography collection. A user reading a biography is likely interested in reading more biographies of similar kind, so clustering could also be used as a basis for a recommender system [16]. A critical question here is what criteria for similarity to use since there are lots of options available.

To test and demonstrate the potential of clustering in recommending, a recommender system was implemented in SNBF. A similarity between two people was defined as the cosine similarity between the TF-IDF[15] vectors of their biographies. TF-IDF is one of the most fundamental methods used in information retrieval, and gives a kind base line for testing clustering.

To calculate the distance mapping, we first made a SPARQL query collecting all the nouns, adjectives, and verbs in the lemmatized form. The TF-IDF embeddings were generated from these texts. The similarity map was constructed by adding a link between a pair of people if the cosine similarity between their TF-IDF vectors exceeded a pre-defined threshold value. The recommending system on the project page queries for and shows the candidates in ascending order by distance. The recommender system was implemented using the Gensim Library[16] for Python.

The results of clustering was evaluated by manually checking the linkage of a small set of people with first encouraging results. The system is capable of clustering people who share common characteristics, e.g., it forms clusters of politicians, architects, military personnel, etc. On the other hand, in cases of people that have very short bios, or when they do not belong to any specific larger group, the concluded recommended links were not so obvious.

Use Case 3: Network Analysis. Network analysis [20] can be used to study connections of individuals within a specific community. The biographical data

---

[13] http://seco.cs.aalto.fi/projects/dcert/ accessed: 13 August 2018.

[14] http://developers.google.com/maps/ accessed: 13 August 2018.

[15] http://www.tfidf.com/ accessed: 13 August 2018.

[16] https://radimrehurek.com/gensim/ accessed: 13 August 2018.

can be used to construct social networks to analyze the patterns of relationships, composition and activities of people in their own historical context. For this purpose, the SPARQL endpoint can be utilized to first select a target group of people with respect to desired criteria, such as time of birth, gender, or profession. From the query results, it is easy to construct social networks based on different criteria, such as family or business relations, references or co-location in biography texts, and so on. Social networks can finally be analyzed using standard network metrics and visualization tools.

For example, the SPARQL query of Fig. 4 finds people born in the 20th century and their professions. The query results can be used to construct a network of people based on the HTML links between the biographies, showing connections between the persons. A network of (cf. Fig. 5) is then created and shown using Gephi[17], illustrating the clusters of professions that are shown in different colors. The modularity, degrees, PageRank, HITS, and different centrality measures [18] can be calculated from the network to find our central figures of the community and their roles.

In Fig. 5, we have a network of people constructed using the query in Fig. 4. In this network people are divided into clusters by their professions. The black dots represent professions that have not been included in the list of professions in the query. Other colors represent professions that are described in the picture. The node size is based on the PageRank measure estimating the centrality of a node. The highest PageRank values indicate that the person references and is frequently referenced in other biographical texts. The clustering in the network indicates that the biographies make reference to people of the same vocation. The politicians, rulers, and presidents are highly clustered among themselves whereas the musicians are split to two groups representing classical and popular music.

Use Case 4: Linguistic Analysis. The linguistic data created by the pipeline can be used to study not only the protagonists and groups of them but also how the biographies have been written. When historians write texts, they arrange, interpret, and generalize from facts and events using their own style and words. By assessing biographies by looking at the use of vocabulary it is possible to (1) find and analyze differences between authors as well as (2) differences between groups of biographies written by different authors. For example, what kind of differences in wordings are there in use when describing women and men, or politicians in different parties?

To facilitate linguistic analysis and comparison of bios, a separate application view was implemented in the SNBF portal. This view utilizes the data produced by the NL pipeline. A faceted search interface, using facets such as authors, time periods, vocations, titles, genders, places, and last names, is used for focusing the analysis on different target groups of bios. By selecting facet categories, the underlying SPARQL query is modified and the application renders the query result as a linguistic analysis of the target group bios. The analysis is represented as a table that lists the verbs, common nouns, adjectives, and proper nouns

---

[17] https://gephi.org/ accessed: 13 August 2018.

```
PREFIX xsd: <http://www.w3.org/2001/XMLSchema#/>
PREFIX categories: <http://ldf.fi/nbf/categories/>
PREFIX gvp: <http://vocab.getty.edu/ontology#>
PREFIX crm: <http://www.cidoc-crm.org/cidoc-crm/>
PREFIX dcterms: <http://purl.org/dc/terms/>
PREFIX sources: <http://ldf.fi/nbf/sources/>
PREFIX nbf: <http://ldf.fi/nbf/>
PREFIX foaf: <http://xmlns.com/foaf/0.1/>
PREFIX skosxl: <http://www.w3.org/2008/05/skos-xl#>
PREFIX skos: <http://www.w3.org/2004/02/skos/core#>
SELECT ?from ?to ?weight WHERE {
  BIND(1 as ?weight) {
    SELECT distinct ?from WHERE {
      { ?from a nbf:PersonConcept . }
      ?from foaf:focus/^crm:P98_brought_into_life/nbf:time/gvp:estStart ?birth .
      FILTER (?birth >="1900-01-01"^^xsd:date)
      ?from dcterms:source sources:source1 .
      ?from foaf:focus/nbf:has_category ?category .
      FILTER (?category IN (categories:c133, categories:c44, categories:c41, categories:c46, categories:c131,
categories:c61, categories:c51, categories:c43, categories:c12) )
    } ORDER BY DESC(?birth)
  }
  SERVICE <http://ldf.fi/nbf-nlp/sparql> {
    ?structure <http://ldf.fi/nbf/biography/data#docRef> ?from .
    ?paragraph dcterms:isPartOf ?structure .
    ?paragraph dcterms:referenced ?link .
    ?link <http://ldf.fi/nbf/biography/data#anchor_link> ?target_link .
  }
  ?to nbf:formatted_link ?target_link .
  ?to skosxl:prefLabel/skos:prefLabel ?label .
  ?to foaf:focus/^crm:P98_brought_into_life/nbf:time/gvp:estStart ?birth2 .
  FILTER (?birth2 >="1900-01-01"^^xsd:date)
}
```

Fig. 4. SPARQL query for constructing a network of people

used in the bios with their frequencies. Moreover, two independent separate faceted search views are shown in parallel in the application, so that the user can compare the language used in two target groups. For example, it is possible to compare how (1) writers vs. (2) artists in the first half of the 19th century are described linguistically. The list of adjectives for writers has words, such as "scientific", "political", and references to different languages. For artists the most common adjectives are related to nationalities, countries, and artistic styles, such as "romantic" and "realistic".

Through these facets the user can also get general statistics such as the number of documents by period of time, or the amount of words in these documents to understand better the division and length of the documents.

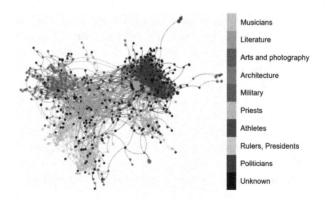

Musicians
Literature
Arts and photography
Architecture
Military
Priests
Athletes
Rulers, Presidents
Politicians
Unknown

Fig. 5. Network analysis of historical people clustered by their profession

In addition to word frequency analyses, there are also other ways for analyzing the bios linguistically. For example, tag clouds for content summarization, concordance analysis of word contexts, and topic modeling with visualizations could be incorporated in the linguistic analysis view application on top of the SPARQL endpoint.

4   Discussion

Contributions and Related Work. NL pipelines for transforming text into knowledge graphs have been created, e.g., in FRED [21], NewsReader [24], and BiographyNet [2]. The pipeline presented in this paper is the first one for Finnish. A distinctive feature of the pipeline is that the whole text, word by word, is transformed into RDF form, retaining also full linguistic information of the texts. We envision that based on such a rich representation, higher level systems for knowledge extraction, named entity recognition with semantic disambiguation, relation extraction, and event extraction, can be implemented more easily, and interesting linguistic research question can be answered, too, as exemplified in our last use case. Yet another contribution of this paper is to present novel use cases for using textual biography collections as Linked Data, supported by working demonstrators. Especially, the paper discussed (1) utilizing faceted search and browsing, combined with data analysis and visualizations, for biography and prosopography, (2) biography clustering for knowledge discovery and recommender systems, (3) the network analysis, and (4) the linguistic analysis of biographical texts.

Each of the use cases opens new wide avenues for studying biographical dictionaries and collections as data, providing new insights into history and cultural heritage research. There are lots of research publications related to faceted search and browsing, data analysis, visualization, prosopography, clustering, network analysis, and linguistic analysis. Instead of discussing these fields of research in detail, our main point was to show, with the support of actual implementations, that by transforming biographies into Linked Data and by publishing the data as a Linked Data service, these technologies and software available can be combined and reused in the new setting of biography and prosopography research in promising ways. The proposed ideas can be applied not only in SNBF but also in other national and other biographical dictionaries, such as the Oxford Dictionary of National Biography[18], USA's American National Biography[19], Germany's Neue Deutsche Biographie[20], Dictionary of Swedish National Biography[21], Biography Portal of the Netherlands[22], and BiographyNet[23].

Future Work. In the future, we plan to publish more detailed accounts of the use cases, presented only shortly in this paper, in more focused research

---

[18] http://www.oxforddnb.com/ accessed: 13 August 2018.
[19] http://www.anb.org/ accessed: 13 August 2018.
[20] http://www.ndb.badw-muenchen.de accessed: 13 August 2018.
[21] https://sok.riksarkivet.se/Sbl/Start.aspx accessed: 13 August 2018.
[22] http://www.biografischportaal.nl/en accessed: 13 August 2018.
[23] http://www.biographynet.nl/ accessed: 13 August 2018.

papers. The Semantic National Biography of Finland will be launched as an open national on-line data service and a semantic portal in September 2018, completing the work that started in 2013 with a first spatio-temporal demonstrator [10] for biographies based on events. We will continue to work and upgrade on methods described above after the publication.

Acknowledgements. Our research is part of the Severi project (http://seco.cs.aalto.fi/projects/severi accessed: 13 August 2018), funded mainly by Business Finland.

References

1. Chiarcos, C., Fäth, C.: CoNLL-RDF: linked corpora done in an NLP-friendly way. In: Gracia, J., Bond, F., McCrae, J.P., Buitelaar, P., Chiarcos, C., Hellmann, S. (eds.) LDK 2017. LNCS (LNAI), vol. 10318, pp. 74–88. Springer, Cham (2017). https://doi.org/10.1007/978-3-319-59888-8_6
2. Fokkens, A., et al.: Biographynet: extracting relations between people and events. In: Europa baut auf Biographien, pp. 193–224. New Academic Press, Wien (2017)
3. Gardiner, E., Musto, R.G.: The Digital Humanities: A Primer for Students and Scholars. Cambridge University Press, Cambridge (2015)
4. Hakosalo, H., Jalagin, S., Junila, M., Kurvinen, H.: Historiallinen elämä - Biografia ja historiantutkimus. Suomalaisen Kirjallisuuden Seura (SKS) (2014)
5. Haverinen, K., et al.: Building the essential resources for Finnish: the Turku Dependency Treebank. Lang. Resour. Eval. **48**, 493–531 (2014). https://doi.org/10.1007/s10579-013-9244-1. Open access
6. Heath, T., Bizer, C.: Linked data: evolving the web into a global data space. Synthesis Lectures on the Semantic Web: Theory and Technology, 1 edn. Morgan & Claypool, Palo Alto (2011). http://linkeddatabook.com/editions/1.0/. Accessed 13 Aug 2018
7. Hellmann, S., Lehmann, J., Auer, S., Brümmer, M.: Integrating NLP using linked data. In: Alani, H. (ed.) ISWC 2013. LNCS, vol. 8219, pp. 98–113. Springer, Heidelberg (2013). https://doi.org/10.1007/978-3-642-41338-4_7
8. Hitzler, P., Krötzsch, M., Rudolph, S.: Foundations of Semantic Web Technologies. Springer, Heidelberg (2010)
9. Hyvönen, E.: Publishing and Using Cultural Heritage Linked Data on the Semantic Web. Synthesis Lectures on the Semantic Web: Theory and Technology. Morgan & Claypool, Palo Alto (2012)
10. Hyvönen, E., Alonen, M., Ikkala, E., Mäkelä, E.: Life stories as event-based linked data: case semantic national biography. In: Proceedings of ISWC 2014 Posters & Demonstrations Track. CEUR Workshop Proceedings, October 2014. http://ceur-ws.org/Vol-1272/. Accessed 13 Aug 2018
11. Hyvönen, E., Ikkala, E., Tuominen, J.: Linked data brokering service for historical places and maps. In: Proceedings of the 1st Workshop on Humanities in the Semantic Web (WHiSe), vol. 1608, pp. 39–52. CEUR Workshop Proceedings (2016). http://ceur-ws.org/Vol-1608/#paper-06. Accessed 13 Aug 2018
12. Hyvönen, E., Leskinen, P., Heino, E., Tuominen, J., Sirola, L.: Reassembling and enriching the life stories in printed biographical registers: norssi high school alumni on the semantic web. In: Gracia, J., Bond, F., McCrae, J.P., Buitelaar, P., Chiarcos, C., Hellmann, S. (eds.) LDK 2017. LNCS (LNAI), vol. 10318, pp. 113–119. Springer, Cham (2017). https://doi.org/10.1007/978-3-319-59888-8_9

13. Hyvönen, E., Leskinen, P., Tamper, M., Tuominen, J., Keravuori, K.: Semantic national biography of Finland. In: Proceedings of the Digital Humanities in the Nordic Countries 3rd Conference (DHN 2018), vol. 2084, pp. 372–385. CEUR Workshop Proceedings, March 2018. http://www.ceur-ws.org/Vol-2084/short12.pdf. Accessed 13 Aug 2018

14. Hyvönen, E., Tuominen, J., Alonen, M., Mäkelä, E.: Linked data Finland: a 7-star model and platform for publishing and re-using linked datasets. In: Presutti, V., Blomqvist, E., Troncy, R., Sack, H., Papadakis, I., Tordai, A. (eds.) ESWC 2014. LNCS, vol. 8798, pp. 226–230. Springer, Cham (2014). https://doi.org/10.1007/978-3-319-11955-7_24

15. Ikkala, E., Tuominen, J., Hyvönen, E.: Contextualizing historical places in a gazetteer by using historical maps and linked data. In: Proceedings of Digital Humanities 2016, Short Papers, pp. 573–577 (2016)

16. Jannach, D., Zanker, M., Felfernig, A., Friedrich, G.: Recommender Systems: An Introduction. Cambridge University Press, Cambridge (2011)

17. Leskinen, P., Hyvönen, E., Tuominen, J.: Analyzing and visualizing prosopographical linked data based on short biographies. In: Biographical Data in a Digital World 2017 (BD 2017), Linz, Austria, November 2017. http://ceur-ws.org/Vol-2119/paper7.pdf. Accessed 13 Aug 2018

18. McSweeney, P.J.: Gephi network statistics. Google Summer Code, pp. 1–8 (2009)

19. Mäkelä, E.: LAS: an integrated language analysis tool for multiple languages. J. Open Source Softw. 1(6) (2016). https://doi.org/10.21105/joss.00035. Accessed 13 Aug 2018

20. Otte, E., Rousseau, R.: Social network analysis: a powerful strategy, also for the information sciences. J. Inf. Sci. 28(6), 441–453 (2002)

21. Presutti, V., Draicchio, F., Gangemi, A.: Knowledge extraction based on discourse representation theory and linguistic frames. In: ten Teije, A. (ed.) EKAW 2012. LNCS (LNAI), vol. 7603, pp. 114–129. Springer, Heidelberg (2012). https://doi.org/10.1007/978-3-642-33876-2_12

22. Pyysalo, S., Ginter, F.: Collaborative development of annotation guidelines with application to universal dependencies. In: The Fifth Swedish Language Technology Conference (2014)

23. Roberts, B.: Biographical Research. Understanding Social Research. Open University Press (2002)

24. Rospocher, M., et al.: Building event-centric knowledge graphs from news. Web Semant. Sci., Serv. Agents World Wide Web 37, 132–151 (2016)

25. Shultz, K.: What is distant reading? New York Times, 24 June 2011. https://www.nytimes.com/2011/06/26/books/review/the-mechanic-muse-what-is-distant-reading.html. Accessed 13 Aug 2018

26. Tuominen, J., Hyvönen, E., Leskinen, P.: Bio CRM: a data model for representing biographical data for prosopographical research. In: Proceedings of the Biographical Data in a Digital World 2017 (BD2017). CEUR Workshop Proceedings (2018). http://ceur-ws.org/Vol-2119/paper10.pdf. Accessed 13 Aug 2018

27. Verboven, K., Carlier, M., Dumolyn, J.: A short manual to the art of prosopography. In: Prosopography Approaches and Applications. A Handbook, pp. 35–70. Unit for Prosopographical Research (Linacre College) (2007)

28. Wu, Y., Sun, H., Yan, C.: An event timeline extraction method based on news corpus. In: 2017 IEEE 2nd International Conference on Big Data Analysis, pp. 697–702. IEEE (2017)

Maintaining a Linked Data Cloud
and Data Service for Second World
War History

Mikko Koho[1]([⊠])[iD], Esko Ikkala[1,2][iD], Erkki Heino[1], and Eero Hyvönen[1,2][iD]

[1] Semantic Computing Research Group (SeCo), Aalto University, Espoo, Finland
mikko.koho@aalto.fi
[2] HELDIG – Helsinki Centre for Digital Humanities, University of Helsinki,
Helsinki, Finland
http://seco.cs.aalto.fi, http://heldig.fi

Abstract. One of the great promises of Linked Data is to provide a
shared data infrastructure into which new data can be imported and
aligned with, forming a sustainable, ever growing Linked Data Cloud
(LDC). This paper studies and evaluates this idea in the context of the
WarSampo LDC that provides a data infrastructure for Second World
War related ontologies and data in Finland, including several mutually
linked graphs, totaling ca 12 million triples. Two data integration case
studies are presented, where the original WarSampo LDC and the related
semantic portal were first extended by a dataset of hundreds of war
cemeteries and thousands of photographs of them, and then by another
dataset of over 4450 Finnish prisoners of war. As a conclusion, lessons
learned are explicated, based on hands-on experience in maintaining the
WarSampo LDC in a production environment.

1 Introduction

This paper studies the fundamental process of building the Web of Data [6] by
incrementally aggregating and aligning new datasets into a Linked Data Cloud
(LDC). The focus is in particular on publishing and using Cultural Heritage
Linked Data on the Semantic Web [8].

We first overview previous research related to the problem of maintaining
ontologies and linked data. Based on this, a typology of change propagation
in interlinked Resource Description Network (RDF)[1] graphs is presented. Two
practical case studies are discussed where a new dataset is integrated into the
WarSampo LDC [9], which contains a dynamic ontology infrastructure and a
collection of Linked Open Data about Finland in the Second World War (WW2).
In both cases, change propagation scenarios are discussed, with lessons learned
explicated. As a conclusion, guidelines for integrating a new dataset into an LDC
are outlined.

---

[1] https://www.w3.org/RDF/.

© Springer Nature Switzerland AG 2018
M. Ioannides et al. (Eds.): EuroMed 2018, LNCS 11196, pp. 138–149, 2018.
https://doi.org/10.1007/978-3-030-01762-0_12

The main contribution of this paper is to address the linked dataset maintenance problem on an LDC level. The paper contributes also by explaining how the new datasets can be shown to the end user as new application perspectives and through enriching other existing application perspectives with additional data.

WW2 data is of great interest not only to historians, but to potentially hundreds of millions of citizens globally whose relatives participated in the war, creating a global shared trauma. However, data about the WW2 is scattered in various organizations and countries, written in multiple languages, and represented in heterogeneous formats. WarSampo [9] provides a novel infrastructure for publishing WW2 data as LOD. The infrastructure supports integrating new datasets into WarSampo, by extending both the DOs and the MDSs. Published in 2015, WarSampo is to our best knowledge the first large scale system for serving and publishing WW2 LOD on the Web. WarSampo is a part of the global LOD cloud[2], and was awarded with the LODLAM Challenge Open Data Prize in 2017.

The data is served on an open data service[3], which enables anyone to build applications that use the data via standard APIs. The WarSampo semantic portal uses the data service to provide different perspectives to the WW2 LOD as customized web applications. New perspectives can be added in a flexible way to provide views to new data, or to answer new research questions with existing data.

The War Cemetery perspective is an in-use application on the Semantic Web: it was published in November 2017 and got 57000 users in one week after that. The Prisoners of War perspective will be published later in 2018. In total, the WarSampo data service was used by 130 000 different users through the WarSampo semantic portal[4] in 2017.

2   Related Work

The problem of maintaining ontologies and linked data have been studied extensively, but mostly from a point of view of editing and managing evolving ontologies and data, not on an LDC level as in this paper. Early works on this line of research include, e.g., [11,15]. In [3,20], the problem of managing a set of interlinked hierarchical RDFS thesauri is discussed. Ontology evolution, and the propagation of changes caused by it, has been discussed in [23] and [25].

Umbrich et al. [24] have surveyed solutions to detect, propagate and describe changes in Linked Open Data resources and datasets. Requirements and approaches are studied for different use cases, e.g. link maintenance and vocabulary evolution. These linked data dynamics are explored also in [2,16]. Handling broken links in Linked Data is discussed in [22].

---

[2] http://linkeddata.org.

[3] http://www.ldf.fi/dataset/warsa.

[4] https://sotasampo.fi/en/.

In addition to the global LOD cloud, other LDCs have previously been presented, like Lexvo [17] and the MIDI LDC [18].

A framework for integrating heterogeneous OpenCourseWare data repositories into a Linked Data publication is presented in [21]. A framework and tool for data fusion, conflict resolution, and quality assessment of Linked Data graphs is presented in [19]. Knoblock et al. [12] presented lessons learned in integrating heterogeneous data from 14 museums into a Linked Data publication, harmonizing data with CIDOC CRM[5].

An overview of the WarSampo data service and semantic portal has been presented in [9]. A core dataset of WarSampo, the casualties of war, and its application in digital humanities research is presented in [14]. Using the war cemetery data in prosopographical research is discussed in [10]. Overview of the Prisoners of War case study with preliminary results have been published [13], with a comparison of different online publishing approaches. Named entity linking in WarSampo was studied in [7]. This paper provides a new view to this line of research from an LDC management point of view.

3   Anatomy and Maintenance of Linked Data Clouds

An LDC consists of a set of graphs. Data is interlinked across graphs by mappings and direct references to URIs in other graphs. We differentiate the graphs into two major categories based on their usage: *metadatasets* (MDS) and *domain ontologies* (DO). MDSs describe objects or other things in an application domain in terms of a metadata schema [4], such as Dublin Core or CIDOC CRM. Collection metadata in libraries, museums, and archives, or their harmonized aggregated versions are typical examples of MDSs. DOs define the basic concepts used in populating the MDSs and are shared by them. DOs include, e.g., ontologies for subject matter concepts (keyword thesauri), places, people, times, and events. The generic, domain independent structure and semantics of DOs and MDSs are defined by a set of shared domain independent vocabularies, such as RDF(S), SKOS, and OWL. Data linking in an LDC is based on making references to shared domain independent vocabularies, domain specific DOs, and mappings.

We call a set of DOs used for populating a set of MDSs in an application domain the *ontology infrastructure*. In many cases, DOs, MDSs, mappings, and domain independent vocabularies are published as one homogeneous triple mass. If there is no separation of DOs and MDSs into graphs, the distinction between them can be vague. An example of this is DBpedia[6], where resources are separated by namespaces, but this distinction is insufficient, since typically one graph can use a variety of different namespaces. A key observation underlying this paper is that from a data management point of view, DOs, MDSs, and mappings are different from each other, and it makes sense to keep them separate in order to support different kind of maintenance operations.

---

[5] http://cidoc-crm.org.
[6] http://dbpedia.org.

An important property of a graph is *independence*: we define a graph independent if it does not make a reference to (i.e. links to) resources in other graphs. For example, SKOS keyword thesauri are often independent DOs making only `skos:broader/narrower/related` references to concepts within the same concept scheme.

A Typology of Change Propagation. A graph can change through changes in its resources. The following three change types are the most fundamental: (1) *Addition.* A new resource is added into the graph. (2) *Modification.* A resource is modified in terms of its properties. (3) *Removal.* A resource is removed from the graph. Based on the primitive changes, more complex changes can be modeled as sequences of more primitive ones, such as moving a resource from a graph into another. The primitive changes may occur in a DO or an MDS, and may have an effect in related DOs or MDSs [23]. We have identified the following four principal cases of change propagation needs between graph types. Here the notation $X \rightarrow Y$ means that a change in a graph X creates a potential need for a change in a graph Y that makes a reference to X.

1. **DO→MDS.** In all cases, linkage based on probabilistic entity linking, from an MDS to the DO, needs to be revalidated. **Addition:** An addition in the DO usually doesn't create a need for change propagation to MDSs. However, when a new DO resource is introduced in an MDS, the linkage from the MDS to the DO is broken since the new resource is not there in the DO. **Modification:** no additional effect. **Removal:** The MDSs can get corrupted by having URI references to removed URIs. The affected MDSs need to be fixed.
2. **DO→DO.** If the changed DO is independent, there are no change propagation needs. Otherwise change propagation is needed as in case DO→MDS.
3. **MDS→DO.** **Addition:** If DOs cover the values used by the MDS, there is no effect. Otherwise the DOs may need to be updated accordingly. **Modification:** usually no effect. If a new value not in a DO would be needed as a property value in the MDS, the DO may need to be updated accordingly. **Removal:** no effect, unless a DO makes a reference to the MDS. This may happen, e.g., when an event ontology makes a reference to an artifact collection database.
4. **MDS→MDS.** Changes between MDSs are propagated as in MDS→DO.

Practical examples of the change propagation scenarios are presented in the use cases in Sects. 5 and 6.

4 Maintaining the WarSampo Linked Data Cloud

Creating the WarSampo ontology infrastructure has been a dynamic process, involving several people working with up to seven datasets at the same time. The metadatasets and domain ontologies have been constantly evolving, which often causes existing entity matching to be invalidated.

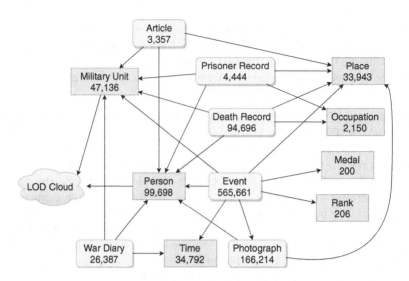

Fig. 1. The main metadatasets (yellow, rounded corners) and domain ontologies (green rectangular boxes) of WarSampo. (Color figure online)

Figure 1 shows the main MDSs and DOs of WarSampo, after the data model changes caused by the case studies presented in this paper. Each MDS and DO shows the number of individual entities belonging to the corresponding class(es). The arrows depict the direction of linkage, which is normally from the MDSs towards the DOs that have been used in annotating the entities. There is also linkage to the global LOD cloud.

The WarSampo LDC is centrally maintained, even if it is based on data from distributed sources. This means that DOs can adapt to changes that are needed when integrating new datasets into the LDC, and should do so to better represent their domain. The ontology infrastructure is extended as needed.

Maintaining the WarSampo LDC is different from maintaining the global LOD cloud, where `owl:sameAs` and related mappings between datasets are created, but changes are seldom propagated across the datasets. This is not feasible in our case, since a new piece of information in one graph of the service may require changes in other graphs, too. For example, if a new place or a person is introduced in a new or existing MDS, the Place DO or the Person DO has to be extended before the new data can be aligned.

Integrating data into a dynamic LD environment is challenging. As a DO becomes more complete, covering its domain more accurately, MDSs using that DO may need to redo their entity linking process, to get more accurate linkage. Failing to do so can cause structurally or semantically erroneous annotations [22] to be used. WarSampo employs plenty of probabilistic entity linking, e.g., to the Person, Place and Military Unit DOs, where the DO is not expected to cover all of the information about its domain. The usual case of change propagation in the WarSampo context relates to the invalidation of the entity linking.

Because of the complex change propagations in the dynamic LDC, maintaining the DOs and MDSs directly in RDF format is too laborious and error-prone to implement in practice, especially in a way that a domain expert with little Linked Data expertise could make changes. This is especially true in the case of person instances as they are linked, directly or indirectly, to everything in WarSampo. Modeling even just the basic information of a person entails, e.g., multiple events, such as birth, death, promotions, and so on. It was decided that the domain experts directly maintain the datasets in their native formats (usually spreadsheet files), which can then be easily transformed and integrated into WarSampo, as needed.

5   Case 1: War Cemeteries

In our first case study, a war cemetery dataset was produced and integrated into the WarSampo LDC [10]. Since Finnish soldiers who perished in WW2 were transported back to their hometown for burial whenever it was possible, the local cemetery is a natural starting point for studying the common characteristics and events of the residents of one's hometown in the turmoil of the war.

Starting Point and Source Data. A complete listing of war cemeteries in Finland was not available, but the Casualties MDS, that was previously integrated into WarSampo, includes the name of the cemetery and/or the municipality in which the person is buried. However, the lack of uniform naming conventions and missing coordinates of the cemeteries made it difficult to locate them and to specify the people buried there.

In 2016–2017 the Memorial Foundation of the Fallen and the Central Organization of Finnish Camera Clubs (Suomen Kameraseurojen Liitto ry, SKsL) carried out a project called "War Cemeteries in Finland". Its goal was to locate, photograph, and collect data about all known war cemeteries in Finland. In total 615 war cemeteries were found, accompanied by 2500 photographs.

Workflow. A representative of SKsL manually harmonized the data entry sheets and filenames of the photographs sent by the camera clubs and organized them into one table. Finally the table was converted into WarSampo compatible RDF by using a Python data processing pipeline[7], which (1) handles the matching of existing cemetery names found in the WarSampo death records to cemetery names in the source table, (2) creates new URIs for cemeteries not found in WarSampo, and (3) creates photograph and photography instances according to the WarSampo data model. Whenever there is a need to update the cemetery data, the source table can be edited and the data processing pipeline can be run again to produce new RDF files for WarSampo.

To avoid errors in the data integration, the "War Cemeteries in Finland" project was instructed to start with the same cemetery name listing that was used when the death records were collected into a database. A challenge here was that some of the cemeteries mentioned in the Casualties MDS were unambiguous.

---

[7] https://github.com/SemanticComputing/cemeteries-csv2rdf.

The structure of the project's output table was agreed on beforehand, so that information about one individual cemetery was gathered in one row, with values separated on columns, easing the RDF conversion process. The cemetery data processing pipeline was run multiple times in order to enhance data quality, and a listing of spelling errors, missing photograph files, etc. was sent back to SKsL for making manual corrections to their table.

The cemetery data was integrated into the Place DO, and the cemetery photograph data into the Photograph MDS. The photographs are generally linked to the photography places via a photography event, which has created the photograph. However, photographs of war cemeteries represent the cemeteries, which are modeled as a subclass of the place class. Some military units and people are mapped to entities in the global LOD Cloud, i.e., Wikidata and DBpedia.

Change Propagation. With regard to maintenance, the basic data about the cemeteries remains independent in the Place DO. If the cemeteries in Place DO change, the linkage from the death records in the Casualties MDS need to adjust for the change as according to the DO→MDS case in Sect. 3.

However, the information about the people buried in a cemetery is stored in the Casualties MDS which makes references to the Place DO. Thus, the changes in Casualties or Photograph MDS related to the cemeteries must be propagated to the Place DO according to the MDS→DO case in Sect. 3.

Semantic Portal Changes. The new War Cemeteries Perspective[8] showcases how the integration of cemetery data enriches the existing WarSampo data and vice versa. The perspective has been developed to gain new insights from the casualties data based on the community-level aspect provided by the cemeteries. This approach is useful, because there is not enough data about the casualties to construct detailed life stories of individual soldiers as biographies, but the amount of individuals is large enough to study the data as groups of people using, for example, visualizations.

The user interface of the Cemetery perspective is presented in Fig. 2. The user can browse all cemeteries, or search the cemeteries by name and narrow the results by using the filters on the left. The results can be viewed as a table with basic information about the cemeteries, or on a map which provides a global view of the cemeteries.

A concrete example of the data integration results can be seen in Fig. 2, where the "Number of graves" column is based on the data of the "War Cemeteries in Finland" project, whereas the "Buried people" column shows the total number of death records (collected in the 1980s) that make a reference to the cemetery. The numbers are equal only with 27% of the cemeteries although ideally they should be equal with every cemetery. This gives valuable insight to the data providers to set the records straight.

When the user clicks the name of a cemetery, an information page opens, showing basic information, photographs, and various visualizations based on the property values of the buried people.

---

[8] https://www.sotasampo.fi/en/cemeteries/.

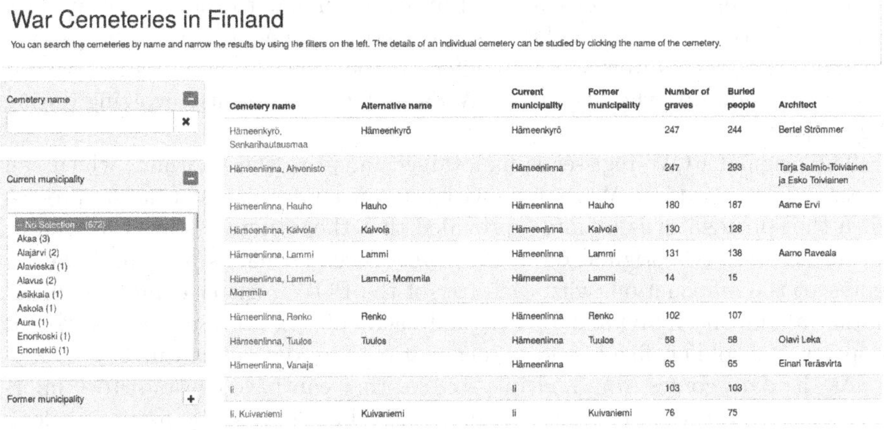

War Cemeteries in Finland

You can search the cemeteries by name and narrow the results by using the filters on the left. The details of an individual cemetery can be studied by clicking the name of the cemetery.

Cemetery name	Alternative name	Current municipality	Former municipality	Number of graves	Buried people	Architect
Hämeenkyrö, Sarkkirihautausmaa	Hämeenkyrö	Hämeenkyrö		247	244	Bertel Strömmer
Hämeenlinna, Ahvenisto		Hämeenlinna		247	293	Tarja Salmio-Toivisinen ja Esko Toivisinen
Hämeenlinna, Hauho	Hauho	Hämeenlinna	Hauho	180	187	Aarne Ervi
Hämeenlinna, Kalvola	Kalvola	Hämeenlinna	Kalvola	130	128	
Hämeenlinna, Lammi	Lammi	Hämeenlinna	Lammi	131	138	Aarno Ruveala
Hämeenlinna, Lammi, Mommila	Lammi, Mommila	Hämeenlinna	Lammi	14	15	
Hämeenlinna, Renko	Renko	Hämeenlinna	Renko	102	107	
Hämeenlinna, Tuulos	Tuulos	Hämeenlinna	Tuulos	58	58	Olavi Leka
Hämeenlinna, Vanaja		Hämeenlinna		65	65	Einari Teräsvirta
Ii		Ii		103	103	
Ii, Kuivaniemi	Kuivaniemi	Ii	Kuivaniemi	76	75	

Fig. 2. Cemetery search in the WarSampo cemetery perspective.

6   Case 2: Prisoners of War

Some 4450 Finnish soldiers were captured as prisoners of war (POW) in WW2 by the Soviet Union. This case study concerns integrating the POW data into the WarSampo LDC.

Starting Point and Source Data. The POW dataset was originally published in a book [1]. Recently, the dataset has been extensively extended, cleaned, and validated by domain experts. A collaboration was set up to publish the data as part of the WarSampo, which was chosen as the primary data publication platform by the stakeholders, which include the National Archives of Finland, and the Association for Cherishing the Memory of the Dead of the War.

The core of the dataset is a register of the Finnish prisoners of war in WW2. The register is formatted as a spreadsheet file, with additional spreadsheet files presenting data about POW camps and hospitals, as well as the primary data sources. The POW dataset contains sensitive information about the individual soldiers, some of whom are still alive. There is an ongoing process to evaluate what information can be published, by the legal experts at the National Archives of Finland. The data will be published in the autumn 2018, at which point the privacy issues should be resolved.

Workflow. The data formatting evolved as a collaboration between the domain experts maintaining the original dataset, and the WarSampo team of Linked Data experts. A data processing pipeline was created[9], that handles data transformation, validation, linking, and harmonization. The pipeline transforms the spreadsheets into RDF, mapping the spreadsheet columns to RDF properties, with possibly multiple values per property, and containing annotations for primary information sources. Automatic linking processes then link the records to WarSampo DOs of military ranks, units, occupations, people, and places.

---

[9] https://github.com/SemanticComputing/WarPrisoners.

The prisoner records were modeled in a way similar to the previously published Casualties MDS [14], and they share common super classes and properties. However, the process workflow was different: the casualty data was received as a static data dump, whereas the POW dataset was constantly evolving during the project.

The original POW register is maintained in spreadsheet format, which can be easily integrated into WarSampo with our automated transformation process when the spreadsheet is updated, provided that the structure stays the same.

For most of the original data, the spreadsheet format is a natural way to represent the information, with each row of the POW register expressing information about one individual soldier, and each column representing a different property of a soldier, like his name, occupation, and date of capture.

As the data comes from multiple sources that can have contradictory information, there is a need to collect all different values for a single property, along with references to the primary data sources. For this purpose, a special cell data format is used that enables to present multiple values and source references in the spreadsheet. The cell formatting is validated during the data transformation process. Also other simple data validation rules are applied to find anomalies during data conversions.

Change Propagation. The POW data introduces the main MDS of POWs, and a DO of war-time occupations. The WarSampo person DO is updated with about 3,000 new person instances. POW camps and hospitals are modeled as part of the Place DO.

The original dataset contains source references for separate pieces of information, which are used in the RDF data model by employing RDF reification for the prisoner records. This is a standard approach to modeling this kind of provenance information on an RDF triple level.

The DOs of military ranks, military units, places (e.g. municipalities, camps and hospitals), occupations and persons provide values for populating the POW MDS. Their linking uses probabilistic entity linking while also original values are stored as literals. All changes in the DOs would require repeating the corresponding entity linking process as according to the case DO→MDS in Sect. 3. I.e. if a new understanding about the historical war-time Occupation DO (cf. Fig. 1) cause two occupations to be merged into one, resulting in the removal of the obsolete one, any linking to the obsolete resources need to be updated.

Adding a new property value in the MDS can propagate the change to related DOs, if the value doesn't exist there (cf. Sect. 3, case MDS→DO). For example, the new value could be a new military rank or a new occupation. When a new POW record is added to the registry, the changes will propagate to the Person DO, either through the linking to an existing person, in which case the person instance is enriched, or through the creation of a new person instance.

The POW records are mapped to the Person DO using probabilistic record linkage [5], where each POW's information is compared with the information in the WarSampo person instances to find matches that have high enough similarity. As the record linkage needs to be able to adapt to changing input dataset, as well as to the changes in the Person DO, a machine learning approach was used, which employs logistic regression based on weighted comparisons of a set of predefined attributes. The weights are calculated based on training data, which is initially acquired from a previous, simpler record linkage implementation, based on manually defined fuzzy matching, and updated manually during linkage iterations. With the machine learning approach, the entity linking process automatically adapts to changes in the POW MDS and Person DO. The linking process needs to be redone when the POW MDS changes.

New person instances are then created for the unlinked POW records and added into the Person DO. With the probabilistic linkage, it is possible that a record is not mapped because there is not enough information about either the POW record, or the person instance, to create a mapping between them. Modifying the information in either the MDS or the DO means that the whole record linkage process should be redone.

Semantic Portal Changes. A new application perspective has been added to WarSampo to explore, analyze, and visualize the information contained in the POW metadataset. The perspective is similar to the earlier casualties perspective, which is used to show information from the death records to the user.

In addition, integrating the prisoners of war data into WarSampo has caused several necessary changes to other parts of the semantic portal. Allowing multiple values for properties with provenance data changes how the information can be presented in a person's home page and how to visualize the data. People's home pages in WarSampo were updated to show information combined from multiple sources (death records, prisoner records, Wikipedia) with source information next to each piece of information.

7 Conclusions

A key lesson learned in our work is that one should make all data transformations and linking into **repeatable, automated processes** to be able to handle change propagation automatically. In the early stages of building WarSampo, the importance of this was not obvious, and for some early WarSampo datasets, the transformation processes were never completely automated. Automating them now would require considerable effort because the datasets have gone through undocumented processes that are not easily repeatable.

The transformation processes should be built using a modular structure, to make the processes **maintainable**, and to enable the reuse of code for other data integration. In a dynamic LDC, the entity linking processes need to be able to **adapt** to common changes in all of the graphs.

Maintenance of an LDC using a complex data model, such as CIDOC CRM, is difficult natively in RDF format. For complex DOs and MDSs, it is easier to update the data in simpler formats, such as Dublin Core, and maintain the transformation processes that build the graphs of the LDC. The complexity of the transformation processes grow as they need to handle the creation or updating of missing or uncertain resources in incomplete DOs shared by multiple MDSs. Simple, independent DOs (e.g. military units, occupations) can be maintained directly in RDF format, whereas more complex DOs like Persons require a different approach.

DOs differ from each other by nature. For example, covering and disambiguating all military ranks is clearly a simpler task than performing the same task with all wartime places. In general, it is not realistic to assume that the DOs completely cover their domain.

Integrating data into a LDC is more laborious than simpler ways of publishing the data in independent data silos. However, the result is an interlinked knowledge base, a Linked Data Cloud, where the interlinked graphs enrich each other, creating a whole that is greater than the sum of its parts.

Acknowledgements. Our work was funded by the Association for Cherishing the Memory of the Dead of the War, the Memory Foundation for the Fallen, the Finnish Ministry of Education and Culture, and the Academy of Finland. The authors wish to acknowledge CSC - IT Center for Science, Finland, for computational resources.

References

1. Alava, T., Frolov, D., Nikkilä, R.: Rukiver. Suomalaiset sotavangit Neuvostoliitossa. Edita, Helsinki (2003)
2. Auer, S., Dalamagas, T., Parkinson, H., Bancilhon, et al.: Diachronic linked data: towards long-term preservation of structured interrelated information. In: Proceedings of the First International Workshop on Open Data, pp. 31–39. ACM (2012)
3. Frosterus, M., Tuominen, J., Pessala, S., Hyvönen, E.: Linked Open Ontology cloud: managing a system of interlinked cross-domain light-weight ontologies. Int. J. Metadata Semant. Ontol. **10**(3), 189–201 (2015)
4. Gartner, R.: Metadata: Shaping Knowledge from Antiquity to the Semantic Web. Springer, Cham (2016). https://doi.org/10.1007/978-3-319-40893-4
5. Gu, L., Baxter, R., Vickers, D., Rainsford, C.: Record linkage: current practice and future directions. CSIRO Mathematical and Information Sciences, Technical report 3/83 (2003)
6. Heath, T., Bizer, C.: Linked Data: Evolving the Web into a Global Data Space. Synthesis Lectures on the Semantic Web: Theory and Technology. Morgan & Claypool Publishers, Palo Alto (2011)
7. Heino, E., et al.: Named entity linking in a complex domain: case second world war history. In: Gracia, J., Bond, F., McCrae, J.P., Buitelaar, P., Chiarcos, C., Hellmann, S. (eds.) LDK 2017. LNCS (LNAI), vol. 10318, pp. 120–133. Springer, Cham (2017). https://doi.org/10.1007/978-3-319-59888-8_10
8. Hyvönen, E.: Publishing and Using Cultural Heritage Linked Data on the Semantic Web. Synthesis Lectures on the Semantic Web: Theory and Technology. Morgan & Claypool, Palo Alto (2012)
9. Hyvönen, E., et al.: Warsampo data service and semantic portal for publishing linked open data about the second world war history. In: Sack, H., Blomqvist, E., d'Aquin, M., Ghidini, C., Ponzetto, S.P., Lange, C. (eds.) ESWC 2016. LNCS, vol. 9678, pp. 758–773. Springer, Cham (2016). https://doi.org/10.1007/978-3-319-34129-3_46
10. Ikkala, E., Koho, M., Heino, E., Leskinen, P., Hyvönen, E., Ahoranta, T.: Prosopographical views to finnish WW2 casualties through cemeteries and linked open data. In: Proceedings of the Workshop on Humanities in the Semantic Web (WHiSe II). CEUR Workshop Proceedings, October 2017

11. Klein, M.: Change management for distributed ontologies. Ph.D. thesis, Free University, Amsterdam (2004)
12. Knoblock, C.A., et al.: Lessons learned in building linked data for the American Art Collaborative. In: d'Amato, C., Fernandez, M., Tamma, V., Lecue, F., Cudré-Mauroux, P., Sequeda, J., Lange, C., Heflin, J. (eds.) ISWC 2017. LNCS, vol. 10588, pp. 263–279. Springer, Cham (2017). https://doi.org/10.1007/978-3-319-68204-4_26
13. Koho, M., et al.: Integrating prisoners of war dataset into the warsampo linked data infrastructure. In: Proceedings of the Digital Humanities in the Nordic Countries 3rd Conference (DHN 2018), vol. 2084. CEUR Workshop Proceedings, March 2018. http://www.ceur-ws.org/Vol-2084
14. Koho, M., Hyvönen, E., Heino, E., Tuominen, J., Leskinen, P., Mäkelä, E.: Linked death—representing, publishing, and using second world war death records as linked open data. In: Blomqvist, E., Hose, K., Paulheim, H., Ławrynowicz, A., Ciravegna, F., Hartig, O. (eds.) ESWC 2017. LNCS, vol. 10577, pp. 369–383. Springer, Cham (2017). https://doi.org/10.1007/978-3-319-70407-4_45
15. Maedche, A., Motik, B., Stojanovic, L., Studer, R., Volz, R.: An infrastructure for searching, reusing and evolving distributed ontologies. In: Proceedings of the Twelfth International Conference on World Wide Web, pp. 439–448. ACM Press (2003)
16. Meimaris, M., Papastefanatos, G., Pateritsas, C., Galani, T., Stavrakas, Y.: Towards a framework for managing evolving information resources on the data web. In: Proceedings of the 1st International Workshop on Dataset PROFIling & fEderated Search for Linked Data, vol. 1151. CEUR Workshop Proceedings, March 2014
17. de Melo, G.: Lexvo.org: Language-related information for the Linguistic Linked Data cloud. Semant. Web 6(4), 393–400 (2015)
18. Meroño-Peñuela, A., et al.: The MIDI linked data cloud. In: d'Amato, C., et al. (eds.) ISWC 2017. LNCS, vol. 10588, pp. 156–164. Springer, Cham (2017). https://doi.org/10.1007/978-3-319-68204-4_16
19. Michelfeit, J., Knap, T., Nečaský, M.: Linked data integration with conflicts. arXiv preprint arXiv:1410.7990 (2014)
20. Pessala, S., Seppälä, K., Suominen, O., Frosterus, M., Tuominen, J., Hyvönen, E.: MUTU: an analysis tool for maintaining a system of hierarchically linked ontologies. In: ISWC 2011 - Ontologies Come of Age Workshop (OCAS), vol. 809. CEUR Workshop Proceedings (2011)
21. Piedra, N., Tovar, E., Colomo-Palacios, R., Lopez-Vargas, J., Alexandra Chicaiza, J.: Consuming and producing linked open data: the case of opencourseware. Program 48(1), 16–40 (2014)
22. Popitsch, N.P., Haslhofer, B.: DSNotify: handling broken links in the web of data. In: Proceedings of the 19th International Conference on World Wide Web, pp. 761–770. ACM (2010)
23. Stojanovic, L., Maedche, A., Motik, B., Stojanovic, N.: User-driven ontology evolution management. In: Gómez-Pérez, A., Benjamins, V.R. (eds.) EKAW 2002. LNCS (LNAI), vol. 2473, pp. 285–300. Springer, Heidelberg (2002). https://doi.org/10.1007/3-540-45810-7_27
24. Umbrich, J., Villazón-Terrazas, B., Hausenblas, M.: Dataset dynamics compendium: a comparative study (2010)
25. Zablith, F., et al.: Ontology evolution: a process-centric survey. Knowl. Eng. Rev. 30(1), 45–75 (2015)

Design of an Interactive Experience Journey in a Renovated Industrial Heritage Site

Maria Gaitanou$^{(\boxtimes)}$, Elli Charissi, Iosifina Margari,
Manolis Papamakarios, Spyros Vosinakis, Panayiotis Koutsabasis,
Damianos Gavalas, and Modestos Stavrakis

Department of Product and Systems Design Engineering,
University of the Aegean, Syros, Greece
{dpsdl4015,dpsdl4120,dpsdl4058,dpsdl3132,spyrosv,kgp,
dgavalas,modestos}@syros.aegean.gr

Abstract. In this paper we present the design of an interactive experience journey at an ex-industrial textile factory. The aim is to enhance the visitors' experience by engaging them in the work processes and flows that were taking place in the actual industrial environment and introduce them to the role of the artifacts and tools involved in real life work scenarios. The development is of the form of a room escaping experience developed on the basis of riddle solving. We used a number of technologies related to interactive systems design such as near field communication, physical computing, sensors, actuators and tangible artifacts.

Keywords: Interactive tour · Escape room · Interactive systems
Physical computing · Tangible interaction

1 Introduction

Heritage, tourism and entertainment are constantly growing sectors currently focusing in the incorporation of interactive technologies for engaging people in rich experiences. In addition, a phenomenon which has grown in popularity in recent years, called "room escaping" gained special attention by those seeking excitement and fun while participating in an active learning experience [1].

The concept of the actual escape room is not new. Although initially it has been largely neglected by the research community, recently, there is a growing interest both among researchers and developers as well as an increased appeal to the general public [2–4]. Real-life escape rooms are live-action adventure games, where the players are organized in groups of two or more people, locked in a room or in a series of rooms, from which they must escape within a pre-defined period [1]. To find their way out, players must solve a number of different puzzles, search for clues and objects scattered in the room and use them to complete specific tasks. Escape rooms are not simply a fun way for players to spend time with their family, friends or colleagues, but more importantly they provide an opportunity to develop organizational and communication skills as well as nurture critical thinking and creativity [2].

© Springer Nature Switzerland AG 2018
M. Ioannides et al. (Eds.): EuroMed 2018, LNCS 11196, pp. 150–161, 2018.
https://doi.org/10.1007/978-3-030-01762-0_13

In this paper our primary goal is to create an interactive, educational and collaborative experience for the visitors of a newly renovated cultural space of a former textile factory (Zisimatos Industry) that has been abandoned since the 80s (1986). The purpose is to create an escape room experience by using interactive technologies based on physical computing and tangible interactions and thus engage the visitors to different scenarios that involve riddles related to the original industry's work processes (Fig. 1).

The objectives of this work include:

Education: highlight the history of the textile industry & the history of the actual textile factory.

Experience: develop interactive experiences for the visitors.

Social engagement: Cultivate the sense of cooperation, teamwork and critical thinking.

Fig. 1. Overview of the Zisimatos textile factory.

1.1   Industrial Cultural Heritage and the Textile Industry of Syros

In the 19th century, Hermoupolis was one of the largest financial centers in Greece, due to the development of shipping and commerce. After the crisis that the local economy suffered due to the expansion of the steamer boats, Syros was no longer a transit center. Cotton-producing industries came to save the city from its financial decline. The cotton-industry was rather extensive encompassing all aspects of cotton manufacturing (yarns, fabrics, facings, socks, handkerchiefs, cloths) [5]. The island's cotton-plants employed a workforce of more than 5,000 workers and were able to meet a significant proportion of the country's needs in cotton. Besides, a part of the plants' production was exported abroad.

1.2   The Industrial Heritage Site: Zissimatos Textile Factory

In 1950, following the dissolution of the company, a commercial & industrial company under the name "G.ZISIMATOS & SONS" was fully renovated and enriched with cutting-edge European equipment used for the production of cotton socks, for men, women and children. In 1960, the factory stopped the production of socks, was renovated again and with the new machines began the production of towels, bathrobes etc. in a wide variety of designs of excellent quality. These products were distributed throughout Greece. The factory had a total power of 167 HP, 19 double looms and 40 workers. After its financial decline in the beginning of 80s, the operation of the factory ceased smoothly in 1986. The factory buildings, complete with their machinery and the leftover tools and equipment used at the time of closure, remained locked since 2017 when the new owner decided to renovate them as an industrial cultural heritage site.

2   Methodology

The design methodology followed an iterative design approach and included close cooperation with the curator and coworkers, as well as in-situ observation and interviews. This design approach was followed for the development of the interactive tour and it can be described with the following intertwined phases.

Research and inquiry (R&I). This phase concerns the research that had to be conducted. This stage lasted 5 weeks and included research on the cognitive background, some indicative related work, survey of the escape room's audience and research on similar technologies.

Design and prototyping (D&P). This phase included an eight-week-long design phase, including designing the tour, choosing the technologies which best fitted our project, designing the prototypes and the riddles.

Evaluation and testing (E&T). This phase of the project included the process followed for conducting the assessment of a low-fidelity prototype, the objectives, the selection of the participants, the results obtained from the evaluation and the final conclusions. It took place in the lab and at the actual site.

3   Research

3.1   Research on Designing Escape Rooms

Escape Rooms represent a new kind of entertainment that has evolved from role-playing, live treasure hunt, and online escape halls where players try to release an avatar by solving puzzles [2, 3].

Many different types of escape rooms are available in various facilities around the world with design concepts varying significantly. Depending on the escape room, players resolutely solve puzzles, that may be spatial, mechanical, linguistic or mathematical. A survey completed in owners of 175 escape room facilities around the world found that 13% had an open model where players solved puzzles in no particular order, 37% had a sequential pattern where the puzzles were drawn in a linear sequence and 45% had multiple sequential paths [2].

Escape rooms are similar to "pervasive games" that move beyond computers to take place on mobiles or other interactive devices [6]. Alternative Reality Games (ARGs) is another type of diffuse game that combines gameplay with real life, often as a form of online storytelling [7–10]. Escape rooms follow the same concept and include a theme that bridges real life and an alternative reality, though to a lesser extent than a game of alternative reality. Cooperation in such contexts has been investigated in several of these games; in general, these games focus on developing trust amongst strangers [11, 12] by creating and exploiting the sense of community [13–15]. Relevant research has indicated that co-operation can help players learn [16], create a common understanding, increase the motivation of players and raise concerns for society and technology.

Researchers have also studied social interaction and feelings during the game. Studies have shown that social interaction (in-situ interaction) is higher when people play against their friends compared to strangers or computer opponents [17, 18]. Feelings of strong social interaction have been associated with user satisfaction and higher levels of stimulation have been associated with playing with a close friend [19]. Higher levels of social interaction can be achieved amongst distributed players when working for a common purpose [18, 20].

3.2 Related Work

In this section emphasis is given on state-of-the-art technologies and related projects. They refer to works implemented for interactive museums and technologies that make the experience of the visitor more interactive.

Interactive museums include *"Sheeptag: An Interactive Museum Exhibition"* a Tangible, Interactive Exhibition for Museums, held in the framework of a thesis in Computer Science and Product Design at the University of Aarhus, 2011 [21]. Sheeptag was put on a permanent exhibition at the Naturhistorisk Museum in Aarhus. The aim of the interactive installation is to assemble the skeleton of an animal by using tangible objects, microcontrollers and a computer application. Each bone has an embedded small RFID tag. The placement of the bone above the red circle indicates the bone in the sheep image on the screen. Also, the corresponding human bone is indicated.

The "Mystery Tour Athens" is another project that features the adventure features of an escape room, but transferring players to the center of Athens. Thus, it offers the possibility to discover important aspects of the historical monuments of the city. To complete the journey, each member of the team is provided with equipment, which also includes an electric vehicle [22].

Technologies that influenced our work include "iPhone RFID Object-Based Media" a prototype of an iPhone media player that uses RFID embedded in physical objects to control media playback [23]. SKÅL is a media player designed for home use that allows the interaction with digital media using physical objects. Interaction takes place by placing different objects in a wooden bowl. The wooden bowl then recognizes the different object, and plays different kind of movies in the TV [24, 25].

3.3 Target Audience

Escape rooms are suitable for a wide set of people. According to research about 37% of the teams are made up of groups of players over 21, about 14% of the players are families with parents and children, while 19% are groups of players under the age of 21. Corporate customers account for about 19% of escape rooms and 11% of teams are couples. What is also interesting, is the results considering the players' gender. Unlike some forms of gambling, escape rooms have drawn players of both sexes. About 70% of the teams are mixed and the other groups are equally distributed amongst males and women.

3.4   Technology Research

We researched a number of technologies including NFC/RFID tags and Beacons for the tokens and the proximity sensing, physical computing platforms, sensors and actuators. NFC/RFID tags were considered for the tokens required to identify the various objects. Beacons used to locate objects in space and identify their relative position with the user while physical computing was the basis for constructing interactions, sensing of the environment and providing system feedback.

For the purposes of this project we used a number of the aforementioned technologies. For the reader we used an Arduino board along with an NFC reader, a buzzer and 2 LEDs used for item recognition. For the interactive table, a second Arduino and another NFC reader with a number of NFC tags for every different object.

4   System Design

The design of the system was divided in five main phases including, the design of the experience journey, the riddles, the workbooks, the interactive technologies and the design and construction of the case of the interactive table.

4.1   The Design of the Interactive Experience Journey

The interactive experience journey was based on the actual production flow of the factory and the order in which the various workstations and tools were arranged. Based on interviews with people who worked in the factory at the time of its operation and desktop research we recorded the actual processes and workflows. For our purposes we distinguished five of the most significant production stages that were representative of the production flow. Based on those we designed the corresponding workbooks and props of the actual workbooks the factory employees owned and used daily. We also designed a distinctive artifact that represented an object/tool for the job[1] (Fig. 2).

4.2   Riddle Design

The next stage in the design process involved the design of the riddles according to the respective workspace and its historical information. Initially, we chose a specific answer that the riddle must conclude with, we brainstormed a number of possible related concepts, we drafted the riddle in terms of metaphors related to the possible

---

[1] https://www.youtube.com/watch?v=2D3ANY0E_Ng&feature=youtu.be.

Experience Journey
Zissimatos Textile Factory

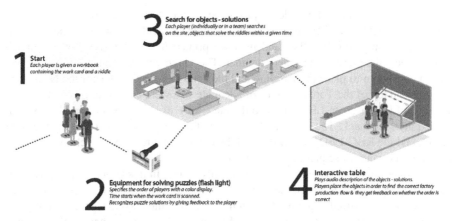

Fig. 2. Experience journey mapping of the textile factory.

concepts of the previous step, and used language techniques such as alliteration and rhyme to make the riddles easier to tell and remember. After designing all riddles, we evaluated them with a group of random students with no prior knowledge on the textile industry. The purpose of the evaluation was to understand the difficulty level of the riddles. In the cases that the participants could not find the right answer, photos from the workspaces were provided so that they could better frame the concept. After the evaluation, changes were made to 3 out of the 5 riddles.

4.3 Workbook Design

For the design of the workbooks, as a reference, we used the real workbooks that have were used in the factory. The same structure was retained, with respect to the data of each worker, but added elements considered essential for the game. Such elements included a map with the indication of each workplace, the riddle, some basic instructions, and the employee card (Fig. 3).

Fig. 3. Player looking through the workbook.

4.4   Prototyping the Interactive Table and Torch

Our system comprised two main components, an interactive table and the tangible torch.

In order to produce a low fidelity prototype for the Torch - the object used to scan items and indicate whether an item is the solution to a riddle - we designed a torch using Creo Parametric by PTC, and then we printed it in a 1:1 scale, in 4 separate pieces. Then, the pieces were glued together. The Torch was designed as a shell, so we had enough room to place the Arduino and the corresponding reader for the NFC Tags inside it. On top of the Torch, 2 holes of adequate size were created to place the LEDs. These 2 LEDs - a green LED and a RGB one - were used to provide the players with the required feedback. The green LED indicated that the player was scanning the right object, and the RBG LED, which showed the colors red, green, blue, yellow and pink, indicated the random sequence of the players.

The final station of the tour was the interactive table. In this table, having solved all the riddles and collected items, the players could "scan" their objects, hear their stories and how they were used in the production flow. Finally, the players were asked to place the items on the table, and re-scan them, this time with the order they think the items were used in the production flow. If the players managed to find the right order of the items, a hidden room was revealed to them and they got to explore it and learn more about the history of the factory (Fig. 4).

Fig. 4. The electronics of the torch prop (left) and the interactive table (right)

5   Evaluation

For the evaluation, we applied standard user testing methods, using low-fidelity prototypes, installed at the actual site of the factory. These included on-site observation, video observation, interviews and questionnaires (Fig. 5).

The objective of the formative evaluation was to obtain useful feedback from designer participants and thus to extract useful feedback with regards to the usability of the system. The evaluation metrics focused on the identification of usability problems, and the overall user experience.

The same procedure was followed for all groups of participants of the evaluation. Initially, some basic information was provided on the design of the game and the use of booklets along with hints about the procedure for recognizing objects. Then, the team entered the evaluation area and each player started playing autonomously by following

Fig. 5. Player during the evaluation trials.

the scenarios related to their profiles. When all the players of the team had solved their riddles, it was time to move to the second part of the game, the table. Next, the players had to scan their items, listen to "story" related to their profile and the production flow they were assigned to. In the following step the participants were prompted by the system to scan the items in the order they thought these fitted the production flow. At this point, the players had an unlimited number of retries in order to find and solve the riddle. Finally, in the case they found the right order, they "unlocked" the hidden room with the actual knitting machines which they could closely examine.

To collect data, we performed on-site observation where we watched and held notes about the navigation of players as well as how they interacted with the game. We also captured the whole evaluation process in video and later did a video observation analysis in order to identify participants' movements and actions. We also handed usability related questionnaires at each evaluation session to all the participants. At the end of the session with the expert participants (professors, designer students) we also performed short interviews in order to collect recommendations about potential improvements and modifications of the prototype.

5.1   Participants

For the purposes of the evaluation we created 4 groups. The first two group had 5 and 4 participants, of ages between 21–23 years old (students) and 28–32 (citizens), respectively. All participants had previous experience with the technologies involved but they had no background about the historical context related to the industrial site. The third group consisted of 4 participants (course instructors) also familiar with the technologies and partially informed about the historical content, the cultural background and the processes and workflows of the factory. Lastly, the fourth group consisted of 5 people identified as "escape room enthusiasts" with special interest in participating in escape rooms for solving riddles. They were partially familiar with the technologies used and unfamiliar of the content and other data related to the site (Fig. 6).

Fig. 6. Player trying to solve her riddle – On the right hand she is holding the torch while on her left hand she is holding her workbook.

5.2   Results and Conclusions

After compiling all the responses and comments we received during the evaluation process, we drew the main results:

- 70% of participants (14 people), argued that they collaborated with other people in their group to find the answers of the riddles, while out of these 14 people, 10 described their collaboration as "fairly good" and 4 of them as "good".
- 95.2% of the participants thought that throughout the game they were able to better understand the production flow of the Textile Factory.
- 42.9% commented that they would not like to use another means to tell the story of the objects.

As regards the most common comments we received:

- The whole process was described as interesting, educational and impressive.
- It was often noted that the process was short in duration and that there was a need for more objects and riddles per workspace.
- There was need for more indications in the recognition object, as well as more indications on the map that illustrated workspaces, as many participants faced problems with their navigation.

6   Issues to Be Improved

The key improvements that we believe that should be implemented in order for the interactive system to be ready for installation are listed below. We also included improvements that we plan to consider in our future work.

As regards the tangible torch, the comments included recommendations to provide a different device to every participant and also incorporate feedback mechanisms (audio and visual) for the riddle responses and the remaining time for solving the riddles. Some users suggested to provide audible notifications for validation of each participant's work card and when a player scans an object (right or wrong object according to their riddle).

The interactive table was recommended to be redesigned so as to aesthetically fit with the factory's arrangement/configuration. The player-table interaction should take place on its surface. Technologies that will be of use would be better placed inside the table and will not be visible. The interactive table should provide for specific spaces for each object to illustrate the factory's production flow in a more comprehensive way (Fig. 7).

Fig. 7. Player using the interactive table during the game

We also received a number of recommendations related to the corresponding post and production flows. These included the creation of more workspaces for better understanding of the factory's production flow, the creation of new workspaces to support more players, to offer more than one riddles at every workspace in order to prolong the game's duration. A gradual escalation of riddles' difficulty was also advised as well as to provide a hint for every object to cater for cases where a player cannot find the answer on the assigned riddle after a period of time.

Acknowledgments. We would like to thank Dimitris Stavrakopoulos for providing access to the factory and valuable information related to project's goals.

References

1. Heikkinen, O., Shumeyko, J.: Designing an escape room with the Experience Pyramid model (2016)
2. Pan, R., Lo, H., Neustaedter, C.: Collaboration, awareness, and communication in real-life escape rooms. In: Proceedings of the 2017 Conference on Designing Interactive Systems, New York, NY, USA, pp. 1353–1364 (2017)
3. Nicholson, S.: Peeking behind the locked door: a survey of escape room facilities. White Paper (2015). http://www.scottnicholson.com/pubs/erfacwhite.pdf

4. Shakeri, H., Singhal, S., Pan, R., Neustaedter, C., Tang, A.: Escaping together: the design and evaluation of a distributed real-life escape room. In: Proceedings of the Annual Symposium on Computer-Human Interaction in Play, New York, NY, USA, pp. 115–128 (2017)

5. Stratton, M., Trinder, B.: Hermoupolis: the archaeology of a Mediterranean industrial city. Ind. Archaeol. Rev. 16(2), 184–195 (1994)

6. Kasapakis, V., Gavalas, D.: Pervasive gaming: status, trends and design principles. J. Netw. Comput. Appl. 55, 213–236 (2015)

7. Benford, S., Giannachi, G., Koleva, B., Rodden, T.: From interaction to trajectories: designing coherent journeys through user experiences. In: Proceedings of the SIGCHI Conference on Human Factors in Computing Systems, New York, NY, USA, pp. 709–718 (2009)

8. Benford, S., Giannachi, G.: Performing Mixed Reality. The MIT Press, Cambridge (2011)

9. Bonsignore, E., Moulder, V., Neustaedter, C., Hansen, D., Kraus, K., Druin, A.: Design tactics for authentic interactive fiction: insights from alternate reality game designers. In: Proceedings of the SIGCHI Conference on Human Factors in Computing Systems, New York, NY, USA, pp. 947–950 (2014)

10. Bonsignore, E.M.: Playing for Real: Designing Alternate Reality Games in Learning Contexts (2016)

11. Bedwell, B., Schnädelbach, H., Benford, S., Rodden, T., Koleva, B.: In support of city exploration. In: Proceedings of the SIGCHI Conference on Human Factors in Computing Systems, New York, NY, USA, pp. 1171–1180 (2009)

12. Benford, S., et al.: The frame of the game: blurring the boundary between fiction and reality in mobile experiences. In: Proceedings of the SIGCHI Conference on Human Factors in Computing Systems, New York, NY, USA, pp. 427–436 (2006)

13. O'Hara, K.: Understanding Geocaching practices and motivations. In: Proceedings of the SIGCHI Conference on Human Factors in Computing Systems, New York, NY, USA, pp. 1177–1186 (2008)

14. Neustaedter, C., Tang, A., Judge, T.K.: Creating scalable location-based games: lessons from Geocaching. Pers. Ubiquitous Comput. 17(2), 335–349 (2013)

15. Neustaedter, C., Tang, A., Tejinder, J.K.: The role of community and groupware in Geocache creation and maintenance. In: Proceedings of the SIGCHI Conference on Human Factors in Computing Systems, New York, NY, USA, pp. 1757–1766 (2010)

16. Bonsignore, E., Kraus, K., Visconti, A., Hansen, D., Fraistat, A., Druin, A.: Game design for promoting counterfactual thinking. In: Proceedings of the SIGCHI Conference on Human Factors in Computing Systems, New York, NY, USA, pp. 2079–2082 (2012)

17. Gajadhar, B., de Kort, Y., IJsselsteijn, W.: Influence of social setting on player experience of digital games. In: CHI 2008 Extended Abstracts on Human Factors in Computing Systems, New York, NY, USA, pp. 3099–3104 (2008)

18. Segura, E.M., Isbister, K.: Enabling co-located physical social play: a framework for design and evaluation. In: Bernhaupt, R. (ed.) Game User Experience Evaluation. HIS, pp. 209–238. Springer, Cham (2015). https://doi.org/10.1007/978-3-319-15985-0_10

19. Mandryk, R.L., Inkpen, K.M., Calvert, T.W.: Using psychophysiological techniques to measure user experience with entertainment technologies. Behav. Inf. Technol. 25(2), 141–158 (2006)

20. De Kort, Y.A.W., Ijsselsteijn, W.A.: People, places, and play: player experience in a socio-spatial context. Comput. Entertain. 6(2), 18:1–18:11 (2008)

21. Rasmussen, J.O.: SheepTag: an interactive museum exhibition. Presented at the Student Interaction Design Research (SIDeR) Conference, Copenhagen, p. 178 (2012)

22. The Mystery Tour Athens—Great Escape Rooms Athens. Great Escape Rooms

23. Timo: iPhone RFID: object-based media in AHO Interaction Design (2009)
24. Martinussen, E.S., Arnall, T.: Designing with RFID. In: Proceedings of the 3rd International Conference on Tangible and Embedded Interaction, New York, NY, USA, pp. 343–350 (2009)
25. Martinussen, E.S., Knutsen, J., Arnall, T.: Bowl: token-based media for children. In: Proceedings of the 2007 Conference on Designing for User Experiences, New York, NY, USA, pp. 17:3–17:16 (2007)

Simulation of an Archaeological Disaster: Reassembling a Fragmented Amphora Using the Thickness Profile Method

Michail I. Stamatopoulos and Christos-Nikolaos Anagnostopoulos[(⊠)]

Social Sciences School, Cultural Technology and Communication Department,
University of the Aegean, 81100 Mytilene, Lesvos Island, Greece
canag@aegean.gr

Abstract. In this paper, we simulate the incredible story of the *Francois Vase,* on a remarkable ancient amphora depicting Achilles and Briseis exhibited in the provincial museum *Sigismondo Castromediano* in Lecce, Italy. A high precision handmade replica of the original red-figure style masterpiece, 50 cm tall, from the collection of the museum in Lecce was built, fully decorated in our laboratory and then intentionally destroyed simulating the archaeological disaster of the *Francois Vase*. The handmade amphora (i.e. replica) was broken in 507 fragments, out of which 148 sherds (or *ostraca*) were offered for digital restoration through the Thickness Profile method on an on-going project.

Keywords: Pottery reassembly · Thickness profile · 3D reconstruction
Sherds

1 Introduction

Reviewing the related archaeological literature, it is obvious that the evaluation and assessment of digital reassembly methods in pottery restoration so far, has been worked out on a small number of sherds (or *ostraca*), ranging from a few pieces up to no more than 30–40 fragments [1–6]. In this paper, we simulate the incredible disaster story of the *Francois Vase* -which was smashed into 638 pieces by a museum guard- on another remarkable masterpiece of an ancient Greek amphora depicting Achilles and Briseis. A high-precision handmade replica of the specific amphora was built, fully decorated in our laboratory and then intentionally destroyed, simulating the archaeological disaster of the *Francois Vase*. The pottery was intentionally broken in 507 fragments, out of which 148 *ostraca* underwent digital restoration through the Thickness Profile method on an on-going project. The Thickness Profile method is a brand new approach [7], the efficiency of which is due to the fact that the important information sought is encapsulated within the *ostraca* and not on their surface. The effectiveness of the method is not reduced by the potential loss of several fragments or the external damage (i.e. colour degradation) on some of them over the centuries. The method has already been successfully tested in varied case experiments on synthetic and real archaeological data, through the use of state-of-the-art technologies with which high-precision measurements were extracted from 3D digital models.

© Springer Nature Switzerland AG 2018
M. Ioannides et al. (Eds.): EuroMed 2018, LNCS 11196, pp. 162–173, 2018.
https://doi.org/10.1007/978-3-030-01762-0_14

2 The Amphora of Achilles and Briseis

2.1 Archaeological Validation

In the provincial museum *Sigismondo Castromediano* in Lecce, Italy, an amphora of ancient Greek ceramic art is exhibited as part (Cat. No. 571) of the permanent museum collection (see Fig. 1). This red-figure style masterpiece, 50 cm tall, is attributed to the painter of the *Berlin Dancing Girl*, an Apulian artist who was active between 430 and 410 B.C. He was called after a calyx krater which depicts a dancing girl and is part of the pottery permanent exhibition in the Antikensammlung museum in Berlin, Germany. In all likelihood, he must have been trained in an Attic workshop located in Kerameikos, Athens, Greece, before working in Apulia, Italy.

Fig. 1. The amphora (Cat. No. 571) in the provincial museum *Sigismondo Castromediano* in Lecce, Italy. The two last photos on the right, demonstrate the handmade replica.

The main scene on the front side of the amphora, narrates a farewell between Achilles and Briseis, while Agamemnon is watching from behind. The Greek names of the three main characters are engraved on the amphora (*ΑΧΙΛΛΕΥΣ*, *ΒΡΙΣΗΙΣ* and *ΑΓΑΜΕΜΝΩΝ*). The scene is delimited by a band of flower motifs on both sides. Achilles stands in the center of the scene looking to the left. He appears nude and holds a cloak in his left hand while offering a phiale to Briseis with his right hand. He wears a Corinthian helmet decorated with a bird and is slightly leaning left on his spear. His round shield rests on his left thigh. Briseis, on the left of Achilles, looks right, towards him. She has a ribbon worn around her head, wears a belted chiton, holds an oinochoe in her right hand and lifts her chiton with the left hand. Agamemnon stands behind Achilles. He is depicted as a bearded man who wears a crown, a laurel wreath and leans on a stick. On the back side of the amphora, two more figures stand on opposite sides of a Doric column, a woman on the right and a man on the left. The woman looks towards left and wears a chiton and a cloak. She bears a laurel wreath. She holds an egg in her left hand and a long band in her right one. The bearded man on the left side looks towards left. He wears a laurel wreath, too. He is dressed in a cloak that leaves his breast naked and he leans on a stick. The rim of the amphora is decorated with egg-shaped motifs. The neck bears two standing lions looking left, on both sides. The handles are decorated with up-turned palmettes. This masterpiece is inspired from the narratives of Iliad. Following the narration of the Homeric poem, the Greeks, right after their first victory against the Trojans, took captives many female priestesses. Achilles fell in love with one of them, Briseis. But Agamemnon decided to keep her as his own mistress causing Achilles anger and his decision to withdraw from battle leaving the Greeks helpless. Despite their efforts to make him return, he only did so, when Ector killed his close friend, Patroclus.

2.2   Building up the Amphora

For the creation of the replica, the available information was limited to a small number of photographs and brief archaeological documentation. The building of the amphora was performed by hand on a wheel, in a Greek ceramic workshop, using liquid clay and then the pottery was baked in an oven. In determining the dimensions of the pottery, even the slight shrinking that would be generated during the baking process, was taken into account. The construction was performed in three separate pieces (main body, neck and base) which were then joined up and baked in the oven. For safety reasons, two copies were made in total to minimize the risk of breaking during baking. The next phase of the project comes to a particularly difficult and complex process in which the amphora (total height 50 cm, main body largest diameter 30 cm, mouth minimum inner diameter 9 cm and neck outer diameter 22 cm) had to be mapped all over its internal surfaces by tracing parallels and meridians (see Fig. 2/top-left). The process was carried out with a complex mechanism that was devised, implemented and applied exclusively by the Greek Cultural Technology Lab of the University of the Aegean, deliberately for the purpose of internal mapping. Internal mapping was considered necessary because this particular amphora, in the largest part of its surface decoration, consisted mainly in large black-coloured areas which would render difficult the demonstration of the results correctness.

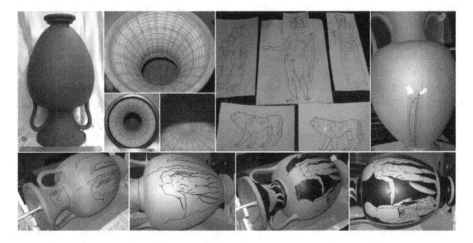

Fig. 2. The building up process. On the top left, the amphora before being baked in an oven.

The amphora was divided internally in 24 vertical areas (based on the 24 letters of the Greek alphabet, A, B, Γ, Δ, E, Z, H, Θ, I, K, Λ, M, N, Ξ, O, Π, P, Σ, T, Y, Φ, X, Ψ, Ω) and 50 horizontal parallels (starting from the 1st parallel on the pottery base, up to the 50th one at the rim of the neck). In all, the amphora was divided -mapped-internally into 1.200 segments (24x50). The amphora weighed 4.780 g. The decoration of the amphora was exclusively performed by the authors of the paper and the only auxiliary visual material was limited to a small number of photographs. The method used to perform the decoration was based solely on stencil techniques. In particular, each main figure to be drawn was initially projected (in 1:1 scale with respect to the original amphora) onto a large flat monitor (using mirror projection) to allow it to be stenciled onto a thick transparent elastic membrane placed on the monitor surface. Thereafter, each of these membranes (see Fig. 2/top-right) were removed and placed upside down (removal of mirror projection) onto the pottery, gently pressed against the clean ceramic surface, leaving the trace of the silhouettes on it. Due to the curvature of such a large object and the deformation (shrinkage) that it appearing in the available photographs, a special filter from a renowned image software was used to stretch the image (e.g. the figures' feet at the bottom of the photos). The same stretching was applied at the lower part of each membrane wherever there was local deformation due to curvature. The outlines of the silhouettes were filled with black color and the amphora was finally covered with a gentle layer of glaze.

2.3   Destroying the Amphora

The amphora was let to perform a free fall from a height of 2.5 m, onto a flat marble surface and it shattered. The whole process was photographed and filmed (see Fig. 3). A related video is available at www.omicron.gr/downloads/SPASIMO.mts.

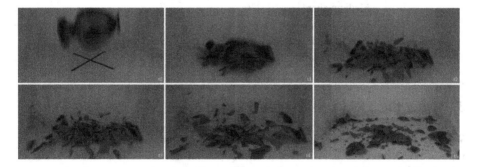

Fig. 3. Some video frames from the amphora breakage.

After the initial breakage, some very large pieces had still preserved the two main silhouettes of the amphora intact, though unintentionally. However, it was considered necessary to break even those large pieces in order to increase the number of available fragments. Eventually, the pottery broke into 507 different pieces. The material that emerged from the crash, was measured, separated, uniquely identified and classified into five different groups, based on the amount of thickness information that it could provide. Of the 507 different pieces (see Fig. 4/right), 350 were very small ones (shells and trimmings), 9 were unprocessable (pottery base and handles) and 148 sherds were usable by the Thickness Profile method (see Table 1). For documentation and further research purposes, the amphora, prior to the breakage, was digitally modeled (3D model) using photogrammetry (see Fig. 4/left).

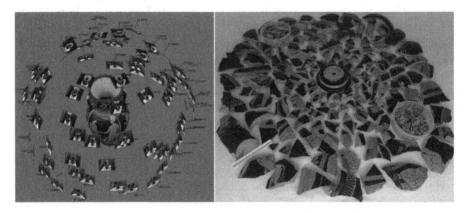

Fig. 4. On the left, a 3D digital model of the amphora. On the right, the 507 pieces after the intentional breakage.

Table 1. Categories of emerged material.

Group	Type of material	Percent of material	Number of sherds
A	Large sherds	18%	18
B	Medium sherds	42%	71
C	Small sherds	15%	59
D	Handles and base	13% (682 g)	9
E	Shells and trimmings	12% (565 g)	350 shells

3   Using the Thickness Profile Method

We display hereafter the results of the digital reconstruction process of the large broken replica of the amphora held in Lecce. Using part of the available abundant material (sherds, thickness measurements, photos, 3D models, reports, etc.), we limit our presentation to the front side of the amphora showcasing only the two main characters, Achilles and Briseis. In total, we recompose and feature the digital results for 35 out of the 148 available amphora sherds to be processed (24% of the overall material). Within this process, we followed exactly the same steps as those taken in the digital Thickness Profile method already applied by the authors on small-scale reconstructions of broken pottery (real and synthetic), in previous papers [7].

Initially, we leveled each sherd by adjusting the inner horizontal traces -that the potter's fingers left on it- between two leveled crosshair beam lasers (see Fig. 8). We then photographed each sherd all around, to obtain sets of photos which we then converted to 3D digital models using the appropriate photogrammetry software. Out of each 3D digital model, we then extracted the vertical plane of the sherd as a sequence of successive thickness measurements (sampling). All the data from the sherds were forwarded into the special software which we had created and the results are presented, analyzed and commented hereafter. After processing the data, it was observed that the large-volume ceramic object had many different cross-section thickness profiles. Intuitively, this resembles many varied *"local thickness profiles"* in large pottery and not just a single cross-section thickness profile that a small pottery might have or even a small number of contiguous sherds (that would belong to a specific pottery area). The various *"local thickness profiles"* did not affect the correctness of the results. A second important observation concerning the large number of medium to small sherds was that they offered similar thickness measurements and raised the rate of wrong matching suggestions. Many small sherds seemed to be stuck in the same thickness values along their vertical plane. This observation is justified by the large size of the amphora, mainly in the large body area, hence the breakage of this area produced many sherds with similar thickness profiles. However, with a small improvement in the calculation algorithm, the success matching rate remained at satisfactory levels. For sherds with varied thickness measurements, the correct hints remained at the same high success rate.

Figure 5 shows all thickness measurements as extracted from the above described procedure. The thickness measurements are displayed exactly as they are processed by the software since they are rounded down to one decimal place. In the same figure, a colour scale mapping for each sherd is displayed representing the thickness measurements in order to help the reader easily identify, at a glance, the appropriate matches. The Thickness Profile method software does exactly the same thing by comparing numbers instead of comparing color variations. Figure 6 shows the front side of the amphora with the two main characters, Achilles and Briseis with the relative placement suggestions as produced by the software. In the same figure, we have centrally embodied the side view of sherd B39 to clearly display and explain the low-level matching between sherd B39 and its surrounding sherds A1, A10 and C31 which drew our attention for an evident, yet astonishing, inconsistence: a detailed observation of the side of B39 reveals a large air-bubble (see Fig. 6/center) which was encapsulated within the liquid clay before baking it and obviously caused the ataxia (possible matching) as shown by the blue indicators (B39 vs A1, B39 vs A10). In the same Fig. 6 on top, we can see the same composition of sherds from the inner side, showcasing the usefulness of internal mapping (1.200 segments, 24x50) carried out in the lab before smashing the amphora. In addition, a thin blue self-adhesive tape has been placed on each of those 35 sherds, to indicate the exact position of the vertical plane as detected through the laser beam alignment. It is noteworthy that those thin vertical blue stripes showcase some sort of *"vertical elegance"* and each of them is arranged in a form of vertical regularity in relation to all the rest and particularly to the neighboring ones. These thin blue stripes were placed on each of the sherds before the handmade reassembly of the back side of the 35 adjacent sherds. This important observation made

Fig. 5 presents the acquired TPs out of 34 pottery sherds. The data are organised in column slots, each headed by a sherd label with its corresponding colour map bar; shorter sherds are stacked beneath within the same slot. The readable numeric values (in mm) are given below, slot by slot.

A14
7,9 7,9 7,9 7,9 7,9 7,9 7,9 7,9 8,0 8,0 7,9 7,9 7,8 7,8 7,8 7,8 7,7 7,8 7,7 7,6 7,6 7,6 7,6 7,5 7,4 7,4 7,4 7,3 7,3 7,3 7,2 7,2 7,2 7,2 7,2 7,3 7,4 7,5 7,5 7,7 7,7 7,8 7,9 8,0 8,1 8,2 8,3 8,6 8,7 8,9 9,2 9,3 9,4 9,4 9,5 9,7 9,9 10,1 10,3 10,5 10,5 10,6 10,7 10,7 10,8 10,9 11,0 11,2 11,2 11,3 11,4 11,5 11,6 11,9 11,9 12,1 12,1 12,1 12,2 12,3 12,5 12,6 12,7 12,6 12,7 12,7 12,7 12,7 12,7 12,7

A10
8,2 8,0 7,8 7,7 7,8 7,8 7,8 7,6 7,5 7,4 7,3 7,4 7,4 7,4 7,4 7,3 7,4 7,4 7,4 7,4 7,4 7,4 7,5 7,6 7,7 7,6 7,7 7,8 7,9 8,0 8,0 8,0 8,0 8,1 8,1 8,1 8,1 8,2 8,2 8,3 8,4 8,2 8,3 8,2 8,0 8,0 7,9 7,9 7,9 7,8 7,7 7,7 7,6 7,6 7,5 7,5 7,5 7,6 7,8 7,8 7,9 8,1 8,2 8,3 8,4 8,5 8,7 8,7 8,8 9,4 9,6 9,6 9,7 9,9 10,1 10,3 10,6 10,8 11,0 11,1 11,2 11,2 11,2 11,4 11,5 11,6 11,7 11,9

B16
7,8 7,9 8,0 8,2 8,1 8,0 7,8 7,8 7,7 7,7 7,7 7,7 7,6 7,6 7,8 8,0 8,2 8,3 8,1 7,9 7,7 7,6 7,6 7,6

B25
10,6 10,5 10,4 10,5 10,4 10,1 9,9 9,6 9,4 9,4 9,1 8,7 8,5 8,3 8,1 8,0 8,1 8,1 8,0

B33
9,2 9,1 9,0 9,0 8,9

C24
8,5 8,6 8,6 8,4 8,4 8,4 8,3 8,3 8,3 8,2 8,1 8,0 7,9 7,9 7,9 7,8 7,9 7,8 7,9 8,0 8,0

C22
12,8 12,8 12,8 12,8 12,8 12,8 12,7 12,6 12,5 12,3 12,2 11,8 11,6 11,4 11,1 10,8 10,7 10,7 10,7 10,6 10,4 10,4 10,2

B34
7,7 7,8 7,7 7,6 7,7

B10
7,7 7,7 7,9 8,0 8,0 7,9 8,2 8,0 7,9 7,7 7,7 7,6 7,5 7,5 7,6 7,7 7,7 7,6 7,6 7,6 7,9 8,0 8,0 7,9 8,1 7,8 8,2

A5
8,1 8,2 8,3 8,4 8,5 8,7 7,6 7,5 7,5 7,4 8,9 9,0 9,1 9,2 9,3 10,0 10,0 10,1 10,1 10,1 9,8 9,6 9,3 9,1 8,8 8,6 8,4 8,3 8,2 8,2 8,3 8,2 8,2

A1
7,5 7,6 7,9 8,0 8,0 7,9 7,8 7,6 7,4 7,3 7,4 7,5 7,8 8,2 8,1 8,1 8,0 8,1 8,2 8,1 8,1 8,2 8,0 8,2 7,9 8,4 8,4 8,4 8,5 8,9 8,9 9,3 9,5 9,9 9,9 9,9 9,8 9,9 8,7 10,1 10,3 10,7 8,7 9,2 10,1 10,1 10,0 9,7 9,9 10,2 10,3 10,8 11,2 11,3 11,7 12,0 12,1 12,3 12,5 12,6 12,7 12,9

C43
7,3 7,3 7,3 7,4 7,4 7,2 7,2 7,2 7,3 7,3 7,3 7,3 7,3 7,3

mm

C12
8,2 8,1 7,9 7,8 7,8 7,7 7,7 7,6 7,6 7,6 7,6 7,8 7,8 7,8 7,7 7,6 7,6 7,6 7,6 7,5 7,5 7,6 7,7 8,0 7,9 7,8 7,9

C41
15,1 15,1 15,1 15,0 14,9 14,7

B68
6,8 7,0 7,1 7,1 7,2 7,3 7,7 7,2 7,1 7,1 7,2 7,3 7,3 7,3 7,5 7,4 7,4 7,3 7,4 7,4 7,6 7,6 7,7 7,8 7,8 7,9 7,8 7,7 7,7 7,8

B45
8,1 8,4 8,7 9,2

C49
7,0 7,2 7,4 7,5 7,6 7,5 7,4 7,6 7,4

A2
8,1 8,1 8,2 8,2 8,2 8,0 7,9 7,8 7,8 7,8 7,7 7,7 7,8 7,8 7,9 7,9 7,9 8,0 8,1 8,1 8,2 8,3 8,4 8,8 9,0 7,7 7,7 7,7 7,8 7,9 9,6 9,7 9,9 10,2 10,3 11,2 11,3 11,7 12,0 12,1 12,3 12,5 12,7 12,8 12,8 12,7 12,8 12,8 12,7 12,8 12,8 12,7 12,8 12,8 12,7 12,9 12,6 11,2 11,6 11,5 11,2 11,1 10,9 10,7 10,6

C28
8,1 8,0 7,9 7,9 7,9 7,8 7,8 7,7 7,5 7,4 7,5 7,5 7,4 7,4 7,5

B39
9,5 9,8 10,0 10,7 10,8 10,9 11,0 11,3 11,6 11,6 11,5 11,3 11,1 11,0 10,8 10,7 10,6 10,5 10,4 10,0 9,7 9,2 8,9 8,6 8,5 8,5 8,5 8,4 8,3 8,3 8,2 7,9 7,8 7,7

B30
11,8 12,1 12,1 12,4

B11
7,9 8,1 8,3 8,4 8,4 8,4 8,3 8,2 8,0 7,9 7,8 7,8 7,8 7,8 7,7 8,1 8,3 8,0 7,9 7,8 7,7 7,7 7,8 7,8 7,6 7,5 7,5 7,7 7,7 7,8 7,9 8,0 8,1 8,2 8,3 8,6 8,7 8,9 9,2 9,3 9,4 9,4 9,5 9,7 10,0 10,3 10,5 10,5 10,6 10,7 10,7 10,8 10,9 11,0 11,2 11,2 11,3 11,4 11,5 11,6

C13
7,2 7,3 7,3 7,3 7,2 7,4 7,4 7,4 7,4 7,4 7,4 7,4

B6
7,9 7,9 7,9 7,8 7,9 8,0 8,2 8,4 8,6 8,7 9,4 9,3 9,4 9,5 9,7 10,0 10,3 10,8 11,0 10,9 10,7 10,5 10,2 9,9 9,9 8,9 8,3 8,2 8,1 8,1 8,2 8,3

A11
10,5 10,6 10,6 10,4 10,2 10,0 10,3 9,9 10,0 9,5 9,0 8,9 8,7 8,7 8,6 8,5 8,5 8,5 8,4 8,3 8,5 8,5 8,3 8,3 8,3 8,3 8,1 8,1 8,0 8,0 8,4 8,4 8,8 8,8 8,6 8,2 8,3 8,5 8,2 7,9 7,7 7,6 7,8 7,9 8,0 7,9 8,1 8,0 8,2 7,8 7,7 7,7 7,4 7,6 7,7 8,0 8,1 8,2 8,3

B15
7,7 7,8 7,9 8,0 8,0 7,9 7,8 7,7 7,6 7,6 7,6 7,6 7,7 7,7 7,8 7,7 7,8 7,8 8,2 8,1 7,8 7,8 7,7 7,6 7,7 7,8 8,0 8,0 7,9 7,8

B58
7,5 7,7 7,9 8,1 8,3 8,5 8,9 9,2 9,5 9,8 9,9 10,1 10,3 10,5 10,7 10,9 11,3 11,5 11,8 12,2 12,4 12,5 12,8 13,1 13,0 12,9 12,8 12,8

C46
7,7 7,8 7,9 8,1 7,8 7,6 7,4 7,4 7,7 8,0 8,1 8,2 8,1 8,1 8,2 8,3

B69
7,3 7,3 7,4 7,6 7,7 7,8 7,9 8,1 8,2 8,4 8,5 8,8 8,6 9,1 9,2 9,2 9,5 9,7 9,9 10,1 10,3 10,5 10,6 10,8 10,9 11,2 11,2 11,3 11,4 11,5

B7
11,9 11,8 11,6 11,4 11,1 10,9 10,7 10,4 10,3 10,4 10,3 10,2 10,3 10,0 9,8 9,9 9,8 9,6 9,5 9,4 8,7 8,5 8,3 8,2 8,1 8,0 8,0 8,0 8,0 8,0 8,1

A4
8,3 8,5 8,5 8,5 8,3 8,3 8,2 8,1 8,0 7,9 7,9 7,9 7,8 7,8 7,9 7,9 7,9 7,8 7,8 7,8 7,7 7,6 7,5 7,7 7,7 7,7 7,8 7,9 8,1 8,1 8,1 8,1 8,2 8,5 8,7 8,9 9,1 9,6 9,8 10,1 10,5 10,8 10,9 10,8 10,6 10,4 10,2 10,1 9,8 9,8 9,8 9,7 9,5 8,9 8,4 8,1 7,9 7,9 8,1

C31
11,2 11,2 11,2 11,0 10,9 10,8 10,5 10,4 10,3 10,2 10,2 10,1 10,0 9,7 9,0 8,7 8,5 8,4 9,3 9,2 8,5 8,5

B60
7,6 7,7 7,9 8,1 8,1 8,3 8,6 8,9 9,3 9,5 9,7 10,2 10,5 10,7 10,9 11,2 11,6 12,1 12,1 12,5 12,6 12,8 13,0 13,3 13,4 13,2 13,2 13,1 13,0 13,0 13,0 12,9 12,8 12,7 12,6 12,5 12,4 12,2 11,8

B8
8,0 8,1 8,1 8,0 8,1 7,8 7,7 7,6 7,7 7,7 7,7 7,8 7,9 7,8 7,9 7,8 8,2 8,2 8,2 8,3 8,4 8,2 8,3 8,4 8,6 8,5 8,3 8,4 8,4 8,4 8,5 8,5 8,5 8,5

mm

Fig. 5. The acquired TPs out of 34 pottery sherds of 148 useful amphora sherds. On the right of each sherd, the corresponding colour map. (Color figure online)

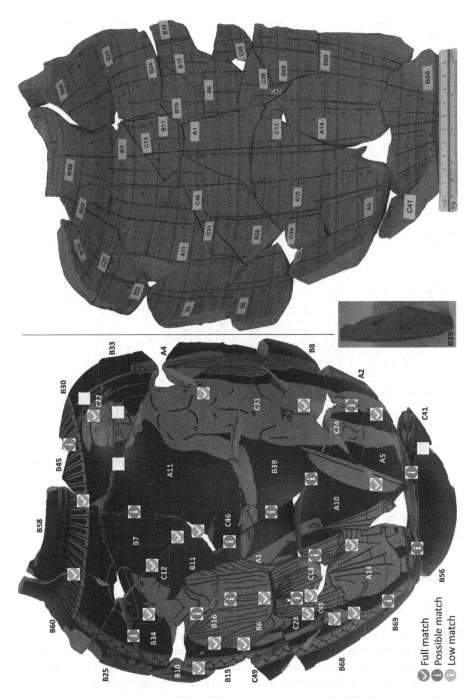

Fig. 6. On the bottom, the reassembly with the suggestions as produced by the software. On the top, the back reassembly side of the 35 sherds. In the center, the side view of sherd B39. (Color figure online)

pair	suggesting position	annotation		pair	suggesting position	annotation
(A2) vs (A5)	in 7,53 56 CH +1mm (M)	REJECT ✓	(B56) vs (A5)	in 8,26 36 CH +25mm (R)	REJECT ⓘ
56/60, 15	out 0,59 40 CH -16mm (oM)	FULL MATCH	36/60, 12	out 1,33 35 CH -49mm (Mu)	POSSIBLE MATCH
(A4) vs (A11)	in 7,35 67 CH +2mm (R)	REJECT ✓	(B56) vs (B69)	in 14,43 36 CH +5mm (R)	REJECT ⓘ
67/68, 15	out 0,36 66 CH -44mm (Mu)	FULL MATCH	36/40, 8	out 1,16 35 CH -33mm (Mu)	POSSIBLE MATCH
(A5) vs (A10)	in 12,98 60 CH +30mm (M)	REJECT ✓	(B58) vs (B45)	in 2,03 37 CH +1mm (M)	LOW MATCH ✓
60/89, 15	out 1,01 59 CH -58mm (Mu)	FULL MATCH	37/51, 15	out 0,51 34 CH -3mm (oM)	FULL MATCH
(A14) vs (A10)	in 0,00 90 CH +0mm ( )	REJECT ✓	(B58) vs (B60)	in 0,78 37 CH +1mm (M)	FULL MATCH ✓
90/89, 49	out 2,74 89 CH -19mm (Mu)	FULL MATCH	37/39, 15	out 0,93 36 CH -1mm (oM)	POSSIBLE MATCH
(B6) vs (A1)	in 0,77 39 CH +17mm (M)	FULL MATCH ✓	(B68) vs (A14)	in 5,41 57 CH +1mm (R)	REJECT ✓
39/63, 15	out 1,23 38 CH -49mm (Mu)	POSSIBLE MATCH	57/90, 15	out 0,32 35 CH -22mm (oM)	FULL MATCH
(B6) vs (B15)	in 5,82 39 CH +5mm (M)	REJECT ✓	(B69) vs (A14)	in 1,02 40 CH +39mm (M)	POSSIBLE MATCH ⓘ
39/43, 15	out 0,58 38 CH -29mm (Mu)	FULL MATCH	40/90, 15	out 1,00 15 CH -25mm (oR)	REJECT
(B7) vs (A11)	in 3,12 46 CH +1mm (M)	LOW MATCH ⓘ	(C12) vs (B7)	in 0,94 27 CH +20mm (R)	LOW MATCH ✓
46/68, 15	out 1,83 41 CH -5mm (oM)	POSSIBLE MATCH	27/46, 7	out 0,38 26 CH -40mm (Mu)	FULL MATCH
(B8) vs (B39)	in 7,22 49 CH +4mm (R)	REJECT ✓	(C12) vs (B34)	in 0,52 27 CH +1mm (R)	POSSIBLE MATCH ✓
49/52, 15	out 0,39 48 CH -37mm (Mu)	FULL MATCH	27/27, 15	out 0,16 24 CH -3mm (oM)	FULL MATCH
(B10) vs (B15)	in 0,51 28 CH +10mm (R)	POSSIBLE MATCH ✓	(C13) vs (A10)	in 0,11 13 CH +9mm (M)	POSSIBLE MATCH ⓘ
28/43, 15	out 0,27 25 CH -3mm (oM)	FULL MATCH	13/89, 12	out 0,56 12 CH -1mm (oM)	REJECT
(B11) vs (A11)	in 0,68 28 CH +41mm (M)	POSSIBLE MATCH ✓	(C13) vs (C28)	in 0,05 13 CH +18mm (M)	FULL MATCH ✓
28/68, 8	out 0,44 27 CH -61mm (Mu)	FULL MATCH	13/30, 15	out 0,00 0 CH +0mm ( )	-
(B11) vs (B7)	in 0,93 28 CH +16mm (M)	LOW MATCH ✓	(C22) vs (B30)	in 1,26 23 CH +8mm (M)	REJECT ⓘ
28/46, 15	out 0,44 27 CH -28mm (Mu)	FULL MATCH	23/30, 15	out 0,58 22 CH -16mm (Mu)	LOW MATCH
(B11) vs (B16)	in 0,60 28 CH +7mm (R)	POSSIBLE MATCH ⓘ	(C22) vs (B45)	in 0,23 23 CH +25mm (M)	FULL MATCH ✓
28/34, 15	out 0,14 15 CH -13mm (oM)	POSSIBLE MATCH	23/51, 15	out 1,12 22 CH -30mm (Mu)	REJECT
(B16) vs (A1)	in 2,05 34 CH +1mm (M)	REJECT ⓘ	(C24) vs (A2)	in 0,67 23 CH +4mm (R)	LOW MATCH ⓘ
34/63, 15	out 0,42 22 CH -12mm (oM)	POSSIBLE MATCH	23/56, 15	out 0,23 16 CH -7mm (oM)	POSSIBLE MATCH
(B16) vs (B15)	in 0,40 34 CH +2mm (M)	FULL MATCH ✓	(C28) vs (A1)	in 2,17 30 CH +1mm (R)	REJECT ⓘ
34/43, 15	out 0,33 33 CH -26mm (Mu)	FULL MATCH	30/63, 10	out 0,66 29 CH -54mm (Mu)	POSSIBLE MATCH
(B30) vs (B65)	in 0,83 30 CH +15mm (M)	POSSIBLE MATCH ⓘ	(C41) vs (B56)	in 0,05 6 CH +10mm (R)	LOW MATCH ⓘ
30/51, 15	out 2,46 29 CH -23mm (Mu)	REJECT	6/36, 15	out 0,00 0 CH +0mm ( )	-
(B33) vs (B45)	in 7,32 29 CH +1mm (M)	REJECT ⓘ	(C43) vs (B68)	in 0,39 26 CH +3mm (M)	FULL MATCH ✓
29/51, 7	out 0,92 28 CH -45mm (Mu)	LOW MATCH	26/57, 15	out 0,18 25 CH -43mm (Mu)	FULL MATCH
(B34) vs (B25)	in 3,06 27 CH +3mm (R)	REJECT ⓘ	(C43) vs (C28)	in 0,32 26 CH +4mm (R)	FULL MATCH ✓
27/29, 15	out 0,63 26 CH -15mm (Mu)	POSSIBLE MATCH	26/30, 15	out 0,09 25 CH -11mm (Mu)	FULL MATCH
(B39) vs (A1)	in 2,42 52 CH +1mm (R)	POSSIBLE MATCH ⓘ	(C46) vs (A1)	in 0,22 18 CH +2mm (M)	POSSIBLE MATCH ⓘ
52/63, 18	out 1,70 51 CH -30mm (Mu)	POSSIBLE MATCH	18/63, 15	out 0,43 17 CH -1mm (oR)	LOW MATCH
(B39) vs (A10)	in 3,38 52 CH +38mm (R)	LOW MATCH ⓘ			
52/89, 19	out 0,37 19 CH -33mm (oM)	POSSIBLE MATCH			
(B45) vs (A11)	in 12,56 51 CH +1mm (R)	REJECT ⓘ			
51/68, 9	out 0,11 9 CH -42mm (oM)	LOW MATCH			

Fig. 7. The suggestions for 38 pairs regarding the two main characters, Achilles and Briseis. All the required data produced by our software displayed for the assistance of the archaeologist.

on such a large number of neighboring sherds taken out of this large amphora has impressed even the authors themselves, since a single image ascertains the validity of the Thickness Profile method.

4   The Thickness Profile Methodology

4.1   Idea of the Method

The Thickness Profile method is based on the matching of consecutive number sequences which represent successive thickness measurements taken out of appropriately positioned vertical cross-sections traced out of the internal parallel lines (see Fig. 8) which the potter's fingers had left on the damp clay during the formation of the pottery [8, 9]. The process resembles the sliding of small thickness profiles along (up and down) on larger thickness profiles. An optimal fitting can be gained solely when the numerical sequence concerning the thickness profile of a small sherd totally fits part of or the whole numerical sequence relating to the thickness profile of a large sherd. This idoneous fitting could be feasible solely in an ideal situation and not with pragmatic data. Besides, our technique relies more on the abundance of thickness measurements rather than on their precision. The Thickness Profile method is actually seeking the ideal "*score*", or in plain words, the fewer differences in the most feasible comparisons. Formally, ideal "*score*" means the minimum sum of the absolute values of the subtractions remainders between the thicknesses of any two tested sherds.

Fig. 8. The orientation procedure between two crosshair beam lasers.

4.2 How the Archaeologist Read the Suggestions from the Software

In order to handle the obtained thickness measured data from the fragments, we have evolved a specific software to make all the required matching calculations. For every two fragments, our software produces two-page report with all the required data to guide the expert archaeologist. In reality, what the program code does, is find and print out the precise matching area (suggesting positions by fields 8–9 and fields 14–15, in Fig. 9) and the human involvement is limited in rightly placing one sherd (referred as

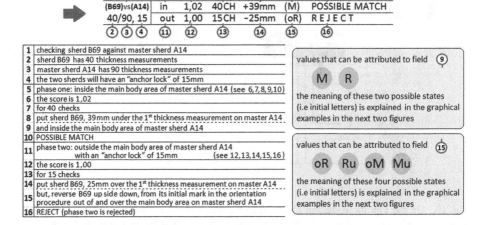

Fig. 9. Legend (key) for the significant pair of lines (B69 vs A14).

slave sherd) on the left side or right side of the other sherd (referred as master sherd). The most significant information in the two-page report is displayed within a pair of lines as indicated and analyzed at Fig. 9 in which, the particular explanations refer to the pair B69-A14 under examination (see Fig. 7/column b/line 6).

4.3   The Algorithm

The software which was specifically designed to process the thickness data out of each sherd consists of four main subsystems, each of which has the following tasks: (1) insertion of all thickness data into appropriate table structures, (2) detection of the best "*score*" through repetitive calculations for each pair, (3) creation of two report pages with all the necessary information for each pair and (4) generation of a summary page, gathering all the results with all the possible couples combination (both true or false). Below, in the next two illustrations, we explain graphically the software steps (see Fig. 10).

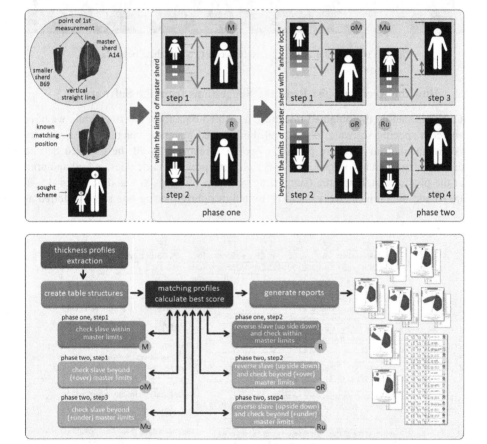

Fig. 10. On the top, the matching phases (graphically) with two sub-steps and four sub-steps respectively (the red arrow is the lock anchor). On the bottom, the software steps inside the core of the algorithm. (Color figure online)

5 Conclusion

We have explained how the Thickness Profile (TP) method was applied for the reassembly of a handmade amphora using 3D digital models out of its *ostraca* and the utilization of their thickness measurements. The outcome of this complex experiment verifies that the new methodology produces reliable results and it can work as an assistive tool for the archaeologist with various kinds and sizes of handmade potteries. It is also important to note that the Thickness Profile method allows the precise reconstruction to be gained with the least human involvement. Our method relies on thickness, a kind of data hosted inside the *core* of the *ostraca* and cannot be significantly altered by soil conditions over the years. In previous papers, our method was tested on authentic ancient fragments and small-sized handmade replicas. In this paper, we have extended our work assessing the method on the fragments of a large scaled replica of a remarkable ancient amphora exhibited in the provincial museum *Sigismondo Castromediano* of Lecce. The results have verified that the Thickness Profile main idea is fully functional, yet a limited customization of the algorithm would be welcomed each time, according to the size and type of the pottery artwork under reconstruction.

Acknowledgements. The authors wish to thank the archaeologist Mrs. Mairy Giamalidi for her valuable archaeological assistance.

References

1. Angelo, L., Stefano, P., Pane, C.: Automatic dimensional characterisation of pottery. J. Cult. Herit. **26**, 118–128 (2017)
2. Huang, Q., Flory, S., Gelfand, N., Hofer, M., Pottmann, H.: Reassembling fractured objects by geometric matching. ACM Trans. Graph. **25**(3), 569–578 (2006)
3. Kotoula, E.: Semiautomatic fragments matching and virtual reconstruction: a case study on ceramics. Int. J. Conserv. Sci. **7**(1), 71–86 (2016)
4. Kampel, M., Sablatnig, R.: Detection of matching fragments of pottery. In: Computer Applications and Quantitative Methods in Archaeology, beyond the artifact digital interpretation of the past, Prato, Italy (2004)
5. Willis, A., Cooper, D.: Bayesian assembly of 3D axially symmetric shapes from fragments. In: Conference on CVPR, Washington, U.S.A., vol. 1, pp. 82–89 (2004)
6. Son, K., Almeida, E., Cooper, D.: Axially symmetric 3D pots configuration system using axis of symmetry and break curve. In: CVPR, IEEE Conference, pp. 257–264 (2013)
7. Stamatopoulos, M., Anagnostopoulos, C.: A totally new digital 3D approach for reassembling fractured archaeological potteries using thickness measurements. Acta IMEKO **6**(3), 18–28 (2017)
8. Toby, S.: Athenian Vase Construction: A Potter's Analysis. The J. Paul Getty Museum, California (1999)
9. Lesley, C.: An Introduction to Drawing Archaeological Pottery, Institute for Archaeologists SHES (2012)

The Orion Pottery Repository – A Publicly Available 3D Objects' Benchmark Database with Texture Information

Andreas Stergioulas[1], George Ioannakis[1], Anestis Koutsoudis[2],
and Christodoulos Chamzas[1(✉)]

[1] Department of Electrical and Computer Engineering,
Democritus University of Thrace, Xanthi, Greece
{andrster, gioannak, chamzas}@ee.duth.gr
[2] Multimedia Department, Athena Research and Innovation Centre,
Xanthi, Greece
akoutsou@ipet.athena-innovation.gr

Abstract. Performance evaluation is one of the main research topics in information retrieval. Evaluation metrics in combination with benchmark datasets (groundtruth) are used to quantify various performance aspects of a retrieval algorithm. In this paper, we present the Orion Pottery Repository, a publicly available and domain specific benchmark database. It is based on open source technologies and contains a total of 160 textured 3D digital replicas of ancient Greek pottery. The dataset offered through the repository can be used for performance evaluation experiments of 3D data retrieval algorithms. Orion's content has been classified according to a pottery shape categorization defined by an in-house developed thesaurus. The repository provides mechanisms that allow a wide range of metadata handling that are based on the CARARE metadata schema which among others it offers the ability to include information related to digitization procedures and their properties.

Keywords: Classification · Retrieval · 3D texture · XML · 3D objects database
Benchmark

1 Introduction

Shape-based classification and content-based retrieval of 3D data is an active topic in research domains such as computer vision, mechanical CAD, cultural heritage and archaeology, molecular biology, paleontology, medicine, etc. [1]. Classification and retrieval experiments are applied on benchmark datasets that compose a strong groundtruth of classified data (in our case 3D objects) in terms of morphological features, shape, color, etc.

In this work, we present the Orion Pottery Repository (http://orion.ee.duth.gr), a publicly available database that currently holds a total of 160 textured 3D digital replicas of ancient Greek pottery which have been classified based on their shape. The replicas in the current version of the database are primarily derived from the database of the Archaeological Museum of Chania while others belong to the Archeological

© Springer Nature Switzerland AG 2018
M. Ioannides et al. (Eds.): EuroMed 2018, LNCS 11196, pp. 174–187, 2018.
https://doi.org/10.1007/978-3-030-01762-0_15

Museum of Abdera. Orion offers to users the ability to expand the contents of the repository by adding their own 3D objects as well as their metadata that comply with the CARARE schema. The reason behind selecting ancient Greek pottery as Orion's theme relies on the fact that ancient Greek pottery and in general pottery is one of the few artefact categories that come with texture, which provides supplemental information in relation to 3D shape. Moreover, morphological features such as a vessel's main body symmetry, are primary features that 3D content-based retrieval algorithms, like the ones that Koutsoudis et al. [2] and Osada et al. [3] proposed, can be exploited to achieve better performance results in terms of retrieval and classification performance.

Since, the 3D objects hosted in Orion derive from the archaeological domain, their categorization dictated the collaboration with archaeologists [4]. One of the main approaches in classifying ancient Greek pottery is based on their use, but this alone would not serve the purpose of this repository. The morphological and technical properties of pottery as well as their decoration are determined up to a certain extent by their intended content and conditions of use and vice versa. Additionally, the attribution of pottery for the execution of certain tasks is determined by their construction features [5]. Thus, such a classification is considered generic and not applicable for shape classification and content-based retrieval. Another classification approach could be based on their illustration technique, but this was also rejected for the same reason. In addition, the presented database can be exploited in other research areas such as classification, retrieval and reconstruction of ancient vases from fragments [6].

Apart from downloading the benchmark dataset, Orion's functionality includes the ability of viewing the 3D digital replica and archaeological information organized according to the CARARE metadata schema. CARARE is a harvesting schema intended to deliver metadata to the CARARE service environment about an organization's online collections, monument inventory database and digital objects [7].

In addition, Orion's registered users can upload their 3D content which can be organized in their own personal collections. This is achieved through a wide range of data management capabilities. Accessing and using Orion's features is performed through a Web-based user interface. Orion is developed using open source technologies such as PHP, AJAX, HTML5, JavaScript, XML, XQuery and eXist-db.

The remainder of the paper is organized as follows: Sect. 2 briefly discusses on recent 3D object benchmarking databases provided to the research community. Section 3 presents a thorough description of the construction workflow related to the Orion Pottery Repository that consists of three parts: *(i)* 3D objects' acquisition, *(ii)* the organization of the cultural heritage metadata and *(iii)* the development of the proposed thesauri. Section 4 further develops the classification of the 3D dataset and finally in Sect. 5 conclusions are drawn and possible future work is discussed.

2 Related Work

The benefits of using a database system (repository) to store and process efficiently digital assets have already been proven by many applications throughout the years. The same also applies for archeological cultural heritage assets. For instance, archeological museums that provided us with 3D digital replicas of their artifacts use a database system to manage such assets in an efficient way. Any categorization of its entries would be considered optimal if it is performed automatically and not manually. Content-based retrieval and classification algorithms can be used to perform such an important and complex task. For the performance evaluation of such algorithms benchmark databases are needed, where both classification and retrieval experiments can be performed. Numerous benchmark datasets have been proposed by different research groups. Many of these have been used in annual competitions such as the SHREC contest [8].

The existence of different benchmark datasets is related to the wide range of applications of 3D content-based retrieval and classification algorithms. For example, in computer architecture, the SPEC benchmarks [9] have been used successfully for evaluating processor performance. For facial recognition there is the GavadDB: 3D Face Benchmark [10]. Additionally, SHREC'07 Protein Retrieval Challenge [11] provides a benchmark dataset of 3D objects that represent proteins structures.

Even though there are numerous benchmark datasets available, there is a limited number of benchmarks that are related to the Cultural Heritage and archaeological domains. Table 1 gathers a few general-purpose benchmark datasets while Table 2 shows domain-specific benchmark datasets. For each dataset, the table contains the domain coverage, the number of objects (cardinality) and whether they provide texture information or not.

In most cases, the texture of 3D objects does not offer essential information for their retrieval or classification. For this reason, the majority of the retrieval or classification algorithms are based on features derived only from their 3D geometry, neglecting the information that is contained in their texture. However, there are cases that texture offers significant information. 3D models of human faces and pottery are such examples. Figure 1, depicts three examples of vases where it is obvious that the texture holds additional vital information. As it can be observed even though the first and third vases belong to the same classification their texture distinguish them from each other significantly. While there is a database for human faces (see Table 2), to the best of our knowledge there is not a database for textured pottery suitable for testing retrieval and classification algorithms. The proposed work attempts to offer such a database. Some of the innovative features of the proposed database are:

- It is domain specific (Ancient Greek Vases).
- All of its models were processed and they are 2D manifolds[1] [12].
- All 3D models have bitmap based texture information.
- There is a proposed groundtruth schema suitable for classified classic antiquity pottery (Sect. 3.3). The repository's GUI offers dropdown lists to assist the classification of new entries. Additional groundtruth schemas will be available for other types of vases.

---

[1] A 3D object is 2D-manifold if it does not contain non-manifold edges or non-manifold vertices nor self-intersections. With the term non-manifold edge, it is implied that more than two triangles share a common edge and a non-manifold vertex implies that two surface sheets are pinched together at this vertex.

Fig. 1. Examples of pottery with texture. From left to right, based on shape, the vases are classified as amphora, lekythos and amphora

Table 1. General purpose benchmark databases for 3D object retrieval

Database	Domain	Number of 3D objects	Texture information
MPEG-7 3D database [13]	General purpose	1,300	No
SHREC'11 track: shape retrieval on non-rigid 3D watertight meshes [14]	General purpose	600	No
NTU 3D model database [15]	General purpose	10,911	Yes
SCULPTEUR prototype dataset [16]	General purpose	300	No
Princeton shape benchmark [17]	General purpose	1,814	No
SHREC - robustness benchmark [18]	General purpose	1,237	No
SHREC - watertight models track [19]	General purpose	400	No
NIST shape benchmark [20]	General purpose	800	No

Even though many benchmark datasets have more 3D objects than Orion, we propose a domain-specific database that deals with textured 3D digital replicas of actual ancient Greek pottery artifacts. Therefore, the Orion enables 3D objects content-based retrieval and classification algorithms to be evaluated on real-world case scenarios offering objective evaluation of their performance, while assisting the development of the recent idea of matching 3D objects at the texture map level.

Table 2. Domain-specific benchmark databases for 3D object retrieval

Database	Domain	Number of 3D objects	Texture information
GavadDB: 3D face benchmark [21]	Faces	427	No
Purdue engineering shape benchmark – SHREC'06 [22–24]	Mecanical parts	180	No
BU-3DFE [25]	Faces	2,400	Yes
SHREC'07 protein retrieval challenge [26]	Proteins structure	>30,000	No
Gallo-Roman figurines [27]	Archaeological	650	No
i3DPost [28]	Movements	8	No
Pottery - bronze age Kotitz cemetery [29]	Pottery	300	No
A 3D pottery content based retrieval benchmark dataset [2, 30, 31]	Pottery	1,012	No

3 Orion Pottery Repository Construction Workflow

Cultural heritage information along with digitization information for each vase, as well as corresponding classification information are stored into an instance of the eXist-db database while with the aid of HTML5, PHP and JavaScript a Web interface enables users to access the benchmark database's capabilities. The query language that enables Web interface-database communication is the XQuery language.

The classification topic will be developed in detail in Sect. 4. It is important to mention that it was performed by expert humans, based on the vase shape, with the collaboration of a specialized archaeologist due to the nature of the database's entries.

3.1 3D Objects Acquisition

Orion currently contains 160 3D objects, obtained under the Creative Commons License from the 3D database of the aforementioned museums, the archaeological museum of Chania [32], and 3D Europeana entries from the archaeological museum of Abdera [33]. This is considered the first version of the dataset and we expect that in the near future users will add more textured 3D models.

3.2 Cultural Heritage Metadata Organization

All information derived from the cultural heritage domain are organized using the CARARE metadata schema (Version 2.0.4). The same schema provides solutions for storing information related to the digitization procedures being followed to create the 3D digital replicas of the pottery artefacts.

The metadata schema was developed by CARARE, a project aiming towards the collection of unique archaeological monuments, architecturally important buildings, historical centers of cities, industrial monuments and landscapes for users of the European digital library Europeana [7]. CARARE was later modified by the European

Program 3D Icons, in order to be more suitable for 3D digital replicas of cultural objects. A set of tools were also provided to allow users to map metadata following the CARARE schema to the Europeana Data Model (EDM which is used to describe the content presented in Europeana).

As in the EDM, there are also entities in the CARARE schema that allow a vast range of information to be described. Such entities are, for example, the top entities of the CARARE metadata schema, which may include a number of entities. The CARARE schema follows an object-centric model for approaching metadata information. Figure 2 presents a visualization of the entities mentioned.

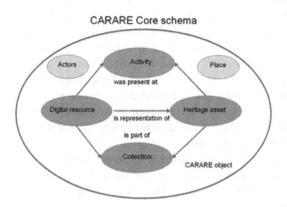

Fig. 2. A basic visualization of the CARARE metadata schema [7]

The second edition of the CARARE metadata schema, as it was developed by the 3D Icons project, dictates the structure of the XML files that are used to hold our database's vases metadata. The top element entities of the schema are presented below [34]:

- CARARE WRAP - Contains CARARE. There may be more than one record that follows the CARARE model.
- CARARE - The CARARE start entity. Includes Heritage Asset, Collection information, Digital Resource and Activity entities:
    - Collection information - contains the description of the collection.
    - Heritage Asset - holds the metadata for a monument, building or cultural object including printed matter and digital objects, including descriptive and metadata management.
    - Digital resource - holds metadata about a digital resource, including its location on the Internet.
    - Activity - contains the metadata for an event or activity related to the heritage asset.

Figure 3 shows the top entities of the CARARE metadata schema version 2.

3.3 Proposed Thesauri Development

As mentioned in Sect. 1 archaeologists contributed for the classification of the dataset.

The taxonomic system applied is based on shape, one of the main criteria for pottery typology. There is a vast amount of pottery manuals, let alone bibliography on specific topics of pottery analysis, useful for endeavors like this. We are mainly based on manuals of Boardman [35–37], Cook [38], Schreiber [39], Trendall [40] and Avramidou and Tsiafaki [41]. We also broadly used the Classical Art and Research Center website of the University of Oxford [42] and the Perseus Digital Library of Tufts University [43].

Variable levels of classification (depths) are used. The first level (depth) of classification is the basic distinction between open (e.g. dish, pinakion/plate, phiale), closed (e.g. amphora, pithos, oinochoe) shapes and small objects. The second level includes all the basic shapes of classical antiquity, whose names are usually associated with their use (e.g. oinochoe from oino- = wine + choē = action of pouring out). A further grading, containing the variations within each shape, constitutes the third level (e.g. geometric oinochoe, lagynos, attic oinochoe etc.), whereas in quite a few occasions the taxonomy reaches a fourth level and an even more detailed typology (e.g. attic oinochoe type I, chous, etc.). We have also included few examples of prehistoric pottery as well as lamps, whose contour renders them a satisfactory criterion for comparison, although technically they are considered minor objects, not pottery. The application of the archaeological taxonomy resulted a total of 147 different categories in which a hosted item can belong. It must be noted that each item may belong to one and only one of those categories.

The goal therefore was to create a thesauri, such as the Getty Research Institute [44] and the European Heritage Network (HEREIN) [45]. The utilization of a controlled vocabulary for describing cultural heritage assets offers great assistance to the various researcher communities, such as content-based retrieval and classification algorithms development, due to the fact that the textual annotation can introduce ambiguities.

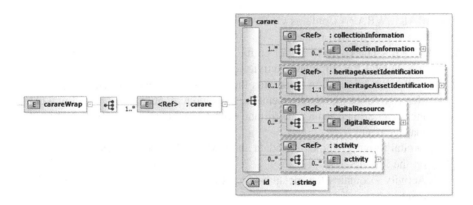

Fig. 3. Top entities of the CARARE metadata schema version 2

4   Classification

According to the classification described above, there are four levels (depths) of classification based on a vase's shape. The first level of classification includes three types of ancient objects: (i) open vases, (ii) closed vases and (iii) small objects. These three main categories are subdivided into a set of sub classifications and those sub classes have two additional levels of classification related again with their shape.

The second level of classification includes the following classes: dish, exaleiptron, kantharos, klepsydra/ water clock, krater, kyathos, kylix, lakaina, lebes/ cauldron, louterion, pinakion/plate, skyphos, stamnos, phiale, alabastron, amphora, aryballos, askos, feeding bottle, lekythos, lydion, oinochoe, pithos, pithamphora, pyriatiri, pyxis, rhyton, hydria, phormiskos, psykter, lamp.

In total, the second level of classification has 31 different categories, whereas the third level has 106 categories. Finally, the fourth level, concerning few selected shapes, has only 29 different categories. Table 3 shows all the different classes that derived from the four-level classification that was applied.

Table 3. Orion vases database classification

First level	Second level	Third level	Fourth level
Open vessels	dish	lekane	
		lekanis	
		plain	
	exaleiptron	plemochoe	
	kantharos	boetian	
		geometric	
		kabeirian	
		plastic	
		one-handled	
		type A	
		type B	
		type C	
	kern		
	klepsydra/water clock		
	krater	geometric	
		volute krater	
		calyx krater	
		column krater	attic
			corinthian
			laconian
			chalkidian
		macedonian	
		bell crater	
		kalathos	
	kyathos		

(*continued*)

Table 3. (*continued*)

First level	Second level	Third level	Fourth level
	kylix	merrythought cup	
		stemless	
		Vroulia type	
		Gordion cup	
		Cassel cup	
		Komast cup	
		laconian cup	
		Droop cup	
		Siana cup	
		band cup	
		type A	
		type A-eye cup	
		type B	
		type C	
		lip cup	
	lakaina		
	lebes/cauldron	on a stand	
		without a stand	
		gamikos	type A
		gamikos	type B
	louterion		
	pinakion/plate	standard	
		stem dish	
		fishplate	
	skyphos	kabeirian	
		kotyle	
		megarian/relief bowl	
		sicelian	
		type A	
		type B	
		chalkidian	
		mastos	
	stamnos		
	phiale		
Closed vessels	alabastron	standard	
		corinthian	
		south italian	
	amphora	amphoriskos	
		geometric	
		west slope	
		neckless/one-piece amphora	nikostheneios
			type A
			type B
			type C

(*continued*)

Table 3. (*continued*)

First level	Second level	Third level	Fourth level
		ionic	pelike
		kados	
		clazomenian	Enmann type
			Knipovitch type
		macedonian	
		loutrophoros	
		neck amphora	apulian (special shape)
			doubleens
			panathenaic
			SOS
			pointed, thasian
			pointed, rodian
			pointed
			pointed, chian
			pointed, Knidian
			pointed, roman
			Nolan
		nestoris/trozella	Ia
			Ib
			IIa
			Iib
			III
		nicosthenic	
		protoattic	
		tyrrhenian	
		stirrup jar	
	aryballos	attic spherical	
		corinthian	pear-shaped
			spherical
			ovoid
		laconian	
		plastic	
	askos		
	lagynos		
	lekythos	standard/cylindrical	
		apoulian	
		squat	
		shoulder	
		globular	

(*continued*)

Table 3. (*continued*)

First level	Second level	Third level	Fourth level
		Deianeira	
	lydion	ionic	
		lydian	
	oinochoe	corinthian	
		cypriotic jug	
		ptolemaic	
		trifoil	standard
			double
		type I	
		type II	
		type III/chous	
		type IV/olpe	
		type V	Va
			Vb
		type VI	
		type VII	
		type VIII	
		type X-beaked	
	pithos		
	pyxis	geometric	
		corinthian	
		nicosthenic	
		type A	
		type B	
		type C	
		type D	
	rhyton		
	hydria	Hadra	
		geometric	
		calpis	
		campanian	
		laconian	
		loutrophoros	
		neck hydria	
	phormiskos		
	psykter		
	feeding bottle		
	pithamphora		
	pyriatiri		
Small objects	lamp		
	censer		
	nest shaped utensil		

Moreover, in order to utilize the shape-based classification, a set of XML files was created where each one represents one category of the classification. Each file has a unique identifier (ID), as well as four other fields indicating the use of the vase of this category, its dating, a paragraph with a short description and a field containing the location of an image an example of a vase of the category appears. There is a total of 147 such files, all complying with the XSD file built to validate the specific XML files.

The parent entity of each XML file starts with the <vase> tag, which includes the id entity that is the vessel category identifier, in *general_type* is contained information about the top class (closed vases, open vases, small items). In *vase_name* the shape is described which is the second level of classification and in the *type* and *type_1* entities respectively the third and fourth level of classification. The description field is a description of a vase in this category, the thumbnail is the URL of the photo, and is also given the option to implement bibliography for the description entity. Finally, in addition to id, all entities can be replicated within an XML and recorded information in different languages. The *lang* attribute is responsible for recording the language in which the information is written in the field.

Figure 4 presents a visualization of the previously described schema.

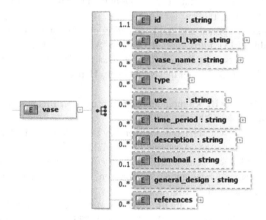

Fig. 4. Classification schema visualization

5   Conclusions

In summary, this paper describes the Orion Pottery Repository, a publicly available benchmark dataset that hosts 3D objects of real ancient Greek vases associated with texture information with the possibility for registered users to download them, along with a groundtruth file, for content-based retrieval and classification algorithms performance evaluation. All data and source code are freely available on the Web (http://orion.ee.duth.gr/).

The main contribution of this work is that we provide textured 3D objects that are also classified based on their shape. We hope that retrieval researchers will use the benchmark in future experiments, further developing content-based retrieval and classification algorithms technology.

Future work for further developing of our benchmark database would be ideal to upload and classify more 3D objects of vases across the different classes that we have suggested in order to make more challenging and objective any performance evaluation using our data.

Acknowledgements. The majority of the 3D objects were obtained gratis from the databases of the archeological museum of Chania and the archeological museum of Abdera, both located in Greece. The tools and libraries used for developing the database and the API were open source code, that are publicly available in the World Wide Web.

References

1. Shilane, P., Min, P., Kazhdan, M., Funkhouser, T.: The Princeton Shape Benchmark. Department of Computer Science, Princeton University (2005)
2. Koutsoudis, A., Pavlidis, G., Liami, V., Tsiafakis, D., Chamzas, C.: 3D pottery content based retrieval based on pose normalisation and segmentation. J. Cult. Herit. **11**, 329–338 (2010)
3. Osada, R., Funkhouser, T., Chazelle, B., Dobkin, D.: Shape distributions. ACM Trans. Graph. **21**(4), 807–832 (2002)
4. Stergioulas, A.: Development and implementation of a 3D object database, Diploma thesis (in Greek) Xanthi (2018). https://goo.gl/zA4Q8o. Accessed 10 Aug 2018
5. Koukouraki, N.A.: Vessels as Purpose Objects-Design of the Documentation System of the Uses of Ancient Ceramics, Master thesis (in Greek) Heraklion (2005). https://goo.gl/m7tJZH . Accessed 10 Aug 2018
6. Willis, A.R., Cooper, D.B.: Computational reconstruction of ancient artifacts. IEEE Sig. Process. Mag. **25**, 65–83 (2008)
7. D'Andrea, A., Fernie, K.: 3D Icons Deliverable D6.1 Report on Metadata and Thesauri (2012). https://goo.gl/YGtqSe. Accessed 13 Aug 2018
8. Shape Retrieval Evaluation Contest (SHREC). http://www.shrec.net/. Accessed 12 Mar 2018
9. Standard performance evaluation corporation (SPEC). http://www.specbench.org/benchmarks.html. Accessed 12 Mar 2018
10. Moreno, A.B., Sánchez, A.: GavabDB: a 3D face database. In: Workshop on biometrics on the Internet COST, Vigo, Spain, 25–26 March, vol. 275, pp. 77–85 (2004)
11. Temerinac, M., Reisert, M., Burkhardt, H.: SHREC'07-protein retrieval challenge. In: Proceedings of Shape Modelling International, Lyon, France (2007)
12. Botsch, M., Kobbelt, L., Pauly, M., Alliez, P., Lévy, B.: Polygon Mesh Processing. AK Peters, Natick (2010)
13. Zaharia, T., Preteux, F.: 3D shape-based retrieval within the MPEG-7 framework. In: SPIE Conference on Nonlinear Image Processing and Pattern Analysis XII, San Francisco, California, pp. 133–145 (2001)
14. Lian, Z., et al.: SHREC'11 track: shape retrieval on non-rigid 3D watertight meshes. In: 4th Eurographics Conference on 3D Object Retrieval, Llandudno, UK, pp. 79–88 (2011)
15. NTU 3D Database. https://goo.gl/gsg6cn. Accessed 15 Mar 2018
16. Goodall, S., et al.: SCULPTEUR: multimedia retrieval for museums. In: Enser, P., Kompatsiaris, Y., O'Connor, N.E., Smeaton, A.F., Smeulders, A.W.M. (eds.) CIVR 2004. LNCS, vol. 3115, pp. 638–646. Springer, Heidelberg (2004). https://doi.org/10.1007/978-3-540-27814-6_74

17. Shilane, P., Min, P., Kazhdan, M., Funkhouser, T.: The Princeton shape benchmark. In: Shape Modeling International, Genova, Italy, pp. 167–178 (2004)
18. SHREC - Correspondence benchmark. https://goo.gl/E96XBt. Accessed 15 Mar 2018
19. SHREC - Watertight Models Track. http://watertight.ge.imati.cnr.it. Accessed 11 Mar 2018
20. SHREC - Structural Shape Retrieval. https://goo.gl/zMNDdd. Accessed 12 Mar 2018
21. Moreno, A.B., Sánchez, A.: GavabDB: a 3D face database. In: Workshop on biometrics on the Internet COST, Vigo, Spain, vol. 275, pp. 77–85 (2004)
22. Jayanti, S., Kalyanaraman, Y., Iyer, N., Ramani, K.: Developing an engineering shape benchmark for CAD models. Comput. Aided Des. **38**(9), 939–953 (2006)
23. National Design Repository. http://edge.cs.drexel.edu/repository. Accessed 10 Mar 2018
24. Shape Retrieval Contest for CAD models. https://goo.gl/i1tRFY. Accessed 10 Mar 2018
25. Lijun, Y., Xiaozhou, W., Sun, Y., Wang, J., Rosato, M.J.: A 3D facial expression database for facial behaviour research. In: IEEE 7th Automatic Face and Gesture Recognition, Southampton, UK, pp. 211–216 (2006)
26. Temerinac, M., Reisert, M., Burkhardt, H.: SHREC'07 protein retrieval challenge. In: Shape Modelling International, Lyon, France (2007)
27. Gorisse, D., Cord, M., Jordan, M. Philipp-Foliguet S., Precioso, F.: 3D content-based retrieval in artwork databases. In: IEEE 3DTV-Conference, Kos Island, Greece (2007)
28. Gkalelis, N., Kim, H., Hilton, A., Nikolaidis N., Pitas, I.: The i3DPost Multiview and 3D human action/interaction database. In: Visual Media Production, pp. 159–168 (2009)
29. Horr, C., Brunnett, G.: Similarity estimation on ancient vessels. In: GraphiCon, Moscow State University, pp. 94–100 (2008)
30. D pottery content based retrieval benchmark dataset. https://goo.gl/pQC2ii. Accessed 10 Mar 2018
31. Koutsoudis, A., Pavlidis, G., Arnaoutoglou, F., Tsiafakis, D., Chamzas, C.: Qp: a tool for generating 3D models of ancient Greek pottery. J. Cult. Herit. **10**, 281–295 (2009)
32. Europeana: Archaeological Museum of Abdera Entries. https://goo.gl/bYBXfQ. Accessed 13 Aug 2018
33. Archaeological Museum of Chania. http://chaniamuseum.culture.gr/. Accessed 13 Aug 2018
34. Fernie, K., Gavrilis, D., Angelis, S.: The CARARE metadata schema, v.2.0 (2013). https://goo.gl/fpA7Rz. Accessed 13 Aug 2018
35. Boardman, J.: Athenian Black Figure Vases: A Handbook, London (1974)
36. Boardman, J.: Athenian Red Figure Vases: The Archaic Period: A Handbook, London (1975)
37. Boardman, J.: Early Greek Vase Painting, London (1998)
38. Cook, R.M.: Greek Painted Pottery, Oxford-New York (1997)
39. Schreiber, T.: Athenian Vase Constructions. A Potter's Analysis, Malibu (1999)
40. Trendall, A.D.: Red Figured Vases of South Italy and Sicily, (World Art) London (1989)
41. Avramidou, A., Tsiafaki, D.: Attica Pottery. Contribution to the contacts of Athens and Thrace, Athens, Kallipos ebook (2015). http://hdl.handle.net/11419/3614. Accessed 7 June 2018
42. Perseus Collection Greek and Roman Materials. http://www.perseus.tufts.edu/hopper/. Accessed 7 June 2018
43. Classical Art Research Centre. https://goo.gl/ViKsvc. Accessed 7 June 2018
44. Bibliography of the History of Art (Getty Research Institute). http://www.getty.edu/research. Accessed 7 June 2018
45. HEREIN: Heritage Network - Council of Europe. https://goo.gl/Uf6yUq. Accessed 7 June 2018

Automatic Identification of Relations
in Quebec Heritage Data

François Ferry[1], Amal Zouaq[2(✉)], and Michel Gagnon[1]

[1] Ecole Polytechnique de Montréal, Montreal, QC, Canada
{francois.ferry,michel.gagnon}@polymtl.ca
[2] University of Ottawa, Ottawa, ON, Canada
azouaq@uottawa.ca

Abstract. Heritage data is often represented in unstructured format, especially textual data. In this paper, our objective is to extract instances of predefined relations between persons and real estates from historical notices in French. Using several vector-based representations and supervised learning algorithms, we build classifiers able to achieve an F-measure between 75% to 85% for relation detection. Our results show that performances are highly dependent on the type of relation, and also on the specific evaluation metrics. Our best results are obtained using a TF-IDF vector representation with a support vector machine classifier or Word2Vec vectors combined with a multilayer perceptron classifier.

Keywords: Relation extraction · Heritage data · Supervised learning Word2Vec · TF-IDF

1 Introduction

With the development of digital technologies in the cultural heritage domain, the automatic population of heritage knowledge bases using information extraction and machine learning techniques is becoming a timely topic [2,9]. In fact, heritage data is often represented as textual data that is not easily exploitable by information systems.

In this work, we present a research project in collaboration with the Quebec Ministry of Culture and Communication (abbreviated as MCCQ in the remainder of this paper) whose global objective is to answer queries related to cultural heritage and more precisely, about people and their particular link with a historic building. For instance, it is currently hard to retrieve *all the architects involved in the construction of religious buildings in Montreal*, despite the fact that this information is available as textual data. All buildings registered in the Repertoire of Cultural Heritage of Quebec have a historical notice, which is a text in French which recounts the lifetime of the building and the people involved with it. This work aims at identifying instances of predefined relations between a person (physical or moral), or group of persons, and a building in these historical notices (in the remainder of this paper we will use *person* to designate any entity

© Springer Nature Switzerland AG 2018
M. Ioannides et al. (Eds.): EuroMed 2018, LNCS 11196, pp. 188–199, 2018.
https://doi.org/10.1007/978-3-030-01762-0_16

occupy : Amédée Robitaille settles in the newly build house.
build: Abner Bagg builds a neoclassical-inspired residence.
design: Henri-Maurice Perrault draws the plans for the new Collège de Montréal. Victor Bourgeau designed the college chapel.
decorate: The interior decorations were made by Emmanuel Briffa. The bas-reliefs of the cinema are by Joseph Guardo.

Fig. 1. Examples of relations by type

[...] The upper floor was laid out in a second phase of work, led by architect **George Browne** in 1848, and was aimed at the eventual installation of City Hall offices in the western part and concert halls in the eastern part. One of the first occupants of these premises was the **Parliament of Canada**, in 1849, which moved there after the fire on the Sainte-Anne market on April 26 during a riot. [...]

Fig. 2. Translation of an excerpt from the historical notice of the Bonsecours Market

that is either a person or a group of persons). These relations describe how a person is related to the building (if he lived in it, if he built it, etc.). Figure 1 describes the target relation types in this study and provides an example for each type. For instance, the relation type *Occupy* expresses the concept of some person or group living in a building, or using it for his/her usual activities.

The text in Fig. 2 is an excerpt of the historical notice of the Bonsecours Market[1], translated from French. It talks about two distinct entities: *George Browne* and the *Parliament of Canada*. *George Browne* co-occurs with the word *architect* which is itself related to the word *led*. It can therefore be reasonably inferred that *George Browne* worked as an architect and as director of works. The proper relation in this case would be *design*. Similarly, we can find a relation between a "moral person", for instance here the *Parliament of Canada*, and the building, which is *occupy*.

The current knowledge base of the MCCQ identifies lists of persons of interest for each historical notice about a building. This work explores the potential of several vector representations, including representations using TF-IDF and word embeddings, coupled with machine learning classifiers, for the accurate classification of heritage relations expressed in French. Unlike the commonly used approaches, our approach doesn't rely on language-specific tools or a particular knowledge base, so it can be adapted to any language.

The paper is structured as follows: first, we present some related work. In Sect. 3, we describe our dataset and our research methodology. Our results are described and discussed in Sect. 4. Finally, we present our conclusions and future works in Sect. 5.

---

[1] http://www.patrimoine-culturel.gouv.qc.ca/rpcq/detail.do?methode=consulter& id=100101&type=bien.

2   Related Work

There has been a significant amount of work for relation extraction in general in the past few years [7,11–13]. However, most of the available systems are, to our knowledge, restricted to the English language. For instance, LODifier [2] is an application to extract RDF triples using DBpedia[2] and WordNet[3]. Entities corresponding to a DBpedia URI are initially recognized using *Wikifier*, which finds Wikipedia links for named entities. Relations between the entities are then detected using a parser and syntactic patterns. Finally, WordNet is used to detect relation semantics, leading to an RDF graph based on DBpedia and WordNet vocabularies. Even though LODifier handles various types of corpora, we cannot use it for two main reasons. First, our texts are in French, which is not supported by WordNet. Secondly, only 5% of the entities in our corpus are matched to a URI in DBpedia.

In the most specific area of digital heritage, [5] proposes to extract events from English texts taken from a relational database that describes archaeological sites. Each site is described by texts about events such as archaeological excavations, studies, etc. The goal is to extract these events using various natural language processing methods, machine learning and an event ontology. Similarly, [8] uses an approach based on named entity detection and parsing to extract relations from texts. Publications about art conservation are analyzed using a domain ontology and serve to automatically populate this ontology. In [4], the authors propose a framework to extract hypernyms, synonyms and other semantic relation patterns from various cultural heritage data sources. Another rule-based approach [1] extracts entities and relations from archaeological reports relying on CIDOC-CRM[4]. This approach uses an already built vocabulary from English Heritage thesauri and glossaries. It also relies on shallow parsing coupled with ontological and terminological domain resources.

Vector space models have also been used in other domains for event and relation detection. For example, [6] proposes a method to identify events in tweets by examining the similarities between words' distribution. Similarly, [3] propose to extract events by aggregating information available in several messages.

In most cases, relation extraction relies on existing knowledge bases, such as DBpedia or specialized ontologies and terminological resources. The majority of the approaches work on the English language. In our project, we rely mostly on historical notices (text) and we do not exploit any knowledge base: we only use our data. Another specificity of our approach is that we target French digital heritage, but these vector space models can be applied on other domains and languages. Our objective is to examine whether it is possible to use an approach based solely on word representations and supervised learning algorithms for automatic relation extraction.

---

[2] https://wiki.dbpedia.org/.

[3] https://wordnet.princeton.edu/.

[4] http://www.cidoc-crm.org/.

3   Methodology

3.1   Dataset Description

For our study, we use the Repertoire of cultural heritage of Quebec[5] as source
of heritage data. This repertoire brings together all the historic buildings and
movable and intangible heritage of Quebec. Here we are only interested in a
subset of this data, that is, the buildings. For each one, the historical notice and
a list of persons that are related to the building are provided. This data includes
16886 *relation instances*, which are pairs ⟨Person, Building⟩ that represent two
entities involved in a relation type. For instance, the pair ⟨George Browne, Parliament of Canada⟩ is an instance of the relation type *design*. Table 1 shows the
distribution of relation types available in the repertoire. As we can see, there
are several under-represented relations. In this work, we restrict ourselves to the
four most frequent types: *occupy, design, build* and *decorate*. Despite the fact
that the relation of type *other* is well represented in the data, it only describes
an unspecific link in a relation instance. It is therefore difficult to use it for
classification purposes.

Table 1. Distribution of the relation instances defined in the repertoire of cultural
heritage of Quebec

Name	Frequency	% of total	Name	Frequency	% of total
Other	7053	42%	Create	27	<1%
Design	5570	33%	Advice	11	<1%
Occupy	1846	10%	Own	10	<1%
Build	1795	9%	Subject	5	<1%
Decorate	502	3%	Engineer	3	<1%
Buried in this place	32	<1%	Edit	2	<1%
Fabricate	28	<1%	Produce	1	<1%

The initial set of considered pairs was composed of 9713 instances of the four
designated relation types. Then we eliminated the relation instances for which
the person was not mentioned in the historical notice of the building. This represented about 60% of relation instances (in most of these cases, the building
did not have any historical notice). Using this initial dataset and some *other*
instances, we selected instances that cover our four relation types and we manually checked and corrected them to form a curated test dataset. These instances
came mainly from the *other* relations, and also from *build, design* and *decorate*
relations. Thus, our test dataset counts 505 instances of relations distributed as
follows: 167 *design* instances, 96 *occupy* instances, 223 *build* instances and 19 *decorate* instances. The remaining relation instances formed our training set, which

---

[5] http://www.patrimoine-culturel.gouv.qc.ca/.

counts 3399 relation instances distributed as follows: 1686 *design* instances, 1040 *occupy* instances, 509 *build* instances and 164 *decorate* instances.

The average length of the historical notices is 2090.28 words with a standard deviation of 1188.74 words. However, this great variability has no impact on our approach, since we are only interested in the sentences mentioning the person involved in a relation instance as explained in Sect. 3.2.

3.2   Dataset Preprocessing

A preliminary observation of the data indicates that, generally, the specific relation between a person and a building is mentioned in the sentences where the person appears in the historical notice of the building. Thus, to classify relations between a person and a building, the idea is to isolate the context (here a sentence) around each mention of the person in the historical notice. It is indeed this context that contains the information used to identify the nature of the relation. Thus we merge all the sentences where the person appears to build a context for that particular relation instance. For example, in the text describing *Bonsecours Market* given in Fig. 2, the context of the *Parliament of Canada* is the sentence *One of the first occupants of these premises was the Parliament of Canada, in 1849, which moved there after the fire on the Sainte-Anne market on April 26 during a riot.* As we can see, this context describes an *occupy* relation between the *Parliament of Canada* and the *Bonsecours Market*.

To summarize, for each relation instance between a person and a building, we extract (i) the label of the relation; (ii) the name and surname of the person involved; and (iii) the historical notice of the building. Then we perform some cleaning of the text. Indeed, each notice describes potentially various relations between the building and several persons. Therefore, while the historical notice describes the relation we are interested in, it might also describe other types of relations. To select only the sentences that interest us, we delete stop words and we keep only the sentences in which the person is mentioned explicitly, i.e. by first and last name, as observed in the majority of our data.

Given a particular relation type, we now have, for each relation instance ⟨Person, Building⟩, a context that corresponds to all the sentences where the person is mentioned in the notice of the building. Indeed, we make the assumption that this context describes the relation of the person with the building. The average length of a context is 28.9 words with a standard deviation of 19.9. This context is then transformed into a vector (a training example). The set of training examples for each relation type forms our corpus, which is used to produce vector representations based on TF-IDF (Section *Sparse Vector based on TF-IDF*) and word embeddings (Section *Word Embedding*).

Sparse Vector Based on TF-IDF. In this vector representation, we consider each training example as a document d. Given that a building is only described in its historical notice (except in a few rare cases), we suppose that a document d describes the relation existing between a given person and a given building.

All the words in the document (except stop words) are weighted using TF-IDF. The method evaluates the importance of a term contained in a document in relation to a set of documents. This metric assigns high weights to terms that are specific to some documents and decreases the weight of very frequent terms in the whole corpus. To evaluate the TF-IDF weight of a term t in a document d, we use the following formula:

$$tfidf_{t,d} = tf_{t,d} \times idf_t \tag{1}$$

where $tf_{t,d}$ is the frequency of the term t in the document d and idf_t is defined as follows:

$$idf_t = log \left[\frac{\text{number of documents} + 1}{(df(t) + 1)} \right] + 1 \tag{2}$$

$df(t)$ being the number of documents where the term t appears. We obtain for each document d a sparse vector of dimension 3651 which is the number of different words in our corpus. The implementation used is *Scikit-learn*[6].

Word Embeddings. Word embeddings are a language modelling technique that maps words to dense vectors of real numbers. The general idea is that words in similar contexts have a close meaning. From a mathematical point of view, this consists of performing an embedding from a vector space whose dimension is the number of words, to a vector space of reduced dimensions. In our work, we chose the Word2Vec algorithm in *Gensim*[7]. We used a pre-trained model based on Wikipedia-fr [10], which represents about 500 million words and 3.6 Go of text. This model relies on the *Continuous Bag-Of-Words* (CBOW) architecture, without lemmatization, and with stopword elimination. The resulting vectors have a dimension of 500.

Using this model, we retrieve the vector representation of each word of our documents. Next, we combine these vectors to produce a document vector using two combination methods.

The first one consists of simply calculating the centroid of the word vectors. By considering the n word vectors $w_{v_1}, w_{v_2}, \ldots, w_{v_n}$ associated to the n words of a document d, respectively, we compute the vector v_d of our document in the following manner:

$$v_d = \frac{1}{n} \sum_{i=1}^{n} w_{v_i} \tag{3}$$

The second method consists of weighting each word vector by the TF-IDF coefficient of the corresponding word in the document and then calculating the centroid of these weighted vectors. Formally, by considering $w_{v_1}, w_{v_2}, \ldots, w_{v_n}$, the n word vectors of document d, and $tfidf_1, tfidf_2, \ldots, tfidf_n$, the corresponding TF-IDF coefficients; then v_d, our document vector, is defined by (4):

$$v_d = \frac{1}{n} \sum_{i=1}^{n} (tfidf_i \cdot w_{v_i}) \tag{4}$$

---

[6] http://scikit-learn.org/.
[7] radimrehurek.com/gensim/models/word2vec.html.

The idea behind the combination of word embeddings and TF-IDF is that both methods provide complementary information. Word embedding allows us to represent the meaning of words, while tf-idf allows us to consider the distribution of these words in the corpus.

3.3   Classification

At the end of the preprocessing step, we obtain two vectors (TF-IDF and word embeddings) for each relation type. The objective of the classification step is to learn a model to automatically classify these relations. For this purpose, we use supervised learning algorithms. These algorithms take as input the document vectors calculated in the previous step and then predict the relations described by each of these vectors. We tried several algorithms (decision tree, k-nearest neighbours, etc.) but we retained in this paper only those that obtained the best results, namely a Multilayer Perceptron (MLP) and a Support Vector Machine (SVM). The classes are our different relation types. We performed a binary classification experiment and a multi-class classification experiment.

In binary classification, we built a binary classifier using the aforementioned algorithms for each possible relation type. To train each classifier, we built one corpus per relation type. For each type, we randomly chose a similar proportion of positive and negative examples. For example, the corpus to train the *design* classifier contains 1686 vectors corresponding to *design* relations and 1686 vectors corresponding to *not-design* relations (other randomly picked relations).

In the multi-class model, we randomly extracted 10 balanced sets containing all four relation types from our training data. We randomly eliminated some instances of the most frequent relations, in order to have the same number of instances for each relation. This reduced the overall training set to 656 relations with 164 instances of each type of relation (*build, design, decorate* and *occupy*). Then we performed a 10-fold cross-validation on our training set.

For implementation, we used the following classes in *Scikit-learn* (see footnote 6):

sklearn.svm.SVC (with linear kernel) and *sklearn.neural_network.MLP Classifier* (with 'adam' optimizer and rectified linear function as activation function).

4   Results

4.1   Binary Classification Results

Training Set Cross-Validation Results. At first, we performed a 10-fold stratified cross-validation on our training set. Our results are presented in Table 2a. The following abbreviations are used: *w2v* stands for Word2Vec; and *w.w2v* stands for Word2Vec weighted by TF-IDF. For each relation, the best results are in bold, and if this result is significantly better than any other results, it is followed by a ∗. To determine if a result is significantly better, we use a post-hoc analysis Tukey test with $\alpha = 0.05$.

By analyzing our results by relation, we show that we have better results for the *decorate* and *occupy* relations while our worst results are with the *build* relation. Now, if we look at our different methods, our weighted Word2Vec method is slightly less efficient than the two others in terms of **accuracy**. TF-IDF word representation seems to perform better with SVM, and Word2Vec better with MLP, and this regardless of the metric. If we compare all our results, we can observe that TF-IDF with SVM obtains a higher **accuracy** for 3 relations out of 4. However, the difference between Word2Vec with MLP and TF-IDF with SVM is slight, and both methods show an **accuracy** between 90% and 96%. In terms of **precision**, TF-IDF coupled with SVM outperforms other configurations for all relations except *occupy* (W2V-MLP). Finally, in terms of **F-measure**, TF-IDF-SVM and W2V-MLP outperform each other in 2 relations out of 4.

Overall, the results of the binary classification on the training set show that, despite higher values obtained with TF-IDF-SVM, these results do not statistically differ from those of W2V-MLP.

Test Results. Our results on the test dataset are shown in Table 2b. Compared to the training set, **accuracy**, **F-measure** and **precision** decrease significantly for all methods, especially for the *occupy* and *decorate* relations, which are the less frequent in our test dataset. For the **recall**, we also observe a drop in performance for the *build* relations. For the other relations, it depends on the used method. With Word2Vec, we observe a better **recall** with the *occupy* and *decorate* relation. While we have pretty good **recall** with these two relation types, we have a low to a very low **precision** for both of them.

4.2   Multi-class Classification Results

Training Set Cross-Validation Results. The results of the multi-class classification on the training set are presented in Table 3a. The performance with the multi-class classification is lower when compared to our previous binary classification results. As before, TF-IDF performs better with SVM while Word2Vec (W2V) performs better with MLP. Furthermore, except in rare cases, Word2Vec weighted by TF-IDF (W.W2V) is outperformed by TF-IDF with SVM and Word2Vec with MLP.

A post-hoc analysis (Tukey test with $\alpha = 0.05$) reveals that in terms of **F-measure**, there are no significant differences between all our methods, except between TF-IDF-MLP and W2V-MLP for the *build* and *design* relations. In terms of **precision**, there are only significant differences between TF-IDF-SVM and W.W2V-MLP for *build* relations. Then, in terms of **recall**, there are no significant differences between all our methods, except for *occupy* relations, where TF-IDF-SVM results significantly outperform all the others. In terms of **accuracy**, there are significant differences between TF-IDF-SVM and TF-IDF-MLP. Finally, in terms of all relation types, the **accuracy** of the TF-IDF-SVM combination significantly outperforms W2V-MLP. Overall, the results on the training

Table 2. Results by relation with our training and test datasets with binary classification: F-score (F), **precision** (P), **Recall** (R) and **Accuracy**.

	(a) Training set						(b) Test set					
	F with SVM			F with MLP			F with SVM			F with MLP		
Relation	tf-idf	w2v	w.w2v	tf-idf	w2v	w.w2v	tf-idf	w2v	w.w2v	tf-idf	w2v	w.w2v
Build	.91	.88	.88	.90	**.92**	.89	**.80**	.75	.74	.74	.77	.74
Occupy	**.95***	.91	.94	.93	.94	.94	.69	.72	.76	**.77**	.73	.70
Design	**.94***	.90	.91	.89	.92	.91	**.84**	.79	.80	.68	.79	.75
Decorate	**.96**	.95	.95	.94	**.96**	.95	.25	.22	**.25**	.18	.23	**.25**
	P with SVM			P with MLP			P with SVM			P with MLP		
Build	**.94**	.89	.90	.91	.93	.90	**.79**	.68	.69	.70	.71	.67
Occupy	.93	.93	.83	.93	**.94**	.93	.54	.59	**.64**	.63	.59	.56
Design	**.95***	.90	.91	.89	.93	.91	**.78**	.70	.71	.58	.71	.63
Decorate	**.98**	.96	.95	.96	.97	.96	**.15**	.13	.15	.10	.13	.15
	R with SVM			R with MLP			R with SVM			R with MLP		
Build	.87	.87	.87	.89	**.91**	.88	.80	.83	.79	.78	**.84**	.83
Occupy	**.97***	.90	.95	.94	.94	.92	.96	.92	.94	**.97**	.96	.94
Design	**.92***	.90	.91	.88	**.92***	.91	**.92**	.91	.92	.81	.90	.91
Decorate	.94	.94	.95	.94	.95	**.96**	.79	**1.00**	**1.00**	.84	**1.00**	**1.00**
	Acc. with SVM			Acc. with MLP			Acc. with SVM			Acc. with MLP		
Build	.91	.88	.89	.90	**.92**	.89	**.82**	.76	.75	.75	.78	.75
Occupy	**.95***	.92	.94	.93	.94	.92	.84	.86	**.89**	**.89**	.87	.85
Design	**.94***	.90	.91	.89	.92	.91	.89	.85	**.99**	.75	.85	.80
Decorate	**.96**	.95	.95	.95	**.96**	**.96**	**.82**	.74	.78	.71	.75	.78

set show that, even if we often obtain better results with TF-IDF-SVM, there are relatively few differences between the various combinations of algorithms and features. As for the binary classification, the results obtained with TF-IDF-SVM do not statistically differ from those of W2V-MLP.

Test Results. Our results are presented in Table 3b. Overall, we note that the SVM-TF-IDF combination outperforms the others for the multi-class classification results on the test dataset. Thus, as for the train dataset, SVM-TF-IDF surpasses the others in terms of **F-measure** and **precision** for the *build* and *design* relations, and in terms of **recall**, for the *occupy* relations. Similarly to the train dataset, we observe that W2V-MLP has good performance too (usually the first or second-best performing classifier).

For the *build* relations, compared to the train dataset, we observe better performance in terms of **F-measure** and **precision**. However, in terms of **recall**, we observe a slight drop of performance. For this relation, we obtain the best results with TF-IDF-SVM. For the *occupy* relations, we obtain the best results with TF-IDF-SVM for the **recall** and **F-measure**, and with W2V-MLP for the **precision**. For the *design* relations, compared to the train dataset, we observe

Table 3. Results by relation with our training and test datasets with multi-class classification: F-score (F), **precision** (P), **Recall** (R) and **Accuracy**.

	(a) Training set						(b) Test set					
	F with SVM			F with MLP			F with SVM			F with MLP		
Relation	tf-idf	w2v	w.w2v	tf-idf	w2v	w.w2v	tf-idf	w2v	w.w2v	tf-idf	w2v	w.w2v
Build	.76	.73	.71	.67	**.78***	.71	**.77**	.73	.73	.68	.74	.71
Occupy	**.84**	.79	.83	.76	.81	.78	**.77**	.74	.57	.71	.77	.72
Design	.84	.81	**.90**	.76	.85	.78	**.85**	.78	.77	.72	.80	.78
Decorate	**.93**	.89	.79	.91	.91	.90	**.55**	.42	.44	.49	.48	0.46
	P with SVM			P with MLP			P with SVM			P with MLP		
Build	**.85***	.77	.74	.74	.81	.72	**.90**	.83	.85	.81	.84	.74
Occupy	.79	**.81**	**.81**	.75	**.81**	.78	.65	.69	.69	.64	**.71**	.35
Design	**.86**	.77	.84	.74	.85	.81	**.86**	.74	.72	.69	.77	.66
Decorate	**.92**	**.92**	.90	.90	.91	.90	.44	.32	.33	.36	.36	**.84**
	R with SVM			R with MLP			R with SVM			R with MLP		
Build	.70	.70	.70	.63	**.76**	.71	**.68**	.65	.63	.59	.66	.62
Occupy	**.92***	.77	.84	.78	.82	.78	**.94**	.98	.81	.80	.84	.79
Design	.83	.87	**.90**	.77	.87	.78	**.84**	.82	.83	.75	.82	.83
Decorate	**.93**	.88	.79	**.93**	.91	.91	.74	.63	.63	**.79**	.74	.68
	Acc. with SVM			Acc. with MLP			Acc. with SVM			Acc. with MLP		
All	**.84***	.81	.81	.78	**.84***	.79	.63	**.72**	.69	.67	.66	.67

similar performance with the TF-IDF-SVM combination for all metrics, and lower performance for all metrics with other methods. Finally, for the *decorate* relations, we observe a drop of performance compared to our training results, and this, for all our methods and metrics. In our test dataset results, this relation has a low **precision** and **F-measure**.

Based on binary and multi-class classifiers, it appears that:

- Globally, on the train dataset, we obtain better performances with the binary classifiers.
- On both datasets (train and test), the TF-IDF-SVN classifier is the best-performing one for most relations and metrics.
- The results on the test dataset are much less regular than on the train dataset, which may be due to the small size òf the dataset and its difference in the proportion of relation instances.

4.3   Discussion and Limitations

Our analysis of the wrong classifications shows us that sentences containing multiple persons and possibly several relations are problematic. In some cases, different relations shared the same contexts, making them indistinguishable. For instance, in the sentence *David Ouellet designed the church and Hubert Morin built it*, our approach cannot indicate whether the builder is David Ouellet or

Hubert Morin. In other cases, the relations were not described in the sentences in which the person was mentioned, or a person was mentioned using a pronoun. To address these issues, we will resort in future work to more advanced processing techniques including syntactic analysis and anaphora resolution. Moreover, we believe that our results can be improved by identifying significant sentences that describe particular relation types using patterns for instance.

Another limitation comes from the classification of the Repertoire of Cultural Heritage of Quebec. Indeed, the current classification does not allow us to have several instances of relations between a person and a real estate. So if someone built and occupied a real estate, then he is registered either in the *occupy* or in the *build* relation but not in both. This leads to two issues. First, as our approach groups all sentences mentioning a person, it is likely that we have considered some training example as belonging to one type of relation while it is also related to another type. For instance, if it is said that *Philippe Poulin built then occupied his house* (which is the registered relation), then with our approach, we might extract text mentioning both relations, while this person is only registered in the repertoire with the *occupy* relation. Thus, we "teach" our algorithms that these sentences describe only an *occupy* relation while they also describe a *build* relation. Our second issue is that if we change the classification to allow a person to have several relations with a building, then the same features will be used for different labels, which points clearly for a need of a more advanced semantic representation of the sentence.

In terms of the effectiveness of the vector-based representations, we noted that the vectors provided to classifiers were sometimes too noisy to classify instances effectively. It is likely that in the case of word embeddings, some noise is induced by the pre-trained model. For instance, "constructor" refers to either an automobile constructor or an edifice builder. Finally, another limitation is that we did not process all the relation types available in the Repertoire of Cultural Heritage of Quebec. Indeed, it is necessary to have a certain amount of training data for the various types. In the future, we plan to extend the set of processed types.

5   Conclusion and Future Work

In this paper, we compared several vector space models for the extraction of predefined relations between persons and heritage buildings by analyzing the historical notices of these buildings. These vector space models are fed as input to supervised machine learning classifiers (binary and multi-class) which have to detect the right type of relations. We showed that the choice of the right method depends on the evaluation metric. Overall, the traditional TF-IDF representation coupled with an SVM classifier obtained the top results in terms of precision, F-measure and overall accuracy. However, these results were not statistically significant compared to the Word2vec representation combined with the MLP algorithm. Thanks to our approach, we managed to reach good results without using any language specific tools or external database, as is it often the case in relation classification.

In future work, we plan to investigate the impact of the pre-trained word2vec model on these results and to train a Word2Vec model on heritage data taken from our corpus and other sources like Wikipedia instead of using a pre-trained model. We also plan to try other word embedding approaches such as GloVe. More importantly, we will try to detect sentences mentioning particular relation types instead of just relying on person and building mentions. This will allow us to deal with the issue of several relation instances between the same couple ⟨person, building⟩ mentioned in the previous section.

Acknowledgements. This work has been funded by the Quebec Ministry of Culture and Communication.

References

1. Vlachidis, A., Tudhope, D.: A knowledge-based approach to information extraction for semantic interoperability in the archaeology domain. J. Assoc. Inf. Sci. Technol. **67**(5), 1138–1152 (2016)
2. Augenstein, I., Padó, S., Rudolph, S.: LODifier: generating linked data from unstructured text. In: Simperl, E., Cimiano, P., Polleres, A., Corcho, O., Presutti, V. (eds.) ESWC 2012. LNCS, vol. 7295, pp. 210–224. Springer, Heidelberg (2012). https://doi.org/10.1007/978-3-642-30284-8_21
3. Benson, E., Haghighi, A., Barzilay, R.: Event discovery in social media feeds. In: Proceedings of the 49th Annual Meeting of the Association for Computational Linguistics: Human Language Technologies, vol. 1, pp. 389–398. Association for Computational Linguistics (2011)
4. Buranasing, W., Phoomvuthisarn, S., Buranarach, M.: Information extraction and integration for enriching cultural heritage collections. In: 2016 11th International Conference on Knowledge, Information and Creativity Support Systems (KICSS), pp. 1–6, November 2016
5. Byrne, K., Klein, E.: Automatic extraction of archaeological events from text, April 2009
6. Doulamis, N.D., Doulamis, A.D., Kokkinos, P., Varvarigos, E.M.: Event detection in Twitter microblogging. IEEE Trans. Cybern. **46**(12), 2810–2824 (2016)
7. Nie, T., Shen, D., Kou, Y., Yu, G., Yue, D.: An entity relation extraction model based on semantic pattern matching. In: 2011 Eighth Web Information Systems and Applications Conference (WISA), pp. 7–12. IEEE (2011)
8. Odat, S., Groza, T., Hunter, J.: Extracting structured data from publications in the art conservation domain. Digit. Scholarsh. Humanit. **30**(2), 225–245 (2014)
9. Petit, J., Boisson, J.C., Rousseaux, F.: Discovering cultural conceptual structures from texts for ontology generation. In: 2017 4th International Conference on Control, Decision and Information Technologies (CoDIT), pp. 0225–0229. IEEE (2017)
10. Schöch, C.: A Word2Vec model file built from the French Wikipedia XML Dump using gensim, October 2016
11. Song, S., Sun, Y., Di, Q.: Multiple order semantic relation extraction. Neural Comput. Appl. 1–14 (2018)
12. Zahedi, M., Kahani, M.: SREC: discourse-level semantic relation extraction from text. Neural Comput. Appl. **23**(6), 1573–1582 (2013)
13. Zheng, S., Jiaming, X., Zhou, P., Bao, H., Qi, Z., Xu, B.: A neural network framework for relation extraction: learning entity semantic and relation pattern. Knowl.-Based Syst. **114**, 12–23 (2016)

Understanding Historical Cityscapes from Aerial Imagery Through Machine Learning

Evangelos Maltezos$^{(\boxtimes)}$, Eftychios Protopapadakis,
Nikolaos Doulamis, Anastasios Doulamis, and Charalabos Ioannidis

Laboratory of Photogrammetry, School of Rural and Surveying Engineering,
National Technical University of Athens, Athens, Greece
maltezosev@gmail.com, eftprot@mail.ntua.gr,
{ndoulam, adoulam}@cs.ntua.gr, cioannid@survey.ntua.gr

Abstract. Understanding cityscapes using remote sensing data has been an active research field for more than two decades. Meanwhile, machine learning provides generalization capabilities compared to hierarchical and rule-based methods. This paper evaluates several machine learning algorithms in order to fuse shadow detection and shadow compensation methods for building detection using high resolution aerial imagery. Three complex and real-life urban study areas were used as test datasets with various: (i) kinds of buildings structures of special architecture, (ii) pixel resolutions and, (iii) types of data. Objective evaluation metrics have been used for assessing the compared algorithms such recall, precision and F1-score as well as rates of completeness, correctness and quality. For both approaches, i.e., shadow detection and building detection, the computational complexity of each machine learning algorithm was examined. The results indicate that deep learning schemes, such a Convolutional Neural Network (CNN), provides the best classification performance in terms of shadow detection and building detection.

Keywords: Shadow detection · Shadow compensation · Building detection
Point cloud · Machine learning

1 Introduction

Urban scene understanding using remote sensing data has been an active research field for more than two decades. Today, building detection has enormously benefited from high resolution aerial imagery datasets [1] and it is useful for several engineering applications [2] such as urban/rural planning, mapping, monitoring and navigation [3, 4]. Although shadows in images have an artistic role, providing a natural scene representation, they also have a destructive role in processing by hiding significant information. Therefore, shadow detection and shadow compensation (also known as shadow removal) is useful for image interpretation, change detection, image segmentation, image classification and matching [5, 6] The key challenge issues in shadow detection are due to diverse orientations of the patterns, self-shadowing, illumination changes, occlusions and the scene complexity. Shadow detection can improve building

© Springer Nature Switzerland AG 2018
M. Ioannides et al. (Eds.): EuroMed 2018, LNCS 11196, pp. 200–211, 2018.
https://doi.org/10.1007/978-3-030-01762-0_17

extraction from urban scenes especially of regions with complex architectural structures [7, 8].

1.1   Shadow Detection, Shadow Compensation and Machine Learning in Cultural Heritage Sites

It has been widely known that the different visible archaeological traces (e.g., soil marks, crop marks, shadow marks and damp marks) are crucial evidence indicating the existence of archaeological remains from high resolution satellite or aerial imagery [9]. These marks generally appear in contrast to surroundings due to different geographical and topographical conditions. Focusing on the cultural heritage sites and historical urban scenes, shadow detection and compensation can highlight significant information contributing to: (i) thematic object recognition and detection (e.g., buildings, specific patterns and significant features, etc.), (ii) road network detection (e.g. grid analysis of ancient cities after the road continuity reconstruction, and filtering them with ancient maps), (iii) serious games, (iv) augmented reality applications, (v) 4D applications (e.g., time series visualisation of ancient cities or reconstructed cultural heritage sites), (vi) relighting objects, (vii) convincing rendering of virtual objects in real scenes, (viii) estimation of building or object height from single imagery or from overlapping shadows, (ix) exploitation of old aerial images and (x) emergency response situations and/or change detection applications associated with damage detection [10–14]. Cultural heritage sites and historical urban scenes consisting of very complex building structures. Thus, the aforementioned tasks are more demanding on such scenes compared to typical cities. On the other hand, machine learning and especially deep learning have recently demonstrated their suitability and potentials for cultural heritage documentation, preservation and protection [15–18].

1.2   Our Contribution

According to our knowledge, a complete and extensive research that explores the performance of machine learning fed by high resolution aerial imagery for shadow detection, shadow compensation and building detection in complex historical urban scenes is missing. A variety of approaches use hierarchical, rule-based methods such objected-based image analysis (OBIA) [19] that are tailored for a particular scene layout and task. Although these approaches extract satisfactory results, they are affected on the parameters used and the features adopted, which are often application dependent. Therefore, they present low generalization capabilities (i.e., robustness against data being outside the training set) since the tuned parameters of one study-area cannot be directly applied to another one. Machine learning techniques are flexible and data driven methods, requiring only training samples to well generalize the properties of each available class. However, in all these approaches shadow modeling is not usually considered, deteriorating urban scene understanding performance.

This paper aims at evaluating the performance of eleven (11) machine learning methods, linear and non-linear, for urban scene understanding using high resolution aerial imagery data. In particular, a fusion of shadow detection and shadow compensation methods for building detection is performed. Performance evaluation is accomplished using objective metrics, measuring both accuracy and computational complexity.

2 Understanding Historical Cityscapes

In this paper, 11 machine learning methods for urban scene understanding (shadow detection and building detection) have been evaluated (see also Fig. 2 for the selected parameters): (i) K-nearest Neighbour (kNN) [20], (ii) K-nearest Neighbour Ensemble (kNN-Ens) [20, 21], (iii) Classification Tree (CT) [22], (iv) Classification Tree Ensemble (CT-Ens) [22], (v) Discriminant Analysis (DA) [23], (vi) Discriminant Analysis Ensemble (DA-Ens) [23], (vii) Naive Bayes (NB) [23], (viii) Random Forests (RF) [24], (ix) Support Vector Machine (SVM) [25], (x) Artificial Neural Networks (ANN) [26] and (xi) Convolutional Neural Networks (CNN) [2].

2.1 3D Geometric Urban Modelling

The aerial images alone are not adequate of providing reliable urban scene understanding due to the fact that some urban objects are usually present similar radiometric (pixel values) intensities, e.g., building rooftops versus roads. For this reason, in this paper 3D geometric information are extracted from the set of aerial images. In particular, we assume that a set of overlapped aerial datasets are available. Then, Dense Image matching (DIM) [27] methods are applied to extract the height (i.e., the depth) of a pixel, which is an important attribute regarding building extraction. The output of the DIM is a 3D point cloud which is geo-referenced using ground control points (GCPs) applying the bundle adjustment algorithm to estimate the positions and attitudes of cameras in triangulation calculations [2]. The normalized Digital Surface Model ($nDSM$) is then estimated, providing a 3D geometric representation of the urban scene. The $nDSM$ is calculated as $nDSM = DSM\text{-}DTM$, where DTM is the Digital Terrain Model (i.e., the bare earth points) and DSM the Digital Surface Model (i.e., the DIM point cloud) [28]. To further improve the classification results, an attribute that models the vegetation characteristics is considered; the Normalized Difference Vegetation Index ($NDVI$), defined as $NDVI = (NIR - R)/(NIR + R)$, where NIR refers to near infrared image band and R to the red image color component. Assembling the aforementioned features together, we create a multidimensional vector that describes the attributes of urban scenes, $f(p) = [I_H(p), I_S(p), I_V(p), nDSM(p), NDVI(p)]^T$ where the I_H, I_S, I_V refers to the HSV color component of the images and $nDSM$ to the normalized height of a pixel. Variable p indicates an image pixel.

2.2 Scene Modelling

The aforementioned multidimensional vector is used for modelling the urban scene, through a supervised learning paradigm. In particular, for every image pixel $I(p)$ a probability mapping is created indicating information associated with the label of each class on a pixel-level framework, $Pr(p) = [Pr_{\omega_1}, \ldots, Pr_{\omega_L}]^T$. Variables Pr_{ω_i} indicate the probability of pixel p to belong to the ith out of the L available classes. Actually, there is a relationship between the input vector $f(p)$ and the probability mapping $Pr(p)$, that is $Pr(p) = g(f(p))$. The unknown relationship $g(\cdot)$ is modelled through a supervised machine learning, as the ones presented above.

2.3 Shadow Compensation

Using the aforementioned urban scene representation, first shadows are detected. For this reason, only the first three components of the feature vector $f(p)$ are considered, that is, the HSV color information of the aerial images. Usually, in complex urban scenes, a typical radiometric compensation by replacing the radiometric attribute of closest areas in not adequate. Thus, the shadows are compensated using the following approach consisting of three steps: (1) **Shadow Segmentation:** First, a region growing algorithm is applied to the areas detected as shadow region by the machine learning classifier. In this way, the shadow regions are labelled as connected components, (2) **Enhanced radiometric compensation:** An enhanced radiometric compensation is applied to the shadow connected components. This is performed using the following algorithm. First, the radiometric information of the neighboring regions around a connected shadow area is modelled through the application of AutoRegressive (AR) filters. Actually, these filters model the textural statistics of non-shadow regions, neighboring to shadow ones. Then, the AR filters are used for compensating the detected shadow regions, improving therefore, urban scene understanding [29] and (3) **Boundary treatment:** To absorb penumbra effects and diffuse reflection zones, especially in the boundary shadow regions, a diffusion process is applied by smoothing the radiometry between the shadow and the neighboring non-shadow regions [5].

3 Experimental Results

3.1 Dataset Description and Evaluation Metrics

Three complex and real-life urban study areas with various: (i) kinds of buildings structures of special architecture, (ii) pixel resolutions and, (iii) types of data were used for evaluation and comparison. The first dataset is the Vaihingen (Germany) orthoimages and DIM point cloud extracted from typical CIR aerial images of pixel resolution of 9 cm and provided by the German Society for Photogrammetry, Remote Sensing and Geoinformation (DGPF) [30, 31]. The second corresponds to the Santorini orthoimages and DIM point cloud extracted from RGB UAV images of pixel resolution of 7 cm. Finally, the third dataset refers to the Zakynthos orthoimages and DIM point cloud extracted from typical RGB aerial images of pixel resolution of 15 cm.

The learning process incorporates: (i) for the shadow detection, the classes of "Shadows" and "Nonshadows" and (ii) for the building detection, the classes "Buildings", "Vegetation" and "Ground". The labelled set includes polygons (samples) of image regions and it is split into three mutually exclusive sets; the training, the validation and the test set. Figure 1 depicts the labelled samples from the three datasets regarding shadow detection. The labelled set was lower than 0.4% and 4.0% of the total dataset for the shadow and building detection respectively for all the study areas. Such percentages indicate particularly small training set. The training set is used to train the network, the validation set to assess the error during training and the test set to benchmark the network performance to data outside the training and validation set. The validation and the training set constitutes of 80% of the total labelled set, while the remaining 20% is the test set. The metrics of recall (Rec), Precision (Pr) and F1-score [26] are used for the evaluation of the shadow detection, while the rates of completeness $C_m(\%) = (100 \cdot ||TP||)/(||TP|| + ||FN||)$, correctness $C_r(\%) = (100 \cdot ||TP||)/(||TP|| + ||FP||)$ and quality $Q(\%) = (100 \cdot ||TP||)/(||TP|| + ||FP|| + ||FN||)$ for the assessment of building extraction [32], where TP the True Positives, FP the False Positives and FN the False Negatives. The reason of using different evaluation metrics in case of building extraction is that we have building reference data to estimate the rates of C_m, C_r and Q. In case of shadow detection, the assessment is performed with respect of the test set.

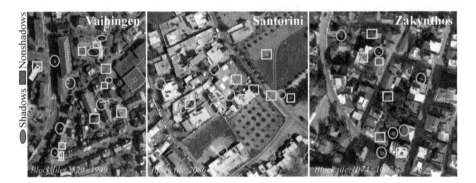

Fig. 1. Labelled samples regarding shadow detection.

3.2   Shadow Detection and Shadow Compensation Evaluation

Figure 2 presents the classification results regarding shadow detection for different classifiers. Figure 3 depicts the performance evaluation regarding shadow detection case. In this figure, we have illustrated: (i) the computational complexity of the training process, (ii) the computational complexity of the classification and finally (iii) the performance evaluation of the classification in terms of Rec, Pr and F1 score. As is observed, the majority of classifiers achieved balanced evaluation performance, with, however, the CNN achieved the best results. Although the computational complexity of CNN is much higher than the compared methods, the use of a better CPU and more RAM capacity can significantly speed up the process.

Additionally, acceleration algorithms can be incorporated [2]. Based on the aforementioned statements, the CNN classifier is adopted in the following for shadow compensation, using the algorithm described in Sect. 2.3. Figure 4 presents the results regarding the shadow compensation algorithm. As is observed, the recovered orthoimages successfully compensates the shadow regions. There are, however, few cases of excessive compensations and radiometric lesions occurred due to: (i) false detected shadows (e.g., associated with nonshadowed objects coloured in black such

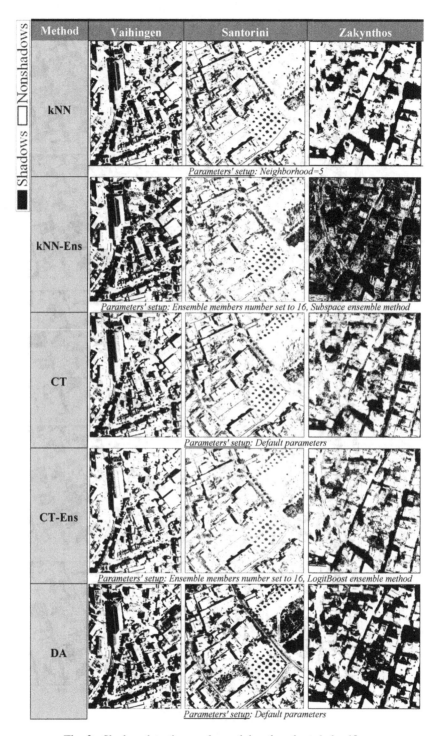

Fig. 2. Shadow detection masks applying the adopted classifiers.

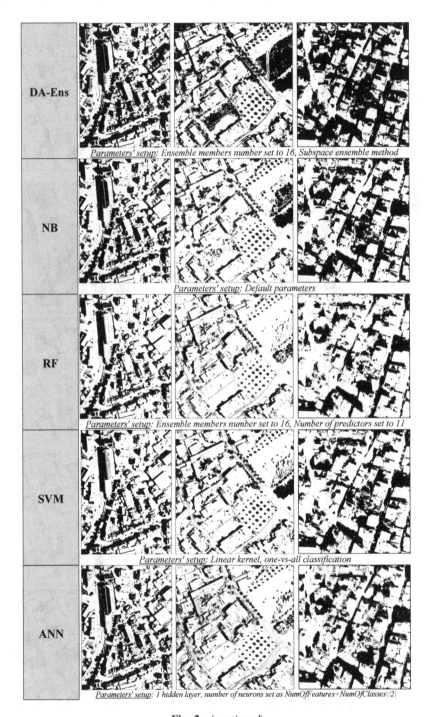

Fig. 2. (*continued*)

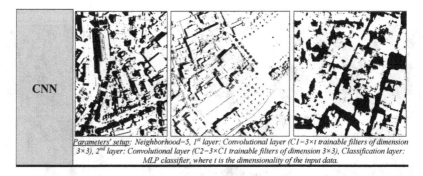

Parameters' setup: Neighborhood=5, 1st layer: Convolutional layer (C1=3×t trainable filters of dimension 3×3), 2nd layer: Convolutional layer (C2=3×C1 trainable filters of dimension 3×3), Classification layer: MLP classifier, where t is the dimensionality of the input data.

Fig. 2. (*continued*)

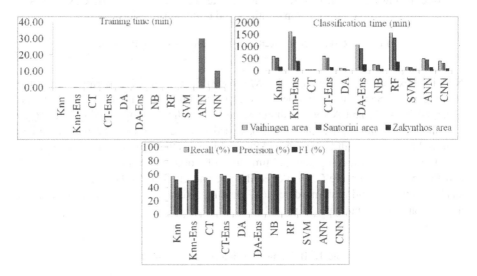

Fig. 3. Metrics and computation time for shadow detection.

cars, solar water heaters or with objects with similar radiometric values with the labelled shadows samples), (ii) missed detected shadows, (iii) limited radiometric information from the neighboring regions (e.g., at dense historical centers with very high buildings, covering all the roads with their shadows) and (iv) local failures during the shadow compensation process. Such cases are challenge for further improvement of the shadow detection and compensation process. The missed shadowed areas that were observed were caused mainly by incomplete collection of labelled samples at these areas.

3.3   Building Detection

Table 1 presents the results of the building extraction for different classification set ups in case that shadow compensation takes place augmented with the *nDSMs* and the

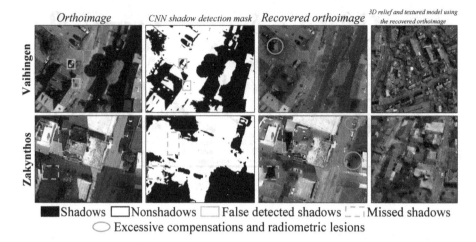

Fig. 4. Results regarding the shadow compensation algorithm.

NDVI index (where is available the *NIR* band). The evaluation performed for the Vaihingen and Santorini areas due to the available building reference data. The DA, CNN, SVM, kNN and ANN classifiers achieved satisfied average quality rates (Q_{av}) i.e., about 75% and higher, indicating balanced C_m and C_r rates. The rest classifiers achieved moderate results. The DA and the SVM seems that satisfy greatly the building detection accuracy vs. computational time tradeoff compared to the CNN (see Table 1 and Fig. 5). However, the CNN proved flexible and efficient for both challenges, i.e., shadow detection and building detection, yielding satisfactory results with a sufficient and reasonable computational time.

Table 1. Building detection per-area accuracies.

| Method | Vaihingen area | | | Santorini area | | | Average |
| | Recovered orthoimage + NDVI + nDSM | | | Recovered orthoimage + nDSM | | | |
	C_m (%)	C_r (%)	Q (%)	C_m (%)	C_r (%)	Q (%)	Q_{av} (%)
kNN	97.5	77.7	76.2	93.1	78.6	74.2	75.2
kNN-Ens	99.8	45.5	45.4	99.8	29.3	29.3	37.4
CT	97.9	71.4	70.4	91.7	80.4	74.9	72.7
CT-Ens	97.8	61.1	60.2	92.4	84.0	78.6	69.4
DA	85.3	86.8	75.6	87.6	88.7	78.8	77.2
DA-Ens	71.8	89.3	66.2	89.2	81.1	73.8	70.0
NB	99.3	63.7	63.5	95.1	79.8	76.7	70.1
RF	98.8	70.4	69.8	92.7	80.9	76.0	72.9
SVM	98.3	75.8	74.8	92.7	81.4	76.5	75.7
ANN	98.3	75.5	74.5	92.8	78.9	74.3	74.4
CNN	97.8	78.6	77.2	92.2	81.0	75.8	76.5

To overcome misclassification problems and therefore to achieve higher success rates, more representative labelled samples can be used to optimize class predictions. In Fig. 6, we also present the impact on the building detection accuracy via CNN by using several configurations of features.

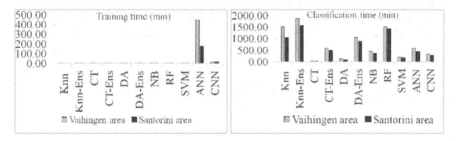

Fig. 5. Computation time for building detection.

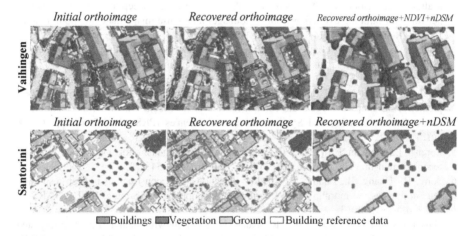

Fig. 6. Impact on the building detection accuracy via CNN and several configurations of features.

4 Conclusions

This paper performs an evaluation for understanding historical cityscapes from aerial imagery through machine learning. To this end, several classification algorithms were employed for shadow detection and compensation as well as for building detection. The shadow compensated orthoimages, combined with additional 3D geometric features and vegetation indices, improves the building detection performance. The DA and the SVM seems that satisfy greatly the building detection accuracy vs. computational time tradeoff compared to the CNN. Thus, they are considered appropriate for "time critical" applications such rapid building extraction or building damage detection in terms of emergency situations. However, the DA and the SVM performed considerably less shadow detection accuracy compared to the CNN. This indicates the potentials and the flexibility of deep learning frameworks to model several classification tasks and very complex problems using particularly small training sets. The CNN is computationally demanding during the training process. To speed up the training process, a workstation with high-end processing power and RAM capacity is needed. Also pre-trained CNN models, can be used to extract sufficient results in reasonable computational time.

Acknowledgments. This research is supported by the European Funded Project of H2020, Terpsichore, under agreement no. 691218.

References

1. Cordts, M., et al.: The cityscapes dataset for semantic urban scene understanding. In: CVPR, Seattle, WA, USA (2016)
2. Maltezos, E., Doulamis, N., Doulamis, A., Ioannidis, C.: Deep convolutional neural networks for building extraction from orthoimages and dense image matching point clouds. J. Appl. Remote Sens. **11**(4), 042620-1–042620-22 (2017)
3. Rottensteiner, F., Sohn, G., Gerke, M., Wegner, J.D., Breitkopf, U., Jung, J.: Results of the ISPRS benchmark on urban object detection and 3D building reconstruction. ISPRS J. Photogramm. Remote Sens. **93**, 256–271 (2014)
4. Doulamis, A., et al.: 5D modelling: an efficient approach for creating spatiotemporal predictive 3D maps of large-scale cultural resources. In: ISPRS Annals of the Photogrammetry, Remote Sensing and Spatial Information Sciences (PRSSIS), II5/W3, pp. 61–68 (2015)
5. Lorenzi, L., Melgani, F., Mercier, G.: A complete processing chain for shadow detection and reconstruction in VHR images. IEEE TGARS **50**(9), 3440–3452 (2012)
6. Song, H., Huang, B., Zhang, K.: Shadow detection and reconstruction in high-resolution satellite images via morphological filtering and example-based learning. IEEE TGARS **52**(5), 2545–2554 (2013)
7. Guislain, M., Digne, J., Chaine, R., Kudelski, D., Lefebvre-Albaret, P.: Detecting and correcting shadows in urban point clouds and image collections. In: 3DV, pp. 1–9 (2016)
8. Hosseinzadeh, S., Shakeri, M., Hong, Z.: Fast shadow detection from a single image using a patched convolutional neural network. In: CVPR, Seattle, Honolulu, Hawaii (2017)
9. Luo, L., et al.: Automated extraction of the archaeological tops of qanat shafts from VHR imagery in Google Earth. Remote Sensing **6**, 11956–11976 (2014)
10. Doulamis, A., et al.: 4D reconstruction of the past. In: SPIE Proceedings, vol. 8795, pp. 1–11 (2013)
11. Kadhim, N., Mourshed, M., Bray, M.: Automatic extraction of urban structures based on shadow information from satellite imagery. In: 14th Conference of International Building Performance Simulation, pp. 2607–2614 (2015)
12. Cerra, D., Plank, S., Lysandrou, V., Tian, J.: Cultural heritage sites in danger-towards automatic damage detection from space. Remote Sens. **8**(781), 1–15 (2016)

13. Zhou, K., Gorte, B.: Shadow detection from VHR aerial images in urban area by using 3D city models and a decision fusion approach. In: ISPRS Annals of the PRSSIS, XLII-2/W7, pp. 579–586 (2017)
14. Kadhim, N., Mourshed, M.: A shadow-overlapping algorithm for estimating building heights from VHR satellite images. IEEE GRSL **15**(1), 8–12 (2018)
15. Llamas, J., Lerones, P.M., Medina, R., Zalama, E., Gómez-García-Bermejo, J.: Classification of architectural heritage images using deep learning techniques. Appl. Sci. **7**(992), 1–25 (2017)
16. Yasser, A.M., Clawson, K., Bowerman, C., Lévêque, M.: Saving cultural heritage with digital make-believe: machine learning and digital techniques to the rescue. In: Proceedings of British HCI Conference, pp. 1–5 (2017)
17. Bassier, M., Vergauwen, M., Van Genechten, B.: Automated classification of heritage buildings for as-built BIM using machine learning techniques. In: ISPRS Annals of the PRSSIS, IV-2/W2, pp. 25–30 (2017)
18. Uhl, J., Leyk, S., Chiang, Y., Duan, W., Knoblock, C.: Exploring the potential of deep learning for settlement symbol extraction from historical map documents. In: UCGIS (2018)
19. Cheng, G., Han, J.: A survey on object detection in optical remote sensing images. ISPRS J. Photogramm. Remote Sens. **117**, 11–28 (2016)
20. Bhatia, N., Vandana: Survey of nearest neighbor techniques. Int. J. Comput. Sci. Inf. Secur. **8**(2), 302–305 (2010)
21. Rokach, L., Schclar, A., Itach, E.: Ensemble methods for multi-label classification. Expert Syst. Appl. **41**(16), 7507–7523 (2014)
22. Farid, D.M., Zhang, L., Rahman, C.M., Hossain, M.A., Strachan, R.: Hybrid decision tree and naïve Bayes classifiers for multi-class classification tasks. Expert Syst. Appl. **41**(4), 1937–1946 (2014)
23. Zhuang, F., et al.: Mining distinction and commonality across multiple domains using generative model for text classification. IEEE TKDE **24**(11), 2025–2039 (2012)
24. Belgiu, M., Drăguţ, L.: Random forest in remote sensing: a review of applications and future directions. ISPRS J. Photogramm. Remote Sens. **114**, 24–31 (2016)
25. Abe, S.: Support Vector Machines for Pattern Classification. Advances in Computer Vision and Pattern Recognition. Springer, London (2010). https://doi.org/10.1007/978-1-84996-098-4
26. Protopapadakis, E., et al.: A genetically optimized neural classifier applied to numerical pile integrity tests considering concrete piles. Comput. Struct. **162**, 68–79 (2016)
27. Remondino, F., Spera, M.G., Nocerino, E., Menna, F., Nex., F., Barsanti, S.G.: Dense image matching: comparisons and analyses. In: Proceedings of Digital Heritage International Congress, pp. 47–54 (2013)
28. Rovithis, E., et al.: LiDAR-aided urban-scale assessment of soil-structure interaction effects: the case of Kalochori residential area (N. Greece). Bull. Earthq. Eng. **15**(11), 4821–4850 (2017)
29. Singh, K.K., Pal, K., Nigam, M.J.: Shadow detection and removal from remote sensing images using NDI and morphological operators. Int. J. Comput. Appl. **42**(10), 37–40 (2012)
30. Rottensteiner, F., Sohn, G., Gerke, M., Wegner, J.D.: ISPRS test project on urban classification and 3D building reconstruction, ISPRS—Commission III—Photogrammetric Computer Vision and Image Analysis Working Group III/4–3D Scene Analysis (2013)
31. Cramer, M.: The DGPF test on digital aerial camera evaluation – overview and test design. Photogrammetrie – Fernerkundung – Geoinformation **2**, 73–82 (2010). http://www.ifp.uni-stuttgart.de/dgpf/DKEP-Allg.html
32. Rutzinger, M., Rottensteiner, F., Pfeifer, N.: A comparison of evaluation techniques for building extraction from airborne laser scanning. IEEE J-STARS **2**(1), 11–20 (2009)

Origin Determination of Mediterranean Marbles by Laser Induced Fluorescence

Valeria Spizzichino[1(✉)], Laura Bertani[2], and Luisa Caneve[1]

[1] FSN-TECFIS-Diagnostic and Metrology Laboratory,
Italian National Agency for New Technologies,
Energy and Sustainable Economic Development, 00044 Frascati, RM, Italy
valeria.spizzichino@enea.it
[2] Italian National Agency for New Technologies,
Energy and Sustainable Economic Development, Guest,
00044 Frascati, RM, Italy

Abstract. LIF measurements have been carried out on marble samples coming from the most famous quarries of the Mediterranean area. Thanks to multivariate techniques and clustering methods the most significative spectral features linked to geographical provenance have found and tested.

The propaedeutic work previously carried out on the reference samples has allowed for the developing of a fast data processing method of LIF data able to provide, in quasi real time, digital images of the artworks where Italian and Greek marbles are marked differently.

Starting from the obtained results, a LIF scanning prototypal system has been used to scan two masterpieces from Roman period interesting for real restoration and archaeological issues: the sculptured group, called Ares Ludovisi (collection of Palazzo Altemps) and the so-called "Two-orant's sarcophagus", housed in the Museum of the Catacombs of San Sebastiano in Rome.

Keywords: Laser Induced Fluorescence · Marble · Scanning system

1 Introduction

Marble has been the main constituent of sculptures and architectural artworks since antiquity. Greeks and Romans were used to extract such material to produce both masterpieces and imposing buildings, as temples or amphitheaters. Several marble quarries have been used since V century B.C., even if there are marble sculptures dated back to the end of IV millennium B.C.

Often the geographical origin of the marble used for a given artwork is meaningful from both historical and archaeological point of view.

The techniques usually used to obtain marble provenance information are based on geochemical methods and petrographic analyses. Anyway, since such techniques are not completely informative by themselves, they are generally coupled to chemical or spectroscopic methods, such as thermal analysis and thermogravimetry, x-Ray diffractometry, x-Ray fluorescence, electron paramagnetic resonance and to chemometric techniques [1–5].

© Springer Nature Switzerland AG 2018
M. Ioannides et al. (Eds.): EuroMed 2018, LNCS 11196, pp. 212–223, 2018.
https://doi.org/10.1007/978-3-030-01762-0_18

Even though in some cases a joined study by these techniques can provide reliable results, sometimes they are limited, also for practical and technical reasons. In fact, they can require sampling and laboratory analyses on every single part of the artwork, if it is not created from a single block.

Laser Induced Fluorescence (LIF) in the last decades has been largely used as spectroscopic characterization method, providing molecular information and a spectral fingerprint of solid or liquid materials [6] in different fields of application, including that of Cultural Heritage [7–10].

In this work LIF measurements have been carried out on marble samples coming from the most famous quarries of the Mediterranean area. Thanks to multivariate techniques and clustering methods the most significant spectral features linked to geographical provenance have been found and tested.

Starting from the obtained results, a LIF scanning prototypal system has been used to scan two masterpieces from Roman period interesting for real restoration and archaeological issues: the sculptured group, called Ludovisi Ares (collection of Palazzo Altemps) and the so-called "Two-orant's sarcophagus", housed in the Museum of the Catacombs of San Sebastiano in Rome.

The preparatory work previously carried out on the reference samples allowed for the developing of a fast data processing method of LIF data able to provide, in quasi real time, digital images of the artworks where Italian and Greek marbles are marked differently.

2   Materials and Methods

2.1   Reference Samples

Ancient Greece was rich in marble quarries from which many valuable varieties of white and gray marbles were extracted. For this reason, the use of marble as a building material has been widespread since prehistoric times and for all Greek and Roman eras.

Examples of precious varieties used in the sculptural works are the Greek marbles Parian, Naxos, Hymettos and Proconnesus and the Italian Lunense (Carrara marble).

Petrographically, the marble is a calcareous rock which, as a result of dynamic or contact metamorphism, has assumed a uniform-grained crystalline structure.

The Parian marble, from the island of Paros, is a very fine saccaroid white marble, very valuable, used in ancient times for works of sculpture and architecture. Naxos is a marble originating from the island of Naxos, the largest of the Cyclades. Similar to the Parian one, but with a larger grain, it is recognized as one of the first used for works of decorative or sculptural nature. Hymettos is a mountain characterized by conspicuous marble deposits slightly green or blue veined, very used in the classical era. Proconnesus marble is a variety of white marble among the most used in the Roman Empire. The variety has a white color, with cerulean shades, uniform or with bluish-gray veins, and presents large crystals. The quarries are located on the island of Proconnesus, in the Sea of Marmara. The first exports of this marble, already used locally, date back to the second half of the first century AD and continued throughout the second and third centuries in the eastern regions of the Roman Empire and along the Danube. In the fourth century it was one of the least expensive marbles of the Diocletian edict and therefore one of the most widespread. The Lunense one, with its gleam and brilliance, has been considered since the antiquity an ideal decorative marble for both artworks and architecture.

In the present work, samples from Carrara, Paros, Naxos, Hymettos and Proconnesus have been characterized by LIF with the final goal to point out the spectral features suitable for a rapid discrimination between Italian and Greek marbles.

2.2 Studied Masterpieces

Ludovisi Ares. The Ludovisi Ares is a Roman copy of a Greek sculpture attributed to Scopas or Lisippo dating from around 320 B.C. The identification of the figure, traditionally considered the god of war, remains doubtful. Recently, however, art historians have supposed it to be Achilles. The sculpture represents a man sitting on a rock with his hands gathered on his left knee and his foot leaning on a helmet. With his left hand he holds the sword and the circular shield is placed down, with the inside facing out. Under the right leg of the god is a small Eros sitting on the ground, while behind the left shoulder appear traces of a figure now lost (see Fig. 1).

Fig. 1. The masterpiece Ludovisi Ares during the *in situ* campaign. The lighting conditions are those in which the LIF measures were performed.

The sculptural group, discovered in 1622, dates back to the 2nd century B.C. and is made of Pentelic marble [11].

Winckelmann (1717–1768) defined the statue as "the most beautiful Mars of antiquity". In fact, the statue has been considered of great value since the moment of its discovery, when a group of collectors entrusted the restoration of the work to Gian Lorenzo Bernini (1598–1680). The sculptor intervened on the sculptural group in various points with additions in Carrara marble [12].

Two-Orant's Sarcophagus. The catacombs of San Sebastiano, located in Rome near the Via Appia, are a vast complex consisting of 12 km of tunnels of tuff and pozzolana. They were the first to be called with the name "catacombs". Initially they played a purely pagan funerary role, with cremation and burial tombs. Some symbols of Christian iconography found in some tombs indicate an early Christian presence, confirming that the transition from the pagan to the Christian phase took place gradually. It can be said that the cemetery was transformed into a place of Christian worship from the moment when the remains of the two apostles Peter and Paul were buried here, even if the archaeological results do not support the hypothesis of the translation of the bodies. The excavations of the original early Christian structure began in the nineteenth century. Many of the finds were recovered during the excavation campaigns carried out during the following decades [13].

Our study focused on the so-called "two-orant's Sarcophagus", a marble sculpture made between the 3rd and 4th centuries AD and preserved in the Sarcophagi Museum located inside the catacomb of San Sebastiano (see Fig. 2). Such artwork is of great importance because of the peculiar figure represented in the central rose. Moreover, archaeologists are still trying to define geographical origin of the three pieces (left, central, right) constituting the sarcophagus to clarify historical trade routes.

Fig. 2. Two-orant's sarcophagus as scanned by LIF system, before the restoration action carried out in the second half of 2017.

2.3   LIF Measurements

Laser-Induced Fluorescence Technique. A LiDAR (light detecting and ranging) fluorosensor, is a remote system based on a laser beam that irradiates a sample and on an optical system that measures the fluorescence spectrum. The analysis of the received optical signal gives information on the spectral properties of the compounds consti-tuting the target surface. The use of lasers instead of other sources is motivated by the ease of building compact systems that produce highly focused, low divergence beams, together with the brightness and the monochromatic excitation of the laser light. The main components of the set-up are a laser excitation source and a spectrum analyzer. Generally, to record fluorescence spectra, a laser operating in the ultraviolet (UV) is used. The laser beam is directed to the sample surface by the use of mirrors or by using an optical fiber. The emitted light is collected with an optical fiber, or collimated with a lens, and directed to the entrance of the spectrum analyzer. For wavelength-resolved fluorescence spectroscopy, the back-scattered radiation is typically dispersed and detected by a spectrometer or by a monochromator coupled with photomultipliers or with an intensified charge-coupled device (ICCD) camera.

For the present study, two different prototypes developed at the ENEA Research Center of Frascati were used: a punctual scanning system (LIFART) and a stand-off image sensor for the first time used in the field of Cultural Heritage.

Punctual Scanning System LIFART. The lidar fluorosensor called LIFART is a remote instrument that can work from a distance to the target up to 10 m. The system details are described in [14]. Just some characteristics are here recalled. LIFART uses a solid-state laser emitting in the UV either at 355 nm or at 266 nm, but for the experiments reported the wavelength at 266 nm has been used.

A coaxial optical design is used to transmit the exciting radiation and to receive the fluorescence signals from the investigated target. The scan point by point is obtained actuating the last mirror with two rotating servo controls operating at high accuracy. The fluorescence radiation is focused at the entrance of a fiber optic linked to a compact QE-Pro Ocean Optics spectrometer, allowing a hyperspectral imaging in the range of 250–947.5 nm with a 2.5 nm bandwidth.

In the present work such system has been used for laboratory tests to obtain fluorescence spectra on reference marble samples.

Stand-Off Image Sensor FORLAB. The second used apparatus, called FORLAB, is a portable apparatus equipped with 8 interferential filters with narrow bands used instead of monochromator and coupled to an ICCD that provides directly fluorescence images at the selected filter wavelengths. If such wavelengths are well chosen, the produced images will be discriminating maps of materials of interest. A motorized delivering optics allows the laser, an excimer laser KrF at 248 nm, to scan spot across the entire area to be investigated from a distance up to 10–20 m. The collecting subsystem is fixed and, as mentioned, connected to the ICCD, characterized by a large field of view (FOV) and conveniently triggered by the laser pulse. The used laser has pulse energy of 16 mJ maximum, pulse repetition rate (prr) up to 500 Hz and pulse duration of 10 ns. The high values of prr of the excimer laser and of speed of the optics movement allow for a very short acquisition time (from 8 to 25 min for complete scan of several square meters, depending on the specific experimental conditions selected). The system is described in more details in [15].

It is, then, clear that a preliminary study is required to obtain fluorescence reference spectra and to individuate filter wavelengths more suitable for the discrimination among interesting materials. Then, to put in evidence the most meaningful spectral features of the materials under analysis, statistic methods such as PCA have been used and clustering techniques have been applied to the whole experimental fluorescence spectra acquired with the LIFART system on reference samples. After that, the stand-off image sensor capabilities have been tested in situ on the two masterpieces described in Sect. 2.2. It was the first time FORLAB was applied to the study of artworks.

3   Tests on Reference Samples and Data Processing

Fluorescence spectra in the range 270–800 nm have been collected on Greek and Italian marble samples in laboratory by LIFART system. For every sample 16 measures in 16 different surface points have been carried out.

On such data a Principal Component Analysis (PCA) has been performed. The first 4 PCs obtained are shown in Fig. 3. From the study of their minima and maxima, listed in Table 1, the wavelengths most useful for a discrimination among different samples have been individuated. They have been, then, used to create ratios and algorithms for a rapid discrimination of materials from data of the stand-off image sensor.

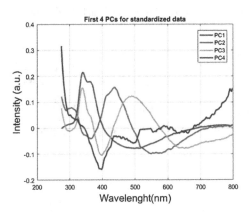

Fig. 3. First 4 PCs for experimental fluorescence spectra on reference samples of marbles.

Table 1. Maxima and minima location for the first 4 PCs shown in Fig. 3.

PC	nm max	nm min
PC1	340	515
PC2	437.5	550
PC3	340	397.5
PC4	790	395.7

After several tests I_{550}/I_{340} vs I_{427}/I_{340} and I_{440}/I_{550} vs I_{340}/I_{550} have been indi-viduated as meaningful parameters. In fact, in the first case, reporting such ratios in a graph data of Italian and Greek marbles get aligned on two different straight lines (see Fig. 4). The equation found for the bisector of the angle formed by them is:

$$y = 0.71x - 0.02 \tag{1}$$

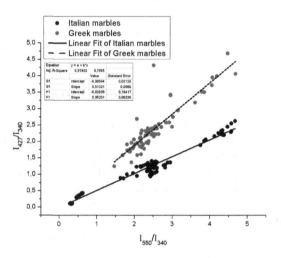

Fig. 4. Fluorescence intensity ratios I_{550}/I_{340} vs I_{427}/I_{340} for Italian and Greek reference marbles.

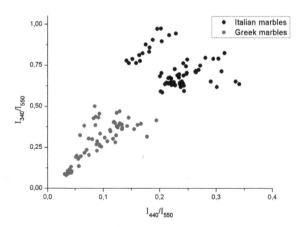

Fig. 5. Clustering of data from fluorescence spectra thanks to the use of the ratios I_{440}/I_{550} and I_{340}/I_{550}

Using the second pair of ratios, two groups of data, completely separated on the Cartesian plane, can be individuated, even if it is not possible to assign to them linear fits, as shown in Fig. 5. This is confirmed by the results obtained by two different clustering methods tested: k-means and a hierarchical cluster tree method. In fact, in both cases all the individual points are well assigned to the two different clusters.

Starting from the obtained results, wavelengths for the filters of the stand-off image sensor have been selected, also on the base of the narrow band interference filters available on the market. Chosen filter are at 445, 376, 340, 315, 290, 415, 532 and 480 nm.

4 *In situ* Measurements and Digital Images Elaboration

The ratios highlighted as significant have also been used for the analysis of the data of marble sculptures from Palazzo Altemps and San Sebastiano catacombs.

In both of these *in situ* campaigns, the stand-off image system FORLAB was used. It does not produce whole spectra but provides fluorescence intensities at the 8 spectral bands above listed. An example of the real-time fluorescence images provided is given in Fig. 6. Therefore, among the available bands, those closest to the wavelength values individuated by PCA and clustering analysis were selected to create digital images.

For the 560/340 vs 427/340 analysis the 532/415 ratio was taken into consideration.

The value 0.71, corresponding to the angular coefficient of the bisector previously found, has been set as threshold for the creation of masks. This method produced good results, shown in figures Figs. 7 and 8, for both sites. To create such images, a mask, where only pixels corresponding to intensity ratio assigned to Greek marbles are yellow, is overlapped to the black and white fluorescence image at 532 nm. In this way it is possible to have information on the present marble origin at a glance. In the background, residual yellow dots are present in some areas, but they do not correspond to areas with real fluorescence signals detection and can be easily removed.

In the case of the Ludovisi Ares, starting from data collected after the cleaning phase carried out by the restorers, the additions in Carrara marble, referable to a restoration of Gian Lorenzo Bernini, are clearly visible and well defined. In particular, the left hand of Ares and the handle of the sword, the head, the leg, the left arm and the quiver of the putto and some areas of the shield are clearly identifiable.

In the case of the sarcophagus, there are no significant differences in the type of marble used for the central part and for the two lateral parts of the sarcophagus. In some areas there are points above threshold that, given their high discontinuity and coincidence with spots partly visible to the naked eye, seem to derive from the presence of foreign materials, probably heart that depresses fluorescence emission simulating the presence of Greek marble because of a lower S/N ratio. In fact, LIF measurements have been carried out before the cleaning and restoration action conducted on the artwork during the second half of 2017.

Digital images with masks created by clustering algorithms on the I_{440}/I_{550} vs I_{340}/I_{550} ratio data have been created too. The obtained results are not as good as those shown in Figs. 7 and 8 (based on the threshold method). The explanation of this can be found in the weight that the values of the selected ratios for background pixels have on

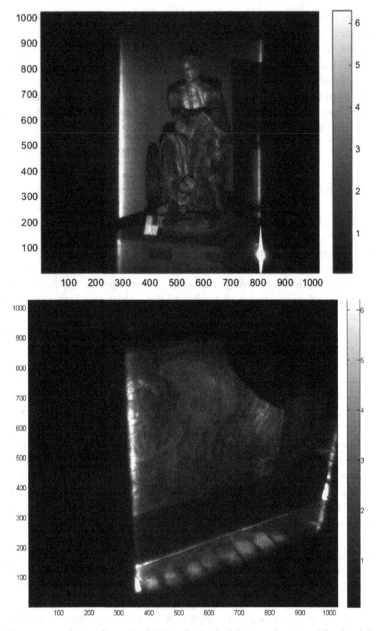

Fig. 6. Fluorescence image filtered at 340 nm for Ludovisi Ares, above, and for the right part of the two orant's sarcophagus below.

the results that can be obtained on the pixels of the artwork surface. So, if for the sarcophagus measurements, where background was very uniform, the results are pretty good and confirm those obtained by the other method, for the Ludovisi Ares results are

R2=532/415 th 0.71

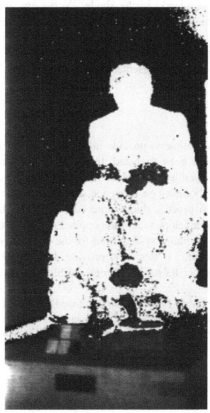

Fig. 7. Frontal view of the Ludovisi Ares after data processing, using the ratio I_{532}/I_{415} as parameter and 0.71 as threshold value for the mask creation. In yellow the points assigned to Greek marbles. (Color figure online)

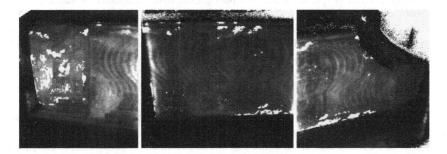

Fig. 8. 3 sections (left, center, right) of the sarcophagus after data processing, using the ratio I532/I415 as parameter and 0.71 as threshold value for the mask creation. In yellow the points assigned to Greek marbles. (Color figure online)

confused. In fact, in the latter case, the background was definitely patchy, with areas in strong light and areas completely in the shade. Works are in progress to make this method more general and suitable also for measurement carried out in environments with complex backgrounds. Moreover, in the future other different methods for data dimensionality reduction and clustering, such as spectral clustering [16], will be tested and compared to those used and presented in this work.

5   Conclusions

The ability of the LIF technique to provide information on the geographical origin of Mediterranean marbles has been analyzed. In particular LIF has been used to distinguish Italian and Greek marbles used since antiquity for art and architectural works. A preparatory study in laboratory on reference samples has allowed to individuate the meaningful algorithms to process fluorescence data and provide origin information. Two methods have been developed and then applied on LIF data obtained on two real masterpieces by a stand-off image system used for the first time on the field of Cultural Heritage. Such system could, in this way, provide, in quasi real time digital images with masks indicating where Italian and Greek marbles are located.

Acknowledgements. The authors would like to thank the Directors of Palazzo Altemps and the Sarcophagi Museum of San Sebastiano catacombs to make accessible studied artworks and the restorers S. Cascioli, D. Papetti, L. Ruggeri for their support and collaboration. This research was supported by the Latium Region under grant agreement lr13, n.1031.

References

1. Polikreti, K., Maniatis, Y.: A new methodology for the provenance of marble based on EPR spectroscopy. Archaeometry **44**(1), 1–21 (2002)
2. Attanasio, D., Armiento, G., Brilli, M., Emanuele, M.C., Platania, R., Turi, B.: Multi-method marble provenance determinations: the carrara marbles as a case study for the combined use of isotopic, electron spin resonance and petrographic data. Archaeometry **42**(2), 257–272 (2000)
3. Gatta, T., Gregori, E., Marini, F., Tomassetti, M., Visco, G., Campanella, L.: New approach to the differentiation of marble samples using thermal analysis and chemometrics in order to identify provenance. Chem. Cent. J. **8**, 35 (2014)
4. Gaggadis-Robin, V., Pojani, I., Polikreti, K., Maniatis, Y.: Provenance investigation of marble sculptures from Butrint, Albania. In: Gutiérrez Garcia-M, A., Lapuente Mercadal, P., Rodà de Llanza, I., (eds.) Proceedings of the IX ASMOSIA Conference: Interdisciplinary Studies on Ancient Stone 2009, Documenta, vol. 23, pp. 310–321. Institut Català d'Arqueologia Clàssica, Tarragona (2012)
5. Lloyd, R.V., Tranh, A., Pearce, S., Cheeseman, M., Lumsden, D.N.: ESR spectroscopy and X-Ray powder diffractometry for marble provenance determination. In: Herz, N., Waelkens, M. (eds.) Classical Marble: Geochemistry, Technology, Trade. NATO ASI Series (Series E: Applied Sciences), vol. 153, pp. 369–377. Springer, Dordrecht (1988). https://doi.org/10.1007/978-94-015-7795-3_39

6. Corcoran, T.C.: Laser-induced fluorescence spectroscopy (LIF). In: Baudelet, M. (ed.) Laser Spectroscopy for Sensing, pp. 235–257. Woodhead Publishing, Cambridge (2014)
7. Farsund, Ø., Rustad, G., Skogan, G.: Standoff detection of biological agents using laser induced fluorescence—a comparison of 294 nm and 355 nm excitation wavelengths. Biomed. Opt. Express **3**(11), 2964–2975 (2012). https://doi.org/10.1364/BOE.3.002964
8. Palmer, S.C.J., et al.: Ultraviolet fluorescence LiDAR (UFL) as a measurement tool for water quality parameters in turbid lake conditions. Remote Sens. **5**, 4405–4422 (2013)
9. Cecchi, G., et al.: Fluorescence lidar technique for the remote sensing of stone monuments. J. Cult. Herit. **1**, 29–36 (2000)
10. Spizzichino, V., Angelini, F., Caneve, L., Colao, F., Corrias, R., Ruggiero, L.: In situ study of modern synthetic materials and pigments in contemporary paintings by laser-induced fluorescence scanning. Stud. Conserv. **60**, S178–S184 (2015)
11. Bombardi, S.: Alcune osservazioni in merito al rinvenimento dell'Ares Ludovisi. Archeol. Class. **52**, 323–342 (2001)
12. Faldi, I.: Note sulle sculture borghesiane del Bernini. In: Bollettino d'arte, XXXVIII, ser. IV, pp. 140–146 (1953)
13. Ferrua, A.: La basilica e la catacomba di San Sebastiano. Catacombe di Roma e d'Italia 3. Pontificia Commissione di archeologia sacra (1990)
14. Colao, F., Fantoni, R., Fiorani, L., Palucci, A., Gomoiu, I.: Compact scanning lidar fluorosensor for investigations of biodegradation on ancient painted surfaces. J. Optoelectron. Adv. Mater. **7**(6), 3197–3208 (2005)
15. Spizzichino, V., Caneve, L., Colao, F.: Stand-off device for plastic debris recognition in post-blast scenarios. Challenges **7**(23), 1–12 (2016)
16. Ng, A.Y., Jordan M.I., Weiss, Y.: On spectral clustering: analysis and an algorithm. In: Advances in Neural Information Processing Systems, pp. 849–856 (2002)

Personalized Heritage Museum Guide
for Married Immigrant Women

Hyeweon Kim[iD] and Jeongmin Yu[(⊠)][iD]

Department of Cultural Heritage Industry,
Graduate School of Convergence Cultural Heritage, Korea National University
of Cultural Heritage, Buyeo-gun, Chungcheongnam-do, Korea
{20182046, jmyu}@nuch.ac.kr

Abstract. This paper presents a novel heritage museum guide framework that provides personalized digital heritage contents to help understand the culture of immigration country. Particularly, this framework focuses on helping married immigrant women in a situation of social exclusion to easily understand a different culture heritage easily by providing similar digital heritage contents of her home country. To develop this guide framework, the following core steps are integrated: (i) collect data, such as logs, Facebook feeds, and frequency of app usage from a users' smartphone, (ii) build users preference profiles through the analysis of collected data, (iii) display similar digital heritage contents of their home country via a head-mounted mixed reality display. From the proposed framework, we expect that the framework will make it easier to understand unfamiliar cultural heritage to married immigrant women who is having difficulty adapting to immigration. Furthermore, her children also can utilize these contents to understand and learn their mother's culture, which can create an empathy between the mother and her children.

Keywords: Married immigrant women · Heritage museum guide
User preference profile · Mixed reality

1 Introduction

A role of a conventional museum is to preserve heritages and provide an experience through the act of viewing. Recently, the needs of visitors changed and so did museums also through various perspectives, such as social inclusion [1–3] and interpretation of museum experience [4–8]. Among the perspectives of museums, this paper focuses on social exclusion (i.e., contrary to the social inclusion), which means the social disadvantage and relegation suffered by marginalized people. To deal with the problem of social exclusion, museums have a duty to provide an assistance to people in social exclusion.

On the other hand, in terms of interpretation of museum experience, [4] museums have a role in education and should to offer the appropriate interpretations to visitors using interactive services [5–8].

To provide interpretation of museum experiences to visitors interactively and individually, museum guides have adopted the state-of-the-arts devices. For instance,

© Springer Nature Switzerland AG 2018
M. Ioannides et al. (Eds.): EuroMed 2018, LNCS 11196, pp. 224–235, 2018.
https://doi.org/10.1007/978-3-030-01762-0_19

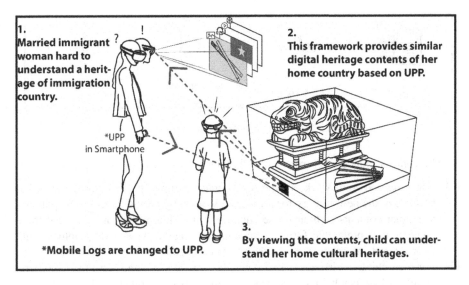

1.
Married immigrant woman hard to understand a heritage of immigration country.

*UPP
in Smartphone

2.
This framework provides similar digital heritage contents of her home country based on UPP.

3.
By viewing the contents, child can understand her home cultural heritages.

*Mobile Logs are changed to UPP.

Fig. 1. Illustration of the proposed conceptual museum guide.

smartphones are used for museum guides due to their powerful advantages such as 2D display, mobile, and hand-held characteristics [8, 9]. As another device, head-mounted display (Optical See-Through Head-Mounted Display: OST HMD) is being recently used for museum guides based on its natural user interface (NUI) [10–12]. Although various types of state-of-the-arts devices are adopted, the provided digital contents do not frequently meet visitors' specific interests [13]. As an alternative, a recommendation system that consider user preferences is one of the ways to meet visitors' needs. By using this system, visitors are provided with categorized digital contents in heritage museums [14].

However, even using recommendation systems, these museum guides present serious some problems. (i) The existing museum guides take no account of a married immigrant woman who has a difficulty adapting to unfamiliar countries. (ii) Although museum guides provide personalized digital contents, they do not provide consider a preferable the type of contents of users (i.e., type of contents are given to users in a predefined manner). (iii) The existing museum guides provide not personalized contents but representative contents of main visitors.

To address these problems, we propose a novel heritage museum guide framework that provides personalized preferable type of contents based on a user preference profile (UPP) for married immigrant women. To implement the proposed framework, the following main steps are integrated systematically: (i) collect data steps with logs, feeds of Facebook, frequency of app usage from a user's smartphone, (ii) design the user preference profile by analyzing the collected data, (iii) display similar digital heritage contents of their home country in form of preference contents via a head mounted mixed reality display (Fig. 1).

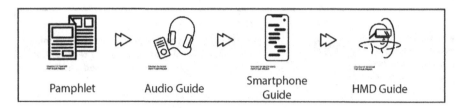

| Pamphlet | Audio Guide | Smartphone Guide | HMD Guide |

Fig. 2. Paradigm shift of museum guide.

The contributions of this paper are followings.

(1) The proposed framework is expected to make it easier to understand unfamiliar heritage of the new country for immigrant women by providing the corresponding to similar contents of their home countries. In addition, they are provided these contents in a preferable form of contents (text, audio, video, 3D graphics) with their interest information, particularly, child education.

(2) For their children also get shared contents to understand and learn their mothers' culture, which can help to create an empathy between mothers and their children. Through this, their children can be developed unique traits that is understanding two cultures. And they can belong to the mainstream of society due to developing their traits.

The remainder of this paper is organized as follows. Related works are briefly introduced in Sect. 2. In Sect. 3, our proposed framework is presented. In Sect. 4, our initial implementation is presented. Lastly, discussions and conclusions are presented in Sect. 5.

2 Related Works

In this section, we introduce briefly the issues faced by married immigrant women when using conventional museum guides. Then, we overview the paradigm shift of museum guides which is shown in Fig. 2.

2.1 Adaptation of Married Immigrant Women

Married immigrant women settle down and live in countries completely different from their home countries. Although the number of married immigrant women is increasing all over the world, they still live in social exclusion, which people suffer not only in their home living but also in the public services. They have struggled to adapt to heterogeneous cultures and have been studied since they are under different stresses from those of indigenous people [15]. The biggest difficulty is to adjust to an unfamiliar country [16]. To solve this problem, the National Museum of Korea ran program for multicultural families since 2007 [17]. However, as the program is temporary, the museum needs a permanent system to serve married immigrant women. Furthermore, married immigrant women have shown a great interest in raising their children [18–20]. Particularly, married immigrant women hardly know their children's school curriculum and education contents, such as (i) when and what contents child learn, (ii) why they learn about such subjects, and (iii) other related education contents, such as outdoor education and books. Even a reversal of roles occurred between mothers and their children because married immigrant women can't speak a second language properly [18]. Difficulty adapting to society is not ended in the generation of mothers, being passed on to children, who have difficulty belonging to the mainstream society because they can't be properly educated.

It is important to help them make their social lives easier, since the number of married immigrant women is increasing. Museums have to solve this from the perspective of social inclusion.

2.2 Museum Guides

Many related works presented that museums prepare the interpretation to visitors using interactive devices. The ICOMOS Charter defines the basic principles for interpretation and presentation of cultural heritage. According to the charter, interpretation refers to the full range of activities to increase public perception and understanding of cultural heritage [5]. Freeman stated: "Based on my experience with interpretation, it is an educational activity to use schematic media to represent the meaning and relationship of the subject." [21]. According to [22], the interpretation is divided into "professional" and "public" levels. In particular, the public level was first interpreted by experts, and filtered information of cultural heritage is presented to the public according to various factors, such as context and type of media. According to the NMCI Horizon project report 2013, the importance of high-quality media (images, audio, video, virtual reality, etc.) related to heritage in terms of collaboration among institutions for resource sharing has increased [23]. However, the method of interpreting and transmitting cultural heritage according to the traditional process can be conveyed unilaterally from an expert to a viewer, or the limits of the determinant can be excluded from various perspectives. To solve the shortcomings of traditional methods, many museums present an interesting interpretation to visitors through various devices and methods, especially using smartphones instead of audio guides due to their advantage of having sensors. [9] explains that whereas smartphone for guide systems have shown an increase in using QR codes (800%), which some researches use at museum guide [24–26], iPad tours (200%) which are been at tablet PC (In [12] paper, they present an interactive museum guide can find and instantaneously retrieve information about the item of interest using a standard tablet PC), and applications (151%) [3, 27, 28], the number of traditional audio guidance systems has reduced to by one-fifth. The main functions of museum mobile guide systems are informational service and multimedia. More specifically, texts, images, sound, and video offered through the museum mobile guide systems provide a rich interpretation of the displays and exhibitions [29]. The [30] paper proposed a multimedia application for museum guides that helps visitor's learning experience. In addition, [31] presented an effect of mobile devices as a museum guide that allow visitors obtain information about the exhibition [31].

A recommendation system or recommender system was originally defined as 'people provide recommendation as inputs, which the system then aggregates and direction to appropriate recipients' [29]. The interest in this area still remains high because it constitutes a rich-problem research area and because of the abundance of

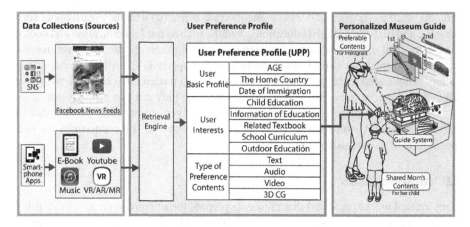

Fig. 3. The proposed heritage museum guide framework.

practical applications that help users to deal with information overload and provide personalized recommendations, content, and services to them [32]. Previous existing research shows that allow visitors to interact through an automatic museum guide system. [14] proposed a recommendation for children that uses a sensing board, which can rapidly recognize the type and location of multiple children, then giving the children audiovisual feedback. Other researches [33, 34] proposed the combination of related people and tags on the internet SNS to recommend social media items or taste-related domains. So we also use SNS through smartphone that recommending items related to a user's activity. Then we can get good quality of recommendation results.

The contributions of proposed framework are: (i) Personalized contents based on UPP helps married immigrant women understand unfamiliar heritage by comparing each heritage in real-time. (ii) Information about user's interests is sent to a married immigrant woman's Facebook newsfeed, so that they refer to them when they educate their children. (iii) Children can understand their mother's culture, develop empathy, and have an opportunity to understand differences. These contributions make married immigrant women adapt overall (both at home and in society) well. Section 3 shows the flow of the proposed museum guide system framework in regular order.

3 Proposed Framework

In this section, we explain the proposed heritage museum guide framework using illustrations from a specific situation.

First step illustrates how to collect data and what kinds of data are collected. In next second step, explain about the user preference profile. In last third step, we show how the system works for a multicultural family in the heritage museum.

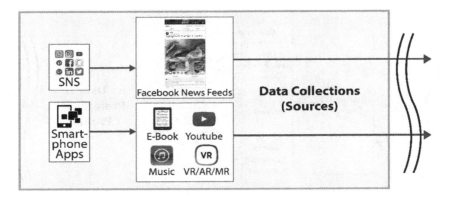

Fig. 4. Data collections of overall framework.

3.1 System Diagram of Heritage Museum Guide

Figure 3 shows the proposed overall system diagram of the personalized heritage museum guide. The flow consists of three steps. First, a smartphone is used to obtain relevant user data, such as logs and, Facebook feeds. Then, a retrieval engine is used derive the UPP. Lastly, users are provided with personalized preferred contents, which can be displayed in a virtual environment. Personalized contents help married immigrant women understand unfamiliar heritage by offering familiar heritage information. Children also watch shared contents. In addition, it provides information of a married immigrant woman's interests based on UPP. The whole process of personalizing a heritage museum guide for married immigrant women is presented in the form of a black box. Each detailed step is given in detail the following subsections.

3.2 Data Collections

In the first step (Fig. 4), two types of user data obtained through a smartphone were considered: the user's SNS and apps. Users' SNS (e.g. Facebook) have many useful information to make UPP. SNS have users' basic profiles and their own feeds, reflecting their interests. Another component to be used are users' smartphone apps. Frequency of app usage can reveal what types of contents users like the most. Summing up, it is possible to find basic users' profiles and interests through SNS their preferred content type through frequency of apps usage (e.g. text, audio, video, and 3D interactive contents). Each component is processed to become quantitative data by using retrieval engine that is used to obtain the relevant information in step 2.

3.3 User Preference Profile

In the second step (Fig. 5), we derived the UPP from the first step. To obtain the UPP, step 2 proceed using a retrieval engine. Through the retrieval engine, data collections were transformed into meaningful UPP. So UPP includes user basic profiles, interests, and the type of preferred content. For example, in a users' basic profile unit, it is

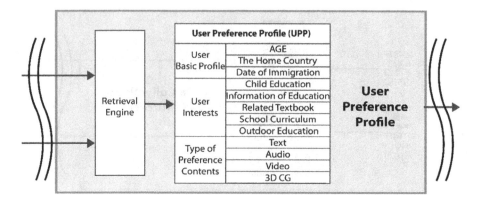

Fig. 5. UPP of overall framework.

possible to find their age, home country, and date of immigration. This information can be used to know about their culture and how much time has passed since their immigration. User interests are given through their SNS activities, such as sharing, liking, and commenting feeds. As examples of user interests, a woman is interested in child education, information of education, related textbooks, school curriculum, and outdoor education. Lastly, type of preferred contents can be known through frequency of app usages. That includes text, audio, video and interactive 3D CG (Computer Graphic: CG). For example, if a married immigrant woman is a long-term user of YouTube application, her preferred video types are appropriate as a form of contents. If user uses 3D applications such as AR (Augmented Reality: AR), VR (Virtual Reality: VR) and 3D contents frequently, she is expected to prefer to see 3D CG. Preferred types of text can be discovered depending on how many document files (Doc, Word, etc.) are available or uploaded on user's smartphone. Whether the user uses e-book or not also can be an indicator. Audio types can be grasped through music apps. Like this, by analyzing the frequency of app usage, we can determine user's preferred type of contents and other custom information.

3.4   Heritage Museum Guide Using Mixed Reality

Figure 6 illustrates how UPP is used in the last step. For example, there is a married immigrant woman who has difficulty understanding immigration heritage at heritage museum. Our system consists of a computing unit for computation, an OST HMD for visualization and a smartphone for a UPP of married immigrant women.

Using OST-HMD, a married immigrant woman is provided with two UPP-based services: a museum guide and user-related interests.

First, a married immigrant woman gets familiar heritage contents similar with unfamiliar heritage collection. Contents on OST-HMD can be compared and contrasted, so that they can compare each cultural heritage in real time with their children. For example, Fig. 6 shows, a married immigrant woman watching two contents of Korean cultural heritage: one named "Au" which seems an animal statue, and other named "Park". However, a heritage like an animal doesn't a statue but an instrument

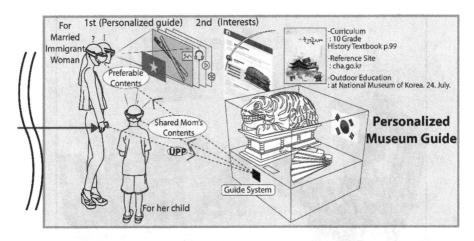

Fig. 6. Personalized heritage guide for a married immigrant woman.

using when plays "Jeryeak" which played for "Jongmyo Jerye" or "Jongmyo Daeje" a rite held for worshipping the ancestor kings and queens of the Joseon Dynasty in Jongmyo Shrine, Seoul, South Korea. Jongmyo Jerye and Jeryeak were designated as the first South Korean Masterpiece of the Oral and Intangible Heritage of Humanity by UNESCO in 2001. Although Au is an important Korean heritage, even Korea natives find it hard to know immediately that it is an instrument (it can be played by scratching a tiger's back). Park is also an instrument played by striking both sides simultaneously, and it is used with the Au. Situation like these (difficulty in proper interpretation) has happened with married immigrant women more than native people. Based on our framework, married immigrant women can compare and contrast each country's heritage. And it can show any type of contents she wants. When she looks at the contents on OST-HMD, personalized contents are displayed automatically, and then the type of contents can be re-selected by her married immigrant women. Particularly, 3D interactive contents can be rotated and enlarged using the drag and multi-touch gestures. In Fig. 6, a married immigrant woman from Vietnam sees a Vietnam cultural heritage instrument named "Sênh tiền" which is played like the Au. And she can also choose the recommended type of contents based on the UPP she wants.

Second, after admiring the cultural heritages, she can get information of her interests on UPP. In Fig. 6, the 2nd shows Facebook news feed with information of interests. Interests of child care, related textbooks, school curriculum, and outdoor education are uploaded on her SNS. The curriculum indicates when a child learns this heritage and where is written in textbooks. Using reference sites, they can get more information related to Au. Furthermore, a married immigrant woman can know about outdoor education related to Au. Therefore, a married immigrant woman gets a chance to educate their children as native mothers do.

Her children are provided with the same contents as mothers' not children preferred contents. Because this moment is to understand their mother culture indirectly and build empathy with their mother by sharing the same contents. Thus, they can grow up with having advantages which mean that they can belong to mainstream society.

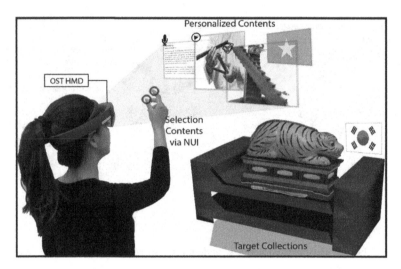

Fig. 7. Tentative implementation of proposed heritage museum guide.

Because children have special talent to understand differences between the cultures of both countries culture.

4   Initial Implementation

This section presents an initial and some expected results based on the implementation of the proposed museum guide. Figure 7 shows the initial implementation of this work.

In the initial implementation, a smartphone is used to get a users' data and OST-HMD for interactive with touchable 3D images and a computing unit to overhand personalized preferable contents. The OST-HMD device is the Microsoft Hololens, which enables people to interact with augment object in real-time by touching and dragging. Thus, we can even observe a cultural heritage's back in detail that is hard to see when using the existing museum guide.

In order to send smartphone's UPP to guide system, it is over handed through short-range wireless communication (e.g. Li-Fi, Wi-Fi etc.). This procedure occurs automatically when a user reaches cultural heritage collections.

In Fig. 7, a user wearing an OST-HMD can control the personalized information in augmented reality. First, a user gets contents refer to a familiar heritage of their home country. Thus, the user can compare an unfamiliar heritage with a familiar heritage, and the type of contents is shown in her favorite type of contents. From this, the user can perfectly get preferred information. If user want to have more knowledge and other type of contents, she can choose other contents instantly just by dragging and touching. Besides of the first suitable contents, there are contents which shows the same heritage in different type.

5 Discussions and Conclusions

Our contributions are the following.

(i) Our novel heritage museum guide enables a married immigrant woman to get personalized contents based on UPP. Based on UPP, it helps visitors to understand unfamiliar cultural heritages by comparing with a familiar heritages provided with preferable contents type. It is not possible in the conventional museum guides. Using OST-HMD, a married immigrant woman interacts with 3D AR contents (familiar heritage) which can be enlarged and rotated using NUI. This ease of use and suitable type of contents can help immigrant women understand an unfamiliar heritage and immigration country's culture more than before. After understanding an unfamiliar heritage, she can be got information related to her interests on her SNS. Therefore, when she educates their children, she can utilize this education information like native mothers do.

(ii) By using this guide, she can solve her interests related to her children. They also have time to understand each other, because they spend time together simultaneously sharing heritage contents. In addition, her children experience indirectly the heritage of their mother's home country. Before this time, it was hard for children to learn about their mothers' culture. This system allows children to develop traits that are different from natives' children. They can belong to the mainstream of society due to developing their unique traits.

Through this research, we discuss issues on the proposed personal heritage museum guide. In the proposed framework, our all the virtual contents and information are saved in the computation (i.g. museums prepare amount hardware). However, this method has a limit of hardware capacity. Fortunately refer to the NMCI Horizon project report 2013, we can overcome this limit. The report suggested that high-quality media (images, audio, video, virtual reality, etc.) related to the heritage were increasingly important in terms of collaboration among institutions for resource sharing [22]. From this point of view, according to the NMCI Horizon project, our framework is feasible in near future.

Acknowledgements. This research is supported by 2018 Support Project for Academic Research in Korea National University of Cultural Heritage.

References

1. DCMS. Centres for Social Change: Museums, Galleries and Archives for AJI (2000)
2. DCMS. Arts and Sport: Policy Action Team 10: A report to the Social Exclusion Unit. RCMG. 2000. Museums and Social Inclusion. The GLLAM Report (1999)
3. Wang, C.S., Su, W.T., Guo, Y.C.: An augmented reality mobile navigation system supporting iBeacon assisted location-aware service. In: Proceedings of the 2016 International Conference on Applied System Innovation, pp. 1–4. IEEE (2016)
4. Wikipedia.org. https://en.wikipedia.org/wiki/Museum#cite_note-5. Accessed 13 June 2018

5. http://icip.icomos.org/downloads/ICOMOS_Interpretation_Charter_ENG_04_10_08.pdf. Accessed 13 June 2018
6. Fleming, D.: The politics of social including. In: Dodd, J., Sandell, R. (eds.) Including Museums, pp. 18–19. RCMG, University of Leicester (2001)
7. Sandell, R.: Social inclusion, the museum and the dynamics of sectoral change. Mus. Soc. 1 (1), 45–46 (2003)
8. Sagar, P., Shraddha, L., Amruta, M., Netra, P.: Smart guide – an approach to the smart museum using android. IRJET (Int. Res. J. Eng. Technol.) 5(2), 652–655 (2018)
9. Tallon, L.: Museum & mobile survey 2012. Pocket-proof & learning-times (2012). http://www.museumsmobile.org/survey-2012/
10. Pollalis, C., Fahnbulleh., W. Tynes, J.: HoloMuse: enhancing engagement with archaeological artifacts through gesture-based interaction with holograms. In: TEI, pp. 565–570 (2017)
11. Azuma, R., Baillot, Y., Behringer, R., Feiner, S., Julier, S., MacIntyre, B.: Recent advances in augmented reality. IEEE Comput. Graph. Appl. 21(6), 34–47 (2001)
12. Azuma, R.: A survey of augmented reality. Presence 6(4), 355–385 (1997)
13. Bay, H., Fasel, B., van Gool, L.: Interactive museum guide: fast and robust recognition of museum objects. In: Proceedings of the First International Workshop on Mobile Vision (2006)
14. Kusunoki, F., Sugimoto, M., Hashizume, H.: Toward an interactive museum guide with sensing and wireless network technologies. In: MTE2002, Vaxjo, Sweden, pp. 99–102 (2002)
15. de Nelly Salgado Snyder, V.: Factors associated with acculturative stress and depressive symptomatology among marred mexican immigrant women. Psychol. Women Q. 11, 475–488 (1987)
16. Newman, L.V.: The expatriate adjustment process; implications of the cross-cultural context on learning the environment following a work-role transition. Unpublished Doctoral dissertation, University of Illinois at Urbana-Champaign (2000)
17. Museum homepage. http://www.museum.go.kr/site/child/archive/post/archive_1710. Accessed 13 June 2018
18. Orellana, M.F.: Translating Childhoods: Immigrant Youth, Language, and Culture. Rutgers University Press, Princeton (2009)
19. Wall, K., José, J.S.: Managing work and care: a difficult challenge for immigrant families. Soc. Policy Adm. 38(6), 591–621 (2004)
20. Weedon, C.: Feminist Practice and Poststructuralist Theory, 2nd edn, pp. 313–314. Blackwell Publisher Ltd., Oxford (1997)
21. Tilbern, F.: Interpreting our heritage: principles and practices for visitor services in parks, museums, and historic places. University of North Carolina Press 35(2), 261–263 (1958)
22. Fitch, J.M.: Historic Preservation: Curatorial Management of the Built World. University of Virginia Press, London (1990)
23. Johnson, L., Becker, S.A., Freeman, A.: NMC Horizon Report: 2013 Museum Edition, NMC (2013)
24. Australian First in Museum Access for Deaf Australians at the National Sports Museum. http://travability.travel/blogs/nsm.html. Accessed 13 June 2018
25. Constantinou, V., Loizides, F., Ioannou, A.: A personal tour of cultural heritage for deaf museum visitors. In: Ioannides, M., et al. (eds.) EuroMed 2016. LNCS, vol. 10059, pp. 214–221. Springer, Cham (2016). https://doi.org/10.1007/978-3-319-48974-2_24
26. Wolff, A., Mulholland, P., Maguire, M., O'Donovan D.: Mobile technology to support coherent story telling across freely explored outdoor artworks. In: Proceedings of the 11th Conference on Advances in Computer Entertainment Technology, pp. 11–14. ACM (2014)

27. Brighton Museums App (2017). http://brightonmuseums.org.uk/discover/smartphone-apps/. Accessed 13 June 2018
28. Wu, S.C.: U-museum and u-learning: on development of National Palace Museum's mobile apps. Int. J. Serv. Technol. **9**(4), 261–278 (2016)
29. Economou, M., Meintani, E.: Promising beginnings? Evaluating museum mobile phone apps. In: Rethinking Technology in Museums Conference Proceedings, pp. 26–27 (2011)
30. Alexandri, E., Tzanavara, A.: New technologies in the service of museum education. World Trans. Eng. Technol. Educ. **12**(2), 317–320 (2014)
31. Paternò, F., Santoro, C.: Exploiting mobile devices to support museum visits through multimodal interfaces and multi-device games. In: WEBIST, vol. 1, pp. 459–465 (2007)
32. Littlestone, N., Warmuth, M.: The weighted majority algorithm. Inf. Comput. **108**(2), 212–261 (1994)
33. Guy, I., Zwerdling, N., Ronen, I., Carmel, D., Uziel, E.: IBM Research Lab.: Social Media Recommendation based on People and Tags (2010)
34. Burke, R.: Hybrid recommender systems: survey and experiments. User Model. User-Adapt. Interact. **12**(4), 331–369 (2002)

Personality Analysis of Social Media Influencers as a Tool for Cultural Institutions

Vassilis Poulopoulos[1]([envelope]) [iD], Costas Vassilakis[2] [iD], Angela Antoniou[2] [iD],
George Lepouras[2] [iD], and Manolis Wallace[1] [iD]

[1] [logo] Knowledge and Uncertainty Research Laboratory,
University of the Peloponnese, 221 31 Tripolis, Greece
{vacilos,wallace}@uop.gr
[2] University of the Peloponnese, 221 31 Tripolis, Greece
{costas,angelant,gl}@uop.gr
http://gav.uop.gr

Abstract. Nowadays, more and more cultural venues tend to utilize social media as a main tool for marketing, spreading their messages, engaging public and raising public awareness towards culture. It comes to a point where the massive of content in social media makes it a tedious procedure to contact the appropriate audience, the people that would really be stimulated by cultural information. In this notion, we assume that establishing conversations of high impact can possibly guide the cultural venues to audiences that can benefit more. These conversations usually include the so called influencers, users whose opinion can affect many people on social media; the latter usually referred to as followers. In this research paper we examine the characteristics of the influencers that can affect the procedures of a cultural venue on social media. The research is done within the scope of "CrossCult" EU funded project.

Keywords: User modeling · Personality traits · Influencers
Cultural informatics · Social media

1 Introduction

The main goal of contemporary museums is to stimulate the senses and activate different cognitive and affective processes, like high order thinking and reflection, desire to know, emotional arousal and more [2–5]. In order to achieve it, they carefully plan exhibition themes and layouts and select objects so as to crate a certain venue ambiance; all to ensure that visitors are engaged and appreciate the overall quality of the museum experience [1]. In parallel, it is a fact that nowadays the cultural institutions tend to widely use technology and its tools to attract people, spread their message and stimulate senses. This can lead to support to the visitor experience before, during and after the visit with different

© Springer Nature Switzerland AG 2018
M. Ioannides et al. (Eds.): EuroMed 2018, LNCS 11196, pp. 236–247, 2018.
https://doi.org/10.1007/978-3-030-01762-0_20

technological solutions spanning from museum websites, to mobile devices and social media [1, 6, 7].

These applications not only provide easy access to different types of content, but they also allow the visitor to have active participation. In parallel, an increasing number of cultural venues support innovative procedures during the visits in order to offer an enhanced experience to their audience. What can really affect the way cultural institutions act is a further analysis of a procedure that can be initiated during the visit and continue as a post-visit interaction; the latter not necessarily including only visitors but a broader audience of people willing to interact with the venue. In other words, the cultural institution can benefit from visitors that can act as ambassadors of the stimulation of feelings and the sharing of the visit experience.

However, some people are more influential than others in spreading the museum message and affecting others' behavior. The personalities of different people and their influential role, like opinion leading, are studied in fields like marketing [12]. Recently, and due to the enormous dissemination of social media, people that are influential are also studied within the framework of social networks [13]. The sharing of experience in everyday life is widespread in a global online world through social media [8] and cultural experiences are no exception. This trend is such that people tend to seek information in the social media about events, things to do or interesting places to visit and a number of people seek advice from "experts" in the field or dominant individuals in order to maximize their experience [9]. By recognizing an expert in the field who can be transliterated as an influencer it is possible to understand the effect this person might have on others [10, 11].

Influencers can affect others in multiple ways, from making a venue known to others and motivating others in visiting, to initiate discussions about cultural heritage, to create communities and keep people engaged, to even set trends. What influencers can or cannot do is of significant importance to cultural institutions, not only because they want to know what influencers might think and do, but also because they would themselves benefit from becoming influencers and key players in social life and social media. In addition, as the scope of an exhibition or generally a cultural institution is to spread a message, the uncontrollable situation of altering the message or spreading a different unwanted message on social media, is something that institutions should be aware of. Therefore, the present work aims at analyzing the personality of the visitors of cultural venues and the discussions that emerge around cultural heritage. We focus on establishing the personality of the influencers and their impact to other visitors, as well as identifying the characteristics of influential discussions. We particularly target the personalization procedure that can be based on the influencers (people and discussions) for each visitor in order to further activate and engage them. Our research is based on the pilot procedures of "CrossCult" EU Project through which we create ad-hoc social networks, where visitors can interact in real time either before, during the venue visit or even after visit. We examine the personality of the visitors that emerge as influencers, the characteristics of posts that turned into important discussions and the way a cultural institution can benefit from this analysis. By performing the research and analysis on the procedures of fast and profitable message spreading through the social media, the cultural spaces have access to footprints they never used before. The role of this identification is crucial for cultural heritage as it can play an active role in the everyday life of people and thus raise the awareness, spread to the masses and engage larger audiences. The structure of the paper is as follows. The next section presents the related work that is done in the specific area, while Sect. 3 presents in detail our research methodology. Section 4 presents our experimental procedures and the next section presents a discussion on the founding. We conclude with future work and remarks.

2   Related Work

The term "influencer" is not novel, but has revived due to its extensive use in social media. In general the influencer is a person that can affect the opinion, the life stance, or the way of thinking and the attitudes of a number of people [20]. This can be done either on purpose, or due to the person's position either in social life or the workplace, or just due to long time media exposure [13]. Common influencers among others could be people like athletes, rock stars, actors, models, politicians, mentors, etc., however, research shows that everyone could be an influencer under certain circumstances [13].

From a technical perspective, establishing the influencers is a procedure that is related to analysing quantitative parameters such the number of posts of a user, the number of likes and comments of other users, the times it is reposted and - if possible - the post reach. Past research has focused on different ways to identify social media influencers. For example, [21] applied a dynamic diffusion model to find influencers in specific discussions and to predict others from different topics, but within a specific time frame. Dedicated algorithms have been also used that measure different variables to spot influencers for a particular product [22]. In addition, it is equally important to recognize how influencer actions and traits are perceived by others. For this reason, a technique was developed to identify the perceived attributes of social media influencers and assist organizations to improve their social media presence [20].

To the authors' best knowledge, there is very little research concerning social media influencers for cultural heritage. A 2012 study [24] revealed a gap in the use of technology and public outreach between high and popular culture. From their definitions, high culture is considered to be of great esteem by sophisticated or higher educated people, while popular culture is referred - as a term - to art that interests the general masses. As such, it seems that popular culture reaches social media users better, whereas high culture is behind in the use of new technologies. In this light, systematic use of technology and social media for high culture is still limited and as a result, the present work, wishes to be among the first to explore the field of influencers in culture and important cultural conversations in social media. Therefore, the current work focuses on identification of the type of personality of the Cultural Influencer.

Finally, the innovation and the importance of the present work lays in the empowerment of the cultural institution in playing an active role in influencing the cultural discussions and trends, identifying individuals and tendencies that can significantly affect and shift the focus of cultural attention, thus making them play a targeted active role in cultural technology and social networks.

3   Research Methodology

The experimental procedure is initiated after a visit in the Archaeological Museum of Tripolis (Greece); visitors were asked to participate in discussions on a Google document, in order to ensure collaboration, as well as Facebook discussions in order to retrieve influencer-related actions. Participants could choose between different discussion topics, all relevant to their museum visit including:

- "Nudity in antiquity and today". During their museum experience, visitors had learnt about the symbolism of the naked body in antiquity.
- "Appearance as a comedy element in Classic Greek cinema", a topic relevant to the museum information they had accessed about appearance of statues.
- "Comparing images", where participants had to compare two images of women from Sicily. The first images showed young Romans wearing bikinis and playing a ball game. This was a mosaic from Villa Romana del Casale di Piazza Armerina (Sicily - 4c AD) [30]. The other image, showed contemporary nuns in Sicily. In another discussion about image comparison, images of ex votos were used from Christian contemporary churches (Catholic, Orthodox) and ancient ones from archaeological museums. The conversation is presented in Fig. 1.

The conversation presented in Fig. 1 is performed in Greek language and some of its "influencing parts" include the following conversation/facts:

- arguing about the assumption that the less science can help the more a superior power is activated and the fact that human beings rely on "transactions" with the superior power only when they are desperate
- conversation about game populous (the player had the role of gad) and reactions of what it reminds
- long, engaging, and provocative conversation about existence of special body parts in the ex votos and what could be their meaning

The discussion topics were carefully selected with the help of humanities experts, in order to initiate conversations where the participant would have the ability to support totally different opinions on the same issue and find followers, supporters and people with different or opposed opinion. The issues are totally related to personal opinions and both the positive or negative opinions on the topics can find huge fans or enemies. This particularity enables more vivid conversations and enhances participation as they are intriguing. Participants were given one (1) week to complete their discussions; and after they completed their discussions, participants were asked to complete a personality test. While the conversations on social media can last more or less "forever" we selected a period of time (seven days after the initialization of the conversation) in order to collect the information up to this time.

Fig. 1. Facebook conversations

3.1 Personality Test

In order to understand the characteristics of people, information about participants' personalities was collected. The DiSC personality test was applied [25], which identifies 4 main personality dimensions:

- Dominance: How people handle situations and cope with problems
- Influence: Describes how people communicate, interact and relate to other people
- Steadiness: Includes aspects like perseverance, consideration for others and their problems, patience etc. that comprise one's individual temperament
- Compliance: How people approach and arrange their activity, procedures and responsibility

DISC is used to improve work productivity [27], teamwork [29] and communication [26], since it shows how people relate to others and to tasks. In addition, past research has used DiSC in predicting the formation of ultimate groups, task performance and members' satisfaction and positive emotions [28]. Therefore, it was also used in our experimental procedure in order to predict people's personality characteristics, as these will emerge through cultural conversations. Each participant in the conversations was provided with an online form including the DiSC personality test in which each one had to answer a series of questions and was kindly asked to submit the results of the tests. A sample result of the disc personality test is depicted in Fig. 2.

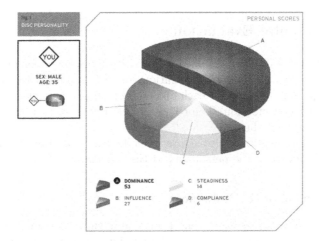

Fig. 2. DISC personality sample answer

As already mentioned the public conversations can provide us with important information about which user acts as an influencer but in the end what is really important is the actual personality of the user.

3.2   Reflection Analysis

Reflection analysis allowed the "in depth" qualitative viewing of the collected data. The number of times reflections occur, as well as types of the reflections are recorded and reported.

For the reflection analysis, the Soren [15] taxonomy of cognitive changes in dealing with cultural content, was used. Visitors described these changes in five ways:

– opportunity to have experiences with authentic objects
– unexpected experience and/or highly emotional experiences
– new attitudinal/cultural understanding
– motivation to become more proactive
– idea of infinity/lasting phenomena (how certain phenomena are relevant to people of different societies and times)

In addition, the Bloom taxonomy and its revised version was also used [16,17]; [18], since reflection could be also treated as an upper level learning process [19]. In particular, the taxonomy describes 6 levels for high-level cognitive processes like memory, understanding/comprehension, application of knowledge, analysis, evaluation, and creativity. These processes are also hierarchically structured from lower (memory) to higher (creativity). Thus, using the two taxonomies (i.e. Soren's, Bloom's), the collected data were qualitatively analysed to reveal their reflection potential.

4   Experimental Evaluation

The experimental procedure included a live visit at the Archaeological Museum of Tripolis, followed by online conversations on topics related to the visit and also a DISC personality test for each of the research participants. Furthermore, analysis on the conversations helped us obtain information about reflections generated throughout the text.

From the aforementioned procedure we collected data in order to study our main research question: the personality of the influencer.

4.1   Personality of the Influencer

In order to establish the users that act as influencers, we primarily identify the influencing discussions/comments. Discussing on social media, influencing comments are texts that have a significant number of (sub)comments, followed by large number of reactions, such as likes and emoticons (emojis). Furthermore, we collect information regarding the personality of the participants in order to study possible correlations between users' personality and influencing texts. Table 1 presents the results of the DISC personality test for the participants that accepted to participate in the personality assessment.

Table 1. Personalities of participants

Dominant	Influencing	Steady	Compliant
5	10	7	2

In addition to locating influential discussions and identify participants' personalities, the algorithm described in [14] was also applied, to find "bonds" between users. This would allow the recognition of influencing people among the participants in the conversation, even before the conversation analysis. According to [14], there is a tendency, in social network users, for higher responsiveness in recommendations made by the friends having the highest *tie strength* with them (or, recommendations that are based on those friends' data, as long as this fact is communicated along with the recommendation). Tie strength is a directed measure and its calculation is based on the number of posts made on the social network within a time frame. More specifically, the tie strength between two users i and j is computed as:

$$W_{i,j} = \frac{C_{i,j}}{C_i} \tag{1}$$

where C_i represents the number of social media articles (either "original" ones or reactions/comments to other articles) posted by user i within a time period, and $C_{i,j}$ represents the number of posts made by user i within the same time period and are either aimed at user j (i.e. user j is explicitly mentioned in the recipient list of the post) or constitute reactions to posts made by user j.

According to the previous, we are able to find strong bonds between users and in that way recognize influencing persons between the participants. The outcomes of the process proved that it seems that some reactions in the conversations are related to strong bonds (a person always reacts - likes - the posts of another person).

Having the knowledge of the participants, their personality, the connection between them, the conversations and the reactions within each conversation we are, finally, able to locate influencing texts and make the interconnection with the corresponding personality. Figure 3 presents examples of typical texts that are considered to be influential.

Fig. 3. Influencing texts

We assume that the people that either initiated a conversation or a thread (a comment in a conversation) that included the characteristics described above (likes, comments, user reactions, reflections etc.) can be considered as influential individuals. We furthermore connected the influencing texts with the personality of the people that produced to the text. Results are present in the following table.

From the above analysis, it seems that it not only people with high Influence personality traits that produce interesting and influential discussions but is also people with mixed types that combine Influence and Dominance (Table 2).

Table 2. Number of interesting texts based on personality

Personality	# of interesting texts	# of people
Influencing only	3	2
Dominant only	2	2
Steady only	2	2
Influencing & dominant	12	4

5   Discussion

Performing the DiSC personality test on the participants we concluded that leading personalities high in Dominance or Influence are not by themselves adequate to influence cultural discussions. Our study revealed that the most influential individuals are the ones of a mixed type of leading traits that combine Dominance with Influence. However, the present work focused on the study of qualitative data and as such the sample size was limited. In addition, all data came from Greek participants and a cultural bias might be affecting the results. Nevertheless, the present work revealed the importance of the personality of the participant in cultural discussions in social media. The exact characteristics of the influencing personalities remain to be studied with a larger and international group. Future works should focus on more cultural discussions and collect data from various participants of different cultural backgrounds.

In addition, it was observed that in cultural discussions, background knowledge on the subject is very important. In this light, it is now only the personality characteristics of the person but also the knowledge on the subject that matter. It seems that an influencer combines both background knowledge and specific personality traits. The two combined seem necessary to produce interesting and influential discussions. At this point it is important to note that is the perceived background knowledge that seems important which might differ from actual knowledge. In other words, it is not what you know but what others think you know. Perceptions of background knowledge together with specific personality characteristics, in this case high Dominance and Influence, seem to create the necessary environment for an influential cultural discussion.

Furthermore, it is possible to relate conversations with strong reflections to influencing people, which, combined with the previous discussion leads to the fact that people that are able to generate emotions through their saying or writing can easily become influencers in cultural related conversations.

6   Conclusions and Future Work

Possible cultural biases might have affected our results as explained above, due to the nature of the work and the background of the participants. Our future work will analyse cultural discussions from people of different cultural backgrounds.

In addition, we will proceed with manipulation of the discussion team composition. In other words, we will ask people of only leader personalities (Dominance, Influence) or people of non-leader personalities (Steadiness, Compliance) to participate. Chatbots can be included in the formation of the teams, programmed in a way that mimics certain personality types, while in parallel researchers can possibly intervene in the conversations in order to provide evidence about manipulation of a cultural related conversation. This manipulation will allow us to study discussions of teams with different compositions of personalities. Once the personality traits that affect cultural discussions are clearly identified, cultural institutions can ask curators of certain personality traits to participate, or do it in an automated manner with the use of specially programmed chatbots. Moreover, we will proceed in the creation of specific guidelines to be followed by cultural institutions that wish to increase their impact on social media through reflection enhancement.

Finally, our future works includes application of the outcomes of our experimental procedures to real life organizations and more precisely cultural institutions. More specifically, a platform is implemented that can identify topics that are related to the cultural institution's context and are in parallel "hot" or "trending" topics. By establishing them we try to apply advertising principles by intervening texts with reflection within relevant conversations and we measure the affection on the discussion and the engagement of people. The latter can be of extreme importance for the public awareness towards cultural heritage related issues, as well as the increase of the engagement of more people to cultural spaces.

Acknowledgment. This work has been partially funded by the project CrossCult: "Empowering reuse of digital cultural heritage in context-aware crosscuts of European history", funded by the European Union's Horizon 2020 research and innovation program, Grant#693150.

References

1. Falk, J.H., Dierking, L.D.: The Museum Experience Revisited. Left Coast Press, Walnut Creek, 416 p. (2013). ISBN 978-1-61132-044-2
2. Maslow, A.H.: A theory of human motivation. Psychol. Rev. **50**(4), 370–396 (1943)
3. Duncan, S., Barrett, L.F.: Affect is a form of cognition: a neurobiological analysis. Cogn. Emot. **21**(6), 1184–1211 (2007). https://doi.org/10.1080/02699930701437931
4. Harmon-Jones, E., Gable, P.A., Price, T.F.: Does negative affect always narrow and positive affect always broaden the mind? Considering the influence of motivational intensity on cognitive scope. Curr. Dir. Psychol. Sci. **22**(4), 301–307 (2013)
5. Harmon-Jones, E., Harmon-Jones, C., Amodio, D.M., Gable, P.A.: Attitudes toward emotions. J. Pers. Soc. Psychol. **101**(6), 1332 (2011)
6. Sheng, C.W., Chen, M.C.: A study of experience expectations of museum visitors. Tour. Manag. **33**(1), 53–60 (2012)
7. Economou, M., Meintani, E.: Promising beginning? Evaluating museum mobile phone apps (2011)

8. Kietzmann, J.H., Hermkens, K., McCarthy, I.P., Silvestre, B.S.: Social media? Get serious! Understanding the functional building blocks of social media. Bus. Horiz. **54**(3), 241–251 (2011)

9. Panahi, S., Watson, J., Partridge, H.: Social media and tacit knowledge sharing: developing a conceptual model. World Acad. Sci. Eng. Technol. **64**, 1095–1102 (2012)

10. Morris, M.R., Teevan, J., Panovich, K.: What do people ask their social networks, and why?: a survey study of status message Q&A behavior. In: Proceedings of the SIGCHI Conference on Human Factors in Computing Systems, pp. 1739–1748. ACM, April 2010

11. Trusov, M., Bodapati, A.V., Bucklin, R.E.: Determining influential users in internet social networks. J. Mark. Res. **47**(4), 643–658 (2010)

12. Gnambs, T., Batinic, B.: A personality-competence model of opinion leadership. Psychol. Mark. **29**(8), 606–621 (2012)

13. Bakshy, E., Hofman, J.M., Mason, W.A., Watts, D.J.: Everyone's an influencer: quantifying influence on twitter. In: Proceedings of the Fourth ACM International Conference on Web Search and Data Mining, pp. 65–74. ACM, February 2011

14. Bakshy, E., Eckles, D., Yan, R., Rosenn, I.: Social influence in social advertising: evidence from field experiments. In: Proceedings of the 13th ACM Conference on Electronic Commerce, pp. 146–161 (2012)

15. Soren, B.J.: Museum experiences that change visitors. Mus. Manag. Curatorship **24**(3), 233–251 (2009)

16. Anderson, L.W., et al.: A Taxonomy for Learning, Teaching and Assessing: A Revision of Bloom's Taxonomy. Longman Publishing, New York (2001)

17. Artz, A.F., Armour-Thomas, E.: Development of a cognitive-metacognitive framework for protocol analysis of mathematical problem solving in small groups. Cognit. Instr. **9**(2), 137–175 (1992)

18. Bloom, B.S., Engelhart, M.D., Furst, E.J., Hill, W.H., Krathwohl, D.R.: Taxonomy of Educational Objectives, Handbook I: The Cognitive Domain, vol. 19, p. 56. David McKay Co Inc., New York (1956)

19. Daudelin, M.W.: Learning from experience through reflection. Organ. Dyn. **24**(3), 36–48 (1997)

20. Freberg, K., Graham, K., McGaughey, K., Freberg, L.A.: Who are the social media influencers? A study of public perceptions of personality. Public Relat. Rev. **37**(1), 90–92 (2011)

21. Peng, W., Sun, T.: U.S. Patent 8,312,056. U.S. Patent and Trademark Office, Washington, D.C. (2012)

22. Booth, N., Matic, J.A.: Mapping and leveraging influencers in social media to shape corporate brand perceptions. Corp. Commun.: Int. J. **16**(3), 184–191 (2011)

23. Fan, W., Gordon, M.D.: The power of social media analytics. Commun. ACM **57**(6), 74–81 (2014)

24. Colbert, F., Courchesne, A.: Critical issues in the marketing of cultural goods: the decisive influence of cultural transmission. City Cult. Soc. **3**(4), 275–280 (2012)

25. Scullard, M., Baum, D.: Everything DiSC Manual. Wiley, London (2015)

26. Sugerman, J.: Using the DiSC® model to improve communication effectiveness. Ind. Commer. Train. **41**(3), 151–154 (2009)

27. Krueger, D.: Characteristics of the female entrepreneur. J. Bus. Entrep. **12**(1), 87 (2000)

28. Lykourentzou, I., Antoniou, A., Naudet, Y., Dow, S.P.: Personality matters: balancing for personality types leads to better outcomes for crowd teams. In: Proceedings of the 19th ACM Conference on Computer-Supported Cooperative Work and Social Computing, pp. 260–273. ACM, February 2016

29. Lykourentzou, I., Naudet, Y., Vandenabeele, L.: Reflecting on European history with the help of technology: the CrossCult project. In: Proceedings of the 14th Eurographics Workshop on Graphics and Cultural Heritage, pp. 67–70. Eurographics Association, October 2016

30. Villa Romana Del Casale. http://www.villaromanadelcasale.it. Accessed Aug 2018

Study of Effectiveness of Treatment by Nanolime of the Altered Calcarenite Stones of the Archeological Site of Volubilis Site (Morocco)

Dalal Badreddine[1,2(✉)], Kévin Beck[1], Xavier Brunetaud[1], Ali Chaaba[2], and Muzahim Al-Mukhtar[1]

[1] LAME Laboratory, University of Orleans, 8 rue Léonard de Vinci, 45072 Orléans, France
dalal.badreddine@etu.univ-orleans.fr
[2] ENSAM Meknès, University of Moulay Ismail, Marjane II – Ismailia BP 15290 Al Mansour, Meknes, Morocco

Abstract. Volubilis is the major archaeological site of North Africa, built in the 3rd century B.C. Unfortunately, the city, classified as a UNESCO world heritage, is affected by several forms of degradation that threaten its sustainability and durability. The main stone of the site, the calcarenite stone, shows many deterioration patterns (sanding, scaling and alveolization) that require immediate interventions of consolidation. In this paper, we subjected stone samples to artificial aging to simulate actual alteration. Then, degraded samples have been treated with commercial nanolime (CaloSil). Nanolime treatment proved to be efficient to recover most of the damage resulting from artificial aging, but also generated a change in color. Using a less concentrated nanolime could limit the aesthetic impact of the treatment.

Keywords: Artificial aging · Nanolime · Consolidant · Volubilis

1 Introduction

Volubilis is the largest archaeological site in North Africa, inscribed on the World Heritage List since 1997 [1]. It is located about thirty kilometers north of Meknes in Morocco (Fig. 1) and is built on the slopes of the Zerhoun massif, on an area of 42 hectares, on the edge of a vast plain.

It was founded in the 3rd century BC by the Mauritanian kingdom, then became an important outpost of the Roman Empire and one of the richest sites of its time in North Africa. During this period, the site reached its maximum expansion with the construction of several notable public monuments. At the fall of the Roman empire, the city was abandoned and then conquered by the Arabs in the 7th century. Idris the 1st, founder of the first Moroccan dynasty, settled there before choosing the city of Fes as capital.

In 1915, archaeological excavations and restoration of the site began [2], discovering more than 20 hectares of the city [3]. The site contains a monumental center,

M. Ioannides et al. (Eds.): EuroMed 2018, LNCS 11196, pp. 248–258, 2018.
https://doi.org/10.1007/978-3-030-01762-0_21

Fig. 1. Geographical situation of the archaeological site of Volubilis

which gathers great public and administrative monuments (the Capitol, the Basilica, the Triumphal Arch and the Forum), a district surrounding the Triumphal Arch and two residential districts (in the north-west and the south) in which we found prestigious houses like the house of Venus. Furthermore, the entire western part of the site has not been searched yet.

Unfortunately, the site is in an advanced state of degradation. An in-situ survey revealed many deterioration patterns, especially on the main stone used that is the calcarenite stone. Based on the glossary illustrated figures of alterations of the stone produced by ICOMOS [4], the main alterations found on the site are:

- Biological colonizations (lichens): it forms colored overlays on the stone surfaces and produces acids that can react with the calcite in limestone (Fig. 2).
- Detachments and losses of material (Figs. 3, 4 and 5): these alterations are manifested in the form of sanding that induces a detachment of the stone grains, alveolization and scaling.

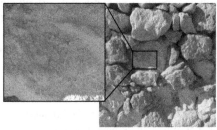

Fig. 2. Biological colonizations (Color figure online)

Fig. 3. Sanding

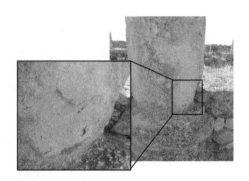

Fig. 4. Alveolization   **Fig. 5.** Scaling

The three latter patterns are very damaging as they induce a loss of calcarenite material. Calcarenite stone has undergone more than 2000 years of exposure to aggressive environmental conditions. In addition to natural factors (wind, temperature variation, rain…), anthropogenic factors (pollution, vibrations, vandalism …) accentuate its deterioration and degradation. Moreover, incompatible previous restoration works led to the transfer of destructive salts (gypsum and halite) into the stone [5]. While it is easier to replace some of the deteriorated stones with new fresh ones retrieved from quarries close to the site, some parts are very hard to replace: either due to the inaccessibility of the said-stones, or to the impact this replacement would have on the monument's authenticity and especially for the carved parts (like capitals and columns). These critically weakened parts need to be treated in situ, by using consolidating methods and materials that needs to be efficient, compatible and durable.

In the past, the use of organic consolidants such as alkoxysilanes, acrylics and epoxy resins was very common in restoration treatments. However, it was proved to have low chemical compatibility with the calcareous stones, and a low durability, which may cause more degradation of the stones [6, 7]. Other types of consolidant used are inorganic consolidants, like the traditional lime water. While it is more compatible with calcareous stones, it is not very efficient as it ensures a weak penetration depth of the lime particles. Due to the low solubility of calcium hydroxide in water (1.7 g/L), many successive applications are necessary to achieve a real consolidation, which may enhance the transfer of destructive salts into the stones [6–8].

In the past decade, alcohol dispersions of calcium hydroxide commonly known as nanolime, were introduced in cultural heritage conservation as an alternative to the traditional consolidants. It consists of very small particles of $Ca(OH)_2$, with an average diameter of 150 nm, suspended in alcohol (ethanol, isopropanol and n-propanol) [9]. So far, nanolimes have been tested on mural paintings, renders and porous building materials. When a substrate is treated with nanolime, calcium hydroxide is precipitated in the pores of calcareous materials as the alcohol evaporates. After carbonation, it replaces the lost binder or matrix in natural stone recovering the superficial cohesion of the substrate. The nanolime has the advantage of being compatible with calcareous stones and more efficient, as the small particle size of nanolime allows greater penetration into the pores and the higher surface area/volume ratio allows for greater reactivity [9].

In addition to mural paintings and renders [10, 11], nanolime treatments have proven to be efficient for the pre-consolidation and recovery of the superficial cohesion of building materials like Maastricht stones [12–14] and lime based mortars [14] which are a highly porous materials. For this study, we considered the nanolime as a consolidation treatment of altered calcarenite stones. The calcarenite stone is very heterogeneous and has a low porosity that varies from 14% to 26%, it requires a different treatment protocol. In fact, the efficiency of a nanolime treatment depends on the protocol of application, that should be developed based on the physical-chemical characteristics of the material [6].

In this paper, we reproduced the alterations observed in situ by subjecting stone specimens to different accelerated aging protocols. After that, the degraded samples have been treated with nanolime. The efficiency of the protocol used in this study was assessed by non-destructive laboratory tests: surface hardness test to assess the superficial cohesion and colometric measurements.

2   Materials

2.1   Calcarenite Stone

Calcarenite stone, also called «molassa», is a beige-yellowish calcarenite limestone rich in terrigenous material and large bioclasts [3]. It contains mostly calcite (86%) and quartz (13%) [5], and represents over 60% of the volume of the building stones used on the site of Volubilis. It was used in most of the site's monuments, as a rubble of masonry, in columns and in some architectural elements.

Due to its apparent heterogeneity, we differentiate 3 litho-facies of the calcarenite stone with different physical, hydraulic and mechanical properties [15] (Fig. 6 and Table 1).

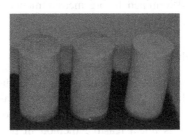

Fig. 6. The three facies of the calcarenite stone: yellow (left) intermediate (middle) and white (right) (Color figure online)

Table 1. Calcarenite stone properties

	Porosity (%)	Capillary water absorbtion coef ($Kg/m^2/h^{0.5}$)	Ultrasonic velocity (m/s)	Surface hardness (HDL)
White calcarenite	15 ± 1	0.59	2178 ± 205	381 ± 31
Intermediate	19 ± 2	2.03	2751 ± 501	378 ± 39
Yellow calcarenite	26 ± 4	3.72	2936 ± 130	296 ± 10

For this study, calcarenite specimens (4 × 4 × 4 cm) were drilled from sound blocks extracted from the main original quarry at Ain Schkor.

2.2   Treatment Product

We used for this study the commercial nanolime CaloSil E50, developed by IBZ-Salzchemie GmbH & Co for consolidating calcareous historic materials. The product contains $Ca(OH)_2$ particles dispersed in ethanol with a concentration of 50 g/l. The particle size ranges from 50 to 150 nm.

3   Methods

3.1   Accelerated Aging Test

Three aging tests were used:

- Thermal shock aging test: specimens of the intermediate litho-facies of the calcarenite stone were subjected to successive cycles of drying and immersion in water. Each cycle consists of drying the samples in an oven for 18 h at a temperature of 250 °C followed immediately by immersion in water at $T \sim 0$ °C for 6 h.
- Freeze-thaw cycles: specimens of the intermediate litho-facies of the calcarenite stone were saturated with water and then placed in a freezing chamber at −18 °C for 24 h. Afterwards the samples were immersed in water at 20 °C for 6 h.
- Salt crystallisation tests were carried out on specimens of all three lithofacies of the calcarenite stone. Cubic specimens (4 × 4 × 4 cm) underwent successive cycles where they are immersed in a 14% solution of Na_2SO_4 for 2 h and then dried in an oven at 105 °C for 22 h, according to the norm NF EN 12370 [16]. The weight of each test sample was determined before measurements, and after each cycle, the resulting weight loss was determined.

3.2   Application Procedure

One crucial aspect for the success of consolidation is the application procedure. For this study the product was applied by brushing to reproduce actual treatment in situ. In fact, while the application of a consolidant by capillary absorption is widely used as standard laboratory method, it is not a feasible method in practice. In situ application usually involves methods such as brushing, injection, spray, pouring [12–17].

The nanolime treatment was applied three times to the altered stones. Due to the low porosity of the stone used (17%), a higher number of applications would not be as effective as the pores would be very quickly filled with $Ca(OH)_2$ particles especially with the highly concentrated CaLoSiL E50. We waited 3 h between two successive applications. This time was measured in a preliminary test as the time required for the evaporation of the ethanol. The specimens were then placed in a climatic chamber with controlled temperature and humidity (20 °C/76% HR) to enhance the carbonation process.

The tests for the assessment of the effectiveness of the treatment were done after 28 days.

4   Results and Discussion

4.1   Accelerated Aging Test

The first two aging tests were very destructive to the calcarenite stone. After only two cycles of each of the protocols, the stone specimens cracked (Fig. 7). On some samples, the cracks are light and extend only on one side. For the rest the cracks are larger and affect two faces. Unfortunately, we could not reproduce the alterations observed on the site with these two protocols.

Fig. 7. Fissurated calcarenite specimens (4 × 4 × 4 cm) after thermal shock and freeze-thraw aging tests

For salt crystallization aging protocol, the test was done twice. In the first time, after 14 cycles the specimens were in an advanced state of degradation and were too weak to be treated (Fig. 8).

Fig. 8. Altered calcarenite specimens (4 × 4 × 4 cm) after 14 cycles of the salt cristalization aging test

The second time, we stopped the test after 7 cycles when visible alteration by the loss of material started appearing especially on the yellow and intermediate lithofacies (Fig. 9). The average mass variations of the samples of the three facies during the test are presented in Fig. 10.

During the first three cycles of the test, the dry mass of the samples increases due to the precipitation of salt in the pores. The dry mass decreases after the fourth cycle for the yellow facies and the fifth for the intermediate facies, in contrast to the white facies whose mass increases slightly but continuously until the end of the test. The white facies stays completely unaltered, even with 14 cycles of the salt crystallization test.

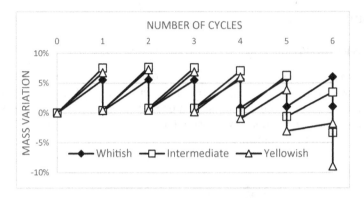

Fig. 9. Average mass variation of the three facies during the salt crystallization test

The yellow and intermediate were altered in a similar way as in situ. On the yellow facies sanding has been observed (Fig. 11), whereas on the intermediate it is rather an alveolization as the yellow parts got altered while the white parts remained intact (Fig. 11). In this study, we focused only on the samples altered by the salt crystallization aging test.

Fig. 10. Calcarenite specimens (4 × 4 × 4 cm) before salt crystallization test: white (left), intermediate (middle) and yellow (right) (Color figure online)

Fig. 11. Calcarenite specimens (4 × 4 × 4 cm) after salt crystallization test : white (left), intermediate (middle) and yellow (right) (Color figure online)

4.2   Treatement with Nanolime

All the faces of the calcarenite specimen studied were treated with nanolime as they were all affected by loss of material. We measured the weight of the samples before and after each application as well as the quantity of nanolime absorbed (Fig. 12).

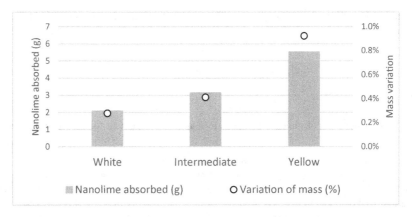

Fig. 12. Variation of mass of calcarenite specimens after treatment and quantity of nanolime absorbed

The variation of mass is due to the precipitation of calcium hydroxide particles in the porosity of the specimens. This variation is proportional to the quantity of nanolime absorbed by the stone during the treatment and to the porosity of the facies treated. The fact that the white calcarenite absorbs less product is not a problem since it is the least altered facies of the calcarenite stone.

The efficiency of the treatment was assessed by two laboratory tests: surface hardness and colorimetry; The surface hardness of the calcarenite facies was measured using a Piccolo 2 durometer. Ten measurements were taken at 10 different points of each pair of parallel faces and then averaged.

Table 2. Values of surface hardness before and after treatment

	Sound specimens	Before treatment	After treatment	Δ
White calcarenite	381 ± 31	342 ± 21	372 ± 2	9%
Intermediate	378 ± 39	358 ± 51	387 ± 46	9%
Yellow calcarenite	296 ± 10	262 ± 36	297 ± 42	13%

The Table 2 represent the evolution of the average of the surface hardness in the samples treated (before and after treatment with the nanolime). It is noted that yellow calcarenite samples have a lower hardness compared to white calcarenite. After treatment, the surface hardness of all samples increases. The increase is more important for the yellow calcarenite and reaches 13% compared to the white and intermediate calcarenite that only achieve an increase of 9%.

The colorimetric values were expressed in the CIE space L*a*b*, where L* is the brightness/darkness coordinate, a* the red/green coordinate (+a indicates the red and −a green), and b* is the yellow coordinate/blue (+b indicating yellow and

−b blue). The color change on the surface (ΔE) was calculated using the following equation:

$$\Delta E = \left((\Delta L)^2 + (\Delta a)^2 + (\Delta b)^2 \right)^{1/2}$$

Table 3. Values of colorimetric values before and after treatment for the three lithofacies

	L*			a*			b*			ΔE
	Before treatment	After treatment	Δ	Before treatment	After treatment	Δ	Before treatment	After treatment	Δ	
White	83.37	86.86	4%	2.81	3.76	34%	13.98	9.33	−33%	5.938
Intermediate	73.65	80.18	9%	4.56	2.76	−39%	19.18	9.04	−53%	12.193
Yellow	69.72	74.31	11%	7.33	3.76	−49%	23.54	9.33	−60%	16.273

As can be seen from Table 3, all specimens demonstrated an overall colour change (ΔE). The color change is proportional to the porosity of the samples and is greater that 5 for all three lithofacies, which represents a risk of aesthetic incompatibility [18]. For all the specimens, we noticed a small increase in the L* value which implies a lightening of the samples. The increase is proportional to the porosity of the samples and is due to white deposits on the surface of the stones which means that part of the nanolime absorbed is carbonated in the surface (Fig. 13). This could be resolved by reducing the concentration of the product used, or by preventing the quick evaporation of the ethanol.

Fig. 13. Calcarenite specimens (4 × 4 × 4 cm) before (left) and after (right) treatment with nanolime (Color figure online)

When compared to the values of surface hardness of unaltered calcarenite specimen we can say that the treatment by nanolime is efficient, it replaces the lost binder in the stone and increases the surface hardness that has decreased after the accelerated aging tests. However, the white coloration observed on the surface can be a problem as it is not acceptable in conservation interventions [19].

5 Conclusion and Perspectives

This paper presented the results of a study to determine the effect of the use of nanolime to consolidate the altered calcarenite stones in the archeological site of Volubilis in Morocco. The main alterations observed at the site induce a loss of calcarenite material (sanding, scaling and alveolization). To test the consolidation efficiency of nanolime, we reproduced these patterns of alteration in the laboratory, by subjecting calcarenite specimens to artificial aging tests.

With salt crystallization aging test, we could reproduce two of the three patterns: alveolization and sanding. These specimens were then treated with a commercial nanolime CaloSil E50. Results show that the treatment is efficient as it increases the superficial cohesion of the altered stone, which increases its surface hardness. From an aesthetic point of view, the treatment leaves a white haze that is usually not accepted in conservation intervention. As perspective, another nanolime product with low concentration can be tested to see if it would mitigate the change of color of subtract.

References

1. UNESCO, Inscription: site archéologique de Volubilis, Maroc (1997). http://whc.unesco.org/archive/1997/whc-97-conf208-17f.pdf
2. Al-Mukhtar, M., et al.: Preservation and valorisation of Morocco's ancient heritage: Volubilis. In: Ioannides, M., Fink, E., Moropoulou, A., Hagedorn-Saupe, M., Fresa, A., Liestøl, G., Rajcic, V., Grussenmeyer, P. (eds.) EuroMed 2016. LNCS, vol. 10059, pp. 160–167. Springer, Cham (2016). https://doi.org/10.1007/978-3-319-48974-2_18
3. Dessandier, D., et al.: Atlas of the ornamental and building stones of Volubilis ancient site (Morocco). In: BRGM (2008)
4. ICOMOS-ISCS, Illustrated glossary on stone deterioration patterns, https://www.icomos.org/publications/monuments_and_sites/15/pdf/Monuments_and_Sites_15_ISCS_Glossary_Stone.pdf (2010)
5. Aalil, I., Beck, K., Brunetaud, X., Cherkaoui, K., Chaaba, M., Al Mukhtar, M.: Deterioration analysis of building calcarenite stone in the House of Venus in the archaeological site of Volubilis (Morocco). Constr. Build. Mater. **125**, 1127–1141 (2016)
6. Borsoi, G., Lubelli, B., Van Hees, R., Veiga, R., Santos Silva, A.: Understanding the transport of nanolime consolidants within Maastricht limestone. J. Cult. Herit. **18**, 242–249 (2016)
7. Ferreira Pinto, A.P., Delgado, R.J.: Stone consolidation: the role of treatment procedures. J. Cult. Herit. **9**, 38–53 (2008)
8. Hansen, E., et al.: A review of selected inorganic consolidants and protective treatments for porous calcareous materials. Rev. Conserv. **4**, 13–25 (2003)
9. D'Armada, P., Hirst, E.: Nanolime for consolidation of plaster and stone. J. Archit. Conserv. **18**(1), 63–80 (2012)
10. Borsoi, G., Tavares, M., Veiga, R., Santos Silva, A.: Microstructural characterization of consolidant products for historical renders: an innovative nanostructured lime dispersion and a more traditional ethyl silicate limewater solution. Microsc. Microanal. **18**(5), 1181–1189 (2012)
11. Giorgi, R., Dei, L., Baglioni, P.: A new method for consolidating wall paintings based on dispersions of lime in alcohol. Stud. Conserv. **45**(3), 154–161 (2000)
12. Borsoi, G., Lubelli, B., Van Hees, R., Veiga, R., Santos Silva, A.: Application protocol for the consolidation of calcareous substrates by the use of nanolimes: from laboratory research to practice. Restor. Build. Monum. **22**, 99–109 (2017)
13. Slizkova, Z., Frankeova, D.: Consolidation of porous limestone with nanolime, laboratory study. In: 12th International Congress on the Deterioration and Conservation of Stone Columbia University, New York (2012)

14. Daehne, A., Herm, C.: Calcium hydroxide nanosols for the consolidation of porous building materials – results from EU-STONECORE. Herit. Sci. **1**, 11 (2013)
15. Aalil, I.: Contribution to the study of the built heritage: methods of diagnosis of the pathologies of structures and means of restoration. Case study: archeological site Volubilis in Morocco. Ph.D. thesis, University of Orleans (France) and University Moulay Ismail (Morocco) (2017)
16. NF EN 12370: Test methods for natural stones - Determination of resistance by salt crystallisation test (1999)
17. Doehne, E., Price, C.A.: Stone Conservation: An Overview of Current Research, 2nd edn. The Getty Institute, Los Angeles (2010)
18. Rodrigues, J.D., Grossi, A.: Indicators and ratings for the compatibility assessment of conservation actions. J. Cult. Herit. **8**, 32–43 (2007)
19. Niedoba, K., Slízková, Z., Frankeová, D., Lara Nunes, C., Jandejsek, I.: Modifying the consolidation depth of nanolime on Maastricht limestone. Constr. Build. Mater. **133**, 51–56 (2017)

3D Digitization, Reconstruction, Modelling and HBIM

Research and Communication of Urban History in 4D Using Historical Photographs – A Status Report of the Research Group UrbanHistory4D

Ferdinand Maiwald[1(✉)], Kristina Barthel[1], Jonas Bruschke[2],
Kristina Friedrichs[2], Cindy Kröber[1], Sander Münster[1], and Florian Niebling[2]

[1] TU Dresden, Media Center, Strehlener Straße 22/24, 01217 Dresden, Germany
ferdinand.maiwald@tu-dresden.de
[2] University of Würzburg, Human-Computer Interaction, Am Hubland,
97074 Würzburg, Germany

Abstract. This contribution shows the work of the junior research group UrbanHistory4D within one year. It explains the different technical and educational approaches when working with media repositories composed of diverse historical data. The group covers technical aspects like photogrammetry, information sciences and Augmented Reality (AR) as well as humanistic topics like history of art, user case and educational studies. In detail, different photogrammetric techniques, various image repositories, a user case study and possibilities of knowledge transfer are evaluated. The main focus in the first year was the development of two prototype applications – a 4D browser interface and an AR application – supported by the different fields of studies. These applications are still refined considering the results of the varying research topics. As an outcome the contribution presents a part of the project organization which plays an important role when working in such interdisciplinary groups.

Keywords: UrbanHistory4D · Junior research group
Historical images · Media repositories

1 Introduction

Historical images, plans and maps are the main source of research in the field of history of architecture [6,32,33,42]. These sources also form a central part in the field of digital humanities. As part of a still ongoing digitization a lot of this data has been stored in large digital repositories. Difficulties that arise with these new media storages are e.g. finding and identifying relevant and meaningful research data. Additionally, contextualizing, comparing and visualizing the data is still a difficult task for researchers. Not least because of the varying, sometimes inconsistent or even completely missing metadata [12].

The eHumanities junior research group UrbanHistory4D, supported by the German Federal Ministry of Education and Research (BMBF), focuses on

M. Ioannides et al. (Eds.): EuroMed 2018, LNCS 11196, pp. 261–270, 2018.
https://doi.org/10.1007/978-3-030-01762-0_22

research questions concerning building/city history as well as transfer of knowledge of the historical city of Dresden. The investigation and development of methodical and technological approaches that join vast repositories of historical media and their contextual information in a spatial and temporal four dimensional model is the main focus of the research group.

The data will be structured, annotated and presented to researchers as well as to the public in a 4D browser application. Another part of the research focuses on the development of an Augmented Reality (AR) tool as a base for information, a research tool and for the transfer of historical knowledge. The prototype database consists of approximately 230,000 digitalized historical images and plans of the historical city of Dresden.

2   Use of Technology and Results

In the following the technological approaches of the junior research group are presented. The research is structured in three different subchapters explaining photogrammetric, user access and knowledge transfer challenges. The forth subchapter shows the effects of the interdisciplinary group on project organization.

2.1   Using Photogrammetric Methods for the Analysis of Historical Image Data

To get a visual access to large image repositories different photogrammetric tools can be useful. They range from an automated sorting of images using context-based image retrieval (CBIR) through the temporal and spatial orientation of images in a virtual environment to the generation of complex historical 3D models.

The potential of historical images lies in the documentation of knowledge but also in the restauration of completely destroyed objects [11,15]. Oriented historical images can also give a yet unknown view of buildings and details that were not present by just using the two dimensional images and that can be visualized and explored in a 3D space. It is even possible that further details can be uncovered in that spatial context. Classical analytic photogrammetry has been supported by digital image analysis since approximately 20 years.

Additionally, the technologies get more and more automatized not least because of machine learning methods. Considering image repositories, a lot of photogrammetric approaches are used when working with recent photography [1,20,37,38]. But also single buildings (or single cities) are modeled using historical data [35,39]. Difficulties that arise when working with historical images are e.g. the missing information about camera, location and time stamp of the image. Image artifacts, huge radiometric image differences and a low scan resolution make a large impact on automatic photogrammetric multi-view stereo (MVS) reconstruction [2].

Thus, photogrammetric techniques have to be adapted to make it possible to work with historical images. Against this background the junior research

Fig. 1. Noisy "historical" point cloud generated only using historical images of the Crown Gate of the Dresden Zwinger.

group tries to customize the Structure from Motion (SfM) method. While this method is already highly developed when working with recent images it is still not possible to align historical images, i.e. images that are very individual and often have large differences in e.g. illumination.

Therefore, it is difficult to find matching points in two or more images with classical approaches like the Scale-Invariant Feature Transform (SIFT) [26]. Still, after testing a lot of different historical image sets combined with the orientation data of recent images using Agisoft PhotoScan, the creation of one single historical 3D model was possible [29] (see Fig. 1). Nonetheless, the junior research group wants to improve the algorithms so that not only a few images can be matched by chance. Ideas that we are currently working on are the matching of shapes and lines in historical images since in man-made environments a lot of these structured objects are visible and likely to be matched [16,24,28]. A first approach has shown the possibility to match quadrilaterals in historical images [41] (see Fig. 2). In a next step those could be useful for the creation of simple historical wireframe models when only few historical images are available [19].

Another topic the project addresses is the calculation of an exterior orientation, i.e. the spatial location of the photographer (camera) in space. Thereby, we use a simple model (LOD2) of the city of Dresden, look for homologue points in model and image, and calculate the approximate position with the direct linear transformation (DLT). Finding similar points in model and images is a difficult task that is not yet completely solved by algorithms. When the approximate camera parameters are known for some images it is planned to use a bundle adjustment to get accurate coordinates.

Fig. 2. Matches between two historical images showing building facades. Homologue points in the two images were matched using quadrilaterals.

2.2   Usage and Access of Image Repositories in the Field of Research in the History of Architecture

Digital repositories fulfill very diverse purposes in the humanities as well as in a frame of museum or touristic transfer. Even aspects in the field of information sciences are important topics [30]. The technical possibilities in these repositories allow art and architectural historians to use a clearly larger amount of data for their research. One important result of the first year of the junior research group is a broad list of existing image repositories and their score in regard of the demand of the work of architecture historians. It is often necessary for scientists to compare and spatialize their sources [3] and also to understand the relation of image source and the presented image [31].

With a user's perspective on image repositories the success of the searching process depends on the knowledge of the user and the usability of the web platform [21]. Users put emphasis on e.g. efficient search and filtering algorithms as well as an intuitive graphical user interface (GUI) and the general navigation on the website [3]. Depending on the group of users a documentation with metadata [4,27] or a basic introduction into the topics and information is requested. In empirical studies the junior research group interviewed 15 students on topics like the search and usage of images. In the following, these interviews were evaluated analytically.

The results showed that the searching process is essentially influenced not only by the presented image contents but also by corresponding textual descriptions and suggestions/links pointing to further resources [5]. The searching strategy changes during the searching process from (a) an undirected browsing through (b) an examination of the inventory for the purpose of a broad overview to (c) the target-oriented search for specific contents and topics. These insights were the basis for the conception and prototypic development of a 4D browser interface intended for the temporal and spatial search in media repositories (see Fig. 3), which is a remarkable challenge [14]. A quite challenging task in the first phase was the semantic connection of data and, for the visualization temporally and spatially presented information. Consequently, the browser application has to display a complete and complex city model that varies over time including images and metadata. With a view to further developments the junior research group wants to test strategies of presenting a large amount of datatypes [34], different application programming interfaces (API) and possibilities to let users interact with the depicted information (see Fig. 4).

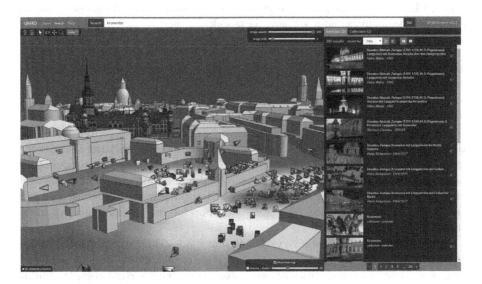

Fig. 3. Prototype application showing the 4D browser with different models of the city municipality (LOD1, LOD2) and images of the city of Dresden.

2.3   Knowledge Transfer of City History Using Augmented Reality (AR)

A spatial and temporal placement inside a three dimensional city model as well as in a AR application is the main focus of the junior research group. The focus lies on a transfer of knowledge of the history of the city for research as well as for the public. For the city of Dresden this could be e.g. the destruction of almost

Fig. 4. Closer look on the prototype showing thumbnails of oriented historical images, interaction possibilities and a low level 3d model.

all historical buildings in World War II and the following reconstruction with its particular design choices.

In the last years various AR applications which are used in urban space have been developed around the world [22,36,43]. Research describes the user requirements of touristic AR applications [17,44], their user acceptance [10,18], their educational potential [23] as well as the potential of sensitizing the user for the aspects of the history of culture [7]. Compared to this, only few works bother with the educational effects on the user [9]. Research on integration of pedagogic and motivational strategies in educational AR applications and deduced design choices is still missing. The junior research group intends to close this gap in its studies.

From a technological point of view different modes of interaction with data of historical sciences have been tested and proved [7,8,25,40,45]. Important questions are: How can possibilities of user interactions with virtual complex buildings and their associated information be designed? Is it possible to use common user interactions with a mobile phone in an AR application? Furthermore, the junior research group analyzed and categorized mobile AR applications for the transfer of knowledge with a view on the design choices. In a next step this shall be the basis for an AR application prototype (see Fig. 5).

2.4 Effects on Project Organization

Considering the described areas of research, a lot of different people from diverse backgrounds are working together in the context of the project. These topics have to come together when aiming at a joint project goal. Therefore, a shared

Fig. 5. Augmented reality visualization in an urban environment (mockup).

vision for the project was developed by the whole junior research group. Also, the exchange plays an important part in such a diverse team. For this reason, communication takes not only place inside of the group but also with an extended set of experts. These discussions are helping to focus the single issues while sharing the knowledge to other members of the team.

Additionally, presentations are held on national and international conferences and later made accessible for the whole consortium. Bilateral discussions between project members are an important element for narrow coordination and an agile development of the prototypes. Those have already been shown to an expert community [13] and in any time soon, these applications will be presented to additional users to identify issues not yet solved by the junior research group.

3   Conclusion and Outlook

This contribution shows different research parts in the junior research group UrbanHistory4D. It presents the work of the first year. The research topics are not only presented from a technical point of view but also from possible user perspectives and educational purposes of the application prototypes. It is planned to refine the prototype applications according to the results of the different study areas. In comparison to other projects, the junior research group works almost exclusively with historical data and thus tries to establish new methods for browsing historical image repositories.

But what is the conclusion after one year of research in the junior research group? Besides the presented work within the different research topics an important task is the generation of interfaces between these topics. This task is continuous throughout the whole project phase and should never be neglected. In the practice of our work different elements like a shared vision of the project results, a narrow coordination and an agile workflow have been established. Thus, this contribution presents not only research results but also strategies of interdisciplinary group work.

Acknowledgements. The research upon which this paper is based was part of the junior research group UrbanHistory4D's activities which has received funding from the German Federal Ministry of Education and Research under grant agreement No 01UG1630.

References

1. Agarwal, S., et al.: Building Rome in a day. Commun. ACM **54**(10), 105–112 (2011)
2. Ali, H.K., Whitehead, A.: Feature matching for aligning historical and modern images. IJ Comput. Appl. **21**(3), 188–201 (2014)
3. Barreau, J.B., Gaugne, R., Bernard, Y., Le Cloirec, G., Gouranton, V.: Virtual reality tools for the west digital conservatory of archaeological heritage. In: Proceedings of the 2014 Virtual Reality International Conference, p. 4. ACM (2014)
4. Bentkowska-Kafel, A., Denard, H., Baker, D.: Paradata and Transparency in Virtual Heritage. Ashgate Publishing, Ltd., Farnham (2012)
5. Bruschke, J., Niebling, F., Maiwald, F., Friedrichs, K., Wacker, M., Latoschik, M.E.: Towards browsing repositories of spatially oriented historic photographic images in 3D web environments. In: Proceedings of the 22nd International Conference on 3D Web Technology, p. 18. ACM (2017)
6. Burke, P.: Augenzeugenschaft: Bilder als historische Quellen. Wagenbach, Berlin (2003)
7. Chang, Y.L., Hou, H.T., Pan, C.Y., Sung, Y.T., Chang, K.E.: Apply an augmented reality in a mobile guidance to increase sense of place for heritage places. Educ. Technol. Soc. **18**(2), 166–178 (2015)
8. Chung, N., Han, H., Joun, Y.: Tourists' intention to visit a destination: the role of augmented reality (AR) application for a heritage site. Comput. Hum. Behav. **50**, 588–599 (2015)
9. tom Dieck, M.C., Jung, T.: A theoretical model of mobile augmented reality acceptance in urban heritage tourism. Curr. Issues Tour. **21**(2), 154–174 (2018)
10. tom Dieck, M.C., Jung, T.H., Tom Dieck, D.: Enhancing art gallery visitors' learning experience using wearable augmented reality: generic learning outcomes perspective. Curr. Issues Tour. 1–21 (2016)
11. Falkingham, P.L., Bates, K.T., Farlow, J.O.: Historical photogrammetry: bird's paluxy river dinosaur chase sequence digitally reconstructed as it was prior to excavation 70 years ago. PLoS One **9**(4), e93247 (2014). https://doi.org/10.1371/journal.pone.0093247. https://www.ncbi.nlm.nih.gov/pubmed/24695537
12. Friedrichs, K., Münster, S., Kröber, C., Bruschke, J.: Creating suitable tools for art and architectural research with historic media repositories. In: Münster, S., Friedrichs, K., Niebling, F., Seidel-Grzesinska, A. (eds.) UHDL/DECH -2017. CCIS, vol. 817, pp. 117–138. Springer, Cham (2018). https://doi.org/10.1007/978-3-319-76992-9_8

13. Friedrichs, K., Münster, S., Niebling, F., Maiwald, F., Bruschke, J., Barthel, K.: Digitale bildrepositorien - wirkliche arbeitserleichterung oder zeitraubend? In: 5. Jahrestagung der Digital Humanities im deutschsprachigen Raum (DHd2018). vol. 5, pp. 30–33. Georg Vogeler (2018)

14. Gouveia, J., Branco, F., Rodrigues, A., Correia, N.: Travelling through space and time in Lisbon's religious buildings. In: Digital Heritage, 2015. vol. 1, pp. 407–408. IEEE (2015)

15. Grün, A., Remondino, F., Zhang, L.: Photogrammetric reconstruction of the Great Buddha of Bamiyan, Afghanistan. Photogramm. Rec. **19**(107), 177–199 (2004)

16. Hamid, N., Khan, N.: LSM: perceptually accurate line segment merging. J. Electron. Imaging **25**(6), 061620 (2016). https://doi.org/10.1117/1.jei.25.6.061620

17. Han, D.-I., Jung, T., Gibson, A.: Dublin AR: implementing augmented reality in tourism. In: Xiang, Z., Tussyadiah, I. (eds.) Information and Communication Technologies in Tourism 2014, pp. 511–523. Springer, Cham (2013). https://doi.org/10.1007/978-3-319-03973-2_37

18. Haugstvedt, A.C., Krogstie, J.: Mobile augmented reality for cultural heritage: a technology acceptance study. In: 2012 IEEE International Symposium on Mixed and Augmented Reality (ISMAR), pp. 247–255. IEEE (2012)

19. Hofer, M., Maurer, M., Bischof, H.: Efficient 3D scene abstraction using line segments. Comput. Vis. Image Underst. **157**, 167–178 (2017)

20. Ioannides, M., et al.: Online 4D reconstruction using multi-images available under open access. ISPRS Ann. Photogramm. Remote Sens. Sapt. Inf. Sci. II-5 W **1**, 169–174 (2013)

21. Kemman, M., Kleppe, M., Scagliola, S.: Just Google it-digital research practices of humanities scholars. arXiv preprint arXiv:1309.2434 (2013)

22. Kounavis, C.D., Kasimati, A.E., Zamani, E.D.: Enhancing the tourism experience through mobile augmented reality: challenges and prospects. Int. J. Eng. Bus. Manag. **4**, 10 (2012)

23. Kysela, J., Štorková, P.: Using augmented reality as a medium for teaching history and tourism. Procedia-Soc. Behav. Sci. **174**, 926–931 (2015)

24. Li, K., Yao, J.: Line segment matching and reconstruction via exploiting coplanar cues. ISPRS J. Photogramm. Remote Sens. **125**, 33–49 (2017). https://doi.org/10.1016/j.isprsjprs.2017.01.006

25. Livingston, M.A., Ai, Z.: The effect of registration error on tracking distant augmented objects. In: Proceedings of the 7th IEEE/ACM International Symposium on Mixed and Augmented Reality, pp. 77–86. IEEE Computer Society (2008)

26. Lowe, D.G.: Distinctive image features from scale-invariant keypoints. Int. J. Comput. Vis. **60**(2), 91–110 (2004)

27. Maina, J.K., Suleman, H.: Enhancing digital heritage archives using gamified annotations. In: Allen, R.B., Hunter, J., Zeng, M.L. (eds.) ICADL 2015. LNCS, vol. 9469, pp. 169–179. Springer, Cham (2015). https://doi.org/10.1007/978-3-319-27974-9_17

28. Maiwald, F., Schneider, D., Henze, F., Münster, S., Niebling, F.: Feature matching of historical images based on geometry of quadrilaterals. ISPRS - Int. Arch. Photogramm. Remote Sens. Spat. Inf. Sci. **42**(2), 643–650 (2018). https://doi.org/10.5194/isprs-archives-XLII-2-643-2018

29. Maiwald, F., Vietze, T., Schneider, D., Henze, F., Münster, S., Niebling, F.: Photogrammetric analysis of historical image repositories for virtual reconstruction in the field of digital humanities. Int. Arch. Photogramm. Remote Sens. Spat. Inf. Sci. **42**, 447 (2017)

30. Münster, S.: Entstehungs-und Verwendungskontexte von 3D-CAD-Modellen in den Geschichtswissenschaften, pp. 99–108. TUDpress, Dresden (2011)

31. Münster, S., Jahn, P.H., Wacker, M.: Von plan-und bildquellen zum virtuellen gebäudemodell. zur bedeutung der bildlichkeit für die digitale 3d-rekonstruktion historischer architektur. Bildlichkeit im Zeitalter der Modellierung. Operative Artefakte in Entwurfsprozessen der Architektur, des Designs und Ingenieurwesens, pp. 255–284 (2017)

32. Paul, G.: Von der historischen bildkunde zur visual history. Visual History: ein Studienbuch. Göttingen: Vandenhoeck und Ruprecht, pp. 7–36 (2006)

33. Pelletier, L.: Architectural Representation and the Perspective Hinge. MIT Press, Cambridge (2000)

34. Samuel, J., Périnaud, C., Gay, G., Servigne, S., Gesquière, G.: Representation and visualization of urban fabric through historical documents. In: 14th Eurographics Workshop on Graphics and Cultural Heritage, pp. 157–166 (2016)

35. Schindler, G., Dellaert, F.: 4D cities: analyzing, visualizing, and interacting with historical urban photo collections. J. Multimed. **7**, 124–131 (2012)

36. Smirnov, A., Kashevnik, A., Shilov, N., Teslya, N., Shabaev, A.: Mobile application for guiding tourist activities: tourist assistant-TAIS. In: 2014 16th Conference of Open Innovations Association (FRUCT16), pp. 95–100. IEEE (2014)

37. Tuite, K., Snavely, N., Hsiao, D., Tabing, N., Popovic, Z.: Photocity: training experts at large-scale image acquisition through a competitive game. In: Proceedings of the SIGCHI Conference on Human Factors in Computing Systems, pp. 1383–1392. ACM (2011)

38. Voulodimos, A., Doulamis, N., Fritsch, D., Makantasis, K., Doulamis, A., Klein, M.: Four-dimensional reconstruction of cultural heritage sites based on photogrammetry and clustering. J. Electron. Imaging **26**(1), 011013 (2016). https://doi.org/10.1117/1.jei.26.1.011013

39. Wahbeh, W., Nebiker, S.: Three dimensional reconstruction workflows for lost cultural heritage monuments exploiting public domain and professional photogrammetric imagery. ISPRS Ann. Photogramm. Remote Sens. Spat. Inf. Sci. **IV-2/W2**, 319–325 (2017). https://doi.org/10.5194/isprs-annals-IV-2-W2-319-2017

40. Walczak, K., Cellary, W., Prinke, A.: Interactive presentation of archaeological objects using virtual and augmented reality. In: Proceedings of the 36th Annual Conference on Computer Applications and Quantitative Methods in Archaeology, Budapest, Hungary (2008)

41. Wang, L.: Line segment matching and its applications in 3D urban modeling. Thesis (2010)

42. Wohlfeil, R.: Das bild als geschichtsquelle. Historische Zeitschrift **243**(1), 91–100 (1986)

43. Yovcheva, Z., Buhalis, D., Gatzidis, C.: Smartphone augmented reality applications for tourism. e-Rev. Tour. Res. (eRTR) **10**(2), 63–66 (2012)

44. Zaibon, S.B., Pendit, U.C., Bakar, J.A.A.: User requirements on mobile AR for cultural heritage site towards enjoyable informal learning. In: 2015 Asia Pacific Conference on Multimedia and Broadcasting (APMediaCast), pp. 1–7. IEEE (2015)

45. Zöllner, M., Becker, M., Keil, J.: Snapshot augmented reality-augmented photography. In: In Proceedings of the VAST 2010. Eurographics Ass. Citeseer (2011)

3-D Survey and Structural Modelling:
The Case of the San Giovanni Baptistery
in Florence

Grazia Tucci[(⊠)], Alessandro Conti, and Lidia Fiorini

GeCO Lab, DICEA, Università di Firenze, Via S. Marta 3, 50139 Florence, Italy
grazia.tucci@unifi.it

Abstract. In 2013 the preliminary interdisciplinary studies for the maintenance of the facades of the Baptistery of Florence included a complete survey of the building. Like in the case of the previous most recent surveys, its geometry was studied with the most up-to-date technologies available. The 3-D model, integrated with the contributions by the other research groups, allowed new hypotheses on its construction and, in particular, a more accurate tuning of the structural models.

Keywords: Survey methodologies · Geomatics · TLS
Cultural heritage documentation · Cracking pattern · Damage assessment
FE model · Masonry domes

1 Introduction

The creation and sharing of a detailed and reliable three-dimensional model in geometric and metric terms is a necessity that is increasingly more felt within interdisciplinary research groups on cultural assets. The 3-D model allows all the actors to refer the information to a common reference system and then to use and compare the contributions and the results coming from the different disciplines. This is even more evident when the research concerns complex or poorly documented buildings [1].

The San Giovanni Baptistery in Florence is certainly a well-documented monument, but scholars are still debating many of its controversial aspects.

The techniques of automated acquisition of spatial information gathered under the name of Geomatics have recorded a remarkable evolution in recent years and are now mature disciplines capable of dealing with cases of any scale and complexity. It is also possible to effectively manage the complete 3-D acquisition of large buildings, having as its only physical accessibility limits, those of availability of time and human and technical resources [2]. In these cases, the availability of new methods of acquisition and data processing not only makes it possible to obtain new forms of representation in two or three dimensions, but also allows for carrying out new or more detailed investigations in the various research fields [3]. For this reason, knowledge of the geometry of the Baptistery of Florence has gradually become more in-depth thanks to the application of the most up-to-date survey methods and exploitation of the most innovative instrumental survey technologies available.

© Springer Nature Switzerland AG 2018
M. Ioannides et al. (Eds.): EuroMed 2018, LNCS 11196, pp. 271–280, 2018.
https://doi.org/10.1007/978-3-030-01762-0_23

In 2013, on occasion of the preliminary investigations for the most recent maintenance interventions of the external stonework, a 3-D survey was carried out which produced a complete high-resolution point model. From this it was possible to obtain a series of 2-D printouts of the interior and the exterior consisting of orthoimages, which realization was described in a previous contribution. The survey was used by the other research groups and integrated with further specialist contributions. This paper re-examines the surveys of the Baptistery, observing in particular how more and more detailed geometric information has made it possible us to deepen knowledge of the statics of the building and to interpret its damages.

2   The Surveys from 1938 to 1999

The Baptistery is one of the oldest and most representative buildings in Florence, the origins of which are still controversial. Also for this reason, it is one of the cases to which the most up-to-date survey techniques available have been applied over the years. By limiting himself to the surveys of the twentieth century, Rodolfo Sabatini carried out a survey campaign from 1938 to 1944 [4]. On that occasion, Guglielmo de Angelis D'Ossat suggested using the topography to determine the exact curvature of the dome. This task, which was very challenging with the available tools because the corners are covered up by the mosaics, was carried out measuring only six points of a corner between two sails with the triangulation technique.

In 1973, Pietramellara [5] carried out what is considered to be the last survey of the Baptistery conducted according to the traditional criteria. Due focusing in particular on the structural and constructive aspects of the building (she mentions the iron tie-rod but without representing it) and to the relationship with the archaeological context, it also shows, in three maps and a cross-section, the overall conformation of the building. Nevertheless, the large-sized plans, printed on different scales and without any measurements (with the mere presence of the metric scale), lack any indications about the survey method used. It is however evident that it was conducted with direct measurements, as can be seen from the substantial correctness of the plans compared to the considerable errors in the cross-section, due to the difficulty of measuring large heights with traditional instruments.

Among the surveys coordinated by Rocchi Coopmans de Yoldi [6, 7] in the 1980's and 1990's, that of Corsucci, Dalzocchio and Pedini [8] still used traditional measuring methods, despite highlighting, with indications of the measurements, a growing attention to the metadata of the survey operations, that is, the information useful for reconstructing and possibly testing the survey itself.

The plan of Prisca Giovannini's survey, the most recent (1995) among those that make extensive use of direct measurements, is almost exactly consistent with the one we obtained with the instrumental survey [6]. The backgrounds of the cross-section, especially in the rendering of the walls viewed in a foreshortened manner, instead highlight the limitations of the manual rendering. It is interesting to note however, that during this survey campaign, instrumental acquisitions were also carried out by exploiting different technologies.

Lamberto Ippolito provided a photogrammetric survey of the internal façade of the northern side, including the situation of the cracks (Fig. 1). In 1998, Walter Ferri instead performed a photogrammetric survey of the dome from which an orthoimage of the intrados in a towards the zenith view was obtained, accompanied by three series of profiles taken from the numerical model [6].

New measurements using topographic instrumentation were made by Paolo Aminti (1989) and Luca Giorgi (1995) [6]. These concern the corners of the intrados of the dome, and in the last case, also a corner of the building from ground level up to the top of the lantern. With respect to the Sabatini survey, the more innovative Galileo Siscam G. T.S. system was used for the detailed survey which made it possible to perform triangulations using two total stations (the first equipped with a laser pointer for tracing the point to be collimated with the second one). The connection of the two total stations to a PC made it possible to interactively control the results and any collimation errors [6].

In 1999, Gabriella Caroti and Gabriele Fangi were the first to use a laser scanner in the Baptistery for a survey of the geometry of the dome. The tool used (MDL Quarryman Ace300), was primarily designed for geological and mining applications. 12,000 points were acquired over the entire dome, a much lower number than that achievable with current laser scanners (capable of acquiring up to a million points per second), but much larger than what had been obtained so far in all previous surveys. It is worth mentioning here that, in the same experiment, the scanned data were compared with those specifically measured with another tool for those innovative years: the Topcon GTP1002 reflectorless total station, which allowed for measuring the distance of physically inaccessible points – providing they were visible – due to not requiring a retro-reflective prism like the tools used previously [6].

The new survey can be compared with the previous ones only from a qualitative point of view, because the original drawings are not available and, even in the case of instrumental surveys, information on data processing is missing. Summarising, the previous surveys are generally accurate, except in inaccessible areas. The main difference with the new survey is the availability of a dense and uniform sampling of the building, which allows to choose later the desired section plan.

3   The 2013 Survey

In 2013, in view of the operations for cleaning the external surfaces, the Opera del Duomo signed an agreement with the University of Florence for increasing the knowledge of the building for the conservation project. The study of the metric and morphological aspects was entrusted to the GeCO Laboratory of the Department of Civil and Environmental Engineering [9].

The survey of such a complex building as the Baptistery required a meticulous design, due to both intrinsic factors (geometry of spaces, dimensions and furnishings, areas acquirable only with provisional works), and extrinsic factors (presence of tourists and vehicles, museum and cultic requirements). Based on these, the topographic network and acquisition methods were designed, and in order to ensure future reusability of the data, particular attention was paid to the storage of data and metadata, with the creation of a backup of the raw data and the intermediates during each phase.

Please refer to the article by Tucci et al. [10] for a more detailed description of the data acquisition and processing, the main phases of which are summarised below.

3.1 Topographic Control Network

A topographic control network was created which was calculated and adjusted in a local reference system. Each survey station was permanently marked and witness diagrams were set up to allow for subsequent geo-referencing operations, and if necessary, any testing or monitoring operations. For the alignment of the external scans, approximately 100 control points were measured, some for alignment calculations and others for verifying and validating the results. Natural points were chosen in order not to conceal the surfaces with targets visible in the printouts.

In order to guarantee the metric precision that derives from referencing based on known coordinate targets without compromising the completeness of the description of the surfaces, two scans were performed from the same location: the first without targets on the scene and the second with targets measured with the total station. The latter, taken as a reference for the scan alignment, was then deleted from the printouts.

3.2 Detailed Survey

A Z+F 5010C scanner was used to perform 16 scans (one for each side and edge) from approximately 15 m with a resolution of 3 mm on the building, also acquiring the RGB values from the same scan point. For the upper parts and the roof, another 5 scans were carried from ground level and 11 from the surrounding buildings.

For the outdoor survey, it was necessary to operate in the early hours of the morning and temporarily limit the work area to avoid the presence of traffic and tourists. The indoor survey was performed in parallel with the same Z+F scanner and a Leica Geosystems HDS6000 scanner, for use where the low light did not allow acquisition of the RGB values. 241 scans were carried out: 34 from the ground floor, 42 in the *matroneo* (women's gallery), 55 in the attic, 94 on the stairs and 16 on the extrados of the dome (the latter were carried out from scaffolding).

3.3 Data Management and Output

All the scans were aligned in the topographical reference system by means of the targets and natural points mentioned above. The point model obtained, consisting of over 14 billion points with an average sampling step of from 3 to 12 mm, constitutes a digital replica that can be interrogated in order to produce traditional graphic outputs in orthogonal projections and also 3D printouts.

3.4 Horizontal and Vertical Cross-Sections

As is well known, a section line is obtained by vectorising a thin slice of points, however, for obtaining a plan or section according to the typical architectural design criteria, a single section plane is not sufficient: in fact, in order to create 4 maps and 4 sections, 20 complete slices were carried out, as well as many other partial sections for describing the structure in its entirety and full articulation.

Fig. 1. Photogrammetric restitution of the cracks pattern, (in red, by Ippolito 1997), superimposed on the GeCO survey (2013). (Color figure online)

3.5   Visible Elevations and Elements

The visible surfaces of the sections and elevations were rendered with orthoimages of the point cloud. These photorealistic representations show the point model in orthogonal projections, without the perspective effects of a photograph, and they have the same metric reliability as a traditional technical drawing. The high resolution of the scans produced such a dense point cloud that it resembles a continuous surface and which was rendered according to orthogonal views, with a resolution of less than 5 mm per pixel. In the images obtained, the RGB and intensity channels were filtered to optimise their readability, with the best parts chosen for each one, and finally, the chromatic and tonal balancing of the resulting mosaic was carried out.

The level of detail with which the elevations and sections of the Baptistery were produced is the one required for their correct and satisfactory reproduction on paper on a scale of 1:50. In expressing the resolution of the data detected with laser scans, it is necessary to differentiate the geometric aspect which refers to the spacing between adjacent points, from the chromatic aspect that depends on the characteristics of the camera incorporated in the instrument. In any case, by using the same instrumental settings, the resolution is greater on the surfaces closest to the scanner compared to those further away, and in the survey of the buildings (at least in the event, which is extremely frequent, of the impossibility of performing scans from raised positions), this involves a resolution that decreases from ground level up towards the roof. For this reason, in the Baptistery survey the scan settings have been optimised in order to obtain printouts in the scale required in the highest area of the elevations.

3.6   Surface Models

In a few of the portions, surface models were also implemented which consisted of a mesh that accurately reproduces the surfaces detected. This form of continuous description, unlike the discrete point model, can be viewed interactively on a computer or reproduced using digital building techniques, thus obtaining physical models that maintain the metric reliability of the digital models [11].

The availability of a complete database of high-density spatial coordinates makes it possible to extract all the desired graphic representations, even when not initially foreseen, providing a reference of known quality for monitoring any possible variations over time.

4   The Digital Survey as an Interpretation Tool

When compared with the previous surveys, this new one is characterised by a particularly high resolution (i.e. the average distance between one point and its neighbours). In fact, the technique via which this survey was conducted made it possible to record all the surfaces with a resolution of a few millimetres. The 3-D model constitutes a digital replica that allows to carry out systematic controls and far-reaching evaluations, without every time having to reach hardly accessible areas to carry out investigations and inspections, as shown by the subsequent examples.

4.1   Construction Techniques and Reuse of Materials

Starting from the point model of a sector of the extrados of the dome on the southern side, the statistical analysis of the measurements of the bricks was performed by first recording the larger elements with an average length of 43.8 cm ($\pm$1.4 cm). If these correspond to full bricks laid as stretchers, this measurement is therefore congruent with that of the greater side of a Roman *sesquipedalis* brick (29.6 cm $\times$ 44 cm). Starting from this initial feedback, we analysed the distribution of the stretcher and header bricks (Fig. 2). The presence of numerous elements with very variable intermediate measurements can be associated with the use of cut bricks, which supports the hypothesis that the bricks installed in the dome were re-used.

Moreover, the investigation only concerned a small portion of a single slice of the dome and therefore gives us nothing more than a possible clue, because in order to attain an adequate level of certainty, it would be necessary to extend the study to larger portions of the extrados.

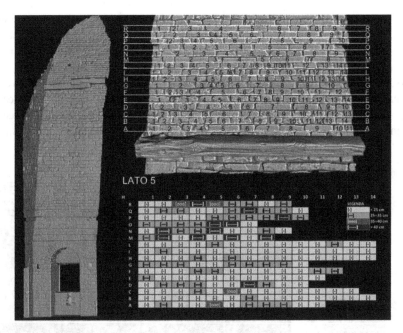

Fig. 2. A sector of the extrados of the dome (left) and statistical analysis of the measurements of the bricks.

4.2 Identification of the Instability and Structural Restraining Measures

3-D models may represent the background for the visualisation of various phenomena: for example, in the structural field it has been possible to visualise the deformation of the walls by means of displacement maps of these with respect to vertical planes used as a reference. When the northern, eastern and southern walls (those characterised by the presence of doors) were examined, it was found that they all have a span of about 5 cm on the outside between the second floor and the attic, just underneath the strip without any marble lining, inside which there is an iron tie-rod that was inserted in 1514. There is a corresponding bulge at the same height on the internal face of the masonry, even if of a smaller size. On the façades, an out-of-plumb of a few centimetres was also detected towards the outside, although hardly appreciable in view of the articulated shape of the elevation [12].

Within the context of the research in which the new surveys and the 3-D model were implemented, other working groups were carrying out simultaneous investigations in the field of monument stability. The new historiographic researches on the interpretation of the crack pattern, the new numerical models, and the investigations on the materials, correlated on the same geometric model, have allowed us to deepen our knowledge of the static conditions and instability of the building [12].

As is already known, the Baptistery has various groups of main fissures which have been detected along the internal edges of the dome, on the axis of the northern, eastern and southern perimeter walls, and on the vertical walls on the western side, above the arch of the *scarsella* (rectangular apse). These types of cracks are recurrent in domes; those around the edges are a consequence of the elastoplastic deformations of the sails that generate tensile stress in the corners, while those on the sides are caused by the thrust of the dome which tends to widen its own perimeter setting. Although some cracks are up to 5 cm wide, many are barely visible due to being covered by the repairs were carried out in remote times and no longer progressing (Fig. 3). This indicates that the cracks had already appeared in past eras when the instability must have seemed even more alarming. In fact, as in many other masonry domes, the tensile stresses in the Baptistery were contained with tie-rods [12].

Fig. 3. Orthoimage of the East façade and detail of a marble wedge covering a crack.

The wooden tie-rods visible in the attic of the extrados of the dome must have been installed during the construction, and investigations on the wood have ascertained that it was partly replaced in the middle of the thirteenth century. This suggests that the cracks were already evident and that the tie-rods was no longer adequate. In 1514, an additional iron tie-rods was installed, positioned around the external perimeter in the area of maximum thrust, which effectively prevented the advancing of the instability.

4.3   3-D Geometrical Modelling

By focusing attention on the use of the geometric model for the definition of the structural behaviour of the building and the interpretation of the instabilities detected, it can be observed how despite the inevitable uncertainties in the modelling of historical buildings, the Finite Element Method (FEM) can be considered among the most reliable tools for the construction of valid numerical models for describing the overall behaviour of ancient masonry structures. The transition which from the survey and geometric modelling leads to structural geometry is essential for defining the reliability of the numerical model. In spite of the obvious simplifications, the more accurate the information of the geometrical survey, the greater the reliability of the results obtained from the numerical models. Over the last few decades various models have been defined for describing the structural behaviour of the Baptistery. The models drawn up by Carlo Blasi and Riccardo Papi in the 1990's and in 2004, made it possible to interpret the cracks visible on the intrados of the dome and on the arch of the *scarsella*. Since 2010 Gianni Bartoli and Michele Betti have perfected additional numerical models (based on the geometry inferred from historical surveys and from Carla Pietramellara's survey) for conducting modal analyses validated by comparison with experimental data acquired with the interferometric radar technique, as well as for studying the behaviour of the monument under the action of its own weight [13].

The results of the analyses have confirmed what was already known, highlighting the strong tensile stresses at the corners between the sails of the dome and in a tangential direction at the level of the *matroneo* and the attic. Nevertheless, these numerical models were not able to detect any tensile stresses capable of justifying the presence of cracks on the axis of the three doors of the Baptistery. In order to arrive at a possible interpretation of these cracks, new numerical models have been implemented thanks to the use of the geometric model from 2013. Due to being developed with a definition of the structural elements more in line with the actual geometry of the building, they have been used to conduct parametric static analyses for shedding light on the alteration of the stress flows whenever the elastic modulus attributed to the various parts of the structure varies. It has therefore been verified how by appropriately reducing the elastic module attributed to the ring-beams at the same height as the *matroneo* and the attic, the tensile stresses were concentrated in the areas in which the cracks that can be observed in the Baptistery occurred [14].

5   Conclusions

Each survey is a historical document, because testifies both to the consistency of a building and to the state of the knowledge and available technologies. Consequently, no survey is conclusive: even what appears to be exhaustive today can be updated in the future with additional analyses and more up-to-date methods. A survey is "an open system of knowledge" that brings together all relevant data and whose creation involves multiple expertise. A 3-D model can be re-used as a base to reference in a BIM model every kind of data, as example building a database of marble cladding for the maintenance of the building.

Acknowledgements. This work has been carried out under the GAMHer project: Geomatics Data Acquisition and Management for Landscape and Built Heritage in a European Perspective, PRIN: – Bando 2015, Prot. 2015HJLS7E.

References

1. Bitelli, G., et al.: Metric documentation of Cultural heritage: research directions from the Italian GAMHER project. Int. Arch. Photogramm. Remote Sens. Spat. Inf. Sci. - ISPRS Arch. **42**, 83–90 (2017). https://doi.org/10.5194/isprs-archives-xlii-2-w5-83-2017
2. Tucci, G., Bonora, V.: Il rilievo della Basilica del Santo Sepolcro a Gerusalemme. In: Atti della 14a Conferenza Nazionale ASITA, pp. 1643–1648 (2010)
3. Tucci, G., Bonora, V.: Geomatic Techniques and 3D Modeling for the Survey of the Church of the Holy Sepulchre in Jerusalem. In: Proceedings XXIII CIPA Symposium, Prague, Czech Republic, 12/16 September (2011)
4. Sabatini, R.: La curvatura e la costruzione della cupola del battistero. Palladio V–VI, pp. 159–163 (1943)
5. Pietramellara, C.: Battistero di S. Giovanni a Firenze. Rilievo e studio critico. Polistampa Firenze (1973)
6. Rocchi Coopmans De Yoldi, G.: S. Maria del Fiore. Piazza Battistero Campanile. Il Torchio, Firenze (1996)
7. Rocchi Coopmans De Yoldi, G. (ed.): S. Maria del Fiore e le chiese fiorentine del Duecento e del Trecento nella città delle fabbriche arnolfiane. Alinea, Firenze (2004)
8. Corsucci, S., Dalzocchio, M., Pedini, L.: Nuove acquisizioni sulla Fabbrica del Battistero di S. Giovanni in Firenze. Bollettino Architetti. Bimestrale di architettura ed economia edilizia **13**(III), 1–17 (1986)
9. Tucci, G., Bonora, V., Conti, A., Fiorini, L., Riemma, M.: Il rilievo digitale del Battistero: dati 3D per nuove riflessioni critiche. In: Gurrieri, F. (ed.) Il Battistero di San Giovanni: conoscenza, diagnostica, conservazione. Atti del Convegno internazionale, pp. 104–117. Mandragora Firenze (2017)
10. Tucci, G., Bonora, V., Fiorini, L., Conti, A.: The Florence baptistery: 3-D survey as a knowledge tool for historical and structural investigations. Int. Arch. Photogramm. Remote Sens. Spat. Inf. Sci. - ISPRS Arch. **XLI-B5**, 977–984 (2016). https://doi.org/10.5194/isprsarchives-xli-b5-977-2016
11. Cignoni, P., Montani, C., Scopigno, R., Rocchini, C.: A general method for preserving attribute values on simplified meshes. In: Proceedings Visualization 1998 (Cat. No. 98CB36276), pp. 59–66 (1998)
12. Ottoni, F., Blasi, C., Betti, M., Bartoli, G.: The effectiveness of ancient "hidden" tie rods in masonry dome preservation: San Giovanni in Florence. In: Van Balen, K., Verstrynge, E. (eds.) Structural Analysis of Historical Constructions – Anamnesis, Diagnosis, Therapy, Controls. Taylor & Francis Group, London (2016). https://doi.org/10.1201/9781315616995-264
13. Fratini, M., Pieraccini, M., Atzeni, C., Betti, M., Bartoli, G.: Assessment of vibration reduction on the Baptistery of San Giovanni in Florence (Italy) after vehicular traffic block. J. Cult. Herit. **12**, 323–328 (2011). https://doi.org/10.1016/j.culher.2011.01.003
14. Bartoli, G., Betti, M., Torelli, G.: Damage assessment of the Baptistery of San Giovanni in Florence by means of numerical modelling. Int. J. Mason. Res. Innov. **2**(2–3), 150–168 (2017). https://doi.org/10.1504/ijmri.2017.085955

3D Documentation and Visualization
of the Forum Romanum:

The DHARMA Forum Project

Krupali Krusche(⊠)

University of Notre Dame, Notre Dame, IN 46556, USA
Kuplekar@nd.edu

Abstract. Documenting large scale sites like the Roman Forum, in Rome, Italy can become a mammoth task. While there is a set methodology for traditional documentation of large sites, as the one developed by Giacomo Boni in the early 1900's, there is very little standardization in the field of digital documentation and cataloguing or making the digital data user friendly for various purposes of conservation of large site. This paper presents the methodology and techniques used by the University of Notre Dame School of Architecture DHARMA team to digitally document for the first time the Forum Romanum, Rome, Italy between 2010 till 2015.

The complexity of site, terrain, and the data to be collected, were supported through three major segments that can be useful for any on-site documentation project. These include (1) Pre-site, (2) On-site and (3) Post-site methods. Employing a comprehensive approach—including 3-D laser scanning, hand measuring, photogrammmetry, and Gigapan technology—the team thoroughly documented the current state of this World Heritage site. Laser scanning was central to this effort, and the details of its implementation contributed to time and terrain effective methods are discussed in this paper. The team working on this project included architects, archeologists, computer engineers and students from various disciplines.

The team's post-site production efforts resulted, most notably, in a highly-accurate point cloud model that can be manipulated for various educational and scholarly uses. These were further transformed to create user friendly outputs including 2D drawings and 3D visuals comprising a 3D app.

As many scholars from different disciplines get involved in the field of digital documentation, it becomes increasingly important to create a methodology of operation that can be described as best practices in the field for large scale sites of great historical value. This study takes the knowledge known in our field over centuries and combines the results of latest technologies to get us the best of both worlds.

This project was done in collaboration with Soprintendenza Speciale per il Colosseo e l'Area Archeologica Centrale di Roma with support from Dr. Patrizia Fortini. Special thanks goes to Luke Golesh and Ryan Hughes who worked on creating the working documents for digitally capturing this site referred to in parts in this paper. Access support was also given by Prof. Dr. James Packer in the initial stages of this project. The project has been supported over the years through funding from the Office of Research, School of Architecture, and the Nanovic Institute at the University of Notre Dame. Computing knowledge was shared by Center of Research Computing and the Academic Digital Media teams. Technical equipment was provided by Leica Geosystems in Italy.

© Springer Nature Switzerland AG 2018
M. Ioannides et al. (Eds.): EuroMed 2018, LNCS 11196, pp. 281–300, 2018.
https://doi.org/10.1007/978-3-030-01762-0_24

Keywords: 3D laser scan · Digital documentation · Roman forum

1 Introduction

Originally initiated in July 2010, the Digital Architectural Historical Research and Materials Analysis (DHARMA) lab from the University of Notre Dame's School of Architecture was granted permission from the then, *Soprintendenza Speciale per i Beni Archeologici di Roma*[1] to document the western half of the Forum Romanum,[2] Rome, Italy, a part of the World Heritage site of the Historic Centre of Rome [1, 2]. In 2012, this project was extended to cover the Forum Romanum in its entirety from the Colosseum up to the Tabularium (except for the Temple of Jupiter which partially embedded in the lower sections of the Capitoline Museum.

The need to document the site arose based on complex nature of its terrain and the large variety of monuments found on the site. The change in grade from the present day ground level created an added complexity to the given problem. Need was seen to comprehensively document the site in its entirety. What resulted from this survey was the most comprehensive data on the site since its documentation when it was first excavated over a hundred years ago.[3] And the first ever time where sectional relationship of the site was understood and studied.

The project was born out of ongoing research to recreate the Forum site circa 330AD [3]. As the project took shape, it became apparent that the DHARMA team would be making a unique contribution both to the fields of architecture and archaeology. While the team's primary objective remained in line—viz., to ascertain with laser-accuracy the locations and relationships of the monuments within the Forum—it would also introduce digital, 3-D visualization into the analysis of the Forum (see Fig. 1). What's more, a comprehensive strategy and best practice, utilizing digital and traditional surveying technologies, would be undertaken, seeking to marry the benefits of manual attention to the site with the precision of digital surveying.

In order to do a comprehensive job with documentation of the site it became quickly clear that a pre-site study would have to be initiated. The study comprised of collecting, reviewing and analyzing previous scholarships in the field and their

---

[1] Soprintendenza Speciale per i Beni Archeologici di Roma has been recently converted to the Soprintendenza Speciale per il Colosseo e l'Area Archeologica Centrale di Roma by bringing the central part of historic Rome under one umbrella under the direct supervision of the Ministero dei beni e delle attività culturali e del turismo (MiBACT).

[2] The survey focused particularly on the most ancient of the *fora*, the Forum Romanum, from its westernmost edge at the Tabularium to the Temple of Vesta. Accordingly, the authors, when referencing the multiplicity of *fora* built during the Late-Republican and Imperial periods of ancient Rome, will speak of the 'Roman Forum;' when referencing the particular forum that is the focus of this study, the term 'Forum Romanum,' or simply the 'Forum,' will be used.

[3] Giacomo Boni was the director of excavations in the Forum Romanum. Boni directed and documented this important project from 1898 until his death in 1925. Thus creating the most comprehensive documentation of the site till date. He did extensive studies in the stratigraphy of the Forum.

Fig. 1. A final complete model of the Roman Forum after cleaning and unifying all points. The façade of the Tabularium towers in the distance; the three standing columns of the Temple of Castor and Pollux occupy the bottom left corner; and the hexastyle porch of the Temple of Antoninus and Faustina occupies the bottom right corner. Source: DHARMA

contributions including their weaknesses. This was followed with a plan to execute an onsite survey that would form the bases of this project and provided a critical overview of the history of documentation of the Forum Romanum.

Aware of the benefits and limitations of the extant documentation, the best practice for preplanning and fieldwork are discussed in detail. For the on-site work the DHARMA team was divided into four groups.[4] The post-site processing of data has been the most extensive and lab intensive part of the project. These include issues related to data management and the variety of results and quality of documentation available in the field based on the density of the point cloud and thus the resolution of the data collected.

The paper concludes with an analysis of the strengths and weaknesses of digital documentation, in light of the team's comprehensive survey.

---

[4] The original survey team in 2010 included (a) a digital survey group, composed of two graduate research assistants, Luke Golesh and Ryan Hughes, employing a Leica Geosystems ScanStation laser scanner; (b) traditional survey group, composed of four undergraduate assistants, Larissa Esmilla, Elizabeth Fuller, Kaitlyn Smous, and Lon Stousland, applying time-honored techniques of hand-measuring (c) a photogrammetry group, helmed by Prof. Dr. Selena Anders and supported by the undergraduate assistants; and (d) an ultra-high resolution photographic group, led by an undergraduate assistant, Ben Keller, using a GigaPan Systems EPIC Pro robotic camera mount under the guidance of Paul Turner.

Two further expeditions (2012, 2013) included teams like Prof. Giovanna Sandusky Lenzi, Dr. Christopher Sweet, Dr. James Sweet, and Ryan Hughes and undergraduate assistants Sharon McGolrick, Mason Roberts, Olga Bryazka, Keaton Bloom, Stephanie Escobar, and Taylor Stein. Offsite support for app and 3D design was provided by Markus Krusche, and Dr. Kristina Furse Davis. All surveys were conducted under the leadership of Prof. Dr. Krupali Krusche.

2 Pre-site Study

Beyond the need to physically record the site is the need to generate the research question based on which the systematic approach of the documentation can be conducted. Thus it becomes crucial to study all the information one can collect about the history of the site. In the case of the Roman Forum, beyond the history of creation of the site was the knowledge to understand who and when had ever documented this site and using what techniques. Vital parts of the study of history of site include:

1. Method of construction of the monument/monuments.
2. Key transformations to the site with a systematic timeline of changes made.
3. Overlay of those changes to create layered map of the site.
4. Specific questions regarding the site that can be resolved through onsite research during the documentation of the monument/monuments.

2.1 History of the Site

The history of the Roman Forum is vast. Countless scholars have provided insights into the creation, evolution and slow decline of this site. On such sites with extensive histories, the forum having one longer than 2900 years, it can be difficult to account for all aspects of historic evidence.[5] The Roman Forum has a unique identity in the history of antiquity and that of the Rome. Not only because it of its historic, cultural and political significance but also because of the manner in which each generation of leaders left a permanent mark on the architectural reminisce of the place. Each time transforming and making it their own, but at the same time leaving admix of monuments and structures that are today collectively known as the Roman Forum. This makes the understanding of the Forum even more convoluted today as one is not dealing with a given timeframe completed complex like those of Trajan, and etc. Thus to comprehend the collective history of over 1000 years of built history and more than 1700 years of ruins can be an uphill task.

Most historians start describing the history of Rome from the time Romulus found Rome as its first king in 753 B.C. [4]. Archeological evidence suggests the initial start of Rome was on the Palatine Hill and at these foothills. These foothills were inhospitable marshland until with the engineering skills of probably the Etruscans to drain the area were applied by the Romans in the mid-sixth century B.C. This converted and created the new public center between the Palatine and Capitoline Hill becoming the political, administrative, legal, commercial and religious centre of Rome – the Roman Forum. The current state of the Forum Romanum, in contrast to its richness in the Republican and Imperial periods of ancient Rome, is surprisingly bare. Invisible within the extant ruins lies a complex history of destruction, excavation, and reassembly.[6]

---

[5] While the Forum history has been identified as started with the creation of Rome around 753BCE, new evidence suggests 900BCE existence of initial start of the Forum. Look at the study and excavation notes of Dr. Patrizia Fortini for the Lapis Niger.

[6] Most notably, the Porticus of the Dei Consentes, the Shrine of Juturna, and the Temple of Vesta are contemporary reconstructions in which ancient fragments have been carefully combined with modern materials in order to evoke something of the monument's original character.

2.2   History of Documentation of the Site

The multiplicity of hands and minds at work in the Forum should not, however, be understood to undermine the value of a thorough documentation of its current state. Rather, it underscores the importance the Forum has held for various peoples over the course of centuries. This history (and the history of scholastic analysis, in particular) is what demands attention here [5].

Since the early renaissance, countless architects and archeologists have chosen the Roman Forum as the subject of their analyses. These early efforts continue to prove valuable today, as they depict state of the site prior to the profound interventions belonging to the Renaissance and twentieth century [6]. Remarkable measured drawings of ancient Roman buildings were made by Giovanni Dondi and Ciriano d'Ancona in the late fourteenth century; none of their existing documentation efforts, however, depict the Forum. This accomplishment belongs to Giuliano da Sangallo. In 1465—the date marked in his sketchbook—he depicts the Arch of Septimius Severus (in perspective, plan, elevation, and molding detail) as well the presumed west façade of the Basilica Aemilia [7, 8].

Documentation efforts continued into the sixteenth century. Étienne du Pérac's *Vestigi dell'antichita di Roma* boasts thirty-nine engravings, the culmination of thirty years of archeological study. Of these studies, two small scale maps and numerous perspective plates offer views of the Roman Forum alongside reconstructions [9].[7] Antonio Dosio's drawings of the Roman Forum include both sketches and detail drawings of the individual monuments—*viz.*, the Arch of Septimius Severus, the Temple of Castor and Pollux, the Temple of Saturn, and the Temple of Vespasian—and perspective views of the Forum in its entirety [10]. Finally, Andrea Palladio, although principally recognized by archaeologists for his documentation of Roman Baths, made a number of detailed observations the Forum's monuments. These drawings include measured plans, elevations, and molding and capital profiles of the Arch of Septimius Severus; multiple plans (including a process plan), partial section, elevation, perspective, and molding profile of the Temple of Antoninus and Faustina; plan, elevation, and molding and capital profiles of the Temple of Saturn; a detailed plan, elevation, and section of Temple of Vesta; and a cornice detail of the Basilica Aemilia [11].[8]

Measured drawings of the seventeenth century continued to improve the documentary accuracy. Searching for a regularized modular system of ancient Roman architecture, Antoine Babuty Desgodetz, in 1682, presents a volume of astonishingly

---

[7] After their discovery in the early twentieth century by Thomas Ashby, the drawings of Étienne du Pérac (also known as the Codex du Pérac) were very difficult to obtain. In 1960, however, Amilcare Pizzi published a volume containing these drawing with an introduction by Rudolf Wittkower.

[8] Alongside an impressive body of built work, Andrea Palladio made a number of significant contributions to the field of architecture—most notably, the illustrations for Daniele Barbaro's commentary on Vitruvius' De Architectura and his own treatise, I Quattro Libri dell'Architettura are two publications by Andrea Palladio. The original illustrations of the first (1570) edition of the "Four Books" have been made readily available in a recent MIT publication.

detailed drawings of the existing monuments of ancient Rome [12].[9] Each of the Forum monuments in his study were minutely delineated: the smallest module on a plate being the slightest molding, which was then rounded to the nearest $1/12^{th}$ fraction. This system ensured precise measurement of detail. (For example, the *apophysis* of the capital of the Temple of Antoninus and Faustina measures one module and the lower facia is 12 7/12ths.)

Following Desgodetz, French architects of the late-eighteenth and early-nineteenth centuries, who won the Grand Prix de Rome through the Ecole de Beaux Arts, conducted continual analyses of the Forum. Precise water-colored, measured drawings were required of these *pensionnaires* as well as reconstructions. Although the reconstructions are not always reliable, the renderings remain inexhaustibly useful for their careful visualization of the existing condition of the monuments [13–15].[10] Also during this time, George Ledwell Taylor and Edward Cresy produced a compilation of architectural reconstructions of the major monuments of Rome in plan, elevation, and detail, each drawn with minute particulars and accompanied by precise measurements. Their 1874 edition, updated by George Ledwell Taylor, was one of the most authoritative accounts of the major monuments of Rome and the Roman Forum at the time [16].

Notable publications by Rodolfo Lanciani, Samuel Ball Platner and Thomas Ashby, and Alfonso Bartoli in the late nineteenth and early twentieth century digest new information from excavations and archeological analyses. The most extensive amount of work on the Roman Forum was done by architect Giacomo Boni who excavated, documented, maintained and restored major works in the Roman Forum from 1898 until his death in 1925 [17]. More recent publications, such as Filippo Coarelli's *Il Foro Romano* and *Lexicon topographicum urbis Romae* [18, 19]; Eva Margareta Steinby's *Lexicon Topigraphicum Urbs Roma*; and monument-specific volumes sponsored by the *Soprintendenza Speciale per i Beni Archeologici di Roma*, collect a vast array of measured drawings and documents of the Forum's current state. The most current and accurate publications focus largely on a specific monument or site within the Forum.[11]

---

[9] While Desgodets advertised his work as having the most detailed and accurate drawings ever produced on the Forum, observations of the DHARMA team's documentation reveal significant discrepancies between some of Desgodets' renderings and the artifacts on site.

[10] In his introduction to Ruins of Ancient Rome, Fillipo Coarelli writes:

"The result (of the Prix de Rome) is a body of drawings that, despite their unreliable reconstructions, often offer us invaluable records in diagrams, cross sections, and perspective views. This is not only because they provide irreplaceable images of Roman monuments made while the monuments were generally in better conditions but also because many times they are the only reliable sketches that were ever made. Their graphic quality is generally infinitely superior to the best produced in our own technological age...."

[11] For example: Cairoli Fulvio Giuliani with Patrizia Verduchi's surveys of the central Forum area; G. Foglia with G. Ioppolo's elevations, plans and overhead plans of the Temple of Saturn and surrounding context; K.A. Nilson and C. Persson with Inge Nielsen and Birte Poulsen's Temple of Castor and Pollux; Stefano de Angeli's Temple of Vespasian; G. Pala's Tabularium; G. Ioppolo with G. Foglia's Tabularium; ADSAR with M. Cecchini's Temple of Divus Julius; F.O. Shulze's Temple of Divus Julius which includes five elevations; A.M. Ferroni's Temple of Concord; H. Bauer's Basilica Paulli; R.T. Scott with Groma's Temple of Vesta; and F. Bianchi's Temple of Antonius and Faustina.

2.3   Unanswered Questions

Despite this overwhelming wealth of information, there are aspects of the study on the Forum that still need documentation to help understand the site in a comprehensive manner:

1. An overall map of the Roman Forum from the Colosseum to the Tabularium. While there are many plans on the Roman Forum, generally these lose accuracy at the scale of the full site. The most accurate plan available to date is that done by Giacomo Boni. This drawing is now close to around a 100 years. And many parts of the site have changed since the earliest excavations.
2. An understanding of how much the site has detoriated since it was first excavated and documented.
3. An accurate understanding of the relationship of the monuments to each other and their sectional placement in relation to the city ground line as it exists today.

Thus the DHARMA Forum project over the last eight years represents a major advancement to the information now available in terms of both documentation and visualization. Existing documentation (plans, elevations, perspectives, and photographs), while remarkable in its meticulous detail, is displayed in isolation and published limitedly, failing both to give a sense of the individual monument's contribution of to the Forum's urban function as well as creating all-but-inevitable restrictions to the access of that scholarship.

2.4   Setting a Research Goal

The DHARMA Forum Project compiles each of the monuments into a single, three-dimensional, highly-accurate, and measurable model. What's more this digital model has the potential of global distribution, allowing researchers remote access to the raw data. Regarding visualization, the Forum Project too has its merits. While in visualization the reconstruction of the Roman Forum by the ULCA Cultural Virtual Reality Laboratory (CRVLab), [20] is a valued contribution in the field, is beyond the scope of this study. The whole project is based on the concept of reconstructing a visual sense of how the Forum may have been but does not contain actual first hand field work and measurements of the site [21]. Instead, the DHARMA Forum Project's scope—i.e., attempting no reconstruction of the site—is more limited than that of the CRVLab, its production of a three-dimensional, measurable model is exceptional. Thus, it can be said that the DHARMA Forum Project opens up a new area of research that lies between the increasingly separate disciplines of documentation and visualization, managing to combine the precision natural to the former and the comprehensibility provided by the latter.

3   On-site Data Collection

3.1   Pre-site Planning

Before the survey group arrived in the Forum, a number of important observations were made that profoundly influenced the nature of the DHARMA team's site-work. Before each site visit, in preparation for the Forum Project, the digital survey group made a number of practical and methodological decisions that would shape its work on site. The first of these sought to balance the size of the Forum site (approximately 250 m × 150 m) with the equipment the team had at its disposal. The team was divided into four groups, (a) a digital survey group, employing multiple long range Leica Geosystems scanners;[12] (b) traditional survey group, applying time-honored techniques of hand-measuring (c) a photogrammmetry group, working on 2D elevational captures of the monuments on site; and (d) an ultra-high resolution photographic group, using a GigaPan Systems EPIC Pro robotic camera mount and Nikon professional D5 digital camera [22, 23].[13,14]

Given these resources, an early plan was to scan the site from the outside corners— *i.e.*, establishing four scan positions outside the site, from which long-range, detailed scans would be made. However, field tests on the campus of the University of Notre Dame demonstrated that such extreme scans produced significant inaccuracies in the

---

[12] A laser scanner is an automated surveying apparatus that uses Light Induced Detection and Ranging (LIDAR) technology to collect precise measurements of an object's location. These coordinates are recorded in the form of a "point cloud" that reproduces an object's shape by converting its spatial geometry into thousands, if not hundreds of thousands, of individual points, each with x,y, and z coordinates. This paper concentrates on the 'time of flight' type of laser scanner, the properties of which are specifically suited to historic and archeological documentation of large sites. The Cyra Technologies Cyrax 2400, designed by Ben Kacyra, became the first time of flight scanner with limited production in 1998. It consisted of a single high-speed laser beam that has a return signal at the same angle of coincidence capturing data via oscillating lightweight mirrors. Leica Geosystems acquired Cyra in 2001 and has since highly improved the scanner's performance and rate of data capture.

[13] Although not discussed at any length in the present paper, these traditional techniques were critical to the DHARMA team's work on the Forum. While ultimately playing a role supplemental to that of the digital survey, these techniques provided irreplaceable experiences of the Forum site. A comparative evaluation of digital and traditional techniques may be found in the Conclusions section below.

[14] Gigapixel Panorama, or GigaPan, image is a super-large, digital, panoramic photograph, which is composed of a series of smaller digital images. This method of data capture allows GigaPan to capture expansive vistas and simultaneously achieve astonishingly high levels of detail. GigaPan technology, initiated by Carnegie Mellon University and NASA Ames Intelligent Systems Division's Robotics Group, functions by using three basic systems: GigaPan Imager System, Stitcher software, and the GigaPan website. The GigaPan Imager is a pivoting robotic camera mount used to install the digital camera and to auto click images based on a selected window frame, set zoom, and with a specified number of vertical and horizontal images. The GigaPan Stitcher software is a custom-designed to combine these large sets of digital images with the least amount of parallax and best exposure levels in order to create the final ultra-high resolution panoramic image. The GigaPan website is the platform, by providing both the unique storage capacities required to handle these data-rich images and the viewing features (most significantly, pan and zoom) necessary to take advantage of their richness, needed to host such data files.

data. And, indeed, this observation was supported by fellow researchers' data. While the scanner can acquire measurements upto 300 m distance, these measurements are significantly influenced by two factors: (1) object reflectivity and (2) laser divergence.[15]

Regarding reflectivity, the manufacturer of the scanner, Leica Geosystems, itself states that the 300 m range is only suitable for objects with surface reflectivity of at least 90%.[16] Given the variety of terrain and materials that the team would encounter at the Forum, this factor alone was significant enough to invalidate the plan for long-range scans. In addition, the laser beam used in digital scanning to acquire x, y, z coordinate data is susceptible to "divergence" at greater distances. The Leica long range scanner projects a laser spot size of 6 mm on an object 50 m distance from it,[17] far below traditional error margins [24]. At 300 m, however, the laser spot size becomes sizably over 2 to 3 cms in diammeter. This fact, alongside experience of far greater errors in long-range field tests, proved remote scanning as incompatible data collection on site in the project. And, in light of these factors, the *practical* range of the scanner for accurate, long-range, remote measuring was established at 50–100 m.

In addition to the constraints posed by equipment, time too was a factor. The team had been granted a relatively short window of time at each visit by the *Soprintendenza* to access the site without restriction—*especially with a high number of tourists visiting the site everyday*. While undoubtedly short, this restriction did not unduly affect the project, given the scanner's facility at data capture (approximately 1000 points to 50,000 + points per second). This rate of acquisition far exceeds that of a person working by hand (approximately 500 points per person per *day* ratio). A digital survey was the most fitting methodology for the project by far.

More significantly, the DHARMA team developed a time-saving, scanning technique, during preplanning. This technique divided a single scan position into many different scans based on the scanned objects' distances from the scanner. What might be called the "normative," or static, method of scanning would set the resolution for a specific distance and apply these settings globally. The result of such a method is the desired resolution at the specified distance, but *only* at that distance. Objects farther from the scanner are acquired with far less detail, and, likewise, objects nearer to the scanner acquire far higher (and potentially unnecessary) density of information. For simple objects that are equidistantly placed, this differential in resolution may prove unimportant, but for such a vast site, the potential for overpopulation was immense.

Rather than using such a broad stroke methods to capture the complexity of the Forum site, the team found that it was far more effective to make multiple, smaller scans from a single scan position, the resolutions of which were tailored to the various distances of the objects in view. The method employed could be likened to a collage. It captured the same field of vision as the previous method, yet it did so through a plurality

---

[15] Comprehensive, technical information, including comparative analysis- both lab and field tested- is available from the symposia from the International Scientific Committee for Documentation of Cultural Heritage (CIPA), and in the Journal of the International Society of Photogrammetry and Remote Sensing (ISPRS).

[16] A datasheet of the Leica Geosystems ScanStation model laser scanner is available for download at CyArk website at http://archive.cyark.org/leica-scanstation-data-sheet-blog.

[17] This is according the Leica Scanner datasheet (see CyArk) and uses a Guassian laser.

of scans, each *adapted* to the desired density of information while simultaneously reflecting the scanned objects' positions in relation to the scanner (see Fig. 2).[18]

Fig. 2. Adaptive scan method: this point cloud image of the Temple of Antoninus and Faustina illustrates the DHARMA team's "adaptive" scan method. The color bands (added for the purposes of this illustration) demarcate individual scans, with five scans composing the final model of this monument. In order to maintain a 1.5 × 1.5 cm point density, the distance from scanner to object was measuredfor each scan and the resolution altered accordingly. Source: Luke Golesh (Color figure online)

Such "adaptive" scans are far more efficient than "static" scans in terms of the amount of data acquired and time spent acquiring it, both of which were factors in the Forum project.[19] That said, the sensitivity of adaptive scans is achieved *only* by the increased effort and attention on part of the scanner's operator. The team is convinced, however, that the project would not have been completed to the desired detail and in the time allotted had this method been unavailable.

---

[18] An example of this method may is available from the team's work of the Forum. With the scanner located at ground level, the top of the entablature of the Temple of Antonius and Faustina was a much greater distance from the scanner, than its base. We thus divided a scan that reflected a1.5 cm × 1.5 cm resolution of a distance of 28 m (the distance to the top or the entablature) down a third of the column shafts. The second scan was of the middle third of the column shafts. A 1.5 cm × 1.5 cm resolution was again used but at a distance of 25.5 m (the farthest distance within this scan). A third scan of the base of the shafts, a 1.5 cm × 1.5 cm resolution was acquired at 17 m. Finally, ground scans were taken and 13 m and 6.5 m.

[19] This static method of data collection could, indeed, be considered a deficiency of current scanner technology. A future growth of the technology may include "dynamic" resolution, in which the scanner is capable of acquiring a uniform resolution for the model regardless of object distance.

3.2   Collection of Data

The DHARMA team's first site day is always dedicated to additional planning, prepared to alter a number of its preliminary considerations during actual on-site adaptability. During this time, the team generally has found that the site supported many of its early conclusions and complicated others. Once on site at the forum, it became all-the-more apparent that the long-range, external scans were not feasible. The terrain of the forum—largely obscure when viewed in plan—rises 12 m from the central square to the western temple platforms. Further topographical variation results from the monument's massive bases. Given that the scanner can only acquire data for objects within its field of vision, the team had to work from the ground, in and among the ruins, using multiple vantages to capture a thorough and coherent model. (see Figs. 3 and 4). The most effective implementation of the scanner demanded that the team suppress its desire to capture any grand vistas—which the final model would provide—and instead attend to topographical nuance of the site and each monuments' composition.

Fig. 3. Single scan/multiple scan comparison: these two images of the Temple of Saturn juxtapose the information captured from a single scan position (top). Source: Luke Golesh

As the Forum supported some of the team's commitments, it complicated others. These difficulties too rested largely in the complexity of terrain and material on site. As the team intended to employ HDS targets to unite the data gathered from individual scan positions, the same difficulties of reflectivity and divergence that manifested during the offsite field tests was re-encountered at the Forum.[20] An ideal distance between scanner and target of 50 m was proposed, according to previous field-work and Leica's recommendation. In light of this restriction and the information that the team wished to capture, it was decided that the site would be divided into five basic sections. These could be roughly described as (1) the western temple precinct, (2) the Basilica Iulia, (3) the central square and Basilica Aemilia, (4) the eastern temple precinct, and (5) the Temple of Castor and Pollux. Proceeding in this manner, the targets provided the control points, while the scanner rotated around them capturing the

---

[20] While it is possible, albeit challenging, to register individual scanworlds without targets during post-processing, the team insisted upon the accuracy and convenience natural to target-based registration.

Fig. 4. Image of that of the final model (bottom). The partiality first image illustrates the necessity for additional scans from different vantages. Those portions of the monument obscured from the scanner's initial view are sought out in the subsequent scan positions. Source: Luke Golesh

desired data within the chosen section. Furthermore, great care was taken to ensure all six targets would be used in each section, and at least four of these targets would be visible from any given scan position. Thus, if one target had an error, there would still be an absolute minimum of three targets to link between two scan positions.

At this time, it was also decided that the digital survey would begin at the westernmost corner of the Forum, on the platform of the Porticus of the Dei Consentes, and work its way east. Yet, despite these critical decisions, the exact number of scans was left undecided, as were the total number of target locations required to fashion the point cloud model. The team's previous experience with the scanner made clear that such articulations of scanner movement were not only unnecessary but potentially obstructive. Rather, as long as the team remained conscious of its goal—a comprehensive, 3-D model of the Forum Romanum—the exact steps it took to reach it need not be specified. The scanner's software interface, Cyclone, further assisted this approach, as the team was able on a daily basis, after field work, to view the data gathered from each scan position and assess its contribution to the entire model.

3.3   Strategic Site Layout

Once the work had begun, the DHARMA digital survey team required seven, twelve-hour days to acquire the data to model the Forum Romanum. The survey began at the westernmost corner of the site and proceeded eastward, scanning the major monuments and open spaces of the ancient site.[21] This survey covered an area of approximately

---

[21] More precisely, the site was traversed, capturing the major monuments, in the following order: the Porticus of the Dei Consentes (scan position 1), the façade of the Tabularium; the Temple of Saturn; the Temple of Vespasian; the Temple of Concord; the Arch of Septimus Severus; the Basilica Iulia; the open, central space (the east and west rostra, the small monuments around the latter, and the Diocletianic columns); the Curia; the Basilica Aemilia; the Temple of Divus Iulius; the Temple of Antoninus and Faustina; the Regia; the Temple of Vesta; and the Temple of Castor and Pollux (scan pos 27).

250 m × 150 m, requiring 27 scan positions (composed of over five hundred individual scans) and 40 target locations only for the western half of the forum (see Fig. 5).[22]

From the platform of the Porticus of the Dei Consentes, a central position was chosen for the scanner (scanworld 1). Also at this time, all six targets were placed in its field of vision. These targets too had to be visible from the other scan positions intended for this section—viz., scanworlds 2–8. Given the critical importance of the targets, a number of considerations went into their exact placement: (1) distance, (2) dispersal, and (3) potential interference. Again, in accordance with existing standards, the ideal distance from scanner to target was 50 m. Confronted with the size of the site, however, this ideal was ultimately extended to a practical target range of 70 m.[23] Another consideration for target placement was dispersal. Dispersing the targets at over a greater area and varying their elevation as much a possible would further ensure accuracy when the scan positions were linked. Lastly, the targets had to be strategically separated from the typical tourist routes lest aberrations occur in the gathered data.

As the scanner moved from the Porticus platform to that of Vespasian, the targets were again acquired, and the new data visible from that position was added to the database. This process of target acquisition and data infill was repeated until the team had acquired a comprehensive survey of the western temple precinct. In order to progress further into the Forum, the targets had to be moved into the next section, the Basilica Iulia. At that point, the relationship between scanner and targets was inverted —i.e., rather than the scanner pivoting around the targets, the scanner would now be used as the control, or "pivot," for the targets. First, the scanner would acquire the targets from the previous section. The targets were then carefully placed in the subsequent section, rescanned, and named in accord with their new location. The scanner, having acquired the necessary data from its "pivot" position, would then proceed as before, moving around the site using the targets as the control. Employing this method —pivoting between targets and scanner— the team was able to use six HDS targets to document the entire site. Ultimately, this process required six "pivot" scan positions[24] and seven target groupings.[25]

In some cases, additional scan positions were added to obtain information from uniquely complex monuments. For instance, scan positions were not been planned for the western temple precinct; however, observing the data in the field, it became clear that they were necessary to capture more fully the western façade of the Arch of Septimius Severus and the platform of the Temple of Concord. This process of self-analysis enabled the team to make the necessary adjustments to the successive scans

---

[22] A 1.5 cm × 1.5 cm "adaptive" resolution was implemented in order to produce a final model with accuracy up to 1/2 in.

[23] Accuracy, as proven by field tests at the University of Notre Dame, was no problem at this extended range.

[24] As seen in Fig. 5, the pivots occurred at scan positions 8, 14, 19, 24, 25, and 26.

[25] The massive base of Temple of Castor and Pollux and relatively flat topography surrounding it forbade simple capture. In addition to those already planned, two pivot scans and ten target locations were required to acquire the necessary data.

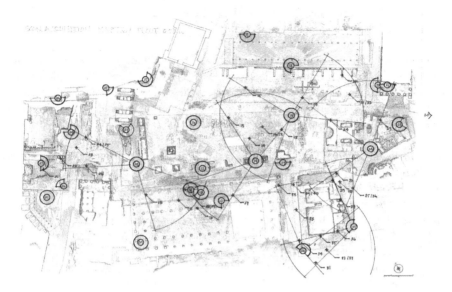

Fig. 5. Scan positions and target locations: this plan displays the scan locations (circled with red numbering) with their associated scope (represented by the second circle). The larger arcs represent pivot locations, displaying the two general areas of targets that each captured. The target locations (rendered in blue) were placed in such a manner as to be unobstructed by the monuments. Source: Ryan Hughes (Color figure online)

and collect all the desired data. In addition to being able to analyze its data in the field, the team was able to register the collected data—i.e., create a digital model out of the information acquired from individual scan positions—in order to further check for any inaccuracies or missing information. This check was conducted each evening after the site, and it proved both an important verification of the daily work and, ultimately, a confirmation of the Project's completion.

4   Post-site Work

4.1   Processing and Creating 3D and 2D Outputs

The DHARMA Forum Project's dataset is formidably large. During field-registration, it became increasingly apparent that the sheer size of the model would make the model difficult to visualize and edit. And, indeed, compiling the data into a single, clear, unified model was a sizable task. Back at the University of Notre Dame, the digital survey team registered the data in its entirety using Leica's Cyclone, a software program designed specifically for viewing, editing, and modeling of 3-D point clouds. Approximately 500 million data points comprise the unified, point cloud model. This registration confirmed the success of the team's field tactics, as only two target locations reported with major errors (see Figs. 6 and 7). Once these comparatively large aberrations were omitted from the registration, the average error for the model was 2 mm, far smaller than the chosen resolution.

Fig. 6. Target accuracy: slight differentiations in target location between the various scanworlds become apparent in this extreme close-up of the vertex. Here less than 5 mm of variation occurs in the acquired location of target no. 4 for seven of the western temple precinct's eight scanworlds. Source: Luke Golesh

Fig. 7. Target error: on two occasions, target locations were captured incorrectly by the scanner. Here, again target no. 4, an unexplained acquisition error from scanworld 7 placed the target vertex over 1 m from its actual location. However, redundant use of targets in every section of the Forum allowed simple deletion of the errant data prior to modeling. Source: Luke Golesh

The next step was to eliminate the unwanted information, or noise, from the model. The primary source of noise was in the constant flow of tourists. Aside from a few instances, tourists were moving during scans and made for little problems with our data. They were, however, visual obstructions in the model. Deleting this noise was simplified as people were limited to paved walking areas. Within the Cyclone software, an operator could hide all other points besides the walkway. Once hidden, deciphering

Fig. 8. Path before cleanup Source: Luke Golesh

Fig. 9. Path after cleanup: while noise doesn't necessarily create data problems in the model, it can be a major visual distraction. The top image shows the model before noise was removed, while the image on the bottom has been "cleaned." Source: Luke Golesh

between wanted and unwanted data points, it was much easier and the model achieved a greater visual clarity (see Figs. 8 and 9). Individual parts of the 3D model could be isolated for a more detailed study (see Fig. 10).

Having registered and unified the point data into a model, the team was able to measure with precision every aspect of the Roman Forum captured by the scanner. This model can be navigated in real time, viewed as one would on site, as well as frozen, in order to examine an area in detail. Additionally, the point data has been cross

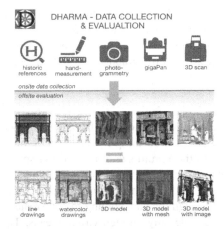

Fig. 10. Date processing: all mediums used on pre and on-site are collected and studied to generate various forms of outputs. The chart above indicates the various outputs from the documentation of Arch of Septimus Severus. Source: Kristina Furse Davis

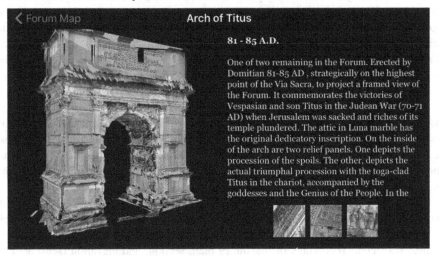

Fig. 11. App on the monuments of Roman Forum: out of the multiple outputs of this project, one output is the 3D app (release planned in spring 2019) for the monuments on the site. The app allows exploration of individual monuments with free spin, rotate and zoom ability. Source: Kristina Furse Davis

referenced and combined with data collected through the three other methods employed by the team for site collection (see Fig. 10).[26] This were converted into line drawings and into common computer aided design (CAD) software for further uses. [27]

---

[26] A more detail report on the methods employed to create integrated methods of study are seen under, Krusche, K. reference articles.

[27] While importing the model into these software programs is possible, the large size of the model currently requires hefty processing power.

A new app and other visual material on the Roman Forum are presently being prepared with combined results of scan data with Gigapan photograpy to create highly accurate photoreal visualization (see Fig. 11). In short, there is a vast potential for visualization of cloud data, both orthographic and three-dimensional.

5   Conclusion

The DHARMA Forum Project would not have been possible without digital surveying technology. The laser scanner was uniquely capable of maneuvering through the complex terrain inherent to the Forum site at a proficient speed with neither compromise in accuracy of data nor undue impact on the ancient site.[28] Most importantly, an easily-comprehensible 3-D model of the Forum Romanum was produced. The unfamiliar viewer can move through the site, coming to appreciate the site from renowned perspectives and those possible only through virtual means. The scholar can measure and manipulate the model as suits the purposes of his or her analysis.

It is critical to note, however, that many important observations, which would have been overlooked by the digital survey, were recorded during the hand surveying of the site by the DHARMA team. Proper use of the laser scanning technology often requires the operator's full attention. The site is viewed inevitably at a removed sense, through a laptop screen; it is not engaged at a physical level. This approach changes the paradigms of the documentation and design processes in historic preservation. With this paradigm shift, the forensic element in historic building documentation can be lost. In comparison, an act of hand measurement can't but bring one into contact with the artifact or monument.

There is no universal tool to document these sites, and we have to find ways in which a combination of these techniques together with hand measuring (still as the most important way of handling and understanding the site) can produce the most accurate and advance results. Together with digital scanning technology, field documentation and photography can be an effective tool for evaluation in both the preservation and conservation of historic resources.

Since its time on the Forum, the DHARMA team has continued converting scan data into both more traditional, orthographic formats for architectural analysis as well as pioneering 3-D visualization methods. Regarding the former, the team produced scaled, watercolor renderings of the site in plan, section, and elevation (see Fig. 11). These drawings, while produced primarily from the digital scan data, were deeply informed by all of the survey methods utilized on site. Regarding the latter, the team (in cooperation with the Center for Research Computing) aims to create an ultra-high resolution, photo-real model through a merger of the laser scanner's point cloud and GigaPan panoramic images. Success in this endeavor could provide the archeologist, art historian, architect, and non-professional alike an intimate experience of a remote— even inaccessible—site. These are but a few of the potential applications of the laser scanner in conjunction with the mainstays of historic research: the hand-measurement and the photograph.

---

[28] More recent scanning devices, with each new generation of Leica scanners, have greatly increased the speed of data capture with associated benefits and drawbacks.

References

1. Watkin, D.: The Roman Forum. Harvard University Press, Cambridge (2009)
2. United Nations Educational, Scientific, and Cultural Organization (UNESCO) World Heritage Convention Homepage, http://whc.unesco.org. Accessed 02 Aug 2018
3. Gorski, G., Packer, J.E.: The Roman Forum: A Reconstruction and Architectural Guide. Cambridge University Press, New York (2015)
4. Martin, T.R.: Ancient Rome, from Romulus to Justinian, pp. 43–50. Yale University Press, New Haven (2012)
5. Steinby, M.E.: Lexicon topographicum urbis romae. Quasar, Rome (1993)
6. Claridge, A.: Rome: An Oxford Archaeological Guide. Oxford University Press, New York (1998)
7. Bignamini, I.: Archives and Excavations: Essays on the History of Archaeological Excavations in Rome and Southern Italy from the Renaissance to the Nineteenth Century, pp. 15–22. The British School at Rome, London (2004)
8. Borsi, S.: Giuliano da sangallo: I disegni di architettura dell'antico. Officina, Rome (1985)
9. Pizzi, A., (ed.) Le Antiche Rovine di Roma Nei Disegni di du Pérac, Milano (1990)
10. Portoghesi, P. (ed.): Giovanni Antonio Dosio: Roma Antica e I Disegni di Architettura Agli Uffizi. Officina Edizioni, Rome (1976)
11. Zorzi, G.: I Disegni delle Antichità di Andrea Palladio. N. Pozza, Venezia (1959)
12. Desgodets, A.B.: Les édifices antiques de rome, dessinés et mesurés très exactement. Chez Iean Baptiste Coignard, Paris (1682)
13. Coarelli, F.: Ruins of Ancient Rome: The Drawings of the French Architects Who Won the Prix de Rome 1786–1924. Getty Publications, Los Angeles (2002). Massilimano, D. (ed.)
14. D'Espouy, H., Blatteau, J.W., Sears, C.: Fragments from Greek and Roman Architecture: The Classical America Edition of Hector d'Espouy's Plates. W.W. Norton and Company, NewYork (1981)
15. Packer, J.E.: Digitizing Roman Imperial architecture in the early 21st century: purposes, data, failures, and prospects. JRA Suppl. Ser. **61**, 309 (2006)
16. Taylor, G.L., Cresy, E.: The Architectural Antiquities of Rome. Lockwood, London (1874)
17. Boni, G.: Le recenti esplorazioni nel Sacrario di Vesta, Tipografia della R. Accademia dei Lincei (1900)
18. Coarelli, F.: Il Foro Romano, 2 v. Quasar, Rome (1983–1985)
19. Coarelli, F.: Lexicon topographicum urbis Romae. Quasar, Rome (2004)
20. Digital Scholarships Collection, UCLA Cultural Virtual Reality Lab (CVR Lab). http://wayback.archive-it.org/7877/20160919152126/http://dlib.etc.ucla.edu/projects/Forum/. Accessed 02 Aug 2018
21. Frischer, B., Abernathy, D., Giuliani, F.C., Scott, R.T., Ziemssen, H.: A new digital model of the Roman Forum. JRA Suppl. Ser. **61**, 162–182 (2006)
22. Krusche, K., Kapp, P.H.: Documenting National and World Heritage Sites: The need to integrate Digital Documentation and 3D Scanning with Traditional Hand Measuring techniques. SMARTDoc Symposium, Philadelphia, Pennsylvania (2010)
23. Gigapan. http://gigapan.org/. Accessed 02 Aug 2018
24. Hughes, K.E., Louden, E.I.: Bridging the Gap: Using 3-D laser Scanning in Historic-Building Documentation. APT Bull. **36**(2/3), 37–46 (2005)

25. Krusche, K., Sweet, C.: Documenting National and World Heritage Sites: The need to integrate Digital Documentation and 3D Scanning with Traditional Hand Measuring techniques. 3D Digital Documentation Summit, National Center for Preservation Technology and Training, National Park Service, U.S. Department of the Interior (2012)
26. Krusche, K., Sweet, C., Sweet, J., Turner, P.: History in 3D: New Virtualization Techniques for Innovative Architectural and Archeological Scholarship and Education. Computer applications and quantitative methods in Archaeology Conference. University of Southampton, UK (2012)

The Reconstruction of Urartu Buildings of Altıntepe in Virtual Environment

The Temple Altıntepe Virtualization Example

Serap Kuşu[✉]

Istanbul University, Ordu Cad. No: 6, Laleli, Fatih, 34134 İstanbul, Turkey
serapkusu@gmail.com

Abstract. In Altıntepe region of Erzincan, Turkey, a temple complex, religious buildings, Apadana, city walls, a drainage system, and many more functionally unidentified architectural remains were unearthed during the excavations which took place between 1960 and 2014.

One of the most remarkable of these buildings is the temple complex. The temple, only the foundation of which has survived today, was virtually reconstructed in 2013, in the light of the archaeological data. The reconstruction was based on the imagery of the temple with towers, found on Urartian stone and bronze plates. The visualization process of the temple consisted of a number of different stages.

In the first stage, the buildings in the Urartu citadel, and the latest data on the architectural plans and the debates of these were evaluated. Previous trials of 3D reconstruction of the buildings contributed greatly to our project. The details on the reliefs of Urartian, Assyrian, and other contemporary cultures, and the publications on these were evaluated and utilized.

In the second stage, the obtained data was transferred to virtual environment. The temple was 3D-modeled with the help of the software 3D Max, AutoCAD and V-Ray.

Then the model was textured and rendered, and the reconstruction was finalized. As a result, the architectural data obtained from the Urartian and Assyrian reliefs, and the archaeological data obtained from the field were combined, which led to a better understanding of the Urartian temple architecture.

Besides, this project yielded technical data and suggestions about the reconstruction of the existing remains. In the end, the visualization of the virtual city is posted public in YouTube "Urartu Kentleri Canlanıyor". (Serap Kuşu

Urartu Kentleri Canlanıyor, https://youtu.be/geuSAGZdDuE (2014)

Keywords: Digital archaeology · 3D reconstructions in archaeology
Urartian kingdom

© Springer Nature Switzerland AG 2018
M. Ioannides et al. (Eds.): EuroMed 2018, LNCS 11196, pp. 301–311, 2018.
https://doi.org/10.1007/978-3-030-01762-0_25

1 Altıntepe Citadel

Altıntepe Fortress was founded on one of the volcanic cones in the northeastern part of Erzincan plain, which is surround-ed by high mountain ranges (Fig. 1). This natural hill is located 14 km from the city center and rises 60 m above the plain level. It first came to the forefront with the plunder of two graves in 1938 and 1956. In 1959, excavation at the site started under the super-vision of the late Prof. Tahsin Özgüç from Ankara University (Özgüç 1966; Özgüç 1969). Excavation continued until 1968 and revealed

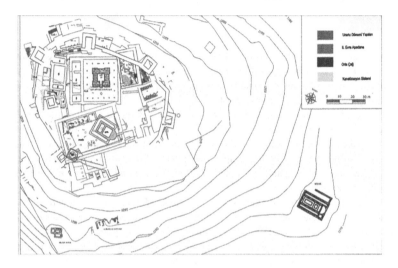

Fig. 1. The Plan of the Inner Fortress of Altıntepe (Karaosmanoğlu 2011: 367)

Fig. 2. Altıntepe Citadel (http://www.bik.gov.tr/tarihi-altintepe-kalesi-turizme-kazandirilacak/.)

architectural features and small finds that belonged to the Urartian period. Finds from the excavation were evaluated in many articles and in a two-volume work. The Urartian buildings discovered at Altıntepe contributed greatly to Anatolian archaeology and are regarded as important examples of the culture which they represent. On top of the 200 m wide hill are the citadel gate and walls, which were destroyed by the late Eastern Roman walls, the temple-palace, apadana, and the storage building immediately outside the walls. On the southern slope of the hill an open-air temple and three underground stone grave chambers are located (Fig. 2. Reference source: http://www.bik.gov.tr/tarihi-altintepe-kalesi-turizme-kazandirilacak/.). The project at Altıntepe, which began in 2003 reached its seventh season in 2009. In the second term of excavation and restoration work we have reached important conclusions (Karaosmanoğlu, et al. 2008: 497; Karaosmanoğlu 2011: 366; Karaosmanoğlu, et al. 2013: 138) (Fig. 3).

Fig. 3. Urartian Temple of Altıntepe (Karaosmanoğlu 2011: 372)

2   The Archaeological Data

The first ideas on the construction of Urartian temples were used as a source from the relief of Khorsabad (Fig. 4). The shape of the temple, pyramidal roof, boilers in front of the temple and shield on the wall has been a source of inspiration for the reconstruction of Urartian temples to many researchers (Botta and Flandin 1849: 141; Barnett 1982: 369–370). In later years, the architectural description on the stone and bronze reliefs from the Adilcevaz, Toprakkale and other Urartian centers, describes the type of architecture as tower buildings which is different than the reliefs from Khorsabad (Fig. 5). It is also understood that those buildings have several floors, and there are often crenellated towers, windows and arched doorways. This description of architecture is often seen to repeat on the reliefs in different Urartian centers (Barnett 1950: Res. 1; Bilgiç and Öğün 1967: 7; Kleiss 1982: 55; Seidl 2004: 146).

Fig. 4. The Relief of Khorsabad (Botta and Flandin 1849: Pl. 141).

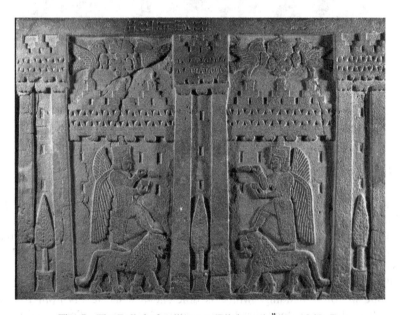

Fig. 5. The Relief of Adilcevaz (Bilgiç and Öğün 1967: 7).

3 The Reconstruction of Temple in Altıntepe

Three basic questions are vital for the 3D reconstruction of Urartian buildings: What have we done, how have we done, and why have we done? The answer to the first question is that we have tried to define the architectural style and size of Urartian buildings. We have stated the methods and techniques we have used while we have planned the Urartian buildings, as the answer of the second question. And, for the third question, we have explained the archaeological and scientific data shaping the Urartian buildings.

- In this framework,
- We have evaluated the archaeological data,
- We have examined the technical possibilities thought to have been used in the construction process,
- We have analyzed the 3D projects carried out about this issue.

We have tried to reconstruct the living spaces found on Altıntepe citadel and the upper parts of these buildings, which did not survive to this day, corresponding to the historicity and the archaeological fabric in the virtual environment, using 3D visualization software.

4 The Process of 3D Reconstruction

The process of 3D reconstruction of the buildings consists of these steps:

The modelling of the buildings in 3D Max software with the help of the data prepared in AutoCAD software.

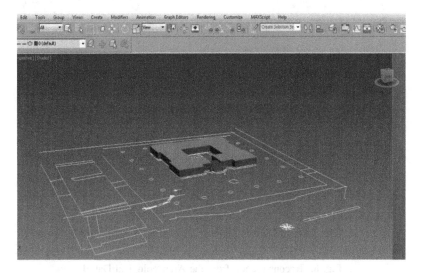

Fig. 6. The First Process of 3D Modeling

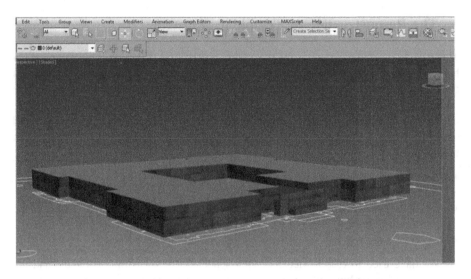

Fig. 7. The Second Process of Stone in Covering 3D Modelling

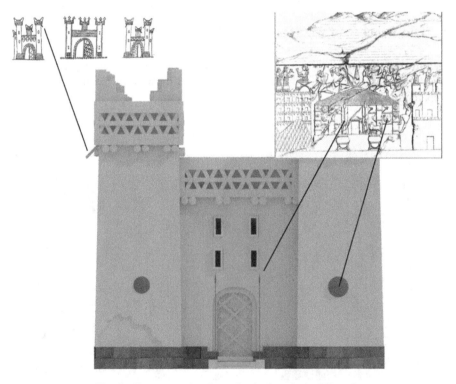

Fig. 8. Reconstruction from the Archaeological Data I

- Covering the models with their own texture and the achievement of the most realistic appearance, enhancing the angles and the realistic appearance of the models using cam and light,
- Rendering the prepared stage and creating files in the suitable picture formats,
- Adding effects to the files in picture formats using Photoshop software, and finishing with the suitable picture formats.

The first part of our 3D visualization project is the reconstruction of the Urartian temple. The architectural plan of the temple is based on stone and metal reliefs of Urartian origin. Architectural motifs repeated on most of those reliefs are such:

- Structures contain towers higher than the façade,
- Beam ends sticking out are visible on the towers and the façade, and they are arranged with regular distances.
- Patterned bands are visible on towers and façades.
- The main building and the towers contain rectangular windows.
- The doors are arched.

We have suggested a temple model with one tower on each corner. We started our Project by transferring the square temple plan drawn on AutoCAD software to 3D Max software and redrawing it (Fig. 6).

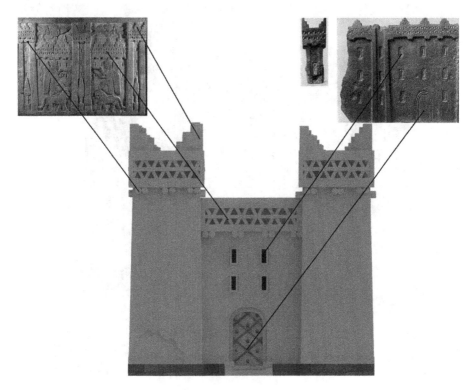

Fig. 9. Reconstruction from the Archaeological Data II

We raised this two dimensional model one point 1.15 m which is the height of the stone foundation surviving to this day. This foundation consists of three rows of basalt stones, and continues along the temple plan as horizontal stone rows. We photographed all sides of the temple in order to give stone texture to the foundation of our model. We virtually fixed the broken, damaged, and lost parts of the stones with the help of Photoshop software, and created the suitable texture to cover the model. We applied the stone texture to all four sides of the one point 1.15 m high mode (Fig. 7). After the necessary corrections we made using 3D Max software to create the suitable appearance, we enhanced the model in order for it to look realistic. There are different opinions about the height of the temple of Altıntepe. We reconstructed the temple with the total height of fourteen meters (Karaosmanoğlu 2011: 367). This is an estimated height. The actual height might differ. We designated the height of the main building as ten meters, and the height of the towers added to the main building as four meters. In this way, we created a temple model with four towers.

There are different opinions about the height of the temple of Altıntepe. We reconstructed the temple with the total height of fourteen meters (Karaosmanoğlu 2011: 367). This is an estimated height. The actual height might differ. We designated the height of the main building as ten meters, and the height of the towers added to the main building as four meters. In this way, we created a temple model with four towers (Figs. 8 and 9).

Fig. 10. The Reconstruction Urartian Temple I

Fig. 11. The Reconstruction Urartian Temple II

Fig. 12. The Reconstruction Urartian Temple III

We used mudbrick, stone, and wood textures for the covering of the model. At the excavations carried out in the Urartian borders, it is discovered that the upper part of the temples were made of mudbrick. With the help of this information, we applied a plastered mudbrick appearance to the upper part of our temple model (Figs. 10, 11, 12, and 13). We added wooden gargoyles to the towers. Thus, we finished our Urartian temple model in the virtual environment. With similar techniques, we virtually reconstructed the temple complex, the palace structure, the mansion, the warehouse, and the defensive walls.

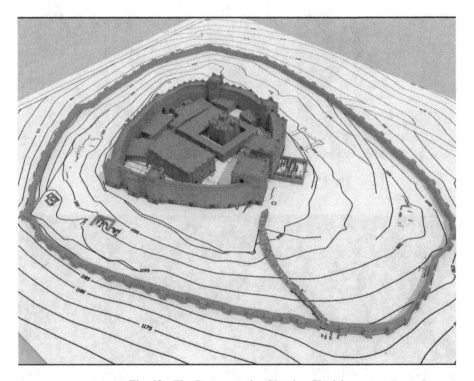

Fig. 13. The Reconstruction Urartian Citadel

5 Conclusion

Thus, we have presented the architectural functions, shapes, and features of the main structures constituting the center of a city. In this way, we have had the opportunity to examine the connection and similarities of those buildings. We have analyzed how the archaeological data obtained have influenced this project, and also the similarities and the differences of similar projects. This is the first time Urartian buildings have been studied in a virtual environment. The measurements and textures of the buildings have been transferred into the digital environment with the help of various software, making it possible to comprehend them in a more realistic and complete way.

References

Barnett, R.D.: The excavations of the British Museum at Toprak Kale near Van. Iraq **1**, 1–43 (1950)

Bilgiç, E., Öğün, B.: Adilcevaz Kef Kalesi Kazıları 1965 - Second Season of Excavation at Kef Kalesi of Adilcevaz. Anadolu (Anatolia) **9**, 1–20 (1967)

Botta, P.E., Flandin, E.N.: Monument de Ninive I-III, Paris (1849)

Karaosmanoğlu, M.: Erzincan Altıntepe Kalesi / Erzincan Altıntepe Fortress. In: Köroğlu, K., Konyar, E. (eds.) Urartu: Doğu'da Değişim/Transformation in the East, pp. 366–371. Yapı Kredi Yayınları, İstanbul (2011)

Karaosmanoğlu, M., Can, B., Korucu, H.: Altıntepe Urartu Kalesi 2006 Yılı Kazı ve Onarım Çalışmaları. In: 29. Kazı Sonuçları Toplantısı, pp. 497–514 (2008)

Karaosmanoğlu, M., Korucu, H., Yılmaz, M.A.: Altıntepe Urartu Kalesi 2011 Yılı Kazı ve Onarım Çalışmaları. In: 34. Kazı Sonuçları Toplantısı, vol. 1, pp. 137–146 (2013)

Kourtzellis, J., Sampanikou, E.: The contribution of 3D representations in the study and promotion of archaeological data: the case of the temple of Messa in Lesvos. In: Sampanikou, E. (ed.) 2nd International Conference on image science "Gazing into the 21st Century". Department for Image Science (DIS), Danube University, Goettweig (2008)

Köroğlu, K.: Urartu: Krallık ve Aşiretler. Urartu: The Kingdom and Tribes. In: Köroğlu, K., Konyar, E. (eds.) Urartu: Doğu'da Değişim/Transformation in the East, pp. 12–55. Yapı Kredi Yayınları, İstanbul (2011)

Morgan, C.L.: (Re)Building Çatalhöyük: changing virtual reality in archaeology. Archaeol. J. World Archaeol. Congr. **5**, 448–484 (2009)

Özgüç, T.: The Urartian Architecture, Anatolia VII (1963)

Özgüç, T.: Altıntepe I, Mimarlık Anıtlları ve Duvar Resimleri-Archhitectural Monuments and Wall Paintings. Türk Tarih Kurumu, Ankara (1966)

Özgüç, T.: Altıntepe II Mezarlar, Depo Binası ve Fildişi Eserler. Türk Tarih Kurumu, Ankara (1969)

Sequeira, M.L., Morgado, L.: Virtual archaeology in second life and opensimulator. J. Virtual Worlds Res. **6**, 1–16 (2003)

Web Sites: http://www.bik.gov.tr/tarihi-altintepe-kalesi-turizme-kazandirilacak/

A New Enhancement Filtering Approach for the Automatic Vector Conversion of the UAV Photogrammetry Output

Maria Alicandro[1]([✉]) [iD], Donatella Dominici[1] [iD],
and Paolo Massimo Buscema[2,3]

[1] University of L'Aquila, Via Giovanni Gronchi, 18, 67100 L'Aquila, Italy
maria.alicandro@univaq.it
[2] Semeion Research Center of Sciences of Communication, Via Sersale 117,
00128 Rome, Italy
[3] Department of Mathematical and Statistical Sciences, University of Colorado,
Denver, CO, USA

Abstract. In the last decades the photogrammetry has undergone interesting innovation, both in terms of data processing and acquisition mode, to allow obtaining detailed 3D models useful for complete survey and important support for the management and recovery of cultural heritage and buildings. However, despite recent developments, the main photogrammetry outputs are raster data (ortophoto and DEM) and point clouds characterized by high informative content, but they are not typically extracted automatically. Automated feature detection is yet manual, time-consuming procedure and an active area of research. The raster to vector conversion is not direct, but transformations must be performed on the input data to convert the pixel values into features. Always, segmentations are preceded by filter technique to remove noise and to improve the conversion phase. However, remote sensing data and especially UAV photogrammetry output are the most complex to treat because of their heterogeneity (presence of different objects and shapes), the nature of sensor used and the different scale. In this work we experiment new enhancement filter to improve the automatic extraction of vector information for a UAV photogrammetry results of the facing walls of eminent church, symbol of the city of L'Aquila, the" Basilica of Santa Maria di Collemaggio".

Keywords: Photogrammetry · UAV · Segmentation · Filter enhancement

1 Introduction

The photogrammetric process, combining the Computer Vision [1–3] and UAV technology [4–7], allows to obtain different metrically correct and georeferenced products, such as 3D models, point clouds, orthomosaics and Digital Elevation Models (DEMs), able to describe in a particular and continuous way the investigated object. However, by their nature, these data do not allow to derive the information about the characteristics of surveyed objects in a quantitative manner (total built area, areas and lengths of details, measurements, material characteristics, etc.), because any point or pixel (depending on the output returned) corresponds to a different information that must be queried

© Springer Nature Switzerland AG 2018
M. Ioannides et al. (Eds.): EuroMed 2018, LNCS 11196, pp. 312–321, 2018.
https://doi.org/10.1007/978-3-030-01762-0_26

individually. The raster to vector conversion is not direct, but transformations, namely segmentation, must be performed to convert the pixel values into features. Segmentation consists of partitioning images into distinct and homogeneous regions based on a distinguishable characteristic. The grouping into regions (clusters) is based on criteria of homogeneity and discontinuity between the values of pixels [8]. The segmentation algorithms derive from the Pattern Recognition and Computer Vision for the analysis of images in different application fields: from medicine to telecommunications. Different types of segmentations have been proposed, each one is used for different purposes and applicable to several types of images. In geomatics, the main segmentation algorithms can be divided into two categories: *pixel-oriented*, based on individual pixel classifications and may be unsupervised or supervised, and *object-oriented*, which instead are able to group characteristics by aggregation in similar regions or polygons. In this case, different strategies are used: point-based, edge-based, region-based or combined. The *object-oriented* techniques are more suitable to extract edge. To improve the segmentation phase, several filter are used for better reading of data [9, 10]. The filtering process tends to create less noisy separation thresholds for contours detection and many algorithms used for this purpose are derivative filters, as Robert, Prewitt, Sobel filters, Canny algorithm and the Laplacian filters (Zero Crossing) [11]. However, remote sensing data are the most complex to treat [12] because of their heterogeneity (presence of different objects and shapes), the nature of sensor used and the different scale.

The literature provides several approaches to obtain vector data in the field of remote sensing. In [12] the main advantages and limitations of object-oriented segmentation techniques to multispectral images are analysed. Another case is reported in [13] for the thematic classification of Worldview2 images, characterized by 8 spectral bands and a geometric resolution of 0.5 m. Other examples are based on the same approach for the restitution of land use and forest maps, always through the treatment of multispectral data from satellite [14, 15]. Another interesting application example for the extraction and vectorial reconstruction of buildings starting from DEM data proposed by [16] among the analysis of the roof discontinuity plans performed on data with a geometric resolution of 1 m coming from LIDAR techniques.

When these techniques are applied to data coming from the close-range photogrammetry, characterized by a very high geometric resolution (centimetre) and a low radiometric resolution (referring especially to amateur camera), the results of classifications cannot be being so satisfying and failing in vectorization. In this work, we present a new approach to improve the vectorialization of the particular mosaic of the main façade of an important cultural heritage. In order to achieve this aim, we analysed how to enhance the separation threshold using a new approach based on experimental filters: Active Connection Matrix (ACM) developed by the Semeion Research Centre for the Science of Communication and until now experimented only in medical field.

2   Case Study "Santa Maria of Collemaggio"

2.1   Test Area and Photogrammetry Survey

The survey involved "Santa Maria of Collemaggio" (see Fig. 1), a medieval church, the most important religious site of L'Aquila (Italy). It was carried out with a mini UAV Anteos A2-Mini/B equipped by a Canon S100 digital compact camera (see Table 1).

Fig. 1. Test area.

The main steps to obtain a metric 3D model are discussed in [17, 18] and in this section the main characteristics are summarised. The survey includes three phase: flight planning, data acquisition and elaboration steps. Starting from the knowledge of the relationships that exist between the characteristics of the sensor (focal length and sensor size), the flight altitude/distance and the Ground Sample Distance (GSD), two flight have been planned with a vertical route to reconstruct the church facades. Two different distance have been planned due to the particular configuration of the site: the first flight was carried out to survey the principal façade, characterised by a large space in front of it, and a second one to survey the "Holy Door" side, where the presence of an escarpment limits the distance of the photograms' acquisition. The parameter are reported in Table 1.

Table 1. (a) Sensor parameters and instrument and (b) Flight parameters.

(a) Sensor parameters and instrument				(b) Flight parameters	1st flight	2nd flight
Type of UAV			Mini-UAV	GSD	1 cm	0,36 cm
			Quad-copter	Distance from facade	30 m	10 m
Optical sensor	Camera		Canon S100	Overlapping	90%	90%
	Resolution		12 MP	Waypoints	14	277
	Focal length		5.2 mm			
	Sensor	Width	7,6 mm			
	Dimensions	Height	5,7 mm			
	Pixel dimension		1.9 μm			

The flights can be executed following the pre-imposed route to acquire 291 images to cover the entire church. In addition, in order to complete the survey design and to georeferenced the final 3D model in the following step, 52 natural Ground Control Points (GCPs) easily identifiable and well distributed on the structure were also measured in a local reference system using a Total Station TS30. In order to georeference the final model with respect to the ETRF00 reference system, a framing network was measured with the GNSS technique in static mode.

The data elaboration has been carried out using Agisoft Photoscan [19] which allows to obtain the 3D model following the Structure From Motion workflow [20] and the Dense Matching approach. This new approach permits to obtain the values of camera calibration in an automatic way [21] considering those values as variables in the resolution of the collinearity equations. Further information of the elaboration steps are explained in [18]. The main results of the of the photogrammetric elaboration are the georeferenced 3D model, ortophoto and DEM (see Fig. 2).

Fig. 2. Photogrammetry results: orthomosaic, depth map and 3D model.

2.2   ACM Elaboration

The edge extraction of the facade mosaic using the object-oriented segmentations and filters requires a clear separation threshold that is still a critical issue. To enhance the threshold distinction, a new approach has been tested, using experimental filters: Active Connection Matrix (ACM) developed by the Semeion Research Centre for the Science of Communication and until now experimented only in medical field. The images, whit this algorithm, are considered as a connected matrix of elements that develop over time. Two new variables are added to the original images: the local connection between the pixels ω and the time t according to the equation:

$$PIXEL^{originale}(x_1, x_2, x_3, x_D) = PIXEL^{ACM}(x_1, x_2, x_3, x_D, w, t) \tag{1}$$

These systems remodel any digital image through three operations:

1. Transform the original image into a connected pixel network;
2. Apply to the connected pixel networks the original brightness of the pixels and/or their connections t;
3. Terminate when the cost function is satisfied that is when the transformation process stabilizes. The ACM systems are subdivided into three classes according to the variables, the pixel connection, the units or both that are considered constrained/unconstrained [22].

For the aim of this work, the New Constraint Satisfaction Networks (New CS), which is a fixed connection system, allowed to obtain a binary image and a good threshold distinction. The analysis was performed on 2D images. A two-dimensional image can be expressed as a pixel matrix according to Eq. (1), in which the radiometric values are considered the evolutionary units *(u)* in the ACM systems and the active array of connections is defined through the following system of equations:

$$
\begin{aligned}
u_{i,j}^{[n+1]} = f(u_{i,j}^{[n]}, u_{i-1,j-1}^{[n]}, u_{i,j-1}^{[n]}, u_{i+1,j-1}^{[n]}, u_{i-1,j}^{[n]}, \\
u_{i+1,j}^{[n]}, u_{i-1,j+1}^{[n]}, u_{i,j+1}^{[n]}, u_{i+1,j+1}^{[n]}, \\
w_{(i,j),(i,j-1)}^{[n]}, w_{(i,j),(i-1,j-1)}^{[n]}, w_{(i,j),(i+1,j-1)}^{[n]}, w_{(i,j),(i-1,j)}^{[n]}, \\
w_{(i,j),(i+1,j)}^{[n]}, w_{(i,j),(i-1,j+1)}^{[n]}, w_{(i,j),(i,j+1)}^{[n]}, w_{(i,j),(i+1,j+1)}^{[n]})
\end{aligned} \tag{2}
$$

and

$$
\begin{aligned}
w_{(i,j),(i-1,j-1)}^{[n+1]} &= g(u_{i,j}^{[n]}, u_{i,j-1}^{[n]}, w_{(i,j),(i-1,j-1)}^{[n]}) & w_{(i,j),(i-1,j-1)}^{[n+1]} &= g(u_{i,j}^{[n]}, u_{i,j-1}^{[n]}, w_{(i,j),(i-1,j-1)}^{[n]}) \\
w_{(i,j),(i,j-1)}^{[n+1]} &= g(u_{i,j}^{[n]}, u_{i-1,j-1}^{[n]}, w_{(i,j),(i,j-1)}^{[n]}) & w_{(i,j),(i,j-1)}^{[n+1]} &= g(u_{i,j}^{[n]}, u_{i-1,j-1}^{[n]}, w_{(i,j),(i,j-1)}^{[n]}) \\
w_{(i,j),(i+1,j-1)}^{[n+1]} &= g(u_{i,j}^{[n]}, u_{i+1,j-1}^{[n]}, w_{(i,j),(i+1,j-1)}^{[n]}) & w_{(i,j),(i+1,j-1)}^{[n+1]} &= g(u_{i,j}^{[n]}, u_{i+1,j-1}^{[n]}, w_{(i,j),(i+1,j-1)}^{[n]}) \\
w_{(i,j),(i-1,j)}^{[n+1]} &= g(u_{i,j}^{[n]}, u_{i-1,j}^{[n]}, w_{(i,j),(i-1,j)}^{[n]}) & w_{(i,j),(i-1,j)}^{[n+1]} &= g(u_{i,j}^{[n]}, u_{i-1,j}^{[n]}, w_{(i,j),(i-1,j)}^{[n]})
\end{aligned} \tag{3}
$$

$$
\forall u_{i,j}^{[n]}; \forall w_{i,j,x+k,j+z}^{[n]}
$$
$$
|(i,j,x+k,j+z) \in I_x^G = \{(i,j,x+k,j+z)|0 < dist(i,j,x+k,j+z) \le G\}
$$

with fixed initial value $u_{i,j}^{[0]} = u_x^{[0]}$; $w_{(i,j)(i,j,x+k,j+z)}^{[0]} = w_{x,xs}^{[0]}$.

Subscript *x* is the pixel position *i; j*, while subscript *s* is the pixel position respect to a neighborhood I_x^G of radius G. G is the pixel's number, neighborhood to the central pixel.

In fixed connection systems, units or pixels evolve at each processing cycle *(n)* on values calculated in the previous cycle using fixed connections:

$$
u_{i,j} = u_x^{[n+1]} = f(u_x^{[n]}, \ldots, u_{xs}^{[n]}, \ldots, w_{x,xs}^{[0]}) \tag{4}
$$

Where $w^{[0]}_{x,xs}$ represents the connection between the pixel $x = (i; j)$ and its neighbour $xs = (i + k; j + z)$ calculated at time 0.

2D image becomes a matrix whit R rows and C columns, in which each cell is an autonomous unit $u_{i,j} = u_{i,j}^{[0]} = u_x^{[n]}$, connected with the 8 units of its neighbourhood with symmetrical weight $w_{(i,j),(i+k,j+z)}^{[0]} = w_{x,xs}^{[0]}$. The Automata Rule (AR) algorithm defines the connection among pixel through non-linear transformations of the different brightness of the pixels. Considering that each unit can assume [0; 1], a parameter is defined to control the connections strength σ, making the algorithm sensitive to differences in the images and can take values between $0 \le \sigma \le 2^N$, with N the discrete number of brightness levels that each unit can assume in the range of data values (for example 2^8). Thus, the Gaussian transformation relative to brightness values among adjacent pixels is defined:

$$R_{(i,j),(i+k,j+z)} = e^{-(\sigma u_{i,j} - \sigma u_{i+k,j+z})^2} \tag{5}$$

Defined its minimum value $\varepsilon = e^{-\sigma^2}$, it is possible to scale and add a constant therefore the value of the projection can take a value into $[-c; c]$ (for example $c = 5$) simplifying the calculations and obtaining:

$$R'_{(i,j),(i+k,j+z)} = \frac{c}{1-\varepsilon}(2 * R_{(i,j),(i+k,j+z)} - \varepsilon - 1) \tag{6}$$

The value of connections is defined through a hyperbolic tangent:

$$w^{[0]}_{(i,j),(i+k,j+z)} = w^{[0]}_{(x,x_s)} = Tanh(R'_{(i,j),(i+k,j+z)}) \tag{7}$$

The AR defines connections as close to 1 if the brightness values of the connected units are similar and tends -1 the more they are not [22].

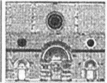

Fig. 3. Automata Rule with different σ; from left to right: $\sigma = 10$, 15, 20 and 40.

In Fig. 3 are reported several analysis varying σ: For weak connections ($\sigma = 10$), there is a loss of information, while for high σ, the strength of connection between the pixels tends to create very noisy images. Therefore, $\sigma = 15$ was chosen as the final AR value.

Once defined the connections, New Cs algorithm determines the evolution of pixels. The New CS is a changed version of the Constraint Satisfaction Networks [23] and the central idea is to consider each pixel-agent of the matrix a "hypothesis", which can be gradually "true" or "false", in ratio to the brightness value of each pixel agent.

The cost function of the New CS system tends to "make true" the hypothesis of the matrix:

$$Maxf(Pixel) = f(Pixel) = \frac{1}{2} * \sum_x \sum_{I_x} u_x * u_{x_s} * w_{x,x_s} \tag{8}$$

where: $Pixel$ = all pixels; x = position of central pixel; I_x = neighbourhood; u_x = value of central pixel $[0; 1]$; w_x; x_s = x e x_s connection.

The optimization rule of each pixel is based on Boolean functions, NOT (XOR), AND and CONTEST. The following Eq. 9 is for the NOT (XOR) function:

$$(u_x u_{x_S}) + (\overline{u}_x \overline{u}_{x_S}) = State; \tag{9}$$

The parameter that allows to define the binary image is the number of cycles (C). Below, some images and their histograms of the orthophoto processing for cycles 1, 30, 60 and 100 are shown (See Fig. 4).

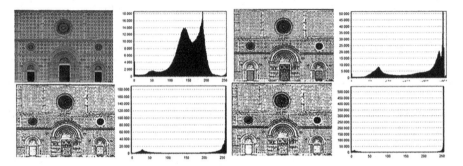

Fig. 4. New CS elaboration. On the left the orthophotos; on the right the histograms. upper left c: 10, bottom left c: 30; upper right c: 60; bottom right c: 100. Values of grayscale pixels from 0 to 255 in x axis, while in the y axis are shown the pixel numbers of the image. Ordinate scale is different, but is not confusing because the objective is to highlight the separation of the pixel's distribution within the binary image.

To create the final vector the image was processed using the ArcSCAN tool in the GIS environment (see Fig. 5).

Fig. 5. Vector conversion ArcSCAN.

The image, however, was not the full resolution orthophoto due to the limit of the software, but the resolution was 2 cm. To evaluate the impact of the resolution, the partial mosaic, with a full resolution (1 cm) was further analyzed with the same parameters (see Fig. 6).

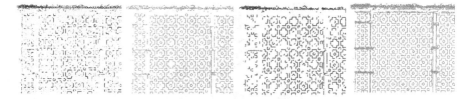

Fig. 6. Vectorization to the original resolution. From left to right, the image changes according to σ: upper left $\sigma = 10$ upper right σ: 15; bottom left σ: 20; bottom right σ: 30.

Finally, a further test was performed varying the neighbourhood of pixels with the creation of greater connections. In Fig. 7 the results performed for the values I = 2, I = 3 and I = 4, in which the neighbourhood of pixels are respectively 24, 48 and 80.

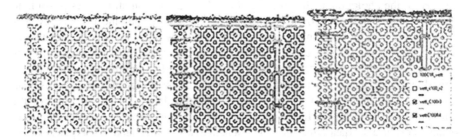

Fig. 7. Vectorization varying I. In particular, the images have been overlapped to highlight the differences. From left to right: I = 1 and I + 1 = 2; I = 2 and I + 1 = 3; I = 3 and I + 1 = 4 and I = 3 and σ = 20.

2.3   Results

As discussed above, the identification of a clear threshold of separation with classical filters to convert raster to vector data is not well defined. The New CS algorithm allowed to define a threshold for a raster to vector conversion. The connection with pixels is determine with the AR algorithm by σ parameter. It can be concluded that the increase of σ makes it possible to increase the visible details but with the maximum limit of 30, in which an increase of noise is observed. Once defined the connection with pixels, the New CS algorithm permit to obtain a binary image operating on C parameter. Furthermore, the output of the elaboration is influenced by the initial resolution image (see Fig. 6): it can be seen that, with equal processing parameters, increasing the resolution of the half, some details are not visible. This is due to the "weaker" constraints imposed by the connections (σ) that are established between the adjacent pixels and the central pixel. Finally, different neighbourhood I has been investigated to evaluate their influence on elaboration. Also in this case, increasing I, t there are more details but also an increase of noise. A good compromise is the result obtainewith σ = 20 and with I = 3 (see Fig. 8).

Fig. 8. Overlapping between I = 3 and σ = 20.

3 Conclusion and Future Developments

The strong automation in photogrammetry and the use of UAV acquisition platforms allowed to the photogrammetry to come back. The automation still makes possible to obtain precise 3D model for the purposes of the survey, but the outputs, even if characterised by a high information content, do not allow direct automatic extraction of descriptive information (features). For this reason, we investigated procedures for the vector conversion of the high information content of photogrammetric data, characterised by a very high geometric and a low radiometric resolution. To achieve this goal, innovative algorithms of ACM have been tested that have allowed to improve the threshold distinction for the future vector conversion. The vector conversion allows to obtain more usable data simplifies the exchange with other analysis applications in different fields of application. The next step will be to perform further quantitative investigation on the obtained results to validate the data. New analysis will be performed to improve the approach and to treat several type of data (for example thermal, multispectral, 3D point clouds, etc.) and ACM filter tested.

References

1. Barazzetti, L., Forlani, G., Remondino, F., Roncella, R., Scaioni, M.: Experiences and achievements in automated image sequence orientation for close-range photogrammetric projects. In: Remondino, F., Shortis, M.R. (eds.) (2011). https://doi.org/10.1117/12.890116
2. Furukawa, Y., Ponce, J.: Accurate, dense, and robust multiview stereopsis. IEEE Trans. Pattern Anal. Mach. Intell. **32**(8), 1362–1376 (2010)
3. Hirschmuller, H.: Stereo processing by semiglobal matching and mutual information. IEEE Trans. Pattern Anal. Mach. Intell. **30**(2), 328–341 (2008)
4. Dominici, D., Baiocchi, V., Zavino, A., Alicandro, M., Elaiopoulos, M.: Micro UAV for post seismic hazards surveying in old city center of L'Aquila. In: FIG Working Week 2012 Knowing to Manage the Territory, Protect the Environment, Evaluate the Cultural Heritage, Roma (2012)
5. Piras, M., Taddia, G., Forno, M.G., Gattiglio, M., Aicardi, I., Dabove, P., et al.: Detailed geological mapping in mountain areas using an unmanned aerial vehicle: application to the Rodoretto Valley, NW Italian Alps. Geomat. Nat. Hazards Risk **8**, 1–13 (2016)

6. Aicardi, I., Chiabrando, F., Lingua, A.M., Noardo, F., Piras, M., Vigna, B.: A methodology for acquisition and processing of thermal data acquired by UAVs: a test about subfluvial springs' investigations. Geomat. Nat. Hazards Risk **8**, 1–13 (2016)
7. Baiocchi, V., Dominici, D., Mormile, M.: UAV application in post-seismic environment. Int. Arch. Photogramm. Remote Sens. Spat. Inf. Sci. **XL-1/W2**, 21–25 (2013)
8. Matta, S.: Review: various image segmentation techniques. Swati Matta/(IJCSIT) Int. J. Comput. Sci. Inf. Technol. **5**(6), 7536–7539 (2014)
9. Roushdy, M.: Comparative study of edge detection algorithms applying on the grayscale noisy image using morphological filter. GVIP J. **6**(4), 17–23 (2006)
10. Shrivakshan, G.T., Chandrasekar, C., et al.: A comparison of various edge detection techniques used in image processing. IJCSI Int. J. Comput. Sci. Issues **9**(5), 272–276 (2012)
11. Maini, R.: Study and comparison of various image edge detection techniques. Int. J. Image Process. **3**(1), 12 (2009)
12. Schiewe, J.: Segmentation of high-resolution remotely sensed data-concepts, applications and problems. Int. Arch. Photogramm. Remote Sens. Spat. Inf. Sci. **34**(4), 380–385 (2002)
13. Baiocchi, V., Brigante, R., Dominici, D., Milone, M.V., Radicioni, F.: Multispectral automatic feature extraction methodologies comparison. In: Proceedings of 33rd EARSeL Symposium (2013)
14. Chirici, G., Di Martino, P., Garfì, V., Ottaviano, M., Tonti, D., Giongo Alves, M., et al.: Tecniche avanzate di cartografia degli ambienti forestali su base tipologica in italia centrale. In: Atti del Terzo Congresso Nazionale di Selvicoltura. Accademia Italiana di Scienze Forestali, Taormina (2009)
15. Pastore, V., Sole, A., Telesca, V.: Classificazione object-oriented e tecniche di segmentazione per la derivazione di cartografia di uso/copertura del suolo multiscala (2010)
16. Forlani, G., Nardinocchi, C., Scaioni, M., Zingaretti, P.: Building reconstruction and visualization from lidar data. Int. Arch. Photogramm. Remote Sens. Spat. Inf. Sci. **34** (5/W12), 151–156 (2003)
17. Dominici, D., Alicandro, M., Massimi, V.: UAV photogrammetry in the post-earthquake scenario: case studies in L'Aquila. Geomat. Nat. Hazards Risk **8**, 1–17 (2016). https://doi.org/10.1080/19475705.2016.1176605
18. Dominici, D., Alicandro, M., Rosciano, E., Massimi, V.: Multiscale documentation and monitoring of L'aquila historical centre using UAV photogrammetry. ISPRS - Int. Arch. Photogramm. Remote Sens. Spat. Inf. Sci. **42W4**, 365–371 (2017). https://doi.org/10.5194/isprs-archives-xlii-5-w1-365-2017
19. User Manuals. http://www.agisoft.com/downloads/user-manuals/. Accessed 20 Apr 2018
20. Westoby, M.J., Brasington, J., Glasser, N.F., Hambrey, M.J., Reynolds, J.M.: Structure-from-Motion'photogrammetry: a low-cost, effective tool for geoscience applications. Geomorphology **179**, 300–314 (2012)
21. Fraser, C.S.: Digital camera self-calibration. ISPRS J. Photogramm. Remote. Sens. **52**(4), 149–159 (1997). https://doi.org/10.1016/S0924-2716(97)00005-1
22. Buscema, P.M.: Sistemi ACM e Imaging Diagnostico. Springer, Milan (2006). https://doi.org/10.1007/88-470-0444-6
23. McClelland, J.L., Rumelhart, D.E.: A simulation-based tutorial system for exploring parallel distributed processing. Behav. Res. Methods Instrum. Comput. **20**(2), 263–275 (1988). https://doi.org/10.3758/BF03203842

The Spatial Form of Traditional Taiwanese Townhouses: A Case Study of Dihua Street in Taipei City

Tung-Ming Lee[(⊠)]

Department of Interior Design, China University of Technology,
56 Sec. 3 ShingLong Rd., 116, Taipei, Taiwan
tmlee@cute.edu.tw

Abstract. In this study, a survey was conducted on traditional townhouses in historic districts in Taiwan. To investigate the development process of townhouse architecture, this study used the townhouses in the historic district of Dihua Street in Taipei as research samples and conducted on-site mapping surveys and interviews. To determine the overall conservation environment of historic districts, this study conducted on-site surveys in Taipei City's Dihua Street, Taipei County's Sanxia Old Street, and Taoyuan County's Daxi Old Street. Data collected during on-site surveys were analyzed and compared, and these results served as a crucial reference for this study.

Keywords: Monument · Historical building · Group of historical buildings
Townhouse architecture · Reuse

1 Background and Objective

Most of Taiwan's existing traditional settlements were preceded by towns during earlier periods of Taiwanese development. As a result, such traditional settlements have a rich history of business activity. In addition, because of the previous dependence on water transportation, most of these historical settlements were port towns. On the basis of their functionality and popularity, most traditional Taiwanese buildings in these towns and settlements were townhouses [1].

For this reason, most traditional buildings observed in Taiwanese cities are townhouses. Examples of settlements that emerged in the early period of Taiwan's development include Tainan-Fu and Lugang in the south of Taiwan, and Tamsui, Dihua Street, Wanhua, Sanxia, Daxi, and Hukou in the north of Taiwan, where townhouse architecture is prevalent [2].

To investigate the preservation of historic districts in Taiwan, it is necessary to conduct an in-depth investigation and case study of a single area. In addition, to thoroughly understand these buildings, their architectural form and characteristics must be discussed. The aim of this study was to conduct a case study of Dihua Street to comprehensively examine the establishment and transformation of townhouses with arcade, the context of their formation, and relevant urban policies. In addition, this study discussed policies aimed at the preservation and revitalization of Dihua Street.

© Springer Nature Switzerland AG 2018
M. Ioannides et al. (Eds.): EuroMed 2018, LNCS 11196, pp. 322–333, 2018.
https://doi.org/10.1007/978-3-030-01762-0_27

A novel perspective was adopted to view Taiwan's historical townhouses, and research findings were compared with information on the historic district to provide a novel approach to considering the preservation and revitalization of cultural assets. This study aimed to provide guidance and inspiration for the preservation and revitalization of historic districts throughout Taiwan, and its results are expected to invigorate efforts toward historic district preservation throughout Taiwan (Fig. 1).

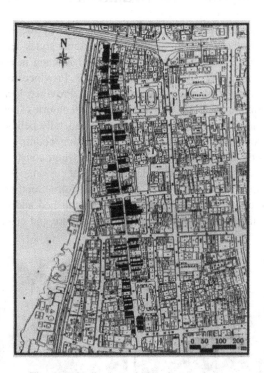

Fig. 1. Distribution of historic townhouses

2 Research Subject and Scope

Dihua Street features a large number of historical buildings and is famous for its Chinese New Year shopping area. In particular, Sect. 1, Dihua Street located between Nanjing West Road and Taipei Bridge has 320 street-facing townhouses (149 houses on the east side while 171 houses on the west side); most of these buildings were constructed prior to 1950, with a historic style and diverse facade designs. Townhouses constructed after the 1950s were influenced by the shophouse style, which was emerging in Taiwan at the time. These townhouses that were constructed later had relatively dull, uniform facade ornamentations, and most facades were decorated using simple methods such as cement paving, granolithic paving, and ceramic tiling. As a result, the townhouse facades that had been known for their diversity began to lose their grandeur and were overshadowed by pre-1950s buildings.

After an on-site survey and analysis, 156 buildings were selected whose facades have rich decorative features. These selected townhouses have not only a historical style but also unique characteristics, making them effective samples for studying townhouse architecture and comparing different types of townhouse architecture.

3   The Origins of Townhouse Architecture

The emergence of townhouses was primarily influenced by the architectural style of urban districts in southern China. Similar architectural styles can be found in the following places: Quanzhou, Fuzhou, Gulangyu, and Xiamen in Fujian Province and Guangzhou, Taicheng, and Macau in Guangdong Province in southern China; Shaoxing, Nanxun, and Zhuangshizhen in Zhejiang Province located on the south-eastern coast of China; in addition to Southeast Asian countries such as Singapore and Malaysia and China towns worldwide (Fig. 2). It is generally believed that immigrants often bring their hometown lifestyles to the destination countries and often use the architectural styles of their hometowns as blueprints when constructing homes in the new locations, while also adapting their designs to local customs. Although the form of Taiwanese townhouse architecture was transmitted from Southern China, the Taiwanese townhouse architecture had already been established and characterized by its distinctive style in the context of Taiwan's unique culture and customs [3].

Fig. 2. Waterside arcade buildings and River Town in Jiangnan, China

Subsequently, this architecture was influenced by the opening up of Taiwanese ports by the Qing Dynasty, whereupon European and American companies established operations on the island, leading to the construction of a substantial number of colonial-style foreign commercial buildings. In addition to the existing Minnan-style architecture, towering Western-style facades were constructed, and given the perception that modernization was equated with Westernization, Westernization became a milestone in the development of townhouse architecture. Subsequently, because of improvements in architectural techniques and materials, townhouses constructed completely using Western building methods emerged, and Westernization became an indispensable element of townhouse architecture.

During the period of Japanese rule in Taiwan, the development of townhouse architecture underwent a new stage. The Japanese colonial government constructed many official government buildings, characterized by the mannerist style, to consolidate its dominant status. Given the influence of the mannerist architecture on public buildings, townhouse architecture style was also affected. Many Taiwanese architects applied what they had learned during their participation in the construction of the public buildings to the construction of private buildings; this phenomenon represents another milestone in the development of townhouse architecture. At the same time, the Office of the Taiwan Governor-General effectively used its authority to construct new districts, such as the Ben Ding (本町) (Between present-day Chongqing South Road and Hengyang Road; Fig. 3) street development project. Furthermore, street development projects for the areas in front of train stations were formulated as a part of railway construction programs, and these projects all adopted brick construction with baroque-style facades for town-houses, which inspired the building designs in the Taiwanese society at the time. Subsequently, urban reform projects were implemented around Taiwan, wherein buildings were demolished to conduct road-straightening or road-widening projects. During the reconstruction of townhouse facades, baroque-style facades were chosen due to the influence of the aforementioned street development projects [4].

Fig. 3. Ben Ding District in the 1920s

4   Traditional Taiwanese Townhouse Architecture

Townhouses are common in Taiwan, and are mostly found in commercial settlements or cities. The main function of these buildings is to host business activities; they differ from another architectural style, courtyard houses (*heyuan*), which primarily serve agricultural purposes. The architectural foundation of a townhouse is characterized by a width of approximately 5.45 m (18 chi [1 chi ≒ 0.303 m], which is equal to 1 *zhang* [3.03 m] and 8 chi), giving such buildings the colloquial name zhangbacuo (meaning houses measuring 1 zhang and 8 chi). These buildings are typically quite long, 30–40 m on average, with some reaching 50–60 m. These townhouses typically have a narrow doorway but deep rear, with three structures built on the foundations, called "*di'yi jin*" (first area), "*di'er jin*" (second area), and "*di'san jin*" (third area); additionally, these structures may be separated by courtyards called "*tian jing*" or "*shen jing*."

Because the layout of a townhouse is long and narrow, the interiors of these structures were dependent on courtyards for lighting and ventilation. The typical townhouse layout was called "San jin," meaning the entire townhouse is divided into three areas from the front to the rear. A common floorplan could be arranged in the following order: arcade → first area → courtyard → second area → courtyard → third area. In this layout, the arcade corridor links each neighboring unit and runs along the entire street [5].

Regarding the townhouse architecture of Dihua Street, these buildings can be divided into five categories according to their structure and the facade style. In the following section, these categories are described according to the decade in which they appeared [6].

4.1 Minnan-Style Townhouses

Along with the formation of settlements in 1851, the three buildings constructed by Lin Lantian (Fig. 4) at this time are the Minnan-style architecture. This type of townhouses mainly consists of one-story bungalows, constructed primarily from wood and supplemented by earthen bricks or Minnan bricks. Although the fronts of these buildings have arcade, they lack ornamented facades, and the fronts of these buildings do not have any decorative features. Because most early residents of Dihua Street were from the Minnan region, and because trade relations were primarily with the Minnan region at the time, the form of early-period townhouses exhibited a traditional Minnan style (Fig. 5) [7].

Fig. 4. The Lin Lantian Residence   **Fig. 5.** Minnan-style townhouses

The unique characteristic of this type of townhouses is that its arcades are hidden within the main body of the buildings. That is, one section of the building serves as an arcade for public use. Because these buildings were one-story bungalows with relatively low floor heights, their facades are almost entirely obscured by eaves, leaving their features difficult to discern from the outside. During this period, the external appearance of buildings was not considered important, so no decorative designs were implemented. The arcade of this type of townhouse was also hidden within the building, resembling a dark corridor. In addition to serving as pedestrian walkways, arcades also functioned as display spaces for shop owners' products or workspaces. Arcades were seen as private spaces provided for public use.

Minnan-style townhouses are the earliest form of townhouse architecture, and their two-dimensional layout constitutes this architecture's original form. The typical layout of townhouses is the three-area form. In this approach, the central courtyard functions not only as a courtyard but also as a kitchen, toilet, or warehouse, and may serve a variety of purposes [3].

4.2   Imitating-Western-Style Townhouses

Imitating-Western-style townhouses appeared in the 1870s, and similar to Minnan-style townhouses, used mainly wooden constructions supplemented by earthen bricks or Minnan bricks. Most of these buildings originally had a one-story structure and might be expanded to be a two-story structure. The most prominent feature of these buildings was the use of Minnan bricks to construct facades that imitated the Western-style architecture (Fig. 6) [8].

This type of townhouse had facades on the front of the building for ornamental purpose to obscure the original Minnan style. The number of stories was typically increased from one to two. Additionally, the parapets at the roof top were adorned with gables mainly for decorative purpose. Although facade ornamentation only focused on the shop name, windows, or the arcade entrance, a trend of building ornamentation was initiated, which was primarily influenced by the colonial-style architecture built by foreign companies.

Although the imitating-Western-style townhouses intended to imitate Western-style buildings, they still preserved the traditional layout of three divisions, similar to the Minnan-style architecture. The most marked difference between these two styles is that imitating-Western-style townhouses have more stories, meaning the buildings must have stairs for building access. However, because each structure within a building site has its own staircase, each can be considered as an independent building.

4.3   Western-Style Townhouses

The Western-style townhouses emerged in the 1890s. After Taiwan entered the period of Japanese rule, a new era of changes in construction techniques and materials began. Because of the establishment of the Taiwan Brick Manufacturing Company (or Taiwan Renga Kabushiki Kaisha in Japanese), Taiwan began producing fair-faced bricks with standardized specifications ($23 \times 13 \times 6$ cm). Together with the introduction of reinforced concrete structures, these developments led to the emergence of buildings with a completely Western style. The overall structures of Western-style townhouses were constructed with fair-faced bricks, and most buildings were either two or three stories tall. This style continued the Western imitation trend of using Western-style facade decorations but increased the number of decorations, and the decorations were increasingly delicate and complex. The emergence of this type of townhouse architecture also marked the formal start of a new historical era of townhouse architecture in which the traditional Chinese-style architecture shifted toward structures that primarily followed the internationally popular Western style of architecture (Fig. 7).

The external appearance of Western-style townhouses is almost identical to that of imitating-Western-style townhouses; however, these buildings are different in that they were constructed according to Western construction methods. They also maintained the layout of three divisions, with independent staircases and entrances for each of the three structures. Apart from increasing the number and elegance of decorations, the only other change exhibited by Western-style townhouses relates to the more prominent style of their gables and elaborate gable ornamentation. In their construction, architects of Western-style townhouses abandoned the previous mixed construction method that primarily used wood; instead, their construction mainly used bricks. In some of these buildings, reinforced concrete was used to construct beams and columns for increased strength. Because of advancements in building methods, three-story buildings also began to emerge during this period.

Fig. 6. An imitating-Western-style townhouse

Fig. 7. Western-style townhouse architecture

4.4   Baroque-Style Townhouses

The baroque style of townhouse architecture appeared in the 1900s. Most buildings with this style were constructed using a combination of fair-faced bricks and reinforced concrete and were generally three-story buildings. Their facade ornamentations tended to be complex, magnificent, and protruding baroque-style decorations. Although these structures were built between 1900 and 1940, they are referred to as baroque-style townhouses because of their resemblance to the Baroque style that emerged in Europe between the 16th and 18th centuries, and to the Neo-Baroque style that was popular during the second half of the 19th century (Fig. 8).

Due to environmental changes and large-scale construction of Japanese government buildings in Taipei, a considerable number of "official buildings" were built. These buildings were mostly built in the Japanese mannerist style, with the main design being the European renaissance style. They were adorned with many foreign-style orna-mentations. Representative buildings of this style include the well-known Office of the Governor-General (the present Presidential Office Building) and Governor-General's official residence (the present Taipei Guest House).

In addition, the buildings designed by Ichiro Nomura and Tetsuro Nakagori, the architects of the Office of the Governor-General, in Ben Ding (Between present-day Chongqing South Road and Hengyang Road) in 1914 used mainly brick constructions, and their facade decorations primarily included renaissance-period European-style ornaments. At this time, buildings with arcades featuring brick arches became the standard for private townhouses. These facts led to the rapid development of town-house architecture in Taiwan. A substantial number of baroque-style townhouses emerged in the district of Dihua Street. Among these, in addition to purely European-style baroque townhouses, Taiwanese-style baroque buildings were also constructed by Taiwanese architects (Fig. 9). The two styles of buildings exhibit their own unique charms.

This type of townhouse architecture is unique due to the complexity of its facade ornamentation and its use of many ornate and protruding baroque-style decorations. Baroque-style buildings use mixed constructions composed of brick and reinforced concrete and are primarily three stories tall. The layout of three divisions that had been in use since the Qing Dynasty was altered to a certain extent during this period. The independent structures were originally linked by the first-floor courtyard; however, in the baroque-style buildings, the structures were connected by the above-ground cor-ridors at the second and third floors. Therefore, the courtyard gradually lost its original function and evolved into something more similar to an open space. However, the layout of this style maintained a vestige of the three-division layout.

Fig. 8. European baroque-style townhouse

Fig. 9. Taiwanese-style baroque townhouse

4.5 Modern-Style Townhouses

In Taiwan, modern-style townhouse architecture emerged during the 1910s. Most buildings of this style were reinforced concrete structures with three or more stories. The modern style abandoned the complex decorations favored by baroque-style townhouses, instead primarily using clear, simple, and modern architectural forms. In the 1930s, the trend of internationalism rapidly influenced buildings in the district of Dihua Street. All the buildings built in modern style were three or more stories, and their structures were composed of reinforced concrete. The spatial layout of these buildings departed considerably from the original three-division layout. The inclusion of a courtyard depended on the judgment of each developer, and most buildings adopted lobbies with high ceilings instead of courtyards, and the separation of each structure became less distinct. In addition, with the use of reinforced concrete structures and advanced construction methods, windows and other openings were no longer restricted to original strategies such as designing these openings by dividing the building into three or five equal parts. As such, the forms of these buildings could be designed more freely (Fig. 10).

Fig. 10. Modern-style townhouse

Fig. 11. Chinese New Year Market in Dihua st.

5   Current Status of and Vision for Townhouse Preservation

Since the formation of the Dadaocheng district in 1851, it has experienced three historical eras: the Qing Dynasty, the period of Japanese rule, and the Republic of China. From a small commercial port on the bank of the Tamsui River, Dadaocheng developed into a trading hub for northern Taiwan and subsequently became Taiwan's commercial center. Under the rapid pace of economic development, Dadaocheng's noteworthy status has already been replaced by other emerging districts of Taipei. However, the status of its most essential area, Dihua Street, remains unshaken; it is still a wholesaling hub for groceries, Chinese medicines, and textiles (Fig. 11).

Dihua Street is a historic district with foreign characteristics. When entering Dihua Street, buildings on both sides tower over the road, giving the sensation of a traditional Taiwanese market. Most buildings along the streets are three or more stories tall, with traditional Minnan-style bungalows interspersed among them. These building have varied facade styles, ranging from Western-themed colonial styles, renaissance-themed baroque styles, and international styles, with diverse and distinctive decorative features. Dihua Street is not only characterized by its wide variety of styles; the ever-changing skyline formed among the connected townhouses gives it a distinct charm. Furthermore, the arcade that stretches for several kilometers along Dihua Street and links the activities of the district is a unique feature.

The dimensions involved in the future development of conservation areas are extensive. In addition to the advancement of the techniques used for preserving heritage areas, the dimensions of land use, urban planning, construction land use, site conservation, and economic issues are key topics that merit further discussion. The practice of area conservation must also consider topics including operations management, and safety and disaster prevention. Accordingly, governmental and civil resources should be integrated to propose projects for developing conservation areas in the future. Therefore, the future development of conservation areas must focus on the local residents' lives and on operations management, and safety and disaster prevention (Fig. 12) [2].

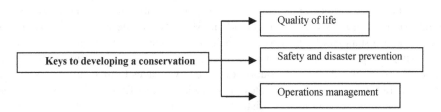

Fig. 12. Three keys to developing a conservation area

In recent years, much attention has focused on cultural landscape, which is a cultural asset that can reflect the relationships between and the universal value of human life, culture, and land use. A cultural landscape generally does not entail a building or a construction complex; nevertheless, it is associated with universal value and thus is a critical cultural asset to preserve. Because the scope of a cultural landscape is generally large, the concept of conservation area development must be applied to preserving cultural landscapes. The conservation of cultural landscapes is a new domain that is key to developing conservation areas and critical to formulating new directions and topics for conservation area development, which are critical to executing initiatives for preserving cultural landscapes and successfully developing conservation areas [2].

The New Orientations for Conservation Area Development in the Twenty-first Century.

a. Conservation of the Outstanding Universal Value of Monuments: A Central Initiative and Goal of Conservation Area Development.
b. Both Prominent Monuments and Common Ancient Buildings Must Be Preserved to Realize the Practical Significance of Conservation Area Development.
c. Monument Conservation Is No Longer Limited to Preserving Monumental Cultural Heritage Sites: Industrial Heritage Is Extensively Emphasized in Recent Years and Is Critical to Conservation Area Development.
d. Reducing the Impact of Contemporary Construction in Monument Complexes: Crucial to Concretizing and Expanding Conservation Areas, Protecting the Urban Fabric, and Structuring Urban Development Programs.
e. Conservation of a Cultural Landscape that Emphasizes and Reflects Human Life and Culture and Land Use: A New Direction of and the Key to Successful Conservation Area Development.

6   Conclusions

In recent years, with Taiwan's rapid economic development, Taipei has continued to develop at a fast pace. As such, historic districts such as Dihua Street and Wanhua District have gradually lost their original importance and have entered a period of decline. Dihua Street has lost its status as Taiwan's commercial center; the wholesaling industry concentrated here has carried on the district's rich heritage of business activity [2].

Townhouse architecture is a major legacy of traditional Taiwanese society; a similar architectural style cannot be found anywhere else in the world. The wisdom of Taiwan's ancestors can be observed in each design detail of the townhouse architecture. This is especially so in the arcade of townhouses; only Taiwan has such a high concentration of arcades. The corridors connected by arcades form an artery linking the entire district, which closely integrates the historic district. Taiwan currently faces the major issue of preserving historic districts. By discussing Dihua Street's townhouses, the need to preserve monuments and maintain historic districts was highlighted.

Awareness of and support for monument preservation has risen in recent years. Taking northern Taiwan as an example, considerable attention has been paid to the "old street" settlements of historic communities such as Dadaocheng and Wanhua in Taipei City; Taipei County's Tamsui and Sanxia; Taoyuan County's Daxi; and Hsinchu's Hukou, either through strong government intervention for preservation or spontaneous civil preservation efforts. Regardless of the method of preservation or the place being preserved, there have been equally strong voices in support of and against preservation, making it difficult to reach a consensus. As such, the preservation of historical buildings and historic districts across Taiwan faces substantial challenges.

Because traditional townhouses and historic districts are intertwined with one another and form a mutual and complementary relationship, one cannot be adequately preserved without the other. In addition, the uniqueness of townhouses lies in their interconnectedness with neighboring buildings and the diverse and distinctive decorations. Therefore, townhouses are distinct from ordinary monuments or historical buildings, as the preservation of a single building does not achieve the goal of preservation. Only by preserving the entire historic district is it possible to preserve the essence of traditional townhouses. Thus, this study argues that the preservation of individual buildings is not appropriate for townhouses. Rather, it is necessary to approach the preservation of such buildings from the perspective of entire historic districts. It is hoped that through the preservation of the entire district, it will be possible to fully preserve the beauty of Taiwan's traditional townhouses.

Stakeholders must step outside the traditional framework for monument preservation and no longer view the preservation of monuments as the starting point for preserving tradition. Instead, the concept of preservation should be abandoned and replaced with the concept of revitalization. The revitalization of areas has become an alternative path for preservation; promoting the revitalization of historic districts indirectly promotes their preservation. In this approach, the narrow thinking behind traditional monument preservation is abandoned along with considerations of which preservation projects are more important. A more pragmatic and feasible method is to stand together with local residents and work for the future of a historic district, thereby realizing preservation and revitalization. Only through this approach can historic districts recover from their decline and start again, moving away from their dark pasts and into a bright future.

References

1. Lee, T.M.: A study of development planning for conservation areas in Taiwan. In: ICCAE 2016 (2016)
2. Lee, T.-M., Yen, A.Y.: Future development plans for conservation areas in Taiwan. In: Ioannides, M., et al. (eds.) EuroMed 2016. LNCS, vol. 10059, pp. 81–88. Springer, Cham (2016). https://doi.org/10.1007/978-3-319-48974-2_10
3. Lee, T.M., Yen, Y.N.: A study for the future development direction of historical conservation areas in Taiwan. In: The 13th Session of the Conference on the Science of Conserving and Reusing Cultural Properties (Ancient Remains, Historic Buildings, Settlements, and Cultural Landscapes) (2010)
4. Lee, T.M., Yen, Y.N.: A preliminary study of historical conservation areas in Taiwan. In: The 10th Session of the Conference on the Science of Conserving and Reusing Cultural Properties (Ancient Remains, Historic Buildings, Settlements, and Cultural Landscapes) (2007)
5. Lee, T.M.: Study of spatial and facade character of town-house in traditional town area, Taiwan. Research Project Report of Architecture and Building Research Institute, Ministry of the Interior, Taiwan, R.O.C. (2005)
6. Lee, T.M.: Study for generally conservation and sustainable development of traditional town area in Taiwan. Research Project Report of Architecture and Building Research Institute, Ministry of the Interior, Taiwan, R.O.C. (2004)
7. Lee, T.M., Hatano, J.: The design and formative background of town-houses. J. Archit. Plann. (Trans. AIJ) **547**, 237– 242 (2001)
8. Lee, T.M., Hatano, J.: The history of arcade (Din-A-Ka) in Di-Hwa Street, Taipei City. In: The 2nd International Symposium on Architectural Interchange in Asia. Biol., vol. 147, pp. 195–197 (1998)

A Digital Workflow for Built Heritage: From SCAN-to-BIM Process to the VR-Tour of the Basilica of Sant'Ambrogio in Milan

Banfi Fabrizio[1]([⊠]), Stanga Chiara[2], and Raffaella Brumana[1]

[1] ABC Department, Politecnico di Milano, Piazza Leonardo da Vinci 32,
Milan, Italy
{fabrizio.banfi, raffaella.brumana}@polimi.it
[2] DAStU Department, Politecnico di Milano, Piazza Leonardo da Vinci 32,
Milan, Italy
chiara.stanga@polimi.it

Abstract. The latest information technology developments have enabled the creation of novel virtual experiences favouring an increasingly higher level of information connected to the 3D reconstruction. Building Information Modelling (BIM), 3D cloud services and virtual/augmented reality (AR-VR) projects are the most applied methods to transmit the wealth of built heritage from both the geometrical and informative points of view. In this paper, we present a holistic workflow to integrate the most applied digital techniques with the aim of creating the highest quality-immersive solutions starting from an accurate 3D survey. Thanks to a new SCAN-to-BIM method that transfer the morphological and typological characteristics of the surveyed building to a shared cloud system, it will be possible to support specialists in the documentation and preservation of historical uniqueness of the basilica of Sant'Ambrogio in Milan (Italy) with a new level of information sharing. Finally, a new digital experience based on next-generation technologies has been offered to the cultural tourism. Thanks to the development of a virtual tour that embeds different multimedia data (360° photos, photos, virtual notebook, description, video, audio etc), it has been possible to create a digital history for one of the greatest examples of the historic Italian architecture.

Keywords: SCAN-to-BIM · Modeling · Grade of generation (GOG)
Accuracy · Digital history · Virtual tour · Disseminating heritage information

1 Introduction

Information and Communication Technology (ICT) is quickly revolutionizing the Architecture, Engineering and Construction (AEC) Industry thanks to the development of new methods and tools to digitally recreate existing buildings. Moreover, ICT developments are determining a significant renewal of diverse interdisciplinary sectors such as design, restoration and preservation of historic buildings. The traditional techniques of graphical representation and building management are being revisited and updated with new knowledge of appropriate use of next-generation instruments to

© Springer Nature Switzerland AG 2018
M. Ioannides et al. (Eds.): EuroMed 2018, LNCS 11196, pp. 334–343, 2018.
https://doi.org/10.1007/978-3-030-01762-0_28

transform the process of computing information in digital data. This change of methods and tools represents a real revolution from both economic and production perspectives.

In recent years, advanced knowledge developed by research centers on 3D survey [1], digital photogrammetry [2], advanced techniques for high precision Non Uniform Rational Basis-Splines (NURBS) surface generation [3], generation and management of complex 3D models in digital environmental [4], virtual tours [5–8] have led to a substantial progress in both practical and theoretical terms. In the digital field, one of the most common applied method is the SCAN-to-BIM process, which represents the surveyed reality in a digital environment. Thanks to a faithful digital reconstruction of the artefact detected with Terrestrial Laser Scanning (TLS), it has been possible to expand the information system of the building and improve the bi-directional relationship between model and information in the digital environment. The connection of each type of data to the model has allowed the substitution of simple processes based on CAD drawings with an articulated model capable of describing both morphologically and typologically the built heritage in a digital hub. The computational power of information in new BIM-based systems and the digitization of historical and material data has led to investigate many innovative solutions, improving several types of analysis, such as the rehabilitation process of the historic building [9], the monitoring of historic infrastructure [10] and the structural finite element analysis [11]. In this context, one of the main fields of research is the three-dimensional modelling, which represents the key to connect different disciplinary sectors, bringing the traditional building management techniques to a new level of development.

2 Related Words and Research Objectives

While in the 90s we witnessed manual drawing techniques being quickly replaced by 2D CAD representations, the last decade has shown how the BIM can easily substitute the CAD application with a three-dimensional information representation that achieves new levels of automation in the building digitization. On the other hand, the future will almost certainly be characterized by the innovative developments in the field of virtual/augmented reality and in real-time building management, which will bring BIM to new levels of visualization for the built heritage. For this reason, this research has investigated the most innovative techniques of 3D modelling, offering a method that interacts with accurate H-BIM, new modelling languages and immersive digital and state-of-the-art virtual reality solutions.

Thanks to the application of new grades of generation (GOG), accuracy (GOA) oriented to create proper SCAN-to-BIM models [12] and the integration of a virtual notebook [13], a digital workflow has been developed embedding 3D survey, AF-BIM, cloud service, VR/AR technology and a digital virtual tour of the Basilica of Sant'Ambrogio in Milan. In particular, thanks to the integration of 360° photos, descriptive texts for every single area and web links for navigation of AF-BIM in the implemented virtual tour, it has been possible to develop a digital history of the church for mobile phones that can be integrated through immersive augmented reality devices. The proposed workflow is based on a three-step methodology (Fig. 1):

1. Combining geometric and material information obtained in different 3D surveying campaigns with a process of information digitization in a virtual notebook that highlights the historical phases subtraction process.
2. Improving the 3D reconstruction of a historic building (SCAN-to-BIM method) by new grade of generation (GOG) that maintains the high level of detail (LOD) of complex 3D parametric objects, such as complex vaulted system, irregular walls and historic decorations, keeping a grade of accuracy (GOA) of 1–2 mm and using a cloud system easily able to shares the wealth of embedded and linked data in BIM, such as material information, historical research, building construction techniques, computing and BIM database via new virtual visualization solutions.
3. Implementing a virtual tour based on the use of all digital data, such as the virtual notebook, BIM of the church, 360° photos, video/audio, 3D animations, textual descriptions and digital links to the cloud system.

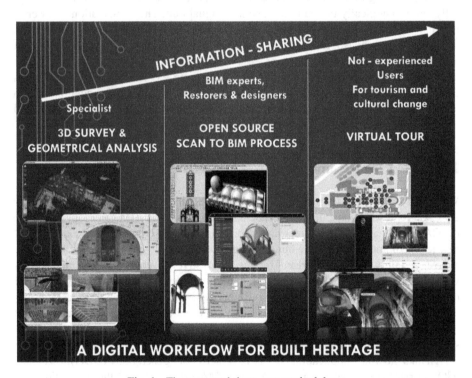

Fig. 1. The proposed three-step methodology

3   Research Methodology

The Basilica of Sant'Ambrogio in Milan is one of the greatest monuments in the city and a well-known building, studied by several authors. Its importance is related not only to Archbishop Ambrogio, an important figure in the Christian communities of the late fourth century but also to its long-lasting construction history, made of reconstructions and restorations. The basilica was founded by Archbishop Ambrogio on a former funerary area in the late fourth century, then it went through many changes, starting from the Romanesque reconstruction to the nineteenth works till the ones of the twentieth century, after the damages of the Second World War. The basilica was part of Ambrogio's project to make Christianity part of the urban spaces, together with the Basilica of San Simpliciano, San Nazaro and San Dionigi (demolished in the late eighteenth century), approximately located at the four-cardinal point of Milan. Although some scholars in the past talked about the church as a *unicum*, one of the greatest example of the Romanesque architecture in Lombardy [14], a more recent publication refers to the basilica as an 'interrupted temple' [15] underlining the great long-lasting constructive history and depicting some peculiar aspects of each historical phase.

This research was carried out by correlating the data coming from the geometrical laser scanning surveys with the historical-archival ones, developing the 3D model to represent the constructive hypothesis and creating an H-BIM for the transmission of the acquired data and the intangible meanings of this great monument. The challenge was not only to analyze a well-known building that has been extensively studied in the literature, but also to realize a 3D model that could capture all the geometrical and spatial complexity of the church, and to connect the acquired historical data to the H-BIM in the digital history of the church.

3.1 An Integrated Digital Documentation for the Basilica of Sant'Ambrogio in Milan: From the Historical-Geometrical Analysis to the N-D Virtual Notebook

The goal of the virtual notebook of the basilica is to convey the great amount of information through the H-BIM, developing a mobile application for smartphones and tablets for touristic purposes. The paper presents the methodology used in the research both from the historical and technological (laser scanner, photogrammetry, HBIM) points of view, using the history of the vaults as a *file rouge* to show the main transformations of the church. The word 'notebook', in Italian *taccuino,* has been used as a key idea and a tool to organize the collected data. *Taccuino* in Italian has two meanings: it is both the book of plain paper to write on and the title of a collection of works, made of different and fragmented pieces [16]. This ambivalence well represents the way we conceived the digital history of the church: the research tries to unveil not-yet-fully understood aspects, showing them in their fragmented entirety and in correlation to the transformations occurred to the church. The word *taccuino* also recalls the old architectural album, such as the 'sketchbook' by Villard de Honnecourt (twelfth century), used to collect drawings and annotations about buildings, mechanical devices, and engineering constructions. Regarding Sant'Ambrogio, the *Carnet de Voyage* [17] by the Alsatian architect Fernand de Dartein has been a reliable source for the study of the nineteenth-century restoration. We correlate the historical drawings and documents with his *planches*, which represent the geometrical survey of the basilica, in order to better understand the nineteenth-century interventions. However, De Dartein was not the only one who recorded these works: at the same time architect Landriani [18], who worked side by side with De Dartein, the German architect Hübsch and the abbot of the church Rossi [19] kept track of these events with drawings and chronicles that were later published.

In this research, the study of the basilica was supported by a methodological approach that allowed to analyze each aspect through a strict correlation between 'direct' (geometrical survey and Building Archeology analysis, accomplished with laser scanner and photogrammetric image acquisition) and 'indirect' sources (historical and archive research, documents, photos, drawings) (Fig. 2). Although offering a conventional report of the monument, starting from its foundation to the present day, the research borrowed from archaeology the idea of a 'subtraction excavation process': the analysis starts from the current arrangement and goes back to the previous ones. By doing this, the church, with all the richness of its past events and transformations, becomes the main source of information and it can be seen in a new light, avoiding fixed knowledge framework and highlighting its constructive, material and geometrical aspects.

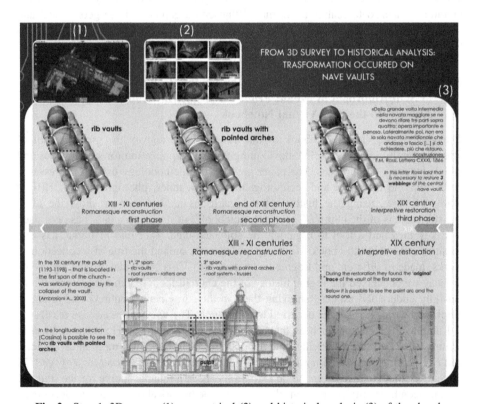

Fig. 2. Step 1: 3D survey (1), geometrical (2) and historical analysis (3) of the church

3.2 Grade of Generation (GOG) and Accuracy (GOA) Applied to the 3D Reconstruction: From a 'Subtraction Excavation Process' to the SCAN-to-BIM Model

Contrary to its apparently homogeneous appearance, the basilica that we can see today is the result of overlapping historical layers, and consequently, the 3D model of this study takes into consideration this concept. The vaulted system of the Basilica of Sant'Ambrogio is made of different vault components, characterized by singular geometrical origins and shapes, constructive techniques and historical phases. The mosaic dome of San Vittore in Ciel d'Oro is probably the most known and ancient vault of the church (late fifth century). Then, there are the groin vaults of the aisle, *matronei*, crypt and the Ansperto Atria, realized in different periods. The nave is characterized by great rib vaults; the *chevet* has a dome, made of eight irregular webbings, realized on an octagonal *tiburio*; the Narthex is characterized both by rib and barrel vaults. Another well-known part of the basilica is the *Canonica* (rectory) by Bramante, characterized by two barrel vault with lunettes.

These vaults, apparently homogeneous at their intrados at a first sight, hide a historical background of reconstruction and restorations that is the reason why their dating remain imprecise, at least until the existing studies will be intertwined with material laboratory analysis.

A laser scanner survey was performed into the entire basilica (nave, aisles, chapels, crypt, San Vittore in Ciel d'Oro, Bramante's rectory, Ansperto Atria, bell towers). It was possible to use thermo camera in the Bramante's *Canonica* to acquire some images of the brick arrangements of the vaults. That is why it was necessary to set different Level of Detail, according to the amount and reliability of the acquired information, i.e. the church has a LOD more accurate than the elements realized for the hypothesis and reconstructions [20]. In particular, thanks to the application of a SCAN-to-BIM method based on new GOGs, an AF-BIM that corresponds to the reality detected by the TLS was created. The analysis of construction techniques, the exact digital reconstruction of complex elements, such as vaults, arches, irregular walls and decorative elements, the linking of information to the model and the automatic creation of digital databases have been supported by the scaled-up application of GOG 9 and 10 for complex elements. In particular, the slicing technique (GOG 9) and the automatic interpolation of the scan's points for the generation of irregular NURBS elements (GOG 10) has allowed the creation of AF-BIM with a GOA of about 1/1.5 mm (Fig. 3).

The subsequent parameterization of the NURBS model in Autodesk Revit has permitted the integration of different types of information to 'new' 3D objects (not present in the standard BIM libraries), such complex vaults and historic elements. Finally, thanks to the conversion of BIM databases to Excel sheets and Microsoft Access databases, restorers, architects and engineers will be able to directly manage the data connected to the model.

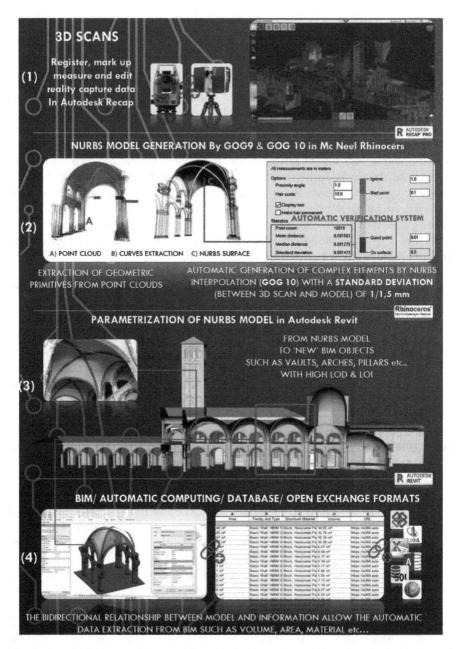

Fig. 3. Step 2: (1) Import 3D scans in Autodesk Recap allowed the point cloud cleaning and save the scan in .pts format; (2) NURBS Model generation by GOGs (9–10); (3) The proper definition of 3D exchange formats allowed the parametrization of the NURBS model in Autodesk Revit, maintaining a high GOA; (4) Automatic computing of the model quantities and material information automatically allowed the information transfer in external databases

3.3 The Virtual Tour of the Basilica of Sant'Ambrogio: From AF-BIM to a Digital History of the Church

A leap forward was made thanks to the creation of a virtual tour combining a large amount of data in a single immersive environment. The development through a web application [21] allows one to reach a larger public not particularly involved in professional disciplines but interested in cultural and touristic activities. Thanks to the implementation of a system that provides the connection of 360° photos, video/audio and 3D animation with their textual description, and digital links to the cloud system, tourists and new users can discover the cultural heritage of the building through a new immersive environment.

Unlike the cloud system, the virtual tour is not just a 'treasure chest' of the entire basilica, but a new product that combines different levels of knowledge with a more playful interaction mode of the building. In particular, the development of the virtual tour allowed to link photos, 360° photos and videos with each other, giving a sense of continuity between a distinct multimedia source.

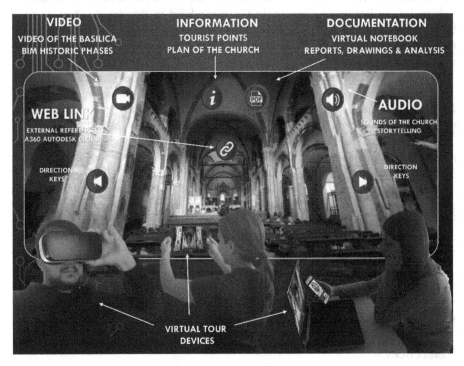

Fig. 4. Step 3: the development process of the virtual tour of the Basilica of Sant'Ambrogio in Milan, Italy

Descriptive texts and links to BIM cloud were integrated into the system through the implementation of functions commonly called hotspots. These functions have allowed the automatic creation of buttons that can be activated in the immersive environment.

Figure 4 shows how from a simple 360° image you can reach any type of digital data (photo, video, audio, historical description, the developed virtual notebook etc):

- The information and documentation functions allowed us to upload descriptive texts for every single object displayed, tourist information, the virtual notebook, reports, drawings analysis of the church.
- The video and audio functions allowed the link of multimedia data for each type of device (VR headset, mobile and desktop).
- The web link function permitted to link the Autodesk A360 cloud, display the BIM and connect the virtual tour to external references and web links.
- The direction keys function enabled us to create a continuous experience among all uploaded multimedia data.

4   Result and Conclusion

The open access virtual tour of the Basilica of Sant'Ambrogio allows us to embed the richness of the intangible elements and values related to the church, showing them through the collected data (virtual notebook, drawings, HBIM, 360° photos, textual description, audios/videos, web-links etc) in a new digital environment, easily accessible and understandable even to non-experts.

Starting from the correlation of the historical data with the geometrical-dimensional ones and the creation of the virtual notebook, the study emphases the importance of H-BIM, whose accuracy was guaranteed by the application of new grade of generation (GOG) that kept a high Level of Detail of the complex SCAN-to-BIM objects.

The presented A360 application offered an open-source web-based system for project content, enabling to share data and statistics, monitor developments and facilitate the exchange of best practices.

From a critical point of view, the virtual tour can be implemented with the new paradigms of the digital interactivity, in a more immersive environment, thanks to the latest generation applications that create new virtual experiences, 3D animations and digital simulations. The main aim is to improve the integration of different type of data, making the BIM-based information system more effective.

Future studies will go further in this direction and the next step is to achieve an immersive mixed experience (VR-AR) that will embed different multimedia files and that will be used both by experts and tourists to study and discover one of Italy's most famous basilicas.

References

1. Slob, S., Hack, R.: 3D terrestrial laser scanning as a new field measurement and monitoring technique. In: Hack, R., Azzam, R., Charlier, R. (eds.) Engineering Geology for Infrastructure Planning in Europe, pp. 179–189. Springer, Heidelberg (2004). https://doi.org/10.1007/978-3-540-39918-6_22
2. Yastikli, N.: Documentation of cultural heritage using digital photogrammetry and laser scanning. J. Cult. Herit. 8(4), 423–427 (2007)

3. Terzopoulos, D., Qin, H.: Dynamic NURBS with geometric constraints for interactive sculpting. ACM Trans. Graph. (TOG) **13**(2), 103–136 (1994)
4. Volk, R., Stengel, J., Schultmann, F.: Building Information Modeling (BIM) for existing buildings—literature review and future needs. Autom. Constr. **38**, 109–127 (2014)
5. Bimber, O., Raskar, R.: Spatial Augmented Reality: Merging Real and Virtual Worlds. CRC Press, Boca Raton (2005)
6. Ioannides, M., Martins, J., Žarnić, R., Lim, V. (eds.): Advances in Digital Cultural Heritage, vol. 10754. Springer, Cham (2018). https://doi.org/10.1007/978-3-319-75789-6
7. Graham, K., et al.: The VR kiosk. In: Ioannides, M. (ed.) Digital Cultural Heritage. LNCS, vol. 10605, pp. 324–336. Springer, Cham (2018). https://doi.org/10.1007/978-3-319-75826-8_26
8. Azhar, S., Hein, M., Sketo, B.: Building Information Modeling (BIM): Benefits, Risks and Challenges (2008). http://ascpro.ascweb.org/chair/paper/CPGT182002008.pdf. Accessed Jan 2013
9. Brumana, R., et al.: HBIM challenge among the paradigm of complexity, tools and preservation: the basilica Di collemaggio 8 years after the earthquake (L'aquila). Int. Arch. Photogramm. Remote Sens. Spatial Inf. Sci. **42**(2w5), 97–104 (2017)
10. Banfi, F., Barazzetti, L., Previtali, M., Roncoroni, F.: Historic bim: a new repository for structural health monitoring. Int. Arch. Photogramm. Remote Sens. Spatial Inf. Sci. **42**(5w1), 269–274 (2017)
11. Barazzetti, L., Banfi, F., Brumana, R., Gusmeroli, G., Previtali, M., Schiantarelli, G.: Cloud-to-BIM-to-FEM: structural simulation with accurate historic BIM from laser scans. Simul. Model. Pract. Theory **57**, 71–87 (2015)
12. Banfi, F.: BIM orientation: grades of generation and information for different type of analysis and management process. Int. Arch. Photogramm. Remote Sens. Spatial Inf. Sci. **42** (2/W5), 57–64 (2017)
13. Stanga, C., Spinelli, C., Brumana, R., Oreni, D., Valente, R., Banfi, F.: An ND virtual notebook about the basilica of S. Ambrogio in Milan: information modeling for the communication of historical phases subtraction process. Int. Arch. Photogramm. Remote Sens. Spatial Inf. Sci. **42**, 653 (2017)
14. Peroni, A.: Tradizione e innovazione in S. Ambrogio romanico. In: Bertelli, C. (eds) Il Millennio Ambrosiano, vol. 1–2, pp. 156–172. Electa, Milan (1987)
15. Gatti Perer, M.L.: La basilica di S. Ambrogio: il tempio ininterrotto. Vita e Pensiero, Milan (1995)
16. Encyclopedia Treccani. http://www.treccani.it/vocabolario/taccuino/
17. Bella, T.: La basilica di Sant'Ambrogio a Milano. L'opera inedita di Fernand de Dartein. Jaka Book, Milan (2013)
18. Landriani, G.: La Basilica Ambrosiana fino alla sua trasformazione in chiesa lombarda a volte. Hoepli, Milan (1889)
19. Rossi, F.M.: Cronaca dei restauri e delle scoperte fatte nell'insigne basilica di S. Ambrogio dall'anno 1857 al 1876. Tipografia S. Giuseppe, Milan (1884)
20. Banfi, F.: Building information modelling – a novel parametric modeling approach based on 3D surveys of historic architecture. In: Ioannides, M., et al. (eds.) EuroMed 2016. LNCS, vol. 10058, pp. 116–127. Springer, Cham (2016). https://doi.org/10.1007/978-3-319-48496-9_10
21. VTClick. http://www.vtclick.com. Accessed 08 Aug 2018

BIM Modelling of Ancient Buildings

Andrea Scianna[(✉)], Giuseppe Fulvio Gaglio,
and Marcello La Guardia

GISLAB ICAR (High Performance Computing and Networking Institute),
National Research Council of Italy, University of Palermo, Viale delle Scienze,
Edificio 8, 90128 Palermo, Italy
andrea.scianna@cnr.it, gfulvio.gaglio@gmail.com,
marcellolaguardia87@libero.it

Abstract. In the last years, new procedures on design and management of constructions, based on 3D standardised models of building elements, have been proposed. It's the case of Building Information Modelling (BIM) applications, that, differently from CAD ones, allow to work with libraries of 3D parametrical objects (smart objects) describing geometric, structural and material properties of building elements. This methodology is based on the Industry Foundation Classes (IFC) model, that represents a global standard for the building data exchange. Initially used for the design of new architectures, BIM methodology has been even more considered also for the management and the conservation of historical buildings, thanks to the possibilities of implementation of semantic information of 3D objects, guaranteed by the connection with the external database. At the same time, the lack of regular surfaces and standardised objects are relevant problems that nowadays strongly limit the use of BIM for Cultural Heritage (CH). Anyway, in recent times, the study of parameterised objects has opened new perspectives for BIM applications on historical buildings (HBIM). The present work shows the last achievements on this topic, focusing the problems derived from the application of BIM methodology to CH. In fact, the irregular shape of ancient architectural components, the wide variety of architectural languages that characterise historical buildings, the presence, sometimes, of different stratifications, are clear examples of the difficulties of implementing HBIM methodology for CH.

Keywords: HBIM · Cultural heritage · Archaeology · Geospatial DB
Survey · 3D modelling

1 Introduction

The digital revolution that is affecting our era, with the huge amount of data that can be shared and/or exchanged anywhere and at any time, has also affected the building construction world with the advent of the Building Information Modelling (BIM). This term refers to a methodology or process through which it is possible to develop and manage digital representations of buildings, infrastructures and, more generally, built places. In fact, according to BIM methodology, it's possible to take in account not only the geometric information of building components but also information concerning

© Springer Nature Switzerland AG 2018
M. Ioannides et al. (Eds.): EuroMed 2018, LNCS 11196, pp. 344–355, 2018.
https://doi.org/10.1007/978-3-030-01762-0_29

their physical characteristics, functionalities and mutual relationships. Although BIM design has taken place in recent years, it had been conceptually proposed about 40 years ago (Eastman et al. 2008). One of the first examples was, in fact, the prototype of Charles M. Eastman who, in 1975, theorised a unique three-dimensional model to describe the construction elements, also useful for the estimation of quantities and materials, associated with an external database (Eastman 1976).

BIM software, available today on the market, favour the sharing of models and related information through the network, thus encouraging collaboration between the various actors involved in the life cycle of constructions. These applications were created for the design of new building (as-designed BIM), based on parametric elements connected to each other through a hierarchical structure of "smart objects" (Garagnani 2013).

Through BIM technology, the use of shared models among different professional figures, with different skills, allows obtaining continuously updated diachronic information (Garagnani et al. 2016). Therefore, this methodology is dedicated not only to the planning and design of an architectural or engineering work but also to its management, maintenance and monitoring (Volk et al. 2014).

Then, the application of this methodology to existing building assets (as-built BIM) has become of fundamental importance, adding information related not only to design but also to current conditions and structural changes over time (Huber et al. 2011). The use of the as-built BIM approach, therefore, represents a particular interesting solution for CH, to manage the information related to the individual 3D components of the monument (Saygi, Remondino, 2013). The BIM applications for historical architecture are much more complex because ancient buildings contain elements and materials having geometries that cannot be represented with standard software libraries (Logothetis et al. 2015). Furthermore, due to its history and to long life, CH tends to change over time as a result of the use, natural deterioration and collapse of structures. A BIM model of a historic building (HBIM model) could also contain dynamic information that, for example, thanks to sensors and control signals, could support the conservation of the structure. This application allows finding the presence of a possible structural problem, such as a collapse or a fracture. In this way, it's possible to analyse the 3D model avoiding the physical exploration of the construction.

This paper deals with the evaluation of approaches that allow the creation of HBIM model of architectural heritage, starting from 3D laser scans and photogrammetric techniques, called 'Scan to BIM' (Baik 2017). HBIM methodology allows providing not only a visual description of the monument but also the implementation of a smart database of semantic information concerning its conditions, materials and history (Scianna et al. 2014). This information can be used, for example, to support the design of a possible restoration intervention, helping the operators involved in the subsequent management and monitoring phase. The possibilities offered by HBIM methodology are strongly linked to the correct decomposition of the structures, based on in-depth studies. It's necessary, in fact, the creation of an abacus of the constructive elements.

Although the modelling of historical architecture has been sufficiently explored by many scholars, its architectural and compositional variety, over time, requires and will still require considerable study work to define the methods of structuring models useful for applications not originally provided for BIM design. Hence to model historical buildings, a comparison with IFC standards (Laakso, Kiviniemi 2012) should be initially made to understand which elements are already included in IFC and which ones can be assimilated to those already present.

2 From BIM to HBIM

In the field of building design, the construction industry has increasingly focused on the use of digital models that go beyond the simple geometric representation of construction elements. Between them, the most complete and validated model is IFC which BIM methodology is based on. Considering the BIM approach applied to historic buildings, called HBIM as mentioned above, the advantages of this methodology would be many: remote control of external and internal parts of the architecture, planning of restoration operations, structural analysis, interactive 3D representations for cultural and educational uses. All this through a single final model. On the other hand, the complexity of historical buildings leads many problems on HBIM applications. It's necessary to take care of the different needs of this methodology, to focus all of the limits and the issues linked to HBIM applications:

– the necessity of a systematic standardisation of every part of the building, useful for the implementation of specific libraries dedicated to CH. These could be considered a particular example of Digital Libraries (Ioannides et al. 2017);
– the necessity of making a classification of the architectural elements, dividing the structure into categories at different hierarchical levels and creating a database for the inclusion of new libraries;
– the modelling and parametrisation of new smart objects that represent the architectural elements of historical buildings. In fact, the complexity of these structures needs an in-depth knowledge of historic construction techniques and advanced modelling skills.

During the experimentation carried out for different study cases, it's been possible to individuate a workflow for the creation of a complete HBIM model (Fig. 1):

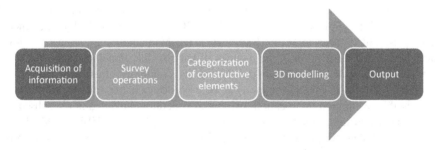

Fig. 1. The workflow for the creation of an HBIM model.

– acquisition of information;
– survey operations;

- categorisation of constructive elements;
- 3D modelling;
- output.

The first phase of acquisition of necessary information regarding each historical building is fundamental for the choice of the next survey operations and also for making a correct decomposition of the structure. Survey operations are necessary for the geometrical reconstruction of the point clouds, that, together with the decomposition of the structure in macro-categories, categories and subcategories of elements, are the basis for the construction of the 3D model. Even if the BIM was thought of as a multipurpose model, that should cover each building over its whole life cycle, and for supporting each kind of processing, the modelling phase depends on the choice of the output model required. In fact, different user needs require different model outputs, and, consequently, different modelling techniques.

In the following section of the paper some interesting issues encountered in the application of the workflow will be analysed:

- the difficulties encountered in the part of the workflow between survey operations and the generation of the 3D model;
- the complexity of the categorisation of constructive elements, necessary for the creation of a library of "smart objects" and the correct modelling of a building;
- the difficulties in modelling and parametrisation of single architectural elements connected with the output to realise.

3 From Survey Operations to General Model

Data collected using the most modern survey instruments and related techniques allow generating models that geometrically describe the building in a very accurate way. They are the starting point for the next modelling phase of the building. Some software and plug-ins, such as Agisoft Photoscan ®, Pix 4D mapper ®, Bentley Context Capture ® and FARO ® VirtuSurv, also allow the semi-automatic creation of 3D models passing through processing of point cloud. However, in all of these cases, the 3D meshes generated from point clouds hold only geometric information. Instead, to correctly create smart objects, it's necessary to store not only their whole geometry but also semantic information on materials properties (specifications). These information are required to describe the shape of a smart object and to consider its function and its relationship with other elements (relational system). Nowadays, the complete automatic generation of building elements from a point cloud is almost not possible. The point cloud can be assumed mostly as a spatial reference for the drawing of geometric parts of building elements whose semantic description can be associated with.

The above considerations have been tested also in a study case regarding the participation to the benchmark activity issued by the Italian Society of Photogrammetry and Topography (SIFET) concerning the "restitution of 3D/HBIM models from point clouds obtained with UAV surveys or terrestrial laser scanning" of the Fornace Penna (an historical industrial building located in Sicily).

Starting from the point cloud, it's been necessary to create a 3D model retracing the shape given from the cloud. In this case, only walls and pillars have been taken from existing libraries. In fact, walls and pillars can be easily adapted to the real ones thanks to the possibility of managing profiles and sections and by assigning materials.

New families of openings, ad-hoc created, have been parametrised to be adapted to the real ones and have been inserted into the library. The difficulty in parameterising the individual segments that make up an opening led to the creation of a family for each opening so that BIM appears less productive. In fact, the openings of the building showed very small differences in size, although they could look the same at first glance. Even for openings with collapsed elements, dedicated families have been created (Figs. 2, 3 and 4).

Fig. 2. Visualization of the BIM modelling of walls of the Fornace Penna over its point cloud.

Hence, this case study highlighted some problems that can be resumed in:

- the lack of specific libraries of smart objects for historic buildings as the great variety of architectural shape requires designers to create new libraries on a case-by-case basis;
- the existence of some limitations in modelling and parameterisation of certain constructive elements;
- the absence of a comprehensive classification of the construction elements of historic buildings supported by semantic data.

4   From the General Model to the Classification of Its Elements

One of the main features of the BIM software is the presence of a parametric objects library described in IFC standards. This kind of library helps very much architects and engineers during the design and the management of buildings. However, despite its vastness, the elements included in software libraries, as said before, not always meet the design and management needs, requiring the creation of specific components for each design case, especially in the case of CH. In fact, doesn't exist a complete

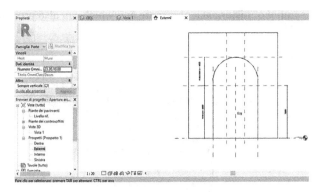

Fig. 3. An example of a parametrisation of an arc opening in BIM.

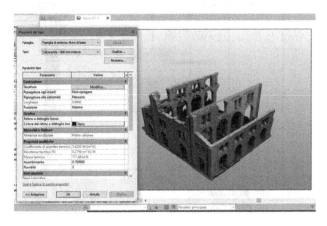

Fig. 4. Visualization of information about a selected element of the Fornace Penna BIM model.

database of ancient smart objects to use as a basis for modelling, that could give essential advantages of reducing times and costs during operations. However, this kind of library must meet specific requirements to be exploited in the same way as those already present within the software. Hence, modern software libraries propose, for new constructions, a very detailed categorisation of the components of the building organism. In Autodesk ® Revit or Graphisoft ® Archicad, for example, it's possible to find a distinction between architectural elements, structural elements and plant engineering. After this, it's possible to find a subdivision that identifies the classes of objects that allow access to the default library and then load the chosen components in the project.

So, the first problem to be faced for the creation of a standard library of elements belonging to the historical building heritage is precisely the breakdown of the building itself. This technique could allow achieving a global knowledge of the artefact. For example, it's possible to apply this technique to a Greek temple, a structure that can be considered as a symbol of historical architecture and which can also provide interesting methodological considerations (Fig. 5).

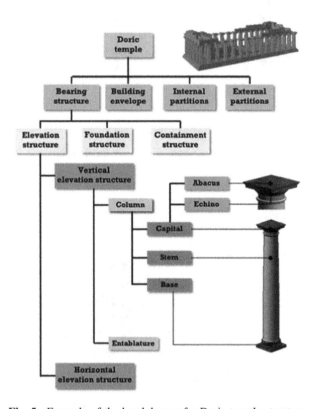

Fig. 5. Example of the breakdown of a Doric temple structure.

The decomposition to follow derives from the classification of the modern technological building system. So it's possible to divide the parts of a building into macro-categories, categories, micro-categories of elements and technical elements. The components constituting each piece of CH should be grouped and classified according to their function, also identifying a further internal subdivision. For example, the technical element "Column", which in turn is composed of other parts, can be found within the micro-category "vertical elevation structure". This last is part of the "Elevation structure" category, which in turn is contained in the macro-category "Bearing structure".

Thanks to this decomposition of the structure, it's possible to associate elements such as columns and lintels with the corresponding modern structural elements. So, they are insertable, through appropriate modelling, within the database, creating a new library of structural elements. For other components such as metopes and triglyphs, the association is not immediate, and it requires an in-depth study of the evolution of historical construction techniques. According to Vitruvius, for example, the triglyphs were used to cover the heads of the wooden beams in the first temples, the metopes instead had the function of filling the gaps between the beams. Furthermore, metopes were all different from each other, because they were also decorative elements used to tell stories. With the subsequent adoption of the stone elements, these parts remained, becoming canonical elements and completing part of the entablature (Washburn 1919; Jones 2002).

This example is useful for underline that the knowledge of the origins and functions of historical elements are fundamental for the association to smart objects already present in the software and for the application of the modelling techniques. It's also important to consider, during modelling, the way in which the elements should be inserted in the overall model and the task or role they have to play.

5   Modelling and Parametrising Objects

The stage of modelling is very delicate and complex. In particular, in the case of BIM, it is important to take care about of some fundamental aspects during the creation of objects belonging to a larger and articulated system.

As seen before, the correct use of HBIM methodology needs the analysis and the breakdown of the architectural structure, where every element should be implemented into a specific library of smart objects related to a particular architectural language.

Despite the proposals of some authors on the creation of a library of historical elements based on the manuscripts of Vitruvius and Palladio and on the books of architectural patterns of the Eighteenth Century, nowadays only a few things have been realised and only in relation to specific cases (Dore et al. 2015). In many historical buildings, besides, apart from differences caused by degrades or for subsequent alterations, it's possible to find differences between similar elements caused by their handmade production. This aspect greatly increases the difficulty of parameterisation of the geometrical elements that compose these buildings.

Anyway, the implementation of different databases, based each one on different architectural languages and containing a hierarchic categorisation of elements, could allow creating an HBIM model in a good level of detail (LoD).

Furthermore, according to BIM, it's important to consider that the same architectural elements could be reproduced with different modelling techniques. Even if BIM born to cover all the aspects and phases of the construction sector, the choice of the best method depends on the final use that has led the model creation. For example, in Revit, an element finalised only to 3D representation or metric calculation can be freely modelled with no limits to surface configurations. Instead, an element finalised to structural analysis (e.g. a pillar), to obtain an association with the analytical model, is obliged to be constrained on both ends to other structural elements (like beams) and to follow a regular path.

The example of modelling here proposed uses a typical column of a Doric temple. In the exposed case it's been used the creation of nested families. They are families containing other families to better manage the parameterisation of the various parts of the objects. With the help of the Book of architectural patterns "the Classical Order of Architecture" by Robert Chitham (Chitham 1984), the column was divided into small parts. The dimensions of each piece have been related to a base unit located in the diameter of the column itself (Aubin, 2013). A key element was the use of profile families containing a two-dimensional closed circuit. In this case, the drawing of the sections of the elements that composed the column has been used. These were then inserted from time to time in a "pillar" family where extruding, path sweeping and solid revolutions were applied. In this way, the typical behaviour of a pillar has been associated with the column, in order to create an analytical model useful for a possible automatic structural analysis (Figs. 6 and 7).

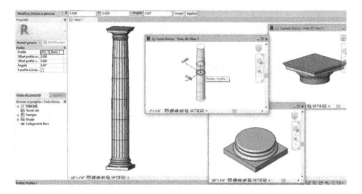

Fig. 6. Nested family "column" containing three families: capital, shaft and base. Each family includes profile families.

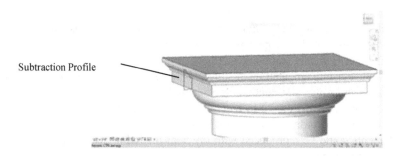

Subtraction Profile

Fig. 7. Modelling and parametrisation of a Doric capital using a profile family in BIM.

The comprehension of the modelling techniques of the column has been very important for the application to a real case, starting from a point cloud obtained during survey operations. Software in facts allows the extraction of different profiles, obtained from point cloud sections.

In this way, the modelled object can be adapted to the real one by varying the base parameter and updating the profile families with the measurements obtained from the survey. This technique allows also representing any degraded elements acting directly on the nested families with solid operations. However, as the case study shows, it's necessary to have a deep knowledge of the modelling techniques that the software makes available. The same techniques also vary depending on the constructive element to represent (Figs. 8 and 9).

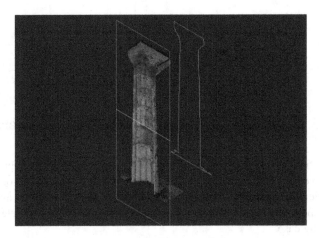

Fig. 8. Section of the column extracted from the point cloud.

Fig. 9. Point cloud, HBIM model and analytic model of the column.

Considering the previous case of the Fornace Penna, the construction of the model was also finalised to develop a structural analysis of the building. This requirement needed to take care especially of connections between walls opportunely inserting the external static constraints. Furthermore, as described before, the choice of the correct modelling methods for the creation of arcs, windows and pillars, highlighting the differences between different kinds of stones, was a fundamental aspect for making a correct structural analysis of the building. About this aspect, it's necessary to clarify that the level of definition that characterises the HBIM model isn't compliant with

Fig. 10. A structural analysis result of a Fornace Penna facade from the BIM model.

monitoring infinitesimal movements of structures. Anyway, HBIM representation is useful for preventing imminent collapses and for planning restoration works (Fig. 10).

More difficulties appear, then, in the case of more complex elements and with more particular shapes; this aspect necessarily requires the use of custom elements to be defined case by case.

6   Conclusions

This paper investigates some critical issues in the making of HBIM representations of CH. The HBIM process is seen, here, as a set of procedures that starts from the collection of data up to the final creation of a complex 3D model of the building full of semantic information. After a definition of the reasons and the advantages that motivate an approach of this kind to the historic architecture, some technical problems have been presented in relation with some study cases. Indeed, while the survey stage is today enough advanced thanks to available technology, the modelling stage of the HBIM process is still problematic and not well defined. Most of the problems are related to the uniqueness of each existing building and/or its components. This uniqueness is due to the handmade production of the historical construction elements, the presence of degradation, the irregular shape of some constructive elements and decorations, and the vast variety of architectural languages on CH. Each of these features makes difficult the realisation of a standard library of CH smart parametric objects.

Moreover, the construction of these libraries needs a standard classification of the parts of historical buildings, but this operation isn't always simple for the reasons indicated before. The categorisation of the components of an ancient building requires an exploration of the old construction techniques to allow an association between their behaviour and the corresponding function of the structural elements formerly inside the BIM software. So, the diffusion of HBIM methodology needs still more technical insights that will be explored in future works.

References

Aubin, P.F.: The doric column, Chap. 8. In: Renaissance Revit: Creating Classical Architecture With Modern Software, pp. 209–242 (2013)

Baik, A.: From point cloud to jeddah heritage BIM nasif historical house – case study. Digit. Appl. Archaeol. Cult. Herit. **4**, 1–18 (2017)

Chitham, R.: The Classical Orders of Architecture, pp. 54–59. Elsevier Ltd. (1985)

Dore, C., Murphy, M., McCarthy, S., Brechin, F., Casidy, C., Dirix, E.: Structural simulations and conservation analysis -historic building information model (HBIM). In: The International Archives of the Photogrammetry, Remote Sensing and Spatial Information Sciences, vol. XL-5/W4, pp. 351–357 (2015)

Eastman, C.: General purpose building description systems. Comput.-Aided Des. **8**(1), 17–26 (1976)

Eastman, C., Teicholz, P., Sacks, R., Liston, K.: Foreword. In: BIM Handbook: A Guide to Building Information Modeling for Owners, Managers, Designers, Engineers, and Contractors. Wiley (2008)

Garagnani, S.: Building information modeling and real world knowledge: a methodological approach to accurate semantic documentation for the built environment. In: Digital Heritage International Congress (DigitalHeritage), Marseille, France, pp. 489–496 (2013)

Garagnani, S., Gaucci, A., Govi, E.: ArchaeoBIM: Dallo scavo al Building Information Modeling di una struttura sepolta. Il caso del tempio tuscanico di Uni a Marzabotto. In: Archeologia e Calcolatori, vol. 27, pp. 251–270 (2016)

Huber, D., Akinci, B., Adan, A., Anil, E., Okorn, B., Xiong, X.: Methods for automatically modeling and representing as-built building information models. In: Proceedings of NSF Engineering Research and Innovation Conference, Atlanta, Georgia (2011)

Iloannides, M., et al.: Mixed Reality and Gamification for Cultural Heritage, pp. 161–199. Springer, Switzerland (2017). https://doi.org/10.1007/978-3-319-49607-8

Jones, M.W.: Tripods, Triglyphs and the origin of the Doric Frieze. Am. J. Archaeol. **106**(3), 353–390 (2002)

Laakso, M., Kiviniemi, A.: The IFC standard – a review of history, development, and standardization. J. Inf. Technol. Constr. **17**(2012), 134–161 (2012)

Logothetis, S., Delinasiou, A., Stylianidis, E.: Building information modelling for cultural heritage: a review. ISPRS Ann. Photogramm. Remote. Sens. Spat. Inf. Sci. **I-5/W3**, 177–183 (2015)

Saygi, G., Remondino, F.: Management of architectural heritage information in BIM and GIS: state-of-the-art and future perspectives. Int. J. Herit. Digit. Era **2**(4), 695–713 (2013)

Scianna, A., Gristina, S., Paliaga, S.: Experimental BIM applications in archaeology: a workflow. In: Ioannides, M., Magnenat-Thalmann, N., Fink, E., Žarnić, R., Yen, A.-Y., Quak, E. (eds.) EuroMed 2014. LNCS, vol. 8740, pp. 490–498. Springer, Cham (2014). https://doi.org/10.1007/978-3-319-13695-0_48

Volk, R., Stengel, J., Shultmann, F.: Building information modeling (BIM) for existing buildings – literature review and future needs. Autom. Constr. **38**, 109–127 (2014)

Washburn, O.M.: The origin of the Triglyph Frieze. Am. J. Archaeol. **23**(1), 33–49 (1919)

Accessing and Understanding Cultural Heritage Through Users Experience Within the INCEPTION Project

Federica Maietti$^{(\boxtimes)}$ ⓘ, Emanuele Piaia ⓘ, Giuseppe Mincolelli ⓘ,
Roberto Di Giulio ⓘ, Silvia Imbesi ⓘ, Michele Marchi ⓘ,
Gian Andrea Giacobone ⓘ, and Silvia Brunoro ⓘ

Department of Architecture, University of Ferrara, Via Ghiara 36,
44121 Ferrara, Italy
{mttfrc, piamnl, mncgpp, dgr, mbsslv, mrcmhl, gcbgnd,
brnslv}@unife.it

Abstract. The interdisciplinary EU funded project INCEPTION – *Inclusive Cultural Heritage in Europe through 3D semantic modelling*, coordinated by the Department of Architecture of the University of Ferrara, is focused on bringing together innovative 3D modelling and ICT applications and professionals involved in different fields of Cultural Heritage. The aim is to increase knowledge, enhancement and dissemination through 3D digital models in order to promote the inclusiveness and accessibility of European assets. In this direction, a Stakeholder Panel with different skills in the field of Cultural Heritage has been involved leading the research toward effective strategies to increase use and reuse of digital models. These strategies are aimed at maximizing the impact of using digital data for cultural heritage applications involving a wide range of non-expert and expert users, starting from specific requirements for processing, managing, delivering cultural heritage information to a broad audience. A co-design workshop has been organized involving Stakeholders in order to investigate on their requirements and expectations, to obtain information that could be useful for the User Centered process of definition of INCEPTION's main outcomes and functionalities.

Keywords: Digital cultural heritage · User centered design · Accessibility

1 Introduction

The INCEPTION project, "Inclusive Cultural Heritage in Europe through 3D Semantic Modelling", started in June 2015 and lasting four years, aims at developing advanced 3D modelling for accessing and understanding European cultural assets. One of the main challenges of the project is to close the gap between effective user experiences of Cultural Heritage via digital tools and representations, and the enrichment of the scientific knowledge.

The project is developed through a strong synergy among the Consortium Partners and the Stakeholder Panel, an assembly of European institutions, already involved during the project preparation phase with the aim of directing research toward those

M. Ioannides et al. (Eds.): EuroMed 2018, LNCS 11196, pp. 356–365, 2018.
https://doi.org/10.1007/978-3-030-01762-0_30

strategies needed by "end users" and institutions to increase knowledge, enhancement and dissemination through digital models.

During the project development, several activities and meetings have been arranged in order to strengthen the Stakeholders' role within INCEPTION and to learn from Stakeholders about their needs and expectations [10]. The interest of Stakeholders for 3D modelling and learning about cultural heritage assets' significances via digital media guided the project progress and strongly influenced the type, content and applicability of final products.

In order to apply a User Centered Design methodology to the project of the INCEPTION's User Experience (UX), the last Stakeholders meeting was organized in June 2018, and it has been conceived as an interactive workshop. The main aim was to focus effectively on two topics: new tools for modelling Cultural Heritage, and how to make Heritage more accessible and understandable by different kind of users.

1.1 INCEPTION Project Overview

As part of 3D integrated survey applied to Cultural Heritage, digital documentation is gradually emerging as effective support of many different information in addition to the shape, morphology and dimensional data. The contribution of INCEPTION in increasing knowledge is based on the improvement and optimization of data collection processes and the development of semantically enriched 3D models, accessible by different Cultural Heritage experts, users and different disciplines through an open-standard Semantic Web platform [1].

Among several related projects dealing with Heritage 3D modelling, INCEPTION is relevant and differentiates from these projects because it is focused on heritage "spaces" (complex architectures and sites), on semantic enrichment - creating 3D models for multiple purposes, needs and level of knowledge of the end-users – and on the collection of all information in a unique Platform [2].

The overall project workflow starts from requirements (what kind of data, information and visualization issues can be collected and managed by a 3D model according to specific users and needs), the integrated data capturing and holistic heritage documentation, the semantic enrichment via 3D modelling in H-BIM environment, and the models deployment and valorization through the INCEPTION platform. Model formats accessible by the platform to the users are openBIM formats, and textured models (Collada files). 3D models are based on open standards in the BIM, GIS, Semantic Web and point cloud area (including IFC - ifcOWL, gbXML, CityGML, E57, etc.) [3].

According to the overall INCEPTION workflow, the H-BIM modelling procedure starts with documenting user needs, including experts and non-experts.

The identification of the Cultural Heritage buildings semantic ontology and data structure for information catalogue allows the integration of semantic attributes to 3D digital geometric models for management of heritage information within the INCEPTION platform. So the main innovations under INCEPTION will be delivered through an open standard platform to collect, implement and share digital models. Platform interface and functionalities will allow users to download and upload models, work with H-BIM models with different level of details, enrich contents and information linked to geometric models in an interoperable way and explore a wide range of data and contents.

1.2   Stakeholders Involvement Toward a Broad Accessibility of 3D Digital Models

The INCEPTION project established a broad Stakeholder Panel with participants of different countries, disciplines and potential professional users, involved in several stages of the project, starting from the analysis of needs and requirements. A part of the Stakeholder Panel has been involved more closely providing Demonstration Cases, supporting the consortium in data collection for data modelling and on-site or off-site demonstration activities [9].

The INCEPTION platform is already structured through a general architecture, and a first prototype has already been elaborated based on the macro-needs analysis carried out in the first phase involving users and Stakeholders and developed through the definition of invariants and technological and system constraints [4].

According to Human Cantered Design's principles, an iterative process has been applied to the first prototype in order to evaluate and implement it together with users and Stakeholders for new versions' development.

The objective is not only to gain opinions on the current state of development of the INCEPTION platform by users, but also and above all to participate with them in the experimentation and re-elaboration of the opportunities offered by the platform as defined through the first analyses [5].

The aim of this activity, which takes the name of Co-Design, is to understand if the first prototype allows the understanding of the instrument, if this understanding allows a greater awareness on the needs focused during the first analysis, and if this awareness helps to reconsider the structure of the current prototype, improving it.

The purpose is not only to analyse the requests of users and Stakeholders, but also to work together to the design of a new set-up of the platform, so that it responds to needs that have not yet been identified, and it's easy to navigate and interesting for each type user, common visitors or specialized technicians.

2   Co-design Workshop

2.1   Definition of Co-design Experiences

Co-design is a well-established approach to creative practice, particularly within the public sector. Co-design is often used as an "umbrella" term for participatory, co-creation and open design processes [8].

The co-design approach enables a wide range of people to make a creative contribution in the formulation and solution of a problem. A key tenet of co-design is that users, as "experts" of their own experience, become central to the design process.

A wide range of tools and techniques are available to support the co-design process. Potential solutions can be tested through prototyping and scenario generation techniques. Two techniques are usually applied:

- Storytelling/Storyboards is a tool that helps visualizing the experience that the user will experience through the design of key passages for a type of story usage [7].

- The Experience Map is a visual map that graphically describes the experiences through the different steps and touchpoints. The compilation of the map is exploding on different floors all the steps that the user does, so that they have a unified view from the top of the experience.

2.2 The INCEPTION Co-design Workshop

Six Stakeholders participated in the Co-Design workshop, from different countries (Italy, Belgium, Slovenia, Greece, Spain and Germany) and from different Heritage fields. Members from institutions such as the Geodetic Institute of Slovenia, the General Hellenic Archives-Historical Archives of Epirus, the Institute of Cultural Heritage of Spain, the firm Energy Efficient Architecture Renovation Conservation, the Italian Association of Local and Institutional Museums, the Institute for Diagnostics and Conservation of Monuments in Saxony, represented several skills and expertise.

The aim of the Co-Design workshop was to create an informal experience (Fig. 1) to exchange considerations regarding INCEPTION functionalities within the platform, providing a specific service able to fulfil different needs of different user categories. To gather information about users' needs, the collaborative work session with INCEP-TION Stakeholders allowed pointing out what kind of tools and facilities they would need to achieve requirements and opportunities.

Fig. 1. In order to gather personal information from the Stakeholders in a confidential way and establish a mutual knowledge, a sort of game was developed in which each participant indicated in a card its own data and interests, using an imaginary identity.

During the first step, Stakeholders were asked to be not so closed to reality, in order to outline an overall picture of user needs through an inclusive and dynamic parallel session. In this first phase, the Co-Design session involved all Stakeholders around a worktable. Thanks to the presence of a moderator, every participant became familiar with the activity of brainstorming, namely a creative technique based on associations of ideas. Every single member was stimulated to freely share his/her own suggestions and

Table 1. Summary of the results gathered during the Co-design workshop.

	Contents	User experience	Interface
Tourist and specialized users	Hyperlinks to external platforms	Storytellers to relate the real site and the virtual model	Accessibility and inclusion even to people with special needs or disabilities
	Update the models with related data and information	Possibility to print virtual models into 3D physical models	Intuitive and hierarchical interface
	Examine the model in different historic periods	Knowledge about building by showing historical events	Information available even on smartphone and by AR
Governments and decision makers	Information about events and exhibitions and info about the physical place	Bridge the gap between real and virtual experiences	Do not waste time to find data during researches
	Download models for related activities	Make users updated on last modifications of their visited models	Provide users the % of browsed elements of a visited model
	Reliable data for scientific researches	Provide augmented reality during a visit	Give users few and clear information
Technicians and professionals	Split the elements of a building in order to visualize different historic phases	Keep in memory information already visited Real-time work sharing	Private area for not accessible models and filter research bar
	Store data of previous interventions and documents available even on mobile devices	Download 3D models with different scales of details	Timeline of interventions and last updating
	Interoperability among several external databases	See missing parts of the buildings	Comprehension of different parts that compose the building

opinions about the topics of INCEPTION's platform, in term of functionalities, graphic interface, etc. Every single idea was transcribed by the design team on many post-its and sorted on a specific whiteboard. Only at the end of brainstorming activity, the performed work was discussed and analysed, making a qualitative and quantitative selection and organization of the developed ideas.

It was chosen to consider three main significant user categories: *tourists and specialized users* (*academic and researchers*), *governments and decision makers*, and *technicians and professionals*. The criteria for defining users were based on the concept of inclusion and on the maximum possible spread of 3D models for different uses applied to the knowledge and conservation of Cultural Heritage.

Thoughts, comments and ideas resulting from the brainstorming among partners and Stakeholders were collected in three categories:

- contents,
- user experience and
- interface,

where "contents" are data and information relevant according to the opinion of the Stakeholders; "user experience" are opportunities in browsing 3D digital models and interacting with specific information; and "interface" are all the possible platform functionalities (Table 1 and Fig. 2).

Fig. 2. View of the co-design workshop.

3   INCEPTION Platform Interface and Accessibility

Within Co-Design session, a journey map was defined. INCEPTION platform has a high number of functions and different modalities of interaction, so the card-sorting methodology was applied to represent schematically the complex architecture of the web platform in a user centered approach, facilitating shared representations of work through a tactile and visible experience of the possible interaction tools. Thanks to Stakeholders different skills, different feedbacks from wide-ranging experiences, abilities and needs were collected. Different contents of the INCEPTION platform were hierarchized and it was analyzed what interaction modalities were more usable for final users, in order to reach an intuitive and accessible navigation.

The workshop tried to define tools able to improve user experiences for a first interaction with the INCEPTION platform. To do this, many "cards" were processed and printed, representing through icons and drawings every single operation that the user can perform inside the system. To make the process more practical and accessible, tools were divided into 4 macro groups:

- Cards for the functions related to the BIM model (zoom, clipping planes, change shades, walkthrough, pan, rotate, filter elements, etc.);
- Cards for the functions related to video (play 360°, rotate 360°, rotate, download and upload, etc.);
- Cards for the functions related to the use of images (full screen, zoom, etc.);
- Cards for the functions related to data loading and uploading (download, upload, open metadata).

Then some white cards were printed for each macro group, in order to be able to implement the hypothesized tools based on the specific needs of the Stakeholders involved and increase the available functions. The aim was to create a visual graphic map allowing users to understand and move the tools at their disposal, to imagine a possible conceptual map of tools for knowledge/modification/implementation of the platform [6] (Fig. 3).

Fig. 3. View of some of the used cards.

During this phase, an experience map was elaborated with the aim of understanding the most appropriate and suitable tools for platform navigation and exploration by different users, and to point out possible weaknesses, trying to find accessible and inclusive solutions. Thanks to this methodology, it was also possible to analyze the information flows between activities, making the navigation experience more efficient. The tools considered more relevant are related to basic actions to be performed on the model, such as visualize and download videos and images, select elements of the model, measure distances or surfaces or move within the model. "Missing" cards from the first survey were not related to operational tools to be applied to the model, but rather to a better contents organization, information flows and navigation.

How to understand and interact with the information shown by the INCEPTION platform interface and how to make it easier to navigate is a relevant point outlined for basic users. Navigation can be carried out by two different ways of interaction: through the 3D model or by customizing contents through research filters. At the first browsing, training instructions may be useful on how to use the platform, as well as a location bar to find buildings to visit. To provide information, it is possible to either receive personal data of users by filling in a short initial questionnaire or by data obtained from previous navigations or already present in the INCEPTION database (user profiling). An additional functionality suggested as relevant is the possibility to run virtual guides: it is useful to know how long the experience is before starting it or to provide both a short and full version and a list of visited or favorite models.

Fig. 4. Proof of concept of a 3D model case of data access to the platform; on the left, possible interactions (BIM model, point cloud, images, documents, videos, etc.).

For each building, a window showing available functions should be useful, also based on different devices (laptop, smartphone, tablet, etc.). Additional suggestions are related to different interfaces for any single typology of users, and the possibility to receive news when models are updated (Fig. 4).

Regarding expert users, the discussion was focused mainly on the creation of contents: who can upload files to be approved by expert evaluators in order to deliver only reliable models, through a moderator who approves the files and authorizes to proceed with the upload. The possibility to have some guidelines explaining how to upload the file with its specific characteristics is a point stressed several times.

Every user should be able to upload data, materials and information in relation to BIM models. The opportunity to relate many developers who work together on a single file updatable in real time, without having multiple copies of the object, is an additional requirement.

At the end of the workshop, the participants were asked about their perceptions. The general feeling was that the Co-design represented an intensive work session where everyone was feeling free to express the own point of view, with the aim of enriching the users' and Stakeholders' perspectives within the INCEPTION project. The organization of the Co-design Workshop was effectively focused on objectives set by the team, both for obtaining information needed for the application of the User Centered Design process, and to strengthen the sense of being part of a group of people with different backgrounds working for the same purpose.

4   Conclusions

User needs collected during the co-design workshop were grouped and classified in some subgroups more specifically related to the optimization of the platform. Of course, the needs of every user category may interact and influence each other. Requirements have been discussed and pointed out to design different interfaces for each user target. The visitor's interface should be simple and intuitive, and provide immersive experiences according to the user needs in an open access environment.

About technical users, the interface should provide a filter research area in order to avoid wasting time in searching needed information. Technical users need specific and technical tools to be used in their work, so the system should provide a better support in performing their activities rather than focusing on virtual expositions. For decision makers, it is more interesting to provide scientific and reliable sources, involving at the same time touristic users through the activities promoted by the public institution itself. The requirement to provide an easy-to-use platform for upload and download files has been highlighted, as the availability of a private area in order to protect data to be shared with specific partners but not publicly. For the visitor/tourist it would be useful to analyze a tool set that could improve knowledge and involvement of people by virtual experiences. Virtual reality guides are positively considered, but it is crucial providing experiences based on different historic periods and related contents. Through a different user experience map, expert users debated on the importance of policies for data management, data reliability and guidelines for downloading and uploading files.

Based on these results, the platform interface and content management are being updated. The verification of this advanced prototype will be the focus of the next Stakeholders workshop, in November 2018.

Quantitative results on platform interface and accessibility will be delivered after the project conclusion, when the platform will be populated with several heritage models, as well as an estimation of usability of different platform functionalities.

Acknowledgments. The project is under development by a consortium led by the Department of Architecture of the University of Ferrara. Academic partners of the Consortium, in addition to the Department of Architecture of the University of Ferrara, include the University of Ljubljana (Slovenia), the National Technical University of Athens (Greece), the Cyprus University of Technology (Cyprus), the University of Zagreb (Croatia), the research centers Consorzio Futuro in Ricerca (Italy) and Cartif (Spain). The clustering of small medium enterprises includes: DEMO Consultants BV (The Netherlands), 3L Architects (Germany), Nemoris (Italy), RDF (Bulgaria), 13BIS Consulting (France), Z + F (Germany), Vision and Business Consultants (Greece).

This research project has received funding from the European Union's H2020 Framework Programme for research and innovation under Grant agreement no 665220.

References

1. Maietti, F., et al.: Heritage fruition through 3D semantic modeling and digital tools: the INCEPTION project. In: IOP Conference Series: Materials Science and Engineering, vol. 364, p. 012089 (2018)
2. Di Giulio, R., Maietti, F., Piaia, E., Medici, M., Ferrari, F., Turillazzi, B.: Integrated data capturing requirements for 3D semantic modelling of cultural heritage: the INCEPTION protocol. Int. Arch. Photogramm. Remote Sens. Spatial. Inf. Sci. **42**(2/W3), 251–257 (2017)
3. Bonsma, P., et al.: Handling huge and complex 3D geometries with semantic web technology. In: IOP Conference Series: Materials Science and Engineering, vol. 364, p. 012041 (2018)
4. Maietti, F., et al.: Roadmap for IT research on a Heritage-BIM interoperable platform within INCEPTION. In: Borg, R.P., Gauci, P., Spiteri Staines, C. (eds.) Proceedings of the International Conference SBE Malta, pp. 283–290. Gutenberg Press, Malta (2016)
5. Di Giulio, R., Maietti, F., Piaia, E.: 3D documentation and semantic aware representation of cultural heritage: the INCEPTION project. In: Catalano, C.E., De Luca, L. (eds.) Eurographics Workshop on Graphics and Cultural Heritage, pp. 195–198. The Eurographics Association (2016)
6. Davis, F.D.: Perceived usefulness, perceived ease of use, and user acceptance of information technology. MIS Q. **13**, 319–340 (1989)
7. Kankainen, A., Vaajakallio, K., Kantola, V., Mattelmaki, T.: Storytelling Group - A co-design method for service design. Behav. Inf. Technol. **31**(3), 221–230 (2010)
8. Pallot, M., Kit, B., Senach, B., Scapin, D.: Living lab research landscape: from user centred design and user experience towards user cocreation. Hal archives-ouvertes (2011)
9. Mincolelli, G., Marchi, M., Imbesi, S.: Inclusive design for ageing people and the internet of things: understanding needs. In: Di Bucchianico, G., Kercher, P.F. (eds.) AHFE 2017. AISC, vol. 587, pp. 98–108. Springer, Cham (2018). https://doi.org/10.1007/978-3-319-60597-5_9
10. Mincolelli, G.: Customer/User Centered Design. Analisi di un caso applicativo. Maggioli, Rimini (2008)

Digital Interpretation and Presentation for Monuments Built by ARCHES - Take Kinmen Area Heritage as an Example

Wun-Bin Yang[1,2], Jihn-Fa Jan[3], Tsung-Juang Wang[1], Yi-Chou Lu[2], Chiao-Ling Kuo[4], and Ya-Ning Yen[2(✉)]

[1] National Taipei University of Technology, 1, Sec. 3,
Zhongxiao E. Rd., Taipei 106, Taiwan
[2] China University of Technology,
56, Sec. 3 ShingLong Rd., 116 Taipei, Taiwan
{wunbin, alexyen}@cute.edu.tw
[3] National Chengchi University, 64, Sec. 2, Chih-Nan Road, Taipei 116, Taiwan
[4] Research Center for Humanities and Social Sciences, Academia Sinica,
Taipei 115, Taiwan

Abstract. Conserving and preserving the national heritage reflects important cultural stewardship and the application of ARCHES provides for robust international interoperability of this heritage. In recent years, Taiwan has promoted protection and management of historic architecture and cultural heritage, through completion of a series of databases and inquiry platforms for the cultural heritage. However, there remains a significant digital divide between domestic integrated digital data exchange performance and international standards. Hence, Taiwan is focusing on integrating multi-source digital data and database exchange services with complete ontologies and taxonomies in conjunction with the latest global developments. This study constructs ontological metadata for registration and designation of historical architecture. The ontology, based on the CIDOC CRM, is used to import the contents of the current national cultural heritage database in Taiwan to build the ontology model of registration and designation of historical architecture; and the results are displayed through the network platform. The results indicate that new interpretative data models can improve mutual exchange of information and attain the purpose of heritage educational promotion. The metadata structure is built by using the ontology model according to international standards. It provides a positive structure for conveying Taiwan cultural heritage throughout the world.

Keywords: Ontology · Cultural heritage · Historic architecture
CIDOC CRM · Arches

© Springer Nature Switzerland AG 2018
M. Ioannides et al. (Eds.): EuroMed 2018, LNCS 11196, pp. 366–375, 2018.
https://doi.org/10.1007/978-3-030-01762-0_31

1 Introduction

The Bureau of Cultural Heritage, Taiwan Ministry of Culture is heavily invested in promotion of the national cultural heritage. The information model for the current National Cultural Heritage Database (NCHDB) is constructed according to the international standard Dublin Core (DC). DC contains 15 core items. Each item has a specific taxon or ontological meaning. NCHDB regulations provide for robust consultations with expert stakeholders as to metadata information for methods of cultural heritage preservation and cultural heritage guidelines [1]; then the NCHDB maps the cultural heritage data fields to relative core elements of DC for building the Taiwan cultural heritage metadata model.

Concomitant with maturation of Internet technology and data exchange requests, the concept of Linked Open Data (LOD) was proposed and is now in wide use [2]. LOD means data can be created, connected and used at the network level. Thus, data will have multiple values, and such data can be linked to each other. In comparison with new technology and emerging concepts, the DC cultural heritage database metadata requires data exchange increase, field level expansion and review of the design concept. In 2001, the Taiwan Library Act provisions provided for "Regulations in Metadata Format" but the system was not robust enough with only 15 core DC items insufficient to support the needed complicated metadata structure.

Ontology can be used to describe and express professional knowledge with accuracy, brevity and clarity, along with formal definitions and descriptions, conceptualization of certain fields [3]; and then describing the relationship between the concepts and ideas. An ontology is a model expressing the relations and perspective of certain fields. This study constructs the metadata according to the ontology of the ICOM CIDOC Conceptual Reference Model (CIDOC CRM). The main purpose of CIDOC CRM is to implement data exchange and integration between cultural heritage data and diverse sources, so as to achieve semantic interoperability [4], improving shortcomings of the DC core, and promoting the relevance and presentation of Taiwan cultural heritage database metadata.

At present, the Taiwan national cultural heritage database in Taiwan constructs metadata through interviews requested by the Ministry of Culture. However, the metadata does not meet international standards, and has resulted in follow-up data exchange difficulties and an unclear concept of the whole model. Doerr mentioned differences between the cultural heritage field and information engineering make it arduous to build a complete conceptual model [5]. Since introduction of CIDOC CRM in 1995, ISO21127 has emerged as the leading integrated cultural heritage ontology standard. Though it might be insufficient for in some instances; most of the core concepts are fully elucidated in the model.

Cultural heritage preservation is highly diverse, multicultural and multilingual, so appropriate inclusive usage mandates holistic metadata standards for content. Carrascal et al., adopted CIDOC CRM to build a cultural heritage database in Cantabria, Spain. They noted the area is replete with diversified cultural heritage types including man-made and natural products [6]. Information for each item involves different sources, carriers, and formats. The project integrated the information according to the

CIDOC CRM standard over a wide range able to integrate the data from different sources. In addition, many items for cultural heritage ontology are extended by implication from CIDOC CRM. For example, In 2017, Vlachidis et al. developed the ontology based on the European CrossCult Project, demonstrating the challenges and outcomes of semantics and inference of cultural assets [7]. In 2014, Hu et al. developed an ontology for the intangible heritage of Pan Wang Festival in China, focusing on the activities conducted in CIDOC CRM [8]; Pramartha et al. established the ontology of Indonesia's Bali culture and web portal for the KULKUL system in 2017, but it still does not incorporate the concept of a 3D building model [9]. CRMdig focuses on digital data and the sources [10]. FRBRoo elucidates the basic semantics of bibliography [11]. CRMarchaeo applied the standard for archaeological surveying [12]. Niang et al., designed an ontology model to manage and display heritage preservation based on CIDOC CRM [13]. The ontology structure adopted the concept of the life cycle and added three fields for monument investigation, heritage and persons. Later, they applied the new ontology to a building information model; combining the building components and ontology for physical heritage maintenance. This study shows the application and importance of the CIDOC CRM for architectural heritage management.

In summary, the CIDOC CRM covers a wide range of levels and has been successfully applied to a variety of contexts to construct metadata with a uniform format and international standard. Thus, it can assist in building Taiwan's heritage preservation data with high exchangeability, interoperability and fully elucidated structure. In addition, it can help to build 3D digital technology, promote data integration efficiency among different sources, and provide a basis for international integration and heritage access harmonization.

2 Life Cycle of Cultural Heritage

At present, the Taiwan national cultural heritage website was revised September 1, 2016, and published online. The total number of entries and accessions registered is listed in Table 1 [14]. The metadata consists mainly of cultural heritage registration information. However, to preserve the life cycle information for various types of cultural heritage, the concept of the life cycle (as Fig. 1) and corresponding regulations to formulate suitable metadata fields are deployed.

In Phase 1 of the life cycle, heritage registration is undertaken. The content includes basic information of cultural heritage entries to meet the requirements for administration and education. Phase 2 involves information on the various investigational research, maintenance/repair/restoration, reuse plans and, heritage preservation/conservation. Phase 3 focuses on recording and managing information to maintain complete digitalized information for cultural heritage accessions to the platform. The purpose of designing the whole database is to fulfill requirements for administrative requests, digitalized preservation, knowledge management, and expectations for promoting additional value of cultural heritage through mining cultural heritage Big Data. The metadata fields supra were made according to users' requests. It did not consider the follow-up data exchange phase so the fields for cultural heritage exchange were insufficient, and the core values were not included, either.

Table 1. Taiwan cultural heritage entries (2018.5)

Category	Type	Quantity	Total
Tangible heritage	Monument	903	2389
	Historic building	1364	
	Settlement	13	
	Archaeology site	47	
	Cultural landscape	61	
	Memorial building	1	
	Antiquities	1726	1726
Intangible heritage	Traditional art	184	485
	Traditional crafts	135	
	Folk custom	166	

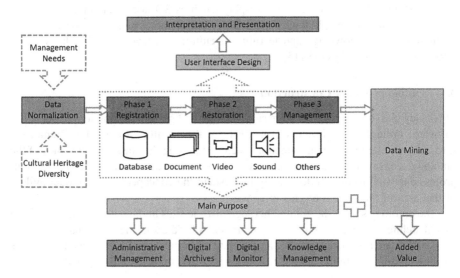

Fig. 1. Concept map of full life cycle

This study deploys CIDOC CRM to promote overall database exchangeability and ensure the data structure's accuracy, brevity and clarity. In addition, the ontology model is written with reference to the Ontology Web Language (OWL). The user can browse the web page directly, understand the overall model of the metadata and will not be restricted to only limited information accessibility. The ontology model can ensure overcoming the digital divide and offering functionally relevant understanding of Taiwan's national cultural heritage for all stakeholders.

3   Digital Interpretation

This study is divided into three parts. Part I, deploys the ontology concept of CIDOC CRM, as to standards and correlation for the cultural heritage database metadata. Such parts include:

a. Inviting cultural heritage digitalization experts to conduct interviews to understand their viewpoints regarding metadata and actual operational phases in accordance with the model.
b. Process cross-checking for the metadata fields in the current Taiwan national cultural heritage database with the entities in the CIDOC CRM. Ensure use of CIDOC CRM as an interface foundation is feasible.
c. Construct the ontology model. The ontology model is used to present the definition and correlation for each class in the cultural heritage database.

Part II adds 3D models or image display (such as 3D laser scanning, photogrammetry model, panoramic photography and UAV aerial photography) for specific fields, promoting user's knowledge and learning of cultural heritage. Part III relates to the ARCHES navigation system [15].

3.1   Ontology Model Construction

This study used the Protégé software suite to build and present the ontology model. The software, Protégé, was developed in 1991 by the Stanford Center for Biomedical Informatics Research. Its main functions include building the class and relevance of the ontology, constructing the ontology model, presenting the model structure for non-professional staff to be able to quickly understand the concepts that the model builder of that area of the system desires to convey.

The ontology shows the cultural heritage historic sites in the ontology model (phase 1) and architecture components. The primary class for the specified list (phase 1) model is 14, which are associated with the appropriate properties, and its associated properties are shown in Fig. 2. In the model, each class is corresponds to an Entity and actual use

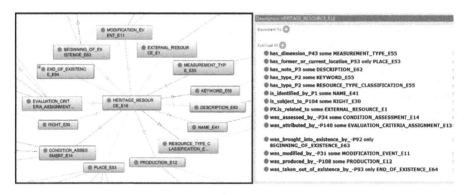

Fig. 2. Ontology model (list information)

demands as determined by CIDOC CRM; also the classes are expanded to different Entities. For example, the status investigation for the component in Fig. 3 indicates recording current status investigation results of the component including description of the investigation, date, types, administration suggestions and threats. Different classes can be connected through the CIDOC CRM, which allows each Entity to fully preserve its original intentions. Meanwhile, each entity can be read and used by the computer, allowing for empowered and inclusive data exchange.

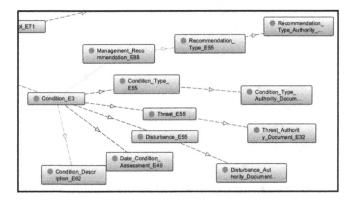

Fig. 3. Ontology model for historical architecture "condition"

3.2 Metadata Mapping

This study deploys the Arches-HIP system to undertake data presentation to guide the completed ontology model into the Arches-HIP and build the relative Authority Documents. Then, these are imported into the system platform to ensure feasibility by constructing the basic data test for the ontology model.

Table 2. Comparison table for database field and Arches-HIP

	Field name	Field code	Data type	Arches-HIP
1	Serial number	assetid	int	EXTERNAL XREF.E42
2	ID	caseId	int	EXTERNAL XREF.E42
3	Case type	otherAssetsType	nvarchar	HERITAGE_RESOURCE_ USE_TYPE.E55
4	Case name	caseName	nvarchar	NAME.E41
5	Case nickname	caseAliasName	nvarchar	NAME.E41
6	Case english name	caseEnglishName	nvarchar	NAME.E41
7	Register reason	registerReason	nvarchar	REASONS.E62
8	Date of publication	registerDate	nvarchar	DESIGNATION_OR_ PROTECTION_FROM_DATE.E49
.	....	....	....	....

After building the metadata model of cultural heritage supra, each class is mapped to different classes (Table 2) in Arches-HIP, including Heritage Resources, Heritage Resources Group, Activity, Historical Event, Actor and Information Resources. For the insufficient part, a corresponding Scheme (Fig. 4) is built in Arches-HIP directly and new authority document added for selection in the drop-down menu [16].

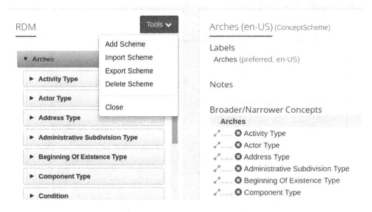

Fig. 4. RDM page for the new added scheme

4   Digitization Presentation

The ARCHES system deployed in this study is mainly for the Qionglin area (Fig. 5) in the island of Kinmen adjacent to historic China on the Asiatic mainland, but now appertaining to Taiwan. The Tsai Lineage Temple (Fig. 6), a prime example of the traditional value of filial piety, is taken as an example for interpretative data content of architectural cultural heritage. The content of the metadata converts current cultural heritage data (phase 1) in Taiwan from demand-oriented (with data structure limitations) into the metadata model based on the adopted Ontology. In the data exchange phase, such changes greatly enhance the capability for file export and communication.

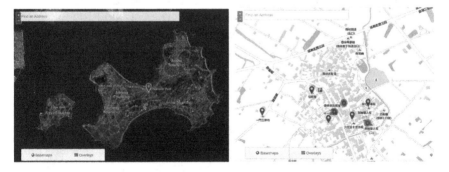

Fig. 5. Kinmen area base map

Fig. 6. Web user interface for the Tsai Lineage Temple

For example, the existing NCHDB shows the relevant basic information about each of the monuments, and the information of the builder or craftsman of the monument has not been linked to each case, thus, the specified historical case cannot be found through relevant craftsman during the search. However, through the establishment of ontology, the unidirectional correlation of previous data can be strengthened and improved, and the visual presentation of ARCHES system will also enhance the cognitive function of users on query and learning maps as well (Fig. 7).

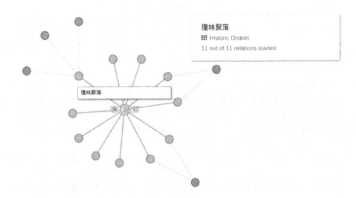

Fig. 7. Visual presentation of ARCHES

5 Conclusions and Future Suggestions

This study builds a metadata and ontology model meeting the requirements of international data exchange standard and promoting the functions of data exchange. At present, the Taiwan government has begun to review the "standardization" for the database and the interpretation materials. The Ministry of Culture emphasizes that the restoration of cultural assets should be extended to the historical memory, and it can use the function of cultural science and technology to achieve the internationalization of local culture. This study can be linked to the requirements mentioned above, and the establishment of interpreting data based on international standards could be used as the basis for future international integration, effectively reducing the cost-benefit of development and future data exchange.

Heritage metadata in the Chinese language can also map to the fields and content as listed in the Entities and Properties in CIDOC CRM. Although administrative records will concomitantly increase, most of the metadata can be mapped. After importing the ontology model, the ARCHES presentation system allows the user to understand the concept of the model through directly browsing the web pages. The platform framework also saves much manpower. In addition, it can export data with multiple network languages for various purposes. Currently, the specified list phase of the monument in NCHDB can correspond to the Arches-HIP class; however, it is still necessary to expand the relevant categories for the re-use and maintenance phases in the future in order to meet the information required at each phase and to enhance the content required by different users.

The second phase will perform a relevance study between the cultural heritage ontology data and the 3D models. It will offer references and suggestions for future data exchange requirements for Taiwan's national cultural heritage; and should gradually improve the operability of cultural heritage browsing systems for the public and enhance the promotion of cultural heritage education and international integration.

Acknowledgements. This study is sponsored by the Bureau of Cultural Heritage, Ministry of Cultural for 2018 Research and Development Project Plan (107-6).

References

1. Ministry of Culture.: Cultural heritage preservation act. Ministry of Culture (2016)
2. W3C eGov Wiki.: Linked Open Data. https://www.w3.org/egov/wiki/Linked_Open_Data. Accessed 30 May 2018
3. Pattuelli, M.C.: Modeling a domain ontology for cultural heritage resources: a user-centered approach. J. Am. Soc. Inf. Sci. Technol. **62**(2), 314–342 (2011)
4. Crofts, N., Doerr, M., Gill, T., Stead, S., Stiff, M.: Definition of CIDOC CRM version 5.0.2 (2010)
5. Staab, S., Studer, M.: Handbook on Ontologies. Springer, Heidelberg (2009). https://doi.org/10.1007/978-3-540-92673-3
6. Hernández, F., Rodrigo, L., Contreras, J., Carbone, F.: Building a cultural heritage ontology for Cantabria. In: Annual Conference of CIDOC, pp. 1–14 (2008)

7. Vlachidis, A., Bikakis, A., Kyriaki-Manessi, D., Triantafyllou, I., Antoniou, A.: The CrossCult knowledge base: a co-inhabitant of cultural heritage ontology and vocabulary classification. In: Kirikova, M., et al. (eds.) ADBIS 2017. CCIS, vol. 767, pp. 353–362. Springer, Cham (2017). https://doi.org/10.1007/978-3-319-67162-8_35
8. Hu, J., Lv, Y.C., Zhang, M.: The ontology design of intangible cultural heritage based on CIDOC CRM. Int. J. U-E-Serv., Sci. Technol. 7(1), 261–274 (2014)
9. Pramartha, C., Davis, J.G., Kuan, K.K.Y.: Digital preservation of cultural heritage: an ontology- based approach. In: The 28th Australasian Conference on Information Systems (2017)
10. Doerr, M., Theodoridou, M.: CRMdig: a generic digital provenance model for scientific observation. In: TaPP 2011 3rd USENIX Workshop on the Theory and Practice of Provenance, Heraklion, Greece (2011)
11. Le Boeuf, P.: A strange model named FRBROO. Cat. Classif. Q. 50(5–7), 422–438 (2012)
12. Doerr, M., et al.: CRMarchaeo: modelling context, stratigraphic unit, excavated matter. In: 29th CRM-SIG Meeting, Heraklion, Greece (2013)
13. Niang, C., et al.: Supporting semantic interoperability in conservation-restoration domain: the PARCOURS Project. ACM J. Comput. Cult. Herit. 10(3), 16:1–16:20 (2017)
14. National Cultural Heritage Database Management System. https://nchdb.boch.gov.tw/. Accessed 30 May 2018
15. Arches, What is Arches?. https://www.archesproject.org/what-is-arches/. Accessed 16 Apr 2018
16. Farallon Geographics.: Arches-HIP Documentation release 1.0. Chap. 3, pp. 13–19 (2017)

HBIM in Cultural Heritage Conservation: Component Library for Woodwork in Historic Buildings in Taiwan

Y. M. Cheng[1] , C. C. Mou[1], Y. C. Lu[2], and Y. N. Yen[2(✉)]

[1] Department of Civil Engineering and Hazard Mitigation Design, China University of Technology,
56 Hsing-Lung Road, Section 3, Taipei 116, Taiwan, ROC
yingmei@cute.edu.tw
[2] Department of Architecture, China University of Technology, 56 Hsing-Lung Road, Section 3, Taipei 116, Taiwan, ROC
alexyen@cute.edu.tw

Abstract. The aim of this study is to propose an application framework of HBIM for historic buildings in Taiwan with a focus on defining the components of historic buildings, component attributes, and the relationship between the components and restoration data. The information is then imported into a database and presented in a visualized model. Issues explored include definition of components and the process of generating component library for historic buildings with an emphasis on traditional woodwork. The case study is on Huangxi Academy. To generate the component library, regulations must be established to define structural components of historic buildings and the component types must be categorized. The structure of Huangxi Academy is divided into 5 areas with individual elements and the components are classified into one of the three categories, family component with parameters, family component without parameters, and custom component. In addition, for create basic visual effects for each component with data pertaining to renovation, the LOD 300 model is suggested for this project.

Keywords: BIM · HBIM · Historic building · Revit

1 Introduction

1.1 HBIM

BIM (Building Information Modeling) is wildly used in the Architecture, Engineering and Construction (AEC) industry. It improves the accuracy and efficiency of information transfer during the construction life cycle. In recent years, a large number of research studies have discussed the use of BIM in the preservation of heritage/historic building, and named it HBIM (Heritage/Historic Building Information Modeling). Comparing to BIM, HBIM emphasizes more on the data behind the heritage building and modeling technique for as-built structures. The generation of HBIM involves the

© Springer Nature Switzerland AG 2018
M. Ioannides et al. (Eds.): EuroMed 2018, LNCS 11196, pp. 376–385, 2018.
https://doi.org/10.1007/978-3-030-01762-0_32

analysis of information concerning the history and renovation of the historic buildings, especially on the relationship between the parameters of the model and the historical information. However, there are major challenges for HBIM projects. Often times, the original construction drawings for historic buildings are missing. The structures are often in the state deterioration due to natural factors, or they have been renovated and modified. These structures often have unique features and historical significance. The component parameters are also distinct. It is difficult to use the component library within the current BIM framework to complete the model. Therefore, researchers must first survey and measure the building components using laser scanning and photogrammetry, etc. Then they may refer to literature concerning historic structures to build the models. In addition to modeling techniques, it is also necessary to consider attributes concerning the renovation of components to convey the information for each component more clearly. For example, the ontology method is adopted to clarify the common terminology of each historical component, its attribute, and correlation. In short, to provide accurate information to different stakeholders at different stages of a project life cycle, it is critical to consider the role of these components in HBIM, which is to define how the building components and the data behind them can be integrated and presented.

Research on HBIM includes modeling techniques that help build precise models quickly [1–7]; definition of model information [8–11]; applications of HBIM [12–15]. In the AEC industry, BIM users often choose different Level of Development (LOD) at different stages of project life cycle to enhance communication depending on the level of detail or the subject area a model element has been developed for. The LOD specification utilizes basic LOD definitions developed by the AIA for the AIA G202-2013 Building Information Modeling Protocol Form and is organized by CSI Uniformat [16]. Banfi [5] proposed GOG, GOI and GOA to give significant support to the process of building upgrades, focusing on reading and the proper use of models for as-built BIMs.

1.2   Application of HBIM on Historic Buildings in Taiwan

This project is supported by the Ministry of Culture in Taiwan, and the aim is to propose a HBIM framework for historic buildings within the country. Recent research on HBIM focuses on the refinement of 3D models. However, in respect to the value of historic buildings, the documentation and background of each building element deserve more attention. Details related to the building should also be included, such as the shape of the elements, names of the artisans, as well as renovation period and process in addition to the basic information, historic registry and background of the building. It is necessary to preserve all relevant information on historical building elements, which may be passed down for future generations. For this reason, HBIM is defined in this project as an information management tool during the life cycle of historic buildings with a 3D model. The focus of this paper is on the process of generating component library for historic buildings with traditional woodwork in Taiwan. It is important for the future development of this project. The core issues explored in this project are as follows.

- Definition of components: the building components should be separated into individual element unit in order to present complete historical traces of each building component. For example, there are different history and renovation records associated with each "dougong" (tou-kung, bracket set), beams, and pillars, and each should be treated as a different individual unit.
- Definition of component attributes: the component attributes include the dimensions, materials, surface decoration, time, names of the artisans, tools used, and renovation record of all repairs made. The attributes should be determined based on needs during different stages of the project life cycle.
- Definition of association: the association is created in order to give the elements of the building, their relationships, and the renovation details common vocabulary. The association also identifies the interrelationships within and among the category and class to establish basic data description, and explore the possibility of data validation and integration. Ontology and CIDOC CRM is adopted to redefine building components and basic/repair information.
- Data is imported into the database and presented in a visualized model.

2 Huangxi Academy

In Taiwan, historic buildings include cultural/educational monuments, temples, residential structure, ancient tombs, and so on. This research is trying to create a breakdown of the structure of Huangxi academy (cultural/educational monument) to analyze the building elements, and create the component library with Autodesk Revit. Huangxi academy (Fig. 1) was built in 1888. It is a historic city monument located in Dadu District of Taichung City. It was once an important gathering place for the scholar and officials in Dadu, Longjing, and Wuri. During the Japanese Occupation period, it was used as a national elementary school. Currently, it is mainly a tourist attraction and place of worship.

Huangxi Academy is a traditional building with the double-square layout and a courtyard separating the front and back. The width of the building is seven "kaijian" (a traditional measuring unit), which is about 28 meters wide. The depth is approximately 30 meters. The spatial layout from the outside in includes shanman (front gate), courtyard, baidian (hall of worship), main hall (lecture hall), east and west chambers, and connecting hallways (Fig. 2). Building materials include red brick tiles, granite, bluestone and Cunninghamia lanceolata (China-fir).

3 HBIM Component Library

BIM is based on components (parametric objects) that are stored in object library with information. Currently, most BIM applications deal with new buildings. The predefined libraries or tools for modelling historic buildings are limited. In this project, a reusable parametric library objects for historic buildings are created with an emphasis on traditional woodwork. The components and 3D model are created using Autodesk Revit,

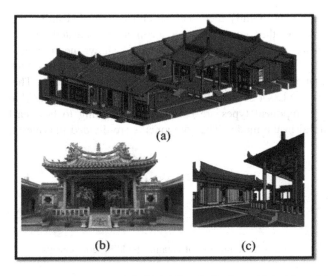

Fig. 1. Huangxi academy: (a) 3D model, (b) baidian (hall of worship), (c) partial 3D sections.

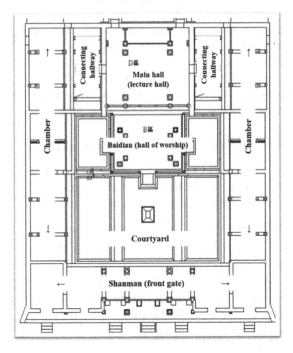

Fig. 2. Layout of Huangxi Academy, including front gate, courtyard, hall of worship, main hall, chambers and connecting hallways

in which RFA files are family files that can either be loaded into a project or saved externally. To allow other projects to use the components created for this project, most of the components are created as RFA file. Figure 3 shows the process of building the components. The 2D CAD of Huangxi Academy provided by the Center for Cultural Sites Rehabilitation and Development is used as the reference basis. The drawings are created with FARO Laser Scanner Fo-cus3Dx130 based on on-site field measurements. In Fig. 3, the component types are categorized according to how each component would be utilized in the model. The components are divided into the three following classifications.

Fig. 3. The process of creating building components.

- **Family component with parameters:** this classification applies when a component is used repeatedly in the project and the size needs to be modified for different positions.
- **Family component without parameters:** this classification is for a component that is used repeatedly in the project without modification to the size. This classification also applies when the component is used only one time in this project, but it is a general component which can be used in other projects.
- **Custom component:** components are under this category when they are used only one time and cannot be used for other projects.

3.1   Regulations for Defining Building Components of Historic Buildings

In order to define the regulation for building components, historic references concerning the structure, conservation and restoration records international studies And experts in related fields were consulted. The regulations are defined as follow:

- Regulations for distinguishing building components (as shown in Fig. 4):

    a. Start form the front of the building, and progress along the main axis of the building. For example, shanmen → tianjing → baidian → zhengdian (front gate → courtyard → hall of worship → main hall).
    b. Distinguish every truss from the outside to inside, from front to back and from the left to right in every building space.
    c. From the lowest building component under the truss, identify every interval at different height.
    d. In every height interval, follow the same principles (from outside to inside, from front to behind and from left to right) to identify every building component.
    e. If one building component crosses multiple intervals, choose the first interval that it connects.

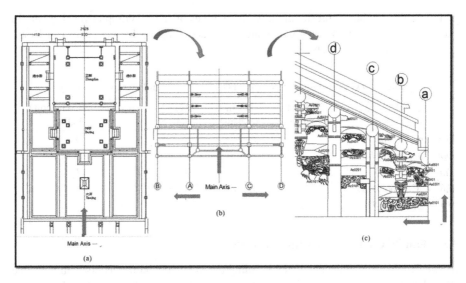

Fig. 4. Regulation for defining building components: (a) plan of a Minnan style historic buildings, example of rule a, (b) example of rule b, (c) profile of a truss, example of rule c-d.

- Regulations concerning the definition of building component as one or multiple elements in the BIM model:

  a. When the exact position in need of restoration on the building component cannot be predicted, the entire building component should be treated as one element. For example, it is impossible to predict which part of a wall would need restoration since the position of possible cracks on a wall would be unpredictable. For this reason, the entire wall is regarded as one element.

  b. The building component has a significant cultural or historical significance. For example, if the imprint, pattern or inscription on one roof tile is different from the others, this tile would be regarded as one element. Otherwise, all roof tiles should be considered one building element.

  c. The building component consists of a series of elements, such as rafters under the roof. If none of the rafters has been modified or restored, all rafters would be regarded as one element.

These regulations are established based on the case of Huangxi Academy. However, traditional Minnan buildings come in many forms. The modeling process would vary for different structures and for different needs, especially if special circumstances apply.

3.2 Building Components in Each Area of Huangxi Academy

The structure of Huangxi Academy is divided into five areas: Front gate, hall of worship, main hall, chamber, and connecting hallway. According to the regulations stated in Sect. 3.1, the breakdown of special building components is shown in Table 1, including the numbers representing how many types of special components there are in each area. Some custom components are specifically created for the project in Revit, and are not included in Table 1.

Table 1. Types of building components in each area in Huangxi Academy.

	Front gate	Hall of worship	Main hall	Chamber	Connecting hallway
Tong (main beam)	2	3	3	0	0
Dou (supporting bracket)	9	12	5	3	1
Ying (roof beam)	3	3	3	1	1
Family Components without parameters	58	41	44	13	36

3.3   Family Components with Parameters

In order to improve efficiency when building the 3D model, components with the same shape but different sizes are selected as family components with parameters. In the case of Huangxi Academy, four family components with parameters are created. They are round supporting bracket, square supporting bracket, major beam and roof beam. Figure 5 shows these four components with the parameters where the size may be modified entirely or partially. For example, users may modify the diameter of a roof

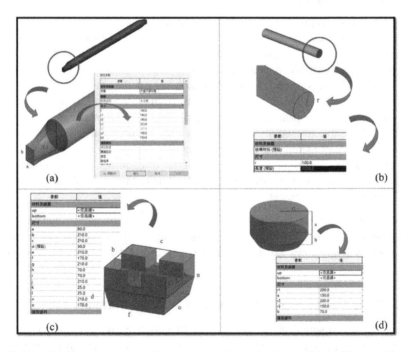

Fig. 5. Four family components with parameters: (a) major beam, (b) roof beam, (c) square supporting bracket, (d) round supporting bracket.

beam (b) by changing the value of parameter r and change the size of the rectangular tip of the tenon (a) by changing the value of parameters a and b. Figure 6 shows 12 different sizes of the square brackets in the hall of worship.

Fig. 6. 12 square supporting brackets in the hall of worship.

3.4 Family Components Without Parameters

In addition to the family components with parameters, most of the components are created in RFA file, but the parameters are not set at this point. Users may set parameters depending on their projects needs at any time. Twenty-three structural elements are created for Huangxi Academy, and each is further developed based on the

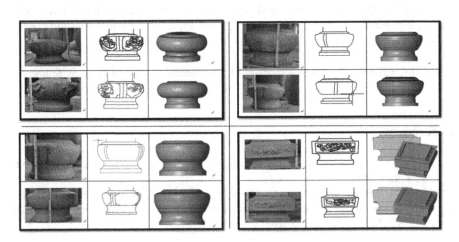

Fig. 7. Column base in the hall of worship

type of form variations. Figure 7 shows eight types of the structural element, column base, in the hall of worship.

4 Conclusion

This article discusses the process of building component library for historic buildings with Huangxi academy as the example.

- Before building the component library and 3D model, building components/elements within the historic building must be separated and categorized into appropriate element units. Depending on the information necessary for the future database, ways of separating and categorizing the components may vary.
- The components must be appropriately classified, and the parameters must be examined to determine whether they are necessary. This will be beneficial for the management of the component library, and make the components more applicable and usable for future projects.
- In order to create visual effects for each component with data included, such as information pertaining to renovation, LOD 300 is recommended. A lower model may not generate as much detail. However, if a higher model is used, building the model would be more time consuming given the intricate nature of traditional woodwork. Additionally, the 3D model will be available online with links to the database for browsing. A model with too much detail will reduce the browsing speed.

HBIM can record, present and transfer data behind elements of historic buildings. Comparing to conventional digital archiving technology, HBIM records both the information pertaining to the entire building as well as the individual structural element. This is important to the conservation of historic buildings. The article discusses the process of building component library for woodwork on historic buildings in Taiwan. However, the creation of component library is only the beginning. The ultimate goal for this project is to establish a comprehensive database for historic buildings. Additional issues should be further explored, including how to define and classify the data behind each element, and redefine the relationship among the data sets.

Acknowledgements. This study is sponsored by the Bureau of Cultural Heritage, Ministry of Cultural for 2018 Research and Development Project Plan (107-5).

References

1. Murphy, M., McGovern, E., Pavia, S.: Historic building information modelling (HBIM). Struct. Surv. **27**(4), 311–327 (2009)
2. Hichri, N., Stefani, C., DeLuca, L., Veron, P., Hamon, G.: From point cloud to BIM: a survey of existing approaches. ISPRS - Int. Arch. Photogramm. Remote Sens. Spat. Inf. Sci. XL-5/W2, **XL-5/W2**, 343–348 (2013)

3. Barazzetti, L., Brumana, R., Oreni, D., Previtali, M., Roncoroni, F.: True-orthophoto generation from UAV images: implementation of a combined photogrammetric and computer vision approach. ISPRS Ann. Photogramm. Remote Sens. Spat. Inf. Sci. **2**, 57–63 (2014)

4. Pöchtrager, M., Styhler-Aydın, G., Döring-Williams, M., Pfeifer, N.: Automated reconstruction of historic roof structures from point clouds – development and examples. In: 26th International CIPA Symposium 2017, Ottawa, Canada (2017)

5. Banfi, F.: BIM orientation: grades of generation and information for different type of analysis and management process. Int. Arch. Photogramm. Remote Sens. Spat. Inf. Sci. - ISPRS Arch. **42**, 57–64 (2017)

6. Prizeman, O.E.C., Sarhosis, V., D'Altri, A.M., Whitman, C.J., Muratore, G.: Modelling from the past: the leaning southwest tower of caerphilly castle 1539-2015. ISPRS Ann. Photogramm. Remote Sens. Spat. Inf. Sci. **4** pp. 221–227 (2017)

7. Nony, N., et al.: Protocols and assisted tools for effective image-based modeling of architectural elements. In: Ioannides, M., Fritsch, D., Leissner, J., Davies, R., Remondino, F., Caffo, R. (eds.) EuroMed 2012. LNCS, vol. 7616, pp. 432–439. Springer, Heidelberg (2012). https://doi.org/10.1007/978-3-642-34234-9_44

8. Niang, C., Marinica, C., Leboucher, É., Bouiller, L., Capderou, C.: An ontological model for conservation-restoration of cultural objects. In: International Congress on Digital Heritage, pp. 157–160 (2015). https://doi.org/10.1109/digitalheritage.2015.7419476

9. Cacciotti, R., Blaško, M., Valach, J.: A diagnostic ontological model for damages to historical constructions. J. Cult. Herit. **16**, 40–48 (2015)

10. Acierno, M., Cursi, S., Simeone, D., Fiorani, D.: Architectural heritage knowledge modelling: an ontology-based framework for conservation process. J. Cult. Herit. **24**, 124–133 (2017)

11. Messaoudi, T., Véron, P., Halin, G., DeLuca, L.: An ontological model for the reality-based 3D annotation of heritage building conservation state. J. Cult. Herit. **29**, 100–112 (2018)

12. Niang, C., Marinica, C., Leboucher, É., Bouiller, L., Capderou, C., Bouchou, B.: Ontology-based data integration system for conservation-restoration data (OBDIS-CR). In: Proceedings of the 20th International Database Engineering & Applications Symposium, IDEAS 2016, pp. 218–223 (2016). https://doi.org/10.1145/2938503.2938545

13. Quattrini, R., Pierdicca, R., Morbidoni, C.: Knowledge-based data enrichment for HBIM: exploring high-quality models using the semantic-web. J. Cult. Herit. **28**, 129–139 (2017)

14. Banfi, F., Fai, S., Brumana, R.: BIM automation: advanced modeling generative process for complex structures. ISPRS Ann. Photogramm. Remote Sens. Spat. Inf. Sci. **4**, 9–16 (2017)

15. Yen, Y.-N.: A CH based integrative management framework on the value priority aspect. In: Ioannides, M., Fritsch, D., Leissner, J., Davies, R., Remondino, F., Caffo, R. (eds.) EuroMed 2012. LNCS, vol. 7616, pp. 841–848. Springer, Heidelberg (2012). https://doi.org/10.1007/978-3-642-34234-9_90

16. BIMFORUM (2018). http://bimforum.org/lod/#_ftn2

Panoramic Image Application
for Cultural Heritage

Maarten Bassier$^{(\boxtimes)}$, Tijs Deloof, Stan Vincke, and Maarten Vergauwen

Department of Civil Engineering, TC Construction - Geomatics, KU Leuven,
Leuven, Belgium
{maarten.bassier,tijs.deloof,stan.vincke,maarten.vergauwen}@kuleuven.be
https://iiw.kuleuven.be/onderzoek/geomatics

Abstract. Advancements in remote sensing and communication technology caused a surge in new methods to capture and share information about tangible heritage. The documentation of these monuments
is vital to the conservation process. However, current workflows generate an immense amount of information and often fail to properly relay
the context of the scene. Additionally, the distribution of information
between different stakeholders is paramount in preventive conservation.

The goal of this research is to provide heritage experts with the tools to
better capture and communicate information about heritage sites. More
specifically, an image recording workflow is presented to rapidly acquire
a series of panoramic images of the scene and present them accordingly.
An online web application is created based on an existing viewer that
allows even unskilled users to access the data and intuitively visit the
site. The proposed application can be used to distribute information to
stakeholders and supports decision makers to constitute a suitable treatment if necessary. Furthermore, the panoramic viewer and accompanying
map can be used as a backbone to link to other data such as 3D models,
orthographic images and so on.

Keywords: Cultural heritage · Image documentation · Visualisation
Google API

1 Introduction

Cultural heritage experts are continuously looking for new techniques to better
preserve and manage our tangible heritage. An important aspect in the process
of conservation is the documentation of the as-is conditions of the exterior of
objects and monuments. This includes the gathering and recording of all pertinent data, both metric and non-metric, of the current state of the asset. This
documentation is crucial in the examination of the asset and allows experts to
gain a better understanding of the history and context of the recorded entities.
More specifically, the acquired information is used for the purpose of pathol-
ogy detection, visualization and conservation planning [1]. Furthermore, an

© Springer Nature Switzerland AG 2018
M. Ioannides et al. (Eds.): EuroMed 2018, LNCS 11196, pp. 386–395, 2018.
https://doi.org/10.1007/978-3-030-01762-0_33

Fig. 1. Overview traditional images taken of a church attic with poor lighting conditions. The bottom right image depicts the lighting panel used to generate the artificial lighting for the omni-directional camera.

accurate and realistic documentation is required to constitute a proper treatment in preventive conservation.

The recent advancements in sensor and communication technology give access to new ways for heritage experts to share information with interested parties. A crucial aspect of the information distribution are tools to intuitively communicate the current state of a monument. Typically, this is performed with a set of images and textual documents. However, these are hard to interpret as the vocabulary is often field specific. Also, the field of view of the imagery is often limited and the location of the images is unknown. E.g. the images taken in Fig. 1 are challenging to interpret as no geospatial information is present. They might be taken in the same section or in consecutive sections. Furthermore, the lighting conditions are a major obstacle in the proper documentation of the environment. The emphasis of this work is to investigate to which extend existing tools can be applied to better communicate and document heritage information. More specifically, we look to provide an intuitive tool to visualize and distribute information about monuments that is accessible by both experts and novices.

The remainder of this work is structured as follows. The background and related work are presented in Sect. 2. In Sect. 3, the heritage application is proposed. A real test case is shown in Sect. 4. Finally, the conclusions are presented in Sect. 5 along with a discussion about the future work.

2   Background and Related Work

The acquisition of imagery for the documentation of heritage sites is widely adopted in the industry. It is not uncommon for heritage projects to capture tens of thousands of images of every detail and object in the scene. As the project expands, the number of images quickly becomes overwhelming [2]. An important factor in the number of images being generated is the Field of View (FoV). Typical cameras with 18 mm to 55 mm lenses generate a multitude of images compared to fish eye lenses or omni-directional cameras. Not only does this result in increased file sizes, it also raises confusion in the project as there is significantly more data being generated. Several researchers have proposed methods to cope with the problems of photographic documentation. A popular approach is the use of panoramic imagery. For instance, Jusof et al. [3] acquire High Dynamic Ranging (HDR) panoramic imagery in caverns and visualize it in a webbrowser for documentation purposes. The emphasis of their work is on the creation of imagery near the quality of the human eye [4]. As the focus is on detailing, their Gigapixel imagery approach is time-consuming and needs post-processing to properly create the panoramic imagery. We propose a similar workflow but propose a swift and easy to use workflow that combines cheap sensors and lighting techniques to rapidly capture the scene. Fan et al. [5] also use HDR panoramic imagery to create an immersive heritage environment and provide an offline database to visualize the data. While being faster, they do not provide a spatial component to help orientate the viewer. Currently, most applications still require the semi-automated stitching of the data which slows down the process significantly [6,7].

Another interesting application of image documentation is the production of 3D models and orthographic imagery [8,9]. This involves photogrammetric processes that compute the relative orientation of the imagery with respect to each other based on the overlap. The process of building a 3D model from images involves the dense matching of overlapping pixels which is computationally challenging [10]. In general, these techniques are used to document a portion of the scene or a specific object [11]. For instance, Chiabrando et al. [12] use airborne and close-range photogrammetry to produce orthophotos of a project. Pierrot-Deseilligny et al. [13] use a similar approach and also use the images to create 3D models. Reconstructions of entire buildings are also proposed but typically these are based on Terrestrial Laser Scanning (TLS) [1,14,15]. Images from online repositories are also used for 3D reconstruction. Makantasis et al. propose a method to extract useful imagery from freely available data sets and successfully reconstruct entities in 3D [16]. The resulting models can be computationally burdening and often require proprietary software. They are better fit for specific heritage applications opposed to the general information distribution to all parties. 2D plans are easier to use and interpret but are also labor intensive to produce [17]. In our applications, we propose the use of a simplistic 2D plan together with an immersive viewing application for intuitive information interpretation. Also, we focus more on providing a tool to represent a general overview of the entire site with a minimal effort instead of highly detailed deliverables. By doing so, we provide an easy to use platform that allows for the referencing of other information. For instance, our panorama application can be augmented with links to a 3D viewer that allows the visualization of 3D models. We believe that this is a valuable workflow since it is important to know first where an object is located before going into detail. This is especially important in heritage applications due to the complex spatial relations between the objects.

An application closely related to our work is a virtual tour. Over the years, several researchers have proposed solutions for the production of virtual tours of heritage sites. Martinez-Grana present a virtual tour application using Google earth and QR codes [18]. They provide a digital environment that the user can intuitively traverse through along with several hyperlinks that reference to locally acquired imagery. Gonzalez-Delgado et al. [19] provide a similar environment and link a database of non-metric information to the presented imagery. Google Indoor Street View is also proposed. Bonacini et al. [20] investigate this technology to create a virtual tour of museums. Similar to our approach, they capture panoramic imagery at key locations and link it through the Google API. These applications provide an immersive data visualization platform and a set of functionalities. Gaming engines and visualization tools are also successfully employed to communicate information to both experts and novices [21]. Serious games are an interesting alternative [22–25] but these applications typically focus on interaction while our application aims to visualize information.

3   Methodology

In this section, we propose our application for the purpose of heritage documentation and visualization. The emphasis is on a fast and easy to use procedure to capture heritage sites. Additionally, we provide an online platform that allows stakeholders to intuitively interact with the information from any location. In the following paragraphs the used method and procedure to set up such an environment are further elaborated.

3.1   Data Acquisition

As previously stated, the emphasis of this research is on the creation of a fast and easy workflow to produce an immersive environment for the purpose of visualization. As the goal is to create an online platform, the amount of data should be kept to a minimum. Also, the heritage application should provide a general overview of the site. In order to comply with these requirements, the use of panoramic imagery is proposed. An omni-directional camera is used to capture imagery at keypoint locations in the project. Figure 3 depicts an example spread of the panoramas over a site in order to capture al the relevant information. Additionally, a simplistic map of the project is constructed either by hand, existing plans or automated procedures. The location of each panorama is marked in the map and used as input for the viewer. A multitude of omni-directional cameras is commercially available depending on the quality requirements of the project. In this application, we choose an inexpensive and easy to use sensor.

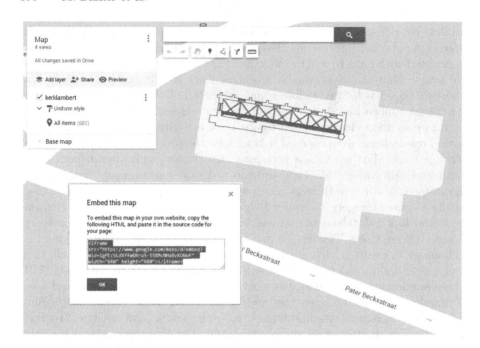

Fig. 2. Overview Google Maps creation tool with .KML drawing integration and HTML handle for public sharing [26].

3.2 Visualization

The used platform is based on an existing successful viewer. More specifically, the Google API [26] is used as a basis for our application. An HTML based website is created with the following components: an interactive map, a viewer and some navigation functionalities.

Map. The map component of the application is based on the Google Maps API (Fig. 2). First, a simplistic plan created by hand measurements or prior plans is georeferenced and transformed to a .KML file. Next, Google Maps is used to create a custom map that includes both the target area and the imported plan. The resulting map handle or ID is embedded into the HTML-code of the website.

Viewer. The panoramic viewer is initialized by the *google.maps. StreetView-Panorama* function (Fig. 3). The viewer is given a tileSize and a worldSize equal to the size of the panoramic images. Each panorama is declared as a variable with a unique ID, description, latitude and longitude. A center heading is also defined with respect to the topographic north. The *getCustomPanorama(pano)* controls the interface with the interactive map. In case a panorama location is selected, the appropriate panoramic image is loaded into the viewer.

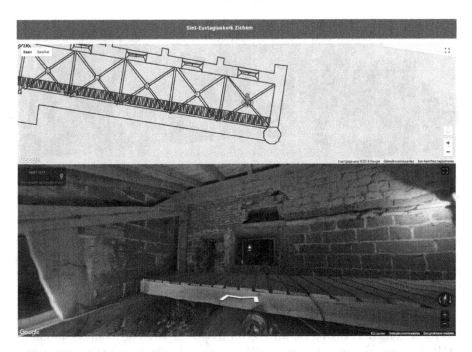

Fig. 3. Overview viewing application developed with the Google API including the map (above), viewer (bottom) and navigation tools (white arrows) [26].

Navigation. The navigation functions of the viewer are defined by the white arrows in the panorama viewer that indicate the presence of nearby other panoramic images. The arrows can be used to quickly traverse through the scene. An adjacency graph is constructed that links each panoramic image to its neighbors. A white direction arrow is created for each neighbor controlled by the *link* function. The heading of each arrow is defined by the relative geospatial positioning of each neighboring image projected onto the panoramic viewer. Additionally, one can also use the search function to locate a specific panoramic image based on the description of the individual variables.

4   Experiments

A realistic test case is presented for the application testing. The Sint-Eustachius church is a Romanesque church built between 1300 and 1500. It was constructed in several stages and was altered multiple times. It has both elements of the Romanesque and the Gothic building period and has a rich history. Unfortunately, the church is in a dire state. The iron sandstone, which is the main building material, has deteriorated drastically over time. In the context of a heritage conservation project, the historic significance of the church was investigated. More specifically, there was the need to visualize the different construction phases of the church based on a visual inspection of the attic above the

Fig. 4. Overview test case Sint-Eustachius church with target attic depicted in red ©https://www.google.be/maps. (Color figure online)

northern nave (Fig. 4). The attic is little more than a crawling place with no lighting and numerous repetitive sections (Fig. 1). Documentation attempts with conventional photography resulted in poorly lit, highly confusing imagery which failed to capture the overview of the space.

The developed panoramic application served as a visualization tool to support the presentation of the history of the structure. The attic was acquired with the Ricoh Theta S. Placed on a tripod, this pocket sized 360°camera produces 14MP imagery through its two 12MP cameras. As the image stitching is performed onboard, no post-processing is required. In total, 20 panoramic images were captured. A challenging aspect was the absence of proper ambient lighting. As no lights were present, artificial lighting was provided. Aside from several spots, a lighting panel was used for homogeneous lighting placed directly underneath the sensor (Fig. 1 bottom right). Figure 3 depicts the resulting imagery of the Ricoh supported by the artificial lighting. Overall, it is observed that, even though the lighting conditions are not perfect, the lighting was appropriate for the documentation of the scene and that the lighting panel properly distributes homogeneous light for the omni-directional camera.

The acquired imagery was imported in the application along with the existing plans of the attic. The directional arrows for the navigation were manually set based on the relative position of the imagery on the map. The interactive map with the plan and the viewer were integrated through the use of the google API. The resulting viewing application was hosted on an external server, making the data available to all stakeholders at the following url: http://www.cantico. be/Zichem/Zichem. The viewer was used to support the historic evaluation of the church. It provided much needed context for the discussion of the different building stages and hypotheses. Also, it supported the discussion concerning the potential treatments as the attic could be intuitively traversed with the viewer.

5   Conclusion and Future Work

In this paper, a visualization application is presented for heritage purposes. The emphasis of the work is on providing an intuitive and comprehensive way to distribute information about tangible heritage to the different stakeholders. Opposed to traditional photographic documentation workflows which are prone to confusion and misinterpretation, we propose the use of georeferenced 360° panoramic images. An omni-directional camera is used on a tripod along with a lighting tile for homogeneous ambient lighting to rapidly capture the site. The resulting imagery is integrated with a map of the site and geolocated. Based on the Google API, we propose an online platform that allows the viewing of the imagery with an interactive map. An immersive panorama viewer is implemented along with navigation tools to intuitively traverse the scene.

From the experiments is derived that the proposed workflow is a valuable tool in communicating historic information to the stakeholders. Also, it can function as a support tool for decision makers to judge upon the best suited treatment of the asset. Overall, the panoramic application provides a more immersive and comprehensive data experience than a set of photos and text documents. In future work we will continue to investigate the opportunities of using the online viewer not only for visualization but also for interaction purposes. Functionalities such as geotagging, pathing and linking the application to a GIS or Building Information Model might be invaluable for content handling.

Acknowledgment. This project has received funding from the European Research Council (ERC) under the European Un-ion's Horizon 2020 research and innovation programme (grant agreement 779962), FWO PhD fellowship 1S11218N and the Geomatics research group of the Department of Civil Engineering, TC Construction at the KU Leuven in Belgium. The application is developed together with Profiel cvba.

References

1. Logothetis, S., Delinasiou, A., Stylianidis, E.: Building information modelling for cultural heritage: a review. ISPRS Ann. Photogramm. Remote Sens. Spat. Inf. Sci. **2**(5/W3), 177–183 (2015). https://doi.org/10.5194/isprsannals-II-5-W3-177-2015. http://www.isprs-ann-photogramm-remote-sens-spatial-inf-sci.net/II-5-W3/177/2015

2. Galatsanos, N.P., Chin, R.T.: Digital imaging for cultural heritage preservation. IEEE Trans. Acoust. Speech Signal Process. **37**(3), 415–421 (1989). https://doi.org/10.1109/29.21708

3. Jusof, M.J., Rahim, H.R.A.: Revealing visual details via high dynamic range gigapixels spherical panorama photography: the Tempurung Cave natural heritage site. In: Proceedings of the 2014 International Conference on Virtual Systems and Multimedia, VSMM 2014, pp. 193–200 (2014). https://doi.org/10.1109/VSMM.2014.7136690

4. Roussou, New Heritage: New Media and Cultural Heritage. Technical report. Routledge, London and New York(2008)

5. Fan, J., Fan, Y., Pei, J.: HDR spherical panoramic image technology and its applications in ancient building heritage protection. In: Proceeding 2009 IEEE 10th International Conference on Computer-Aided Industrial Design and Conceptual Design: E-Business, Creative Design, Manufacturing - CAID and CD 2009, pp. 1549–1553 (2009). https://doi.org/10.1109/CAIDCD.2009.5375018

6. McCollough, F.: Complete Guide to High Dynamic Range Digital Photography. Scitech Book News (2008). http://books.google.com/books?id=6jK_jXsWZXsC&pgis=1

7. Vincent, M.L., DeFanti, T., Schulze, J., Kuester, F., Levy, T.: Stereo panorama photography in archaeology: bringing the past into the present through AVE-cams and immersive virtual environments. In: 2013 Digital Heritage International Congress, October 2013. https://doi.org/10.1109/DigitalHeritage.2013.6743783. http://ieeexplore.ieee.org/lpdocs/epic03/wrapper.htm?arnumber=6743783

8. Costamagna, E., Spanò, A.: Semantic models for architectural heritage documentation. In: Ioannides, M., Fritsch, D., Leissner, J., Davies, R., Remondino, F., Caffo, R. (eds.) EuroMed 2012. LNCS, vol. 7616, pp. 241–250. Springer, Heidelberg (2012). https://doi.org/10.1007/978-3-642-34234-9_24

9. Hassani, F.: Documentation of cultural heritage techniques, potentials and constraints. Int. Archiv. Photogram. Remote Sens. Spat. Inf. Sci. - ISPRS Archiv. 40(5W7), 207–214 (2015). https://doi.org/10.5194/isprsarchives-XL-5-W7-207-2015

10. Robleda, P.G., Pérez, R.A.: Modeling and accuracy assessment for 3D-virtual reconstruction in cultural heritage using low-cost photogrammetry: surveying of the "santa maría azogue" church's front. Int. Archiv. Photogram. Remote Sens. Spat. Inf. Sci. - ISPRS Archiv. 40(5W4), 263–270 (2015). https://doi.org/10.5194/isprsarchives-XL-5-W4-263-2015

11. De Reu, J., et al.: Towards a three-dimensional cost-effective registration of the archaeological heritage. J. Archaeolog. Sci. 40(2), 1108–1121 (2013). https://doi.org/10.1016/j.jas.2012.08.040

12. Chiabrando, F., Donadio, E., Rinaudo, F.: SfM for orthophoto generation: awinning approach for cultural heritage knowledge. Int. Archiv. Photogram. Remote Sens. Spat. Inf. Sci. - ISPRS Archiv. 40, 91–98 (2015). https://doi.org/10.5194/isprsarchives-XL-5-W7-91-2015

13. Pierrot-Deseilligny, M., De Luca, L., Remondino, F.: Automated image-based procedures for accurate artifacts 3D modeling and orthoimage generation. Geoinform. CTU FCE 6, 291–299 (2011). https://doi.org/10.14311/gi.6.36. https://ojs.cvut.cz/ojs/index.php/gi/article/view/2687

14. Murphy, M., McGovern, E., Pavia, S.: Historic building information modelling - adding intelligence to laser and image based surveys of European classical architecture. ISPRS J. Photogram. Remote Sens. 76(March), 89–102 (2013). https://doi.org/10.1016/j.isprsjprs.2012.11.006

15. Fritsch, D., Klein, M.: 3D preservation of buildings - reconstructing the past. Multimed. Tools Appl. 77(7), 9153–9170 (2018). https://doi.org/10.1007/s11042-017-4654-5

16. Makantasis, K., Doulamis, A., Doulamis, N.D., Ioannides, M.: In the wild image retrieval and clustering for 3D cultural heritage landmarks reconstruction, vol. 75. Western Michigan University (2016). https://doi.org/10.1007/s11042-014-2191-z

17. Yastikli, N.: Documentation of cultural heritage using digital photogrammetry and laser scanning. J. Cult. Herit. 8(4), 423–427 (2007). https://doi.org/10.1016/j.culher.2007.06.003

18. Martínez-Graña, A.M., Goy, J.L., Cimarra, C.A.: A virtual tour of geological heritage: valourising geodiversity using google earth and QR code. Comput. Geosci. 61, 83–93 (2013). https://doi.org/10.1016/j.cageo.2013.07.020

19. González-Delgado, J.A.: Virtual 3D tour of the Neogene palaeontological heritage of Huelva (Guadalquivir Basin, Spain). Environ. Earth Sci. **73**(8), 4609–4618 (2014). https://doi.org/10.1007/s12665-014-3747-y, http://www.scopus.com/inward/record.url?eid=2-s2.0-84925482646&partnerID=tZOtx3y1

20. Bonacini, E.: A pilot project with google indoor street view: a 360° tour of "Paolo Orsi" Musuem (2015). https://doi.org/10.2423/i22394303

21. Carrozzino, M., Bergamasco, M.: Beyond virtual museums: experiencing immersive virtual reality in real museums. J. Cult. Herit. **11**(4), 452–458 (2010). arXiv:1011.1669v3. https://doi.org/10.1016/j.culher.2010.04.001

22. Anderson, E.F., McLoughlin, L., Liarokapis, F., Peters, C., Petridis, P., de Freitas, S.: Developing serious games for cultural heritage: a state-of-the-art review. Virtual Real. **14**(4), 255–275 (2010). https://doi.org/10.1007/s10055-010-0177-3

23. Chen, S., Pan, Z., Zhang, M., Shen, H.: A case study of user immersion-based systematic design for serious heritage games. Multimed. Tools Appl. **62**(3), 633–658 (2013). https://doi.org/10.1007/s11042-011-0864-4

24. Mortara, M., Catalano, C.E., Bellotti, F., Fiucci, G., Houry-Panchetti, M., Petridis, P.: Learning cultural heritage by serious games. J. Cult. Herit. **15**(3), 318–325 (2014). https://doi.org/10.1016/j.culher.2013.04.004

25. Dörner, R., Göbel, S., Effelsberg, W., Wiemeyer, J. (eds.): Serious Games - Foundations, Concepts and Practice. Springer, Cham (2016). https://doi.org/10.1007/978-3-319-40612-1

26. Google Developers, Google API (2018). URL https://developers.google.com/

Cultural Heritage Digitization and Copyright Issues

Athina Chroni[(⊠)][iD]

Ephorate of Antiquities of West Attika, Ministry of Culture and Sports,
20 Paramythias st., 10435 Athens, Greece
athina.chroni@gmail.com

Abstract. In recent years, it has become common knowledge that culture is the main component for people's creative communication as well as for the elimination of social differences and political contradictions, the encounter for people of different racial, ethnic, religious hues in a common place, leading thus to the achievement of world peace.

Furthermore, the field of culture under proper management, can contribute substantially to improving the economic conditions of different countries, considering the multiple fields of production and dissemination potential of diverse cultural products which, combined with the explosive and rapid growth of telecommunications and the internet, create a considerable number of new jobs.

As a result: the growing interest in this sector. However, the legal framework in which the digitization and management of cultural heritage should develop is not always clear enough or, even when it is clear, it is overturned by modern trends, which, for the sake of technology, become massive.

It is therefore important to know basic relevant notions and principles for navigating and acting in a politically correct way in the vast and diverse universe of civilization: the present study constitutes an attempt both to specify the notions of cultural heritage and copyright, as well as to detect the possibilities and limitations of digitization and management of cultural heritage as defined by the current legal framework.

The aim is the succinct quote of the afore-mentioned, in order that this project will serve as a concise manual easily understood and useful mainly to people not specialized in law.

Keywords: Cultural heritage · Tangible · Intangible · Digitization
Intellectual property rights · Copyright · Greek legislation
European Union legislation · Open sources

1 Cultural Heritage

1.1 Cultural Goods: Tangible, Intangible, Natural and Digital Cultural Heritage

According to Law No **1103/1970, Ar. 1**[1] «as cultural goods are considered those that, religious or secular, are determined by each State as important for archaeology,

---

[1] This is a Convention with the force of law, signed in Paris on November 17, 1970 between the Member States and accepted by the General Conference of the United Nations Organization for the Instruction, Science and Education.

© Springer Nature Switzerland AG 2018
M. Ioannides et al. (Eds.): EuroMed 2018, LNCS 11196, pp. 396–407, 2018.
https://doi.org/10.1007/978-3-030-01762-0_34

prehistory, history, philology, arts or science» and are determined in detail in Ar. 4 of the same Law. [43] It becomes thus clear that until 1970, the notion of cultural goods is restricted exclusively to **_tangible_** *cultural goods*, a notion that will be enriched several years later, by including the **_intangible_** *cultural goods* as well, as is apparent from the **Law No 3028/2002, Ar. 2, Par. e**:«As **_intangible cultural goods_** are meant to be expressions, activities, knowledge and information, such as myths, customs, oral traditions, dances, performances, music, songs, skills or techniques that are testimonies of traditional, folk and scholar culture.» [43].

The intangible cultural heritage as a motivating force of cultural diversity is extremely fragile. In recent years, it has received international recognition and its rescue has become one of the priorities of international cooperation, thanks to the leading role of the **UNESCO**[2] towards the adoption of the **Convention for the Safeguarding of Intangible Cultural Heritage** [44].

The term «**natural** cultural heritage» determines the natural environment as it is composed of landscapes, flora and fauna, scientifically known under the term «biodiversity», as well as geological data including mineralogy and paleontology, under the scientific term of «geological diversity». The **Convention Concerning the Protection of the World Cultural and Natural Heritage** [17] adopted by the UNESCO in 1972 links the cultural heritage with the natural environment, assessing and thus setting the monuments of nature with the monuments of human civilization at the same hierarchical level.

As to the term «**digital** cultural heritage»: it concerns the cultural material produced in digital form or digitized for preservation purposes.[3]

1.2   Cultural Heritage Protection

General

Cultural heritage is the cultural imprint of the long-running course of man. Being formed under the influence of various time and place components (environmental data, geomorphology) acquires manifestations, firstly interpreted as ways of solving and satisfying the daily needs of man for his survival in the early stages of his appearance (artifacts for hunting, agriculture, livestock farming). However, on a second level, after having performed their initial function, man, will start to explore their aesthetic extensions and make specific choices, expressed through the notion of *art*. Over the centuries and the following increasing of human population spread at the same time to various geographic lengths and widths on earth, these artistic choices determine the respective group of people, initially at a family or group level, evolving to a race, nation and, finally, state level, acquiring thus a specific semantic value. Cultural heritage crystallizes and expresses the collective memory on local terms, as well as on

---

[2] United Nations Educational Scientific and Cultural Organization.

[3] The present study was implemented within the framework of the Postgraduate Program Studies «Advanced Informatics and Computing Systems/Digital Culture»/University of Piraeus, Subject «Copyright and Digital Media» under the supervision of Vagena E., Ph.D., Lecturer of the Course and Legal Counselor at the time at the Hellenic Copyright Organization and Associate Professor Vergados D., PhD.

global terms, since the local is the minimum piece of the broader mosaic of mankind's cultural activity and production.

The *World Heritage Center*, established in 1992, is the UNESCO monitoring center and coordinator at the same time for all *World Heritage Issues* [42, 45, 46].

Cultural Heritage and Greek Legislation

At this point, the Greek law is quite clear: «In order to ensure the protection of their cultural goods, the Member States of the present Convention undertake to establish in their territory one or more Services for the protection of cultural heritage.» (**Law No 1103/1970, Ar. 5**) [43].

«1. The protection of cultural heritage aims at preserving the memory for the sake of present and future generations and the upgrading of the cultural environment. (**Law No 3028/2002, Ar. 1**) [43].

2   Copyright

2.1   Definition

«*Copyright* is called the right that the legal order confers to the author of a spiritual work on this specific work. *Copyright* is called as well all the relevant institution, that is, the set of rules that regulate this right.» [4 pp. 145, 9 pp. 6] The initial holder of the *economic* and the *moral* right in a work shall be the author of that work. (**Law No 2121/1993, Ar. 6**) [31, 32, 39].

Orphan Works: «are works that are protected by intellectual property rights and/or related rights and whose beneficiaries have not been identified or even if identified, have not been located in spite of a diligent search from the part of the orphan works' use operators» [31].

Copyright shall last for the whole of the author's life and for seventy (70) years after his death, calculated from 1st January of the year after the author's death. (**Law No 2121/1993, Ar. 29**) [39].

After the expiry of copyright protection, the State, represented by the Minister of Culture, may exercise the right of recognition of the author's paternity, as well as the right of protection of the integrity of the work deriving from the moral right.

2.2   Copyright Legislative Framework

The need for the establishment and configuration of a copyright legislation arose due to technological evolution, the rapid development of which, especially nowadays, made possible the reproduction of works without the intermediary and the remuneration of their original author. National legislations worldwide are moving under two systems:

- the **European**: it has an individual character and the protection of the author appears to stem from an absolute natural right of the author (*droit d' auteur, Urherberrecht*),
- the **Anglo-American**: it makes use of the term *copyright* and it is based on author's right to prevent other persons from copying the original work that he has created [3 pp. 23, 9 pp. 4].

«In Greece, the first complete law on copyright was the **Law No 2387/1920**, while only in **1993**, after a three-year legislative process, the **Law No 2121** for the protection of copyright and related rights has been voted and constitutes the main source of copyright legislation in Greece. Greece's national legislation is in line with the European Community *acquis*.» [9 pp. 4–5, 38, 39].

Copyright Object of Protection

According to **Law No 2121/1993, Ar. 2, Par. 1**: «The object of the copyright legislation is the *work* which is meant as any *original intellectual creation of speech, art or science, expressed in any form.*» [39].

It is worth noting that «the law protects not only the original works but also the derivative works and the collections. Derivative works are therefore considered the works that have resulted from revision, modification, adaptation, in general, from the «conversion» of an existing work (original) or of folk tradition expressions.» [9 pp. 7].

Cases of Non-protected Works

According to **Law No 2121/1993, Ar. 2, Par. 5**, [39] the following are not protected:

- the official texts expressing the exercise of state authority,
- the expressions of folk tradition,
- news and simple facts.

All the afore-mentioned are not protected in their original form but only if they are processed, for example in the case of publishing a relevant collection.

In addition, ancient works are not protected under the Law No 2121/1993 because their term of protection has expired. However, they are protected under specific legislation, namely under Law No 3028/2002 «regarding the protection of antiquities and cultural heritage in general.» [1 pp. 45, 4 pp. 145, 9 pp. 8].

Databases and Webpages

Greek legislation, by the **Law No 2819/2000, Ar. 2, Par. 2a**, [19] incorporated the **Not. 21 Preamble to European Community Directive 96/9/EC:** in order that a *database* is protected under the copyright legislation, it is required that the choice or the arrangement of its content is an intellectual product [2, 8, 9 pp. 11, 26].

A work is protected equally either it is embedded on a material medium, or it is located digitally on a *website*. The use of any work uploaded on the Internet is subject to the provisions of the law just as when it is available in any form other than the network [9 pp. 13].

3   Recording, Documentation and Registration of Tangible and Intangible Cultural Heritage

Regarding the specific sector, which might be characterized as the cutting-edge controversial point nowadays, the Greek legislation is detailed and clear, as follows:

Law No 3028/2002, Ar. 3 & 4: [43]

- The monuments are recorded, documented and registered in the National Archive of Monuments, kept at the Ministry of Culture.

- A Presidential Decree, issued upon a proposal by the Minister of Culture, regulates the organization and operation of the National Archive of Monuments and defines the way of recording the monuments, the way of protecting data, the conditions under which the right of access to the afore-mentioned for research and other purposes should be exercised, as well as any necessary detail.

Law No 3028/2002, Ar. 5: [43]

- The Ministry of Culture is concerned for the recording in written form, as well as in sound, image or sound and image media materials, the recording and documentation of intangible cultural goods of the traditional, folk and literary culture, which are of a particular significance.

Later, in the framework of the measures for the protection of cultural goods the **Law No 3658/2008-Government Gazette A-70/22-4-2008** [43] establishes within the Ministry of Culture an administrative unit at the level of Directorate, titled «Directorate of Documentation and Protection of Cultural Goods», which is subject to the General Directorate of Antiquities and Cultural Heritage (**Ar. 1**) [35].

4   Digitization - Definition

By using the term «digitization» of a cultural good, tangible or intangible, it is meant to create a relative digital substitute. All products coming from a digitization organized at a state level plan and following specific standards, form the *digital cultural reserve* of the state. Given that «Europe's cultural and scientific resources are a unique public wealth that shapes the collective and growing memory of different societies», [5, 11, 25] we become aware of the important role that the digitized cultural resources may play, being flexible in management and diffusion.

4.1   Objectives of Digitization

Having as a starting point the Greek legislation regarding the protection of cultural heritage, and according to the organizational structure of the Ministry of Culture and Sports, as uploaded on the relevant website, [34] «strategic objectives of the General Directorate of Antiquities and Cultural Heritage are the following:

(a) Formulating and supervising the policy for the protection, rescue, discovery, preservation, highlighting and promotion of the cultural heritage of Greece, both tangible and intangible,
(b) Coordinating, supervising and ensuring the proper and efficient function, ensuring the proper administration and accountability, achieving specific goals, **simplifying the administrative procedures of the Ministry of Culture and Sports Services subject to the General Directorate.**»

According to the organizational structure of the Ministry of Culture and Sports [36] «the operational objectives of the Directorate of Modern Cultural and Intangible Cultural Heritage are the following:

(a) The implementation of a policy to preserve and highlight intangible cultural heritage,
(b) The implementation of a policy to promote cross-cultural issues in the field of culture,
(c) The protection and highlighting of movable monuments of modern cultural heritage,
(d) The implementation of a museum policy for the museums of modern culture (supervision and scientific assistance, recognition - certification, promotion and application of modern museological approaches).»

4.2 Applicable Digitization Rules on Case-Guiding Principles

The digitization of cultural heritage at state planning level is governed by clear guiding principles which are developed in the relevant legislative texts. Specifically, according to **Law No 2557/1997, Ar. 6,** «Cultural Heritage highlighting and promoting, Museum Policy - Research Institutions» (: «Museum policy is designed and implemented by the Ministry of Culture»), [18] and to **the Law No 3028/2002, Ar. 4 & 5.** [43][4].

5 Digitization Products Management

«The Fund of Archaeological Proceeds collects, manages and allocates its resources in general to serve the objectives pursued by the General Directorate of Antiquities and Restoration of the Ministry of Culture and Sciences.» (**Law No 736/1977, Ar. 1 & 2**) [33].

Returning to the **Law No 3028/2002, in particular Ar. 46, Par. 4**: «By decision of the Minister of Culture and Sports, issued after an opinion of the competent Council on a case-by-case basis, shall be determined the terms, the conditions, the service institution and the procedure for granting production, reproduction and dissemination permissions to the public, either institutions or persons, other than those of the Ministry of Culture and Sports and the Fund of Archaeological Proceeds, by any means and media, including information and communication technology, copies and imaging (photographs, videos) of monuments belonging to the State, immovable monuments located in archaeological sites and historic places or stand-alone, as well as of movable monuments located in museums or collections of the State. The relevant license is granted to natural or legal persons against a fee paid to the Fund of Archaeological Proceeds. Concerning those copies that are available to the public it is forbidden to bear the stamp of the Fund of Archaeological Proceeds. The production, reproduction and dissemination to the public either of copies or of imaging, aiming to a direct or indirect economic or commercial purpose, without authorization, shall be punishable by the penalty described in Par. 1, Ar. 66. The production of casts and identical copies of movable monuments located in museums or collections of the State is performed only by the Fund of Archaeological Proceeds.» [43].

---

[4] See par. No 3 of the present paper.

5.1   Possibilities and Constraints of Creating-Managing-Disposing Cultural Heritage Digitization Products

It is worth mentioning at this point that in recent years new types of licenses are configured:

1. The *GNU GPL* [28, 29] open source licenses: this is a series of licenses that sprang from the world of free software and allow their distribution, use and modification to as many people as possible with the obligation of distributing the source code always when distributing the software [9 pp. 42, 20, 27, 37].
2. The *Creative Commons (CC)* [12, 13] licenses: these are framework conventions that are free of charge and concern the provision of protected works on the Internet. The validity of these licenses has been confirmed by courts in Spain and the Netherlands. [9 pp. 43, 12, 14, 40] The use of the *CC* licenses creates a clear legal framework regarding the terms of exploitation of each work. They are offered free of charge on the Internet, they are not exclusive, they allow the exchange of works via the Internet, and their use does not require the beneficiary to be completely forfeited from the exploitation rights of his work. These licenses **do not provide for the possibility of revocation**, i.e. the author is not able to cancel a posteriori the *CC* license if the work has already been released [15, 16].
3. The *Copyleft* licenses: they grant freedom to use, modify, and distribute an intellectual work, with the limitation that each copy or derivative work will be distributed under the same license of use by granting the same freedoms. This limitation does not contradict the freedoms provided and which render the work free content [10].

Additionally, in modern times, the rapidly evolving digital technology combined with its relatively low cost both of hardware and software, the development of web-based crowdsourcing platforms of diverse cultural content, which are based on the creative contribution and collaboration of people from all over the world (*Wikimedia Commons* [47] for example), as well as the existence of web-based platforms for the dissemination of digitized cultural goods, free of charge or on a fee (*Open Heritage by Google Arts & Culture* [30], *3dwarehouse* [41] for example), has clearly made possible the creation and dissemination of digital substitutes of cultural goods by non-state actors without the control of the competent authorities.

This is an activity with the highest growth rate, which, as it is clear, «violates» the legally correct frame, without necessarily allowing negative criticism. The data therefore change, a fact that renders imperative the recognition and acceptance of the current situation in terms of legislation, as well as their reciprocal harmonization.

5.2   Cultural Heritage and European Union

The **Directive of the European Union of 27/10/2011** [23], aiming at optimizing the benefits of digital technology for the economic growth, the creation of new jobs and the improvement of the quality of life of the European citizens and regarding the «Digitization and online approach to cultural material and digital preservation», indicates as necessary and urgent the digitization and online presentation of the European cultural heritage on the *Europeana* [21] web-based platform: the digital library of the European Union, which offers access to more than 19 million digitized items. It was launched on November 20, 2008 (Directive, Par. 14). The aim is to digitize the entire European cultural heritage by the year 2025 (Directive, Par. 15) and encourages the re-use of digitized material for both commercial and non-commercial purposes, **provided that the rights relating to copyright are respected** (Directive, Par. 7). Furthermore, it highlights the need for the private sector to be involved in the implementation and completion of the specific project (Directive, Par. 9). Moreover, the European Union Directive of 24/05/05 proposes solutions regarding *orphan works* (Directive, Par. 12). The statement concerning the need for the respective digital maintenance aiming at the preservation of the digitized cultural material, is characteristic (Directive, Par. 16).

5.3   Cultural Heritage, Modern Production and Management Models

Culture is dynamic in nature: consequently, cultural heritage is a perpetual process.

With this reasoning, the Portal of the hotel «Asteras Vouliagmenis», in Athens, Greece, a project by the architects Sakellaridou R. and Papanikolaou M., constructed in 2008 and having become an emblematic landmark of the area, although just 10 years old, has been characterized «Monument of Modern Cultural Heritage» at the beginning of 2018 [7].

Consequently, it is worth asking ourselves and reflecting on what is to be born in terms of modern cultural heritage, in any artistic style, always having as criterion the respective decisive cultural imprint in contemporary time: public and private works, graffiti, street artists, art produced with new technologies, music cultures of the last decades are just some examples. Will they be treated as individual author's works or altogether as a cultural heritage content and which should be the respective legislative framework? Where is the dividing line that defines the distinct (?) regions between author and cultural heritage? **This question is partly answered by Par. 11 of the European Union Directive of 27/10/2011: «Only part of cultural material [23]**[5] **retained in libraries, archives and museums belongs to the category of public use (*public domain*), in the sense that it is no longer protected by copyright, while the rest (cultural material) is protected by copyright. Given therefore that rights are the key to further activation of creativity, Europe's cultural material should be digitized, made accessible and maintained with full respect for the whole copyright framework.»** Noteworthy is the statement of Par. 13 of the same E.U. Directive on the protection of the public domain in order that the relevant cultural material remains accessible to the public: it is thus proposed to avoid the use of watermarks or other protection measures for *public domain cultural material*, as evidence of ownership or origin.

Regarding the afore-mentioned, an excerpt from the interview of architect Sakellaridou R. is very characteristic: «**After its implementation, the architectural work**

---

[5] According to Par. 1 of the EU Directive of 27/10/2011, the following are defined as cultural material: printed material (books, magazines, newspapers), photographs, museum objects, archival objects, audio and audiovisual material, monuments and archaeological sites.

leaves the hands of its creator. It is delivered to the collective. It is a painful, like all, act of adulthood. The work now belongs to something wider and more important than its author.» [7].

Furthermore, the European Union on its official website concerning the *Digital Single Market* [22]: emphasizes the special significance and importance of digitizing the cultural goods, given that they breathe a new life, while at the same time the citizens have now unprecedented opportunities to access cultural material and vice versa, the state actors and the institutions multiple ways for handling and disseminating this information and the digital products. *Virtual Museums* do not require the visitors' physical presence. *Augmented* and *Mixed Reality* further improve the experience of the virtual visitor. Under this perspective, the General European Commission Directorate for Communications Networks, Content & Technology has conducted extensive policy coordination as well as funding actions to supplement Member States' cultural policy in areas of digitization and online access to cultural material and digital preservation.

Additionally, in the framework of the components that exercise pressure and may affect States' policy regarding the management of both the cultural material itself as well as its digitization products, it is imperative at this point the reference to the three different cultural heritage management models:

- the ***material-based approach/The Venice Charter for the Conservation and Restoration of Monuments and Sites*** (Icomos, 1964), emphasizing the material/fabric, which is considered important mainly from the historical, archaeological, scientific and aesthetic aspect,
- the ***values-based approach/The Burra Charter for the Conservation of Places of Cultural Significance*** (Icomos Australia, 1999), emphasizing the values attributed to cultural heritage by different interest groups of people. As «value» is considered to be the legitimate interest of a group of people in cultural heritage, this group including the whole community.
- the ***living heritage approach***, a model not universally applicable. It is aiming mainly at the «living cultural heritage», namely cultural heritage that still exists today and is further developed on the basis of the continuity of the initial connection of the society with its cultural heritage [6 pp. 38–48].

It is noteworthy that the UNESCO World Heritage Center initially followed the *material-based approach* model but then adopted the *values-based approach* model.

6   Conclusion

The digitization of cultural heritage followed by the dissemination of the respective digital products, highlighting local cultural identities and at the same time contributing to the acquaintance with the «foreign», will be the catalyst for the creative approach of different ethnicities. It has also become clear that in modern times new technologies have enabled the massive and rapid production, management and dissemination of digitized cultural goods, a fact that clarifies the need to change the respective legal framework in Greece and to align it with modern trends and prospects, so that the legislative framework becomes more flexible and open, under conditions, embodying thus the spirit of democracy in its cultural dimension, and rendering, consequently, cultural heritage digital products available to the public.

The afore-mentioned brief citation of the Greek and European legislation, concerning the notions of cultural heritage and the relevant digitization copyright issues, renders clear enough the possibilities and limitations of digitization and management of cultural heritage, as defined by the current legal framework cross-referenced with modern social trends and crowdsourcing platforms as well, implying at the same time the urgent need for a new alignment of law, technology and society. The presented study's originality and novelty of highlighting and interpreting only the basic legislative principles on the specific issue, turns it out to a concise manual easily understood and useful to people coming from various scientific fields, not necessarily the law.

The declaration of the year 2018 as «**The European Year of Cultural Heritage**», following a decision by the European Parliament and the Council of the European Union (**Decision E.U. 2017/864/17-5-2017**), [24] forms an excellent opportunity to mobilize up to these reflections.

References

1. Kallinikou, D.: Copyright and Related Rights. 2nd edn. Sakkoulas A, Athens (2005). Καλλινίκου, Δ.: Πνευματική Ιδιοκτησία και Συγγενικά Δικαιώματα. 2η Έκδοση, Σάκκουλας Α, Αθήνα (2005)
2. Kanellopoulou-Boti, M.: Information Law. Issues of Intellectual property, Patents, Library Science and Advertising. Nomiki Bibliothiki, Corfu (2004). ISBN 960-272-255-X. Κανελλοπούλου-Μπότη, Μ.: Το Δίκαιο της Πληροφορίας. Ζητήματα πνευματικής ιδιοκτησίας, ευρεσιτεχνίας, βιβλιοθηκονομίας, διαφήμισης. Νομική Βιβλιοθήκη, Κέρκυρα (2004). ISBN 960-272-255-X
3. Kotsiris, L.: Copyright Legislation. 4th edn. Sakkoulas A, Athens (2005). Κοτσίρης, Λ.: Δίκαιο Πνευματικής Ιδιοκτησίας. 4η Έκδοση, Σάκκουλας Α, Αθήνα (2005)
4. Koumantos, G.: Copyright. 8th edn. Sakkoulas A, Athens (2002). Κουμάντος, Γ.: Πνευματική Ιδιοκτησία. 8η Έκδοση, Σάκκουλας Α, Αθήνα (2002)
5. Papatheodorou, T.S.: Digitization. Laboratory of High Performance Information Systems, Patras University, Patras (2003). Παπαθεοδώρου, Θ.: Ψηφιοποίηση. Εργαστήριο Πληροφοριακών Συστημάτων Υψηλών Επιδόσεων, Πανεπιστήμιο Πατρών, Πάτρα (2003)
6. Poulios, I., et al.: Cultural Management, Local Society and Sustainable Development. Hellenic Open University, The Greek Academic Libraries Association, National Technical University of Athens, Athens (2015). Πούλιος, Ι., et al.: Πολιτισμική Διαχείριση, Τοπική Κοινωνία και Βιώσιμη Ανάπτυξη. Ελληνικό Ανοικτό Πανεπιστήμιο, Σύνδεσμος Ελληνικών Ακαδημαϊκών Βιβλιοθηκών, Εθνικό Μετσόβιο Πολυτεχνείο, Αθήνα. ISBN 978-960-603-444-2 (2015). www.kallipos.gr. Accessed 06 Aug 2018
7. Sakellaridou, R.: Point of View: Reflections on the Astir Palace Vouliagmeni Gate. Kathimerini Newspaper (27/02/2018). Daily Publications S.A., Athens (2018). Σακελλαρίδου, Ρ.: Άποψη: Σκέψεις για την Πύλη του Αστέρα Βουλιαγμένης. Εφημερίδα Καθημερινή (27/02/2018), Καθημερινές Εκδόσεις Α.Ε., Αθήνα (2018). http://www.kathimerini.gr/950857/article/politismos/polh/apoyh-skeyeis-gia-thn-pylh-toy-astera-voyliagmenhs. Accessed 06 Aug 2018

8. Sinodinou, T.: Copyright Issues and New Technologies: The user-author relationship. Sakkoulas A, Athens-Thessaloniki (2008). Συνοδινού, Τ.: Πνευματική Ιδιοκτησία και Νέες Τεχνολογίες: Η σχέση χρήστη-δημιουργού, Σάκκουλας Α, Αθήνα-Θεσσαλον ίκη (2008)

9. Vagena, E.: Introduction to Copyright Legislation. Specific Technology Issues (Informatics and Internet). 20 Years of Implementation of Greek Law No 2121/1993 on Intellectual Property and Related Rights. Intellectual Property Protection Union – Greek Unit of Association Littéraire et A. Nomiki Bibliothiki, Corfu (2014). Βαγενά, Ε. Εισαγωγή στο Δίκαιο της Πνευματικής Ιδιοκτησίας. Ειδικότερα Θέματα Τεχνολογίας (Πληροφορικής και Διαδικτύου). 20 Χρόνια Εφαρμογής του Ν 2121/1993 για την Πνευματική Ιδιοκτησία και τα Συγγενικά Δικαιώματα. Ένωση Προστασίας Πνευματικής Ιδιοκτησίας – Ελληνικό Τμήμα της Association Littéraire et A. Νομική Βιβλιοθήκη, Κέρκυρα (2014). ISBN 978-960-562-346-3

10. Copyleft Wikipedia. https://el.wikipedia.org/wiki/Copyleft. Accessed 06 Aug 2018

11. CORDIS Community Research and Development Information Service. http://cordis.europa. eu/guidance/archive_en.html. Accessed 06 Aug 2018

12. Creative Commons. https://creativecommons.org/. Accessed 06 Aug 2018

13. Creative Commons Greece. http://www.creativecommons.gr/. Accessed 06 Aug 2018

14. Creative Commons Press Releases. http://creativecommons.org/press-releases/entry/5822. Accessed 06 Aug 2018

15. Creative Commons Wikipedia. https://el.wikipedia.org/wiki/Creative_Commons. Accessed 06 Aug 2018

16. Creative Commons Lisence Wikipedia. https://el.wikipedia.org/wiki/Creative_Commons_ license. Accessed 06 Aug 2018

17. Cyprus National Commission for UNESCO. http://www.unesco.org.cy/Index.aspx? Language=EN. Accessed 06 Aug 2018

18. Digital Platform of Greek Codified Legislation. Ψηφιακή Πλατφόρμα Ελληνικής Κωδικοποιημένης Νομοθεσίας. https://www.e-nomothesia.gr/kat-arxaiotites/n-2557-1997. html. Accessed 06 Aug 2018

19. Digital Platform of Greek Codified Legislation. Ψηφιακή Πλατφόρμα Ελληνικής Κωδικοποιημένης Νομοθεσίας. https://www.e-nomothesia.gr/kat-athlitismos/n-2819-2000.html. Accessed 06 Aug 2018

20. District Court of Frankfurt Am Main Judgement. http://archive.li/nL1xa, http://www.gpl-violations.org/news/20060922-dlink-judgement_frankfurt. Accessed 06 Aug 2018

21. Europeana Collections. https://www.europeana.eu/portal/en. Accessed 06 Aug 2018

22. European Commission Digital Single Market Policy. https://ec.europa.eu/digital-single-market/en/digital-cultural-heritage. Accessed 06 Aug 2018

23. European Commission Digital Single Market Strategy. https://ec.europa.eu/digital-single-market/sites/digital-agenda/files/en_4.pdf. Accessed 06 Aug 2018

24. EUR-Lex Access to European Union Law. https://eur-lex.europa.eu/legal-content/EN/TXT/? uri=CELEX%3A32017D0864. Accessed 06 Aug 2018

25. EUR-Lex Access to European Union Law. http://eur-lex.europa.eu/legal-content/EN/TXT/? uri=LEGISSUM:l24226a. Accessed 06 Aug 2018

26. European Union (EU) Directive No. 96/9/EC of the European Parliament and of the Council, of 11 March 1996 on the legal protection of databases. http://www.wipo.int/wipolex/en/text. jsp?file_id=126789. Accessed 06 Aug 2018

27. Free Open Source Software. http://www.ellak.gr/. Accessed 06 Aug 2018

28. GNU Operating System. https://www.gnu.org/licenses/gpl-3.0.en.html. Accessed 06 Aug 2018

29. GNU General Public Lisence Wikipedia. https://en.wikipedia.org/wiki/GNU_General_Public_License. Accessed 06 Aug 2018
30. Google Arts & Culture Open Heritage. https://artsandculture.google.com/project/cyark. Accessed 06 Aug 2018
31. Hellenic Copyright Organization European Directives. http://www.opi.gr/index.php/genikes-plirofories-pi. Accessed 06 Aug 2018
32. Hellenic Copyright Organization Law 2121/1993. https://www.opi.gr/index.php/en/library/law-2121-1993. Accessed 06 Aug 2018
33. Hellenic Republic Ministry of Culture and Sports. https://culture.gr/el/ministry/SitePages/archeol_law.aspx?iID=181. Accessed 06 Aug 2018
34. Hellenic Republic Ministry of Culture and Sports General Directorate of Antiquities and Cultural Heritage. https://www.culture.gr/el/ministry/SitePages/viewyphresia.aspx?iID=1304. Accessed 06 Aug 2018
35. Hellenic Republic Ministry of Culture and Sports Directorate of Cultural Goods Documentation and Protection. https://www.culture.gr/el/ministry/SitePages/viewyphresia.aspx?iID=2442. Accessed 06 Aug 2018
36. Hellenic Republic Ministry of Culture and Sports Directorate of Modern Cultural and Intangible Cultural Heritage. https://www.culture.gr/el/ministry/SitePages/viewyphresia.aspx?iID=1724. Accessed 06 Aug 2018
37. JBB Rechtsanwälte Law Firm. http://www.jbb.de/en. Accessed 06 Aug 2018
38. Law 2387/1920. Νόμος 2387/1920. https://el.wikisource.org/wiki/%CE%9D%CF%8C%CE%BC%CE%BF%CF%82_2387/1920. Accessed 06 Aug 2018
39. Law No 2121/1993. https://www.opi.gr/index.php/vivliothiki/2121-1993. Accessed 06 Aug 2018
40. Première mention des CC dans une décision de justice en Espagne. http://lists.ibiblio.org/pipermail/cc-fr/2006-February/000744.html, https://archive.li/wwZGW. Accessed 06 Aug 2018
41. 3D Warehouse. https://3dwarehouse.sketchup.com/. Accessed 06 Aug 2018
42. UNESCO. https://whc.unesco.org/. Accessed 06 Aug 2018
43. UNESCO Database of National Cultural Heritage Laws. http://www.unesco.org/culture/natlaws/index.php?. Accessed 06 Aug 2018
44. UNESCO Greece Intangible Cultural Heritage. http://www.unesco-hellas.gr/gr/3_5_2.htm. Accessed 06 Aug 2018
45. UNESCO Greece World Cultural Heritage. http://www.unesco-hellas.gr/gr/3_5_1.htm. Accessed 06 Aug 2018
46. UNESCO World Heritage List. https://whc.unesco.org/en/list/. Accessed 06 Aug 2018
47. Wikimedia Commons. https://commons.wikimedia.org/. Accessed 06 Aug 2018

The First Attend for a Holistic HBIM Documentation of UNESCO WHL Monument: The Case Study of Asinou Church in Cyprus

Kyriacos Themistocleous[1(✉)], Marinos Ioannides[2], Simos Georgiou[2], and Vasilis Athanasiou[2]

[1] Department of Civil Engineering and Geomatics,
ERATOSTHENES Research Centre, Cyprus University of Technology,
Saripolou 2-6, Achilleos 1A Building, 3036 Limassol, Cyprus
k.themistocleous@cut.ac.cy
[2] Digital Heritage Research Laboratory, Department of Electrical Engineering,
Computer Engineering and Informatics, Cyprus University of Technology,
Arch. Kyprianou 31, 3036 Limassol, Cyprus
{marinos.ioannides, simos.georgiou,
vasilis.athanasiou}@cut.ac.cy

Abstract. The study examines the documentation of the Asinou Monument within the auspices of the H2020-SC6-R&I-INCEPTION project. The project focuses on the use of innovative 3D modelling of cultural heritage through an inclusive approach for 3D reconstruction of monuments, as well as the built and social environments over time. The project will enrich European identity by examining how European cultural heritage evolves over time. Therefore, data acquisition techniques and 3D reconstruction and modelling methodologies for data processing were examined using the Asinou Church as a case study. Asinou Church is a 11th century church located in the Troodos Mountains of Cyprus, which is a UNESCO World Heritage Site. This unique monument contains some of the finest Byzantine wall paintings in Cyprus which date between the 11th to the 17th century. Their outstanding historical value is very exceptional and makes their documentation a great challenge for the present ICT technologies. Different multimodal techniques, such as photogrammetry, laser scanning, image processing, video and audio were used for the data acquisition of all detailed features of the tangible building and the intangible story (liturgy). Following, the information was processed to create a 3D model in order to document the church using Building Information Modeling (BIM). The church was digitally reconstructed in a 3D BIM model, where it was then processed to produce a Heritage Building Information Model (H-BIM) in order to create a prototype for a holistic documentation and further study.

Keywords: H-BIM · EU-H2020 INCEPTION · Digital cultural heritage
Remote sensing · BIM · 3D model · UNESCO WHL · 3D reconstruction
Asinou Church

© Springer Nature Switzerland AG 2018
M. Ioannides et al. (Eds.): EuroMed 2018, LNCS 11196, pp. 408–414, 2018.
https://doi.org/10.1007/978-3-030-01762-0_35

1   Introduction

The study examines the documentation of the Asinou Monument within the auspices of the H2020-SC6-R&I-INCEPTION project for the development of a prototype cloud digital platform to interact with the end-user within a series of visual data and metadata regarding the monument.

The INCEPTION project[1] focuses on using innovative 3D modelling of cultural heritage through an inclusive approach for 3D reconstruction of artefacts, as well as the built and social environments over time. This outstanding project will enrich European identity by examining how European cultural heritage evolves over time. INCEPTION provides state-of-the-art 3D reconstruction by utilizing innovative procedures for 3D laser survey, data acquisition and processing. In this way, the accuracy and efficiency of 3D capturing is improved through the integration of Geospatial Information, Global and Indoor Positioning Systems (GIS, GPS, IPS) through hardware interfaces and software algorithms. The INCEPTION methods are used to create 3D models that are easily accessible and interoperable with different hardware and software. As well, the INCEPTION project has developed an open-standard Semantic Web platform for Building Information Models for Cultural Heritage (HBIM) that will be implemented in user-friendly Augmented Reality (VR and AR) operable on mobile devices.

In this case study, the semantic development of the different entities and objects that make up the construction of the Asinou Church and the interior, including wall frescoes and the 3-D space create a knowledge base for the research of the Asinou Church. The idea of using digital technology to document cultural heritage in all aspects, both tangible and intangible heritage within a structure, creates a dynamic repository and valuable resource to better understand the cultural heritage monument, as end-users will have the ability to access the information from the digital platform at any time [1–5].

Different techniques, such as photogrammetry, laser scanning, drones, video and images were used for the data acquisition of all features of the church, which were then processed to create a 3D model and document the church using Building Information Modeling (BIM). The church was digitally reconstructed in a 3D BIM model, which was then processed to produce a Heritage building Information Model (H-BIM) in order to create an information database for further study.

2   Study Area

The study area is the monument of Panagia Phorbiotissa, also known as Asinou Church (Fig. 1), which is a small 11th century church dedicated to the Virgin Mary. The church is located in the north foothills of the Troodos Mountains of Cyprus, which is a UNESCO World Heritage Site [6]. The monument was built at the end of the 11th century and was a monastery church until the end of the 18th century, when it was abandoned. The church consisted of a vaulted single-aisled nave and the narthex that

---

[1] www.inception-project.eu.

was added in the second half of the 12th century. The structure was built with mud mortar and has experienced frequent collapses and reconstructions.

Fig. 1. The Panagia Phorbiotissa monument - Asinou Church

The interior of the church is entirely covered with over 100 frescoes from the 12th–17th Century and are considered some of the best examples of Byzantine mural paintings in Cyprus. Many of the original wall-paintings from the 12th century, are in the apse of the Holy Bema and the west wall of the church, which suffered damages especially from earthquakes. During the 14th century, the conch of the apse was rebuilt and the external buttresses were added The narthex was redecorated in 1332/3 following strong Frankish influences [7].

3   Methodology

Following a phase of a detail data acquisition procedure (geometry, materials, etc.) a Building Information Modelling (BIM)[2] is used for design and management of projects in the built environment industry. BIM is a collaborative model where multiple team members can work on a project at the same time. BIM provides a multi layered, multi-dimensional, multi-disciplinary, parametric, smart and informative digital model of a project.

Building Information Modelling (BIM) workflows provides the capability to document cultural heritage buildings in order to facilitate the existing building model

---

[2] https://en.wikipedia.org/wiki/Building_information_modeling.

structure with the information collected from the cultural heritage building in order to create an integrated HBIM (Heritage Building Information Model) (Fig. 2).

Fig. 2. HBIM strategy

HBIM includes all the information and parameters from the cultural heritage building, including building components, structural elements, materials and semantic information. The development of such an information management model was the basic tool in order to construct and develop the H-BIM of the Asinou Church.

In the Asinou Church case study, the BIM workflows and the BIM 3D model were developed using 3D laser scans, point clouds and UAV data of the topography of the church [6, 8]. Using BIM software, the survey data, together with the data from the laser scanners' millions of data points and images from the site were used to process the data and develop a point cloud of the church [9]. The point cloud to BIM modelling utilizes state-of-the-art technology to convert the point cloud and laser survey data into accurate 3D BIM models (Fig. 3). Point cloud to BIM modelling are considered to be more accurate than traditional surveys using measuring tools. The 3D BIM model created from laser scan and UAV data was integrated with the building semantic data, providing information, such as construction materials, condition, color, texture, etc.

Fig. 3. 3D model elevation, generated by point cloud (Color figure online)

The 3D BIM model resulted from the survey data using laser scanners and photogrammetry documented the existing condition of the Asinou Church with a scale of 1:1 in order to integrate all the metadata collected from the building. The methodology used to document the church included:

1. 3D building documentation of the existing church (3D)
2. Date/time of construction of different aspects of the church (4D)
3. Quantity of the materials and structural elements (5D)
4. Model analysis and sustainability evaluation of the space and climatic conditions (6D)
5. Conservation and rehabilitation management (7D).

Figure 4 features the 3D development of the HBIM model.

The resulting 3D HBIM has the ability to manage all the building information as a church and as a cultural heritage monument. The HBIM approach for documenting such cultural heritage monuments is the solution for managing tangible and intangible information that creates the narrative of the monument. The HBIM acts as a source of information which provides valuable data without the need of visiting the monument [5]. Figures 5 and 6 both feature sections of the model.

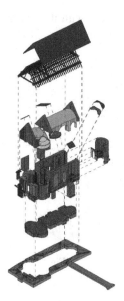

Fig. 4. 3D development of the model

Fig. 5. 3D model section

Fig. 6. Section of 3D HBIM

4   Results

The first phase for the process of documenting, creating and implementing the methodology of BIM for cultural heritage monuments provides the opportunity of capturing the cultural heritage information for managing a HBIM holistic approach. In the case of the Asinou Church, the presence of the Byzantine frescoes in the interior space created the need for the collection of data in order to integrate the story of each

Fig. 7. Frescoes inside Asinou Church (Color figure online)

fresco into the building information regarding image, geometry, color, texture, etc. The entire church was modeled using HBIM so that all the frescoes covering the walls and ceiling of the church could be documented (Fig. 7).

The next step to the use of information is to extract that information to the user by using augmented and virtual reality technologies, thereby provided an added-value experience to the visitor.

Acknowledgements. The project is funded by the European Union EU- H2020-SC6-R&I-INCEPTION project, contract# 665220.

References

1. Sotirova, K., Peneva, J., Ivanov, S., Doneva, R., Dobreva, M.: Digitization of cultural heritage – standards, institutions, initiatives, Chapter 1 (2012)
2. IFLA/UNESCO: IFLA/UNESCO Manifesto for Digital Libraries (2010)
3. Crane, D.J.: Creating services for the digital library. In: Online Information 1996, Proceedings of the International Online Information Meeting, London, 3–5 December 1996, pp. 397–401 (1996)
4. Bachi, V., Fresa, A., Pierotti, C., Prandoni, C.: The digitization age: mass culture is quality culture. challenges for cultural heritage and society. In: Ioannides, M., Magnenat-Thalmann, N., Fink, E., Žarnić, R., Yen, A.-Y., Quak, E. (eds.) EuroMed 2014. LNCS, vol. 8740, pp. 786–801. Springer, Cham (2014). https://doi.org/10.1007/978-3-319-13695-0_81
5. Arnold, D.: Excellence in Processing Open Cultural Heritage D. 1. 12 - Publishable Final Activity Report (2008)
6. Themistocleous, K., Ioannides, M., Agapiou, A., Hadjimitsis, D.G.: The methodology of documenting cultural heritage sites using photogrammetry, UAV and 3D printing techniques: the case study of Asinou Church in Cyprus. In: Proceedings of the Third International Conference on Remote Sensing and Geo-information of Environment, 16–19 March 2015, Paphos, Cyprus (2015a)
7. http://www.mcw.gov.cy/mcw/DA/DA.nsf/All/AB4501039DBBC4ABC22571990031F7A8? OpenDocument
8. Themistocleous, K., Ioannides, M., Agapiou, A., Hadjimitsis, D.G.: A new approach for documenting architectural cultural heritage: the case study of Asinou Church in Cyprus. In: Proceedings of the International Conference on Sustainability in Architectural Cultural Heritage, 11–12 December 2015, Limassol, Cyprus (2015b)
9. Oreni, D.: From 3D content models to HBIM for conservation and management of built heritage, pp. 344–357. Springer, Heidelberg (2013)

Digital Cultural Heritage – Smart Technologies

Smart Tourism Routes Based on Real Time Data and Evolutionary Algorithms

Mário Amorim[1]([⊠]) , Adriana Mar[1] , Fernando Monteiro[1],
Stella Sylaiou[2], Pedro Pereira[1] , and João Martins[1]

[1] CTS – UNINOVA Department of Electrical Engineering,
Faculty of Science and Technology, Universidade NOVA de Lisboa,
2829-516 Caparica, Portugal
{m.amorim, am.jesus}@campus.fct.unl.pt,
fernando.j.c.c.monteiro@gmail.com,
{pmrp, jf.martins}@fct.unl.pt
[2] School of Social Sciences, Hellenic Open University, Patras, Greece
sylaiou@gmail.com

Abstract. Tourism is an industry that has been growing rapidly in the last few years and it is expected that it will continue to grow. Due to the evolution of technology, mobile applications are being increasingly used in all kinds of industries, being one of them tourism. Presently there are already a few mobile applications used to increase the experience of the user when visiting a place, but these mobile applications lack some important features. This paper describes the development of a mobile application with integrated routing algorithms used to increase the experience of the tourists when visiting the city of Avila, Spain. The tourist will have at their disposal real time information about all the monuments available for visit, a full set of predefined circuits with different visit times and degrees of difficulty and also the possibility to create an optimized or personalized circuit combining the user preferences such as visiting time and number of monuments to visit.

Keywords: Tourism · Mobile applications · Routing algorithm
Real time data · Optimized route

1 Introduction

Tourism is one of the branches that has been growing more rapidly both in the number of tourists and in terms of tourist infrastructure. This growth has created the need for greater investment by cities not only in the restoration and preservation of monuments but also in the creation and improvement of support infrastructures for tourists [1].

In Europe, tourist activity is a source of considerable economic income that has been increasing in recent years. In Portugal, in 2016, there was a 1.4% increase in GDP (Gross Domestic Product) as shown in [2]. It also represents one of the largest sources of employment in major European cities. In [3] it is shown that in Spain between 2014 and 2015 there was an increase of around 13% in the number of jobs linked to tourism.

© Springer Nature Switzerland AG 2018
M. Ioannides et al. (Eds.): EuroMed 2018, LNCS 11196, pp. 417–426, 2018.
https://doi.org/10.1007/978-3-030-01762-0_36

With the increase in the number of tourists and infrastructures, it is difficult for tourists to decide which tourist spots to visit and to collect information on these points due to the wide variety of sources. On the other hand, the available information about the main tourist attractions is not real-time information often finding itself outdated.

Not only tourists, but also municipalities have logistical problems in infrastructure control such as the number of daily visitors, occupancy rate and waiting times, among other factors, where real-time information is currently non-existent. Another problem encountered by the municipalities is the high number of possible platforms for sharing information about tourist attractions, making it increasingly difficult to concentrate the information in a single place accessible to all tourists [4].

In view of the panorama described previously, this work intends to develop a mobile application for tourists in order to improve their experience. The mobile application developed in the framework of SHCity project will have as a pilot area the historic city of Avila, Spain, due to its geometry and distribution of the main historical points that helps the development and testing of this application.

The remain of the manuscript is organized as follows. Section 2 introduces the evolution through the years of tourist mobile applications as well as some of the existing tourist mobile applications used on the experience phase. In Sect. 3 it is presented the architecture, the main features of SHCity mobile application and the architecture of the optimization algorithm used. Section 4, the highlight goes to the development of SHCity mobile application and its optimization algorithm. Section 5 contains the results of the developed applications with some examples of its functionalities. Finally, conclusions are offered in Sect. 6.

2   Tourist Mobile Applications

This section introduces the evolution of mobile applications, more specifically applications related with tourist activity. It also explains the different stages experienced by tourists when travelling. After this explanation a review of the existing mobile apps used to improve the tourist experience when visiting a location is offered.

2.1   Evolution of Tourist Mobile Applications

The development and use of mobile applications have been growing over the last few years. Since the first App Store appeared in July 2008, mobile applications are increasingly being used in various industries and activities as reported in [5].

According to [6], approximately 3.9% of the total number of active applications in the Apple App Store in 2017 are tourism-related applications, making tourism the seventh most popular category.

These applications can be divided into five stages of travel experienced by the tourist as represented in Fig. 1, going from the choice of destination to the sharing of experience.

The experience phase, which is fundamental for the tourist, aims to provide information about the public transport network, the main points of interest and static

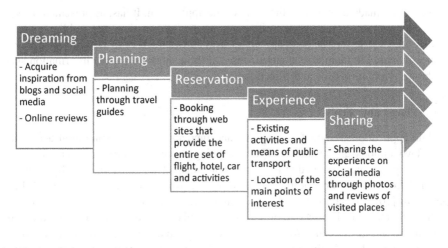

Fig. 1. Five stages of travel experienced by tourists. Adapted from [7].

information about these places. Some of these applications also have GPS directions to guide the tourist and use the application as a platform for interaction between different users.

2.2 FindNatal

FindNatal is a mobile application available for IOS and Android created in 2014 that aims to enrich the experience of tourists when visiting the city of Natal, Brazil. It was created to work independently and offline, presenting in its current version the following functionalities as described in [8]:

- English and Portuguese as available languages;
- Displays for each attraction photos, description, location, email, web page and opening and closing times;
- Shows from the current location of the user, which route must be followed to reach the selected destination;
- Sends an alert when the user is 500 m from a tourist point;
- Allows the user to evaluate both the points of interest visited and the city. This assessment can be made at the level of public cleanliness, safety, accessibility and tourist services.

This application is used not only to assist the tourist in finding the main points of interest, but it also shows the main bars, restaurants and hotels of the city.

2.3 SMARTAPPCITY

This is the first mobile application available in Spain that brings all the services of the city together on a single platform. Through a partnership with the municipalities or private entities, the data is provided by the entities and inserted into a database and subsequently made available to the users of the application. It has, as presented in [9] a great amount of services such as tourism, traffic information and public transport among others. The service dedicated to tourism allows the user to view in a list or on a map which are the main tourist attractions. All these attractions have information such as the description, photos and directions.

2.4   Places and Trails

Mobile application designed to motivate and increase touristic exploration across the UK. Two options are available. The first being designated Places, where the main historical points are presented in list form or on a map. These locations can be manually selected from the list or a notification can be sent when the user is near one of these points. In [10] it is said that each point has information such as pictures, description, audio and video file. The second option is Trails, where, in list form, the available trails are shown, and users can also add their own trails, making them available for other users to enjoy. When offline, the application has illustrative maps to guide the tourist along the trails.

2.5   Edinburgh – World Heritage City App

Edinburgh WHCT mobile application has four pre-defined circuits with audio guide, where the user can choose the circuit from a list containing the four pre-defined circuits. In [11] it is explained that each of the circuits has a brief description and some photos of the places that the user can visit. The user can also add comments and photos of the visited places. The user is also able to send a postcard to other users, promoting interaction between the users of the application. It also has an interactive game with a set of objectives, where the user that can achieve more goals and visit more places has the highest score, which is stored in a table along with the scores of the other participants [12].

2.6   Norwich: Heritage City

Mobile application developed to share with the users the history of the buildings of Norwich, England. It has as presented in [13] a list and a map with the historical monuments available to visit, each with a brief description and photos, sending a notification when the user is near one of these monuments. It also contains a description of the city of Norwich with some historical facts about the city and an online notebook where the user places badges won from visiting the city historical buildings, thus motivating the user to explore and visit the city.

2.7   Comparison

Table 1 shows the comparison between the existing mobile applications briefly explained in the subchapters above, and SHCity mobile application presented in this work.

Table 1. Comparison between the different mobile applications.

	FindNatal	SMARTAPPCITY	Places and trails	Edinburgh-WHCT	Norwich: Heritage City	SHCity
Real time information about each attraction	✗	✓	✗	✗	✗	✓
List of tourist attractions	✓	✓	✓	✗	✓	✓
Custom circuits	✗	✗	✗	✗	✗	✓
Audio guides	✗	✗	✓	✓	✗	✓
Directions	✓	✗	✗	✗	✓	✓
Pre-defined circuits	✗	✗	✓	✓	✓	✓
Information about each attraction	✓	✓	✓	✗	✓	✓
Evaluation of each attraction	✓	✗	✗	✗	✓	✗

When analyzing Table 1, it is verified that there are already some applications to support the tourist experience, some with more functionalities than others. Of all the mobile applications analyzed only SHCity has custom circuits, that means, none of the other applications allows the user to select monuments to include in a circuit. As for real-time information, apart from SHCity, only one other application has this functionality, providing real-time meteorological and traffic information to its users.

As for the SHCity mobile application, it can be concluded that in comparison with the others it is the most complete in terms of functionalities. It stands out in relation to the other ones by the use of real-time information such as occupation, waiting time, temperature and time of visit, information that will be provided to the mobile application by a set of sensors existing in all the main points of interest of the city.

3 SHCity Mobile Application Architecture

With the ambition to improve the tourist experience when visiting the city of Avila, Spain, a mobile application was developed. This application intends to give the user in a simple and intuitive way different functionalities represented in Fig. 2, that will improve his visit to the city. It also has four different languages available such as Spanish, Portuguese, French and English.

The architecture of the mobile application is divided into four main functionalities, being them:

- **Monuments/Places List** - A list of all the monuments available for visit is shown, along with the accessibility information of each monument. These monuments can also be represented in a location map, where in both cases the user can choose one

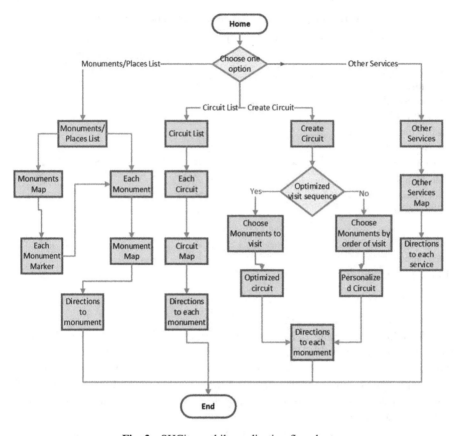

Fig. 2. SHCity mobile application flowchart

of the monuments available. When a monument is chosen, photos, a brief historical explanation and real time information is shown. The user then has the option to get directions from his current location to the chosen monument.

- **Circuit List** - A list of predefined circuits with different durations and degree of difficulty is shown, these circuits were developed by the municipality of Avila along with the cities tourism officials. When one of these circuits is chosen, photos and information about the circuit is shown, the user can then choose to see the circuit in a location map and start the visit.
- **Create Circuit** - In this option the user has the possibility to create his own circuit. The user can choose between an optimized or a personalized circuit. In the first case after picking out witch monuments to visit, an optimized circuit using a routing algorithm is created, saving the user the most amount of time possible. In the personalized circuit option, the user selects the monuments by order of visit, obtaining in the end a circuit with the chosen order. In both cases, the total duration and distance is shown and when the circuit is started the mobile application shows directions to each monument.

- **Other Services** - Here the user can see the location on a map of the main pharmacies, hospitals and green areas located near the monuments available for visit. Directions to the service location are also available.

The optimized circuit explained above, is based on a routing algorithm developed with the objective of saving the most amount of time possible when visiting the city. As represented in Fig. 3, this algorithm receives user information such as the time available for the visit and real time information about the monuments that the user has chosen, such as visiting time, waiting time and the walking duration between monuments.

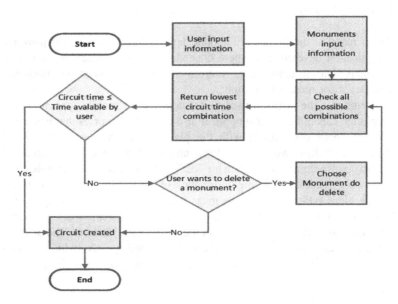

Fig. 3. Routing algorithm flowchart

Using evolutionary algorithms with the user input information and the monuments information, the algorithm checks all possible combinations and returns the combination with the lowest time. It then verifies if this time is lower than the time provided by the user. If it is, the optimized circuit is created, if not the user is provided with the option of deleting a monument. If he doesn't want to delete a monument a circuit is created with the original monuments. If the user wants to delete a monument, the algorithm starts again but without the deleted monument, therefore obtaining a lower circuit time.

3.1 Evolutionary Algorithms

The evolutionary algorithm tries to find the best solution between the available possible solutions for a certain problem. These algorithms are presented as methods that use basic principles of evolutionary theory and genetics, based mainly on the survival paradigm of the fittest [14].

In our case we need an algorithm that given some initial parameters is able to give in a short period a solution that is considered satisfactory. To obtain these results we used genetic algorithms, this is a robust algorithm that regardless of the initial parameters, satisfactory solutions are always given. Using recombination operators, a network of solutions is created, then the best solution is given. The advantage of this evolutionary algorithm in comparison with others is that it does a less exhaustive search, saving a lot of time and at the same time giving a solution that is viable.

4   Implementation

With the increase in the number of mobile applications, several new platforms for mobile application development where created. After some research, two stood out from the many that currently exist, Android Studio and Outsystems. Both are well known and exist for quite a long time.

Outsystems was the platform used to develop SHCity mobile application because of its simplicity, capabilities and support. It also has online courses that help beginners grow and get more comfortable with the platform which was really helpful and motivating. The platform works with blocks and all of the styles where created using CSS. It also allows communication whit REST API´s, which was in this case very helpful, not only to get the real time information of the monuments but also to connect with Google Maps API, which are the maps used in SHCity. These maps restrict the use of some functionalities such as the avoidance of stairs, narrow streets or elevated areas. The algorithm was also developed in the Outsystems platform. The development of the algorithm was made with blocks of conditions, which made it difficult to include some of the specifications that where set in the beginning of the project.

5   Application Results

With SHCity mobile application we are able to increase the experience of the tourist when visiting the city of Avila, Spain. As represented in Fig. 4, the user is able to get real time information and directions about all the monuments in the monuments/places list option. The user is also given the total distance and duration from the current location to the monument selected. As the user walks, a stick figure will follow the user´s location so that the user can guide himself throw the correct path.

When the user wants to create its own circuit two options are given, optimized or personalized circuit creation. In both cases as represented in Figs. 5 and 6 the total circuit time and duration is given and then the user will be able to get the directions in order, to each of the monuments chosen.

Analyzing Figs. 4 to 6, we can see a simple and intuitive mobile application that stands out from the ones that already exist in the area, going from the real time information provided to the user to the creation of optimized and personalized circuits which take in account this real time information.

Fig. 4. Monuments/places list option

Fig. 5. Create optimized circuit option

Fig. 6. Create personalized circuit option

After analyzing these results, we came to the conclusions that some improvements can be done. The most significant one is the use of a different development platform that allows the development of a stronger and more versatile algorithm. Allowing the user to save some circuits and share them with other users is also a functionality that will improve the functionality of SHCity mobile application. Other improvements will be suggested by users during the mobile application test phase.

6 Conclusions

From the research conducted it was clear that many studies and projects were already developed addressing mobile applications for the tourism industry, in this particular case applications used to improve the user experience. The literature review has allowed to identify these mobile applications and its main features.

The work presented in this paper aims to improve the tourist experience when visiting the city of Avila, Spain. Comparing with the different mobile applications, SHCity has all the main features that were considered important to the tourists when visiting a city. In order to highlight SHCity mobile application from the others we use real time information about the occupation rate and waiting time, information that is also used to create the optimized routes, improving like no other application the tourists experience. From the results presented this application is very simple to use but with a high level of functionality and features that meet the need of the tourists.

References

1. Sequeira, T.N., Nunes, P.M.: Does tourism influence economic growth? A dynamic panel data approachy. Appl. Econ. **40**, 2431–2441 (2008). https://doi.org/10.1080/00036840600949520
2. INE (National Institute of statistics): Estatísticas do Turismo 2016 (2017)
3. Hidalgo, C., Maene, O.: The nature of spain's international cultural tourism throughout the economic crisis (2008–2016): a macroeconomic analysis of tourist arrivals and spending. Economies **5**, 32 (2017). https://doi.org/10.3390/economies5030032
4. Wang, D., Park, S., Fesenmaier, D.R.: The role of smartphones in mediating the touristic experience. J. Travel Res. **51**, 371–387 (2012). https://doi.org/10.1177/0047287511426341
5. Christian, M.: Mobile application development in the tourism industry and its impact on on-site travel behavior. 65 (2015)
6. Statista: Most popular Apple App Store categories in January 2018, by share of available apps (2018). https://www.statista.com/statistics/270291/popular-categories-in-the-app-store/. Accessed 16 Apr 2018
7. The Five Stages of Travel. http://think.withgoogle.com/insights/embeds/five-stages-of-travel/index.html
8. Oliveira, J., Cacho, A., Moura, B., et al: FindTrip : Um Aplicativo Móvel para o Turismo Inteligente na Cidade do Natal. Univ Fed do Rio Gd do Norte – UFRN (2014)
9. Smartappcity SMARTAPPCITY. http://smartappcity.com/en/
10. Audio Trails 2018 audiotrails.co.uk. http://audiotrails.co.uk/welcome-native-app-platform/
11. Morrow, K.J.: Bus. Oppor. **1**, 288–296 (2001)
12. Edinburgh World Heritage Edinburgh - World Heritage City App. https://www.ewht.org.uk/visit/edinburgh—world-heritage-city-app
13. Norwich V heritagecity. http://www.heritagecity.org/about-us/norwich-heritage.htm
14. Fonseca, C.M., Fleming, P.J.: An overview of evolutionary algorithms in multiobjective optimization. Evol. Comput. **3**, 1–16 (1995). https://doi.org/10.1162/evco.1995.3.1.1

Art Nouveau Danube Digital Repository

Franc J. Zakrajšek[✉] and Vlasta Vodeb[iD]

Urban Planning Institute of the Republic of Slovenia, Ljubljana, Slovenia
{franc.zakrajsek,vlasta.vodeb}@guest.arnes.si

Abstract. The paper presents the development and the implementation of the Art Nouveau digital repository as a part of Art Nouveau Danube project. The digital repository functions as a common content point of Art Nouveau heritage in Danube region and is connected with other cultural portals. The repository supports the research, preparation of studies and other project activities. On the other side, the repository is accessible to general public for tourism and education. It contains information on movable, immovable and intangible Art Nouveau heritage from whole Danube region in different forms (3D objects, videos, texts, photos, descriptions). Metadata sources are re-use and enrichment of Europeana metadata and new digitalization and documentation of Art Nouveau heritage in this region.

Keywords: GIS · Mobile app · Europeana · Digital cultural heritage Art Nouveau

1 Background

Art Nouveau movement begun in Western Europe at the turn of the 19th and 20th centuries. The movement exposed new ideas in art, reflecting needs of modern life. The movement is "a multifaceted artistic phenomenon. In brief, the main characteristic of the best Art Nouveau creations is that each represents a so-called Gesamtkunstwerk. This refers to works of art created according to a unified programme and existing as a joint product of several fields of art. Architecture, fine and applied arts are obligatory, in combination also with other disciplines, such as interior and graphic design, scenography, music, and fashion." [1] In work of architects most common elements are portraying the nature and expressing national histories and folk art. The architects of movement experimented in use of new constructing materials for buildings and decorations, redefined functionality of spaces, applied new technical and structural building solutions and spatial concepts. Their architecture still provokes emotions and that is the reason to be appealing and realized.

The core centres of Art Nouveau creations in Western Europe are Brussels, Barcelona, Budapest, Paris, and Vienna. Brussels is recognized as Art Nouveau centre through works of Victor Horta, Henry van de Velde and Paul Hankar. Art Nouveau in Paris at the fin de siècle was the only style expressed in architecture and also internal design. Vienna became the centre of Secession architecture and art after 1895. Barcelona and Budapest developed their own Art Nouveau architectural language with

© Springer Nature Switzerland AG 2018
M. Ioannides et al. (Eds.): EuroMed 2018, LNCS 11196, pp. 427–436, 2018.
https://doi.org/10.1007/978-3-030-01762-0_37

Antonio Gaudí in Barcelona and with Ödön Lechner's in Budapest. Torino, Riga and Aveiro represent important Art nouveau centres in Europe's periphery. Turin became the Italian capital of the Stile florale with many residential buildings and tombstones designed in this style. Riga is famous for being a city with the largest number of Art Nouveau buildings. Aveiro is known by the decorations of street facades with ceramic tiles, ironwork balconies and floral mouldings. Influences of Wiener Secession, Hungarian style and mixture from Western Europe can be found also in architectural creations through whole Danube region (Fig. 1). For some nations in this region Art Nouveau style even contributed to the formulation of national identity.

Fig. 1. Selected Art Nouveau buildings from Danube region

Several important architects working in Danube region gained education in Technical College, Wagner School and School of Decorative Arts in Vienna. They spread the Wiener Secession architectural principles through the Danube region. Otto Wagner is recognized as the father of modern European architecture. He advocated a breakaway from historicist architecture, and introduced functional architecture that suits practical needs of modern people. His ideas are implemented in Slovenia and Croatia. Wagner's influence is found also in Bulgaria through the works of Georgi Fingov. Another group of architects followed Ödön Lechner or Hungarian Style. Lechner is an author of some Budapest iconic buildings. The use of modern materials and decorations with Zsolnay tiles inspired by old Magyar and Oriental folk art are most important characteristics of Hungarian variation of Art Nouveau. Most buildings influenced by Lechner can be found in central Danube region. In wealthy cities in Austro-Hungarian Empire Era in Slovakia, Serbia and Romania many impressive buildings were built under his influence. After the World War II those cities declined and some of them started to renovate Art Nouveau buildings only in last decade. Through the region several other architects implemented ideas and principles of Art Nouveau movement also from France and other European styles. Branko Tanazević from Serbia transformed Hungarian Style. The abundant opus of Daniel Renard in Romania reveals the influence of the French school École des Beaux-Arts. László Székely designed modern Timişoara in different styles and under various influences. Kálmán Rimanóczy connected Art Nouveau and eclecticism. Naum Torbov, the master of floral decoration, Kiro Marichkov and Petek Momchilov, who planned some symbolic buildings in Sofia are considered to be most representative Bulgarian Art Nouveau architects [2].

2   Art Nouveau Danube Project

Art Nouveau digital repository has been developed in the framework of the project Art Nouveau: Sustainable protection and promotion of Art Nouveau heritage in the Danube region.[1] The project brings together experts from Austria, Bulgaria, Croatia, Hungary, Slovenia, Serbia and Romania. Many jewels of Art Nouveau architecture, decorative and applied arts in Danube region have only been partially researched and their potential for urban and tourist development is not sufficiently exploited. Taking into account the common roots of the Art Nouveau movement, a common transnational approach is encouraged in the effective preservation, renovation and revitalization of this valuable heritage. The goal of the Art Nouveau project is to reveal, digitize and promote this heritage through Art Nouveau Danube digital repository (AND digital repository) and Art Nouveau Danube mobile app (AND mobile app). Figure 2 presents the main parts of the project.

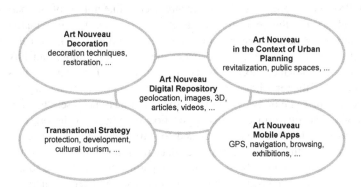

Fig. 2. Art Nouveau Danube project parts

[1] The project is financed by The Danube Transnational Programme (http://www.interreg-danube.eu/, last accessed 2018/06/29).

3   Art Nouveau Danube Digital Repository

AND digital repository is the indispensable part of Art Nouveau Danube project and functions as a common content point for Art Nouveau heritage in Danube region. It presents standardized and interoperable heritage descriptions, photos, and 3D models on interactive geographical map and is linked to other cultural portals and Europeana (European Digital Library). Partners are using the repository to conduct researches, prepare studies, and strategy for Art Nouveau heritage preservation in the region. Upon completion of the project, it will remain available as a knowledge base for professionals and for everyday use as an online tool for tourism, research and education.

The challenge and motivation of the AND digital repository was the need for its rapid development, merging Europeana resources with requirements of Art Nouveau Danube project, and the lack of heritage documentation data. The results are satisfactory as far as the experts are concerned. Repository offers potentials to observe, compare, and analyze this heritage for whole Danube region via single interactive geographical map. The originality is simplicity of the repository. Each object in the repository contains geographical coordinates, link to national heritage portal and link to Europeana.

3.1   Approach

The first step in developing the repository was to define metadata schema. The schema ought to be simple and understandable also for project participants who had less experience in cultural heritage documentation. However, on the other side the metadata ought to be complaint with Europeana Data Model, RDF, Dublin Core, ISO 19115, CIDOC-CRM and Inspire Directive to ensure secure integration of the partners' different metadata into the repository (example in Fig. 4). Let us emphasize three important attributes: accurate geographical coordinates up to 5–10 m in real world, link to national portal where user can find detail metadata description, and link to Europeana as an international context of observed digital object. First step is followed by the implementation of the repository. ICT web platform with database management system has been developed in cloud environment. Such approach increased the efficiency and reduced costs. The platform contains application for ingestion the original metadata into the repository for local institutions and for Art Nouveau passionate. The special focus was given to the enrichment of metadata with geographical coordinates. Once this technical background has been ensured, the partnership proceeded to the ingestion of the content into the repository. Ingestion followed strict technical rules to assure compliance with standards and interoperability for re-use by any stakeholder, also by local administrations [3–7].

The repository contains data from three sources: re-use of available resources from the Europeana portal, the existing data from local institutions and others, preparation of additional digital resources by project partners and Art Nouveau passionate, digitalization of analogue Art Nouveau objects by project partners (Fig. 3).

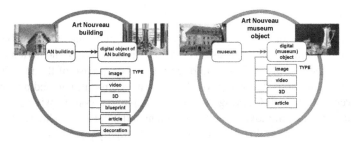

Fig. 3. Art Nouveau Danube digital repository structure

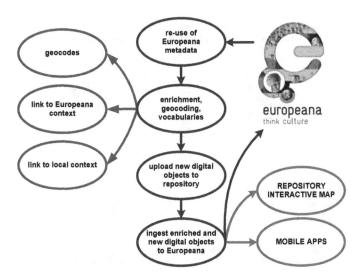

Fig. 4. Data flow in Art Nouveau Danube digital repository

In order to complete ingestion of digital metadata for whole Danube region (for example Serbia, Romania and Bulgaria have not any data in Europeana) also the digitalization was needed. Special efforts were made for partners to understand the process of digitization. Its understanding is important for creating quality and sustainable digital objects. The process can be divided into three phases: preparation – capturing – optimization. The important element of this process and development of repository was also solving copyrights issues and quality control [8, 9].

3.2   Results

The web application for updating and use of AND digital repository has been developed and implemented, and is in use by project partners (http://and.civitat.com). The user interface consists of mapping and querying tools. The use of the map is intuitive with basic GIS functions like zoom-to-all, zoom-in, zoom-out, pan and a possibility to switch seven base layers. Clicking on an item displays a pop-up with thumbnails of movable, tangible and immovable cultural content at that location. The link to refine the search in pop-up redirects the user to a page with a highly powerful search capability. Registered users can also create, edit metadata and upload digital objects. Currently there are 16.434 digital objects in the repository (Figs. 5 and 6).

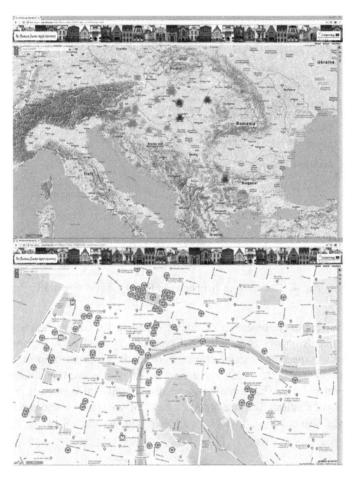

Fig. 5. Overview and detail map in Art Nouveau Danube digital repository

Description of AN building
(uirs, Slovenia, Trgovina Urbanc / Store Urbanc)

40462		uirs		Slovenia		2764		ANB

Title	Trgovina Urbanc / Store Urbanc
Description	Trgovina Urbanc / Store Urbanc, also House of Urbanc, Centromerkur, Galery Emporium; style: Secession; Restavratorski center ZVKDS (2009-2010), Fredrich Sigmundt (architect; 1902-1903); EŠD: 397; Ljubljana, Slovenija
Classifications	Secession (Slovenian Art Nouveau)
People	architects: Sigmundt, Fredrich
Time	1902-1903
Place	Ljubljana, Slovenija
	14,5065427	46,0518715	1
ViewAtLocal	http://www.eheritage.si/Digital.aspx?ID=21secesija_KVRTYLJILQVWENLNYGHKLUTQFHMNMR
ViewAtEuropeana	http://www.europeana.eu/portal/record/2026119/Partage_Plus_ProvidedCHO_eheritage_si__Zavod_za_varstvo_kulturne_dedi__ine_Slovenije__Urbanisti_ni_in_titut_Republike_Slovenije_SI_MK_AN
Institution	eheritage.si, Urbanistični inštitut Republike Slovenije
Language	Slovenian
Updated by	uirs
Updated on	09.05.2018
Partner	uirs

Fig. 6. Example of form for metadata description in Art Nouveau digital repository

4   Art Nouveau Danube Mobile App

One of the use of the AND digital repository is a mobile application. The AND mobile app has been developed as an essential tool for efficient and advanced tourist promotion of Art Nouveau heritage in the Danube region. The app contains data on Art Nouveau architectural heritage (buildings and digital objects of those buildings), and Art Nouveau museum objects. User can retrieve information about the building and photos of its exterior, interior, articles about the building and 3D models. The app enables GPS navigation, identification of individual building, and allows browsing information on digital objects. The target audiences are tourists, scholars and local residents to recognize and learn about this heritage, understand the history and its values. At present, the prototype version on Android platform is launched. The app is in testing phase. Beside the GPS location, the app takes into account also the azimuth direction of mobile device and recognizes nearest Art Nouveau building in this direction, and then displays building's digital objects (screenshots in Fig. 7). IOS and web mobile versions are planned to be developed in the next step. First comments from end users (tourists, scholars and citizens) are positive. Users especially like the intuitive interface with map that orientates towards Art Nouveau building they are watching and easily get an overview or detail information on it.

AND mobile app has been developed with the open source and free technology. Main components are PostgreSQL 9.3 [10] with PostGIS extension [11], Geoserver 2.4 [12], .NET 4.5 [13], Openlayers 4 [14], Google Maps API 3 [15], jQuery 3 [16], Sketchfab 3D [17].

Fig. 7. Art Nouveau Danube mobile app

5   Lessons Learnt

1. Combining the re-use of Europeana data and ingestion of additional or missing data ensures that whole region is sufficiently covered, the data are ready to be used within the project, and outside the project, are accessible for specialists, architects, conservators, urban planners, and general public.

2. Europeana is a comprehensive resource not only for metadata and digital objects, but also for knowledge on copyright issues, documentation, interoperability and digitalization standards and recommendations.
3. The bottleneck of re-use of Europeana metadata is that they rarely includes geographical coordinates especially with the accurate geolocation, therefore the enrichment is needed.
4. Using simplified EDM for metadata is a good approach when the participants involved have less experience on digitization and ingestion of digital cultural heritage.
5. Participation of local experts in the process of metadata enrichment with geolocation and controlled vocabularies is crucial for satisfying results as they know the details of local cultural heritage. The accurate facts are essential in order to end users are to trust and use the AND mobile app.

6 Further Work

The AND digital repository and AND mobile app is going to be regularly maintained and updated. AND digital repository automatically feeds AND mobile app. The stable platform is required in order to allow project partners and other users to upload and use metadata in the future.

The appealing nature of Art Nouveau heritage raised the interest among cities and tourist organizations. The API for other mobile apps of cities, tourist guides, booking systems and similar is going to be developed.

References

1. Pirkovič, J.: Art Nouveau in Western Europe. In: Vodeb, V. (ed.) Art Nouveau in the Context of Urban Planning. Urban planning Institute of the Republic of Slovenia, Ljubljana (2018)
2. Vodeb, V.: Introduction. In: Art nouveau valovanje: arhitektura v Podonavju: katalog mednarodne razstave ob svetovnem dnevu dediščine Art nouveau 2018, Ljubljana, Dunaj, Zagreb, Budimpešta, Subotica, Beograd, Oradea, Sofija = Waves of art nouveau: architecture in Danube region: catalogue of the international exhibition world day Art nouveau 2018, Ljubljana, Vienna, Zagreb, Budapest, Subotica, Beograd, Oradea, Sofia. Urbanistični inštitut Republike Slovenije, Ljubljana (2018)
3. Europeana data model: version 5.2.7. (2014). https://pro.europeana.eu/files/Europeana_Professional/Share_your_data/Technical_requirements/EDM_Documentation/EDM_Definition_v5.2.7_042016.pdf. Accessed Dec 2017
4. Directive 2007/2/EC of the European Parliament and of the Council of 14 March 2007 establishing an Infrastructure for Spatial Information in the European Community (INSPIRE). Official Journal of the European Union, L 108/1, 25 April 2007 (2007)
5. Zakrajšek, F.J., Vodeb, V.: Art Nouveau Danube digital repository: metadata description, v.1.1. Technical report, European Union Interreg Danube Programme, Project Art Nouveau (2017)

6. Zakrajšek, F.J., Vodeb, V.: eCultureMap – Link to Europeana Knowledge. In: Bolikowski, Ł., Casarosa, V., Goodale, P., Houssos, N., Manghi, P., Schirrwagen, J. (eds.) TPDL 2013. CCIS, vol. 416, pp. 184–189. Springer, Cham (2014). https://doi.org/10.1007/978-3-319-08425-1_20

7. Zakrajšek, F.J., Vodeb, V.: Reuse of Europeana metadata for geo-location services. In: 2015 Digital Heritage International Congress, Granada, Spain. IEEE Press, Danvers (2015). https://doi.org/10.1109/DigitalHeritage.2015.7419612

8. Kenney, A.R., Rieger, O.Y., Entlich, R.: Moving Theory into Practice: Digital Imaging for Libraries and Archives. Cornell University Library, New York (2003)

9. Iglésias, D.: D 3.1.1 Digitised material (first release). Technical report, Europeana Photography, The Europeana Publishing Framework, Europeana Content Re-Use Task Force (2013)

10. PostgreSQL. https://www.postgresql.org/

11. PostGIS: Spatial and Geographic objects for PostgreSQL. http://postgis.org/

12. GeoServer. http://geoserver.org/

13. Microsoft .NET Framework 4.5. https://www.microsoft.com/en-us/download/details.aspx?id=30653

14. OpenLayers. https://openlayers.org/

15. Google Maps API. https://cloud.google.com/maps-platform/maps/

16. jQuery. https://jquery.com/

17. Sketchfab 3D. https://sketchfab.com/

A Consortium Blockchain System for Verifying Digital Contents on Traditional Costumes

Eun-jin Kim🆔 and Jeongmin Yu$^{(\boxtimes)}$🆔

Department of Digital Heritage Industry,
Graduate School of Convergence Cultural Heritage,
Korea National University of Cultural Heritage,
Buyeo-gun, Chungcheongnam-do, Korea
{dodaik, jmyu}@nuch.ac.kr

Abstract. Many countries and organizations have an archive database for the digital preservation of cultural heritage. As recording cultural heritage data becomes more common, the importance of a reliable database is emphasized. However, if the verification of the produced digital heritage content is not correct, continuous errors are yielded in their applications and cultural heritage is misinterpreted. In this paper, we propose a consortium blockchain system for verifying digital cultural heritage contents. Blockchains, which have been applied to various fields recently, are a distributed data storage technology proposed by *Satoshi Nakamoto*. Blockchains are attracting attention as a technique for creating and storing reliable records owing to its property that it cannot be arbitrarily changed. We propose a verification system that is organized by three expert groups for assessment: researchers, curators, and artisans. The three expert groups review the digital heritage content and finally approve the content via a consensus process. To this end, the approved digital content is created as a block and stored in a blockchain record. We expect that the proposed consortium blockchain system will obtain efficiency and reliability in the screening process by leaving a reliable record of the digital content.

Keywords: Consortium blockchain · Digital contents of cultural heritage
Verification system · Smart contract

1 Introduction

Many countries and institutions have archived their cultural heritage digitally for preservation and opened it up to the public [1, 2]. The most important role of digital heritage is for it to be shared to satisfy the public interest for heritage of humanity. For example, the Smithsonian museums in the United States provide 3D digital content on cultural heritage in their collections [3]. Europeana is a digital library project in Europe that provides digital content from libraries, museums, art galleries, and archives throughout Europe [4]. The government of South Korea conducted a project for discovering and digitizing a cultural heritage and provided it to the public via the web [21].

The shared digital cultural heritages are widely used for cultural archetypes and applications, but not all contents are verified correctly. The cultural heritage registered

© Springer Nature Switzerland AG 2018
M. Ioannides et al. (Eds.): EuroMed 2018, LNCS 11196, pp. 437–446, 2018.
https://doi.org/10.1007/978-3-030-01762-0_38

in the digital archive must clearly verify the uncertainties that may arise in the reconstruction and recording of the contents, and then transmit them to the user [5]. The unverified digital heritages yield severe errors in their application contents. Based on this awareness of the problem, the need for the verification of digital contents via selected experts has been raised.

Since the produced digital contents of cultural heritage have historical significance in society, it should strive for long-term preservation without changing its data [8]. Long-term preservation should be associated with the integrity of the data. This is possible through the establishment of reliable databases and institutionalized standards [7].

Recently, blockchains [9] have received close attention as a reliable distributed data storage technology. The blockchain is a technique for storing and distributing replicated data to all nodes participating in the system without using a central server. It is almost impossible to make any changes to the records because the blockchain compares the data of each node from time to time to find the changed part. Thus, the blockchain guarantees the integrity of the data and can maintain a permanent record. Some researchers are aware of their potential as a reliable database and are actively conducting research on this [10]. In addition, smart contracts built into the blockchain enable automated work processes.

However, it is difficult to utilize it in a system that needs to be controlled because of the features that are open to unspecified individuals. The consortium blockchain [15] has been presented to solve this problem. The consortium blockchain is a system that gives promised organizations and individuals the authority to participate in the system and ensures the validity of the agreed contracts. It uses a restricted network, so it is easy to control the system and it can process data quickly. This can therefore be useful for trading platforms or government agencies that require approval.

Until now, the blockchain has been recognized as an efficient data validation system that guarantees integrity. In digital cultural heritage content verification, the blockchain can be used as an important system. Most digital archives currently in use have guidelines for verifying digital content, but without separate protocols. However, content verification through guidelines is inefficient because there are time and location constraints. The system proposed in this paper is quick and efficient because it can execute the protocol online using a smart contract. In particular, the cultural heritage expert agreement system using blockchain for content verification is a newly proposed in the field of cultural heritage.

In this paper, we propose a consortium blockchain system for verifying digital content on traditional costumes. Traditional costume contents should be considered in a comprehensive historical and empirical context. The consortium for the verification of digital heritage content is divided into three groups. The reason for organizing the reviewers into three groups is to avoid the consequences of biased reviews. The three groups are divided into researchers, curators, and artisans (shown in Fig. 1). Each expert group consists of individuals who are officially certified in their research fields. Afterwards, the correctly verified digital contents from experts are registered in the blockchain system. This system ensures the integrity of data and creates reliable content through a review process involving the consensus process of experts.

The following are the contents to be presented in this paper. In Sect. 2, we provide background knowledge about historical research on Korean traditional costumes and blockchains. In Sect. 3, we present the blockchain-based verification system. Finally, in Sect. 4, we refer to the conclusions and the direction of future research.

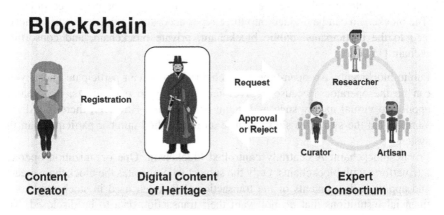

Fig. 1. Overall consortium blockchain for verification of traditional costumes.

2   Background and Related Works

2.1   Blockchain Systems

As e-commerce developed, the central system made transactions possible by guaranteeing individual identity. However, the central system had some drawbacks. The data managed by the central system can be changed by malicious manipulation or hacking. In addition, the system was inefficient because the management costs were high and the transaction stage was complex [16]. As a solution to this problem, *Satoshi Nakamoto* devised the blockchain system in 2008 [9].

The blockchain is a decentralized data distribution storage system. Anyone can participate in the system, and all nodes participating in the system share the same data. It is possible to trade without going through the central server, and it is difficult to arbitrarily manipulate the data. The main characteristics of the blockchain can be summarized as follows [17].

First, the blockchain has a distributed structure. The verified transaction information is generated as a block and stored in the blockchain. At this time, the data is replicated and stored in a distributed node, not in a central server. Since all nodes have the same data, it is possible to trade directly between individuals without going through a central server.

Second, it is difficult to change registered data. Blocks are linked together with the hash value of the previous block. If the data is arbitrarily changed, the hash value of the connection block will change and not be recognized in the system. Therefore, it is almost impossible to change the data because all nodes have to change data at once.

Third, smart contracts enable automation and efficient work processes [11]. The user can make the application through the simple creation of a script embedded in the blockchain. Since it is possible to complete the contract online, it is efficient because it can overcome location restrictions and replace the document and signature required for the contract with a code. Above all, if the condition of the pre-written code is satisfied, the contract is automatically executed so that the business can be processed quickly.

The blockchain can be divided into three types according to the degree of authority granted to the participants: public blockchain, private blockchain, and consortium blockchain [15].

1. Public blockchain: An open-type blockchain. Anyone can participate and anyone can be the operator. Because it gives fair authority to participants, it is mainly applied to virtual money such as Bitcoin or Etherium. However, there is a disadvantage that the system is slow because an unspecified number participates in the system.
2. Private blockchain: A centrally controlled blockchain. One organization operates the platform with blockchains. Only the subject who operates the blockchain creates and approves the contents of the transaction. It is often used in stock markets or financial institutions that do not want their transaction data to be disclosed. The system is fast because one organization participates.
3. Consortium blockchain: A mixed-type blockchain. It is a combination of the public and private blockchains. Only the participants authorized by the system participate and derive a consensus according to certain rules, such as the smart contract. It is used by trading platforms or government agencies that require an agreement between participants. The system is fast because only the participants authorized by the system participate.

This paper proposes a verification system using the blockchain. This system uses the characteristics of the blockchain that store unchanging data and support an efficient transaction protocol. Participants in the system can be divided into content creators and reviewers. This system is best suited to the consortium blockchain because the participants are limited and have to reach a certain consensus. In the next section, we will examine the verification system process in detail.

2.2 Traditional Costumes in Joseon Dynasty

Joseon was the last dynasty of Korea, which lasted from 1392 to 1910. Joseon was a status-driven society based on a strict exemplum. The costumes of the Joseon Dynasty were changed and institutionalized according to the times. The attire regulations were finely organized based on laws and institutions. It is difficult to reproduce the costumes of the Joseon Dynasty because the specific regulations differed according to the situation and ritual.

For example, the *yung-bok* was the official activity attire of the king and officials. The *yung-bok* was worn by distinguishing the color of the clothes and ornaments according to the situation. The regulations on the *yung-bok* of the king and officials appear in *Sang-bang-jeong-rye* and *Sok-dae-jeon*, published in 1750 and 1746, respectively. *Sang-bang-jeong-rye* is a regulation on royal attire. *Sok-dae-jeon* is a legal code compiled in the late Joseon Dynasty to revise and supplement early Joseon Dynasty laws. The legal code includes the rules on the officials' attire.

According to *Sang-bang-jeong-rye*, the king used red-painted official hats made of horsehair (namely, *ju-rip*). The king's official robes (namely, <u>*cheol-lik*</u>) were red and expressed his authority with round patches embroidered with a dragon (namely, *hyung-bae*) on the front and back and both shoulders (shown in Fig. 2).

In *Sok-dae-jeon*, *yung-bok* attire is divided into two categories: *dang-sang-gwan* and *dang-ha-gwan*. *Dang-sang-gwan* was for high-level officials, who closely aided the king, and *dang-ha-gwan* was for lower-level officials. The *yung-bok* attire of *dang-sang-gwan* included red official hats and blue official robes (shown in Fig. 3). The *yung-bok* attire of *dang-ha-gwan* consisted of black official hats (namely, *heung-nip*) and blue-gray official robes in the palace (shown in Fig. 4, left). However, during the royal procession, they had to wear red official robes (shown in Fig. 4, right). Both the king and the officials wore black boots that covered their ankles (shown in Table 1).

In the case of Joseon Dynasty costumes, it is necessary to conduct diverse studies with reference to regal codes, literature, paintings, and relics to reproduce the contents properly. However, content that lacks historical research may be registered in the database. Therefore, it is necessary to verify the contents through the examination of experts in each field for database registration.

Table 1. The *Yung-bok* attire corresponding to social status.

Status	King	A high-level official	Low-level official
Official hats	Red	Red	Black
Official robes	Red	Blue	Blue gray/Red
Footwear	Black	Black	Black
Figures			
	Fig. 2. The king's *yung-bok* [18] (Color figure online)	**Fig. 3.** A high-level official *yung-bok* [19] (Color figure online)	**Fig. 4.** A low-level official *yung-bok* (left): when inside the palace [19] (right): when outside of the palace [20] (Color figure online)

3   Proposed Consortium Blockchain for Verification

The process of the digital contents of the digital heritage verification system is shown in Fig. 5: (i) The content creator registers the digital content on digital heritage and (ii) analyzes the metadata of the content and finds the reviewers in each group and request; (iii) the reviewers send the results of the verification and perform an agreement, (iv) "Three rejections" or "One approval and Two rejections"; they send the modifications and review them again "Two approvals and one rejection"; they review them again or approve them after consultation (v) "Three approvals"; and a block is generated with metadata in the blockchain.

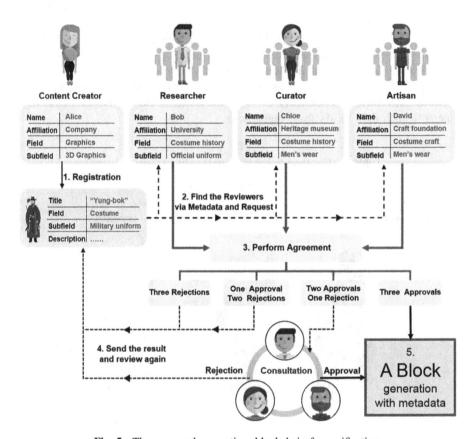

Fig. 5. The proposed consortium blockchain for verification.

Step 1: Register participants and digital contents

Participants (i.e., content creators and reviewers) join the system [13]. The content creators create digital content on heritage and register them in the system. They could be a company or an individual. When joining the system, they select the classification of the participant and enter details such as name, affiliation, field, and subfield (shown in Table 2).

The content creator uploads digital content on traditional costumes to the system for review. Then, they enter the metadata for the content. The items are title, field, subfield, and description. The content name should show the characteristics of the content most clearly, and the relevant fields and subfields should be entered so that it can be connected with the metadata of the reviewers [6]. Finally, a description of the content should be entered so that it can be referred to in the content review (shown in Table 3).

Table 2. Examples of participant information

Classification	Content creator	Reviewers		
		Researcher	Curator	Artisan
Name	Alice	Bob	Chloe	David
Affiliation	Company	University	Heritage museum	Craft foundation
Field	Graphics	Costume history	Costume history	Costume craft
Subfield	2D graphics	Official uniform	Men's wear	Men's wear

Table 3. Metadata of digital contents on digital heritage

Digital content	Item	Substance
Fig. 6. High-level officials' *yung-bok* attire [21]	Name	High-level officials' *yung-bok* attire
	Field	Traditional costume of Joseon Dynasty
	Subfield	Official uniform, Men's wear
	Description	A detailed description of the content

The reviewers are qualified experts who verify the content registered by the content creators. The reviewers are divided into three groups: researchers, curators, and artisans. The researcher group contains researchers who conduct research in each field. The curator group comprises museum curators who are in charge of exhibiting and managing artifacts directly, and the artisan group is composed of nationally certified artisans. The reviewers set up the group to which they belong at the time of sign-up, select the participant classification, and input information including the name, affiliation, related field, and subfield (shown in Table 2).

Step 2: Find the reviewers via metadata and requests

The system finds the best reviewers based on the metadata of the reviewers and digital contents and automatically requests a review. For the sake of fairness in the review, the information on the content creator is not included when the contents are delivered to the reviewer. The method of passing on contents for review uses a public key infrastructure (PKI). By using the PKI, information on the reviewers and creator is protected from other system users [12]. The digital contents to be reviewed are encrypted and transmitted by the public key of the selected reviewer. First, the reviewer checks the metadata of the content and determines whether it can be reviewed. If the reviewer is willing to review it, they decrypt it with their private key; otherwise, they send it back to the content creator.

The reviewer uses their professional knowledge to verify that the digital contents have been reproduced correctly. If the content is reproduced correctly, the reviewer encrypts it using their own private key and sends it to the system, including the public key. On the other hand, if the content is not reproduced correctly, the reviewer attaches the modification, encrypts it with the content creator's public key, and sends it to the system.

Step 3: Perform agreement

The system involved the following consensus process by combining the received results [11].

1. *"Three rejections" or "One approval and two rejections"*: This process includes two cases. The first is three rejections, and the second is one approval and two rejections. The system transmits the result of the review encrypted by the public key to the content creator. The content creator decrypts with the private key and checks for modifications. The contents can be requested to be reviewed again after revising and supplementing them.
2. *"Two approvals and one rejection"*: This process works when two reviewers approve and one reviewer rejects. The system suspends judgments on content and allows the reviewers to exchange their verification results. The reviewers derive a consensus on content through a consultation. If the result of the consensus between the reviewers is rejected, the content can be reviewed again. In contrast, if approved, it creates a block and registers it in the blockchain.
3. *"Three approvals"*: When content is approved by three reviewers, content verification information is generated as a block. The blocks include time stamps, content information, and the content creator and reviewer's private key (shown in Fig. 7). The generated block is registered in the blockchain and becomes the verification data of the digital contents [14].

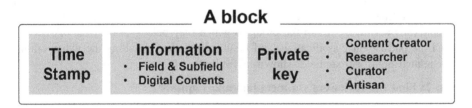

Fig. 7. Elements of a block

In this chapter, we have discussed how to configure a consortium blockchain and verify the digital content of traditional costumes within the system. The digital content verified through this system generates a block and is registered in the blockchain, and the digital heritage contents ensure reliability.

4 Conclusion and Future Works

UNESCO has set up guidelines for the selection of digital content for long-term digital preservation [2]. The purpose of these guidelines is to find preservation value for digital cultural heritage and establish a policy for preserving selected digital heritage. However, it is not easy to distinguish whether the generated digital contents of cultural heritage are worth preserving. Most institutions lack expertise in the historical research of digital content, so they need help from external agencies or experts. The system derives a consensus among the reviewers through smart contracts. The final results are stored and propagated to the blockchain. Information stored in the blockchain cannot be changed intentionally, so information about content authentication remains indefinitely.

Therefore, the content creator is motivated to produce high-quality contents, and copyright can be protected at the same time as the verification. In contrast, those who verify the contents will be cautious about content verification because the authentication information about the work remains. The digital cultural heritage reproduced as a result is expected to have correct historical research and improve the quality of contents.

Thus far, we have discussed the process of digital content verification system based on the consortium blockchain. What has not been covered in detail in this paper will be elaborated in further research. The future research will proceed as follows.

First, when the verification system becomes deadlocked, the system should allow reviewers to share their opinions and draw a consensus. We will construct a detailed consensus protocol on this part in subsequent studies.

Second, regarding the reward problem of the reviewers, after the content review, compensation should be given to the content creator and reviewers. The proposed system in this paper generates a block when all three reviewers approve of the content. However, even if the content is rejected and does not generate a block, compensation for the review should be given. Therefore, it is necessary to research the compensation problem of the reviewers and content creators.

The blockchain is an innovative system that has emerged to solve the trustworthiness problem of information. By applying it to the field of cultural properties, we intend to improve efficiency in preserving and managing cultural properties. Through future research, we expect that the blockchain will be used in various cultural heritage fields.

Acknowledgements. This research is supported by 2018 Support Project for Academic Research in Korea National University of Cultural Heritage.

References

1. UNESCO: Charter on the preservation of the digital heritage (2003)
2. UNESCO: Guidelines for the selection of digital content for long-term digital preservation (2016)
3. Smithsonian 3D.https://3d.si.edu/
4. Europeana collections. https://www.europeana.eu/portal/en
5. Koller, D., Frischer, B., Humphreys, G.: Research challenges for digital archives of 3D cultural heritage models. J. Comput. Cult. Herit. (JOCCH) 2(3), 7 (2009). https://doi.org/10.1145/1658346.1658347
6. Felicetti, A., Lorenzini, M.: Metadata and tools for integration and preservation of cultural heritage 3D information. Geoinformatics FCE CTU 6, 118–124 (2011). https://doi.org/10.14311/gi.6.16
7. Thwaites, H.: Digital heritage: what happens when we digitize everything? In: Ch'ng, E., Gaffney, V., Chapman, H. (eds.) Visual Heritage in the Digital Age. SSCC, pp. 327–348. Springer, London (2013). https://doi.org/10.1007/978-1-4471-5535-5_17
8. Lemieux, V.L.: Trusting records: is Blockchain technology the answer? Rec. Manag. J. 26 (2), 110–139 (2016). https://doi.org/10.1108/RMJ-12-2015-0042
9. Nakamoto, S.: Bitcoin: a peer-to-peer electronic cash system. White paper (2008)
10. Gaetani, E., Aniello, L., Baldoni, R. et al.: Blockchain-based database to ensure data integrity in cloud computing environments. In: Italian Conference on Cybersecurity, Venice, Italy, 17–20 Jan 2017, p. 10 (2017)
11. Christidis, K., Devetsikiotis, M.: Blockchains and smart contracts for the internet of things. IEEE Access 4, 2292–2303 (2016). https://doi.org/10.1109/ACCESS.2016.2566339
12. Zyskind, G., Nathan, O.: Decentralizing privacy: using Blockchain to protect personal data. In: 2015 IEEE Anonymous Security and Privacy Workshops (SPW), pp. 180–184. IEEE (2015). https://doi.org/10.1109/spw.2015.27
13. Lee, W.K., Jin, J., Lee, M.: A Blockchain-based identity management service supporting robust identity recovery. Int. J. Secur. Technol. Smart Device 4(1), 29–34 (2017)
14. Kim, H.M., Laskowski, M.: Toward an ontology-driven blockchain design for supply-chain provenance. Intell. Syst. Account. Financ. Manag. 25(1), 18–27 (2018). https://doi.org/10.1002/isaf.1424
15. Zhu, Y., Riad, K., Guo, R., et al.: New instant confirmation mechanism based on interactive incontestable signature in consortium Blockchain. Front. Comput. Sci. 1–16 (2017). https://doi.org/10.1007/s11704-017-6338-8
16. Tapscott, D., Tapscott, A.: Blockchain Revolution: How the Technology Behind Bitcoin is Changing Money, Business, and the World. Penguin, London (2016). ISBN 9781511357692
17. Buterin, V.: A next-generation smart contract and decentralized application platform. White paper (2014)
18. Woo, Y.: The king's yung-bok attire in sang-bang-jeong-rye (2015). https://blog.naver.com/dndudwp99/220495798524
19. Banquet for the elderly people given at naknamheon (1795)
20. Royal banquet in the year of musin (1848)
21. Culturecontent.com. http://www.culturecontent.com/

eDIRICA: Digitizing Cultural Heritage for Learning, Creativity, and Inclusiveness

Olufemi Samson Adetunji[1,2,3](✉) [iD], Clement Essien[3,4] [iD],
and Oluwatosin Samuel Owolabi[5] [iD]

[1] School of Architecture and Built Environment, University of Newcastle,
Callaghan, Australia
olufemi.adetunji@uon.edu.au
[2] Department of Architecture, Federal University of Technology, Akure,
Akure, Nigeria
[3] NERD Multi Partnerships, Lagos, Nigeria
[4] Department of Electrical Engineering and Computer Science,
University of Missouri, Columbia, USA
u.c.essien@mail.missouri.edu
[5] Department of Architectural Technology, Federal Polytechnic,
Nasarawa, Nigeria
tosinowolabing@gmail.com

Abstract. The integration of information and communication tools to the management of cultural heritage (CH) promotes culture-based creativity, historical learning and awareness, cultural diversity and social cohesion. However, various developing countries are facing challenges due to inadequate infrastructure to support the integration. In Nigeria, for instance, heritage sites are mainly protected for tourism purposes with little focus on the educational purposes and the broader impacts of CH within the community. This paper, therefore, describes the planning stage for the development of eDIRICA, a Web-app tool that incorporates learning, peoples' engagement and creativity to create a new paradigm for the management of cultural heritage in Nigeria. The rationale is to document heritage sites and convert the information into knowledge through the creation of interactive learning modules, collaborative activities and events. Primary information were collected through questionnaire survey of randomly selected school students and teachers. Semi-structured interviews were also conducted for heritage managers of three CHs. The study finds that heritage education is not included in school curriculum, inadequate trained teachers and collaboration between heritage managers and school administrators. Also, young people are interested in engaging and learning about cultural heritage through digital platforms in view to contribute to the development of their communities.

Keywords: Digitization · Cultural heritage · eLearning

This work was supported by the Australian Government Research Training Program Scholarship.

© Springer Nature Switzerland AG 2018
M. Ioannides et al. (Eds.): EuroMed 2018, LNCS 11196, pp. 447–456, 2018.
https://doi.org/10.1007/978-3-030-01762-0_39

1   Introduction

Advancements in information and communication technology (ICT) aided various digital innovations across aspects of human life especially human association with cultural heritage (CH). The development of mobile or portable technology improves the process of obtaining data and information about heritage sites [1]. However, many of the web applications are multi-purpose and meet the demands of users. For instance, Yastikili [2] focused on digital photogrammetry and laser scanning as investigative tools for cultural heritage documentation, while Eisazadah, Houbart, Hallot and Haylighen [3] examined the roles of social media such as Facebook, Instagram and Twitter in the understanding of cultural heritage. Mobile apps and smartphones are also vital to conservation, restoration, documentation and innovations in cultural heritage [4]. The evaluation of websites of museums conducted by Kabassi [5] noted that mobile applications contribute to inspire and provoke curiosity and further understanding of cultural heritage among local people and visitors.

Furthermore, heritage is a vital component of the community, which has to be documented, preserved, and transmitted to future generations. Ocal [6] stated that each generation tends to change what was inherited and new elements are added when heritage is passed from one generation to the other; therefore, heritage education is vital for documentation and preservation of changes that occur across generations. Heritage education is the 'pedagogical process in which people learn about heritage assets' both tangible and intangible in a systematic approach [7]. The approach can be in three forms – traditional, hybrid (blended) or digital. The traditional method involves face-to-face teaching where the teacher uses printed or unprinted, audio or visual teaching materials [8]. While recently the incorporation of ICT leads to the development of hybrid and digital approaches.

The digital approach also involves the use of mobile applications and websites not only to preserve and share information and knowledge but also to reveal the importance of the community to the future generations. The hybrid approach involves the combination of the two (i.e. traditional and digital) approaches. The information and knowledge about heritage are taught in classrooms and available on websites and mobile applications. The use of digital tools in heritage education, however, gives 'multiple possibilities to learn in-situ' and improve access to heritage [7]. Therefore, this paper describes the processes and lessons learnt in the planning stage for the development of eDIRICA (Education through Innovation and Rethinking in Culture and Art), a web application designed with functions and features to educate users (especially the young people) and foster creativity, innovation, and inclusiveness in cultural heritage.

2   The eDIRICA Approach

Limited digital tools focusing on cultural heritage in Africa support the engagement of the people in the management of cultural heritage [9]. Mainly because younger generations believed cultural heritage 'belong to the ancestors' while heritage professionals viewed heritage as 'physical and material' [10]. Also, decision-making and management of cultural heritage are done through a top-down approach with the professionals and governments on top of the chain. However, Council of Europe [11], emphasised participatory approach to CH with communities playing an important role in the identification, ownership, and interaction with heritage. Lim *et al.* [12] bolstered the standpoint of the Faro Convention with emphasis on integrated citizen participation which has become 'ethical obligation and political necessity'. However, providing heritage knowledge through integrated approach helps the community to view heritage as legacy transmitted to the future generations from the predecessors. Heritage education serves as 'vehicle' to disseminate information about heritage across generation, and within and outside the local community. Therefore, the integration of digital tools in heritage dissemination is vital due to the nature of 'always-connected' society.

3 Why Nigeria

Various reports, such as Bloom and Mckinnon [13], Melorose, Peroy and Careas [14], and UNDESA [15] emphasised the importance of the education sector to the dividend of population growth to be realised. By 2030, the population of Nigeria is projected to reach 263 million, indicating 44.1% increase from 2015. In 2010, the youths represented 40–45% but are projected to be 55–60% of the population by 2030. The growth in population creates tremendous strain on the education system and huge demand for education, especially from the younger generation. Also, there is limited content on tangible and intangible heritage in the school (primary and secondary) curriculum in Nigeria. Various human settlements in Nigeria are also experiencing developmental changes with growing demand for land and housing leading to the destruction of multiple heritage buildings and sites [14]. However, various efforts are implemented to re-position Nigeria on the path of sustainable development that includes improving the quality of and access to ICT and education infrastructure. The introduction of mobile communication and the internet in the 1990s helped to improve access to education, especially amidst the younger generation. However, the education sector still experiencing challenges such as inadequate collaboration across different stakeholders, high rate of out-of-school children, and poor interest towards education amidst the younger generation. As a result of this, eDIRICA seeks to improve interests of younger generation towards education through participatory and innovative heritage learning in view to improve awareness and conservation of tangible and intangible heritage in Nigeria.

3.1 Project Aim and Objectives

EDIRICA aims to bridge the gap in documenting cultural heritage to educate and improve interaction, participation and share heritage knowledge amidst people, especially young people through web tools. However, at the planning stage, the objectives are:

1. to identify and assess the opinions of key stakeholders in the integration of digital tools in heritage education in Nigeria
2. to understand the potentials and challenges to the hybrid heritage education
3. to develop project concept and delivery strategy for eDIRICA.

3.2   Methodology

The project administered two different questionnaires to schools students and teachers. Semi-structured interviews were also conducted for heritage managers of three CHs in Nigeria. However, at this stage, the survey focused on public schools within the local communities of the selected CHs. 15 students and five teachers were randomly selected in each of the communities (see Table 1). The student questionnaire (SQ) consists of three parts: levels of interest in and knowledge about CH, and digital literacy, while the teachers' questionnaire (TQ) focused on digital literacy, curriculum content, and level of knowledge in CH. Also, one heritage manager (HM1-3) was selected in each of the three CHs for interview focusing on collaboration and involvement of schools in the management of cultural heritage and perception of hybrid heritage education. A five-point Likert scale (0–4) is adopted to evaluate each factor. Descriptive analysis was also conducted on the survey responses and supported by interviewees' responses.

Table 1. Distribution of respondents

Gender	Students		Teachers	
	N	%	N	%
Male	29	64.44	4	26.67
Female	16	35.56	11	73.33
Total	45	100	15	100

Table 2. Levels of interest and knowledge about cultural heritage

Students		Teachers	
	Mean		*Mean*
Level of knowledge about cultural heritage	1.23	Level of knowledge about cultural heritage	2.35
Satisfaction with heritage information taught in school	1.52	Satisfaction with CH content in school curriculum	1.43
Interest in studying about cultural heritage in school	3.58	Interest in participation in heritage education and related activities	3.62

3.3   Findings and Discussion

Levels of Interest and Knowledge about Cultural Heritage. 84.44% of the student respondents have not visited any CH, and 13.33% visited CH more than two years ago. On the other hand, less than 7% had the opportunity to visit CH through tours organised in their schools. However, more than 76% indicated lack of opportunity to participate in tours, unaffordable visitor access fee and little/no knowledge about CH as reasons for not visiting CH. 66.67% of the teachers revealed that heritage education is not offered in their schools and 73.33% gained minimal knowledge about CH through their family transfer or reading of books related to CH. In Table 2, more students and teachers express a low level of knowledge CH. Also, HM2 responded that '...*less number of schools organise excursions to cultural heritage for their students, and even during the holiday period, few school-age children visit the cultural heritage'*. This serves as reasons for schools not organising tours. However, more teachers and students indicated strong interest to participate in heritage education and related activities. The heritage managers revealed that '*little efforts are made by governments to make cultural heritage attractive to visitors'* (HM3).

Digital Literacy. 92% of the student respondents and all the teachers revealed that they use mobile phones. But, more than 76.35% of the students use their phones frequently for calls, text and multimedia messages, social media, taking photos and videos, viewing movies and playing games. When compared with 52.68% of the teachers that only uses their phones frequently for calls and text messages. Also, more than 60% of the students gain access to a computer through *cybercafé* where users need to pay internet access fee. Also, less than 34% of the teachers have access to the internet through their phones or *cybercafé*. The HM1 stated that '*access to ICT technology in cultural heritage is considerably* low'. This was bolstered by HM3 that '*limited steps taking by heritage manager to integrate ICT are mainly done through the social media with few information about cultural heritage available on websites'*. Based on this, more students use the internet predominantly for social networking and games, while more teachers with the phone do not access the internet but for calls and messages.

Deductions. Organising tour is one of the ways of learning as information and knowledge inherent in cultural heritage and enhances connection and experiences of students with cultural heritage. Also, students are open to engaging with information through the internet, but the level of digital literacy is low amidst the teachers. Heritage education is also not included in the school curriculum, and heritage educators are inadequate in schools. However, many schools are lacking adequate ICT technologies that can improve the teaching methods used in the schools.

3.4 Project Concept and Framework

eDIRICA, a web application, developed to serve as e-learning platform for heritage education to improve citizen engagement and participation in the management of cultural heritage in Nigeria which is vital to the current approach to heritage management in Nigeria. Government institutions at both federal and state levels are the main actors with conflicting interests. At the federal level, the National Commission for Museums and Monuments (NCMM) coordinates heritage with linkages with Heritage management boards in each of the 36 states. However, there is little or no participation of people in the management of heritage in Nigeria. Also, there is low exploitation of the potentials and benefits of digital applications to promote heritage and integrate the people as the core of the management approach of cultural heritage. Therefore, eDIRICA aims to bridge this gap by providing heritage e-learning platform for people especially the younger generation.

The concept of eDIRICA as shown in Fig. 1 combines education, inclusion and creativity. Education involves gathering historical information about tangible (sites, buildings, artefacts) and intangible (knowledge, symbols, values and meanings) heritage in Nigeria into interactive learning modules and self-assessments. The modules will be delivered through learning games, visual and audio representations. The use of learning games is supported by Anderson et al. [16] that serious gaming is an ideal medium not only for education but also for entertainment especially for younger generation while visual and audio representations provide immersive experiences and improved understanding to students.

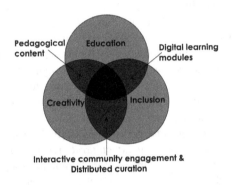

Fig. 1. Concept of eDIRICA

According to Jeannotte [17], cultural heritage is a vital social capital needed for development of civic participation for sustainable communities. Also, Cameron and Kenderdine [18] revealed that cultural heritage defines the identities of individuals and groups and provides shared language through which members of the society communicate. However, Ardissono et al. [19], linked 'inclusion and participation' and 'innovation and creativity' in their study of personalisation in cultural heritage. They noted that cultural heritage presents huge amount of information and knowledge, which needs to be filtered and personalised through inclusion and participation of individuals. In other words, heritage education offers means of improving social inclusion, participation, innovation and creativity through the strengthening of social bonds, integration and solidarity within the society [20].

3.5   Project Features

Blended Learning. In many countries, heritage studies take different forms. For instance, countries such as Turkey delivers heritage studies through formal and informal means to improve the connection of local communities to heritage. Also, in Spain, heritage studies are embedded into history and geography in both elementary and middle schools. However, Australia employs blended learning styles where people have extensive access to heritage information through the traditional face-to-face and digital platforms. Ocal [6] noted that information about cultural heritage is collected and archived electronically in developed countries. When compared to developing countries, heritage education is rather absent at both elementary and secondary levels.

The reasons are: (1) shortages of teachers trained in heritage education, (2) fast-growing demand for education, and (3) inadequate technological development. In Nigeria, for instance, heritage information are stored in printed forms in libraries, physical forms (artefacts, buildings, and sites) in museums and heritage sites. This constitutes a great limitation to peoples' access to heritage information. But, Andersson and Gronlund [9] point out that the implementation of e-learning strategies in developing countries helped to improve access to education. Therefore, eDIRICA serves as an e-learning platform to deliver heritage education to students, especially at primary and secondary levels (see Fig. 2). ICT offers effective ways to access information and knowledge inherent in cultural heritage in Nigeria. Information about cultural heritage in Nigeria will be collected from National Commission for Museums and Monuments (NCMM), Libraries, and community leaders to be developed into thematic modules and delivered on term-based learning system to schools in Nigeria.

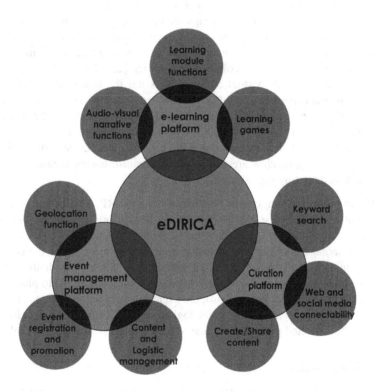

Fig. 2. Features of eDIRICA

Community-Based Distributed Curation. With the explosive growth of digital tools and contents for cultural heritage, there is increasing use of distributed curation (DC) to involve professionals and non-professions in the generation of heritage contents. DC is a participatory process of content generation that involves people (local and non-local), historical properties (artefacts, buildings, and sites), and ICT [21, 22]. For instance, the social media such as Facebook, Twitter, and Instagram used in India, Australia, United Kingdom and France to generate historical contents and promote social actions on heritage. In other words, social media has dramatically influenced people's understanding and interaction with heritage but with challenges of bias and misrepresentation of information [23]. Provision of conflicting historical information is another challenge to DC due to the involvement of amateur participants [24]. Therefore, in other to develop contents for heritage studies, eDIRICA employs community-based distributed curation where informed community members (such as community leaders, chiefs, elders etc.) and professionals will generate contents (in audio and visual forms) and developed into learning modules (see Fig. 2). This approach helps to eradicate inconsistent historical information and preserve original information. Users will be able to share the contents on social media and other platforms.

Interactive Community Engagement. The increasing recognition of the roles of ICT gave prominence to virtual communities in the management of heritage. The virtual community is 'computer-mediated groups sharing common identities and interests' [25]. Based on this, engagements are developed with social software and applications for computer-mediated collaboration to organise events and activities including historical discussions, games, and collaborative stories [25, 26]. However, Greer [27] noted that the focus of the virtual community is not the integration of ICT but for members to interact, participate and engage in activities and events that lead to the empowerment of the community. Given this, eDIRICA considered the dynamics of Nigeria societies with nascent digital literacy to develop community engagement strategies using the digital technology with broader acceptance amidst Nigerians. Community-based approaches are employed to organise events focusing on cultural heritage and mediated by digital tools.

Event Planning and Management Platform. Also, eDIRICA will serve as a platform for planning and organising events and activities focusing on cultural heritage. As supported by Jeannotte [17], strategic planning and organisation of activities and events focusing on heritage contribute to inclusion and sustainability within the community. The planning tools will have distributed functions to allow individuals and groups (such as schools, governmental and non-governmental organisations) to plan, organise, and publicise events and activities. Also, the event platform will include ticketing tools, online and SMS registrations, and event logistics tools. SMS registration is included because of the expected difficulties in access to the internet in some parts of Nigeria.

3.6 Delivery Strategy

At the initial deployment state, eDIRICA will collaborate with relevant local, international, governmental and non-governmental organisations to reach out to selected pilot schools on the UNESCO Associated Schools Networks in Lagos, Nigeria. The objectives for this stage are:

1. to create the essential tools and contents of the e-learning platform
2. to develop a learning framework and modules

3. to explore the impacts of heritage education and community-based distributed curation on people's participation in cultural heritage
4. to collect feedback from users for further updates and improvements to the web platform.

4 Conclusion

The roles of cultural heritage are unlimited; influences social processes and discourses within communities beyond the sites and artefacts but are regarded as identity and discourse of the legacies of the past generations in the present. Therefore, through eDIRICA, present generation would engage and interpret heritage in the context of the developments of the modern days. Also, associations with and management of heritage is made open for the involvement of people with little or non-expertise knowledge about heritage. The e-learning platform supports younger generation, viewed as detached from their heritage, are involved as the focus of the web applications. Individuals regardless of the level of digital literacy will be able to participate actively in activities and events organised to promote heritage within and outside their local communities.

References

1. Ovidia, S.-M.: Heritage conservation in secondary education curriculum a didactic proposal based on the application of ICT. Procedia - Soc. Behav. Sci. **51**, 782–786 (2012). https://doi.org/10.1016/j.sbspro.2012.08.240
2. Yastikli, N.: Documentation of cultural heritage using digital photogrammetry and laser scanning. J. Cult. Herit. **8**, 423–427 (2007). https://doi.org/10.1016/j.culher.2007.06.003
3. Eisazadeh, N., Houbart, C., Hallot, P., Heylighen, A.: The Potential of Digital Tools and Technologies in Architectural Heritage Research for an Inclusive Approach to Built Heritage (2017)
4. Soto-Martín, O., Lodeiro-Santiago, M.: Apps in the practice and teaching of conservation and restoration of cultural heritage. Procedia Comput. Sci. **75**, 381–389 (2015). https://doi.org/10.1016/j.procs.2015.12.261
5. Kabassi, K.: Evaluating websites of museums: state of the art. J. Cult. Herit. **24**, 184–196 (2017). https://doi.org/10.1016/j.culher.2016.10.016
6. Ocal, T.: Necessity of cultural historical heritage education in social studies teaching. Creat. Educ. **7**, 396 (2016). https://doi.org/10.4236/ce.2016.73039
7. Mendoza, R., Baldiris, S., Fabregat, R.: Framework to heritage education using emerging technologies. Procedia Comput. Sci. **75**, 239–249 (2015). https://doi.org/10.1016/j.procs.2015.12.244
8. Ott, M., Pozzi, F.: Towards a new era for cultural heritage education: discussing the role of ICT. Comput. Hum. Behav. **27**, 1365–1371 (2011). https://doi.org/10.1016/j.chb.2010.07.031
9. Andersson, A., Grönlund, Å.: A conceptual framework for E-learning in developing countries: a critical review of research challenges. Electron. J. Inf. Syst. Dev. Ctries. **38**, 1–16 (2009). https://doi.org/10.1002/j.1681-4835.2009.tb00271.x

10. Sobaih, A.E.E., Moustafa, M.A., Ghandforoush, P., Khan, M.: To use or not to use? Social media in higher education in developing countries. Comput. Hum. Behav. **58**, 296–305 (2016). https://doi.org/10.1016/j.chb.2016.01.002

11. Council of Europe: Council of Europe Framework Convention on the Value of Cultural Heritage for Society. Council of Europe Treaty Series, vol. 199 (2005, Council of Europe)

12. Lim, V., Frangakis, N., Tanco, L.M., Picinali, L.: PLUGGY: a pluggable social platform for cultural heritage awareness and participation. In: Ioannides, M., Martins, J., Žarnić, R., Lim, V. (eds.) Advances in Digital Cultural Heritage. LNCS, vol. 10754, pp. 117–129. Springer, Cham (2018). https://doi.org/10.1007/978-3-319-75789-6_9

13. Bloom, D.E., Mckinnon, R.: Program on the G lobal change, pp. 1–21 (2010)

14. Melorose, J., Perroy, R., Careas, S.: World population prospects. United Nations **1**, 587–592 (2015). https://doi.org/10.1017/CBO9781107415324.004

15. UNDESA Population Division: Population 2030: Demographic challenges and opportunities for sustainable development planning. United Nations 58 (2015)

16. Anderson, E.F., et al.: Developing serious games for cultural heritage: a state-of-the-art review. Virtual Real. **14**, 255–275 (2010). https://doi.org/10.1007/s10055-010-0177-3

17. Jeannotte, M.S.: Singing alone? The contribution of cultural capital to social cohesion and sustainable communities. Int. J. Cult. Policy **9**, 35–49 (2003). https://doi.org/10.1080/1028663032000089507

18. Cameron, F., Kenderdine, S.: Theorizing Digital Cultural Heritage: A Critical Discourse. MIT Press, Cambridge (2007)

19. Ardissono, L., Kuflik, T., Petrelli, D.: Personalization in cultural heritage: the road travelled and the one ahead. User Model. User-Adapt. Interact. **22**, 73–99 (2012). https://doi.org/10.1007/s11257-011-9104-x

20. Aldous, J., Hill, R.: Social cohesion, lineage type, and intergenerational transmission. Soc. Forces **43**, 471–482 (1965)

21. Liu, S.B.: Grassroots heritage: a multi-method investigation of how social media sustain the living heritage of historic crises. ProQuest Dissertations and Theses **723**, n/a (2011)

22. Abbassi, Z., Hegde, N., Massoulié, L.: Distributed content curation on the web. ACM Trans. Internet Technol. **14**, 1–15 (2014). https://doi.org/10.1145/2663489

23. Minelli, S.H., et al.: MOVIO: a toolkit for creating curated digital exhibitions. Procedia Comput. Sci. **38**, 28–33 (2014). https://doi.org/10.1016/j.procs.2014.10.006

24. Oomen, J., Aroyo, L.: Crowdsourcing in the cultural heritage domain. In: Proceedings of the 5th International Conference on Communities and Technologies - C&T 2011, p. 138 (2011). https://doi.org/10.1145/2103354.2103373

25. Affleck, J., Kvan, T.: A virtual community as the context for discursive interpretation: a role in cultural heritage engagement. Int. J. Herit. Stud. **14**, 268–280 (2008). https://doi.org/10.1080/13527250801953751

26. Giaccardi, E., Palen, L.: The social production of heritage through cross-media interaction: making place for place-making. Int. J. Herit. Stud. **14**, 281–297 (2008). https://doi.org/10.1080/13527250801953827

27. Greer, S.: Heritage and empowerment: community-based Indigenous cultural heritage in northern Australia. Int. J. Herit. Stud. **16**, 45–58 (2010). https://doi.org/10.1080/13527250903441754

THREADS: A Digital Storytelling Multi-stage Installation on Industrial Heritage

Eriana Panopoulou[(✉)] ⓘ, Konstantinos Kouros,
Aikaterini Pasopoulou, Giorgos Arsenikos, Spyros Vosinakis,
Panayiotis Koutsabasis, Modestos Stavrakis, and Damianos Gavalas

Department of Product and Systems Design Engineering,
University of the Aegean, 84100 Syros, Greece
{eriana.pan, k.kouros, a.pasopoulou,
g.arsenikos, spyrosv}@syros.aegean.gr,
{kgp, modestos, dgavalas}@aegean.gr

Abstract. Storytelling enables us to connect through narratives that create reflections on our experiences. When storytelling concerns cultural heritage, it brings forth tangible and intangible assets that characterize activities and events of the past, which may sensitize visitors of a cultural site. In this paper, we present our cultural storytelling project THREADS, a four-station installation that narrates a story of a worker in a textile factory. The system comprises: (a) a welcome station (an animation on public display) that explains the main story and challenges to visitors, (b) the fabric design station (multi-touch display) where the visitor can create a simple fabric for production, (c) the punched cards station (Arduino mechanism), where the visitor codes their initials to binary form and receives a punched card, (d) the Jacquard production station (gesture-based interface with Leap Motion and Unity), where the visitor uses the card to repair a mechanical loom. THREADS has been installed in an abandoned building of a textile industry, which operated between 1914–1986, and it is now renewed and open to visitors. A preliminary empirical evaluation of THREADS revealed that it is not the variety of technologies that engages users, but a storyline flow that retains their attention and interest.

Keywords: Digital storytelling · Heritage tourism · Industrial heritage
Digital cultural heritage · Textile

1 Introduction

Storytelling has been associated with cultural heritage since the beginning of time, from folklore narration to carrying on a society's cultural identity. Tales of parents, grandparents, and historians about who they/we were, what they did, and how they did it bear the identity of the referred social group. This identity, along with historical artifacts, shapes our own dynamic set of ideas, principals, and beliefs (a culture), and links us to a legacy. To preserve and effectively embrace and pass on cultural heritage, storytellers need inspiring means to capture their listeners' attention and empower their retention. To trigger emotions and experiences, people should be exposed in a rich environment

© Springer Nature Switzerland AG 2018
M. Ioannides et al. (Eds.): EuroMed 2018, LNCS 11196, pp. 457–469, 2018.
https://doi.org/10.1007/978-3-030-01762-0_40

according to the desired context and be allowed to step away from everyday reality [2, 12]. The narration of a story, especially of past events, can be more memorable to the listener if it occurs in a relevant environment with visual impressions [6]. The enriched environment, when complemented by digital media, is able to better communicate cultural heritage related content, providing a more holistic approach [14].

In this paper we present THREADS[1], a multi-stage installation for digital story-telling about industrial heritage, which has been installed in a renewed as a cultural space, previously abandoned textile industry building[2]. The aim has been to assist the soon-to-be-opened venue which will hold a permanent exhibition of textile machinery, products, and employment artifacts, and will promote heritage tourism. Our main design focus has been to raise cultural heritage awareness about the textile firm's past significance.

THREADS utilizes basic storytelling techniques to inform and sensitize visitors regarding the cultural heritage of the textile firm. It takes the visitor on a brief journey on site and narrates basic textile principles, technologies and fabrication processes. The four-station system is installed across from the physical artifacts, allowing a mental connection with the digital plot points and challenges. The storyline starts with the visitor entering the (virtual) factory (station 1) and being welcomed as a candidate worker. The challenge is to go through the production steps (next 3 stations) for the employer to see which is the most appropriate for them to get hired for. The stations challenge the design, coding and repairing abilities of the user, referencing a fabric's design process (station 2), it's break down to binary code (station 3), and the repairing of a weaving machine (Jacquard Loom [13]) (station 4). Through role assignment, visitors are encouraged to learn key historical facts in an engaging manner, making it possible to emotionally connect with the textile factory's behold cultural heritage.

2 Related Work

2.1 Related Interactive Systems

A number of systems utilize multitouch technology to let visitors learn through interacting with the digital content. For instance, the Walls of Nicosia interactive application allows the user to have a virtual tour through the fortifications of Nicosia throughout the centuries [10]. The target audience (children) come across a virtual world application running on a multi-touch table. Such interaction is highly effective for learning performance, combining education and entertainment (edutainment).

An experiential approach is having users take up an active role in the story and participate using natural interactions. Such is the Cycladic sculpture application [18] where users become sculptors and progressively create a statue using the appropriate tools. The application is based on bare hand interactions supported by Leap Motion. Users found the experience positive and engaging, with no significant differences in

---

[1] THREADS Promo video.

[2] Zissimatos Textile Firm of Hermoupolis, Syros island, Greece.

performance between adults and children [9]. This encourages the use of the Leap motion controller for public gesture-based interactions.

Also, the recent hybrid approach trend combines virtual and physical interactive means, offering a mixed reality environment. The Loom [3] project is such an example, comprising a simplified small-scale loom model and a multi-touch screen for digital content and feedback, installed at an industrial museum. Museum visitors can experiment, play and gain awareness about the weaving process by interacting with the loom model whilst observing their "product" on screen. Additionally, a multimedia interface presents information about the loom exhibits of the museum and the textile industry.

Prototyping platforms of other interactive systems were met in the Museomix hackathon, the Holoint installation, and an AR physics puzzle. Museomix aims to create digital artefacts for museums for a personalized the visit [15]. Holoint is a gesture-based VR environment designed for a museum setting [4]. It offers users advanced and engaging interactive opportunities while navigating through ancient Rome (using Leap motion). The AR physics puzzle simulates Newtonian physics according to the placement of physical markers, in a game context [1]. Each marker represents a visual virtual 3D piece of stationary. The user manipulates virtual objects to witness their Newtonian behavior.

The aforementioned technologies served as bases for either the technological or design means that we used in THREADS. Alike technologies and types of interaction, such as the Leap motion sensor, VR environment, the mixed reality and role assignment have been incorporated in our project to attain similar results and experiences. More specifically, we borrow the role assignment from the Cycladic sculpture app, the edutainment and mixed reality approaches from the Walls of Nicosia and Loom projects respectively, the VR and Leap motion elements from the Museomix, Holoint, and AR puzzle systems.

2.2 Overview of Two Approaches for Storytelling

A fundamental formula for story structure has been proposed as "A Hero's Journey" (Archplot or Monomyth) by Campbell [2]. The pattern is spotted in myths across cultures and follows twelve steps to complete the storyline [2, 17], regarding the hero:

0. Status quo: Resting in their home culture.
1. Calling to adventure: An outside figure calls the hero into action.
2. Supernatural aid: Is given tools to help him in his quest.
3. Crossing the Threshold: Embarks on a journey to the unknown.
4. Trials: Is tested in his new surroundings and passes trials to continue.
5. Approach: New mentors and companions help the hero.
6. Ordeal: Experiencing a near death adventure, plunging down into an abyss.
7. Reward: Surviving the darkest moment and getting knowledge/treasure/power.
8. Magic flight: The hero flees from the enemy.
9. Return: Returning to the real world.
10. Resurrection: Arising transformed to the real world.
11. Resolution: Facing the final quest and using all the "rewards" gained to succeed.
12. New Status quo: The hero now rests in a new (self) culture.

To examine a modern perspective of storytelling, we analyzed the branding and marketing implementation of [2] by Sachs [16]. Sachs' contrasts the passive story encountering of people due to broadcast media of the past century, with the active story sharing through social media. In this post-broadcast era, as referred to, people have more control over what ideas they encounter and communicate, hence experiencing a digitally empowered version of oral storytelling. The classic story elements of [2] are defined as symbols for morals illustrated as values of the brand. The hero is the target audience, whereas the brand embodies the mentor or caller figure. Ultimately, storytelling is used in this manner to connect audiences with deeper values (Fig. 1).

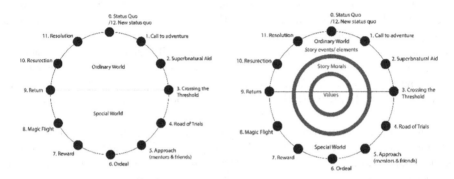

Fig. 1. (Left) Classic model of storytelling (Campbell). (Right) Modern approach for storytelling in branding and marketing (Sachs).

The preceding systems tested technological capabilities, whereas our development level is preliminary and serves the purposes of the creative and cognitive aspects. We found our design for storytelling approach on well-established theories, easily grasped by non-storytellers. Creativity is difficult to mold, yet we attempt to showcase how developers can structure their thinking process in order to bring technology and design in the same grid.

3   Digital Storytelling Approach

3.1   Storytelling Approach in THREADS

To relate the historical importance of the factory to people of the present, we needed to correlate key facts of the industry's historical status and events with current standards. We framed the necessary information on a story path to help visitors understand, recall and better relate to the context. The story form is based on a universal pattern of a protagonist-focused tale (Campbell's model) and on Sachs's framework on storytelling in the post-broadcast digital era. By combining Campbell's classic model with Sachs's framework, we came up with our basic storytelling approach for creating short story-based interactive systems.

To help visitors engage and immerse in the story, the narrative revolves around meaningful content, or else the principal tangible or intangible assets of the cultural site. By combining the classic and modern approaches, along with the idea of real world metaphors, we adopted a simplified approach for creating interactive systems based on storytelling. According to resources and knowhow, design ideas can be prototyped using appropriate technology by addressing key questions about story-telling, cultural content and design elements. The **key storytelling questions** include:

1. Who is the hero?
2. Who is the caller?
3. What is the core value you want to communicate?
4. What are the main artifacts/key touch points?
5. What is the (main) challenge?
6. What is the level of emotional involvement you want for your users?

The **cultural content** includes the main artifacts on site, various visual elements, testimonials, observations of people and the 'character'/mood/essence of the site. The cultural content is identified through contextual research including field visits, obser-vation and interviews. The selection, documentation and curation of cultural content results to the **design elements**. These may be physical or digital and they are about the selected items that are going to appear in the designed system(s). These may include: human figures or characters, physical and digital objects, tools (including interactions and manipulations), scenery, sounds, etc (Table 1).

Table 1. Storytelling approach in THREADS.

Question	Cultural content	Design elements	Notes
Who is the hero?	*Venue visitors*	*On-site user*	*Any visitor*
Who is the caller?	*Factory owner*	*Virtual character*	*Avatar and animation*
What is the core value you want to communicate?	*Industrial heritage*	*Identity of place and people*	*About factory and industry*
What are the main artefacts/key touch points?	*Textiles (fabrics, towels), looms, threads, shuttles, working stations, ...*	*Character of factory owner, punched cards, towels and initials, Jacquard loom and gesture manipulations*	*It is prohibited to touch artifacts; the exhibition area is separated from visitor pathway*
What is the (main) challenge?	*Learn about factory's history and works*	*Three interaction stations (design, code, repair)*	–
What is the level of emotional involvement?	*Medium*	*Intriguing, fun, interesting, learning*	*Beware of nostalgia effect*

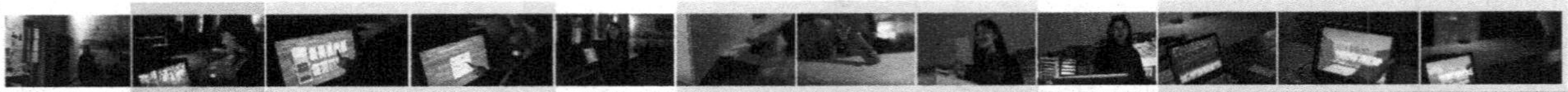

JOURNEY											
USER	User approaches the installation / touches the screen to start	User is been assigned the Role of a potential employee /is challenged to perform following tasks	User moves to next screen/ chooses background color and pattern for his towel design	User chooses his initials to sign the towel	User moves to next station	User inserts blank card into the punching box	User presses button to start punching mechanism/ waits for green light to turn ON (end of punching)	User takes punched card	User moves to next station	User watches "How the Jacquard loom works" video/is instructed how to fix it	User passes shaft through loom (fixesloom)	User is hirred by the employer
SYSTEM	System turns on	System plays introduction video	System hosts Windows App in multi-touch display				System turns on Arduino mechanism /Green ligh lights up when punching mechanism is finnished			System plays Jacquard video foutage/ and interaction tutorial	System uses Unity and Leap motion for game control	System plays hirring video
PRODUCTION PHASES		Welcome phase/ role assignment	Order Phase	Order Phase		Order Phase	Order Phase	Order Phase		Weaving Phase	Weaving Phase	Hirring Phase
HIGHLIGHTS	The system is alined across from the real coresponding artifacts	Animation character as the factory owner /employer	Personalization features	Personalization features				Punched pattern is the initials' form in Binary (0 1) (user initials from previous station)		Emphasis on one artifact		Achivment

Fig. 2. Swim lanes illustrating the visitor journey.

On applying these principals, we recorded content and design elements for THREADS. Our story's "hero" is the venue's on-site visitor regardless of age, and the core value in discussion is industrial heritage found in the venue's and peoples' identity. The main artefacts include weaving tools, machinery, and people presence evidence. The greater challenge is to learn about the factory's history and function. Finally, the emotional involvement affects immersion, visitor experience and learning process, thus we wanted to keep it at a medium level, avoiding nostalgic references [5].

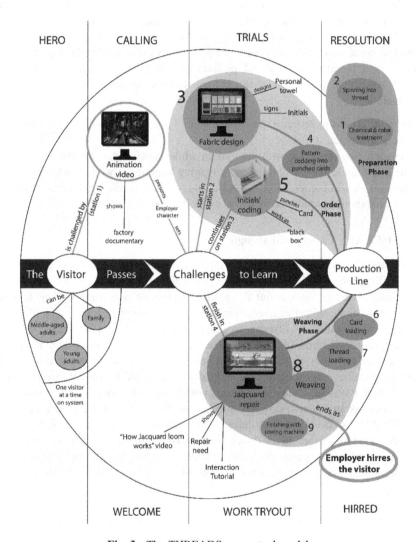

Fig. 3. The THREADS conceptual model.

4 Concept Design

4.1 Pre-design, Research Methods

We employed several research methods to gather sufficient context insight including, desktop research, literature review, field visits, observation, interviews and contextual inquiry [7]. These pre-design, research methods provided us with insights on the history, function and socioeconomic importance of the factory, and helped us distinguish key points of interest of the factory's past function. Since the physical artefacts are not always approachable by the visitors, we opted to place digital artefacts in parallel to the real ones. Stepping into the visitors' shoes, we observed the venue and traced the usual routes one may take through the exhibition. The findings have been analyzed and recorded as a set of preliminary design goals regarding the nature, context, layout and placement of the system. Related to the overall user experience these include:

1. The user should experience the significance of the factory for the local community during its operation.
2. The user should interact with the system while viewing the exhibits.
3. The user should have a playful and engaging experience while learning.
4. The user should comprehend the basic stages of the textile production process.
5. The user should participate in the story as it unravels.

4.2 THREADS Conceptual Design

The THREADS system represents a simplified simulation of the textile production process. When using the THREADS installation, the visitor of the factory needs to pass several challenges to learn about the textile production line (Fig. 3). The first welcoming stage along with three remaining challenges comprise four stages of interaction, each representing a different working station: (1) role assignment, (2) fabric design, (3) punched cards, (4) Jacquard loom repair. The user goes through the process and learns at each station the corresponding action that would occur (Fig. 2). The information is conveyed through varying media and gestural interactions [6] to keep the user engaged. Physically, the user interacts with three touch screens and a wooden box (which contains an Arduino-powered mechanism for creating the punched card).

THREADS is standalone installation located at the main area of the factory and is independent to the other audiovisual or assistive museum devices visitors' might potentially carry. The system does not interfere with the guided tours' content and it encourages visual contact with the actual physical artefact (exhibits) of the factory.

5   System Prototyping

The **first station (Welcome and Role Assignment)** works as an introduction to the forthcoming process (Fig. 4). An animated host character welcomes the user in the factory and narrates a brief history of the textile industry in Syros and its social impact. The host assigns the role of a potential worker in tryout for a job position to the user. As such, the user is required to pass through all the working stations. The character explains the required interaction in the following steps of the process. The first station operates in a 23" inch touch monitor. A live action video introduces the visitor to historical facts about Industrial Syros, and the context of the system, and the host character performs over the video footage, narrating the story to the user. Animation has been used as a narration means since it facilitates learning and helps the user immerse into the presented fictional world [11, 12].

Fig. 4. Animation screenshot.

In the **second station (fabric design)** the visitor is asked to design a towel fabric. By choosing a background color and a design pattern, he generates a virtual prototype of a towel, and then is invited to sign it with his initials. Finally, he is instructed how to use the next station. The App (Fig. 5) is designed as a Windows Application and runs on Universal Windows Platform, in a 23" inch touch monitor. There are 5 UI scenes in total:

SCENE 1: "Welcome" screen, featuring the brand Logo and the "Start" button.

SCENE 2: Fabric design - color and pattern selection.

SCENE 3: Name initial and font selection.

SCENE 4: Fabric preview.

SCENE 5: QR code corresponding to fabric design. Printing of QR code. The initials' information gets stored as a variable sequence (code following).

Fig. 5. The fabric design multi-touch app (second station). (Color figure online)

In the **third station (punched cards)** the user interacts physically with the system to make a punched card. The punching mechanism (Fig. 6) is hidden inside a wooden box, with an insertion slot in the front, a start button and a LED light on top. As instructed, the user takes a blank card from a stack in front of the box, inserts the card in the slot and presses the button. Once done, the LED lights up to indicate that the card is ready and can be removed. The user takes out the punched card and proceeds to the next station. In the card punching station an Arduino board controls two stepper motors, two solenoids, a pushbutton, and one LED light bulb.

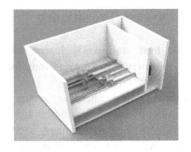

Fig. 6. 3D model of the card punching box.

In the **fourth station (Jacquard repair)** the user needs to repair the Jacquard loom. He is introduced to the basic concepts of the Jacquard loom and is instructed to repair it by repassing the shuttle through its track. Upon completion he is hired as a worker, marking the end of his journey. Animated footage explains the function of a typical Jacquard loom. The user is introduced to a Unity environment with a simplified, virtual loom model (Fig. 7), with an empty shuttle path. The user manipulates the shuttle (dragging along a path) via gestures (pinch) over LEAP motion. The fourth station operates in a 23″ inch touch monitor.

Fig. 7. The loom repair app (fourth station).

THREADS borrows from the Monomyth key plot points for the sake of story flow, immersion, and engagement, as well as Sachs' point of view on the target group embodying the "hero" and the system/brand/venue featured as the "caller". The system introduces the visitor and his role assignment by the animated character as a "hero" character called into adventure by an outside figure (Monomyth steps 0, 1). It features the factory setting and the production line work stations (fabric design, punched cards station, Jacquard repair) as the "new unknown world" and the road of trials (3, 4). Finally, it finishes with the visitor successfully going through the work stations, and being hired as a factory worker, as a correlation to the Reward, and Return (7, 9). Cognition and experience wise, the visitor has learned about the industrial heritage of the factory and gained a piece of its culture (Monomyth's Resurrection 10 and New Status quo 12).

6   Evaluation

We conducted formative evaluations [8] to test the usability of THREADS and gather data for future redesign. There were eleven participants in total, seven students, three academic staff members and the factory's owner. Users have been briefly introduced to the context of the system and then let alone to pursue the steps themselves. Members of the design group made clarifications, when needed. The users have been asked to think-aloud about their experience. At the end of the test, they have been requested to provide answers to a 6-item online questionnaire (Fig. 8). The evaluation has taken place at the university's computer lab. The station apps have been installed on different PCs to simulate the visitor's navigation along the stations.

Most users found the system engaging and relatively easy to use especially at the first two stations. Users reported some concerns regarding their interactions with the Arduino mechanism, which has been a black box to them. Future work in this respect will involve the placement of the mechanism into a plexiglass material. Additionally, some reported usability issues in gesture interaction via Leap motion. Most understood the historical facts (answers to questions 5 and 6). Overall, the users engaged successfully with the system and have had a satisfying experience. They have been able to learn and follow the storyline with no serious problems. Further prototyping and implementation work is expected to smoothen the problems of interacting with mid-air gestures.

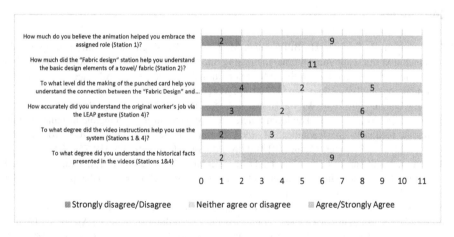

Fig. 8. Participant answers on questions about their experience in THREADS.

7   Conclusions and Future Work

This article introduced THREADS, a four-stage installation and interactive prototype for conveying the cultural heritage of a textile industry. The approach for the design of THREADS has been informed by several approaches on storytelling. The system comprises four stations of various interactive technologies: animated characters, live action footage and animation, multitouch screens, Arduino-powered mechanisms and gesture-based interactions. We investigated to what extent these different technologies could be effectively combined and keep the user interested as the story unfolded. Further work is underway to improve functionality and usability. Passive information passing needs to be simplified and present only the essentials (station 1). Interaction phases need to provide better feedback (station 2), and transparency of events (station 3). Lastly, virtual objects and environment need characteristics of realism to assist the user during the interaction.

The design process is a creative one and can be limited by technological factors. However, by filtering out information and clarifying the essential pieces, it was easier for us to find connecting points, form an information flow and define a user journey. By prototyping and testing the system, we concluded that the variety of technologies and exciting features alone is not what engages the users. Humans retain their attention and interest by following a flow; a storyline. Therefore, despite the technological flaws encountered, users have been able to perceive the context and enjoy the storytelling experience.

Acknowledgements. We thank Dimitris Stavrakopoulos for providing access to the Zissimatos Textile factory and the hosting of on-site activities. We also thank Dr. Pavlos Chatzigrigoriou for providing information and answers regarding the industrial cultural heritage of Hermoupolis, Syros, Greece.

References

1. Buchanan, P., Seichter, H., Billinghurst, M., Grasset, R.: Augmented reality and rigid body simulation for edutainment: the interesting mechanism-an AR puzzle to teach Newton physics. In: Proceedings of the 2008 International Conference on Advances in Computer Entertainment Technology, pp. 17–20. ACM (2008)
2. Campbell, J.: The Hero With a Thousand Faces. Princeton University, Princeton (1949)
3. Dimitropoulos, A., et al.: The loom: interactive weaving through a tangible installation with digital feedback. In: Ioannides, M. (ed.) Digital Cultural Heritage. LNCS, vol. 10605, pp. 199–210. Springer, Cham (2018). https://doi.org/10.1007/978-3-319-75826-8_17
4. Fanini, B., d'Annibale, E., Demetrescu, E., Ferdani, D., Pagano, A.: Engaging and shared gesture-based interaction for museums the case study of K2R international expo in Rome. In: 2015 Digital Heritage, vol. 1, pp. 263–270. IEEE (2015)
5. Frow, J.: Tourism and the semiotics of nostalgia. October **57**, 123–151 (1991)
6. Heiden, W.: Edutainment aspects in hypermedia storytelling. In: Pan, Z., Aylett, R., Diener, H., Jin, X., Göbel, S., Li, L. (eds.) Edutainment 2006. LNCS, vol. 3942, pp. 389–398. Springer, Heidelberg (2006). https://doi.org/10.1007/11736639_50
7. Holtzblatt, K., Jones, S.: Contextual inquiry: a participatory technique for system design. In: Participatory Design: Principles and Practices, pp. 177–210 (1993)
8. Koutsabasis, P.: Human-Computer Interaction. Kleidarithmos (2011)
9. Koutsabasis, P., Vosinakis, S.: Adult and children user experience with leap motion in digital heritage: the cycladic sculpture application. In: Ioannides, M., et al. (eds.) EuroMed 2016. LNCS, vol. 10058, pp. 350–361. Springer, Cham (2016). https://doi.org/10.1007/978-3-319-48496-9_28

10. Michael, D., Zaharias, P., Chrysanthou, Y.: A virtual tour of the Walls of Nicosia: an assessment of children's experience and learning performance. In: VAST: International Symposium on Virtual Reality, Archaeology and Intelligent Cultural Heritage, pp. 9–15 (2010)
11. Morrison, J.B., Tversky, B., Betrancourt, M.: Animation: does it facilitate learning. In: AAAI Spring Symposium on Smart Graphics, vol. 5359 (2000)
12. Mossberg, L.: Extraordinary experiences through storytelling. Scand. J. Hosp. Tour. **8**(3), 195–210 (2008)
13. Posselt, E.A.: The Jacquard Machine Analyzed and Explained. StreetLib (2017)
14. Reunanen, M., Díaz, L., Horttana, T.: A holistic user-centered approach to immersive digital cultural heritage installations: case vrouw maria. J. Comput. Cult. Herit. (JOCCH) **7**(4), 24 (2015)
15. Rey, S.: Museomix: lessons learned from an open creative hackathon in museums. In: European Tangible Interaction Studio (ETIS 2017), vol. 1861, p. 5, June 2017
16. Sachs, J.: Winning the Story Wars: Why Those Who Tell–and Live–the Best Stories Will Rule the Future. Harvard Business Press (2012)
17. Verigakis, N., Stavrakis, M., Darzentas, J.: Educational interactive storytelling for narrative comprehension and recall in dyslexic children: employing a mythic narrative structure. In: Workshop on Interactive Storytelling for Children in 9th International Conference on Interaction Design and Children, Barcelona, June 2010
18. Vosinakis, S., Koutsabasis, P., Makris, D., Sagia, E.: A kinesthetic approach to digital heritage using leap motion: the Cycladic sculpture application. In: 2016 8th International Conference on Games and Virtual Worlds for Serious Applications (VS-Games), pp. 1–8. IEEE (2016)

Documentation Strategy for Intangible Cultural Heritage (ICH) in Cultural Heritage Institutions: Mak Yong Performing Art Collection

Mazlina Pati Khan[1]([✉]) [iD], Andika Abdul Aziz[1,2],
and Khairul Azhar Mat Daud[2]

[1] Universiti Teknologi MARA, Shah Alam, Malaysia
mazlina8001@uitm.edu.my
[2] Universiti Malaysia Kelantan, Bachok, Malaysia

Abstract. United Nations Educational, Scientific, and Cultural Organization (UNESCO) has recognized Mak Yong's Theater Performing Art as a Masterpiece of Oral and Intangible Cultural Heritage (ICH) of Humanity by September 2005 (UNESCO, "Mak Yong Theater", https://ich.unesco.org/en/RL/mak-yong-theatre-00167, (September 28, 2016)). Unfortunately, Mak Yong was declared as an irrelevant form of performing art due to the prohibition in the year 1991 since the Islamic Party of Malaysia (PAS) that took control of the state. It is viewed as being non-compliant to Islamic teachings. Various efforts have been undertaken to protect cultural heritage by collecting and documenting especially in the manifestation of intangible cultural value in order to consolidate and nurture appreciation of the cultural heritage within society. Thus, this study explores the documentation strategy approach obtainable in cultural heritage institutions on preserving and safeguarding ICH collections. A novel qualitative methodological approach was used by employing a case study design; semi-structured interviews were conducted to examine the aperture on the implementation of documenting ICH collection in the National Archives, National Museum, and the National Library of Malaysia.

Keywords: ICH collection · Cultural heritage institution
Information heritage documentation · Records and archives management

1 Introduction

Malaysia is one of the countries that comprise of various cultural heritages where most of them are documented and embedded in several mediums such as artifacts, manuscripts, sculptures, traditional motifs and textile designs, gold craftsmanship and others. To consolidate and nurture appreciation of cultural heritage that is intact with a society, diverse efforts have been taken to protect it, by collecting and documenting cultural heritage is it with tangible or intangible cultural value. Part of these collections have been accumulated and stored in libraries, museums, archives, art galleries and cultural centers which require enormous responsibility in preserving and making them

M. Ioannides et al. (Eds.): EuroMed 2018, LNCS 11196, pp. 470–479, 2018.
https://doi.org/10.1007/978-3-030-01762-0_41

retrievable to the public. Apart from these collections there are also other types of ICH collections such as traditional songs and music, legends poetry and poem, treatment and traditional herbs, oral tradition collections and others which need to be inheritable from one generation to the next.

UNESCO's endeavor throughout the Convention for the 2003 Safeguarding of Intangible Cultural Heritage concerning ICH has seen an expansion due to the response of the vanishing of traditions as a result of disappointment in local cultural reproduction, preservation, and continuation in the globalization age. This has incited Malaysia to get a proclamation of intangible heritage on 25 November 2005, and thus UNESCO declared Mak Yong's Performing Art as the "Third Proclamation of Masterpiece of the Oral and Intangible Heritage of Humanity" in the world. This is an enormous recognition and a huge responsibility to the nation to conserve and preserve it as a world heritage and to make it accessible and profitable to the country.

1.1 Intangible Cultural Heritage (ICH) Documentation

Since the adoption of UNESCO 2003 declaration, safeguarding of intangible cultural heritage has become more efficient and vigorous. The role of local communities, supported by more local governments around the world, and participation of cultural heritage institutions are now actively contribute to safeguard, document and promote their local intangible culture for various purposes. Moreover, Arantes [1] adds that documentation and promotion, which have proven to be useful tools for safeguarding ICH, can also be interpreted as ways of staging or enacting heritage in the world media (photography, film, audiovisual recordings).

There are numerous ICH documentation projects that have been carried out by cultural heritage institution for variety of ICH elements for example a project led by the National Museum of Egyptian Civilisation in documenting Egyptian traditional culture [2]. This project, collaboration with Folk Creativity Centre (FCC), implemented an analysis of collection which includes five main topics, covering different aspects of Egyptian culture. Furthermore, a project of documenting and archiving musical traditions in Western India [3] where it embraces the community's involvement in strengthening audio visual recording collections in Langas Manganiars and Mandolin traditional music. Likewise, another project for documenting Mangyan heritage of Mindoro, Philippines was conducted by the heritage centre [4].

1.2 Documentation of Mak Yong Performing Art

Mak Yong is recognized as an ancient-theatre since the 18th century in Kelantan with forms and features of ritual, stylized acting and dance, vocal and instrumental music, song, creativeness of storyline and formal as well as spontaneous dialogue [5]. It was presented as a royal theatre under the direct benefaction of the Kelantan Sultanate until the 1920s [6]. However, at present Mak Yong has become an unpopular cultural performing art due to the prohibition by the Islamic Party of Malaysia (PAS) in year 1991 since the political party took control of the state due to being inconsistent to Islamic teachings [7]. This progressively dimmed this traditional performance since there are no more heirs who are experts in sustaining this heritage at not just national level but also international level.

Besides safeguarding ICH by performing it to the public such as by using intellectual writing and discussion in seminars and, educational programmes to youngsters, Mak Yong also needs to be documented as part of the heritage conservation for education support, research and access to the originalities of this performance art. According to Chaudhuri [3] various approaches can be applied in documenting ICH involving high technology audio and video recording, visual, movement, presentation and expression of audience in real time. In the meantime, this recording can be stored and preserved at the cultural heritage institution for future reference. However, to engage an authentic and reliable collection or recording of Mak Yong's performing arts or other ICH elements, good documentation strategies of ICH are required to ensure originality and trustworthiness of content and information of the resources. In year 1967, the first documentation of Mak Yong took place when Mubin Sheppard was the Museum Director at the time. He brought an Asian music specialist namely Professor William Malm from Michigan University of United Stated of America to compile, record and document about 11 Mak Yong's stories which consist of 90 h monochrome videotape that took 32 nights [10]. This recording collection was also made a copy to be kept in the national museum. Nonetheless, referring to Mubin Sheppard's letter that was found in the national archive shows that he requested the recording for a recopy because the original collection was involved in a fire disaster at national museum which almost destroyed all museum collection at the time [11]. Unfortunately, no response was received. To date researchers found that, there is no single recording that is fully documented on Mak Yong's performing art is being kept in any repositories in this country. This article will discuss the roles of cultural heritage institutions in documenting the heritage information management through strategies that can be done to achieve a successful documentation project for ICH collection.

1.3   Roles of Cultural Heritage Institution in Preserving ICH

In the case of roles in ICH documentation, periodic reports of States Parties submitted in 2016 reported the current status of the implementation of Convention for the Safeguarding of ICH. It described that various dedicated institutions took the responsibility in collecting and/or holding documentation resources such as museums, archives, libraries, national cultural studies, cultural institutions, galleries and others [12]. It is also reported that currently no comprehensive protocol is available for collection and procedure related to documentation in view of the number and variety of bodies involved in different countries. This report reveals that cultural heritage institutions configure their roles in sustaining the ICH in their country through the process of acquisition, classification, description, storage, preservation, reference services, and advocacy towards offering an enriched cultural heritage to the public. Nevertheless, these various approaches are taken without any overarching methodology in documenting their ICH collection appropriate to them.

In the standpoint of documentation science, it can be said that the relationship among archives, museums, and libraries are "interconnected". The collaboration of the documentation activities among these institutions will initiate responsiveness in sustaining the cultural heritage and enriching the ICH collection. Cox [13] describes this as a multi-institutional collaboration in establishing institutional archival programs rather than being especially dependent on collecting historical manuscripts, setting explicit goals for developing documentation, and merely achieving adequate documentation by analyzing existing records that are often fragmented.

2 Research Methodology

This study adopts a case study research which was to explore the roles of cultural heritage institution in safeguarding ICH collection through documentation strategy. For the purpose of the study data were collected from the three (3) main cultural institutions in Malaysia, namely the National Archives, the National Library, and the Department of National Museum. The method of data collection implemented was personal interview which was conducted through series of semi structured interviews with 13 respondents concerning the documentation and development of the ICH collection in the institutions. According to Jacob and Furgerson [14], interviewing people is the primary method to gather the various aspects of human experience. The research employed NVIVO11 to analyze the data from the respondent interview which contribute to the elements that are embedded in the documentation strategy model such analysis of collection, community involvement, collaboration among institution, response to the changes, strategic planning and creation of new collection.

3 Documentation Strategy for Mak Yong's Collection

Using the documentation strategy model that was applied by previous scholar and practitioner in this field, the researchers were able to identify the elements that were employed and could be supported in the heritage information documentation strategy. Furthermore, the researchers categorized each of these elements into equation groups and organized a checklist of frequency rate of elements according to scholar model. The table (Table 1) below illustrates work that was carried out;

Table 1. Documentation strategies model

Documentation strategy element	Scholar					
	Booms (1972)	F. Gerald Ham (1975)	Linda J. Henry (1980)	Helen W. Samuels (1986)	Hackman & Warnow-blewet (1987)	Richard J. Cox (2003)
(1) Analysis of collection	✓	✓	✓	✓	✓	✓
(2) Community involvement				✓	✓	✓
(3) Collaboration among Institutions		✓		✓	✓	
(4) Response to changes	✓			✓	✓	✓
(5) Strategic planning	✓					
(6) Creation of new collection			✓	✓		

The results from the interview sessions revealed that some of the undertaken documentation strategy elements were impractical such as strategic planning and creation of new collection. Most of the respondents reflected that these elements were impractical nowadays. This can be inferred from a feedback by a respondent (C7) *"... strategic planning nowadays commonly embedded in the process of annual collection analysis; it is because the user request of the heritage collection is too small and we can't see the significance to have different strategic planning for heritage collection"*. Secondly, most of the respondents also revealed that it was unfeasible for the creation of a new collection especially for the heritage documentation because it required complicated process with the highest commitment, as expressed by respondent (B12) who stated that *"not all cultural heritage agency will have an opportunity to create a new documentation for Mak Yong because Mak Yong itself is obsolete, it's hard to find people who really practices it authentically and most importantly not all cultural heritage agencies are capable to develop a new collection, what we can do is practising oral history of Mak Yong"*. It shows that these two (2) elements are unworkable because of the redundancy of work and lack of authentic sources in creating a new collection.

Therefore, this study excluded these two elements and focused on other elements which currently are being carried out for the collection development in cultural heritage institutions. Besides that, the results of the interviews also ascertained two additional elements proposed by most respondents in improving the quality of documenting heritage information in this country. The new elements that are practiced by agencies and proposed by the respondents are Information Heritage Advocacy and National Heritage Centre for managing all of ICH collection.

3.1 Analysis of Collection

The primary context involved in the implementation of documentation strategies for ICH collection consists of the analysis of the collection presented in the repository which also contributes to an acquisition procedure or collection development process that are practiced in these institutions. This process is important in order to examine the current collection reserved in the respective repositories. Besides that, the analysis of the collection should be employed to ensure that every component of Mak Yong is documented efficiently for future generation's reference. Findings from the interviews with the information professionals involved in conducting the acquisition process and the collection development found that a few methods exist in the process of analyzing the Mak Yong collection.

Firstly, special collection research is crucial in ensuring that the process of analysis will be put into action effectively, efficiently and economically. The top management plays important roles in coordinating the work for this purpose. As stated by Newman and Huvila [15, 16] agree that good planning in coordinating a collection analysis can reduce the redundancy of collection and is indicative of the repository and drivers of change in documenting information heritage. As stated by respondent B2, he said that *"... do a deep research on Mak Yong collection and identify the lack of information and write a proposal then it is up to the upper management to decide"*. The research should be put into practice annually for different ICH elements; circuitously all types of

ICH will be documented whether or not they are enclosed with international or national pronouncement.

Besides that, analysis of collection should be equipped with a committee that includes experts and assistants from heritage fields in conducting the process of analysis. The committee should be responsible to conduct a collection survey for the purpose of investigating the gap of heritage information. This action can be done by listing all the collections related to the elements of Mak Yong which can be categorized into a theme such as song and music, stories, presentations, character, spectacle, author or creator, date of deposit and others. From the gaps, the committee would be able to recognize the prospective depositor for collection development purposes, build a relationship with them and provide consultancy in terms of substance in preserving the cultural heritage information for the nation. Moreover, this progression can encourage cultural heritage institutions to conduct an acquisition for the lack of information in Mak Yong elements.

3.2 Community Involvement

The study discovered a few approaches available in gaining community involvement such as actively developing networking with the elite within Mak Yong community for example connoisseurs, high profile figures, public agencies and with in non-elite members of the community such Mak Yong groups performer, culture artist, practitioners and persons. They are enthusiasts of Mak Yong who are involved into transferring knowledge and personal collection and building relationship with community involvement for the purpose of executing its heritage research and documentation. The significance of community involvement in the documentation strategy is vital in encouraging contemporary linkages to one's distinctive cultural past [17].

Contribution of expertise known as knowledge expert that treated as an asset of the relevant Mak Yong community which can be transferred to a cultural heritage institution and developed further [18]. Almost all of respondents agreed that expert involvement is a major channel in documenting vital information about Mak Yong as mentioned by one of respondents that *"they are resources person, meaning that the information from them is most crucial and authentic sources that we should documented"*. This contribution can be made through knowledge transfer such as writing, publication, oral history and knowledge sharing. Furthermore, a good relationship with the expertise is capable of providing a lustrous cultural heritage collection's to the public reference as well as highlighting the significance of this heritage toward national development through the documentation.

In addition, indigenous communities or practitioners who are still enthusiastic about Mak Yong should also take part in this approach. Cultural heritage institutions should play an important role as the medium the between government and these groups in order to contribute to the continuation of their legacy in making Mak Yong as a national and world heritage. Financial initiatives and support from the government and NGO's are able to support the Mak Yong performance and directly nurture the creation of new collection and present prolongation ICH information documentation.

3.3 Collaboration Among Institutions

Collaboration among cultural heritage institutions is actively put into practice given the same circle of directive because they are in the same ministry and given the same mandate which responsible to preserving and disseminating right information to the right people in the right format. The collaborations consist of collection and information resources exchange among agencies, reference services and research consultation regarding the subject matter related to the information held in the cultural heritage. These collaborations are commonly practiced by each cultural heritage institution for cultural heritage collection or other types of collections [19]. Nonetheless for Mak Yong collection has an inactive collaboration between other agencies due to the lack of information resources in the cultural heritage institution itself. According to the respondents, this situation is commonly caused by the feeble management of the authorities and lack of enforcement by the Malaysia National Heritage Act 2005 (Act 645) toward the heritage information management.

Meanwhile, information professional collaboration is a crucial element in formulating a successful documentation strategy because it is a motivation to the systematic and centralized approach in documenting heritage information management. In addition to this, sharing skills among the staff of a cultural heritage institution can offer a better benefit to the government in sustaining the heritage information; it can enrich the agencies with knowledge worker and professional worker in the future. Staff can share their technical skills such as conservators from a museum, library or archives, audio-visual technician staff from archives to other agencies related to the production documentary. This collaboration is also known as the National Blue Ocean Strategy (NBOS) where agencies can exchange their expertise with the staff.

3.4 Response to Changes

Due to the rapid changes in technology, the organizations must narrowly scrutinize the greatest approach of preserving the digital collection so that they will be sustainable even if the technology changes. With regards to the response to changes, all cultural heritage institutions in this country are aware of the need to revolutionize information and collection [20]. Thus, archives and libraries have employed a digitization program for the collection including ICH collection. Specially, the museum is attentive to the development of collection synchronized with the expansion of information communication technology and user information needs.

Based on the findings, it was revealed that two main changes needed to be considered in order to make sure the Mak Yong collection is able to be retained permanently in the nation. Firstly, institutions must respond to current information changes in Mak Yong itself that contribute to the extinction of performance and practitioners. These institutions should engage in the recreation for documenting the originality and authenticity of information resources. The changes in terms of performance structure, costume and accessories design, music, dialogue, storylines and others should be identified in order to construct the changes of information revolution for Mak Yong Performance Arts. Besides that, response to the changes of collection is also significant in documentation strategies especially in the technological stream today. Media storage, device, application and format platform have become more high density in the cultural heritage institutions which are bonded with the eligibility of a physical collection. Nevertheless, Wellington and Huvila [16, 21] state that the advancement of technology can present more advantages because it has created a catalyst for escalating amounts of integrative practice between cultural heritage institutions such as galleries, libraries, archives and museums. The study also revealed that networking among cultural heritage institutions is able to help the ICH collection especially Mak Yong to be preserved through the digital age.

3.5   Information Heritage Advocacy

Consequences to the economic recession at present unswervingly creates struggles for cultural heritage institutions as they are hard-hit by the lessened support from the government, public and private sectors. Thus, the present set of circumstances has made it clear that sound advocacy needs to be at the top of the priority list for cultural heritage organizations [22] especially due to its fragile nature and danger of disappearing ICH. Some notable examples include the loss of dialects and languages, chants, the art of pottery making, and many more.

Most respondents opined that cultural heritage institutions should be more proactive in planning and giving advocacy to the public through creating interactive tools such as early educational cultural heritage syllabus at the primary school, short documentaries and commercials on broadcast channels and others. Nemani [23] suggests that there should be exposure to ICH collection through CD-ROMs and guidebooks, and social media pages; creating short educational films and documentaries; establishing an interactive webpage; and developing educational toolkits and drawing and colouring books for children. It also includes developing advocacy materials such as brochures, posters, calendars, magazines and newsletters to promote work on the safeguarding of ICH. These initiatives directly reduce the needs for fund allocation in dissemination and sustaining ICH to the public.

The benefits of information heritage advocacy include increased awareness, improved depositor relations and networking and the development of new or the expansion of existing ICH collections. The advantages of advocacy events will also increase responsiveness for the respective department, collection acquisitions and development, and the creation of new connections and collaborations with other agencies in sustaining ICH in the country.

3.6   National Heritage Centre

Although most UNESCO state member parties have not assigned a dedicated centre for documenting and preserving the ICH collection they utilize museum, archive, library and other cultural hubs to manage it. However there are also some countries that emphasize a specific institution for managing and preserving information and collection related to ICH [12]. This clearly shows that special care and interest towards ICH collection is carried out by countries that appreciate their cultural value is in line with country development. The findings from the study reveal the need for a specific centre known as the national heritage centre for safeguarding national cultural information including tangible or intangible heritage.

Most respondents agree that the establishment of a national heritage centre is capable of developing a new phase in the documentation of heritage information management where a centralized collection is responsible for collecting and preserving in a solitary hub. Moreover, the centre also plays an active role in the cultural fieldwork network program which is extensively for community participation in cultural heritage management and documentation. There are many expected benefits obtainable from this centre such as systematic cultural heritage information from the ground level as public reference, focused resources storage, holistic management of ICH documentation that will ensure the transmission of social values and safeguarding cultural identity.

4   Conclusion

Documentation of the ICH requires a distinctive methodology contrasted with execution towards heritage sites, monuments, buildings, and nature. ICH, much like language, workmanship, music, and dance, is more complex and requires particular information, knowledge and ability towards preserving it. The treasured and sensitive value needs to be rearranged through cultural heritage expertise that covers prospective dancers, musicians, minstrels, writers, historians, and the local community, and it requires guidelines in documenting their collection systematically. A good documentation strategy in cultural heritage institution reflects the eagerness of the country in sustaining and safeguarding our value of ICH and committed to pass on to the new generation to appreciate it. Finally, all cultural heritage institutions and public can benefit from an enhanced awareness of ICH and the significant aspect of documenting our heritage for better understanding.

Acknowledgement. This research was supported by Ministry of Higher Education of Malaysia under SLAI/SLAB scholarship for PhD level for period September 2015 to Mac 2019. We thank to all that has been involved in provided insight and greatly assisted in this study.

References

1. Arantes, A.A.: Beyond tradition: cultural mediation in the safeguard of ICH. In: The First ICH Researchers Forum of 2003 Convention : The Implementation of UNESCO's 2003 Convention, June 2012
2. Crofts, N.: Grasping the intangible: how should museums document intangible heritage? In: CIDOC 2010: ICOM General Conference, pp. 1–15 (2010)
3. Chaudhuri, S.: Research and documentation as tools for sustaining ICH: archives and community partnership – a case study from India. In: Meeting on Documentation of ICH (2012)
4. Templanza, M.R., Templanza, N.R.: A study of the documentation and archival practices of the mangyan heritage center and the center for mindoro studies. In: The General Conference Congress of Southeast Asian Librarians (CONSAL) XVI. Bangkok, Thailand (2015)

5. Yousof, G.-S.: Mak Yong: The Ancient Malay Dance-Theatre, pp. 108–121. Asian Studies, Quezon City (1979)
6. Kvam, H.: City culture at the crossroads. J. Urban Cult. Res. **3**, 60–69 (2011)
7. Shuaib, A.A., Halid, R.I.R.: The search for the middle path: Islam and the tradisional malay performing arts. UMK Print (2011)
8. Matusky, P.: The significance of preservation: to save or not to save? Tirai Panggung: J. Seni Persembahan **5**, 56 (2002)
9. McCulloch, G.: Documentary Research in Education, History and the Social Sciences. Rutledge Falmer, London (2004)
10. Sheppard, M.: Ma'Yong, The Malay Dance Drama. Malaysian Society for Asian Studies (1969)
11. Sheppard, M.: Ma'Yong. Correspondences, 1959–1993. 2000/0007440. Arkib Negara Malaysia, Kuala Lumpur
12. UNESCO: Examination of the reports of States Parties on the implementation of the Convention and on the current status of elements inscribed on the Representative List of the Intangible Cultural Heritage of Humanity. Addis Ababa, Ethiopia (2016)
13. Cox, R.J.: Documenting localities: a practical model for american archivists and manuscript curators. Libr. Rev. **52**(5), 236–237 (2003)
14. Jacob, S.A., Furgerson, S.P.: Writing interview protocols and conducting interviews: tips for students new to the field of qualitative research. Qual. Rep. **17**(42), 1–10 (2012)
15. Newman, J.: Sustaining community archives (2010)
16. Huvila, I.: Change and stability in archives, libraries and museums: mapping professional experiences in Sweden. Inf. Res. **21**(1) (2016)
17. Kurin, R.: Safeguarding intangible cultural heritage in the 2003 UNESCO convention: a critical appraisal. Mus. Int. **56**(1–2), 66–77 (2004)
18. Manetsi, T.: Safeguarding intangible heritage in South Africa: a critique of the draft national p olicy on living herit age. Int. J. Intang. Herit. **6**, 58–69 (2011)
19. Robinson, H.: Knowledge Utopias: an epistemological perspective on the convergence of museums, libraries and archives. University of Sydney (2015)
20. Manaf, Z.A., Ismail, A., Razlan, N.M., Manaf, A.A, Daruis, R.: Risk management for digital cultural heritage information in Malaysia. In: Proceeding of European Conference on Information Managagement Evaluation, pp. 1–9 (2013)
21. Wellington, S.: Building GLAMour: converging practice between gallery, library, archive and museum entities in New Zealand memory institutions. Victoria University of Wellington (2013)
22. Gwinn, N.E., Valletta, M.: LAMMS and international collaboration. In: ICOMOS Scientific Symposium: Changing World, Changing Views of Heritage: The Impact of Global Change on Cultural Heritage-Technological Change, Malta 2009 (2009)
23. Nemani, S.: Pacific Intangible Cultural Heritage Mapping Toolkit. Secretariat of the Pacific Community (SPC), Suva, Fiji (2012)

The New Era of Museums and Exhibitions

Metadata Standards for Virtual Museums

Stella Sylaiou[1], Elena Lagoudi[2], and João Martins[3(✉)]

[1] Hellenic Open University, Patras, Greece
sylaiou@gmail.com
[2] National Documentation Center, Athens, Greece
elenalagoudi@gmail.com
[3] CTS-UNINOVA and FCT/UNL, Costa da Caparica, Portugal
jf.martins@fct.unl.pt

Abstract. The raison d'être of museums are their collections. Museums' main purpose is to collect, preserve exhibit and interpret the objects of artistic, cultural, historical, or scientific significance for the higher reasons of education, study and enjoyment. Museum objects are information carriers. In the Information and Communication Technologies era information about museum objects is documented, organized and communicated with the help of information systems in virtual museums. Considering the working definition of the ViMM project, a virtual museum (VM) can be considered a digital entity that, considering the museum's specificities, enhances, complements, or augments the museum through interactivity, personalization, user experience and richness of content. The virtual museums' context is organized with the help of metadata, the data about the data. This paper presents the main metadata standards used by virtual museums and the qualitative results of an extensive survey conducted in the framework of the ViMM project for identifying the strengths and weaknesses of the main used metadata standards.

Keywords: Virtual museums · Digital documentation

1 Introduction

Information and Communication Technologies (ICT) used to transform, enrich and enhance the cultural experience have enabled a cultural organizations' dynamic and efficient interaction with their audiences, making knowledge more attractive [1] and spread the knowledge in an educational and entertaining way via virtual museums [2]. The development of ICT in the archaeological documentation and recording, provides valuable help mainly to the problem of organising fragmentary records and knowledge. However, technology can be a double-edged sword in case the produced digital material is not curated and preserved carefully [3] with negative effects to the quality of the cultural content provided. More and more the WWW is used for facilitating interchange and interoperability [4] and disseminating cultural information. The virtual museums seek to make accessible digitised information not only to specialists, but also to the wider academic audience and the general public. The recording and documentation procedures and the databases produced need carefully designed ontologies that use logical models to bring the contents of the virtual museums databases into the

© Springer Nature Switzerland AG 2018
M. Ioannides et al. (Eds.): EuroMed 2018, LNCS 11196, pp. 483–497, 2018.
https://doi.org/10.1007/978-3-030-01762-0_42

Semantic Web. The amount of information can make very difficult for the user to find and retrieve the desired information. The solution to the aforementioned issue is a search system/functionality that can make a personalised search. Thus, virtual museums must (a) achieve the interoperability and allow cross-searching of distributed resources [5] (b) integrate existing cultural research data infrastructures, in a way that distributed datasets and new technologies can be used by researchers as an integral element of the archaeological research methodology [3]. However, almost all large digital repositories consist of/hold a very huge number of documents in several formats. The National Information Standards Organization (NISO) defines the following metadata principles: (a) conformity with community standards, (b) support interoperability, (c) use authority control and content standards, (d) include a well-defined declaration of the usage conditions and terms, and (e) support, for the objects in collections, their long-term curation and preservation [6]. Metadata is a requirement for all the levels of data curation [7]. Past research has demonstrated that embedding metadata helps sustaining a museum visual archive [8]. Semantic heterogeneity between museum data sources can also be explored using top level ontology [9]. In another case, museum collection was integrated with archives and library collections in the repository using an open-source technology (DSpace) and involving the selection of appropriate representations of the objects and the definition of a metadata crosswalk between the original metadata standards and qualified Dublin Core (DC) [10].

The work described in this paper explores the contextualisation and linking of cultural datasets with the help of metadata that make it possible to stimulate the museum research using linked data. Metadata means "data about data". The "meta" prefix comes from the Greek prefix and preposition χμετά-, meaning "after" or "beyond", but it is used in epistemology with the meaning "about". Considering the Metadata concept as the data that can provide information about one or more data aspects, then Metadata can be used in order to recap essential information about that data which can make a lot easier the working and tracking with specific data [11]. Metadata can also be defined as *data describing the context, content and structure of records and their management through time* (ISO 15489-1 s 3.12). Virtual museums, that aim to virtually exhibit and communicate with their virtual visitors, need to use metadata standards authoring, maintaining and managing their exhibitions. This paper will present the results of a survey for metadata and other standards that are likely to be relevant for virtual museums.

The structure of the paper is organised as follows: after a short introduction Sect. 2 refers to the metadata literature review, whereas the Sect. 3 describes the project and its objectives. In Sect. 4 it is described the research contribution and the technical implementation of the research. Finally, a summary of the research results is presented in Sect. 5.

2 Types of Metadata

Museum documentation is related with several aspects that include development and information usage about the objects within a museum collection, as well as the procedures that support its management, so as to make it accessible and available to its users. The main issues that have to be considered, while developing a metadata strategy, are as follows:

- the purpose of the collection;
- its specific objectives;
- its users, what kind of information they need and how they look for them;
- the level of material grading, collection, single entry or both;
- if there are multiple versions and manifestations that need to be defined;
- if the collection and its objects already have legacy metadata;
- what kind of thematic categories include collection and what metadata standards exist in these categories;
- what metadata are used by other or similar organizations and which are the most appropriate of them;
- how rich the description should be and whether it needs to identify hierarchical relationships.

Effective documentation facilitates: (a) collection policies, (b) collection care and accountability, (c) collection access, interpretation and use, and (d) collection research [13]. The list with the main best practices in the area of metadata, in virtual museums, is presented below:

- A European context – The Lund Principles;
- European Museums' Information Institute (EMII) Survey (EU);
- eEurope Digitisation, National Policy Profiles survey;
- NOF-digitise Technical Standards and Guidelines (UK);
- The PULMAN Guidelines (EU);
- EUROPEANA [12];
- Western States Digital Standards Group Standards (USA);
- Getty Research Institute, Getty Vocabularies (all of them online):

  - Art & Architecture Thesaurus [14];
  - Cultural Objects Name Authority [15];
  - Getty Thesaurus of Geographic Names [16];
  - Union List of Artist Names [17];
  - Getty Thesaurus of Geographic Names Online [16].

There are many types of metadata that are mainly relate to the following elements:

- conceptual models (which describe how the information and concepts of a resource are related);
- metadata schemata (comprised of a set of attributes or characteristics were data are defined, e.g. DC).

2.1 Conceptual Models

The conceptual models describe how the information and concepts of a resource are related. They define the entities of description and their relationship to one another [18]:

- **CIDOC-CRM** (10-years old conceptual reference model that provides a formal structure to describe cultural heritage documentation's implicit and explicit concepts and relationships) [19].

- **FRBR** (Functional Requirements for Bibliographic Records) a model to reflect the conceptual structure of information resources in the bibliographic universe, also **FRSAD** (Functional Requirements for Subject Authority Data), **FRAD** (Functional Requirements for Authority Data) and finally **FRBRoo**. FRBRoo is a result of collaboration of the museums with the library's community. It is the International Federation of Library Associations and Institutions, known as IFLA, and the International Committee on Documentation of the International Council for Museums (CIDOC-ICOM) that decided to collaborate with the aim to harmonize the reference models each organization has. It is an ontology which is considered as an extension of CIDOC-CRM. This formal ontology intends to seizure and characterize the fundamental semantics of bibliographic information in order to facilitate the mediation, incorporation and interchange of museum and bibliographic information.
- **Europeana Data Model (EDM).** This Europeana aggregation model is based on use of standards from DC, CIDOC-CRM, FRBRoo and OAI-ORE.

2.2 Metadata Categories and Standards

The metadata categories and standards comprised of a set of attributes or characteristics were data is defined. Table 1 presents the main metadata categories and their functions [20].

Table 1. Main metadata categories and their functions.

Metadata categories	Functions
A. Descriptive metadata	Identification of the material
	Description of the content
	Understanding the context of the material's creation
	Retrieval of the information
	Indexing and classification
B. Administrative metadata	Documenting the chain of custody of digital material (e.g. copyright)
	Documenting changes to the metadata (when the item was digitized)
C. Technical metadata	Describing the digital file technical information
D. Rights metadata	Describing and managing the intellectual property rights
E. Use metadata	Managing user access and any authentication required
	User tracking
F. Structural metadata	Describing the internal structure of complex digital objects and how to navigate between constituent parts
G. Preservation metadata	Describing activities which have been undertaken to facilitate long-term access to the material

There are many different metadata standards for culture, arts and museums. Table 2 presents an overview of the main selected metadata standards.

Table 2. Main selected metadata standards.

Metadata standards	
Cultural metadata standards	**CDWA** (Categories for the Description of Works of Art) [21]; **CCO** (Cataloguing Cultural Objects) [22]; **Dublin Core** [23]; **MARC21** [24]; **UNIMARC** [25]; **MODS** (Metadata Object Description Schema) [26]; **VRA Core** (a data standard used for the description of works and images of culture and art) [27]; **LIDO** (Lightweight Information Describing Objects) [28]; **Object ID** [29]; **SPECTRUM** [30]; **ISAD(G)** (General International Standard Archival Description) [31]; **EAD** (Encoded Archival Description) [32]
Visual metadata	**MPEG-7** (Multimedia content description interface – standard ISO/IEC 15938) [33]
Cataloguing Rules	**AACR2** (Anglo-American Cataloguing Rules, 2nd edition) [34]; **ISBD** (International Standard Bibliographic Description) [35]; **RDA** (Resource Description and Access) [36]
Resource discovery metadata	**TEI** (Guidelines for Electronic Text Encoding and Interchange) [37]
Administrative metadata	**PREMIS** (Data Dictionary for Preservation Metadata) [38]
Standards for authority identification-authoritymetadata	**MARC** (MAchine-Readable Cataloging) standards, in machine-readable format, for authority records [39]; **MADS** (Metadata Authority Description Schema), an XML schema for an authority element set, which could be used to provide metadata about terms (genres, geographic, topics, etc.), events and agents (organizations, people); **EAC** (Encoded Archival Context), an XML schema used for authority records in conformity with ISAAR [40]
Standards for object identification, controlled by an	Legal personality identification systems (person-IDs) and authorities: **CONA** (Cultural Objects Name Authority) [15]; **DAI** – Digital Author Identification, this is a subset of ISNI; **ISAAR (CPF)** – International Standard Archival Authority Record for Corporate Bodies, Persons, and Families (This standard is published by the International Council on Archives) [40]; **ISNI** – International Standard Name Identifier; **LCCN** – Library of Congress Control Number; **NDL** – National Diet Library; **ORCID** – Open Researcher and Contributor ID, this is a subset of the ISNI, which exclusively identifies scientific and other academic authors [41]; **VIAF** – Virtual International Authority File, currently focused on personal and corporate names this is an aggregation of authority files [42] Bibliographic object identification systems and authorities: **DOI** – Digital object identifier; **ISBN** – International Standard Book Number; **ISSN** – International Standard Serial Number; **urn: lex** is used for law-document identifiers, and it is controlled by local law authorities Other identification systems (for generic named-entities) and authorities: **GeoNames** (geographical database available and accessible through various web services, under a Creative Commons attribution license) [43]

(*continued*)

Table 2. (*continued*)

Metadata standards	
Standards for terminology and treasures	Vocabulary of Basic Terms for Cataloguing Costume; **Iconclass**; **AAT** (Art & Architecture Thesaurus)
Standards for Intellectual property rights (IPR)	**ccREL** - Creative Commons Rights Expression Language (provides a framework for expressing rights information for open access web resources. The ccREL metadata record includes simple Dublin Core elements to describe the resource, and additional elements to describe the Creative Commons license that is associated with it. Available in English only) [44]; **DOI** – Digital object identifier (Within the digital environment DOI, standard ISO 26324, is often used as a system for identifying and exchanging intellectual property. It is composed of an exclusive alphanumeric string providing a framework for handling intellectual matter, connecting customers with content suppliers, easing electronic commerce, and assisting automated copyright management for all media types) [45]

3 Research

3.1 Research Questions and Experiential Procedure

In the framework of the ViMM project (https://www.vi-mm.eu/) an extensive survey has been conducted to identify the key metadata, terminology and identifier standards for digital heritage. A questionnaire has been created for exploring the metadata that are used the most by the participant, or the participant's organization, and for identifying the strengths, the weaknesses of selected virtual museum metadata. It has been distributed via a Google form (https://goo.gl/forms/9px9bTSv07VOxZOr2) and sent via e-mail. Seventy-nine questionnaires have been filled by experts and seventy-two of them have been selected for the survey analysis.

3.2 Participants

Firstly, some general information (educational level, years of experience, field of expertise) about the profiles of the participants have been collected. At a percentage of 38% the participants hold a PhD degree, another 59% a Master's degree, whereas 3% of the participant has a Bachelor's degree.

17% of the participants have till five years of experience, 21% have between 6 and 10 years of experience, 24% have between 11 and 15 years of experience, 17% between 16 and 20 years, whereas 21% of the participants have more than 20 years of experience. 52% of the total participants are historians, archaeologists, culturalists and museum curators, while 24% are archivists/librarians, 19% of them are ICT specialists, UX designers and computer scientists, and 5% are architects, civil engineers and urban designers. The above characterization is presented in Fig. 1.

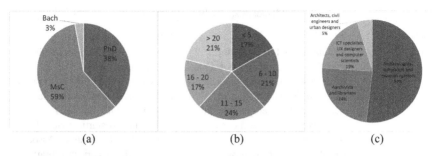

Fig. 1. Survey participant's characterization by (a) academic degree, (b) working experience and (c) working role.

4   Results

Concerning the metadata schemes that the participant, or the participant's organization, uses the majority use the MARC21 (41%). 39% use the Dublin Core metadata schema, 11% uses the CDWA, 2% uses CCO and 7% uses any other scheme, as presented in Fig. 2.

A thematic analysis has been conducted and identified the most common issues and ideas that summarizes the views that have been collected. The survey results for the strengths and weaknesses of the metadata, used by virtual museums, are summarized in the participants' comments presented in Table 3.

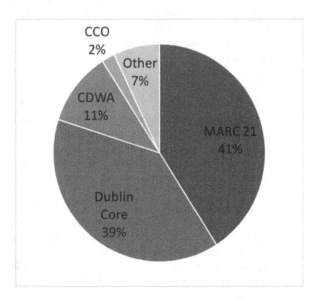

Fig. 2. Most used metadata schemes.

Table 3. Metadata strengths and weaknesses.

Metadata	Strengths	Weaknesses
CCO	- Fantastic tool to guide the selection and formatting of data values used in a metadata schema - It supports the creation of shareable and interoperable data, even across domains, i.e. even across GLAMs. - It offers organization of information for all levels of use	- Difficult time being implemented by museums - It seems to be fairly unknown in libraries and archives despite support by OCLC (http://firstmonday.org/article/view/1628/1543), Visual Resources Association and the American Library Association - There is information that does not cover, e.g. distinguishing place of excavation, following exhibition details of an object or conservation details. But it can be extended performance of artistic output, impact of this (ex. exhibitions, designs) - More nuanced data needs, such as more contextual information about cultural objects, are missing
Dublin Core	- Simple and clear in concept - Comprises all key informational elements - Widely used - High level of data exchange and data harvesting (OAI- PMH) - Applicable to scientific literature interoperability - Simple, straight-forward	- For museum collections needs to be extended (maybe as an application profile or create cross walks with VRA or CIDOC-CRM) - Not so good for arts objects not specific
MARC21	- Universal adoption - Hierarchical information	- Complicated and not human-understandable at its core
UNIMARC	- It is bibliographic with modular structure, widely used (MARC family/MARC21), issued and supported by Library of Congress - Crosswalks to all widely known standards	- It requires higher level of expertise for feeding metadata into the schema - Purely designed for libraries, not to be used for museum objects
VRA Core	- It is designed for museum/art objects and issued by Library of Congress - It has high credibility and it is relatively simple in use - It covers well most aspects and it is multilingual - It crosswalks to other schemas - It has conceptual elements	- It requires higher level of expertise (relatively to Dublin Core) for feeding metadata into the schema - It is still simpler than CIDOC-CRM

(continued)

Table 3. (*continued*)

Metadata	Strengths	Weaknesses
LIDO	- It is used as intermediate schema to EDM (via MINT mapping tool) structured information, clear assignment of rights - Event-oriented - It shows compatibility with museum portals and cultural heritage portals - Greatly structured with an interoperable data exchange schema - It brings into cataloguing the critical notion of unique identifier for data entities, such as concepts, people, things, events, places, and time periods - It can accommodate event-based descriptions, quite comprehensive in that regard	- It is very extensive and not well known in many countries, i.e. in Italy. -It is quite complex, and better documentation and tools should be provided - It has a flat structure and slow up take in the community of museums and aggregators (at least in the US), because it is too rigid as a structure (but that is true of all metadata schemas, as opposed to data models - Used by Europeana, DDB and others; the link http://54.247.69.120/build/movio_musem/en/1/Home fits the considered example
SPECTRUM	- It is a documentation standard, very clearly specifying the process of museums work - Used in Britain, Netherlands, Germany etc.	
EAD	- It has compatibility with archival portals - Concerning its structure; XML is a very hierarchical format, which works well with archival description	- It is quite complex, and software developers are not aware of it - It is not very flexible and thus not as widely adopted as it could be
METS	- It is a container metadata scheme that shows compatibility with library portals - For digital preservation purposes	- It is too narrow to encode unusual non-book materials in libraries
HBIM	- Nowadays interventions on existing buildings are more important, hence this is needed	- It is not truly supported by all software
Iconclass	- It has a very specialized vocabulary that is unique - It has a strong expertise in religious scenes. It has a linked open data version	- The terms have no scope notes - The scope is western culture oriented only

(*continued*)

Table 3. (*continued*)

Metadata	Strengths	Weaknesses
AAT	- It is issued by the Getty foundation; the Getty's controlled vocabularies (AAT but also ULAN and TGN) are widely used and as such are great points of junction between data sets - It is widely used, well structured, easy-to-search and use - It supports uri - It stays up-to-date and it is continuously maintained - It can support ontological structures and permits multilingualism depth and richness - It shows compatibility with other museums, partly translated to German - They are now available for free as linked data resources and they are being translated into many different languages - Besides widely adopted, it is published as linked data for wide use and linking - It is a controlled vocabulary and is adequate for describing and indexing the fine art, decorative arts, and archival materials held by my museum depth and breadth of entries/ideas, structure, compatibility with LOD - Links to records for the chosen schema: http://54.247.69.120/build/movio_musem/en/1/Homeeuropeana http://collections.britishart.yale.edu/vufind/Record/1670871 (used at YCBA as in many other American museums) http://collections.britishart.yale.edu/oaicatmuseum/OAIHandler?verb=GetRecord&identifier=oai:tms.ycba.yale.edu:726&metadataPrefix=lido (LIDO XML showing the AAT and TGN terms)	- Pending on the collection, some additions might be needed (it has beautiful instructions for doing so); however, it is not enough detailed and it is very art-focused - There may still be some equivocalities at the Getty about the Getty vocabularies being concepts or digital representations of true world things/places/people - The contribution process to the Getty vocabulary program is long and complex, which speaks to the quality of the vocabularies, but reduces the volume of contributions; which is unfortunate as their scope is currently limited to western culture mostly - Certain terms can be very complicated; similar terms out of context of their hierarchy may be confused with others; inconsistency in editorial style of terms and headings - Hierarchy is arranged by formal facets rather than by subject - There are limited cross-references and limited ability to represent multifaceted interrelationships - There is not really pertinent information, other than local needs particular to country, region etc.... - They mostly cover western culture only - In terms of the TGN, it does not cover historical or mythological places

(*continued*)

Table 3. (*continued*)

Metadata	Strengths	Weaknesses
LCCN	- It has a worldwide coverage on major names - It Is very reliable, widely adopted and easy-to-use	- It is mainly focused on North America and English speaking people - The alphanumeric structures make them not human-readable
ORCID	- Authority names given by the persons themselves, therefore purely reliable supported by most publishers, includes a wide range of data such as funding and peer review apart of publications - It is used by all major scientific publishing industries.	- It covers only recent names
VIAF	- It is international, widely used and has a linked data version	- It is very library centered
WorldCat/identities	- It provides an overview of books	
DOI	- It is current, web designed, cheap to run, reliable - It refers to a unique document with a permanent digital identifier, even if webpage disappears - Used in most repositories	- It does not cover old material, unless digitized etc.... - Some documents may have been published in different ways
ISBN	- International database highly recognized - International standard, available for search in OPACs ISBN is widely used worldwide (WorldCat is offered as a LOD resource) - Widely-adopted, it's a worldwide standard for book identification	- Very old - All bibliographic resources do not have an ISBN - Long numbers
ISSN	- It recognizes a journal or a book series International standard, available for search in OPACs - Widely-adopted	- Not very significant
GeoNames	- Reliable, complete, rich and international - It has interface to the museum documentation systems - It uses PHP language	- Weak - It provides alternative names (in many cases); it needs older name of a place or the sequence of place name changes - There is no pertinent information, even small towns and hamlets in countries, such as Germany are covered

(*continued*)

Table 3. (*continued*)

Metadata	Strengths	Weaknesses
CIDOC-CRM	- It covers concepts and allows the real "documentation of museum objects" to appear as a logical sequence - It is event-based and it provides lots of flexibility - It is extremely large and it shows comprehensive integrity of concept uses, flexibility, interoperability - Used for LOD modeling (http://edan.si.edu/saam/id/object/1989.68) -It provides: * elements of exhibition and conservation activities, but it can be extended * hierarchical collection descriptions; the concept of a "collection" is also not clearly represented, as museums and archives	-It requires high expertise to use it and feed metadata into the schema - Not widely used yet - Too complex; it is not used any more - Huge and very complicated and there is no community agreement on application; similar things may be modeled differently depending on project/context - It is extremely complex, it expects perfection and precision in knowledge of the museum's collections, when in fact ambiguous, or more generic models would be more useful - Complex to communicate with inexperienced users
Europeana Data Model (EDM)	- European standard, a basic model affordable for any source database structure and widely used - Close to Dublin Core and/or crosswalk available and used by many institutions - It provides interoperability and compatibility with German Digital Library and Europeana and all domain and national aggregators German Digital Library	- Too flat and does not allow mapping to highly complex/rich source databases - At the collection level some extra information might be needed to be recorded - There are missing events (like in LIDO) - Complex and easy-to-use tools for small institutions are missing

5 Conclusions

Research on virtual museums is gathering momentum, nevertheless, there are considerable gaps in the field of virtual museums metadata which in turn offer opportunities for further, related projects. The research has shown that even in cases of widely used metadata standards, such as Dublin Core and CIDC-CRM, it seems that there are some issues, that have to be confronted, e.g. they have to be extended or simplified. There is also need for further enrichment in relation to the terminology pertaining virtual museums. Moreover, most of the metadata schemata used by virtual museums are created for English speaking people. Sometimes information concerning the virtual museums metadata is not always up-to-date and it becomes obsolete. Some of the metadata schema shall become more user-friendly, since they are quite complicated and difficult to be used by the users. In addition to that, there are no metadata schemata for specific virtual museums, e.g. ethnological. As a future work we plan another extensive survey that will provide new insights that will permit us to critically comment on the standards and correlate the metadata standards to the concept of the Virtual Museum, as this is defined by the ViMM project (https://www.vi-mm.eu/2018/01/10/the-vimm-definition-of-a-virtual-museum/).

Acknowledgements. The research was supported by the Virtual Multimodal Museums (ViMM) project, Coordination and Support Action (CSA) funded under the EU Horizon 2020 programme (CULT-COOP-8-2016). The authors would like to thank Effie Patsatzi for her helpful advice on various issues examined in this paper and all the anonymous survey participants for their valuable feedback.

References

1. Kavoura, A., Sylaiou, S.: Effective cultural communication via information and communication technologies and social media use. In: Encyclopedia of Information Science and Technology, 4th edn. IGI Global (2016)
2. Virtual Museum definition, Virtual Multimodal Museums project. https://www.vi-mm.eu/2018/01/10/the-vimm-definition-of-a-virtual-museum/. Accessed 15 May 2018
3. Bekiari, Ch., Doerr, M., Angelakis, D., & Karagianni, F. Building comprehensive management systems for cultural – historical information. In: CAA2014 21st Century Archaeology Concepts, methods and tools, Proceedings of the 42nd Annual Conference on Computer Applications and Quantitative Methods in Archaeology, 7th–8th March 2014, Rethymno, Crete, Greece, pp. 227–234. Archaeopress, Oxford (2015)
4. The ability of multiple systems with different hardware and software platforms, data structures, and interfaces to exchange data with minimal loss of content and functionality. National Information Standards Organization, Understanding Metadata. NISO Press, Bethesda (2004). http://www.niso.org/standards/resources/UnderstandingMetadata.Pdf
5. Aloia, N., et al.: Enabling European archaeological research: THE ARIADNE e-infrastructure. Internet Archaeol. **43** (2017). http://eprints.uwe.ac.uk/34820. Accessed 21 June 2018
6. Moulaison Sandy, H.M., Dykas, F.: High-quality metadata and repository staffing: perceptions of united states–based OpenDOAR participants. Cat. Classif. Q. **54**(2), 101–116 (2016)
7. Sabharwal, A.: Digital Curation in the Digital Humanities, Preserving and Promoting Archival and Special Collections, 1st edn. Chandos Publishing, Oxford (2015)
8. Gillis, S.: Embedding metadata to sustain a museum's visual archive. J. Digit. Media Manag. **4**(3), 217–230 (2016)
9. Hajmoosaei, A., Skoric, P.: Museum ontology-based metadata. In: IEEE Tenth International Conference on Semantic Computing (ICSC), Laguna Hills, CA, pp. 100–103 (2016)
10. Barroso, I., Hartmann, N., Ribeiro, C.: Metadata crosswalk for a museum collection in a thematic digital library. J. Libr. Metadata **15**(1), 36–49 (2015)
11. A Guardian Guide to your Metadata. theguardian.com. Guardian News and Media Limited. https://www.theguardian.com/technology/interactive/2013/jun/12/what-is-metadata-nsa-surveillance#meta=0000000. Accessed 12 June 2013
12. EUROPEANA. https://www.europeana.eu/portal/en. Accessed 28 July 2018

13. International Council of Museums: Statement of principles of museum documentation, 2 November 2016. http://network.icom.museum/fileadmin/user_upload/minisites/cidoc/ DocStandards/principles6_2.pdf
14. Getty Research Institute. Art & Architecture Thesaurus® Online. http://www.getty.edu/ rsearch/tools/vocabularies/aat/index.html. Accessed 28 July 2018
15. Getty Research Institute: Cultural Objects Name Authority® Online. http://www.getty.edu/ research/tools/vocabularies/cona/index.html. Accessed 28 July 2018
16. Getty Research Institute: Getty Thesaurus of Geographic Names® Online. http://www.getty. edu/research/tools/vocabularies/tgn/index.html. Accessed 28 July 2018
17. Getty Research Institute: Union List of Artist Names® Online. http://www.getty.edu/rsearch/ tools/vocabularies/ulan/index.html. Accessed 28 July 2018
18. Idea: Mapping the world of cultural metadata standards. http://www.idea.org/blog/2011/11/ 04/mapping-the-world-of-cultural-metadata-standards/. Accessed 28 July 2018
19. CIDOC: Supporting Museum Documentation. http://network.icom.museum/cidoc/. Accessed 28 July 2018
20. Higgins, S.: Data modelling for analysis, discovery and retrieval Managing. ALA Neal-Schuman, p. 39 (2016)
21. Categories for the Description of Works of Art. http://www.getty.edu/research/publications/ electronic_publications/cdwa/index.html/. Accessed 28 July 2018
22. Cataloging Cultural Objects: A Guide to Describing Cultural Works and Their Images. http://www.cco.vrafoundation.org/. Accessed 28 July 2018
23. Dublin Core Metadata Element Set. http://dublincore.org/documents/dces/. Accessed 28 July 2018
24. MARC 21 XML schema. http://www.loc.gov/standards/marcxml/. Accessed 28 July 2018
25. UNIMARC - Universal MARC format. https://www.ifla.org/publications/node/8716. Accessed 28 July 2018
26. MODS - Metadata Object Description Schema. http://www.loc.gov/standards/mods/. Accessed 28 July 2018
27. VRA Core. http://www.loc.gov/standards/vracore/. Accessed 28 July 2018
28. LIDO – Lightweight Information Describing Objects. http://network.icom.museum/cidoc/ working-groups/lido/what-is-lido/. Accessed 28 July 2018
29. Thornes, R.: Introduction to Object ID: Guidelines for Making Records that Describe Art, Antiques, and Antiquities. Getty Publications Virtual Library (1999)
30. Spectrum UK collection management standard. http://collectionstrust.org.uk/spectrum/. Accessed 28 July 2018
31. ISAD(G) - General International Standard Archival Description. https://www.ica.org/en/ isadg-general-international-standard-archival-description-second-edition. Accessed 28 July 2018
32. EAD - Encoded Archival Description. http://www.loc.gov/ead/. Accessed 28 July 2018
33. Van Hemelrijck, D., Vanlanduit, S., Anastasopoulos, A.A., Philippidis, T.P.: Emerging Technologies in Non-destructive Testing VI: Proceedings of the 6th International Conference on Emerging Technologies in Non-Destructive Testing, Brussels, Belgium, 27–29 May 2015. CRC Press (2015)
34. Anglo-American cataloguing rules. https://archive.org/stream/pdfy-VV-4_m1HVoyDFFrA/ AACR2_djvu.txt. Accessed 28 July 2018
35. ISBD: International Standard Bibliographic Description - Consolidated Edition. De Gruyter Saur, Berlin/Munich (2011)
36. RDA: Resource Description and Access. http://www.rda-rsc.org. Accessed 28 July 2018
37. TEI P3. https://quod.lib.umich.edu/t/tei/. Accessed 28 July 2018

38. PREMIS Data Dictionary for Preservation Metadata. https://www.loc.gov/standards/premis/. Accessed 28 July 2018
39. MARC 21 Format for Authority Data. https://www.loc.gov/marc/authority/. Accessed 28 July 2018
40. Encoded Archival Context for Corporate Bodies, Persons, and Families. http://eac.staatsbibliothek-berlin.de. Accessed 28 July 2018
41. ORCID iD - Open Researcher and Contributor ID. https://orcid.org/about/what-is-orcid/mission. Accessed 28 July 2018
42. VIAF - The Virtual International Authority File. https://viaf.org. Accessed 28 July 2018
43. GeoNames geographical database. http://www.geonames.org. Accessed 28 July 2018
44. ccREL - Creative Commons Rights Expression Language. https://wiki.creativecommons.org/wiki/CC_REL. Accessed 28 July 2018
45. DOI - Digital Object Identifier. http://www.doi.org/. Accessed 28 July 2018

Coroplastic Studies Through 3D Technology: The Case of Terracotta Figurines from Plakomenos, Greece

Dimitra Sarri[1]([✉]) and Effie F. Athanassopoulos[2]

[1] Greek Ministry of Culture, Archaeological Ephoreia of Corinthia,
20007 Ancient Corinth, Greece
dimitra.sari@gmail.com
[2] Department of Anthropology, 816 Oldfather Hall,
University of Nebraska-Lincoln, Lincoln, NE 68588-0368, USA
eathanassopoulos1@unl.edu

Abstract. This paper focuses on the ongoing research of terracotta figurines using a 3D modeling method, laser scanning. The aim is to explore the contribution of 3D technology to the study and dissemination of this particular group of archaeological material. This is a pilot project and it concerns a small selection of figurines from the site of Plakomenos, in Corinthia, Greece. The site was excavated in 2003, by the Archaeological Ephoreia of Corinthia, and brought to light a large number of finds that belong to the archaic period (7th - 6th centuries BCE). Here, we provide a summary of current efforts to digitize the collection using 3D technology and develop a digital database/library to enhance research, dissemination and preservation of this significant collection.

Keywords: 3D modeling · Terracotta figurines · Archaic period
Plakomenos · Greece

1 Archaeological Elements

1.1 The Excavation

A sizeable collection of terracotta figurines came from two rescue excavations undertaken by the Archaeological Ephoreia of Corinthia, Greece, in 1998 and in 2003, at the site of Plakomenos at Leonti. The site is located in the NE Peloponnese, in Corinthia, near the town of Nemea (Fig. 1). Archaeological sites in the vicinity, include: Phlious, a classical city state where excavations have revealed part of the acropolis, and the site of Aidonia, where a cemetery of Mycenaean chamber tombs is

---

This paper reports on the ongoing study of a collection of terracotta figurines of the Archaic period using 3D technology. It is the first time that 3D modeling is implemented in the analysis and publication of archaeological material of this kind from the site of Plakomenos, in Corinthia, Greece. Here, we provide a summary of current efforts to digitize the collection using 3D technology and develop a digital database/library to enhance research, dissemination and preservation of this significant collection.

© Springer Nature Switzerland AG 2018
M. Ioannides et al. (Eds.): EuroMed 2018, LNCS 11196, pp. 498–508, 2018.
https://doi.org/10.1007/978-3-030-01762-0_43

currently under excavation. Further away, to the East, is Archaia Nemea, the site of a Panhellenic sanctuary dedicated to Zeus.

The site was first identified during a surface survey that was carried out by the University of Heildelberg. Rescue excavations followed, which centered on an olive grove and revealed a dense layer of miniature votive vessels and terracotta figurines. The artifacts date to the Archaic period, from the end of the 7th century until the mid-5th century BCE. The preliminary study of the finds indicates that they derive from a votive deposit. They represent dedications to a sanctuary, most likely of Aphodite, as evidenced by a fragment of a black-glazed skyphos with a votive graffito mentioning the name of the goddess. Unfortunately, the exact location of the sanctuary is not yet known. Further investigation of the site is required in order to reveal the architectural and other remains [1].

1.2 The Terracotta Figurine Collection from Plakomenos

The term Coroplastic studies denotes the craft of the coroplast, a modeler of terracotta figurines, which represent a variety of figures of small size. The figurines are made of clay or similar malleable material, such us wax or plaster [2]. The coroplast works the clay with his hands and shapes it using soft tools made of wood and bone or using molds, depending on the type and size of the figurine. Often, a combination of hand-made and mold-made parts are combined to create the final form.

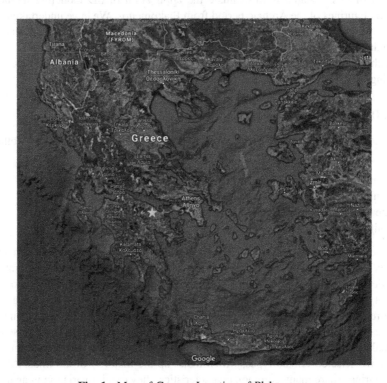

Fig. 1. Map of Greece- Location of Plakomenos

The terracotta figurines are the focus of our research. More than 1500 figurines are preserved nearly complete. They belong to a variety of types. The majority represent female figures. Other common types are naked standing male figures, horse riders, horses and other animals, and models of furniture such as couches. In addition, there are complex scenes such as dancers forming a circle, or similar scenes depicting daily life and religious practices. Most of the figurines are hand-made, while a small number are made in a mold. Another common type combines a hand-made body with a mold-made head. Some have human-like facial features and other bird-shaped faces.

The female figurines belong to two types, the standing and the enthroned form. In most cases, the female figures are seated on thrones that are joined with the figure; the front part of the throne consists of the lower edge of the figure's dress, while the back is supported by two cylindrical legs. They wear a polos on the head, a cylindrical crown, and the hair is shaped in relief. There is a wide variety of decorative elements on their clothes. The simplest decoration consists of a breast-band in relief, while other figurines have additional breast-bands and disc-shaped pins. The jewelry, mainly earrings and necklaces, is also varied. This type of figurine is common in the northern Peloponnese, in the regions of Corinth and Argos [3].

2   The Research Project

The goal of this research is to evaluate the application of 3D modeling methods to terracotta figurines of the Archaic period from Plakomenos. We have undertaken a pilot project, using a laser scanner to produce 3D models of a small sample of figurines. The immediate goal is to evaluate the accuracy and level of detail that can be achieved with this method, and identify shortcomings. Overall, this project examines the value of 3D modeling to the study and dissemination of this particular group of material.

2.1   3D Models-Selection Criteria

The selection of figurines for the 3D modeling procedure was based on the following criteria:

- Document the most common types of figurines
- Document variation of basic features
- State of preservation (selection of well-preserved figurines)
- Significance of a particular type for future archaeological study.

In the initial stage of the 3D modeling process, we selected simple figurines without complex features. In the next phase we worked with figurines that are more elaborate, with added decorative elements. Complex scenes that represent scenes of daily life or rituals have not been included in this pilot project. We plan to focus on these in the near future.

Currently we have produced models of 30 figurines. At first we chose figurines from the most common types, mainly seated females, standing naked males and horse riders. Our goal is to document a representative sample of the Plakomenos collection. Thus, initially we selected female types, which make up the majority of the finds. Although these figurines share many common characteristics, they exhibit variation in anatomical features and decorative details. In addition, there are differences in the clay and surface treatment. The main objective in this initial phase is to produce high fidelity 3D models of the most common types and use the models in the analysis and publication of the material.

Out of the completed 3D models, 14 belong to the female type; they are preserved to a length of 0.09 m. to 0.22 m. The majority are handmade (MN 1345, 1365, 1388, 1432) or of mixed type, with a handmade body and molded head (MN 1398, 1115, 1376, 1120, 1413, 1092, 1095, 1412, 1311), (Fig. 2). Only one of the selected figurines was entirely mold made (MN1329).

Fig. 2. Common types of figurines: hand-made (MN 1432, MN1365) and mixed type (MN 1376)

Also, as part of the pilot study, we selected two female heads of figurines that represent different styles and different time periods, an early archaic (MN 1379) and one of the classical period (MN 1378). A *kourotrophos* figurine (MN 1099), that is a female figure holding a baby in her arms was also selected (Fig. 3). Again, these were selected with the same criteria, to examine the level of detail that can be captured and reproduced in the 3D models.

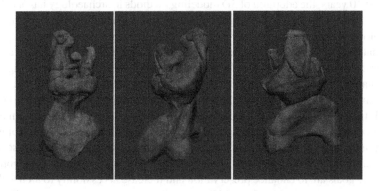

Fig. 3. 3D model of kourotrofos

The standing male figurines are few, only five have been recognized so far in the Plakomenos collection. However they are of particular interest for further study, since they are quite unusual and not paralleled elsewhere in the region except at the site of Phlious [4].Thus, we selected figurine MN 1093 which represents a standing male figure wearing a polos with a disk on the head, and a necklace with a pendant around the neck (Fig. 6). Horse riders are a more common type. Since they are handmade they do not show many face and body details. Still, they exhibit variation in their characteristics. Some of them have long hair, or wear a helmet, and some bear a shield (MN 1098, MN1582). Also, common are animal figurines, primarily horses (MN 1417, MN 1370).

As the research continues, the selected sample of figurines is expanding to include more complex types, such as two dancers (MN 1420, MN 1526), two female figures sitting on the same throne (MN 1309), a standing female with the hands on a round table-top supported by a cylindrical shaft, perhaps kneading bread (MN 1516), two flute players (MN 1344, MN 1560) (Fig. 4), a boat (MN 1112) and a rectangular piece of furniture (MN 1320).

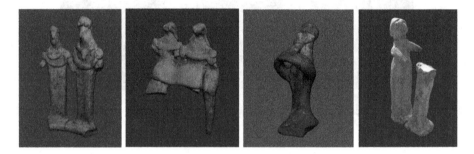

Fig. 4. 3D models of Plakomenos Figurines (MN1420, MN1309, MN1433, MN1516)

3   3D Modeling

3.1   Digitization of Archaeological Collections

In the last 10 years, the adoption of 3D modeling methods in archaeology has accelerated. This new technology has led to the growing digitization of a wide variety of artifacts and archaeological collections [5]. The popularity of 3D models is tied to the many advantages that these new tools offer, such as increased measurement precision, ability to reconstruct artifacts and reunite collections, virtual preservation and ease of digital data dissemination. The 3D modeling of the figurines from Plakomenos started as a pilot project, in order to obtain accurate data for documentation and visualization. We are using a NextEngine 3D laser scanner, a portable, affordable, scanner, which has found many applications in archaeology [6] (Fig. 5). For example, the Virtual Curation Laboratory, at the Virginia Commonwealth University, has been using a NextEngine 3D laser scanner to digitize artifacts from many US historic sites (https://virtualcurationmuseum.wordpress.com/). The goals are to enhance preservation and increase accessibility to archaeological artifacts, through the combination of 3D data collection using scanning and 3D printing

[6, 7]. The Digital Archaeological Archive of Comparative Slavery has produced 3D models of Afro-Caribbean pottery with this scanner (https://www.daacs.org/about-the-database/3d-laser-scanned-artifact-images/). Another research project in Greece is digitizing Bronze Age terracotta figurines from Crete with a NextEngine laser scanner [8].

3.2   The NextEngine 3D Laser Scanner

The NextEngine is equipped with twin arrays of four solid-state lasers. This method is faster compared to others, as the four twin laser arrays allow multiple points to be scanned at once [9, 10]. The NextEngine comes with the ScanStudio HD PRO software, which operates the scanner. This laser scanner is suitable for small to medium-sized artifacts. The artifact is placed on a small turntable that attaches to the scanner. There is an adjustable steel mount and a gripper with a rubber tip to hold the artifact in place. The turntable rotates at fixed intervals or "divisions" that can be defined by the user. Most artifacts require a minimum of 7–8 divisions for a full 360° rotation. The scanner projects laser stripes onto the object to record its surface attributes; it uses a triangulation technique to calculate the distance of each point and generate the 3D point cloud. Each division records a partially overlapping view of the object. Once the 360° rotation is complete, all recorded views are combined automatically into a 3D model. Some parts of the object, those not captured by the lasers in the initial positioning, mainly the top and the bottom, need to be scanned separately and merged with the 3D model. Thus, in most cases, additional views are needed to complete the model. The model requires editing (trimming, aligning, fusing) and, depending on the complexity of the object, recording and editing can take from half hour to two hours, sometimes longer. The editing can be accomplished with the scanner's software, which can align and merge scans, simplify the mesh, fill gaps, etc. Another option is to import the scans into a different software, such as Meshlab, and complete the remaining tasks there.

The NextEngine scanner has twin 3.0 Megapixel CMOS image sensors which record texture in color mode [9]. The texture is not high resolution, it is inferior to the texture produced by image-based methods, such as photogrammetry. There are additional limitations, depending on the object's surface. For example, reflective, very dark or transparent surfaces are not captured well, unless coated with a fine powder. Also, objects with deep recesses or interior surfaces do not produce satisfactory results. Early experimentations with figurines from Plakomenos indicated that figurines with complex features, such as females wearing a veil, which have deep, shaded parts, are not good candidates for this method. Overall, the texture is affected by lighting conditions and by the number of overlapping views that are combined in the final model; multiple views of the same part of the artifact can lead to poor quality texture when aligned. To some extent this is remedied in the final stage, when the model is fused, the mesh is simplified and the textures are blended. Still, the end result is variable and the texture is not always of high quality. Another option is to view the figurine without the texture, which makes subtle surface details visible. A key factor for success is the placement of the object at the appropriate distance from the scanner. The scanner has two focal lengths, macro and wide. There is an extended option but it requires additional software. An object has to be placed between the minimum and maximum distance for each focal length, which requires some experimentation.

The main advantage of the NextEngine scanner is its accuracy. According to the manufacturer's specifications, the accuracy in Macro Mode is ± 0.005 inch (± 0.13 mm), providing a maximum point density of 400 points per inch. The accuracy in Wide Mode is ± 0.015 inch (± 0.38 mm) with a point density of 150 points per inch. Polo and Felicísimo tested the performance of this scanner and found that the mean uncertainty in the Macro Mode is approximately half that of the Wide Mode, at ±0.81 mm and ±1.66 mm, respectively. They concluded that this scanner is a valuable tool for scanning small-medium sized objects. Its uncertainty values are more than adequate for a wide set of applications, such as museums, natural history collections, and digital exhibits.

Overall, the specific traits of the NextEngine 3D desktop laser scanner make it very useful to archaeological research, since it is lightweight, affordable, easy to operate and relatively accurate. In the case of the Plakomenos figurines, this scanner has produced high fidelity models with all their features and imperfections, surface lines, indentations, breaks, etc. The models reproduce the original artifacts in great detail, their facial features, clothes, and hair-styles. Thus, the 3D models can facilitate different types of analysis, especially manufacturing methods, since many figurines combine hand-made bodies with mold-made faces. Currently, the models are available on sketchfab. The original files of the 3D models, created by ScanStudio, are exported into standard formats such as PLY or OBJ files and are uploaded on sketchfab. Our preference is for the Matcap rendering, one of the options available on sketchfab, which highlights the features of the 3D models.

Fig. 5. NextEngine 3D laser scanner

3.3   Virtual Collections and Exhibits

This project complements other digitization efforts that are being undertaken with similar material. Terracotta figurines from the 'House of Orpheus' at Nea Paphos, Cyprus, have been digitized with a ZScanner® 700CX. One of the goals is the application of automated virtual restoration techniques to predict the appearance of the missing parts of digitized fragments. This project is also planning a virtual museum exhibit and additional applications to engage the general public [10, 11]. An assemblage of terracotta and limestone sculptural fragments from the Cypro-Archaic period at Athienou-Malloura, Cyprus, has been digitized using structured light scanning to produce a corpus of 3D models. Structured light scanning provides an accurate record of individual artifacts and can facilitate the identification of joins through details of breakage surfaces and overall morphology [12]. Finally, another collection from Cyprus, from the sanctuary at Ayia Irini, well-known for the large number of terracotta figurines of animals, male-warriors and priests, is being digitized. This project is taking an additional step, using two different methods, laser scanning and photogrammetry, to produce 3D models that combine accurate geometry with photorealistic texture [13]. Overall, this brief literature review demonstrates that 3D modeling is becoming an indispensable tool in the documentation, analysis and dissemination of archaeological collections of terracotta figurines.

4   Preliminary Results

The initial results with the 3D modeling experimentation are encouraging. The 3D laser scanning has produced high fidelity models where the anatomical features and decorative elements are very clear, especially in comparison with 2D photographs. This is an important step for the study of this specific collection and similar collections from other sites. For archaeological research to progress, we should develop methods that allow the detailed examination of the artifacts, and aid classification and documentation of the stylistic variability within each type. Also, the 3D models assist in the study of manufacturing techniques, facilitate measurements, and close inspection of the artifact. The next step is to collect additional data and undertake quantitative analysis of the figurines from Plakomenos. The ultimate goal is to compare them with similar collections of figurines from the broader region. The archaeological data can be supplemented with written sources that discuss the history of the region, or ancient testimonies that provide information on daily activities and rituals of the Archaic era, such as Strabo or Pausanias [14, 15].

Common methods currently in use consist of the examination of the artifacts themselves, taking measurements, photography and section (profile) drawings. 3D technologies can improve these practices and the study of the specific archaeological finds. This ongoing project has already established that the 3D models are superior in comparison with 2D photographs and drawings. The 3D models capture all the details of the figurines which are clearly visible, especially in the Matcap rendering (available on sketchfab). With the 3D model, a high fidelity copy of the artifact is available to the researcher and the viewing experience approximates the inspection of the original artifact. Furthermore, potential errors introduced in drawings or photographs (depending on lighting conditions) are eliminated. The major advantage is that the object/artifact can be rotated allowing the researcher to examine all its sides, take measurements and document stylistic features (Fig. 6).

Fig. 6. Standing male figure

Another substantial advantage is that the researcher can study the material anywhere, outside of the specific museum or storage space where the collection is held. Access to archaeological materials is often restricted, due to distance or other factors, such as museum regulations and hours of operation. Another substantial advantage is that the researcher can examine the digital copy multiple times without handling the artifact. The virtual examination eliminates factors that lead to the deterioration of the artifact, especially when an object is fragile or worn. Thus, these methods can enhance preservation, as the digital copies provide faithful substitutes of the artifacts to the researcher. At the same time, the 3D models facilitate the initial grouping, classification and comparison of the material. Since the Plakomenos figurines are characterized by a wide variety of decorative features, the first step is to establish correlations, develop a typological classification and determine dates for particular types. This whole process is facilitated by the 3D models which can be compared easily.

Furthermore, the large number of figurines in the Plakomenos collection necessitates the development of a database, which will contain all the information, including excavation context and typological characteristics. This database will include the 3D model of the figurine, and provide access to the digital "original" and its state of preservation. The database will facilitate the quantitative and qualitative analysis of the material as well as its interpretation. It will also assist in the identification of partially preserved figurines on the basis of measurements or established typology.

The Plakomenos database will require standardization, which is a key aspect for the creation of an online archive. The first step is to develop a list of terms to classify all of the figurines. Consistent vocabulary terms will be important for searching and examining the collection. We are planning to use open source software such as Omeka, based on the Dublin Core format. These software generate metadata fields that are standardized and simple to fill out. Standardization practices are essential when it comes to creating metadata for archives. Currently the 3D models that are posted on sketchfab provide basic information including typology, brief description, manufacturing method(s), material and dimensions of the figurine. For example, MN 1516 is a female figure standing in front of a high table; it is hand-made, of white clay. Its dimensions are: height 12 cm; width 5 cm.

This information is very useful in order to understand the function of the terracotta figurines and the role they played in religious rituals. Since they were dedications to a deity, in this case Aphrodite, they can provide information about the beliefs and requests of the worshippers. In addition, through the study of manufacturing techniques and the characteristics associated with different workshops, we can discern influences and reconstruct communications between different regions. Thus, we can draw inferences about the social groups who visited the sanctuary and the areas they came from.

A digital archive can solve problems that many archaeologists face, that is the comparison of similar material from different regions. The development of a digital database can streamline the search for artifacts using standardized terms such as a specific type of figurine, a specific region, or certain characteristics. By building a database that brings together material from several regions, it will be possible to identify similar artifacts efficiently and facilitate comparisons. In addition, a digital database will enhance the dissemination of research results and encourage sharing of information between researchers interested in coroplastic studies of the Archaic period.

5 Lesson Learned and Future Plans

Our current experience with 3D laser scanning and its application to the Plakomenos collection has been positive. We have created accurate digital copies of the figurines, which facilitate the study, classification and presentation of the material. So far, we have worked successfully with relatively simple forms of figurines. In the near future we will continue the production of 3D models of a larger number and more diverse forms of figurines. We will experiment with more complex types that are composed of multiple figures or elements in order to evaluate the efficacy of these methods. In addition to laser scanning, we plan to introduce photogrammetry, and compare the results. Photogrammetry is likely to improve the texture of the 3D models. By combining these two methods we expect to produce accurate as well as photo-realistic 3D models. In addition, we are designing a digital database which will include the 3D models of the Plakomenos figurines. The goal is to create a digital library, which will be available online and easily accessible, and will contribute to the study of Archaic terracotta figurines in Greece and the broader region.

Finally, a major advantage of this technology is that it facilitates virtual preservation and digital data dissemination. Thus, artifact analysis and classification, as well as digital preservation, are benefiting from 3D technology. Well-established initiatives such as Digital Antiquity and tDAR, the Archaeology Data Service (UK), and Open Context are providing leadership in the area of preservation, and long-term access to archaeological information. This project, along with other similar initiatives to digitize existing collections of terracotta figurines are offering new research opportunities and, also, are contributing to long-term preservation efforts.

References

1. Aslamatzidou, Z., Sarri, D.: Deposit of archaic shrine in the site Plakomenos Leontiou in Nemea Corinth (in Greek). In: Kissas, K., Niemeier, W.D. (ed.) The Corinthia and the Northeast Peloponnese Athenaia, vol. 4, pp. 397–403. German Archaeological Institute, Loutraki Corinthias (2009)
2. Peppa Papaioannou, E.: Coroplastic Artefacts of Archaeological Museum of Peraius (in Greek). Parousia magasine, Athens (2011)
3. Barfoed, S.: The mystery of the seated goddess: archaic terracotta figurines of the Northeastern Peloponnese. In: Thomasen, H., Rathje, A., Bøggild Johannsen, K. (eds.) Vessels and Variety: New Aspects of Ancient Pottery Acta Hyperborea, pp. 85–105. Museum Tusculanum Press, Copenhagen (2013)
4. Biers, W.R.: Excavations at Phlius, 1924: the votive deposits, Hesperia, vol. 40, pp. 397–423 (1971)
5. Grosman, L., Karasik, A., Harush, O., Smilanksy, U.: Archaeology in three dimensions: computer- based methods in archaeological research. J. East. Mediterr. Archaeol. Herit. Stud. 2(1), 48–64 (2014)
6. White, S.: Virtual archaeology – the NextEngine desktop laser scanner. Archaeol. Int. 18, 41–44 (2015). https://doi.org/10.5334/ai.1804
7. Means, B.K., McCuistion, A., Bowles, C.: Virtual artifact curation of the historical past and the NextEngine desktop 3D scanner. Tech. Briefs Hist. Archaeol. 7, 1–12 (2013)
8. Morris, C., Peatfield, A., O'Neill, B.: Figures in 3D: digital perspectives on Cretan Bronze Age figurines. Open Archaeol. 4, 50–61 (2018). https://doi.org/10.1515/opar-2018-0003
9. Polo, M.E., Felicísimo, A.M.: Analysis of uncertainty and repeatability of a low-cost 3D laser scanner. Sensors 12, 9046–9054 (2012). https://doi.org/10.3390/s120709046
10. Brown, J.: Innovation at home – Inside a 3-D desktop scanner. Electron. Eng. Times 48–49, 26 September 2010
11. Papantoniou, G., Loizides, F., Lanitis, A., Michaelides, D.: Digitization, restoration and visualization of terracotta figurines from the 'House of Orpheus', Nea Paphos, Cyprus. In: Ioannides, M., Fritsch, D., Leissner, J., Davies, R., Remondino, F., Caffo, R. (eds.) EuroMed 2012. LNCS, vol. 7616, pp. 543–550. Springer, Heidelberg (2012). https://doi.org/10.1007/978-3-642-34234-9_56
12. Counts, D., Averett, E., Garstki, K.: a fragmented past: (Re)constructing antiquity through 3D artefact modelling and customised structured light scanning at Athienou-Malloura. Antiquity 90, 206–218 (2016)
13. Vassallo, V.: 3D digital approach to study, analyse and (Re)interpret cultural heritage: the case study of Ayia Irini (Cyprus and Sweden). In: Campana, S., Scopigno, R., Carpentiero, C.M. (ed.) CAA2015: Keep the Revolution Going, Proceedings of the 43rd Annual Conference on Computer Applications and Quantitative Methods in Archaeology, pp. 227–232. Archaeopress, Oxford (2015)
14. Williams, C.: Corinth and the Cult of Aphrodite. In: Del Chiaro, M.A., Biers, W.R. (eds.) Corinthiaca: Studies in Honor of Darrell A. Amyx, pp. 12–24 (1986)
15. Croissant, F.: Identication d'une déesse: questions sur l'Aphrodite argienne. In: Prétre, C. (ed.) Le donateur, l' offrande et la déesse: systèmes votifs dans les sanctuaries de déesses du monde grec: actes du 31e colloque international organize par l' UMR Halma-Ipel, pp. 181–202. Université Charles-de-Gaulle/Lille, Liège (2007)

Tell the Story of Ancient Thracians Through Serious Game

Desislava Paneva-Marinova[1]([✉]) [iD], Malvina Rousseva[2],
Maria Dimova[1], and Lilia Pavlova[3]

[1] Institute of Mathematics and Informatics,
Bulgarian Academy of Sciences, G. Bontchev str. 8, 1113 Sofia, Bulgaria
dessi@cc.bas.bg, mash@abv.bg
[2] Institute of Art Studies, Bulgarian Academy of Sciences,
G. Bontchev str. 6, 1113 Sofia, Bulgaria
malvina.rousseva@gmail.com
[3] New Bulgarian University, Montevideo str. 21, 1618 Sofia, Bulgaria
pavlova.lilia@gmail.com

Abstract. The technological revolution gives innovative learning tools to the teachers and the possibility to deploy new learning approaches for deeper understanding and better demonstration of the learning content. These tools aim to engage the learners in more active participation during the perceiving of knowledge. This paper presents a new learning approach for studying the ancient Bulgarian history and civilization by realize a storytelling in a serious game. The paper makes an overview of "serious games" and their power to seek creative and logical thought, problem-solving, as well as develop a variety of skills and competencies to the learner. It also includes a short presentation of the "digital storytelling" learning method, which successfully helps instructors to motivate students learning, stimulate curiosity, and to make them interested. Finally, the paper provides details for the proposed approach and its design, mainly with respect to target learning aims, expected outcomes and plans for future improvements.

Keywords: Storytelling · Serious games · Gamification
Ancient thracian civilization · Improved knowledge understanding

1 Introduction

The new strategies for teaching and learning point to the investigation and the deployment of workable learning methods and scenarios for better understanding of the learning content and engagement learners in more active participation during the perceiving of knowledge. Good educational results are achieved by storytelling, understanding-by-design, serious educational games, game components, learning-by-authoring, and/or any combinations of them, when the specific learner's needs and wishes are kept in mind and different digital resources (*viz.* cultural, historical, encyclopedic, *etc.*) are contextually used for the target learning purposes.

The needs of the students in high school, the educational requirements, and the current teaching practices inspired the authors to start a long-term consideration of

© Springer Nature Switzerland AG 2018
M. Ioannides et al. (Eds.): EuroMed 2018, LNCS 11196, pp. 509–517, 2018.
https://doi.org/10.1007/978-3-030-01762-0_44

teaching strategies that could improve the current Bulgarian classroom experience. The researchers looked for innovative pedagogical practices with an involvement of the technologies in the learning process [1]. The specific task was to produce an educational "design" plan unfolding current teaching and studying practices in the Humanities, a field with excessive quantity of facts with vague logic often leading to misunderstanding. Moreover, the proposed solution has to be easily transferred to a similar or dissimilar domain.

The paper proposes a new learning approach for better understanding of ancient history and civilization, and especially, the Thracian civilization, by storytelling and serious game combination. Section 2 makes an overview of "serious games" and their power to seek creative and logical thought, problem-solving, as well as develop a variety of skills and competencies to the learner. It also includes a short presentation of the "digital storytelling" learning method, which successfully helps instructors to motivate students learning, stimulate curiosity, and make them interested. Section 3 provides details for the proposed approach and its design, mainly with respect to target learning aims and expected outcomes. The paper ends with some conclusions and further development plans.

2 Serious Games and Digital Storytelling for Education

The "serious games" method is accepted as a research, pedagogic, and evaluative tool in the technology-enhanced education [2]. The students involved in the game must use different skills, competences, and experience to solve the mini games and reach the end.

For the first time Abt introduces the term "serious game" and describes the utilization of situations in and outside the class room in his book "Serious games" [3]. He describes "serious game" as a "game having explicit and carefully crystalized educational purpose, as the main goal is not entertainment". Serious games can elicit significant engagement from learners and further to the effectiveness of the learning process. Education based on serious games generates good levels of comprehension and unconscious processing of content of relatively great difficulty. For example, the integration of ICT in the 6th- and 7th-grade ancient history curriculum would allow – by means of game playing, interactive interface, visualization, video, and animation – to present the material in a fun and accessible way [4]. This integration will make it easier to explain connections, relationships, and influences among ancient civilizations; to demonstrate the continuity of ideas, despite the demise of entire nations, and will improve the students understanding of the evolution of civilization. Serious games play an important role in providing the young learners with orientational literacy and an ability to apply their knowledge in activities different from those practiced at school [5].

Main research questions that we put forwards are: How to activate and stimulate learning through games? How games can increase motivation, engagement, and improved learning outcomes? How to enhance comprehension of content by skillfully executed invisible modern-day methods that students would both accept and welcome? What problems students would find interesting and attractive and how these problems can provoke the desire to learn new things and how the game could be in favor of this? Looking for the adequate solutions, we used our experience and knowledge to find the appropriate combination of storytelling and game that could make the learning content interesting and desirable for the students [6, 7].

Digital storytelling is the practice of using digital technologies to tell a short story [8]. Like traditional narratives, digital stories focus on a subject and feature from a particular point of view. What distinguishes digital storytelling is the inclusion of digital images, text, audio narration, moving image (video), and music. These multimedia narratives tend to be short (2–10 min), personalized reflections which use still pictures or videos of personal artefacts to create short evocative stories/plots. Such digital narratives are an extension of traditional storytelling, providing engaging stories, which can be shared within social/leaning communities.

Digital Storytelling is employed in a range of contexts and for a variety of purposes: self-awareness or discovery; narrative (knowledge management) in businesses; facilitating group understanding; engagement of marginalized sections of society; subject learning and development of subject, cultural or societal resources [9–11]. The digital story genre is perhaps most frequently associated with the telling of personal stories, often of cultural or historical importance to the author [12]. Such stories often focus on interesting experiences, memories of some past event or person or personal journeys to overcome challenges or achieve goals [13]. Robin [8] identifies two other types of digital story – one that informs or instructs and one which examines historical events. We will focus on a story based on historical facts aiming to improve knowledge understanding and to make and educational application of digital storytelling.

Kenny [14] argues that classroom practice that combines use of digital media with the art of story – leveraging both the skills and preferences of digital age students and the inherent human interest in story – is a potentially powerful pedagogy. Digital storytelling can be used to engage, inform, explore and transform, and thereby lends itself to educational contexts. Indeed, as shown by Yuksel et al.'s [15] world-wide survey investigating the use of digital storytelling to support learning. The digital storytelling is used in educational contexts not only to develop subject area knowledge, writing skills, technical skills, and presentation skills, but additionally reflection, language, higher level thinking, social, and artistic skills are also developed.

Digital storytelling, when well-conceived and executed, provides an engaging and powerful account of a 'story' – be it informative, imaginative or reflective. While any well-formed story should achieve this, the integrated visual and audio nature of digital storytelling is particularly potent to generations who have grown up in a social and multi-media world. The nature of the engagement goes beyond mere entertainment, although the value of fun in educational contexts is not to be underrated; using digital storytelling in the curriculum can afford real educational advantages [11]. Firstly, the multi-media nature makes the content of the digital narrative more accessible to technology-centric students, many of whom are alienated from traditional textual forms [13]. Secondly, as researchers such as Burmark [16] have shown, the combination of text integrated with visual images enhances student understanding. The visual component, especially where of a personal nature, helps situate the story within a recognizable context. According to Bruner's theory of situated cognition, this increases the time that students are able to retain and understand information [14] as well as enabling students to better organize information into manageable chunks. Thirdly, the multimedia nature of digital stories encourages active listening.

The stronger educational benefits could arise when students become involved as active learners in the authorship of digital stories. Creating their own digital stories, whether personal, informative or imaginative, requires the student to engage with the structure of storytelling. In developing the story, students must understand the basics of narrative structure as well as grammar. For example, students will need to consider dramatic tension, pacing and narrative flow. Further, as Ohler [17] advocates, authoring of digital stories provides a powerful opportunity for students to develop critical media skills.

3 Storytelling in a Serious Game for Better Thracian History Learning

The proposed combining of storytelling and serious games for a better study of the Thracian history and civilization is the base of *the following learning scenario*:

Established Goals: To learn the concepts, facts and specifics for the Thracian civilization, focusing on the lifestyle, beliefs and traditions of this ancient people leaving on the Balkan Peninsula.

The Content of the Thracian Story: The story in the game is based on a historical and cultural journey through the pictures, texts and mini games placed on the walls of six rooms named after six key aspects/components of the Thracian civilization.

The first room named Thrace illustrates (tells the story of) the geographical locations on the Balkans of the most famous Thracian tribes, their names and essential characteristics, often described by ancient Greek and Latin historians/authors.

The second room named Tomb presents the architectural design of the structures built under earth mounds, the Thracians funerary practices and rituals, and their belief in the immortality of the soul, mentioned by the ancient writers. In this room the students can see the images of well-preserved Thracian cult buildings dated in the 1st mill. BC, artefacts that were part of the funerary gifts and symbols of the ruler's power/reign.

In the third room named Armory the students will learn about the different Thracian weapons, and the traditional armament wrought by bronze or iron. The Thracian warriors were mentioned for first time in the Homer poem Iliad as glorious and invincible soldiers, who preserved their aureole for centuries.

The fourth room is named Herron after the building dedicated to Thracian ruler, priest or heroes declared to be an immortal demigod that regularly restores harmony in the tribe and protects its territories. In the Heroon the students will learn some facts and stories about the Thracian Hero – demigods and their divine powers.

The fifth room of the Thracian history is named Treasure and on its walls are placed images of famous gold and silver treasures used by Thracian kings and the tribal nobility in their everyday life. Coins, jewellery, vessels for feasts and insignia of status give an idea of their wealth and power.

The last room is the Sanctuary and the design of its space illustrates the written and visual information of the Thracian Gods and Goddesses. Their names and appearance are some of the facts that the students need to learn if they want to finish the game successfully.

The data and facts provided in the story derive from ancient documents, architecture, artefacts found during archaeological excavations, and from scholarly research by Bulgarian specialists.

The story is told through a serious game representing a labyrinth of rooms. The game will take you through the rooms of the building uncovered beneath the Ostrusha Mound, located in the Valley of the Thracian Kings near the city of Kazanlak. All the objects, drawings and reliefs are real and were discovered at the time of the archaeological excavations made by scientists. Their position in the building's rooms is the creative decision of the team who prepared the story and the game, but the main purpose is to tell the Thracian story in the most realistic way [18].

The Game Scenario: There are six rooms through which you need to pass: "Thrace", "Tomb", "Armoury", "Heroon" (a temple to an immortalized tribal chief, priest, or hero), "Treasury" and "Sanctuary". To enter the sixth and final room, "Sanctuary," you need to visit the other five, successfully complete all of the mini-games and receive pieces of Thracian treasure as prizes. Picture 1 depicts the West wall in room Thrace and some of its components: images, text boxes, mini-games.

Fig. 1. West wall in thrace room

Game Review: The first version of the educational game *The Thracians* is available in Bulgarian and the multilingual version is under development. The participants can play in a virtual 360° panorama environment consisting of seven scenes (called rooms), one of them is external the others are internal. The game begins outside the tomb. The player can enter through a door and can move and turn with the arrow keys and the 'A, S, D, W' keys on the keyboard, and "look around" with the mouse, too. In each room there are pictures, descriptions, games and doors (see Fig. 1). The pictures and descriptions help to solve the interactive mini-games. Figure 1 depicts a description belonging to a picture on the wall. The doors are initially closed, and they can be opened by solving the mini-games assigned to them.

Game Development: The technological implementation of the storytelling and the game solution are created by the team from the Institute for Computer Science and Control, Hungarian Academy of Sciences (MTA SZTAKI) under the joint project "Development of Software Systems for Multimedia and Language Technologies" of Institute of Mathematics and Informatics, Bulgarian Academy of Sciences and MTA SZTAKI. MTA SZTAKI team developed a multilingual and multiplatform Game Development, Management and Presentation Tool to support the creation of various interactive mini-games and combine them to full-featured games [5]. This Tool has the following components: Game Template Developer, Game Editor, Game Publisher, Game Portal and User Management.

- Game Template Developer: In the game template developer area, game developers can upload the necessary files and program code parts to the Game Server to let them be used by other users of the system. A game template thus consists of the game logic files and the list of necessary parameters with their types, but it does not contain questions, styles and settings.
- Game Editor: The game editor area is the component where the editors can put together the games from the available game templates. First, they select a game template and then they add the necessary question-answer combinations to them, select the desired styles, etc. Although the game could be playable at this state, however, it won't be available to any regular user yet.
- Game Publisher: The game publisher's task is to create game packages from the games created by the game editor. A game package contains at least one game, but in most cases multiple ones are combined. Game packages can be shared among members of a specified group of users who will be able to play the game.
- Game Portal: In the game portal area, the players can see all the game packages assigned to them. They can play any of the game packages and see their scores in rank lists.
- User Management: In the user management area, the administrator of the system can see and manage the user accounts of the Game Server.

By using these components, the main steps of game (or mini-game) development are as follows:

1. *Select mini-game type.* The implemented game types include sliding puzzle, memory game, matching, ordering, crossword, multiple choice question, word search, blind map, etc.
2. *Create game style.* HTML5 together with CSS3 technology was successfully applied for preparing the layout of the games.
3. *Add question pool and the set of game parameters.* The games can be associated with a question pool and customized by different parameters (e.g., size, time limit). Rules can be defined for scoring. During the game on a given platform (e.g. Web, mobile), some of the questions are randomly selected from the pool. Therefore,

different players can play the same game with different questions and the user can play the same game several times without repetition.

4. *Define game languages.* Current release of the game is fully implemented for a Web-based access by PCs. Now, the authors work on a version for mobile phones. This version can be also display on VR headsets.

The images of authentic architectural environment and archaeological artifacts used in the game belong to the private digital library of Prof. Malvina Rousseva, collected by her as an expert on Thracian architecture and culture.

For the next edition authors plans to achieve maximum authenticity in the design of the original burial mound and the building under it by additional media objects *viz.* several 360° panorama pictures of the tomb entrance and the rooms. Authors continue to work on the current release of the game *e.g.* to provide a sound version of the text objects, to add an avatar helping learner during content exploring, to find additional challenges and tasks to the learner, to register for playing online games in competitive way *etc.*

Game Testing: The first version of the game was tested in a class with 9–11 years old students in third and fourth grades, respectively. In the end of the game the students answered 22 questions in an anonymous yes/no questionnaire and were asked to clarify the reasons for their answers. The questions: "Did you enjoy the game?", "Was the content of the game clear to you?" and "Did you learn anything new about the Thracians from the game?" received positive answers. The students show great interest towards the storytelling and game solution that introduced to them the Thracian culture and civilization in this new to the Bulgarian education system method. For the first time instead of reading the textbook they study by playing. After the game and the analysis of the questionnaire a special session with history teachers was organize to clarify the results achieved by the students in their class. The discussion was based on the ten key impediments to applying games in the education identified by Shapiro [20].

The successful results encourage us to think about another educational storytelling & gaming resource connected with the Bulgarian ancient and medieval history. In combination with the appropriate content and story, serious games become an important modern-day educational tool, which reflects both the current state of technology and the learners' social profiles [19].

The authors in collaboration with history instructor-pedagogues, verified the pedagogic and methodological relevance of the approach to the approved educational programs and requirements in Bulgaria.

The content development and game testing are done during the project "Serious Games as Contemporary Tools for New Educational Applications" Contract DSD-2/05.04.2017 between Bulgarian Academy of Sciences and the Institute of Mathematics and Informatics, Activity "Introduction of Contemporary Methods in Educating and Fostering Young Talent" (PMC №347).

Lesson Learned by the Game Authors: The project design had two important impacts on authors creating the game. They improve their professional experience in implementation of new technological solutions for optimizing the educational processes and enrich their knowledge on Balkan ancient history.

4   Conclusions

Digital games are applied widely in various areas closely related to cultural heritage. They provide useful information and increasing appeal and engagement for all user ages, as well as fun and play. The proposed project aims to give opportunities for creation of a more effective and engaging learning process involving students in active knowledge observation of the ancient history. During the game design, the authors follow frameworks and models, used in the tools for maze creation, interactive learning content, and international projects [21–23] for interactive game-based educational practices.

The game *The Thracians* presented here has been implemented by using a flexible game engine. The main advantage of this engine is that the game can be easily customized for different learning domains. The game layout, the structure of the maze, the texture of the floors, walls and ceiling, the pictures on the wall, the presented content and the mini-games can be easily changed via modifying the parameter files which accelerates the development of new games. Key factor in the success of the game is creating high-quality educational content with multimedia items and its easy adaptation to the game environment.

Acknowledgements. This work is partly funded by the Bulgarian Academy of Sciences under the research project № DFNP-17-31/25.07.2017 "Models and Tools to Increase and Customize Visitors' Experiences in a Digital Cultural Content Management System".

This work is also partly funded by the Bulgarian National Scientific Fund under the research projects № DN02/06/15.12.2016 "Concepts and Models for Innovation Ecosystems of Digital Cultural Assets" (web site: http://cultecosys.math.bas.bg), WP2 - Creating models and tools for improved use, research and delivery of digital cultural resources.

References

1. Dimova, M.: Towards models and tools to increase and customize visitors' experiences in a digital cultural content management system. In: Digital Presentation and Preservation of Cultural and Scientific Heritage, vol. 7, pp. 239–242 (2017)
2. Bontchev, B., Paneva-Marinova, D., Draganov, L.: Educational video games for Bulgarian orthodox iconography. In: Chova, L.G., Martínez, A.L., Torres, I.C. (eds.) ICERI2016 9th Annual International Conference of Education, Research and Innovation, Seville, Spain, pp. 1679–1688 (2016). https://doi.org/10.21125/iceri.2016.1374
3. Abt, C.: Serious Games. University Press of America, New York (1970)
4. Slavova-Petkova, S., Dimova, M., Luchev, D.: Learning scenario for better understanding of fairy tales using role-playing and serious games methods. In: Digital Presentation and Preservation of Cultural and Scientific Heritage, vol. 6, pp. 241–246 (2016)
5. Luchev, D., et al.: Game-based learning of Bulgarian iconographical art on smart phone application. In: Proceeding of the International Conference on e-Learning 2016, pp. 195–200 (2016)
6. Slavova-Petkova, S.: Project "Models and applications of serious learning games in education of cultural-historical heritage and national identity". In: Digital Presentation and Preservation of Cultural and Scientific Heritage, vol. 7, pp. 243–248 (2017)

7. Vasileva, M., Bakeva, V., Vasileva-Stojanovska, T., Malinovski, T., Trajkovik, V.: Grandma's games project: bridging tradition and technology mediated education. TEM J. **3**(1), 13–21 (2014)
8. Robin, B.R.: Digital storytelling: a powerful technology tool for the 21st century classroom. Theory Pract. **47**, 220–228 (2008)
9. Benmayor, R.: Digital storytelling as a signature pedagogy for the new humanities. Arts Humanit. High. Educ. **7**(2), 188–204 (2008)
10. Petrucco, C., De Rossi, M.: iNarrare con il digital storytelling a scuola e nelle organizzazioni. Carocci (2009)
11. Roby, T.: Opus in the classroom: striking CoRDS with content-related digital storytelling. Contemp. Issues Technol. Teach. Educ. http://www.citejournal.org/volume-10/issue-1-10/current-practice/article1-html. Accessed 28 May 2018
12. Lambert, J.: Digital Storytelling Cookbook. Digital Diner Press, Berkeley (2007)
13. Gunter, G., Kenny, R.: Digital booktalk: digital media for reluctant readers. Contemp. Issues Technol. Teach. Educ. **8**, 84–99 (2008)
14. Kenny, R.F.: Digital narrative as a change agent to teach reading to media-centric students. Int. J. Hum. Soc. Sci. **2**(3), 186–194 (2007)
15. Yuksel, P., Robin, B., McNeil, S.: Educational uses of digital storytelling all around the world. In: Society for Information Technology & Teacher Education International Conference, Nashville, Tennessee, USA. AACE. http://digitalstorytelling.coe.uh.edu/survey/SITE_DigitalStorytelling.pdf. Accessed 28 May 2018
16. Burmark, L.: Visual presentations that prompt, flash and transform. Media Methods **40**(6), 4–5 (2004)
17. Ohler, J.: The world of digital storytelling. Educ. Leadersh. **63**, 44–47 (2007)
18. Paneva-Marinova, D., Pavlov, R., Luchev, D., Ruseva, M., Bontchev, B.: The first information day: serious games as contemporary tools for new educational applications. In: Digital Presentation and Preservation of Cultural and Scientific Heritage, vol. 7, pp. 283–285 (2017)
19. Paneva-Marinova, D., Iliev, A., Pavlov, R., Zlatkov, L.: Towards increasing and personalizing of user experience in the digital culture ecosystem. Int. J. Appl. Eng. Res. **13**(6), 4227–4231 (2018)
20. Shapiro, J.: Games in the classroom: overcoming the obstacles (2014). https://ww2.kqed.org/mindshift/2014/09/12/games-in-the-classroom-overcoming-the-obstacles/. Accessed 10 May 2018
21. Anderson, E.F., McLoughlin, L., Liarokapis, F., Peters, C., Petridis, P., Freitas, S.: Serious games in cultural heritage. In: Proceedings of 10th International Symposium on Virtual Reality, Archaeology and Cultural Heritage, VAST (2009)
22. Van der Vegt, W., Westera, W., Nyamsuren, E., Georgiev, A., Martínez Ortiz, I.: RAGE architecture for reusable serious gaming technology components. Int. J. Comput. Games Technol. (2016). https://doi.org/10.1155/2016/5680526
23. Westera, W., Van der Vegt, W., Bahreini, K., Dascalu, M., Van Lankveld, G.: Software components for serious game development. In: Proceedings of 10th European Conference of Game-Based Learning, Paisley, Scotland, 6–7 October 2016 (2016)

New Cross/Augmented Reality Experiences for the Virtual Museums of the Future

Geronikolakis Efstratios[1,2(✉)], Tsioumas Michael[3(✉)],
Bertrand Stephanie[4(✉)], Loupas Athanasios[1,2(✉)], Zikas Paul[1,2(✉)],
and Papagiannakis George[1,2(✉)]

[1] Computer Science Department, University of Crete, Voutes Campus,
70013 Heraklion, Greece
{stratosg,papagian}@ics.forth.gr,
loupas.thanos@gmail.com, paul.zikas@ovidvr.com
[2] Foundation for Research and Technology Hellas, 100 N. Plastira Str.,
70013 Heraklion, Greece
[3] Hellenic Ministry of Culture and Sports,
Service of Modern Monuments and Technical Works of Central Macedonia,
Herodotou str. 17, 540 03 Thessaloniki, Greece
mtsioumas@culture.gr
[4] Museology–Cultural Management Department,
Aristotle University of Thessaloniki, University Campus,
54124 Thessaloniki, Greece
bertrandstephanie@gmail.com

Abstract. Mixed Reality (MR) applications and technologies have become quite popular nowadays. They are used in many areas (e.g. Games, Entertainment, Education, etc.). But what about Cultural Heritage? Cultural Heritage is an area that presents a great variety of opportunities for MR applications. These opportunities include storytelling (a way for visitors to learn and retain more information about the exhibitions that they explore), gamified presence (an incentivizing tool to keep them attentive during their visit) and many more. This paper discusses the creation of Cross/Augmented Reality applications for the Industrial Museum and Cultural Center in the region of Thessaloniki, and presents some early results. The region of Central Macedonia has a rich history and its Cultural Heritage is extremely significant. The local importance of Cultural Heritage can be observed in the actions undertaken by local authorities, as well as the region's participation in European Cultural Heritage projects. The creation of Cross/Augmented applications can greatly contribute to the preservation and promotion of Cultural Heritage. These technologies are not only liable to prove very popular with the public due to their current mass appeal; they are likely to shape the Virtual Museums of the future. Overall, the main contribution of this paper is to provide the first bibliographical reference to examine the implementation of Virtual Museums in Cross Reality, Augmented Reality and Virtual Reality using both ARKit and ARCore's latest APIs.

Keywords: Mixed reality · Augmented reality · Cross-reality
Cultural Heritage · Virtual museum · Thessaloniki

© Springer Nature Switzerland AG 2018
M. Ioannides et al. (Eds.): EuroMed 2018, LNCS 11196, pp. 518–527, 2018.
https://doi.org/10.1007/978-3-030-01762-0_45

1 Cultural Heritage in the Region of Thessaloniki

1.1 Digital Cultural Heritage in Thessaloniki

Thessaloniki is one of the most popular travel destinations in Greece. The region's extensive and vivid history has drawn numerous visitors, who choose to travel to this city in order to discover its landmarks firsthand, and experience everything its Cultural Heritage has to offer. Local authorities have taken several steps in order to promote its Cultural Heritage using diverse strategies designed to help visitors explore the region in a more effective and productive way. Towards this goal, numerous websites have been created, including, a website where visitors can find general information about Thessaloniki [1], another that provides information about its history, arts, byzantine arts, exhibitions, as well as photographs, maps and more [2], and finally, several websites dedicated to specific monuments [3].

Amongst the region's Digital Cultural Heritage projects, "Thessaloniki VR" or "Thessaloniki VR (UNESCO Edition)" [4] is a notable example. The project consists of a mobile application for Android and iOS devices, with which users can explore in Virtual Reality (VR), the most important sights of the city, including Kamara, Galerius Palace (Navarino Square), Alatza Imaret, Aristotelous Square, Ladadika, the board-walk, the statue of Alexander the Great and others. This application is a great example of what can be achieved in terms of Digital Cultural Heritage. More applications of this kind, which offer users similar and even more diverse opportunities, are urgently needed.

1.2 The Participation of Thessaloniki in European Cultural Heritage Projects

The region of Thessaloniki has also demonstrated its keen interest in preserving and promoting its Cultural Heritage by participating in European projects like CHRISTA [5–7], Cult-RinG [8, 9] and HIGHER [10].

2 Added Value of Digital Cultural Heritage Projects

2.1 Expansion of Institutional Capabilities

In effect, Digital Cultural Heritage projects implemented through mixed-reality applications are vital to insuring cultural institutions' sustained relevance and renewed public interest and engagement. These projects can provide far more than a supportive role by merely extending existing display formats: for instance, by supplying augmented audio-guides and automated pedagogical programs. Digital Cultural Heritage projects offer the possibility of expanding institutional capabilities by surpassing otherwise intractable limitations related to the material reality of: (a) the exhibits (e.g. conservation issues, lack of availability of unique artworks and artifacts), (b) the infrastructure (e.g. fixed space, circumscribed resources), and (c) the users (e.g. safety and security constraints, limited access – especially when it comes to periphery locations).

2.2 Public Engagement

As a dynamic and responsive display technology endowed with the potential for personalization, MR applications are intrinsically designed to contribute to experience enhancement and content retention. In this way, they increase user enjoyment and education, which are an essential part of any cultural institution's core mission. In addition to advancing these fundamental remits, MR applications also tender the most effective means for cultural institutions to sustain a measure of produsage (user-led content creation) [11] by way of data generated through viewer interaction. These applications can provide inclusive platforms for open source, collaborative and participatory types of knowledge creation towards a cultural commons more in tune with the current network condition than traditional, collection-centered, authoritative modes of content delivery.

3 Mixed Reality Experiences for Interaction with Cultural Heritage

3.1 Mixed Reality Installations

Mixed reality has the potential not only to increase motivation to learn, but also to raise interest in Cultural Heritage [12]. Apart from providing an enjoyable experience, mixed reality installations can facilitate cultural awareness, historical reconstruction and heritage awareness [12]. It can be implemented using a number of different installations. In the specific case under consideration, the only thing that the installations require is a mobile device (phone or tablet). With a phone or tablet, the user (or museum visitor) is able to see augmented 3D models of different exhibits that belong to the museum display, and even a 3D model of the museum itself, and explore both as if he/she was there. As an added benefit, several users (in the vicinity of the user holding the device) can participate at the same time by seeing the results on the shared screen (in contrast with Virtual Reality headsets, where the number of users that can simultaneously use the application is limited due to the restricted number of head mounted displays).

3.2 Storytelling in Mixed Reality

Static visualizations have been traditionally employed to support storytelling in the form of text, diagrams and images [12]. The adoption of dynamic approaches utilizing state-of-the-art 2D and 3D graphics is emerging in an effort to explore the full potential of interactive narration [12]. In comparison with static forms of storytelling, the use of 3D graphics (making text and/or images appear on a 3D object accompanied by an animation, for instance) renders the reading procedure more compelling for the users than straightforward written information. In the case of the specific Cross-Reality applications under consideration, boards with text are used as storytelling elements designed to apprise users of the museum's history whilst simultaneously bringing into focus different exhibits and parts of the museum. The added value of these boards is that users are not only able to view the 3D model of the museum and its exhibits, they are also presented with information pertaining to different aspects of the museum's history, thus contributing to the preservation of the institution's Cultural Heritage.

3.3 Gamified Presence in Mixed Reality

Gamification is different from computer games even if it shares a lot of common theories and practices of development [12]. The most basic objective of gamification is to keep users interested and motivated so that they do not get bored and quit the specific application too soon. When integrated into a Cultural Heritage mobile application, gamification can incentivize users into continuing their exploration of the museum/exhibition by offering mini-games: for instance, asking them to find specific objects/areas inside the museum, and/or providing quizzes to test acquired knowledge. Such applications can motivate even more people to visit museums, and attract children through play. In the case of the applications under review, the quiz room, where users can test their knowledge about the museum, is a gamification element that makes their virtual experience more interesting and fun by rewarding them with a virtual prize if they answer most of the questions correctly. Moreover, the attribution of a score motivates users to revisit the application again in order to improve their personal results. In this way, the added value of these gamification elements is an increase in interest across all age groups, making the applications fun to use, and even inciting users to recommend them to others.

4 The Work in the Industrial Museum and Cultural Center in Thessaloniki

4.1 Brief History of the Museum

The building of the Industrial Museum and Cultural Center in Thessaloniki has a fascinating history. It is the only remaining structure of the "Hamidie" complex, which was founded during the city's last ottoman period (1875) as an Orphanage ("Islahane") and a School of Arts and Crafts. The complex is located in the region of Evangelistria on the eastern side of the city walls, both within and outside the historical city limits. After the liberation of Thessaloniki, the building's ownership passed to the Greek state, which rented out the complex from 1920 onwards in order to accommodate usage commensurate with the workshops that were originally housed in the School [13].

In 1992, the Ministry of Culture and Sports designated the building complex, together with its equipment, as a listed historical monument. In 2011, the project "Restoration of the listed complex of the former School of Arts and Handicrafts ("Hamidie School") and conversion into an Industrial Museum and Cultural Center" was included in the Operational Programme of Macedonia and Thrace as part of the NSRF 2007–2013. The building complex's restoration and reuse were completed in 2015 thanks to funding provided by the Greek state and the European Union.

4.2   Objectives and Means

The Industrial Museum and Cultural Center in Thessaloniki is essentially a museum of its own history and evolution, exhibiting industrial machines and artifacts that were found within, or related to it, in addition to highlighting its own architectural structure as the last building to bare testimony to the late nineteenth century's urban plan of that area. Its objective is to present the history of the technical schools that operated in similar institutions/orphanages, including the techniques of the workshops and the industries that flourished in the second half of the nineteenth century in Greece: namely the history of casting (one of the oldest of these techniques) and the operation of foundries. As required by the initial museological study, it was deemed necessary to present this material in an experiential way in order to convey the education and working conditions of that era, as well as the general operation of the production line, and in particular, the function of the machines, tools and facilities.

The exhibition was created using a wide range of cutting-edge methods derived from modern exhibition principles designed to shape and present the interpretive material both in terms of content and its formulation. The technologies and tools that were used include:

- An immersive reality application installed in a specially designed space, which experientially illustrates the evolution of the late nineteenth century city quarter into today's modern city using 3D mockups to present the different phases of the urban grid,
- An interactive multimedia exhibit (infokiosk), in which the history of technical education is presented in game form,
- QR codes to direct apps on mobile devices to display information about other technical schools of the same era,
- Video projections of interviews with people who worked there describing working conditions and sharing their memories,
- Animation, video and sound of the machines in operation,
- A virtual tour of the museum's facilities and exhibitions offered through the museum's website.

4.3   Integrating MR

The integration of MR in the Industrial Museum and Cultural Center was done after the applied museological study, following the increasing tendency to implement MR in CH/DCH. As project administrator, the Service of Modern Monuments and Technical Works of Central Macedonia embraced modern technologies right from the get go, and further intends to invest in this domain. Indeed, when it comes to preserving and promoting intangible CH – for instance, casting techniques as well as the education and working conditions of specific eras, which are core objectives of the project – the use of MR is virtually the only way of providing in situ visualization and representation.

The vast majority of visitors to the Industrial Museum and Cultural Center are students and people under the age of 45 with a great interest in new technologies. Thus, beside attracting more visitors, using MR supplies the cultural institution with the means to enhance and fulfill its mission of educating, communicating, promoting, and studying the past in an enjoyable and innovative way.

4.4   Apple's ARKit and Google's ARCore Comparison

ARKit and ARCore are SDKs used for augmented reality applications, which differ in implementation. They are based on the following basic features: Motion Tracking, Environmental Understanding and Light Estimation [14]. ARKit (iOS devices) uses a Visual Inertial Odometer (VIO) to achieve Motion Tracking in order to accurately track a position in reference to objects in the real world [14]. Moreover, devices equipped with ARKit can grasp and process the shape of the surrounding environment (horizontal distances) – a function called Environmental Understanding. Finally, Light Estimation enables the cameras of the iOS devices to detect real world area light sources and light the augmented reality objects accordingly [14]. Conversely, ARCore (android devices), uses Inertial Measurement Unit (IMU) to track and interpret data. In a different manner, this SDK also measures the shape, build and features of the surrounding objects to detect and identify the right position and orientation of the Android device in use [14]. ARCore implements Environmental Understanding and Light estimation in a similar way to ARKit.

The main differences between these two SDKs involve floor mapping and accuracy. ARCore provides richer floor coverage, able to manage larger maps [15]. ARKit only stores the most recently captured location data, limiting the stability with which a scene can be re-localized [15]. Moreover, it appears to be a little more accurate in differentiating between horizontal and vertical surfaces [15]. It is superior at recognizing walls and floors as it gathers more feature points by moving around the room. As a result, ARKit and ARCore are two very good SDKs, each with their own advantages and disadvantages. The choice between both really depends on the application. In the case of the applications described in this paper, the ARKit version is potentially more accurate when it comes to placing the portal on a floor in the real world due to its accuracy, when compared to ARCore.

4.5   Cross-Reality Application for the Exploration of the Museum

A mobile application currently under development for the Industrial Museum and Cultural Center in Thessaloniki consists of a visit in cross-reality. In other words, this application is essentially a Virtual Museum. It targets people that cannot travel to Thessaloniki or visit the museum but still want to explore the contents of the specific institution. The work that has been completed to date is based on a 3D model of the institution that was provided by the museum officials (Fig. 1).

iOS Version (Using Apple's ARKit)

The first version of this cross-reality experience designed for this specific museum was created using Apple's ARKit and Unity3D. This application is designed for iOS and runs on iPad Pro 10.5-in. The application starts with a portal. When the user walks through the portal with his/her device, he/she is transferred to the entrance of the museum. From that point on, the user can walk with his/her device and explore the

Fig. 1. ARKit version: standing outside the cross-reality museum (left) and being inside one of the museum rooms (right). In both images the mini map can be seen in the lower right corner, displaying the position and rotation of the user (small red square). (Color figure online)

different areas of the museum, as if he/she was there. A number of information points have been added so that when the user gets close to those points, a board appears containing specific information about the museum and its content, thus allowing for the user to learn about the museum's history and discover its exhibits. Collision detection has been added, as well as animations of doors opening and closing when the user walks through them in order to make the experience more realistic. Future improvements to this application might include: adding more animations to the models of several machines to enable users to see what those machines looked like when they were in use; another possible avenue would be to add a virtual 3D character to interact with the users and provide them with information about the museum (storytelling element).

Android Version (Using Google's ARCore)

An Android version of the Industrial Museum and Cultural Center of Thessaloniki's cross-reality application designed for ARCore supported devices [16] is also under development. It is based on the latest AR technologies developed by Google and aims to extend the current device support, making it accessible to more users. Just as the application described above, the same model of the museum is used in order to create a cross-reality portal to the museum as shown in Fig. 2.

The application detects planes in the real word using the built-in camera of the device, giving the end user the ability to place a portal and move through it into the virtual museum. Consequently, the user is able to explore it while differentiating it from the real world, thus conveying a sense of realism at the same time. The next steps in the development of this version of the application involve completely integrating the

Fig. 2. ARCore version: the portal leading to the cross-reality museum (left) and the view of the portal while inside the museum (right).

features of the iOS version, including animations, a mini map for easy transportation through the museum and gamification elements that will offer users a fun and compelling virtual museum experience.

4.6   Augmented Reality Application for the Exploration of the Museum

A second application currently under development is aimed at people who actually visit the museum. This application can only be used inside the museum. It is designed to recognize the room of the museum where the user is located and provide different augmented 3D models (like boards, etc.) containing information related to specific areas of the museum. This application will be made for iOS and run on the iPad Pro 10.5-in.

5   Conclusions

Cultural Heritage is an area where technology has a lot to offer. Computer graphics and Digital Cultural Heritage have the power to give people access and bring them closer to every monument and museum they desire. This is a vital contribution to the preservation of Cultural Heritage. This paper has examined attempts to create such applications for a museum in Thessaloniki. One can only hope that more attempts like these will be made in the future to give rise to Virtual Museums that will enable people to come into contact with Cultural Heritage from their homes with the help of Virtual or Augmented Reality.

5.1   Lesson Learned

It is now clear that more Digital Cultural Heritage applications are needed in the region of Central Macedonia. Such applications are essential, as they greatly contribute to the preservation of Cultural Heritage, by making CH assets available to more people, many of whom would not otherwise have access to them. In terms of the specific Cross-Reality applications under consideration, they provide more people with the opportunity to learn about the museum, its exhibitions and its story, therefore broadening their knowledge while preserving Cultural Heritage.

5.2   Impact and Added Value

These applications (both ARKit and ARCore versions) have a major impact on Digital Cultural Heritage. Specifically, they are able to immerse users in a virtual world, which in this case corresponds to the virtual version of the Industrial Museum and Cultural Center of Thessaloniki. Cross-Reality elements make these applications more interesting by transferring users from the real to the virtual world via a portal that they can place wherever they want. This switch between the real and the virtual world coupled with the user's ability to walk around naturally enhance the feeling of presence, making the virtual experience feel more realistic. The storytelling elements of these applications (boards with information about the museum exhibits) and the gamification elements (the quiz game enabling users to test the knowledge that they acquire during their virtual museum visit in an attempt to score points and win a virtual prize) improve the overall quality of the experience by making it more interesting and more fun. Applications with such elements have a significant impact on people (both adults and children), encouraging the latter to revisit them again with the aim of improving their quiz score and obtaining higher prizes, thus inciting users to recommend the applications to others. A possible future usage of dynamic storytelling elements, like a virtual character [17, 18] guiding users through the museum, might also improve the experience. There are currently a little to none applications of this kind that focus on the region of Central Macedonia, opening up great potential for the future.

References

1. History Center of Thessaloniki. https://tinyurl.com/y8rxy54m. Accessed 20 May 2018
2. Culture Thessaloniki. https://culture.thessaloniki.gr/. Accessed 20 May 2018
3. Galerian Complex. http://galeriuspalace.culture.gr/en/. Accessed 20 May 2018
4. Browsing the city of Thessaloniki from mobile device with Virtual Reality applications. http://www.voria.gr/article/i-thessaloniki-parousiazi-ton-eafto-tis-me-virtual-reality. Accessed 20 May 2018
5. The action plan for the protection and promotion of the cultural heritage of Central Macedonia was presented. https://tinyurl.com/y783cy4w. Accessed 20 May 2018
6. CHRISTA Inauguration meeting in Thessaloniki. https://tinyurl.com/y7hmv679. Accessed 20 May 2018
7. Region of Central Macedonia CHRISTA project. http://www.pkm.gov.gr/default.aspx?lang=el-GR&page=29&projectid=49. Accessed 20 May 2018

8. Region of Central Macedonia Cult-RinG project. http://www.pkm.gov.gr/default.aspx?lang=el-GR&page=29&projectid=60. Accessed 20 May 2018

9. Cultural Routes as Investment for Growth and Jobs. https://www.interregeurope.eu/cult-ring/. Accessed 20 May 2018

10. Region of Central Macedonia HIGHER project. http://www.pkm.gov.gr/default.aspx?lang=el-GR&page=29&projectid=50. Accessed 20 May 2018

11. Bruns, A.: Produsage: towards a broader framework for user-led content creation. In: Proceedings of the 6th ACM SIGCHI Conference on Creativity & Cognition, Washington, DC, pp. 99–106 (2007). https://doi.org/10.1145/1254960.1254975

12. Papagiannakis, G., Geronikolakis, E., Pateraki, M., Lopez-Menchero Bendicho, V., Tsioumas, M., Sylaiou, S., Liarokapis, F., Grammatikopoulou, A., Dimitropoulos, K., Grammalidis, N., Partarakis, N., Margetis, G., Drossis, G., Vassiliadi, M., Chalmers, A., Stephanidis, C., Magnenat-Thalmann, N.: Mixed reality gamified presence and storytelling for virtual museums. In: Lee, N. (ed.) Encyclopedia of Computer Graphics and Games. Springer, Cham (2018). https://doi.org/10.1007/978-3-319-08234-9

13. The Islahane of Thessaloniki. https://tinyurl.com/yday8wzp. Accessed 09 Aug 2018

14. ARKit Vs. ARCore – How they compare against each other? https://www.itfirms.co/arkit-vs-arcore-how-they-compare-against-each-other/. Accessed 11 Aug 2018

15. ARCore vs. ARKit: Which Is Better for Building Augmented Reality Apps? https://www.iflexion.com/blog/arcore-vs-arkit-better-building-augmented-reality-apps/. Accessed 11 Aug 2018

16. ARCore Supported Devices. https://developers.google.com/ar/discover/supported-devices. Accessed 20 May 2018

17. Arnold, D., Day, A., Glauert, J., Haegler, S., Jennings, V., Kevelham, B., Laycock, R., Magnenat-Thalmann, N., Maïm, J., Maupu, D., Papagiannakis, G., Thalmann, D., Yersin, B., Rodriguez-Echavarria, K.: Tools for populating cultural heritage environments with interactive virtual humans. In: Open Digital Cultural Heritage Systems, EPOCH Final Event 2008, Rome (2008)

18. Vacchetti, L., Lepetit, V., Ponder, M., Papagiannakis, G., Fua, P., Thalmann, D., Magnenat-Thalmann, N.: Stable real-time AR framework for training and planning in industrial environments. In: Ong, S.K., Nee, A.Y.C. (eds.) Virtual Reality and Augmented Reality Applications in Manufacturing, pp. 125–142. Springer, London (2004). https://doi.org/10.1007/978-1-4471-3873-0_8

3D Models and Virtual Tours for a Museum Exhibition of Vietnamese Cultural Heritage Exhibits and Sites

Thomas P. Kersten$^{(\boxtimes)}$ (iD)

Photogrammetry and Laser Scanning Lab, HafenCity University Hamburg,
Überseeallee 16, 20457 Hamburg, Germany
Thomas.Kersten@hcu-hamburg.de

Abstract. In this contribution examples of Vietnamese cultural heritage objects of different size and importance, which were reconstructed in 3D from image sequences, in order to manufacture digital (and physical) photo-realistic replicas for an exhibition and for 3D visualisation in virtual applications for museums, are presented. For the "Treasures of the Archaeology and Culture of Vietnam" exhibition selected cultural heritage objects from different museums in Vietnam were digitised in September 2015 using image sequences taken with a digital reflex camera Nikon D800 and documented in detail by the Photogrammetry & Laser Scanning Lab of the HafenCity University Hamburg. The Treasures of Vietnam, which were never exhibited outside of Vietnam, were shown for the first time in Germany in the context of three exhibitions in the cities of Herne, Chemnitz and Mannheim between October 2016 and February 2018. The workflow from 3D object recording and modelling up to visualisation and 3D printing is described. The results of the generated 3D models and their integration in virtual tours of world heritage sites are presented.

Keywords: 3D · Digitization · Meshing · Modelling · Replica
Printing

1 Introduction

Cultural Heritage (CH) objects are important testimonials of our human past. Worldwide, this historical inheritance is today in significant danger due to destruction by war, terrorism and vandalism as well as from the effects of weathering. A substantial number of cultural objects was already transported, sold or destroyed in the past. Examples of the senseless destruction are the large Buddha statues of Bamiyan in Afghanistan [1] and the archaeologically important site of Palmyra in Syria [2]. On the other hand, many CH objects are stored, non-restored or conserved in storehouses and they lose their ornaments or shape over time. In order to avoid the complete loss of all information of this cultural heritage, 3D recording and documentation with modern measuring techniques is an essential and highly successful method. An additional support for this task is the ongoing increased efficiency of Internet and computer technology combined with the rapid development of appropriate computing algorithms in computer vision and photogrammetry. Thus, efficient and flexible reconstruction of the 3D

© Springer Nature Switzerland AG 2018
M. Ioannides et al. (Eds.): EuroMed 2018, LNCS 11196, pp. 528–538, 2018.
https://doi.org/10.1007/978-3-030-01762-0_46

geometry of CH objects is possible for their protection, for future tasks of preservation and for a location-independent presentation.

In most cases the valuable and interesting archaeological finds and exhibits remain in the country of origin due to their significant national meaning, for legal reasons or also due to transport risks. Therefore, procedures and tools must be developed and used to show these unique objects to an interested public abroad. CH objects of different sizes (from coins to complex temple constructions) can be recorded and modelled in 3D from image sequences taken using commercial digital cameras using highly developed software. A camera, a scale bar and a laptop are the components of this so-called low-cost system, which is very useful and which has already been effective for a variety of applications in archaeology, restoration, cultural heritage, visualization, analysis of building construction and their damage, etc. [3–6]. Examples for massive 3D digitization of museum contents and of cultural objects are presented in [7] and [8], while the state of the art and future perspectives of 3D printing is published in [9]. If one considers the fact that the transport and import of structured light systems or laser scanners into a foreign country often causes various bureaucratic as well as sometimes creating transport-technical hurdles, the employment of a camera instead can be an uncomplicated, low expenditure alternative. The use of successful methods, incorporating various applications, and the creation of an optimised workflow for generating 3D models and corresponding 3D prints of Vietnamese CH exhibits are described in this contribution. Furthermore, virtual tours of World Heritage Sites which integrated these virtual 3D models, were developed and presented in the museum exhibitions.

Fig. 1. Announcement of the exhibition "Treasures of Archaeology of Vietnam" in Germany.

2 Photogrammetric 3D Recording

In this contribution five examples of Vietnamese CH objects of different size and importance, which were reconstructed in 3D from images sequences for the generation of digital and physical replicas, are presented (Fig. 2). For the exhibition "Treasures of Archaeology of Vietnam" [10], which visited the German cities Herne (Fig. 1), Chemnitz and Mannheim between October 2016 and January 2018, selected CH objects of Vietnam, which were never previously exhibited outside of Vietnam, were photographed using images sequences and documented in detail. The photogrammetric data acquisition was carried out in specific museums in Vietnam in September 2015. Therefore, all selected objects were photographed from different perspectives and heights using a digital single-lens reflex camera Nikon D800, which has a full format sensor of 36 mm × 24 mm with a resolution of 36 million pixels. Using a stable camera position on a tripod the photographs could be taken with a long focal length (ca. 35 mm or 80 mm) and with a small aperture (f/22) thus allowing a long exposure time and optimal sharpness despite partially unfavourable lighting conditions. Taking the photos with HDR (High Dynamic Range) in an exposure latitude of three photos (over, under and normally exposed), optimal exposure of the object could be guaranteed, since the three photos were already merged to an optimally exposed photo in the camera's on-board computer. During photogrammetric data acquisition calibrated scale bars with lengths of 14 cm, 28 cm and 44 cm were placed around the object, in order to precisely scale the 3D point cloud generated from the photos. During data processing of the different image sequences an accuracy of approx. 0.05 mm could be determined for the scale bars.

In order to completely model an object such as a skull, two image blocks were taken, one of the upper part and one of the lower part. However, using this approach sufficient overlap must exist in object space between both image blocks in order to fully compute a complete model.

Fig. 2. Treasures of Vietnamese Archaeology as CH objects to be recorded – f.l.t.r.: wooden Buddha statue, skull with earring, gold masks, Mukhalinga ("phallus with face") and drum.

3   Image Data Processing and 3D Modelling

In the following the data processing and 3D modelling of the five most important CH objects, which were recorded in Vietnam, is briefly introduced. The evaluation of the image data was carried out using Agisoft PhotoScan from St. Petersburg as follows: After the import of the photos, image orientations and camera calibrations were computed per image block. Therefore, all images were connected to each other by automatic pixel measurements resulting in a sparse 3D point cloud. Correct scaling of the generated 3D point clouds was ensured by precise manual measurement of scale bars in the images. For the case where several image blocks were necessary for object recording, it was essential to first merge all image blocks in one project. For this a (low) resolution mesh was computed and manually cut to generate a mask from object space into image space. This mask represented only the object shape without any disturbing surroundings. Subsequently, all photos of the different image blocks were oriented again using the mask information, so that all photos were oriented in a single common image block. However, if the orientation of all photos was not completely successful, additional tie points could be manually measured in the appropriate photos before a new image orientation was computed. Once successful a dense point cloud of the entire object could be computed without hidden areas. The point cloud could be cleaned, filtered, segmented and meshed directly in PhotoScan. Other options for data processing of point clouds are available with software packages such as Geomagic, CloudCompare or other modelling programs. As a final step the cleaned meshed model was textured with high resolution textures in PhotoScan using the existing photos.

3.1   The Wooden Buddha from South Vietnam

The 3D recording of the first object was a challenge since the wooden Buddha statue is very fragile and relative flat, which made the creation of a connection between both sides (front and back surface) very difficult in the later modelling process. The 190 cm tall Buddha statue, which was discovered in March 2004, is originally from Gò Tháp (Mekong delta, province Đồng Tháp, south Vietnam) and is located in the museum Đồng Tháp in Cao Lãnh. It belongs to the Óc EO culture and it was manufactured in the 2nd century A.D. [11]. A standing setup of the statue for image capture was not possible due to safety reasons. The statue lying on two stools (Fig. 3) was photographed in 378 photos (193 front, 185 back) with the Nikon D800 (f = 85 mm), with both High Dynamic Range (HDR) and normal exposure time from each camera station to ensure quality exposure. Due to the flat geometry of the statue and the configuration of the camera positions for the front and back side of the statue there were only a few over-lapping areas for connecting the two object parts. Therefore, corresponding points in both object parts had to be measured manually to ensure a geometrical correct con-nection of the two photo blocks. The 3D model of the wooden Buddha (Fig. 3 right) was created at four different resolution levels in the file format OBJ, in order to fulfil the different requirements from 3D printing to visualisation: 5 million (368 MB), 2 million triangles (147 MB), 600,000 triangles (52 MB) and 200,000 triangles (23 MB).

Fig. 3.   Camera set up for image acquisition (left) and 3D model of the Buddha head (centre/right).

3.2   A Skull with Earring from Ho Chi Minh City

The second object presented is a skull with earring of the SA Huỳnh culture (Figs. 2 and 4), dated between the 3rd and 1st Centuries B.C. and located in the grave field Giồng Cá Vồ. This item was photographed in the national museum in Ho Chi Minh City. The upper and lower parts of the skull were recorded in two image sequences around the object and from different heights resulting in 193 photos (Fig. 4 left).

Unfortunately, the skull and lower jaw were not firmly connected to each other and collapsed, so that both object parts were photographed lying next to each other after turning the object to take photographs from the opposing side. This mishap made the further data post processing substantially more difficult, since the accurate position of the lower jaw had to be reconstructed now from the first image series of the top side and resultant deformations in the lower jaw had to be corrected. The textured 3D model of the skull (Fig. 4 right) consists of approx. one million triangles, which corresponds to a data volume of 102 Mbyte in ASCII format.

Fig. 4. Camera setup for the recording of the skull with earring (left), skull as triangle mesh (centre) and as textured 3D model (right).

3.3   Gold Masks from South Vietnam

In the museum of the province Bà Rịa - Vũng Tàu two gold masks (size – 10.9 × 4.5 cm and 9.7 cm × 6.0 cm, thickness – approx. 1 mm) were photographed (Fig. 5). These were found as burial objects in two different graves of the 1st century B. C. on the archaeological site Giồng Lớn in South Vietnam. The two sides of the masks were well-documented from different camera positions in 107 and 60 photos, respectively, so that all details were visible. Using these image sequences a surface model of the front and rear sides were computed in each case. These were assembled afterwards as a common 3D model with a data volume of 20 Mbyte (e.g. gold mask 1: 124.249 points and 248.494 triangles). The assembling of the two sides was carried out using four points, which were visible as holes in the corners of each gold mask.

Fig. 5. Camera setup for the recording of the gold mask (left), 3D model of the gold mask in front and back view (centre) and detailed section of the triangle meshing (right).

3.4 Mukhalinga of the Cham Culture

In the museum Mỹ Sơn near Đà Nẵng in central Vietnam (province Quảng Nam), about 30 km southwest of the former port town Hội, a Mukhalinga of the Cham culture (from the 8th century) was photographed with 184 photos from different heights and perspectives. The Mukhalinga ("phallus with face"), an early manifestation of Shiva with the representation of its face, has the impressive dimensions of 1.26 m height, 0.41 m width and 0.41 m depth. For scaling of the image sequence two horizontal and vertical 2 m scale bars were additionally placed into the object area (Fig. 6 left). Using the recorded image data 3D models (Fig. 6 right) were generated at different resolutions for usage in different applications, e.g. such as 3D printing (high resolution) and 3D visualisation on a standard PC (low to very low resolution).

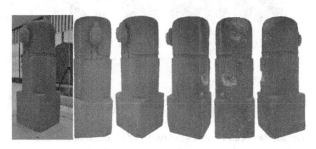

Fig. 6. Photo (left) and 3D model of the Mukhalinga from five different perspectives (right).

3.5 The Bronze Drum from Cổ Loa

A bronze drum of more than 2000 years old from Cổ Loa was photographed with 165 images in the museum of the city of Hanoi. The positions of the camera and one of the two scale bars used are represented in Fig. 7 (left).

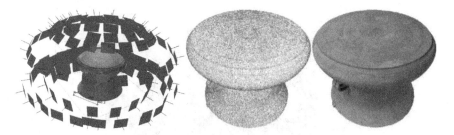

Fig. 7. Configuration of camera positions for 3D recording of the drum (left), triangle mesh (centre) and textured 3D model of the drum (right).

Image orientations and camera calibration were computed in 37 min on a powerful notebook (Schenker XMG 64bit operating system, 32 GB RAM, 2 Nvidia Geforce

GT780M, CPU Intel core i7-4940MX CPU 3.1 GHz), while the computation of a dense point cloud with 42.5 million points took five hours and 21 min. Using these data 3D models (Fig. 7) were derived at different resolutions (Table 1): (a) high resolution (100%) with 8,501,538 triangles and a file size of 940 MB, (b) low resolution (11%) with 945,093 triangles and a file size of 99.7 MB and (c) very low resolution (1.2%) with 100,000 triangles and a file size of only 12.4 MB, which corresponds to a data reduction factor of 83 for the last case. For quality control of the generated 3D models a 3D comparison between the three data sets was computed using the software Geo-magic studio, which confirmed very small average deviations of less than 0.1 mm for the reduced models (Fig. 8).

Fig. 8. 3D comparison between high-resolution (100%) and reduced datasets (11% and 1.2%) of the drum (unit of colour scale in [m]). (Color figure online)

Table 1. Technical specifications for the models of Cổ Loa drum with different resolutions.

Resolution	Data set	# triangle	# MB	Reduction factor
High	100%	8,501,538	940.0	1
Low	2.2%	945,093	99.7	9
Very low	1.2%	100,000	12.4	83

Fig. 9. 3D replicas as exhibits in the LWL Museum for Archaeology in Herne: f.l.t.r. wooden Buddha, skull and Mukhalinga. (Color figure online)

4 Replicas by 3D Printing

For the exhibition "Treasures of the Archaeology of Vietnam" in the LWL Museum for Archaeology in Herne the company ARC-TECH GbR (in Birstein, Germany) manufactured three exhibits (wooden Buddha, skull and Mukhalinga) as 3D replicas (Fig. 9). The replicas were produced at a scale 1:1 by 3D printing using photogrammetric 3D models of the original objects. The skull with earring was printed in monochrome colour (gypsum colour) with a layer stratification of 0.1 mm in a ColorJet Printing procedure lasting approx. 8–9 h using a ZPrinter ProJet 660Pro 3D printer, while PU resin was infiltrated in a generative layer construction method. The wooden Buddha and the Mukhalinga were manufactured in one common job of approx. 30–35 h by sand printing (dark grey) with layering of 0.3 mm, while both objects were processed together in a pressure chamber and printing process respectively. In the printing process PU resin was also infiltrated here, in order to make the replicas more robust and more resistant. The surfaces were later carefully revised and manually coloured by hand, which took approx. 120 h in total.

5 Virtual Tours for World Heritage Sites

For a museum representation of world cultural heritage sites in Vietnam five different sites in central and North Vietnam were developed as virtual tours. These were generated from full-spherical panoramas (360° view) from different camera stations. The panoramic tripod head used for panorama photography was designed in such a way that the camera projection centre always rotates around exactly the same point (Fig. 10 left). For each panorama image a total of twelve photos were taken with a Nikon D800 (fisheye lens Nikkor 10.5 mm) – nine photos with a horizontal rotation of 40° each around the vertical axis as well as one photo looking vertically to the sky and two photos vertically downwards to the ground (Fig. 10 centre). Using the twelve photographs the panorama image was automatically calculated with the software PTGui, which is unwounded on a cylinder (Fig. 10 right). For the calculation of the panorama image the exposure of all photos could be adjusted to each other and disturbing areas could be masked in PTGui.

Fig. 10. Generation of panorama imagery – camera on a panoramic tripod head (left), single photographs for the panorama computation (centre) and computed full-spherical panorama after exposure balancing in PTGui (right).

As an example, the virtual tour of Mỹ Sơn is represented in Fig. 11. This interactive virtual tour contains 31 panoramas in total and shows a full-spherical panorama for each camera station, which offers a 360° view similar to Google Street View. The user sees a panorama at the start of the virtual tour and as an option an aerial photograph or a map as an overview of the world cultural heritage site (switchable on and off), in which all available camera stations are marked (Fig. 11). The panorama can be rotated 360° and zoomed in and out. By clicking on an appropriate arrow as a directional indicator in the panorama or by clicking on spots in the general overview map the visitor can navigate the tour. A radar in the general map (Fig. 11) shows the current perspective view of the panorama, while a compass with north arrow shows orientation in the current position. Additionally, hotspots are integrated as links to images, detailed photographs and drawings of finds as well as texts for explanations or descriptions, music, videos and other user actions such as 3D objects using a XML-based programming language.

With this new technology not only remote places such as world cultural heritage sites can be informatively and interactively demonstrated to interested museum visitors, but also archaeological finds in 3D can be linked to the original site of discovery. For the exhibition "Treasures of Archaeology of Vietnam" in Herne the following further virtual tours were arranged: citadel Hoa Lư with Trường Yên (Ninh Bình), citadel of the Hồ dynasty in Thanh Hóa, the Literature Temple and the citadel Thăng Long in Hanoi (Fig. 11 right). These tours were presented on a large screen at an exhibition wall and controlled by a terminal with trackball device.

Fig. 11. User interface for the virtual tour of the world heritage site Mỹ Sơn with explanations and possible additional information (left) and some virtual tours for world cultural heritage sites in North Vietnam – citadel Hoa Lư at Trường Yên (Ninh Bình) (top right), citadel of the Hồ dynasty in Thanh Hóa (centre right) and the temple of literature (bottom right).

6   Conclusions and Outlook

The methods and systems used in this project successfully demonstrated best practice for recording and 3D modelling of Vietnamese CH objects, so that the requested products for the museum exhibition could be reproduced in the form of appropriate virtual tours and digital and printed 3D replicas. A high-resolution digital SLR camera with the HDR function used on a tripod offers the ideal equipment for photographing with optimal lighting and depth sharpness for projects within museum areas. In addition, high performance portable computers (notebooks) allow on-site flexible and automatic data processing of the recorded image sequences, which ensures rapid quality control of the processes and the generated products. Several applications (e.g. visualisation, Internet, 3D printing) can be realised by automatic generation of textured 3D models at different resolutions using the appropriate data. The software PhotoScan is easy to use also for non-photogrammetric users and it automatically supplies results in a well-defined workflow. However, expert knowledge is meaningful, if not even necessary, for the evaluation of the results (image orientations, camera calibration and triangle meshing).

The combination of 3D models and virtual tours is the first step to a virtual museum, since archaeological finds and sites can be virtually connected to each other, which gives access to remote cultures and exhibits for visitors. Such virtual museums can be composed as interactive learning platforms, so that interested people can playfully acquire information (as serious games), in order to achieve a successful learning effect. This is the modern way of disseminating knowledge. Therefore, modern visualisation tools such as smartphones, tablets or large 3D screens offer an interactive and detailed representation of archaeological objects and exhibits in 3D for all interested users [12].

References

1. Gruen, A., Remondino, F., Zhang, L.: Reconstruction of the great Buddha of Bamiyan, Afghanistan. Int. Arch. Photogramm. Remote. Sens. Spat. Inf. Sci. **34**(5), 363–368 (2002)
2. Wahbeh, W., Nebiker, S., Fangi, G.: Combining public domain and professional panoramic imagery for the accurate and dense 3D reconstruction of the destroyed Bel Temple in Palmyra. ISPRS Ann. Photogramm. Remote. Sens. Spat. Inf. Sci. **3**(5), 81–88 (2016)
3. Remondino, F., El-Hakim, S.F., Gruen, A., Zhang, L.: Turning images into 3-D models. IEEE Signal Process. Mag. **25**(4), 55–65 (2008)
4. Barazzetti, L., Remondino, F., Scaioni, M.: Combined use of photogrammetric and computer vision techniques for fully automated and accurate 3D modeling of terrestrial objects. In: Proceedings of SPIE Optics + Photonics, vol. 7447 (2009)
5. Kersten, T., Lindstaedt, M.: Automatic 3D object reconstruction from multiple images for architectural, cultural heritage and archaeological applications using open-source software and web services. Photogramm. – Fernerkund. – Geoinf. J. Photogramm. Remote Sens. Geoinf. Sci. **6**, 727–740 (2012)
6. Kersten, T.P., Lindstaedt, M.: Image-based low-cost systems for automatic 3D recording and modelling of archaeological finds and objects. In: Ioannides, M., Fritsch, D., Leissner, J., Davies, R., Remondino, F., Caffo, R. (eds.) EuroMed 2012. LNCS, vol. 7616, pp. 1–10. Springer, Heidelberg (2012). https://doi.org/10.1007/978-3-642-34234-9_1
7. Guidi, G., Gonizzi Barsanti, S., Micoli, L.L., Russo, M.: Massive 3D digitization of museum contents. In: Toniolo, L., Boriani, M., Guidi, G. (eds.) Built Heritage: Monitoring Conservation Management. RD, pp. 335–346. Springer, Cham (2015). https://doi.org/10.1007/978-3-319-08533-3_28

8. Hollinger, R.E., et al.: Tlingit-Smithsonian collaborations with 3D digitization of cultural objects. Mus.M Anthropol. Rev. **7**(1–2), 201–253 (2013)

9. Balletti, C., Ballarin, M., Guerra, F.: 3D printing: state of the art and future perspectives. J. Cult. Herit. **26**, 172–182 (2017)

10. Reinecke, A., Mühlenbrock, J.: Schätze der Archäologie Vietnams – Die erste deutsche Vietnam-Ausstellung 2016/17. Antike Welt – Zeitschrift für Archäologie und Kulturgeschichte, 8–11 May 2016. Philipp von Zabern, WBG, Darmstadt (2016)

11. Reinecke, A.: Tempel, Inschriften und frühe Buddha-Figuren aus Holz von Gò Tháp. Frühgeschichte in Südvietnam – die Óc Eo-Kultur. Schätze der Archäologie Vietnams, Begleitband zur Sonderausstellung, p. 599, Nünnerich-Asmus Verlag & Media, Mainz (2016)

12. Tschirschwitz, F., Kersten, T.P., Zobel, K.: Interactive 3D visualisation of architectural models and point clouds using low-cost-systems. In: Ioannides, M., Magnenat-Thalmann, N., Fink, E., Žarnić, R., Yen, A.-Y., Quak, E. (eds.) EuroMed 2014. LNCS, vol. 8740, pp. 268–278. Springer, Cham (2014). https://doi.org/10.1007/978-3-319-13695-0_26

An Augmented Reality Mobile App for Museums: Virtual Restoration of a Plate of Glass

Andrea F. Abate[1][(✉)], Silvio Barra[2], Giuseppe Galeotafiore[1],
Carmen Díaz[3], Elvira Aura[3], Miguel Sánchez[3], Xavier Mas[3],
and Eduardo Vendrell[3]

[1] University of Salerno, Fisciano, SA, Italy
abate@unisa.it, g.galeotafiore1@studenti.unisa.it
[2] University of Cagliari, Cagliari, Italy
silvio.barra@unica.it
[3] Universitat Politècnica de València, Valencia, Spain
madiama84@gmail.com, eaura@crbc.upv.es,
misan@disca.upv.es, jamasbar@upvnet.upv.es,
even@upv.es

Abstract. One of the problems for archaeologic museums is having the opportunity to show most of the objects that they preserve. This is an action they can't afford because of the limitation of exhibition spaces, the high number of artifacts they guard and/or the conditions of the real objects. Nowadays, with the use of cutting-edge 3D technologies, there is the possibility to offer virtual views of objects adding information and enhancing visitor's experience. In this paper, an Augmented Reality app for visualizing restored ancient artifacts is presented. Based on an algorithm that addresses geometric constraints of fragments to rebuild the object from parts, the AR application shows a reconstructed artifact offering the possibility for the user to visualize missing fragments. The app has been demonstrated using a real restored glass plate from the Manises Ceramic Museum, under the context of a research project funded by the Spanish Ministry of Economy, Industry and Competitiveness.

Keywords: Restoration · Mobile app · Augmented reality

1 Introduction

The development of 3D technologies applied to the Cultural Heritage field (CH) has been growing exponentially thanks to the joint efforts of disparate research fields leading to extraordinary results lately. Such a technological cooperation helped growing the conservation, the display and active spreading of the cultural artifact to a public more interested in new ways of knowledge and information. To that extent, these 3D technologies are shaping the way Cultural Heritage is documented and how it is interacted with. The use of laser 3D scanners, the methods of 3D modelling and reconstruction, photogrammetric techniques, 3D printing and computer vision have become powerful tools able to transcend our perception of cultural artifacts [1–4].

© Springer Nature Switzerland AG 2018
M. Ioannides et al. (Eds.): EuroMed 2018, LNCS 11196, pp. 539–547, 2018.
https://doi.org/10.1007/978-3-030-01762-0_47

There is no doubt information and communication technologies are the foundation of the development these news methods of studying and presenting where, tangible objects and/or virtual ones interact with each other improving both documentation and object visualization.

In such a technological context, augmented reality (AR) is a very versatile tool with a great potential for broadcasting the knowledge about Cultural Heritage. As opposed to Virtual Reality, where the user is immersed in a computer-generated virtual world, augmented reality enhances the real world with additional 3D graphics overlapped in the user field of vision. It provides a feeling of immediacy and spatial consistency between virtual and tangible objects [5, 6].

The growing and massive use of AR in museums' environment has been possible thanks the technological evolution of portable devices (such as mobile phones and tablets) [7] and the readiness of geolocation [8–10]. This combination allows users to reach wider information about the cultural object and to interact in a natural and intuitive way without the need of being familiar with new technologies [11]. It is about apps with tangible interfaces that allow handling the virtual object as if it were a real object [12, 13]. To that extent, there have been developed several applications of the use of augmented reality: (a) personal guides or assistants, (b) applications based on the use of tags and (c) augmented virtual reconstructions [14].

In this paper's case, a personal guide using a mobile device like a smartphone or tablet is created. The application overlays computer-generated graphs over the device's camera images, more specifically, the virtual restoration of an archaeological glass plate. The application allows the simultaneous visualization of real and reconstructed parts (missing parts), allowing the visitor the visualization of the complete artifact.

In order to demonstrate the use of the application, a case study have been done using a restored glass plate from the Manises Ceramic Museum.

The goal of this project is to provide an innovative and alternative solution to museums for (1) visualizing objects they preserve and (2) attract more people to archaeologic activities with the use of 3D technology and smart devices that they use every day.

2   Case Study

An archaeological glass plate has been selected for creating an application of AR to show a restoration case study (Fig. 1). This glass plate, from Manises Ceramic Museum´s collection (Valencia, Spain), was recovered from an archaeological excavation made in the city of Manises in 2004. The archaeological artifact dates from 16th and early 17th centuries [15] and was manufactured by glassblowing. It is a small plate measuring just 25 mm height $\times$ 110 mm width, with a variable thickness between 0.8 and 5 mm. Its morphological description shows a deep dish with 10 mm horizontal brim turned edge and a slightly convexed bottom.

Having 3D models of ancient glass artifacts is useful for archaeologists as they can manage these digital models preventing damages in delicate glass objects and giving access to the research community. Additionally, the use of Augmented Reality techniques together with 3D models allow having digital representations of real objects to

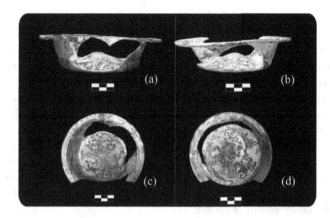

Fig. 1. Plate of glass. Front (a), back (b), top (c) and bottom (d).

be used on a variety of purposes, such as interaction with the artifacts, dissemination and distribution.

When burial environment has deteriorated archaeological glass artifacts due to its sensitive material condition, the use of 3D models became an imperative option.

For the case described in this paper, the glass plate has been affected by high levels of humidity. In particular, because of its alkaline nature, the surface of the plate suffered from this incorrect humidity leading to a rapid dehydration of the material, causing dulling (loss of its original clarity and transparency), iridescence (variegated coloration of the surface of glass), opacity (opaque white, light brown or mottled brownish-black in color), black discoloration (opaque blackened layer on the surface), spontaneous cracking (formation of fractures) and loss from the surface [16]. There were two mechanisms involved: de-alkalization and network dissolution. In addition, the fragility of the plate has led to be highly susceptible to experiment physical damage by mechanical shock. The glass plate appears broken in three fragments creating two extensive mutilation areas in the middle part. The reconstruction of the mutilated areas would imply a quite difficult handmade process, requiring many time and endurance. The glass plate would be on risk of deterioration due to its fragile and weak condition.

To deal with this problem, a solution is provided, by means of a method that recovers missing parts from a 3D model of the glass plate. This restoring process is showed through a mobile application in which the missing parts reconstructed are assembled into the fragile glass plate.

3   3D Digitization of the Object

Two techniques were used in order to register the glass plate: triangulation laser scanner and photogrammetry. First, a 3D model of the glass plate has been acquired by using a laser scanner (Konica Minolta VIVID 900). An opaque surface is needed in order to start the acquisition process with this type of scanner. As the glass plate studied has some reflective/refractive surface areas, a temporal opacifier has been used. The use of cyclododecane on spray over archaeological glass surfaces was established in [17]. It allows the object surface to be covered by an opaque white coat that sublimes at room temperature without leaving residual. The object covered with cyclododecane is placed on a round turntable with a 45° rotation step. Two different positions were used during the acquisition process: one for the top and the other one for the bottom. All three fragments were acquired separately. When 3D geometric models were obtained, then MeshLab was used for an optimization procedure of the models (Fig. 2).

Then, a photogrammetry technique with a Nikon D70 camera and a rotary table was used at 22.5° rotation step. The glass plate was acquired for three times to register the top, the middle and the bottom shape. As the quality of the resulting mesh was better than the one obtained with the scanner, we decided to use it, allowing to keep color texture from photogrammetry. Minor defects found on texture were corrected using a photography editing software.

Fig. 2. 3D digital model of the glass plate obtained by means of a laser triangulation scanner as well as textures taken by using photogrammetry techniques. Mesh (a, c) and texture (b, d).

Three different files are the final result: an "obj" file for the mesh, an "mtl" file, containing the reference to the texture map and its shading properties, and a "jpg"-"png" file with the bitmap of the texture.

4   Virtual Restoration of the Glass Plate

The restoration of the plate was made in two steps: (1) an automatic reconstruction of the glass plate using 3D models obtained from all fragments acquired, and (2) the reconstruction of missing parts by means of a 3D modeling process.

First, an automatic technique was used to reconstruct the glass plate, taking as input all 3D geometric models of the fragments. Thus, fragments are matched one against other, by using the rigid transformation matrices that maximize the contact area between their surfaces. The process takes into account a possible erosion of the fragments, so maybe the best match is not the solution. For these cases, a global reconstruction algorithm is needed to discard the first solution, asking to return other possible matches.

This technique implies two phases: fragments' preprocessing and pairs' searching. The first phase involves lots of comparisons between pairs of fragments, getting results that can be used in as many associations as needed in additional searches. The second phase is considered as an exhaustive strategy of exploration. In order to optimize this, a hierarchical strategy is introduced. This proposed search considers different hierarchical fragment description as Levels Of Detail (LOD). It starts by matching rough representations of fragments. Then, the process refines the most favorable matches until the finest LOD is reached. The search stops at this stage and it returns the resulting alignment [18].

The second step consists on restoring mutilated parts of the plate. To do that, two missing parts were recovered using the methodology developed in [19]. This virtual restoration takes into account the 3D mesh of the plate so two selected areas have been replicated from the 3D model and placed in the gaps.

The different steps for this virtual restoration process are next (Fig. 3):

(a) Analyze the 3D model of the plate and select two areas with similar shape to the missing parts.
(b) Make a duplicate of the selected areas.
(c) Place duplicated areas into gaps.
(d) Adapt implants to the gaps.
(e) Apply a Boolean operation between the original object and the implant to obtain a topography of the fractured area.

As the result of this restoration process, two implants were obtained, allowing the restoration of the damaged object from its visual reconstruction.

Finally, two fragments needed to be textured, by means of a texture map for each model. To facilitate this operation, a reduction on the number of polygons for each mesh representing an implant had to be done. Then the texture map is extracted and the 3D geometric model of the plate was projected against the 2D texture map image [20]. The final 3D texture was obtained by cloning the original texture.

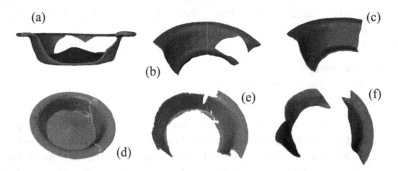

Fig. 3. Results of the process of reconstruction of the missing fragments. (a) 3D digital model of the glass plate, (b) section, (c) section completed, (d) two sections positioned in the missing areas, (e) Boolean and (f) two final implants.

The final result is the virtual model of the glass plate with the virtual reconstruction of missing parts, mesh and texture (Fig. 4).

Fig. 4. The 3D digital model of the glass plate including the missing parts and the texture map. Mesh (a, c) and texture (b, d).

This model has a good accuracy (less than 600 μm, according to manufacturer specifications of scanner) with high resolution texture maps, that makes it perfect for its use in website visualization or AR applications.

The virtual restoration of the glass plate, including the modeling of the missing parts, allows its use for visualization, including software developments that allow interaction with the model, preserving the real artifact during exhibitions.

5   Augmented Reality App Development

As explained before, in order to be used by museums, an Augmented Reality application has been developed so visitors can easily appreciate complete restored archaeological artifacts, including their missing parts. This app is intended to be used as a complement to real ancient objects during their exhibition, and can be downloaded to any individual mobile device.

The AR app development involved the use of three different tools:

– Vuforia AR Platform;
– 3D Graphic Engine Unity 2017 3.1;
– Android SDK.

To let the Vuforia "Object Targets" component recognize an object, it needs the so-called *object data*. Therefore, the application "Vuforia Object Scanner" is used to scan the physical object and creates the Object Data, which includes the data necessary to the definition of the Object Target in the Target Manager. In order to avoid the manipulation of the original glass plate, and because of its fragility, a 3D printed model of the plate obtained from a 3D model have been used (Fig. 5).

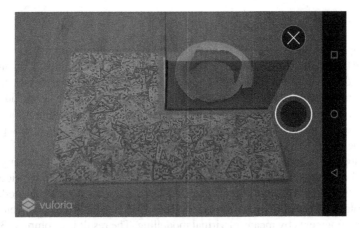

Fig. 5. The object is processed in order to initialize the target.

The scanned object and the Object Data generated were hence added to the Target Manager. This operation will generate a set of files containing the native datasets used for the integration with the Unity3D Vuforia plugin.

Once imported into Unity, the "Guide View Mode" allowed the view of the object and the positioning of the fragments to the proper location. Then, the app was ready to be installed on the Android Mobile.

When using the AR app, once the plate is recognized, the fragments will appear in the proper position. In the leftmost part of the Fig. 6, the plate is positioned over a table: the locations of the missing pieces are clearly visible. In the rightmost part, the application positioned correctly the missing pieces in the proper locations.

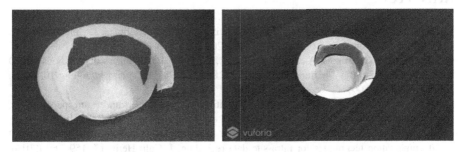

Fig. 6. On the left, the plate which we want to reconstruct the missing pieces. On the right, the missing fragments are positioned in the proper locations.

This way, a virtual restoration of a real archaeological object is performed allowing the user to visualize the complete object including all missing parts.

6 Conclusions

In this paper, an Augmented Reality (AR) based application is introduced for visualization of archaeological artifacts. This app shows the virtual model of an ancient object together with their missing parts, when pointing the mobile device to it. This way, the user can visualize the complete restored object, having a real idea of the restoration process. This software development is proposed as an solution for museums so they can show real artifacts that preserve or as a means to attract people to archaeology.

The app has been tested on a real glass plate from the 16th or 17th century. From a 3D model of this artifact, a virtual restoration process was performed, considering two missing fragments. The procedure began with the acquisition of a 3D model of the original plate, followed by its texturization. Then, the 3D model was completed adding all missing fragments by means of virtual modelling. The result is a complete 3D model of the restored plate.

This way, the 3D model can be used in an exhibition so visitors can download the app and use their own mobile devices to get an idea of how the real glass plate was. Museums can easily use these kind of solutions in order to show their pieces and make people appreciate the work of restorers in an interactive 3D environment.

Acknowledgements. This work is supported by Spanish Ministry of Economy, Industry and Competitiveness, in the context of the research project "R4FA. Desarrollo de un Sistema Integrado de Restauracion, Recomposicion, Restitucion y Representacion de Fragmentos Arqueológicos" (HAR2015-69408-R).

Authors would also like to acknowledge the collaboration of the Manises Ceramic Museum for their cooperation and support to this project, providing access to archaeological artifacts.

References

1. Pieraccini, M., Guidi, G., Atzeni, C.: 3D digitizing of cultural heritage. J. Cult. Herit. **2**(1), 63–70 (2001). https://doi.org/10.1016/S1296-2074(01)01108-6
2. Pavlidis, G., Koutsoudis, A., Arnaoutoglou, F., Tsioukas, V., Chamzas, C.: Methods for 3D digitization of cultural heritage. J. Cult. Herit. **8**(1), 93–98 (2007). https://doi.org/10.1016/j.culher.2006.10.007
3. Balletti, C., Ballarin, M., Guerra, F.: 3D printing: state of the art and future perspectives. J. Cult. Herit. **26**, 172–182 (2017). https://doi.org/10.1016/j.culher.2017.02.010
4. Galeazzi, F.: Towards the definition of best 3D practices in archaeology: assessing 3D documentation techniques for intra-site data recording. J. Cult. Herit. **17**, 159–169 (2016). https://doi.org/10.1016/j.culher.2015.07.005
5. Azuma, R., Baillot, Y., Behringer, R., Feiner, S., Julier, S., MacIntyre, B.: Recent advances in augmented reality. IEEE Comput. Graph. Appl. **21**(6), 34–47 (2001)
6. Krevelen, D.W.F., Poelman, R.: A survey of augmented reality technologies, applications and limitations. Int. J. Virtual Real. **9**(2), 1–20 (2010)
7. Angelopoulou, A., et al.: Mobile augmented reality for cultural heritage. In: Venkatasubramanian, N., Getov, V., Steglich, S. (eds.) MOBILWARE 2011. LNICST, vol. 93, pp. 15–22. Springer, Heidelberg (2012). https://doi.org/10.1007/978-3-642-30607-5_2

8. Krogstie, J.: Bridging research and innovation by applying living labs for design science research. In: Keller, C., Wiberg, M., Ågerfalk, P.J., Eriksson Lundström, J.S.Z. (eds.) SCIS 2012. LNBIP, vol. 124, pp. 161–176. Springer, Heidelberg (2012). https://doi.org/10.1007/978-3-642-32270-9_10

9. Billinghurst, M., Dünser, A.: Augmented reality in the classroom. Computer **45**(7), 56–63 (2012). https://doi.org/10.1109/MC.2012.111

10. Azuma, R., Billinghurst, M., Klinker, G.: Special section on mobile augmented reality. Comput. Graph. **35**(4), vii–viii (2011). https://doi.org/10.1016/j.cag.2011.05.002

11. Mase K., Kadobayashi R., Nakatsu R.: Meta-museum: a supportive augmented-reality environment for knowledge sharing. In: Proceedings of International Conference on Virtual System and Multimedia, pp. 107–110. IEEE Computer Society Press, Japan (1996)

12. Butchart B.: Augmented reality for smartphones. Technical report, JISC Observatory (2011)

13. Villarejo, L., González, F., Oriol, R., Miquel, J.: Introducing augmented reality in cultural heritage studies. ELC Res. Pap. Ser. **8**(8), 6–14 (2014)

14. Ruiz Torres D.: La realidad aumentada y su aplicación en el patrimonio cultural. Ed. Trea, Gijón, pp. 69–118 (2013)

15. Hortelano Uceda, I.: Intervención arqueológica en el solar de la calle Doctor Catalá Díez n° 3 de Manises (l'Orta Oest). Memoria inédita depositada en la Dirección Territorial de Cultural de la Conselleria de Cultura, Educación i Esport (2004)

16. Davison, S.: Conservation and Restauration of Glass, 2nd edn. Butterworth-Heinemann, London (2003)

17. Díaz, C., Aura, E., Sánchez, C., Vendrell, E.: Cyclododecane as opacifier for digitalization of archaeological glass. J. Cult. Herit. **17**, 131–140 (2016). https://doi.org/10.1016/j.culher.2015.06.003

18. Vendrell-Vidal, E., Sánchez-Belenguer, C.: A discrete approach for pairwise matching of archaeological fragments. ACM J. Comput. Cult. Herit. **7**(3) (2014). https://doi.org/10.1145/2597178. Article 15

19. Díaz, C., Aura, E.: Making 3D implants for conservation and restoration of archaeological glass. Virtual Archaeol. Rev. **8**(16), 103–109 (2017). https://doi.org/10.4995/var.2017.5946

20. Guidi, G., Ruso, M., Beraldi, J.-A.: Acquisizione 3D e modellazione poligonale, pp. 294–297. McGraw-Hill Companies, Milano (2010)

Touring the *Forum Adiectum* of *Augusta Emerita* in a virtual reality experience

Emiliano Pérez$^{(\boxtimes)}$ (iD), María José Merchán, María Dolores Moreno(iD),
Pilar Merchán, and Santiago Salamanca(iD)

Escuela de Ingenierías Industriales, Universidad de Extremadura,
Avda. de Elvas s/n., 06006 Badajoz, Spain
{emilianoph,mjmerchan,mdmorenorabel,pmerchan,ssalamanca}@unex.es

Abstract. The current advances of Information and Communication Technologies (ICTs) have created new spaces for the recreational participation, mainly on virtual spaces, which can be considered as one of the main drivers of the cultural and creative production. This paper describes the experience in developing and testing an interactive 3D virtual environment for the *Aeneas* group in the *Forum Adiectum*. 3D models obtained from different sources can be included in this virtual world after a proper adaptation. We aim to demonstrate that this way of showing Cultural Heritage can motivate and facilitate people's learning o our past rather than traditional media.

Keywords: 3D modelling · Digitization · Virtual reality
New learning environments

1 Introduction

The use of Virtual Reality (VR) in cultural heritage has a fundamental objective: to approach the history of the peoples, through their heritage, in a simple way so that their understanding and learning is easier and more attractive for the public. According to Roussou [17] the key issue of Virtual Heritage "is not only to visually represent, in a photorealistic manner, places, monuments or landscapes that do not exist, never existed, or may not be easily experienced but to present these in a meaningful and engaging way, to add the extra touch that will render the representation an experience". To achieve this, it is necessary to create 3D models that faithfully represent what we want to show, and make an application that has a clear and precise learning objective.

There are two ways to obtain 3D models. The first one is based on the application of the Geometry Stage of the standard pipeline of computer graphics [11]. In this way, the 3D models are recreations, more or less exact, of the heritage works that want to be presented in the VR system. For example, Gaitatzes *et al.* [10] present several scenes related to the Hellenic culture: the Bouleuterion (a public building of Miletus) the Temple of Zeus at Olympia, the Magical World of Byzantine Costume and several pieces of ceramics. Anderson in [4] proposes to

© Springer Nature Switzerland AG 2018
M. Ioannides et al. (Eds.): EuroMed 2018, LNCS 11196, pp. 548–559, 2018.
https://doi.org/10.1007/978-3-030-01762-0_48

use computer game engines as a low cost tool for the creation of virtual scenarios that, in the particular case of this work, is a single Pompeian house. Recently, Cristphy *et al.* [8], have presented the virtual reconstruction of Choirokoitia (Cyprus).

VR projects based on 3D models that are recreations of heritage works, have a relevant value as dissemination and teaching systems. In addition, in some situations, it is the only way to be able to make an application of Virtual Heritage. However, the visualization that is achieved with these models is, in many cases, artificial and with not very good quality.

It is not always possible to create virtual worlds using 3D modelling software. For example, the recreation of a sculpture with many details and ornaments could be a very complex task. In this case it is necessary to start from a real model that serves as the basis for the creation of the 3D model for our VR application, and the methods used for the creation of 3D models are those of Computer Vision, unlike the previous ones, where the methods of Computer Graphics were utilized. There are various methodologies to capture 3D data. The most common are: Photogrametry, especially Structure from Motion (SfM) [3], short-range 3D scanners (laser scanners and structured light scanners) and medium/long range (phase-shift and time-of-flight laser scanners) [19]. When short-range 3D scanners are used, creating models for VR applications is not difficult. In [7] a methodology is proposed to carry it out. The problem with SfM and medium/long range scanners is that they provide 3D point clouds, and not 3D meshes or parametric 3D models, which are the models used in VR. From these point clouds, it is usual to create 3D triangular meshes. Nevertheless, in many cases the software and hardware that is used to create the virtual scenes is not able to interact in real-time fluently, making the experience of the users not satisfactory. Recently, Jiménez *et al.* [12] have presented a method in which, the poor visualization of the model, due to the reduction of the triangular mesh, was enhanced by using Normal Maps [9]. They apply it for the visualization of various tumulus. Another strategy utilized to improve the user experience is the creation of "as-is" 3D models, which are parametric models fitted to point clouds. Younes *et al.* [21] use this procedure to carry out the reconstruction of the Roman theater of Byblos. The problem is that, if the heritage pieces to be reconstructed are very complex, this method is not viable.

In this work we present the development of a VR application where we insert 3D models created by using 3D scanners. In particular, we show the reconstruction of the sculptural *Aeneas* group [14] and its location in the *Forum Adiectum* of *Augusta Emerita* (Mérida, Spain). The 3D data were acquired with a short-range laser scanner (Minolta Vivid 910i) for the pieces of the sculptural group, and with a medium-range scanner (FARO LS-880) for the forum. All the 3D models has been processed so that the quality of the visualization and the user's real-time experience is not compromised. On the other hand, the VR application has been designed so that the user learns the cultural context that surrounds the sculptural group and, also, the reconstruction work that was carried out in this singular project.

The structure of the paper is as follows. Section 2 gives the historical context of this paper, and describes the digitization process and the reconstruction proposal developed. Section 3 explains the process to develop our aimed VR application and the results obtained. Finally, some conclusions and future works are drawn in Sect. 4.

2   Digitization of the *Aeneas* group and the *Forum Adiectum*. Proposal for reconstruction

Augusta Emerita, capital city of the Roman Lusitanian province (Hispania), was founded in the year 25 BC. From its beginnings, the creation of public areas and the construction of their monumental buildings inside were undertaken. In this context arose the *Forum Coloniae*, and some decades after and close to it, the so-called *Fori Porticus* or *Forum Adiectum*. Nowadays, a huge amount of its fine decoration has been recovered there, among which we can point out the Aeneas group, so important for Archaeology for being the only one preserved nowadays. It was supposed to be located in one of the room, on a base whose remains can be still seen, although its real location keeps on being an opened hypothesis. [5,15]

The process to recover this important sculptural group was a hard and long-lasting task. Essentially, there were two fragments of large size and about 25 small fragments belonging to two different statues. The first large piece is the middle part of a larger-than-life-size *thoracata* (a Roman statue in military clothes). It comprises the part below the breastplate, the short skirt and the beginning of both legs. The other large fragment includes the chest and the right arm of an old beard man with his head covered. The essential studies of W. Trillmich established the join among these fragments: they would all have belonged to the hypothetical provincial replica the Aeneas group, the most famous one in Rome since it had been exhibited in the *Forum Augustum* [6]. This group represented the generational sequence of the Trojan cycle: Aeneas runs away from Troy with his son, Ascanius, hold by the hand, while Anchises, his old father, incapable of moving fast, is transported on Aeneas' left shoulder (Fig. 1 left).

Some years ago, the authors of this paper undertook the task of proposing a solution for the placement of the retrieved pieces of this group with the final goal of making the reconstitution of this artwork. This task, tough and gruelling when carried out manually, would clearly lead to a final solution with lots of gaps (Fig. 1, right).

In order to solve this acutely complex 3D puzzle, we proposed a hybrid human-computer strategy suitable for archaeological environments [2]. Obviously, the strategy began with the digitization of the existing fragments using short range laser scanner to obtain accurate models. The scanner used was a Minolta Vivid 910. The 3D modelling procedure followed basically consists of two branches for data processing, one for the geometry -registration, integration, and post-processing- and one for the texture -registration, correction, and reconstruction-, that eventually converge to provide the mesh and the texture that compose a single representation of the object: 3D coloured model.

We used our own developed software in this process. The registering of the partial views was implemented through geometrical transformations, as usual, by using the kd-tree algorithm as well as the point-to-point minimization [18]. As for the merging stage, it was performed by means of the renowned mesh zippering algorithm [20]. The output of this second stage is a mesh that fits the surface of the whole object. This single mesh is then processed with the hole-filling technique proposed in [16] in a third stage. With respect to colour, we utilized the information provided by the scanner itself. Every point of each view scanned has its own and only pixel associated in the colour image. We implemented a sequential strategy that permits to control the process of colour merging and to test the result while each new view is added. More information can be found in [1].

Once a digital model was created for each of the fragments, our strategy offered the proposal shown in Fig. 1 right for the placement of the pieces where we generated the missing part of the group by using modelling tools of Blender software and basing its design in other representations of the group and in the studied Roman style of sculptures. Table 1 summarizes some data for the digital models of main figures of the group, numbered as depicted in Fig. 1.

Table 1. Figures for the meshes that compose the virtual scenes and reduction percentage applied to decrease their resolution

Sculpture	#	Views	Surface (dm²)	Volume (dm³)	Original mesh (digitized)		Reduced mesh		Reduction Percentage
					Vertices	Triangles	Vertices	Triangles	
Ascanius	1	165	318.22	125.176	742786	1485571	81489	162994	10.97%
Aeneas	2	183	213.31	168.978	600253	1199949	120223	240442	20.03%
Anchises	3	129	102.97	33.755	341782	683556	127437	254870	37.29%
Designed mesh	4	-	1623.54	258.90	5144199	5143880	299199	595252	5.82%
Fori Porticus	-	25	137024.83	-	12584255	25158531	715742	1428803	5.69%

On the other hand, we wanted to make a model of the *Fori Porticus*, the monumental space where the Aeneas group was located, as said. For the acquisition of the geometrical information, we utilized the laser scanner "Faro LS 880" that provides panoramic views of the scene. The colour information was captured by means of a Nikon D200 camera with Nikon AF DX Fisheye lens.

With the aim of obtaining a high-quality photorealistic model, we applied the method proposed in [13] for splitting the colour integration and the geometry reconstruction phases.

3　VR Application

The main target of the developed VR application is to let the user explore several virtual environments using a VR headset and interact with the pieces that are

Fig. 1. On the left, several objects engraved with the representation of the *Aeneas* group. On the right, proposed reconstruction of the *Aeneas* group, where the numeration corresponds to pieces described in Table 1.

supposed to belong to this sculptural group. Thus, users can be aware of the difficulty of the reconstruction problem and they can also observe the solution proposed by our research group within the context of the project mentioned. To start, we enumerate the different phases of the development process and the particularities associated to each of them.

Basically, all the tasks leading to obtain the VR application can be divided into two main stages: the generation of the 3D elements and the design of the application with a user-friendly interface, as shown in Fig. 2. These two stages are described in the following Sects. 3.1 and 3.2, respectively.

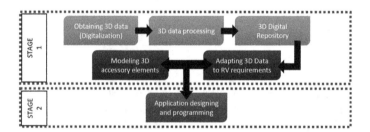

Fig. 2. Schema followed to build the VR application.

3.1 Generation of the 3D Elements

The first step to develop a VR application is to define the virtual environment to be explored. In the present case, it was clear that it was intended to offer the user the chance to navigate through all data, that we had generated related with *Aeneas* group. According to their source and size, these data can be divided into four categories, schematized in Fig. 3,

(a) large elements (*Forum Adiectum*), digitized with the FARO laser scanner.
(b) medium-small size elements (fragments of the *Aeneas* group), digitized with the MINOLTA rangefinder.
(c) medium-sized elements that were modelled to represent the missing parts of the *Aeneas* group in order to complete our reconstruction proposal (Blender software).
(d) medium-sized and large elements modelled for the design of the VR application (virtual museum, tables).

As mentioned before, the data obtained through are stored using two different types of 3D models, point clouds or meshes, depending on the type of scanner used. Likewise, the colour is another parameter stored differently.

The final aim is that all the data compose a virtual world that can be explored in real-time. Regarding that, it should be remembered that VR applications impose some requirements and constraints with the use of 3D data, mainly due to current hardware limitations to represent 3D scenes with texture and light effects in real time. To overcome these stumbling blocks and accomplish that requirements, a 3D adaptation process must be carried out on all the 3D digitized data. Thus, three fundamental parameters can be distinguished, that will condition the process of adapting the data to be usable as elements of virtual environments: (i) type of 3D model, (ii) resolution and (iii) colour of data.

These parameters must be modified and adapted for all the elements composing the virtual world, depending on the category to which each element belongs. The only category whose elements do not need an adaptation process is the category (d). Since these elements are generated from scratch with the objective of taking part of VR scenes, during its modelling stage, all considerations about real time 3D representation must be taken into account. Figure 3 summarizes the relationship between categories and parameters to be adapted.

Next, paragraphs are devoted to explain the process of adapting the data to be used in the VR application, by acting on each of the three parameters described.

Type of 3D Model. The acquired 3D data are represented using different 3D models according to the type of scanner used. On the one hand, the long distance FARO laser scanner, used for elements of category (a), generates a point cloud. On the other hand, the MINOLTA rangefinder scanner, used for elements of category (b), and the modelling software, for elements of category (c), produce triangulated surfaces.

Although it is possible to perform a VR exploration of elements defined by point clouds, it is desirable that the use 3D elements are defined by triangular meshes. First of all, this is because the user's feeling of immersion is not the same if you explore a 3D virtual world whose objects are defined by isolated points that objects defined by surfaces. In the first case, the user would observe, for example, a building whose walls seem to be formed by continuous surfaces from a certain distance, but when he/she approaches, he perceives that the wall is composed of separate points. Secondly, generally, in graphical engines,

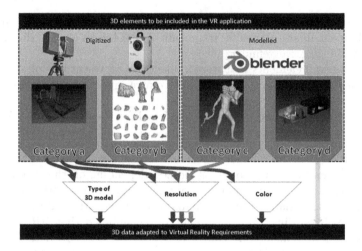

Fig. 3. Categorization of the 3D elements that take part of the virtual scenes and parameters that it is necessary to modify in each category.

the use of triangulated surfaces is required to make use of physical engines. This is necessary for the development of applications in which the user can interact with the scenario (walking, colliding with the elements...).

In our case, the transformation concerning the type of 3D model must be applied to the model of the *Forum Adiectum*: from point cloud to triangulated surface. Before proceeding with the calculation of the surface, given the amount of points in the 3D model of the forum, a process of subsampling is applied so as the number of points and, therefore, the triangulation computation time is reduced. Next, the triangulation is computed. Both tasks are carried out using the Meshlab software. Specifically, the point cloud of the forum initially had 15,000,000 points. After we applied a subsampling of 30% to data the produced point cloud had 4,500,000 points. Then, before the triangulation, we used the tool "Compute normals for points sets" to orient all normals in the point cloud. Finally, the surface reconstruction process was performed using the Screened Poisson method. This reconstruction resulted in a mesh with 8,000,000 triangles.

Resolution. It is clear that the objective of the digitization process is to obtain high quality models, in order to have a digital record of historical heritage elements, not to mention the models that potentially could allow the generation of high precision replicas of those elements. Therefore, the data obtained after digitizing with 3D scanners have a very high resolution. Thus, point clouds are obtained, in the case of the elements of category (a), with a very high number of points per dm^2 and triangulated surfaces, in the case of those of categories (b) and (c), with a large number of triangles per dm^2. This resolution is ideal when you want to create high quality infographies of 3D elements with realistic lighting effects. However, for real-time viewing it becomes a great disadvantage.

In addition, VR also adds the difficulty of visualization from two points of view, one per eye. This means high computational power needs, which entails the use of high performance hardware that, obviously, involves an expensive equipment.

As said, we aimed to develop an application that could be executed in computers with enough power for VR, but not to demand high-end computer of professional level.

Therefore, the next step for the adaptation of the data, is the reduction of the number of triangles, applicable to both the objects of category (a) and those of (b) and (c). The number of triangles that can appear in a virtual environment in real-time depends on several factors, such as the elements that are likely to be viewed simultaneously from one point of view, the texture of the objects, the lighting effects included, the interactions of the physical engines... Thus, the reduction process is applied through the use of the Meshlab "Simplification: Quadric Edge Collapse Decimation" tool. Within the optional parameters available for this tool we have forced it to preserve the topology of the surface, to compute the optimal position of simplified vertices, as well as to clean the resultant mesh after the simplification.

Table 1 summarizes the results obtained after applying this process to some meshes of category (b). An example of the reduction of these meshes are depicted in Fig. 4. It must be remembered that for the forum, a sub-sampling process was applied to the point clouds before approaching the triangulation, so it can be said that the forum is subjected to two processes of resolution reduction.

Fig. 4. Example of the reduction of resolution applied to the *Anchises* mesh: (left) digitized mesh; (right) optimized mesh to VR application.

Colour. Colour is another parameter that has great importance to achieve a realistic representation of the virtual environment. A suitable textured environment can make the difference between making the user have an intense immersive sensation, or not.

Depending on the type of scanner, this information is given in two ways. For the elements of category (a), the RGB information of each of the points that compose the cloud is stored in a 3-component vector and, for the elements of categories (b), (c) and (d), each meshed surface, corresponding to each object, has associated a texture map (a two-dimensional image that stores the colour information for each triangle).

In general, graphics engines work with triangulated surfaces with associated texture maps. A conversion in the colour information is therefore required here for the category (a) data, that is, for the forum. This process is carried out, using the tools Meshlab: "Parametrization Trivial per-triangle" (to map all triangles into equal sized triangles) and "Transfer Vertex attributes to texture" (to assign the color per vertex to the mesh's texture). As a result, an image file, independent from the 3D information file, is generated.

3.2   Results

As said, from a learning point of view, the purpose of the application that has been designed is to present the history of the *Aeneas* sculptural group and its relevance in the Roman world, to show the location of the group in the *Forum Adiectum* and to disseminate the reconstruction process of the *Aeneas* group as well as to estimate the location of said group within the forum.

The software chosen for the design of graphic application is Unity, nowadays very widespread for the generation of VR applications.

Hardware used both for application design and for the application execution are: a high-end PC and a mid-range PC: intel i7-6700K 4GHz 32 GB RAM, NVIDIA GTX1080; and, intel i5-7400 3 GHz 8GB RAM, NVIDIA GeForce GTX 660 Ti. Regarding the HMDs, it has been tested and exhibited, using Oculus Rift CV1, HTC Vive and Lenovo Explorer WMR.

The designed application is composed of three different areas: (i) exhibition area of the individual digitized elements; (ii) exhibition area of the group reconstruction proposal; and (iii) area to explore a real digitized environment, where the proposed location of the group can be observed in its true environment.

The first two areas are part of the same Unity scene, while the third one has been separated to a different scene. Unity loads only one scene at a time, which allows dividing the number of polygons of all elements to be displayed in different scenes, with the decrease in computational load that this entails. Figure 5 represents the structure of VR application with respects to the division in areas and scenes.

For areas 1 and 2, a small building was modelled consisting of two different rooms and their corresponding decorative elements, using the Blender software. On the other hand, as an interface with VR headset and controllers, it was decided to include the Steam VR package. This package, which offers compatibility with the most widely used headsets nowadays (Oculus Rift and HTC Vive HMD), incorporates some scripts in the application to manage VR headsets and its controllers.

Next, each of the areas that compose the VR application will be briefly described:

- **Area 1:** The experience begins in this room, in which the user can move to three tables on which three floating can be read: *Aeneas*, *Ascanius*, and

Anchises. The different pieces discovered for each member of the group are on every table. Among them, only 2 of those pieces are exposed to the visitors and the rest are stored in the warehouses of the National Museum of Roman Art of Mérida. Therefore, two unique experiences are offered to the user: the possibility of interacting with pieces that are not allowed to be touched in real life and the visualization of pieces never exposed to the public.

– **Area 2:** This room is connected to area 1 through a door. It is a diaphanous room in which our proposal for the reconstruction of the *Aeneas* group on a real scale is located at the bottom. The user gradually perceives the real size that the group would have if it existed as he approaches, and he can see the pieces with which the user interacted in Room 1 in a light colour, placed in their proposed position. The rest of the mesh, that does not exist in reality, can be seen in a dark brown colour.

– **Area 3:** The user accesses this area from area 2, at the moment he selects a point labeled with the title "Forum". Basically, in this scene the user virtually visits the forum, and visualizes it on a real scale. Within this scenario, the group reconstruction proposal is placed in its hypothetical original position as mentioned in Sect. 2.

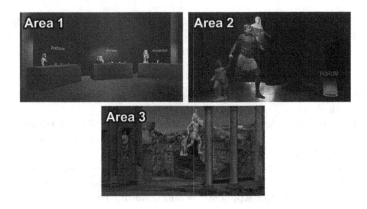

Fig. 5. Scenes in which the VR application is divided: Scene 1 – museum–; Scene 2 –*Forum Adiectum* – (Color figure online)

4 Conclusions

In this paper we have presented the procedure to generate virtual worlds that include 3D models created with the data obtained from very different sources: 3D modelling software, laser scanners and rangefinders.

First, a brief description of the digitization process of *Aeneas* group and *Forum Adiectum* has been exposed. The difficulties of the project to reconstruct the supposed original shape of such group from a limited set of discovered pieces have been pointed out.

Starting from this point, we have described the outline general process to adapt digitized and modelled 3D data, to make it usable in VR applications. Additionally, the different parameters of these data on which to directly act to perform such adaptation have been detailed.

Finally, we have explained the VR application developed to disseminate the reconstruction process and the proposed composition, as well as an hypothesis of its studied location on the *Forum Adiectum*. This application was recently tested during the 2018 international museum day at the ational Museum of Roman Art of Mérida, Spain, where we could check that people explicitly stated a very positive opinion about this experience.

As future works, we plain to make a more exhaustive survey about the use of this technology in order to try to do a comparison between the learning process with and without VR applications.

Acknowledgments. This work has been supported by the project IB16162 from Junta de Extremadura and Fondo Europeo de Desarrollo Regional "Una manera de hacer Europa".

References

1. Adán, A., Dominguez, V., Chacón, R., Salamanca, S., Rodríguez, H.: Creating 3D virtual sculptures from vision and touch technologies. In: Proceedings of the 3rd International Conference on Digital Interactive Media in Entertainment and Arts, pp. 10–12 (2008)
2. Adán, A., Salamanca, S., Merchán, P.: A hybrid human-computer approach for recovering incomplete cultural heritage pieces. Comput. Graph. **36**(1), 1–15 (2012). Cultural Heritage
3. Aicardi, I., Chiabrando, F., Lingua, A.M., Noardo, F.: Recent trends in cultural heritage 3D survey: the photogrammetric computer vision approach. J. Cult. Herit. **32**, 257–266 (2018)
4. Anderson, M.A.: Computer games and archaeological reconstruction: the low cost VR. In: Enter the Past. The E-way into the four Dimensions of Cultural Heritage. Proceedings of Computer Applications and Quantitative Methods in Archaeology, pp. 521–524 (2004)
5. Ayerbe, R., Vera, T.B., García, F.P.: El foro de Augusta Emerita. Génesis y evolución de sus recintos monumentales. Anejos de AespA LIII, Madrid (2009)
6. Barrera, J.L.D.L., Trillmich, W.: Ein wiederholung der Aeneas-gruppe vom Forum Augustum samt ihrer inschrift in Mérida (Spanien). Rheinisches Museum **103**, 119–138 (1996)
7. Bruno, F., Bruno, S., De Sensi, G., Luchi, M.L., Mancuso, S., Muzzupappa, M.: From 3D reconstruction to virtual reality: a complete methodology for digital archaeological exhibition. J. Cult. Herit. **11**(1), 42–49 (2010)
8. Christofi, M., et al.: A tour in the archaeological site of Choirokoitia using virtual reality: a learning performance and interest generation assessment. In: Ioannides, M., Martins, J., Žarnić, R., Lim, V. (eds.) Advances in Digital Cultural Heritage. LNCS, vol. 10754, pp. 208–217. Springer, Cham (2018). https://doi.org/10.1007/978-3-319-75789-6_15

9. Fernández-Palacios, B.J., Remondino, F., Stefani, C., Lombardo, J., Luca, L.D.: Web visualization of complex reality-based 3D models with NUBES. In: Proceedings of the 2013 Digital Heritage International Congress (DigitalHeritage), vol. 1, pp. 701–704, October 2013

10. Gaitatzes, A., Christopoulos, D., Roussou, M.: Reviving the past: cultural heritage meets virtual reality. In: Proceedings of the 2001 Conference on Virtual Reality, Archeology, and Cultural Heritage, VAST 2001, pp. 103–110. ACM, New York (2001)

11. Hughes, J.F.: Computer Graphics: Principles and Practice. Pearson Education, London (2014)

12. Jiménez Fernández-Palacios, B., Morabito, D., Remondino, F.: Access to complex reality-based 3D models using virtual reality solutions. J. Cult. Herit. **23**, 40–48 (2017)

13. Merchán, P., Adán, A., Salamanca, S., Domínguez, V., Chacón, R.: Geometric and colour data fusion for outdoor 3D models. Sensors **12**(6), 6893–6919 (2012)

14. Merchán, P., Salamanca, S., Adán, A.: Restitution of sculptural groups using 3D scanners. Sensors **11**(9), 8497–518 (2011)

15. Nogales, T.: Fora Lusitaniae. Grandes complejos augusteos, imagen de un tiempo nuevo. Gerión. Revista de Historia Antigua **35**(Esp.), 469–486 (2017)

16. Pérez, E., Salamanca, S., Merchán, P., Adán, A., Cerrada, C., Cambero, I.: A robust method for filling holes in 3D meshes based on image restoration. In: Blanc-Talon, J., Bourennane, S., Philips, W., Popescu, D., Scheunders, P. (eds.) ACIVS 2008. LNCS, vol. 5259, pp. 742–751. Springer, Heidelberg (2008). https://doi.org/10.1007/978-3-540-88458-3_67

17. Roussou, M.: Virtual heritage: from the research lab to the broad public. Bar Int. Ser. **1075**, 93–100 (2002)

18. Rusinkiewicz, S., Levoy, M.: Efficient variants of the ICP algorithm. In: Proceedings Third International Conference on 3-D Digital Imaging and Modeling, pp. 145–152 (2001)

19. Sansoni, G., Trebeschi, M., Docchio, F.: State-of-the-art and applications of 3D imaging sensors in industry, cultural heritage, medicine, and criminal investigation. Sensors **9**(1), 568–601 (2009)

20. Turk, G., Levoy, M.: Zippered polygon meshes from range images. In: Proceedings of the 21st Annual Conference on Computer Graphics and Interactive Techniques, SIGGRAPH 1994, pp. 311–318. ACM, New York (1994)

21. Younes, G., et al.: Virtual and augmented reality for rich interaction with cultural heritage sites: A case study from the Roman Theater at Byblos. Digital Applications in Archaeology and Cultural Heritage **5**(December 2016), 1–9 (2017)

A Semantically-Enriched Digital Portal for the Digital Preservation of Cultural Heritage with Community Participation

Cokorda Pramartha[1,2(✉)] ⓘ, Joseph G. Davis[2] ⓘ,
and Kevin K. Y. Kuan[2] ⓘ

[1] Department of Computer Science, Udayana University, Denpasar, Indonesia
cokorda@unud.ac.id
[2] School of Information Technologies, The University of Sydney,
Sydney, Australia

Abstract. Understanding our past can determine our ability to understand the present. Many people associate cultural heritage with the ancient past and history; however, cultural heritage should be seen as a continuous tradition that lives through daily practices. In this paper, we present the details of our research dealing with one aspect of Balinese culture, the Balinese traditional communication system (*kulkul*), undertaken in the Indonesian island of Bali. The central aim of our project was to document, organize, and preserve the relevant *kulkul* knowledge for the benefit of the Balinese community, and the younger generations in particular by designing and developing a digital portal as a dynamic repository. A basic ontology of key *kulkul*-related concepts and terms and their interrelationships that as part of our digital portal was developed to support the semantic searching and browsing of the online portal and related resources. Much of the content for the digital portal was acquired through community-based crowdsourcing and the informants came from the different geographical areas in Bali. Members from the community were invited to contribute their knowledge to enable the online digital portal to evolve into a living repository of Balinese cultural knowledge. The significant number of digital cultural resources uploaded and the substantial growth of the *kulkul* ontology by the community are indicators of the success of this research project. The prototype digital portal is implemented on the cloud to facilitate elastic growth and easy user access to the resources both to read and to add content. Finally, the digital portal was made available online and extensive evaluation was carried out based on responses from selected users drawn from community by letting them use and experience the digital portal in order to evaluate the ease of use and usefulness. The evaluation results suggest that, for the most part, the users perceived the digital portal to be relatively useful and easy to use.

Keywords: Digital portal · Balinese culture · Balinese *kulkul*
Ontology

© Springer Nature Switzerland AG 2018
M. Ioannides et al. (Eds.): EuroMed 2018, LNCS 11196, pp. 560–571, 2018.
https://doi.org/10.1007/978-3-030-01762-0_49

1 Introduction

The loss of cultural knowledge is not just a process that has occurred in the past; it is still happening today when access to traditional resources and traditional ways of life are limited and restricted for the younger generation. Traditional cultural knowledge is the knowledge that has accumulated from the contributions and historical experiences of many generations. It is clear that understanding the traditions of the past in the right context, depth, complexity, and diversity, is to re-affirm cultural identity in the present.

Today, the rapid development and adoption of digital technology such as the Internet and mobile technology have created an opportunity for cultural heritage preservation to be facilitated by these technologies. The digital preservation of cultural heritage offers new and innovative means of digital heritage knowledge representation and to link both the people who possess the heritage knowledge and others who want to acquire that cultural knowledge. Moreover, digital cultural heritage resources open new pathways for scholars, members of the community, and younger generation in particular, to represent, store, refine, maintain, share and continue to contribute to further development of cultural heritage knowledge.

Cultural heritage is an aspect of past experiences that carry important value for a society, and continues to change dynamically with time [1, 2]. Heritage is the opposite of nature, in that heritage is something that has been trained and learnt, while nature refers to the 'original' [3]. It is a form of a man-made heritage that is often context-rich and therefore evolves through a long and complex process rather than by a single action or creation [1, 4].

The tangible objects of cultural heritage are maintained by the material form in which they are encoded, stored, and replicated. A problem encountered in cultural digitisation projects is the preserving of information beyond the actual physical object, such as contextual and cultural practice-related information. Cultural heritage knowledge – specifically, cultural practices and traditions – are changing over time and evolving.

The central goal of this project is to digitally document and share information regarding one aspect of the Balinese cultural heritage – *kulkul*. The *kulkul* system is part of the Balinese traditional communication systems that varies from one Balinese village to another and remain being used in the Balinese community. We transformed the cultural knowledge and related practices into an explicit and digital form, in order for the public to add, refine, and share this knowledge. In this paper, we discuss the methods we employed to design, develop, implement, and to evaluate the semantically enriched digital portal for documenting and sharing one important aspect of Balinese cultural heritage.

2 Digital Portal Design, Development and Implementation

In our previous research, we have gathered a significant amount of information and that has contributed to a detailed understanding of the Balinese *kulkul* system and its diversity through in-depth interview with selected Balinese cultural experts. We have proposed a knowledge classification framework based on the key Balinese cultural principal (*Tri Hita Karana* and *Desa Kala Patra*) to capture, classify, and organise the richness of *kulkul* related knowledge [5]. Drawing from the in-depth interview approach, we came out with the detailed *kulkul* specifications and features. Furthermore, we modelled the *kulkul* domain and developed the *kulkul* ontology in order to provide an abstract representation of the *kulkul* domain knowledge that can assist the users to engage with the computer systems in a meaningful manner [6]. Much of the *kulkul* digital content available in our digital portal was acquired, populated, and organised by the community-based crowdsourcing that came across different regency in Bali [6].

Our digital portal development employed a prototyping method that focused on the full functionality of the key aspects of the final IT artefact. We used the freely available open source tools and integrated them into our digital portal architecture [6]. We developed our platform from scratch with the aim of maximizing the integration between the modules that we prepared in of the each stages of the prototype development. We can break down our application into three main modules that support the following services:

1. Populating content: allows multiple online users to contribute their knowledge by populating detailed content on Balinese *kulkul*.
2. Browsing: allows users to browse through different parts of the ontology by navigating through *kulkul* classification hierarchies.
3. Searching: lets users construct a query relating to one or more attributes of the *kulkul* artefact or practices as inputs, and displays a selected attribute for the output.

It is important that the appearance and level of fidelity of the prototype is accepted by the potential users. During the early stages of the digital portal development, we focused on developing a mid-fidelity prototype with a mock-up graphical user interface (GUI) to demonstrate and communicate the idea, and to provide a draft functionality of the artefact. The medium-fidelity prototyping tools and methods focus on the ease of production as well as the supporting detail of the design for direct manipulation. Also, the detailed information about functionality, navigation, and the layout of the content is presented without involving detail on programming [7]. To realise our artefact, the JustInMind[1] prototyping tools were used to enabled us to simulate and present the prototype either offline (without the Internet connection) or, by uploading the object to the cloud services, users could try and experience it using a web browser over the Internet. In developing the digital portal mid-fidelity prototype using the JustInMind tools, we adopted the steps and method proposed by Engelberg and Seffah [7] (see Fig. 1).

After all the steps and iterations of the prototype design process were completed, we demonstrated the artefact to the researchers for feedback and approval. This was followed by the systematic development of the actual IT artefact.

The digital portal, which has been made available online at http://ccbp.oss.web.id, was developed to ease the task of recording and preserving cultural heritage,

---

[1] https://www.justinmind.com.

specifically of the Balinese *kulkul*, and to enable people to access, share, and contribute to this knowledge. This semantic-enriched digital portal relies heavily on the *kulkul* ontology. The *kulkul* ontology was populated in the previous study through community-based crowdsourcing [6].

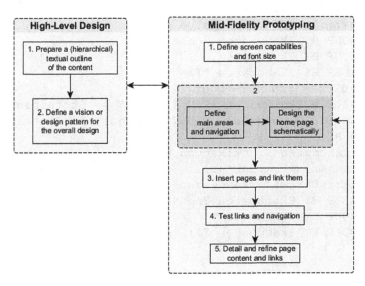

Fig. 1. Mid-fidelity prototyping steps. Adopted from "A framework for rapid mid-fidelity prototyping of web sites" by Engelberg and Seffah [7].

2.1 Browsing Facility

The browsing module that we developed allows the user to explore the *kulkul* information available at the digital portal by following one interesting link to another, usually with a definite objective but without a planned search strategy. Furthermore, using this module allows the user to navigate the browsing activity to a different part of the *kulkul* classification hierarchies.

The front page of this module, as shown in Fig. 2, provides users a summary on the districts, villages and *banjar* in each regency for which content data were inserted and updated by the Community-Based Crowdsourcing we conducted in our previous study [6]. The calculation process calculates the transitive path of object properties in the OWL (thk:isPartOf) and the number of instances in each district (*kecamatan*), village (*desa*) and *banjar* class. Further, the number of instances is classified and organised by regency (*kabupaten*) see the SPARQL query against the RDF triple store below.

```
$result1 = $sparql->query(
  "SELECT ?kabupaten (SUM (?total) AS ?totaldesa)
  {SELECT ?kabupaten (COUNT (?desa) AS ?total)
  WHERE
  {?kabupaten a thk:Kabupaten .
  ?desa a thk:Desa;
  thk:isPartOf* ?kabupaten .}
  GROUP BY ?kabupaten ?desa }
  GROUP BY ?kabupaten
  ORDER BY ?kabupaten ");
$result2 = $sparql->query(
  "SELECT ?kabupaten (SUM (?total) AS ?totalbanjar)
  {SELECT ?kabupaten (COUNT (?banjar) AS ?total)
  WHERE
  {?kabupaten a thk:Kabupaten .
  ?banjar a thk:Banjar;
  thk:isPartOf* ?kabupaten .}
  GROUP BY ?kabupaten ?banjar}
  GROUP BY ?kabupaten
  ORDER BY ?kabupaten ");
```

Fig. 2. Counting the number of district, village, and *banjar*.

2.2   Search Facility

The search facility was developed to give the user flexibility to find the relevant digital resources by constructing multiple criteria for the query. First, the user should select one output query: in other words, what are they looking for. For instance, the user may like to know the location of the *kulkul*, the number of *kulkul* installed at the particular location, the raw material of *kulkul*, and so forth. Second, the user should select at least one input query filter, so the digital portal can search the available resources using the semantic relationships of the constructed query. For example, finding a *kulkul* that is used for *manusa yadnya* activity, installed in Gianyar regency, with has a height of between 150 and 170 cm, and so forth. By giving more criteria for the search, the systems will try to follow the semantic link for each criterion (class, object property, data property and instance) that is available in the digital portal (see program code below for a query example and Fig. 3 shows the graphic user interface of the search facility).

```
SELECT DISTINCT (?tempat as ?output)
{ ?kulkulName thk:numberKulkul 1 .
?tempat thk:hasKulkul ?kulkulName .
?kulkulName thk:isUsedFor ?aktivitas .
?aktivitas a thk:ManusaYadnya .
?tempat thk:hasKulkul ?kulkulName . }
ORDER BY ?output
```

As shown in Fig. 3, the user should select at least one output filter query and can select more than one input filter query in order to construct the semantic query in the digital portal. At the right side of the interface, we print the SPARQL query when the system executes the user query. This output is used for the purpose of research, to check whether the system performs the right query.

Fig. 3. *Kulkul* used for *manusa yadnya* activity where one *kulkul* is installed, in any location.

3   Digital Portal Demonstration and Evaluation

The aim of this evaluation was to understand whether the users found the digital portal useful and helpful from the perspective of learning about the Balinese *kulkul* artefact and related practices. This evaluation was designed to assess users' perceptions of the usefulness and ease of use of the digital portal. Perceived usefulness is defined as "the degree to which a person believes that using a particular system would enhance his or her job performance" [8, p. 320]. Perceived ease of use refers to "the degree to which a person believes that using a particular system would be free of effort" [8, p. 320]. The following sections describe in detail the process of evaluation and analysis.

3.1 Participants and Data Collection

This study was carried out over three months. Participation in the study was voluntary. None of the participants had been involved in any of our previous data acquisition surveys related to this project. Participants were recruited from the student and staff networks of three universities in Bali (Universitas Udayana, UNDIKNAS University and Universitas Pendidikan Ganesha), and other communities in Bali. The Universitas Udayana was chosen for the research because of its reputation as a repository of Balinese cultural knowledge and expertise. The UNDIKNAS was selected because this university is recognised as one of the best private universities in eastern Indonesia, and currently there are more 3,000 students enrolled in this university. The Universitas Pendidikan Ganesha (Undiksha) was chosen because it is the second largest university in Bali and is located on the north island of Bali (Buleleng Regency). Currently, the Undiksha employs around 700 staff and 11,400 active students. Our study intended to involve participants from a variety of backgrounds.

The participant recruitment and evaluation process is shown in Fig. 4. Once the participants agreed to take part in the study, they were put through a short training session using the tutorial video that we provided on the digital portal. The tutorial video outlined the steps required for this study. After viewing the tutorial video, all participants were required to provide their online consent and then conduct a range of browsing and searching tasks using the features and facilities available in the digital portal. Finally, all participants were invited to respond to a small set of questions regarding the usefulness and ease of use of the digital portal.

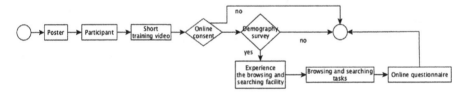

Fig. 4. Evaluation process

The data used in this research was collected using an online questionnaire that we developed, and the data gathered was logged at the portal. The study was carried out over several sessions or days to enable us to improve the performance of the system when the participants reported bugs in the digital portal. Before the evaluation started, all the participants were asked to watch an eight-minute tutorial video provided on our digital portal. The tutorial video informed participants about how the system works and what the participants should do during the study. The tutorial video explained how to use the semantic browsing and semantic searching facilities in the digital portal. The operation of a semantic search is significantly different to the text- and keyword-based search service that is commonly available in many Web applications. For a text-based search, the user types any text string and the system will match it with the available data. However, in our semantic search, the user selects only the available classes and instances that are part of the ontology and the RDF data store

After the above steps were completed, participants were asked to perform two sets of tasks. Firstly, participants were asked to undertake five browsing tasks (exploration of the World Wide Web by following one interesting link to another) on the browsing module (Fig. 5). In each browsing task, participants were required to answer a question by constructing two elements of the query using the digital portal browsing module. Here is an example of the browsing question:

– List two (2) name of villages (*desa adat* or *desa pakraman*) that use *kulkul* for *manusa yadnya* activities.

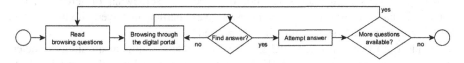

Fig. 5. Browsing task flowchart

Secondly, participants were expected to perform five searching tasks (request for a piece of information from a database) using the digital portal searching module. In order to be able to answer the questions using the searching facility, the participants were required to construct two or more elements of the query as input filters and form one category query from the *kulkul* ontology hierarchy as the output filter (Fig. 6), and follow up by clicking the search button. Here is an example of the searching question:

– List two (2) name of the raw material that uses for *kulkul*, where are *kulkul* installed two (2) in each location, the direction of installing is face to face, and has height 160 cm

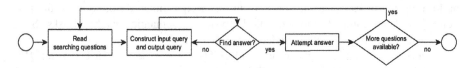

Fig. 6. Searching task flowchart

In the first stage of the evaluation, we performed a pilot study with only 15 participants to see whether the users could successfully complete the task using the digital portal. Based on this small sample of participants, we examined whether significant errors were due to bugs in the system. Using this data, we performed debugging and made some adjustments to the digital portal before inviting more participants to undertake the evaluation.

After performing the browsing and searching tasks, all participants were invited to answer a small set of questions regarding the ease of use and usefulness of the digital portal. We adopted the questionnaire constructed by Davis [8], in which we focused on two dimensions: perceived usefulness (PU) and perceived ease of use (PE). The perceived usefulness (PU) comprised of five items:

1. Using the digital portal would enable me to accomplish tasks more quickly.
2. Using the digital portal would improve my task performance.
3. Using the digital portal would enhance my effectiveness in performing my tasks.
4. Using the digital portal would make it easier to do my tasks.
5. I would find the digital portal useful to finish my tasks.

The perceived ease of use (PE) comprised of three items:

1. I would find it easy to get the digital portal to do what I want it to do.
2. I would find the digital portal to be flexible to interact with.
3. I would be easy for me to become skillful at using the digital portal.

The items are measured using 7-point Likert scale (strongly agree = 7, agree = 6, somewhat agree = 5, neither agree nor disagree = 4, somewhat disagree = 3, disagree = 2, and strongly disagree = 1). Moreover, participants were invited to add further comments and suggestions if they wished.

Aside from two constructs (PU and PE), we added additional questions to determine whether the video tutorial (VT) that we provided helped the participants to understand and perform their tasks:

1. The video tutorial provided is useful for me to understand the use of digital portals.
2. It is easy for me to understand the tutorial video material provided.

The back-translation method [9] was adopted to ensure the reliability of the instrument in different source languages. Thus, all questions in the questionnaires were given in Bahasa as the targeted participants were fluent in Bahasa.

3.2 Data Analysis and Results

A total of 90 participants responded to our invitation. However, we were only able to use 68 usable responses because some of them completed the questionnaires without performing the tasks or did not respond to all the questions. Also, some of the participants did not complete the semantic browsing or semantic searching tasks. Such incomplete data could not be included in the analysis.

Among the 68 participants in our study, 75% were male and 25% female; 91% were Balinese Hindu, 66% part of a Balinese community (*sekaa banjar, sekaa truna truni* and *sekaa gong*) and 94% were university students or had a university degree.

Browsing Tasks
All activities and interactions of the participants with the digital portal, such as the times at which the online user started and finished the tasks, were recorded automatically in the log file. The log file was used to analyse the efficacy of the digital portal and the perceived levels of ease of use and usefulness of the portal information by the participants. On average, participants spent 86 min to complete the given tasks, with a minimum of 15 min and a maximum of 260 min. After the participants finished performing the browsing tasks, we marked each one of the submissions. We classified the marking skim into three categories:

1. Wrong. This score was given when the participant did not give the correct answer to the given task.
2. Partially correct. This score was given when the answer matched any required criteria.
3. Fully correct. This score was given if the participant gave an entirely correct answer to the question.

Using these criteria above, 71% of the participants answered the question correctly, and 11% did not give an answer that was close to the requirement.

Search Task
Similar to the browsing tasks, we marked each of the answers attempted by the participants. We used the same scale (wrong, partially correct and fully correct) as that used for the browsing task to evaluate the answers. On average, 68% of the answers given by participants to the questions using the semantic searching modules were entirely correct, and 15% of the answers were wrong.

Perceived Usefulness and Perceived Ease of Use
After all the participants had completed the browsing and searching tasks, they were invited to answer a small set of questions related to the perceived usefulness and perceived ease of use of the digital portal. To analyse the questionnaire outcomes, the following statistical analyses were conducted using SPSS:

- Kaiser-Meyer-Olkin (KMO) Measure of Sampling Adequacy analysis was conducted to ensure that there was adequate and high variability in the collected data for factor analysis.
- Bartlett Test of Sphericity was conducted to ensure that the items of the instrument were sufficiently correlated.
- Reliability test (Cronbach's alpha) was conducted to find internal consistency among the items.
- One-sample t-test was conducted to determine whether the system is perceived as easy to use and useful.
- Principal component analysis with varimax rotation was conducted on the collected data. This method was used to determine the number of factors or principal components to retain.

Kaiser-Meyer-Olkin Measure of Sampling (KMO) and Bartlett's Test of Sphericity are measures of sampling adequacy that are recommended to check the case-to-variable ratio for the analysis being conducted. The collected data were inspected through KMO with a value of 0.853. High values close to 1.0 indicate that conducting a factor analysis on the data will be suitable. Also, as a rule of thumb, KMO values between 0.8 and 1 indicate the sampling is adequate. The results of the Bartlett Test of Sphericity (approximate chi-square = 358.458, df = 28, sig. = 0.005) with a small value of significance level (less than 0.05) indicated that a factor analysis may be useful and was suitable for the collected data.

The reliability of the items was assessed with Cronbach's alpha. The calculated alpha was 0.922 for perceived usefulness (PU) and 0.833 for perceived ease of use (PE) which is above the minimum threshold of 0.7 [10]. Hence, the reliabilities are deemed sufficient.

For ease of interpretation and to assess users' perception of the portal, we averaged participants' raw scores on each of the above two component items (PU and PE). Also, due to the exploratory nature of this research element, we treated the above scores with the equal weights [11]. The results indicate that the users' perceived usefulness (PU) and the users' perceived ease of use (PE) of the digital portal score was statistically significantly higher than the middle point of 4.0 (see Table 1). Additionally, with more than 91% of the total users responding on the agree scale point the results suggest that generally, the users perceived the usefulness and ease of use with of the digital portal to be positive.

Table 1. One-sample t-test

Constructs	t	df	p	SD	mean
PU	19.605	67	0.005	0.82	5.95
PE	21.493	67	0.005	0.71	5.85
VT	22.491	67	0.005	0.80	6.18

Multimedia Tutorial Resources
As previously noted, we added two additional questions apart from the perceived usefulness and perceived ease of use. These additional questions aimed to assess whether the given video tutorial (VT) helps the user to finish the browsing and searching tasks. Similar to the PU and PE, the reliability of the items was assessed with Cronbach's alpha to find internal consistency between the items. The calculated alpha was 0.835 which is above the minimum threshold of 0.7. Therefore, the reliabilities are deemed sufficient to be used for evaluation.

The result indicates that the users' perceived usefulness of the tutorial video (VT) score was statistically significantly higher than the middle point of 4.0 (see Table 1). Therefore, with more than 95% of the total users responding on the agree scale point, and none of them responding on the disagree scale point, the result suggests that generally the users perceived the video tutorial to be helpful in finishing the given tasks.

Apart from the questions on perceived ease of use, usefulness and multimedia tutorial resources, we added additional questions to capture the individual users' comments and suggestions for further improvements.

The suggestions of the users after they evaluated the digital portal gave us positive feedback that was helpful for making improvements, which we have since made. Furthermore, three participants contacted us to ask whether they could have access to the portal to populate the *kulkul* details for their village, because they saw that some of the *kulkul* details of their village or *banjar* were not entirely populated. They were aware that doing so would help to capture and document their traditions over time, and also to help the next generation to learn more about their heritage.

4   Conclusion

We have presented the details of our research dealing with one aspect of the Balinese cultural heritage, the Balinese traditional communication system (*kulkul*). Our contributions include the development, implementation, and evaluation of the community-based and semantic-enriched digital portal that enable the public to add, refine, and share previously fragmented knowledge about one aspect of the Balinese cultural heritage.

Our study involved 68 participants from three universities and communities in Bali to evaluate the main features of our digital portal (semantic browsing and semantic searching) in term of ease of use and usefulness. The results suggest that, for the most part, the users perceived the usefulness and ease of use of the digital portal to be positive. Furthermore, the requests by some participants of this study to be contributors to add content to the digital portal based on their knowledge of aspects of *kulkul* indicates a positive commentary on the project. Work is ongoing to develop the prototype further and to populate it fully before it can be installed in one of the memory institutions in Bali (e.g. Bali Museum).

Acknowledgements. This project received funding from The Indonesia Endowment Fund for Education (LPDP) [grant no. PRJ-02/LPDP/2013]; and Competitive Research Grant, The Ministry of Research, Technologies, and Higher Education, Indonesia [grant no. 486.24/UN14.2/PNL.01.03.00/2016].

References

1. Harvey, D.C.: Heritage pasts and heritage presents: temporality, meaning and the scope of heritage studies. Int. J. Herit. Stud. **7**(4), 319–338 (2001)
2. McCarthy, M.: Historico-geographical explorations of Ireland's heritages: towards a critical understanding of the nature of memory and identity. In: Ireland's Heritages, pp. 3–51. Routledge (2017)
3. Von Unge, E.N.: When culture becomes heritage. In: Search of the Samdok Discourse of Collecting Contemporary Heritage. Master's Thesis. International Museum Studies. Götemborgs Universitet (2008)
4. Munjeri, D.: Tangible and intangible heritage: from difference to convergence. Mus. Int. **56** (1–2), 12–20 (2004)
5. Pramartha, C., Davis, J.G.: Digital preservation of cultural heritage: Balinese *Kulkul* artefact and practices. In: Ioannides, M., et al. (eds.) EuroMed 2016. LNCS, vol. 10058, pp. 491–500. Springer, Cham (2016). https://doi.org/10.1007/978-3-319-48496-9_38
6. Pramartha, C., Davis, J.G., Kuan, K.K.Y.: Digital preservation of cultural heritage: an ontology-based approach. In: The 28th Australasian Conference on Information Systems, Hobart, Australia (2017)
7. Engelberg, D., Seffah, A.: A framework for rapid mid-fidelity prototyping of web sites. In: Hammond, J., Gross, T., Wesson, J. (eds.) Usability. ITIFIP, vol. 99, pp. 203–215. Springer, Boston, MA (2002). https://doi.org/10.1007/978-0-387-35610-5_14
8. Davis, F.D.: Perceived usefulness, perceived ease of use, and user acceptance of information technology. MIS Q. **13**, 319–340 (1989)
9. Brislin, R.W.: Back-translation for cross-cultural research. J. Cross-Cult. Psychol. **1**(3), 185–216 (1970)
10. Nunnally, J.C., Bernstein, I.H.: Psychometric Theory. 3rd edn. McGraw-Hill Series in Psychology, vol. xxiv, 752 p. McGraw-Hill, New York (1994)
11. Hair, J.F., et al.: Multivariate Data Analysis (5th ed.). 6th edn. Prentice-Hall International, Upper Saddle River (1998)

Towards a Mobile Crowdsourcing System for Collective Memory Management

Konstantinos Koukoulis[(⊠)], Dimitrios Koukopoulos,
and George Koubaroulis

Department of Cultural Heritage Management and New Technologies,
University of Patras, Agrinio, Greece
{kkoukoulis,dkoukopoulos,gkoubaroulis}@upatras.gr

Abstract. Collective memory characterizes the behavior of certain groups of people that form communities inside an urban environment. Quality of life, as a smart city objective, should concern the understanding of diversity, reducing alienation and preservation of people's intangible cultural heritage. In this paper we attempt to give a first answer to such problems proposing and implementing a trustworthy mobile crowdsourcing system for a collective memory management based on the needs of users, specialists or not. We demonstrate a basic usage scenario to show the strength of the implemented services, along with a first system evaluation showing positive results.

Keywords: Collective memory management · Mobile crowdsourcing systems

1 Introduction

"I came to this country as an immigrant shortly before Pearl Harbor. It did not take me long to establish friendships. But I felt for a long time that there was something in my relations with Native Americans that blocked full communication, and that there was a kind of impossible barrier between us". Continuing his narrative, Halbwach argued that collective memory (CM) was a communication barrier [1]. CM is an interpretation of the past that groups of people recognize as commonly shared [2]. Since always people are suffering from displacement. UNESCO is paying attention in the displaced persons due to conflicts, natural disasters or the effects of climate change which often leads to the loss of cultural references [3]. These people are often moving in groups losing the bonds with the tangible cultural heritage. The need to help these groups of people to maintain their bonds to their cultural heritage (CH), both tangible and intangible (ICH) is essential [4]. Nevertheless, they carry with them their ICH along with some memorabilia. Can we manage these memories?

Nowadays, a lot of work is dealing with crowdsourcing (CS) systems [5–8]. A CS system, "employs a multitude of people to help solve a problem defined by system owners" [9, 10] and this trend is getting attention because of its application to various fields [11–13]. Building a CS system faces many challenges, such as people motivation, task assignment, quality control and contribution aggregation [8]. In this work we try to address those challenges proposing a mobile CS system for the efficient management of CM. We are especially interested in displaced people memories. This work

M. Ioannides et al. (Eds.): EuroMed 2018, LNCS 11196, pp. 572–582, 2018.
https://doi.org/10.1007/978-3-030-01762-0_50

aims at the preservation (collection, management and dissemination) of CM facilitating the cohesion of communities of people with shared memories. In particular, we present the design and the implementation of a system that manages CM based on the needs of users, specialists or not. To improve the trustworthiness of the proposed system we apply an extended role-based access control model. Also, we discuss a basic usage scenario to show the strength of the implemented system services. Finally, we perform a first evaluation comparing the proposed system to other implemented systems with CS mobile modules.

2 Related Work

Nowadays there are many systems targeting CH management that use mobile CS solutions [25]. One of the most known ones is "Europeana 1914–1918" where people can upload their stories through a portal [16] and browse this content through a mobile app [18]. [19] focuses on stories of Denmark. People can contribute digitized content and stories connected to a specific place on a map through a portal or a mobile app. Then, users can view and annotate stories and navigate through different areas of interest such as castles and other places of greater historical importance even points of interest such as restaurants and music festivals. In "HistoryPin" the focus is on groups of pins uploaded by members (collections that contain text, images, audio and video items) related to particular places [24]. In [17] an online participatory plat-form for managing cultural content is proposed. The platform allows contributions from various categories of users and can store and display material from all major cultural disciplines. In [20] the implemented system deals with social events of the modern urban life supporting the establishment of an intelligent environment providing specific services which promote crowd management. An urban computing application that allows forming and interacting with the collective city memory is described in [21].

The vulnerability of stored cultural content in unauthorized access is a serious problem in cultural environments that jeopardizes the adaptation of digital applications from cultural experts. Towards the creation of a sense of trust, a lot of research has been done in the field of authorization mechanisms concerning access control in multimedia content [22, 23]. In [22] authors describe an authorization mechanism targeting multimedia content stored in digital libraries. A role-based access control mechanism is applied on mobile guiding services in a cultural environment in [23].

3 User Requirements

To provide a set of system requirements, a three-step procedure was followed. First, we searched the literature for CM management systems [16–21, 24, 26]. We studied the proposed system features concerning preservation, diffusion as well as the type of content of the application. Then, we filtered our results conducting interviews with specialists in the fields of cultural heritage management and history. As a result, we designed a specific questionnaire targeting refugees or their descendants to investigate what they would like in such a system in terms of content and interface functionalities. Analyzing the results, we encoded the desirable system features in Fig. 1.

Main objective
• Should preserve/rescue/promote and disseminate data (P).
• Should satisfy educational needs (P).
• The public should trust the system (P).
• Collect as much material as possible and disseminate data (M).
Environment (friendliness)
• Stories and complementary material should be presented in an attractive and comprehensible manner (P).
• Users should be able to download the provided information (P).
• Stories and complementary material could be displayed in a timeline so that the user can easily have an overview (P).
• Stories should be sorted using ready-made thematic categories, such as recorded (P). testimonials, and photographed documents.
• Finding, downloading and installing the app should be an easy and quick process (M).
• Data recording (of audio, video, images) should be an easy and quick process lacking complexities (M).
• Explanatory captions should exist in each field to understand functionality (M).
• Screen switching and data downloading should be fast (M).
• Help in the form of explanatory videos or messages should exist (P, M).
• Information for application developers should be provided (P, M).
• Should be easy to use (P, M).
Services
• A discussion forum should be present (P).
• Volunteer should manage her/his content (P).
• Experts should be able to comment volunteer data and published stories (P).
• Advanced users can download published content (photos, audio, video) in good quality (P).
• The user can easily register as a volunteer (M).
• Volunteer should be able to publish, unpublish, delete a story (M).
• Volunteer should be able to preview his unpublished stories (M).
• Volunteers should easily upload stories with their accompanying material (audio, images, texts, videos) (M).
• Advanced users should be able to create collections (with stories and digital objects) (P, M).
• Search with simple keyword should be provided (P, M).
• Story viewing should be allowed to simple users (P, M).
• Sharing content to social media should be present (P, M).
• Stories should be accessible with the use of a map (P, M)
• Volunteers and users should be able to see the stories that have been published by all volunteers (P, M).

Fig. 1. User requirements for portal and mobile app (P is for portal and M for mobile app).

4 System Architecture

The proposed CS system is separated in three discrete modules (Fig. 2). The first module contains the system databases and a file system. The second module is the Authorization Access Manager that is responsible for the user's secure access to system data. The third module is the Application Module that consists of a portal and a mobile app used for system interaction with users.

We propose an extended version of role-based access control (RBAC) model [15] aiming at the development of a trustworthy CM management environment where user needs will be satisfied. There are five distinct types/roles of users: *cultural content managers, specialists, regular users, advanced users and volunteers*. Separating users into groups assist the custom service use and data access. Advanced users are allowed enhanced functionality such as participation in a discussion forum, social media sharing and story collection creation. Volunteers can perform regular user operations, submit

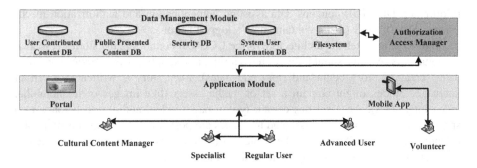

Fig. 2. System design.

new material on the system database and process, publish, and delete their unpublished stories. Specialists are experts in history and cultural heritage who can comment on volunteer posts or rate stories. Cultural content managers are system supervisors, process all posts made by volunteers, while importing their ones. They can also delete content that belongs to volunteers and specialists. Only regular users are unregistered. Volunteers can use mobile services only, while cultural content managers and specialists can use portal services. Only regular users can search and view stories already published by volunteers.

The system content refers to all kind of data that are held in the database concerning stories. The basic content is produced by volunteers. Complementary content is produced by other types of users (advanced users, specialists, cultural content managers). A main content categorization concern user provided content (images, audio, video, text and position data) and composite content (processed generic content and user provided content). The type of content can be text (like story description and caption, names of related persons and a specialist annotation), images (like postcards, family pictures, official documents, letters, personal diaries and maps), video (like documentaries, narrations, films demonstrating ICH [14]) and audio (like testimonials, descriptions, narratives that involve ICH, interviews, songs). Story attributes could be categorized in content, context and model-based attributes. Content-based attributes include thematic attributes (like story title and description, names of persons), images of memorabilia, video containing interviews, audio containing sounds or songs related to the story. Context-based attributes are video, audio and texts that refer to the context of the story (like annotations of specialists). Model-based attributes derive from the model itself. In this case, model-based attributes are related to user roles, viewing rights and data related to social media publishing permission rights permission.

The system collects and disseminates content through data management module databases. User Contributed Content DB (UCC) contains unpublished stories that are provided by volunteers. The story is the main entity. Each story can contain many media data items (images, texts, videos, audio) and related persons. Public Presented Content DB (PPC) contains published volunteer generated data. Cultural content managers manage PPC data (delete, annotate, publish), while specialists only annotate PPC data. Story collections created by advanced users are stored in PPC. System User

Information DB (SUI) contains data assisting authentication and authorization mechanisms. Security DB (SEC) contains user's logged actions.

Figure 3 illustrates the architecture of the UCC DB containing the stories uploaded by volunteers. A story should always have a title, a description (its narration) and also dates (creation, story begin and story end dates). Each story is written in a certain language. Stories might contain a set of media assets (like images of memorabilia, video interviews). An asset has certain type (image, video, audio) and belongs to a specific category. Categories assigned to images are postcard, official document, photo, calendar and letter. Stories may be related to persons and persons may be related to many stories. Also, stories may be related to a location and vice versa.

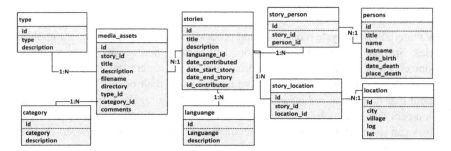

Fig. 3. UCC DB.

The basic permitted operations on data are: view, search, delete, insert, edit, annotate, rate and publish. Searching: Regular, advanced users and specialists can search the published content. Volunteers can search their own content and content published by another volunteer. Cultural content managers can search for any content. Viewing: Volunteers can view data they have inserted in UCC DB. All users, along with volunteers, can view content stored in PPC DB. Inserting: Volunteers can insert data in the UCC DB, specialists can comment and rate. Advanced users can create collections only in PPC DB. Deleting: Volunteers can delete data they own. Cultural

```
INPUT: User request (u, r, s, m, o), the user attributes, services, operations
OUTPUT: ACCEPT or REJECT method:
if (Is_role_regular_user(u, r)) OR (Is_role_advanced_user(u, r))
   OR (Is_role_specialist(u, r)) OR (Is_role_volunteer(u, r))
   OR (Is_role_cultural_content_manager(u, r)) AND (Is_role_operation(s, r))
   then if (constraints_check(u, r, m, s, o))
      then ACCEPT
      else REJECT
else REJECT

Is_role_regular_user(u, r): returns true if user u is authorized for regular_user role else returns false
Is_role_advanced_user(u, r): returns true if user u is authorized for advanced_user role else returns false
Is_role_volunteer(u, r): returns true if user u is authorized for volunteer role else returns false
Is_role_specialist(u, r): returns true if user u is authorized for specialist role else returns false
Is_role_cultural_content_manager(u, r): returns true if user u is authorized for cultural_content_manager
role else returns false
Is_role_operation(s, r): returns true if role r is authorized for service s else returns false
constraints_check(u, r, m, s, o): returns true if user u, service s and a set of multimedia files m satisfy
operation o that is associated with role r else return false.
```

Fig. 4. Authorization control algorithm

content managers can delete data from PPC DB and assign roles to users. Advanced users and specialists can delete their own data from PCC DB. Editing: All users can edit their own data.

Authorization Access Manager. The goal of the authorization manager is to verify whether a user *u*, trying to access a set of multimedia files *m*, using a service *s*, under a certain role *r*, regular user/advanced user/specialist/cultural content manager/volunteer, with permitted actions *a*, is authorized to fulfill its request according to the restrictions enforced by that role. Figure 4 presents authorization control algorithm.

5   System Implementation

A system prototype has been implemented based on free technologies which have a great impact on the internet. An apache server was used to host the portal and a file system for storing uploaded data. All tables were stored in databases using Maria DB. Authorization Access Manager was implemented with the use of PHP stored on the apache server operating with the logic of a RESTful api. System's portal was built as a Single Page Application using Angular2+. The mobile application was created using Ionic Framework. Both mobile app and portal are using Authorization Access Manager to access data securely. The prototype implements the basic usage scenario.

Core services support basic operations for both app and portal. Registration: The creation of new user account where user can apply for a desired role. Authorization: An extended RBAC Model is used. Role assignment is made by cultural content managers (a regular user after registration may become advanced user, specialist or volunteer). Story Search: Regular and advanced users can search using keywords in the story title or the story description field or search via the provided map. Story View: Regular and advanced users have the option of choosing a story and access all associated data. Create collection: Advanced users can create a collection of stories. Rating: Regular and advanced users can rate the published material. Help: Instructional video on the home screen and explanatory texts.

Portal services are necessary for the presentation and processing of the uploaded data. Annotation: Specialists and cultural content managers can comment on stories that are visible to the volunteers. Download: All users can download data items. Edit: Volunteers can edit unpublished stories. Cultural content managers and specialists can edit their comments. Social Media Share: All users can share published content on social networks. Delete: Volunteers can delete their own uploaded material. Specialists can delete their own comments. Culture content managers can delete any content of the PPC DB. Authoring: Cultural content managers can delete irrelevant or offensive stories or unpublish them sending advices for improvement to the volunteers.

App services concern the crowdsourcing of people data. Add Story: The app allows volunteers to contribute stories to the system. Uploaded stories may contain data fields (story title, description and region of origin), media files and related persons. Update an Existing Story: Added stories can be updated by their owners. Texts related to the story can be altered or media files and persons can be added. Publish a Story: Any added story remains unpublished in the UCC DB. When the user chooses to publish a specific story, all related content, is being transferred to the PPC DB and the story is immediately visible to everyone. Unpublish a Story: When a story gets unpublished all data related to the story are transferred to UCC DB and the story is no longer public. Delete a Story: A volunteer can delete an uploaded story from the UCC DB.

5.1 Basic Usage Scenario

This section contains the description of the basic usage scenario. This is done to explore system limits concerning the needs of volunteers and system audience. As a case study we chose to target refugees (and their descendants) that came to Greece in consecutive waves from the Ottoman Empire during the first quarter of 20th century. Those immigration waves did not relate only to Greek nationality citizens of the Ottoman Empire but extending also to other ethnic groups of Asia Minor's peninsula. This incident was traumatic for all the refugees who came to Greece carrying with them very few objects and their traditions from their past lives.

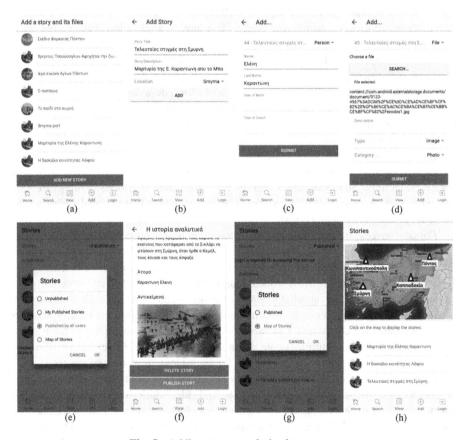

Fig. 5. Adding a story and viewing a story.

A volunteer wants to add a new story along with an image with the use of the app. To do so she/he must login with a proper volunteer account. She/he taps on the "Add" Tab (Fig. 5a) and fills-in the story fields (title, description and location). The location is selected with the use of radio buttons with predefined values resulting from a questionnaire addressed to the system target group. Figure 5b shows all the necessary fields completed and the story is ready to be registered by pressing the "Add" button. At this stage the story has been recorded in the system as unpublished. The volunteer can choose the story and fill in data such as pictures, videos and data about people related to the story. To do so, she/he selects the story. On the top of the screen there is a drop-down menu that helps her/him to add a person or a file. After she/he chooses to add a person, she/he is asked to complete specific fields related to the person (Fig. 5c). She/he then adds an image, chooses "file" from the drop-down menu, selects the file from the phone storage, fills-in information (description, type and category) and submits the file to the system to be added to the story (Fig. 5d). At this moment the story is not yet published. To do that, the volunteer must select the story that is still unpublished (Fig. 5e). After previewing the content of the story, she/he presses on the "Publish story" button (Fig. 5f). The story now is being transferred to the system published stories.

Published stories are automatically accessible to all system users. A regular user wants to seek information related to a certain refugee area. She/he starts the app and taps on the "view" tab at the bottom of the app. All published stories from all users are listed. Search method can be selected using a drop-down menu. "Map of stories" is available on that menu and the user selects it (Fig. 5g). A map showing the basic refugee areas is being displayed and by tapping on the desired area a list of stories develops (Fig. 5h). The story that seeks is at the bottom of the list. Tapping on the story and the containing information is being delivered to her/him.

6   Evalation

Table 1 presents student findings regarding systems mobile features. The proposed mobile system module contains all proposed functionality. The first observation of the team was that the ability to delete uploaded content was not available in all other systems. Of course, a user can delete only her/his own material. Also, the ability to publish content through the app was present in three systems (S3 to S5), while the ability to unpublish content exists only in the proposed system. Some services are popular to most of the systems (microhistories categorization, annotation capability, searching, story viewing, registration, microhistories map, services for non-authenticated users). Video tutorial and create collection service are present only in two systems (S1 and S4). This evaluation process strengthens the hypothesis that CH services can be provided by mobile apps and also validates the adoption of the proposed system services.

Table 1. Evaluation of mobile CS Module: S1 (Proposed System), S2 (Europeana), S3 (1001 Stories of Denmark), S4 (HistoryPin), S5 (Clio), S6 (Par.Aid.S), S7 (Culture Gate).

Services and basic features	S1	S2	S3	S4	S5	S6	S7
Microhistories categorization	✓	✓	✓	✓	✓	-	-
Annotation capability	✓	✓	✓	✓	-	✓	✓
Searching service	✓	✓	✓	✓	✓	✓	✓
Story viewing service	✓	✓	✓	✓	✓	✓	-
Create collection service	✓	✓	-	✓	-	-	-
Rating service	✓	✓	✓	✓	-	-	-
Registration is available	✓	✓	✓	✓	-	✓	✓
Video tutorial is present	✓	-	-	✓	-	-	-
Microhistories map is provided	✓	-	✓	✓	✓	✓	-
Services for non-authenticated are provided	✓	✓	✓	✓	-	✓	-
Inserted material can be published	✓	-	✓	✓	✓	-	-
Inserted material can be unpublished	✓	-	-	-	-	-	-
Inserted material can be deleted	✓	-	-	-	-	-	-

7 Discussion and Conclusion Remarks

This paper presents a CS collective memory management system that handles different types of users from refugees and their descendants to general population, specialized audience and specialists. The proposed system supports memory collection, preservation and dissemination services through mobile or desktop interfaces. The diverse users' needs have been studied thoroughly and formed the basis for the creation of the system design goals. The implemented system was used to demonstrate the strength of system services in real conditions. Evaluation results suggest that the proposed system has all the necessary services to support a basic mobile CS usage scenario concerning fundamental tasks for collective memory management. A big concern of users in CS environments is related to the control access to their own material. Some data should remain private/unpublished, while other data should be published after the owner decides correspondingly. The proposed system addresses this fear applying an enhanced RBAC model. As future work we intend to study the development of educational scenarios regarding local history aiming at the promotion of intergenerational dialog.

Acknowledgments. The authors wish to thank postgraduate students of the Department of Cultural Heritage and New Technologies of Patras University and the members of the refugee community living in our area for their contribution.

References

1. Halbwachs, M.: On Collective Memory. University of Chicago Press, Chicago (1992)
2. Tenenboim-Weinblatt, K., Baden, C.: Collective memory. In: Mazzoleni, G. (ed.) The International Encyclopedia of Political Communication, pp. 1–6. Wiley, Hoboken (2016)

3. UNESCO - 11th session of the Intergovernmental Committee for the Safeguarding of the Intangible Cultural Heritage. https://ich.unesco.org/en/convention. Accessed 21 May 2018
4. UNESCO - Basic Texts of the 2003 Convention for the Safeguarding of the Intangible Cultural Heritage. http://unesdoc.unesco.org/images/0024/002465/246582E.pdf. Accessed 21 May 2018
5. Inzerillo, L., Santagati, C.: Crowdsourcing cultural heritage: from 3D modeling to the engagement of young generations. In: Ioannides, M., et al. (eds.) EuroMed 2016. LNCS, vol. 10058, pp. 869–879. Springer, Cham (2016). https://doi.org/10.1007/978-3-319-48496-9_70
6. Howe, J.: The rise of crowdsourcing. Wired Mag. **14**(06), 1–5 (2006)
7. Oomen, J., Aroyo, L.: Crowdsourcing in the cultural heritage domain : opportunities and challenges. In: Proceedings of the 5th International Conference on Communities and Technologies, pp. 138–149. ACM, New York (2011)
8. Yin, X., Liu, W., Wang, Y., Yang, C., Lu, L.: What? How? Where? a survey of crowdsourcing. In: Li, S., Jin, Q., Jiang, X., (Jong Hyuk) Park, J.J. (eds.) Frontier and Future Development of Information Technology in Medicine and Education. LNEE, vol. 269, pp. 221–232. Springer, Dordrecht (2014). https://doi.org/10.1007/978-94-007-7618-0_22
9. Brabham, D.C.: The effectiveness of crowdsourcing public participation in a planning context. First Monday, **17**(12), 39 p. (2010)
10. Doan, A., Ramakrishnan, R., Halevy, A.Y.: Crowdsourcing systems on the World-Wide Web. Commun. ACM **54**(4), 86–96 (2011)
11. Yuen, M.C., King, I., Leung, K.S.: A survey of Crowdsourcing systems. In: Proceedings of the 2011 IEEE Third International Conference on Privacy, Security, Risk and Trust and 2011 IEEE Third International Conference on Social Computing, pp. 766–773. IEEE (2011)
12. Mahmud, F., Aris, H.: State of mobile crowdsourcing applications: a review. In: Proceedings of the 2015 4th International Conference on Software Engineering and Computer Systems, pp. 27–32. IEEE (2015)
13. Moovit Community, https://www.company.moovitapp.com/. Accessed 21 Oct 2016
14. UNESCO - Intagible Cultural Heritage Domains. https://ich.unesco.org/doc/src/01857-EN.pdf. Accessed 21 May 2018
15. Ferraiolo, D.F., Kuhn, D.R., Chandramouli, R.: Role-Based Access Control, 2nd edn. Artech House, Inc., Norwood (2007)
16. 1914–1918 - Europeana Collections. http://www.europeana.eu/portal/en/collections/world-war-I. Accessed 09 Oct 2017
17. Koukopoulos, Z., Koukopoulos, D.: A participatory digital platform for cultural heritage within smart city environments. In: Proceedings of the SITIS, pp. 412–419. IEEE (2016)
18. Europeana Open Culture. https://play.google.com/store/apps/details?id=com.glimworm.app.europeana&hl=en. Accessed 21 Nov 2017
19. 1001 Stories of Denmark. http://www.kulturarv.dk/1001fortaellinger/en_GB. Accessed 09 Oct 2017
20. Koukopoulos, Z., Koukopoulos, D.: Parades aiding system (PAR. AID. S): intelligent management of carnival parades. In: Proceedings of the 13th International Conference on Intelligent Environments, pp. 6–13. IEEE (2017)
21. Ringas, D., Christopoulou, E.: Collective city memory: field experience on the effect of urban computing on community. In: Proceedings of the 6th International Conference on Communities and Technologies, pp. 157–165. ACM (2013)
22. Kodali, N., Farkas, C., Wijesekera, D.: An authorization model for multimedia digital libraries. Int. J. Digit. Libr. **4**(3), 139–155 (2004)
23. Koukopoulos, D., Styliaras, G.: Design of trustworthy smartphone-based multimedia services in cultural environments. Electron. Commer. Res. **13**(2), 129–150 (2013)
24. Historypin. https://www.historypin.org/en/. Accessed 28 Oct 2017

25. Rodriguez Echavarria, K., Kaminski, J., Arnold, D.: 3D heritage on mobile devices: scenarios and opportunities. In: Ioannides, M., Fritsch, D., Leissner, J., Davies, R., Remondino, F., Caffo, R. (eds.) EuroMed 2012. LNCS, vol. 7616, pp. 149–158. Springer, Heidelberg (2012). https://doi.org/10.1007/978-3-642-34234-9_15
26. Ntalianis, K., Doulamis, N.: An automatic event-complementing human life summarization scheme based on a social computing method over social media content. Multimed. Tools Appl. **75**(22), 15123–15149 (2016)

Digital Cultural Heritage Infrastructure

PHOTOCONSORTIUM: Opening up the Riches of Europe's Photographic Heritage

Valentina Bachi[1], Antonella Fresa[2(✉)], Sofie Taes[3], and Fred Truyen[3]

[1] PHOTOCONSORTIUM, International Consortium for Photographic Heritage,
Via Della Bonifica 69, 56037 Peccioli, Italy
valentina.bachi@photoconsortium.net
[2] Promoter S.R.L., Via Della Bonifica 69, 56037 Peccioli, Italy
fresa@promoter.it
[3] Literary Theory and Cultural Studies - Faculty of Arts, KU Leuven,
Blijde-Inkomststraat 21 PB 3311, 3000 Leuven, Belgium
{sofie.taes,fred.truyen}@kuleuven.be

Abstract. Digitization and crowdsourcing actions are fostered by the European Union for enhancing access and citizens' participation in culture and research. Several experiences are demonstrating how tangible and intangible heritage is moving nowadays from the concept of representing objects to that of safeguarding memories and stories related to those objects. This process means to have richer, more complex and heterogeneous metadata associated to digital objects. To leverage on such richness of information, new approaches for improving searchability/retrievability of digital resources, storytelling and reuse are developing. Also, dealing with crowdsourced contributions of various types poses new challenges for curation and preservation methods in heritage institutions and across separated repositories, where linked objects and resources lie. PHOTOCONSORTIUM, the international consortium for photographic heritage, is exploring the potential of technologies, which can make possible to enrich metadata and utilize photographic heritage at best for different purposes in education, creative industry, and research.

Keywords: Metadata · Digitized photography · Linked thesauri
Multilingualism · Digital collections management

1 Introduction

1.1 About PHOTOCONSORTIUM and Digital Photographic Heritage

PHOTOCONSORTIUM [1] association was established in 2014 with the aim of expanding and enlarging the results of EuropeanaPhotography [2], a project funded by the European Union (EU) in the frame of the Competitiveness and Innovation Programme (CIP) [3]. The wide digitization and aggregation campaign carried out by the project resulted in nearly 500,000 early photography items digitized and made available online. The original partners of that project founded the association to provide a

© Springer Nature Switzerland AG 2018
M. Ioannides et al. (Eds.): EuroMed 2018, LNCS 11196, pp. 585–598, 2018.
https://doi.org/10.1007/978-3-030-01762-0_51

sustainability model, ensuring the long-term maintenance of the project results, and to continue to cope with its initial aims. Since then, the association has grown much, welcoming new members from cultural heritage institutions, archives, professionals and amateurs of vintage photography. PHOTOCONSORTIUM represents a centre of expertise and knowledge on digitization, aggregation of content to Europeana [4], the European digital library, and other digital cultural heritage portals, metadata standards, indexing, cataloguing, controlled vocabularies, and in general best practices for the management of digital archives. The Association is currently acknowledged as the expert hub for photography, also acting as domain aggregator for Europeana. This expertise and knowledge is the core to generate activities, provide services, organise training programs and seminars and participate in new research. The main areas of research for PHOTOCONSORTIUM are, in particular, in the ambit of the role of storytelling and curation to enhance the use and re-use of digital cultural heritage, and the role of rich and dereferenced metadata to improve searchability and interlinking of the digital resources. PHOTOCONSORTIUM is also committed towards smaller and micro institutions and even private collectors and citizens, to support them in sharing their own (private or family) heritage and to contribute to the growth of knowledge that is connected to photographic heritage. By enabling such forms of crowdsourcing, PHOTOCONSORTIUM participates in the process of democratization of culture [5] and explores novel ways to build a gratifying pan-European identity (Fig. 1).

Fig. 1. Band of the battalion, between the two wars, contributor Antonio Ricci, digitized at All Our Yesterdays exhibition and collection days in Pisa in 2014, Promoter Digital Gallery CC BY NC 4.0

1.2   Europeana and the Aggregation Landscape

Europeana, the European digital library, gives access to ca. 50 million digital objects from cultural institutions all over Europe. In 2008, at the launch of Europeana, the rush to digitization of cultural heritage was just open, and no fully developed national platforms were available allowing cultural institutions to expose their data and meta-data to the newly created portal. At the time, two domain platforms, The European Library (TEL) and Video Active (now named EUscreen) were operating, and that was the base Europeana grew on, sourcing metadata from there. In the following years, this original aggregation was supplemented with a number of EU funded aggregation projects. These networks focused on domain/thematic aggregation, with a primary role to help memory institutions in various sectors to digitize and prepare their data for the online presence, for participation to Europeana and, later, for reuse of such digital resources. Among these aggregation projects, some became then independent entities and kept living and operating beyond the end of the EU funding period. The scenario nowadays is rather complex, including national aggregators (platforms with a generalist cultural approach, which allow national cultural institutions to dialogue with Europeana ingestion process), and domain/thematic aggregators for archives, films, photography, audiovisual and sound, together with specific operational fields such as fashion, archaeology and natural history. All these actors talk to cultural heritage institutions (largely museums and archives, but also private collectors and small institutions, and even citizens via collection days), allowing them to prepare their data, both basing on Europeana models and requirements, and taking into account the domain-specific metadata needs.

Although such project-based approach was successful in enlarging the participation in Europeana of cultural institutions of any kind (over 3,700 institutions delivering data to Europeana from all the European countries), unfortunately the result nowadays is far from the optimal. Each project had separate goals, often with different aggregation systems and independent websites/repositories. Data quality often was not appropriately taken into account, nor monitored, as the primary target was on achieving large numbers. In addition, sustainability was not always a priority, and a number of the earliest projects ended without providing solutions for continuity of their services or supporting the preservation or enrichment of the metadata delivered to Europeana. An example of this is a project about photography digitization, the EUROPhoto, which delivered c.1,5 million photographs to Europeana in 2013 and nowadays is no more active, thus resulting in a huge batch of records with broken links in Europeana. Next to the issue of broken links, due to resources that are no more available on the web, Europeana faces the challenge of reviewing the millions metadata currently published on the portal, to upgrade them in a way that the resources are retrievable, searchable, and meaningful for the various categories of users.

A first huge effort was done for the rights/copyright information associated to each resource, which is the top requirement in order to make resources reusable. A long campaign took place for rights labelling, and the result is that today each and every record in Europeana bears a rights indication, so that the user is able to understand what he/she is lawfully allowed to do with the resource found on Europeana. Next step, currently ongoing, relates to the quality of metadata (richness, completeness, multilingualism) and to the quality of the visual representation of the objects (the preview and the thumbnail that are visible in Europeana).

The number and heterogeneity of the aggregators, resulting in non-standardized outcomes, which created some downsides, is now holding a huge potential for supporting Europeana in this crucial task for improving data quality. With the help of the aggregators, particularly the domain and thematic aggregators who have a deep knowledge of both the content providers and the metadata peculiarities in their specialist field, it is possible to analyse the metadata in Europeana and to define appropriate strategies for metadata improvement. This is the ambit of work where PHOTOCONSORTIUM is active together with the other domain and thematic aggregators.

2 State of the Art

Many initiatives and papers have addressed the theme of access to digital cultural heritage, for its use and re-use. This subject has been studied from different angles of research and experimental pilots and it would be out of the scope of this paper to provide a comprehensive discussion of the wide and multidisciplinary range of investigations involved.

However, a few examples of research are listed below as they are considered as the reference framework, where the topics addressed in this paper are positioned. They are: innovative approaches to the issues of right protection [6], reflecting on the role of cultural heritage in a changing world [7], roadmapping citizen science in the cultural sector [8]. Furthermore, the Social Platform named REACH - RE-designing Access to Cultural Heritage for a wider participation in preservation, (re-)use and management of European culture [9] is currently animating the debate about the various declinations that apply to participatory approaches in culture and social innovation.

These areas of research and their results represent the necessary background for PHOTOCONSORTIUM, which participated and is still involved in several linked projects focused on these subjects.

On this basis and in the framework of the above-mentioned state of the art, the following topics are of major importance for the activities of PHOTOCONSORTIUM and its members and are addressed more in detail in the next sections: Storytelling, Metadata curation, Data quality and Multilingualism. These areas are inter-linked and they all refer to the key question of the accessibility to and use/re-use of digital cultural heritage.

Storytelling is considered here as the social and cultural activity of sharing stories. This is a major factor that contributes to the promotion of photographic heritage and to the widest participation of its users, namely photographers, photography enthusiasts, from amateurs to professional curators. Metadata curation, data quality and multilingual search are necessary features to enable storytelling and users' engagement.

2.1   Storytelling and Metadata Curation

There is a deep liaison between storytelling and metadata curation. From one side, metadata curation allows to retrieve more efficiently content of interest for storytelling. From the other side, browsing records in seek for content of interest for storytelling allows to stumble upon problematic records that would need metadata correction or improvement (e.g. typos), or could be easily enriched because missing evident information (e.g. a photo clearly taken in Paris but not tagged as "Paris"). Much of this work has been so far a time-consuming and often tedious manual work: a person sits in front of the screen and looks at thousands of records in the institution's repository. When possible, he/she integrates the metadata with complete, correct or additional information. Now it is evident that cultural heritage institutions, aggregators and other content holders (e.g. stock image libraries) will have high benefits from services and tools that generate/complete metadata in a cost-effective way.

A technology that is rapidly developing is known as 'visual matching annotation'. This is based on algorithms that are able to recognize places, time periods, subjects, and even other specific features as commanded by the user (e.g. "find all the photos that are taken in backlit"). Then, such information is automatically added to the metadata where missing, and/or resources with common metadata are linked, within the same repository as well as across separated repositories. This does not mean that all annotation and curation must be fully automatic from now onwards, as this would deprive the outcomes (both the database of information and the storytelling outputs) of the crucial "human factor". However, once tested and assessed that they comply with a certain level of confidence, the results generated by such automatic services will provide a cost effective way to improve metadata. This will result eventually in a facilitated and often more targeted search, and the linking and contextualization of cultural heritage resources will facilitate the discovery of content, which matches different narrative paths in the storytelling.

2.2   Data Quality and Thesauri

Another effective way of improving searchability of information and metadata consistency is by the use of controlled lists of terms. A photographer's name, if manually added in the metadata, could be mistyped, or could be formatted in different ways - e.g. Holger Damgaard, or Damgaard Holger, or H. Damgaard, or Holber Damgaard - with any other possible combination of typos, and so on. Of course, if the name is mistyped in the metadata, the record will never be retrieved when the search is done with correct spelling.

Although systems and tools to improve consistency and correct typos in a database do exist, as well as search tools that automatically include and search for mistyped terms, it is more efficient to link one's metadata to authority lists, or thesauri, that grant correct and consistent spelling of the term/name, and often provide additional information and a multilingual translation. A number of such specialist thesauri is already available for any sector, and the growing resource of Wikidata is also becoming more and more used, because it allows a certain freedom of adding terms and references when they are missing from other lists.

Furthermore, the controlled list of terms can be provided in multilingual versions, coping with the different national spellings of names, which can be another source of difficulty in the searching activity.

3 Data Quality for Data Reuse

3.1 Europeana DSI – Digital Service Infrastructure

The Trans-European Telecommunications Network part of the Connecting Europe Facility (CEF) Programme aims at delivering interoperability, connectivity and coordination for telecommunication services at European level. A specific area of the work programme is dedicated to supporting projects, which provide efficient solutions for access and distribution of multilingual and multi-domain resources in digital European cultural heritage. Under such framework, since 2014 the projects called Digital Service Infrastructure (DSI) [10] are funded to support Europeana and its aggregation partners, with the objective to improve the Europeana infrastructure. This means to create access, interoperability, visibility and use of European cultural heritage, by the European citizens, cultural institutions and creative enterprises, through the Europeana platform. Now approaching its fourth round of projects, the DSI involved a very wide number of partners and institutions, from all over the EU, all collaborating to improve Europeana as the flagship digital resource in Europe.

PHOTOCONSORTIUM has been a key partner of DSI with a number of good achievements so far and ambitious new objectives for the near future. The major work done relates to metadata and records quality improvements, as illustrated below. However, a huge contribution was delivered to other Europeana initiatives such as the review of terms of the Data Exchange Agreement (DEA) [11], and the realization of a "training playbook" to support aggregators in providing content holders with appropriate information and metadata training for aggregation of content to Europeana portal and collections.

3.2 Europeana Photography Thesaurus

For the EuropeanaPhotography project, a 16-language thesaurus was developed to support metadata encoding for the collections. It covered a series of subject terms and some specific vocabulary to describe photographic technical terms, such as different kinds of print formats, and negative processes. The thesaurus is published as linked data in a SKOS [12] file format. However, a review of this approach is currently ongoing in order to dereference directly more of the subject terms using existing, widely accepted vocabularies like AAT. In a first step the metadata of the Photography collections is updated at the aggregator's side (the MINT tool [13] used by PHOTO-CONSORTIUM) to replace the original thesaurus terms by these linked data pointers. This allows focusing the vocabulary work on the more specific photographic properties. Here we are aiming at two important domains. First, since we uncovered many important yet lesser-known photographers while digitizing early photography throughout Europe, we are building a Photographer's index, which we aim to publish on a public resource such as WikiData or contribute to Getty ULAN. This would enable to support Europeana's efforts to offer entity pages, which will facilitate users to browse through the data. Second, we want to work on true photographic properties of the image, such as balance, fill the frame, lead room, rule of thirds, motion blur, simple, color harmony, framed, leading lines, ... which would allow photo enthusiasts to more effectively explore Europeana's contents on early photography. We also are revising the current photographic technique metadata, as statistics show they were implemented somewhat inconsistently – e.g. a partner might have preferred to describe the photographic process, e.g. 'wet collodion', while another mentions the result, e.g. a 'tintype'. In addition, it would be very helpful to offer a search facet to end-users of Europeana that provides useful periodization of early photography. All these efforts aim to strengthen the usability of Europeana as a portal to explore photographic heritage in its full richness.

3.3   Metadata Enrichment and Metadata Task Force

As mentioned above, PHOTOCONSORTIUM was invited by Europeana Foundation to take part in the DSI-2 project in 2016. The most visible outcome by PHOTO-CONSORTIUM in DSI-2 was the development and curation of the Europeana Photography thematic collection, a sub-website in Europeana portal aiming at highlighting examples and stories related to vintage photography (cfr. 2.4 below). Having in mind the scope of the Europeana Photography thematic collection, the focus of the action in the DSI-2 project was on checking the quality of the legacy datasets originated in the EuropeanaPhotography project (last ingestion in Europeana dating back to 2014, as part of the project funded by the EU). Assessment and improvement of data quality insisted mostly on metadata, and collaboration agreements were established by PHO-TOCONSORTIUM with selected content holders from the network of the association (among which Parisienne de Photographie, Topfoto, United Archives, CRDI/Ajuntament de Girona, KU Leuven, Generalitat de Catalunia, Nalis Foundation). They participated in the project improving the metadata of existing datasets, providing new datasets/items, and participating in the creation of virtual exhibitions, digital galleries and blogs.

In terms of metadata improvements, each content provider was able to perform different actions according to the desiderata for the realization of the Europeana Photography thematic collection. In first place, they provided images and records matching specific requirements for data quality as established in the Europeana Publishing Framework [14]. In particular, a minimum of 800x pixels preview was required for each image, with direct links to the image at the provider's website. Moreover, improvement in accuracy of titles was requested to the content providers, including descriptions and authors/creator information on the legacy data. Finally, licensing was requested to be as open as possible, with non-obtrusive watermarks of even better no watermarks at all. The DSI-2 project continued in the new edition of the DSI-3, active until 31 August 2018, and will continue in the DSI-4 until 2020. As part the action for improving metadata quality, PHOTOCONSORTIUM is committed to raise awareness of the Europeana Publishing Framework, and to promote the upgrade of digitized collection according to different 'tiers' (Table 1).

Table 1. 'Tiers' in the Europeana Publishing Framework

TIER	Technical requirements	Rights specifications
TIER 1	Direct link to object, minimum 0.1 megapixel in size	Any rights statement of Europeana licensing framework
TIER 2	Direct link to object, minimum 800 + pixels wide	Any rights statement of Europeana licensing framework
TIER 3	Direct link to object, minimum 1.200 + pixels wide recommended	Any rights statement of Europeana licensing framework that allow for some reuse
TIER 4	Direct link to object, minimum 1.200 + pixels wide recommended	Any rights statement of Europeana licensing framework that allow for free reuse

PHOTOCONSORTIUM supports and encourages alignment to tier 2, 3 and 4, because of the advantages in terms of visibility of the collections and their accessibility by the targeted users; less invasive forms of image protection like the invisible watermarking technologies or, at least, adoption of non-obtrusive watermarks, to improve usability of the content; and non-restrictive licenses for the digitized images, particularly because this is extremely useful for the creative reuse of digitized content, e.g. in applications for education (Table 2).

Table 2. Sum up of DSI-2 metadata actions

Area of improvement for PHOTOCONSORTIUM partners	Number of records
Larger previews and direct URLs (upgrade to Tier 2–4)	123,846
Metadata improvement, particularly in accuracy of titles, descriptions and authors/creators	11,949
Smaller watermarks than before	35,434
Provision of new content	35,230

The achievement got by PHOTOCONSORTIUM in DSI-2 was relevant, particularly because two important providers – namely, Parisienne de Photographie and TopFoto -accepted to change their original positions about previews and watermarks taken in 2012-2014 during the EuropeanaPhotography project. The changes were with higher resolution previews in the case of Parisienne de Photographie and with the use of a less invasive watermark in the case of TopFoto (as illustrated in the figure below) (Fig. 2). This result is a direct consequence of the launch of the Europeana Photography thematic collection, that showcases the pictures in a more attractive way compared to the general purpose interface of the Europeana portal. It also confirms that the approach 'the more you give the more you get' of the Europeana publishing strategy is effective.

Fig. 2. Example of TopFoto record, one item as published in 2014-2015 and the same item updated in 2017 via PHOTOCONSORTIUM.

The DSI project represents a win-win opportunity for both Europeana and the content providers - particularly because of the possibility of the datasets being included in the Europeana Photography thematic collection generating a wider visibility for the content and its provider, all over the EU and internationally. Furthermore, PHOTO-CONSORTIUM includes a mix of different partners, both public and private organisations, contributing to the project with different opinions and strategies towards the open approach as advocated in the Europeana Publishing Framework. The experience of metadata and workflow improvement established within the DSI project was reviewed by PHOTOCONSORTIUM content providers, and the impact of this action was discussed by the members of the association. It became immediately evident how the metadata improvement in Europeana was beneficial for the content providers.

To capitalize the experience gained in collaboration with Europeana, a dedicated Metadata Task Force was officially created within PHOTOCONSORTIUM and a front-officer was appointed to coordinate the relationships between content providers and the Europeana ingestion team.

3.4   Thematic Collections

As mentioned above, PHOTOCONSORTIUM operates as a thematic aggregator for Europeana: Europe's most trusted portal to Cultural Heritage. Europeana.eu currently holds over 51 million objects provided by thousands of institutions. Unlike Google, Europeana's data and metadata are contributed by professionals and come with a quality and safety guarantee. To make this monumental database more accessible and encourage reuse of its content, Thematic Collections have been established, offering access to well-defined, manually curated, top-quality subsets. These collections are either created in the framework of DSI project and in other CEF Generic Services project PHOTOCONSORTIUM coordinates the efforts toward content selection and curation for two of those Collections: the already mentioned Europeana Photography and another one with a focus on migration.

Europeana Photography: photography.europeana.eu

The thematic platform on photography contains over 1 million high-quality images, and invites visitors to explore its treasures by using the search bar or browsing options.

Furthermore, users are guided through the content more intently via a plethora of curated features, from predefined queries and blog posts, to picture galleries and large-scale exhibitions – all handpicked and narrated by PHOTOCONSORTIUM curators. Masters of early photographers like John Topham, Gaston Paris, Josep Maria Lladó Bausili or Karl Heinrich Lämmel are exhibited at their best in a magnificent digital showcase.

Europeana Migration: migration.europeana.eu

At a time when the word 'migrant' is often accompanied by the word 'crisis', PHOTOCONSORTIUM is joining Europeana in its efforts to show Europe's history of migration in a different light. Through a thematic collection containing a varied range of objects from all over the continent, stories great and small tell the tale of Europe's past and present as a product of many cultural influences. Our heritage shows that Europe is the result of a flow of people and ideas, and that migration is woven through people's everyday lives - from our choice of cuisine to the way we dress. Focusing on the effects of migration on the arts and the sciences in particular, Europeana Migration promises to enlighten and enrich, to surprise and to inspire those who are curious about Europe's shared and multifaceted identity.

4 Future Work

The future work of PHOTOCONSORTIUM will focus on two complementary directions. The former is to develop the concept of accredited aggregator of Europeana, taking the ownership of part of the Europeana mission for the domain of photographic heritage. The latter is the development and testing of novel technological approach to the automatization of metadata generation.

Eventually, both the participation in the Europeana aggregation and the improvement of metadata will contribute to a more efficient and successful curation and storytelling, which represent the ultimate goals for user engagement and exploitation of the results of the work performed by the Association. In this light, PHOTO-CONSORTIUM is committed to continue to widen its communication, using its online website, its channels on the social media, maintaining its collaboration with the *digitalmeetsculture* magazine [15] and through the organisation of workshops, seminars and physical photographic exhibitions.

4.1 Aggregator for Europeana

Beside own association's activities, PHOTOCONSORTIUM intends to maintain its role of photography aggregator and expert hub at service of Europeana, because this opens possibilities for the content providers that belong to the association network. Such possibilities include a bigger visibility and participation in the digitized cultural heritage European landscape, and new technological opportunities for research and improvement of the impact of digitized collections.

4.2   New Projects

"Fifties in Europe Kaleidoscope" is a new project, recently awarded by EC in the 2017 CEF call for Europeana Generic Services, starting in fall in 2018. It is coordinated by KU Leuven, with the participation of PHOTOCONSORTIUM together with several other partners from all over Europe. It has high- technological ambitions and a strong focus on the educational target. Among other outcomes, a MOOC is planned to be released in 2019 and provided online by the participating Universities as part of their educational offer. The scope of the technological research is to develop an intelligent visual similarity search to complement the Europeana core service functionality, applying state-of-the-art deep learning techniques on training photo datasets under the overarching theme of the 1950s in Europe.

The effort to research advanced solutions and technologies for metadata improvement, including automatic identification of information/properties from digital objects, and addition to technical and descriptive metadata, will continue within other projects and proposals to the EU.

A particular interest exists in applying artificial intelligence and visual feature extraction and classification, with expected impact on cultural heritage institutions' workflow, collections visibility and usability, Europeana advances and new possibility of applications in various sectors including education, mental therapy, serious games and others.

4.3   IIIF Standard and PHOTOCONSORTIUM

The International Image Interoperability Framework (IIIF) defines a standardised method of describing and delivering images over the web [16], enabling interoperability across digital repositories.

A Task Force of Europeana worked "to identify the current trends and tendencies towards the handling of the emerging IIIF technology on the part of the Europeana content providers" [17]. It produced a final report [18] providing on the use of IIIF technologies within the Europeana ecosystem. Europeana adopted IIIF into its technical infrastructure, extending "the Europeana Data Model (EDM) to accommodate links to IIIF end-points and manifests. To that end the Europeana service acts as a IIIF reference node serving up IIIF imagery to its interfaces". The challenge is now to make content providers more aware of how to use IIIF to support distribution and use of their digital contents.

PHOTOCONSORTIUM is engaged in the further development of high-end image capturing procedures (via members KU Leuven [19] and CRDI [20]), and image storage and dissemination standards. To this end, it has a liaison with the JPEG standard committees through its member imec/ETRO [21]. PHOTOCONSORTIUM follows in particular the development of multispectrum and reflectance imaging standards which are essential for the capture of early photographic techniques to their full potential. It also follows the JPEG PLENO developments [22] and, on behalf of its members, has liaisons with image rights advocacy groups such as IPTC [23] and CEPIC [24], and is looking in this context into better protection of image integrity and embedded image metadata. For its public oriented activities, in particular its work with cultural heritage institutions, PHOTOCONSORTIUM aims to facilitate among its members the adoption of the IIIF standards and IIIF compliant visualisation solutions. For that matter, encouraging institutions to deliver high resolution images is part of its mission, which is important in light of digital showcases such as Europeana, that support an IIIF viewer for high end images. Providers such as KU Leuven already support IIIF on their own infrastructure [25] (Fig. 3).

Fig. 3. Medamud. Elouet El Ghir Archeologists and guides are on their way to a prehistoric site, collection glass slides KU Leuven, Public Domain Marked.

5 Lessons Learnt, Impact and Added Value

Digital technologies are offering a terrific opportunity to cultural heritage to renew its role in the society. Younger generations, elderly people, researchers, scholars and citizens in general can find a new way to re-appropriating of the heritage belonging to their territories and passed generations. This is particularly true in the case of the photographic heritage, which represents the testimony of the life in the generations that just left, which is a tangible witness of the life of our direct ancestors, and which can provide a concrete contribution to understand our past and the challenges of our present. PHOTOCONSORTIUM has a clear mission that is to improve the discoverability of the heritage of photography in Europe. Improving metadata, content quality, multilingual access and storytelling is part of this mission, looking toward the future steps of moving into a new context where digital cultural content is more accessible and re-usable.

References

1. PHOTOCONSORTIUM Association. www.photoconsortium.net. Accessed 14 Aug 2018
2. EuropenaPhotography website. http://www.europeana-photography.eu/. Accessed 14 Aug 2018
3. Competitiveness and Innovation Programme (CIP). The programme of the EU run from 2007 to 2013 with an overall budget of € 3,621 million. http://ec.europa.eu/cip/. Accessed 14 Aug 2018
4. European Commission. https://ec.europa.eu/digital-single-market/en/europeana-european-digital-library-all. Europeana is the is the European Commission's digital platform for cultural heritage. The platform is available at http://www.europeana.eu/. Accessed 14 Aug 2018
5. Aitamurto, T.: Crowdsourcing for Democracy: New Era in Policy-Making, Committee for the Future, Parliament of Finland (2012). https://cddrl.fsi.stanford.edu/publications/crowdsourcing_for_democracy_new_era_in_policymaking. Accessed 14 Aug 2018
6. Europeana Space project: IP and Europeana Space Pilots: Case Studies (2016). ISBN 9789082636000
7. Borowiecki, K.J., Forbes, N., Fresa, A. (eds.): Cultural Heritage in a Changing World. Springer, Heidelberg (2016). https://doi.org/10.1007/978-3-319-29544-2
8. Civic Epistemologies project: Roadmap for Citizen Researchers in the age of Digital Culture (2015). https://cordis.europa.eu/docs/projects/cnect/4/632694/080/deliverables/001-CIVICE PISTEMOLOGIESRoadmapHandbook.pdf. Accessed 14 Aug 2018
9. REACH project website (2017). www.reach-culture.eu. Accessed 14 Aug 2018
10. Europeana PRO: Europeana DSI-3 (2017). https://pro.europeana.eu/project/europeana-dsi-3. Accessed 14 Aug 2018
11. Europeana PRO: The Data Exchange Agreement (2015). https://pro.europeana.eu/page/the-data-exchange-agreement. Accessed 14 Aug 2018
12. W3C Semantic Web: SKOS Simple Knowledge Organization System (2013). https://www.w3.org/2004/02/skos/. Accessed 14 Aug 2018
13. MINT tool. http://mint.image.ece.ntua.gr/redmine/projects/mint/wiki/Introduction_to_MINT. Accessed 14 Aug 2018
14. Europeana Publishing Framework. https://pro.europeana.eu/post/publishing-framework. Accessed 14 Aug 2018
15. Digitalmeetsculture: Digitalmeetsculture is an online magazine, edited by Promoter S.r.l., freely accessible and published since 2010. www.digitalmeetsculture.net. Accessed 14 Aug 2018
16. IIIF International Image Interoperability Framework. https://iiif.io/. Accessed 14 Aug 2018
17. Europeana PRO: Preparing Europeana for IIIF (2017). https://pro.europeana.eu/project/preparing-europeana-for-iiif-involvement. Accessed 14 Aug 2018
18. Europeana: Report of the Task Force on Preparing Europeana for IIIF involvement (2017). https://pro.europeana.eu/files/Europeana_Professional/Europeana_Network/Europeana_Network_Task_Forces/Final_reports/Preparing%20Europeana%20for%20IIIF%20involvemenet%20TF%20final%20report/report-of-iiif-task-force-2017-final.pdf. Accessed 14 Aug 2018
19. Digital Lab KU Leuven. (in Dutch). https://bib.kuleuven.be/BD/digitalisering-en-document-delivery/digitalisering/digitaal-labo. Accessed 14 Aug 2018
20. Centre de Recerca i Difusió de la Imatge (CRDI). http://www2.girona.cat/ca/sgdap_crdi. Accessed 14 Aug 2018
21. Schelkens, P.: An introduction to JPEG standards for digitizing and archiving applications. Imatge i Recerca: Jornades Antoni Varés (14es: 2016: Girona) (2016)

22. JPEG PLENO. https://jpeg.org/jpegpleno/. Accessed 14 Aug 2018
23. International Press Telecommunications Council IPTC. https://iptc.org/. Accessed 14 Aug 2018
24. Centre of the Picture Industry CEPIC. http://cepic.org/. Accessed 14 Aug 2018
25. KU Leuven Expo Collection. (in Dutch). http://expo.bib.kuleuven.be. Accessed 14 Aug 2018

Digital 3D Reconstruction Projects and Activities in the German-Speaking Countries

S. Münster[1]([✉]), P. Kuroczyński[2], and H. Messemer[3]

[1] Media Center, TU Dresden, 01062 Dresden, Germany
sander.muenster@tu-dresden.de
[2] Computer Science and Visualisation in Architecture, Hochschule Mainz,
Mainz, Germany
[3] Institute for Art History, Julius-Maximilians-Universität Würzburg,
Würzburg, Germany

Abstract. 3D reconstructions are important media to educate and investigate history and to research cultural heritage. Against the background of networking and monitoring activities of the workgroup for Digital Reconstruction of the Association for Digital Humanities in the German-speaking area this paper is dedicated to showcase and systematise a range of current work priorities in the German-speaking countries. It aims on strengthening the image- and object-based research within the framework of Digital Humanities.

Keywords: Digital 3D reconstruction · Cultural heritage · Digital humanities
Survey

1 Introduction

The workgroup "Digital Reconstruction" emerged from the first Annual Meeting of the Association for Digital Humanities in the German-speaking area (25.–28.03.2014, University of Passau) and brings together colleagues who have dedicated themselves to the subject of digital reconstruction from an academic perspective. It currently consists of around 60 people from 29 institutions in the German-speaking region and 4 associated member institutions in Europe (Fig. 1). Basing on previous work about research challenges [1] as well as current projects [2], this article is intended to showcase and systematise a range of current work priorities in the German-speaking countries. It shows the current research focus and makes clear where desiderata are. The aim is to show that within the Digital Humanities there is a significant research area which does work with images, while the majority of Digital Humanities projects still focus on texts.

2 Methodology

The compilation bases on three sources of information:

1. A survey of research perspectives and projects is currently under preparation as part of the book project of the workgroup under the working title "Der Modelle Tugend

© Springer Nature Switzerland AG 2018
M. Ioannides et al. (Eds.): EuroMed 2018, LNCS 11196, pp. 599–606, 2018.
https://doi.org/10.1007/978-3-030-01762-0_52

2.0" [3]. Around 25 articles became part of this book, which describe a large number of recent projects as well as reflect an evolution of digital reconstruction as a field of research.

2. During a poster session held at a workshop of the workgroup in September 2016 current project activties were presented. That workshop provided a clue on current topics as well as an overview of a research landscape.

3. As shown in the following section, several research projects as well as graduation and networking activities are dedicated to mapping, systematize and contextualize digital reconstruction activities.

Fig. 1. Member institutions of the AG Digital Reconstruction

3   Current Research and Work Priorities of Digital 3D Reconstruction

Based on these sources of information, a number of key areas in the field of research of and with digital reconstruction can be identified.

Digital Reconstructions of Specific Artifacts
The still most essential context of an application of digital reconstructions is the creation of digital 3D models of specific cultural-historical objects such as settlement structures, individual buildings or building ensembles, as well as cult objects. This three-dimensional model as well as derived images serve primarily for education, but also increasingly for object-related research. A systematic mapping of projects in this field provdies, for example, the wiki of the workgroup for digital art history, which currently lists 3D models from about 40 locations especially in Germany [4]. Anna Bentkofska-Kafel also maintains a thematically structured overview with a more international focus within the 3D visualization in the Arts network [5]. With a meanwhile 30-year-old history and a multitude of individual activities as well as

caesurae, the scholarly field of digital 3D reconstruction became also the subject of historiographical research. As an example, the dissertation of Heike Messemer investigates relevant milestones in the evolvement of 3D reconstructions from an art history perspective [6].

Methodical Validation

Digital reconstructions do not only employ computer science technologies to deal with humanities issues, but stands in the context of a multitude of different scholarly domains and purposes. In addition to archeology and various tasks of dealing with cultural heritage as focal points of EU funding, specific scenarios in the German research landscape are for example art and architectural history, museology, cultural studies and building engineering [7, 8]. Against this background, there are numerous activities for recording and systematising research and utilization approaches of digital reconstruction [9, 10] as well as focusing on a methodological validation [cf. 11].

Modeling Tools

In focus of digital reconstructions is the formation of a 3D model based on the interpretation of historical sources. In addition, various types of acquired data find their way into such projects, for example in the form of laser scans or photogrammetric reconstructions of existing object parts or as landscape models. A modeling is done on the computer primarily by means of manually operated modeling softwares. A series of projects deals with approaches to simplify these processes by easing modeling tools [12–14] or processes. Others are trying to structure the manual modeling process, to identify common steps into the reconstruction work, and to translate them into digital, ontology-based manuals [15]. To summarize, easy to use workflows and tools are still in the focus of research and tool development and have for a long time been not only a German, but an EU-wide issue. Furthermore, platforms as Sketchfab enabled citizen created models to become visible for a wide public and thereby blur borders between scientific and popular models. This opens up a potential research field regarding the question of how to make clear what a scientific model is [16].

Data and Knowledge Management

Numerous projects focused on data management and particularly the collection and archiving of historical sources, 3D models and visualizations as well as associated meta-, para- and context data. Prominent examples for those projects are EPOCH, 3D-COFORM, CARARE or 3D-ICONS. In addition, many papers deal with fundamental mechanisms of documentation and classification of digital reconstructions [17–19]. Projects such as IANUS, Monarch, DocuVis, OpenInfra or DURAARK have the goal of developing research infrastructures [20–24]. Although these projects differ with regard to the respective addressee group and tool spectrum, questions such as the relationship between model and (explicit) knowledge bases, such as sources are relevant for all endeavors [25, 26]. In contrast to the building industry, which has developed Building Information Modeling (BIM) and an IFC data exchange format in response to digital change, digital humanities have yet to agree on a digital methodology for dealing with 3D models. In this context, Linked Data has become established as future-oriented technology, with knowledge formalization in structured data models and open source with WebGL for web-based visualization of 3D data sets [27]. Closely related, the description of the created models – for example by means of overarching reference ontologies and application-specific application ontologies – is another major field of research [28, 29]. Finally, some research activities deal with the segementation and classification of parts of 3D models from point or polygon clouds [24]. To conclude, the development of virtual research environments is one key area of research and development within a German community, and currently there are numerous – often competing – research infrastructures dedicated to digital reconstruction available, although none have yet been accepted by the majority of researchers.

Presentation
A presentation of 3D reconstructions takes place primarily in the form of rendered images or animation. With regard to the quality of these images, requirements comprise the simulation of materiality and lighting mood, but also heterogeneous probabilities of hypotheses. Current research projects address issues of aesthetics and visual inclusion of varying degrees of hypothesis [30–33], as well as technological issues of interactivity and implementation. Another research issue is the question of the authenticity of digital reconstructions [10]. In terms of accessibility, easy-to-use data viewers – as mentioned in the previous section – are highly demanded by a humanities community [1]. Projects worth mentioning in the field of monument preservation are MonArch [34] and SACHER [35], which enable comprehensive and collaborative management of (digital) cultural heritage and use innovative viewers such as 3DHOP [36]. Within the project ViSIT a virtual museum is being developed to present cultural heritage across borders to tourists [37]. Moreover, rapid prototyping and 3D printing are a comparatively new presentation medium [38], which transforms virtual models into a materiality. A different approach offers a research group of Joerg Maxzin at the Technische Hochschule Deggendorf with the restauration of historical wooden objects with the help of digital technologies [39]. Perception, didactics and presentation in a museum context are further current research topics [40]. Beside common trends like virtual and augmented reality [41] as well as 3D printing, especially the question for a scientifically plausible visualization is a key research field.

Education of Digital Reconstruction Methods
Especially in the field of humanities, general affinity and competency to employ digital research methods are often still poorly developed [42]. Similar to the digital humanities as a whole [43], teaching of production methods, result evaluation and proper use of digital reconstructions to scholars is a major challenge. Consequently, a series of projects and networks focus on learning of digital reconstruction technologies [44, 45] as well as the application of digital reconstruction methods for research and education [eg. 46, 47]. In contrast to Mediterranean countries cultural heritage is only occasionally named as title for study programs in Germany [48], but several study programs on Digital Humanities specifically dedicated to images and objects have arisen during the last years [cf. 49].

Networking Activities
Currently, a scholarly community on digital reconstruction in Germany encompasses a large number of scholars from various disciplinary domains who have until now been insufficiently networked and organized. From this, common hubs for the establishment

and further organisational and methodical development of digital reconstruction as part of the scholarly disciplines of digital humanities and digital cultural heritage are demanded. A first step in this direction was the initially mentioned founding in 2014 of the Digital Reconstruction workgroup, which at European level is accompanied by numerous multinational and mostly thematically focused networks, for example dedicated to virtual museums [50] or color and space of cultural property [51].

4   Conclusion

Quo vadis digital 3D reconstruction? Beside the – still most essential – application of digital reconstructions on specific cultural-historical objects some overarching topics are obvious. According to digital heritage and humanities in general, sufficient data management and infrastructures as well as visualization and education are topics of high relevance. Moreover, with BIM and Linked Data a project independent data structuring became an important research field and potentially enables an exchange and accessibility of models [cf. 52]. While many emphases reflect an international discourse, there are specifics within a German community such as strong links to the history of art and architecture and research methodology as well as aspects *scientificity* in terms of uncertainty or documentation. Since this overview is preliminary and includes primarily activities and protagonists organized in the workgroup Digital Reconstruction, it is an ongoing task to monitor further activities.

References

1. Münster, S., Kuroczyński, P., Pfarr-Harfst, M., Grellert, M., Lengyel, D.: Future research challenges for a computer-based interpretative 3D reconstruction of cultural heritage – A German community's view. ISPRS Ann. Photogramm. Remote Sens. Spat. Inf. Sci. (XXV International CIPA Symposium) **II-5-W3**, 207–213 (2015)
2. Münster, S., Kuroczyński, P., Pfarr-Harfst, M.: Projekte und Aktivitäten im Kontext digitaler 3D-Rekonstruktion im deutschsprachigen Raum. Paper presented at the 4. Jahrestagung der Digital Humanities im deutschsprachigen Raum (DHd 2017), Bern (2017)
3. Kuroczyński, P., Münster, S., Pfarr-Harfst, M. (eds.): Der Modelle Tugend 2.0 – Herausforderungen auf dem Weg zum wissenschaftlichen 3D-Informationsmodell (Arbeitstitel). Heidelberg University Press, Heidelberg (accepted book)
4. Arbeitskreis Digitale Kunstgeschichte Liste digitaler Modelle historischer Architektur. http://www.digitale-kunstgeschichte.de/wiki/Liste_digitaler_Modelle_historischer_Architektur. Accessed 9 June 2014
5. Bentkowska-Kafel, A.: 3DVisA Index of 3D Projects. http://3dvisa.cch.kcl.ac.uk/projectlist.html. Accessed 19 Aug 2016
6. Messemer, H.: The beginnings of digital visualization of historical architecture in the academic field. In: Hoppe, S., Breitling, S. (eds.) Virtual Palaces, Part II. Lost Palaces and their Afterlife. Virtual Reconstruction between Science and the Media, pp. 21–54 (2016)
7. Riedel, A., Henze, F., Marbs, A.: Paradigmenwechsel in der historischen Bauforschung? Ansätze für eine effektive Nutzung von 3D-Informationen. In: Heine, K., Rheidt, K., Henze, F., Riedel, A. (eds.) Von Handaufmaß bis High Tech III – 3D in der historischen Bauforschung, pp. 131–141. Philipp von Zabern, Darmstadt (2011)

8. Burwitz, H., Henze, F., Riedel, A.: Alles 3D? – Über die Nutzung aktueller Aufnahme-technik in der archäologischen Bauforschung. Dokumentation und Innovation bei der Erfassung von Kulturgütern II, Schriften des Bundesverbands freiberuflicher Kulturwis-senschaftler, vol. 5, online publication of BfK-Fachtagung 2012, Würzburg (2012). https://www.b-f-k.de/webpub03/content/vortrag03.html#v03-1. Accessed 24 Sept 2018

9. Münster, S., Niebling, F.: Building a wiki resource on visual knowledge related knowledge assets. In: Spender, J., Schiuma, G., Nönnig, J.R. (eds.) Proceedings of the 11th International Forum on Knowledge Asset Dynamics (IFKAD 2016) Dresden, Germany. 15–17th June 2016, pp. 1606–1618. University of Basilicata, Dresden (2016)

10. Pfarr-Harfst, M.: Typical workflows, documentation approaches and principles of 3D digital reconstruction of cultural heritage. In: Münster, S., Pfarr-Harfst, M., Kuroczyński, P., Ioannides, M. (eds.) 3D Research Challenges in Cultural Heritage II. LNCS, vol. 10025, pp. 32–46. Springer, Cham (2016). https://doi.org/10.1007/978-3-319-47647-6_2

11. Münster, S., Friedrichs, K., Hegel, W.: 3D reconstruction techniques as a cultural shift in art history? Int. J. Digit. Art Hist. 3, 38–60 (2018)

12. Schinko, C., Krispel, U., Gregor, R., Schreck, T., Ullrich, T.: Generative modeling – the combination of knowledge and geometry. In: Der Modelle Tugend 2.0 (accepted paper)

13. Snickars, P.: Metamodeling. 3D-(re)designing Polhem's Laboratorium mechanicum. In: Der Modelle Tugend 2.0 (accepted paper)

14. Havemann, S., Settgast, V., Lancelle, M., Fellner, D.W.: 3D-Powerpoint – Towards a Design Tool for Digital Exhibitions of Cultural Artifacts. Eurographics Association, Brighton (2007)

15. Pfarr-Harfst, M., Wefers, S.: Digital 3D reconstructed models – structuring visualisation project workflows. In: Ioannides, M., et al. (eds.) EuroMed 2016. LNCS, vol. 10058, pp. 544–555. Springer, Cham (2016). https://doi.org/10.1007/978-3-319-48496-9_43

16. Messemer, H.: Entwicklung und Potentiale digitaler 3D-Modelle historischer Architektur. Kontextualisierung und Analyse aus kunsthistorischer Perspektive (Dissertation). (2018, unpublished)

17. Pfarr-Harfst, M.: Documentation system for digital reconstructions Reference to the Mausoleum of the Tang-Dynastie at Zhaoling, in Shaanxi Province, China (Unpublished). o. Ort (2013)

18. Huvila, I.: Perspectives to Archaeological Information in the Digital Society. Institutionen för ABM och författarna, Uppsala (2014)

19. Münster, S., Hegel, W., Kröber, C.: A model classification for digital 3D reconstruction in the context of humanities research. In: Münster, S., Pfarr-Harfst, M., Kuroczyński, P., Ioannides, M. (eds.) 3D Research Challenges in Cultural Heritage II. LNCS, vol. 10025, pp. 3–31. Springer, Cham (2016). https://doi.org/10.1007/978-3-319-47647-6_1

20. Drewello, R., Freitag, B., Schlieder, C.: Neues Werkzeug für alte Gemäuer. DFG Forschung Magazin 3, 10–14 (2010)

21. Bruschke, J., Wacker, M.: Simplifying documentation of digital reconstruction processes. In: Münster, S., Pfarr-Harfst, M., Kuroczyński, P., Ioannides, M. (eds.) 3D Research Challenges in Cultural Heritage II. LNCS, vol. 10025, pp. 256–271. Springer, Cham (2016). https://doi.org/10.1007/978-3-319-47647-6_12

22. Kuroczyński, P.: 3D-Computer-Rekonstruktion der Baugeschichte Breslaus. Ein Erfahrungs-bericht. In: Wissenschaften WZdPAd (ed.) Jahrbuch des Wissenschaftlichen Zentrums der Polnischen Akademie der Wissenschaften in Wien, vol. 3, pp. 201–213. Wien (2012)

23. Kuroczyński, P., Hauck, O., Dworak, D.: 3D models on triple paths – new pathways for documenting and visualizing virtual reconstructions. In: Münster, S., Pfarr-Harfst, M., Kuroczyński, P., Ioannides, M. (eds.) 3D Research Challenges in Cultural Heritage II. LNCS, vol. 10025, pp. 149–172. Springer, Cham (2016). https://doi.org/10.1007/978-3-319-47647-6_8

24. Beetz, J., et al.: Enrichment and preservation of architectural knowledge. In: Münster, S., Pfarr-Harfst, M., Kuroczyński, P., Ioannides, M. (eds.) 3D Research Challenges in Cultural Heritage II. LNCS, vol. 10025, pp. 231–255. Springer, Cham (2016). https://doi.org/10.1007/978-3-319-47647-6_11

25. Hoppe, S.: Die Fußnoten des Modells. In: Frings, M. (ed.) Der Modelle Tugend. CAD und die neuen Räume der Kunstgeschichte, Weimar, pp. 87–102 (2001)

26. Günther, H.: Kritische Computer-Visualisierung in der kunsthistorischen Lehre. In: Frings, M. (ed.) Der Modelle Tugend. CAD und die neuen Räume der Kunstgeschichte, Weimar, pp. 111–122 (2001)

27. Kuroczyński, P.: Virtual research environment for digital 3d reconstructions: standards, thresholds and prospects. Stud. Digit. Herit. 1(2), 456–76 (2017)

28. Homann, G.: Die Anwendung von Ontologien zur Wissensrepräsentation und -kommunikation im Bereich des kulturellen Erbes. In: Schomburg, S., Leggewie, C., Lobin, H., Puschmann, C. (eds.) Digitale Wissenschaft – Stand und Entwickung digital vernetzter Forschung in Deutschland, pp. 33–40. HBZ, Köln (2011)

29. Kuroczyński, P.: Digital reconstruction and virtual research environments – a question of documentation standards. In: Access and Understanding – Networking in the Digital Era, Proceedings of the Annual Conference of CIDOC, Dresden, 06–11 September 2014 (2014)

30. Heeb, N., Christen, J., Rohrer, J., Lochau, S.: Strategien zur Vermittlung von Fakt, Hypothese und Fiktion in der digitalen Architektur-Rekonstruktion. In: Der Modelle Tugend 2.0 (accepted paper)

31. Vogel, G.-H.: Von der Zweidimensionalität zur Dreidimensionalität: wissenschaftliche Rekonstruktion verlorener Architekturen als archäologische und kunsthistorische Wissensbilder vor dem Hintergrund ästhetischer Konzepte der Kunst- und Architekturgeschichte. In: Der Modelle Tugend 2.0 (accepted paper)

32. Lengyel, D., Toulouse, C.: Ein Stadtmodell von Pergamon – Unschärfe als Methode für Darstellung und Rekonstruktion antiker Architektur. In: Petersen, L., von den Hoff, R. (eds.) Skulpturen in Pergamon – Gymnasion, Heiligtum, Palast, pp. 22–26. Archäologische Sammlung der Albert-Ludwigs-Universität Freiburg, Freiburg (2011)

33. Lengyel, D., Toulouse, C.: Darstellung von unscharfem Wissen in der Rekonstruktion historischer Bauten. In: Heine, K., Rheidt, K., Henze, F., Riedel, A. (eds.) Von Handaufmaß bis High Tech III. 3D in der historischen Bauforschung, pp. 182–186. Verlag Philipp von Zabern, Darmstadt (2011)

34. Freitag, B., Stenzer, A.: MonArch – A Digital Archive for Cultural Heritage. In: Vinken, G., Franz, B. (eds.) Das Digitale und die Denkmalpflege: Bestandserfassung – Denkmalvermittlung – Datenarchivierung – Rekonstruktion verlorener Objekte. Verlag Jörg Mitzkat, Holzminden (2017)

35. Apollonio, F.I., Rizzo, F., Bertacchi, S., Dall'Osso, G., Corbelli, A., Grana, C.: SACHER: smart architecture for cultural heritage in Emilia Romagna. Paper presented at the Italian Research Conference on Digital Libraries, IRCDL 2017: Digital Libraries and Archives (2017)

36. 3DHOP – Presenting online high-res 3D models: a crash course. Paper presented at the Digital Heritage 2015, Granada (spain) (2015)

37. n.b. ViSIT: Virtuelle Verbund-Systeme und Informations-Technologien (2016–2019). http://www.phil.uni-passau.de/dh/projekte/visit/ Accessed 13 Aug 2018

38. Grellert, M.: Rapid prototyping in the context of cultural heritage and museum displays. In: Münster, S., Pfarr-Harfst, M., Kuroczyński, P., Ioannides, M. (eds.) 3D Research Challenges in Cultural Heritage II. LNCS, vol. 10025, pp. 77–118. Springer, Cham (2016). https://doi.org/10.1007/978-3-319-47647-6_5

39. Erdmann, L., Hartmann, S., Maxzin, J.: Lukas aus der Asche. Auferstandenes Kulturerbe aus dem 3D-Labor. Kunstverlag Josef Fink, Lindenberg im Allgäu (2016)

40. Grellert, M., Pfarr-Harfst, M.: 25 Years of Virtual Reconstructions. Project Report of Department Information and Communication Technology in Architetcture at Technische Universität Darmstadt. In: 18th International Conference on Cultural Heritage and New Technologies, Vienna, 11–13 November 2013 (2014)

41. Bekele, M., Pierdicca, R., Frontoni, E., Malinverni, E., Gain, J.: A survey of augmented, virtual, and mixed reality for cultural heritage. J. Comput. Cult. Herit. **11**, 1–36 (2018). https://doi.org/10.1145/3145534

42. Albrecht, S.: Scholars' adoption of e-science practices: (preliminary) results from a qualitative study of network and other influencing factors. In: XXXIII. Sunbelt Social Networks Conference of the International Network for Social Network Analysis (INSNA), 21–26 May 2013, Hamburg (2013)

43. Vorstand des Verbandes Digital Humanities im deutschsprachigen Raum, Digital Humanities 2020, Passau (2014). https://dig-hum.de/digital-humanities-2020. Accessed 24 Sept 2018

44. Ioannides, M.: Initial Training Network for Digital Cultural Heritage: Projecting our Past to the Future (2013)

45. Kröber, C., Münster, S.: Educational app creation for the Cathedral in Freiberg. In: Spector, J.M., Ifenthaler, D., Sampson, D.G., Isaías, P. (eds.) Competencies in Teaching, Learning and Educational Leadership in the Digital Age, pp. 303–318. Springer, Cham (2016). https://doi.org/10.1007/978-3-319-30295-9_19

46. Sprünker, J.: Making on-line cultural heritage visible for educational proposes. In: Digital Heritage International Congress (DigitalHeritage), 2013, 28 October 2013–1 November 2013, pp. 405–408 (2013). https://doi.org/10.1109/digitalheritage.2013.6744791

47. Glaser, M., Lengyel, D., Toulouse, C., Schwan, S.: Designing computer based archaeological 3D-reconstructions: how camera zoom influences attention. In: Bares, W., Christie, M., Ronfard, R. (eds.) Proceedings of the Eurographics Workshop on Intelligent Cinematography and Editing EICED 2015, Goslar (2015)

48. Hess, M.: Digitale Denkmaltechnologien. Marktanalyse der angebotenen Studiengänge in Europa   (2017).   https://www.google.com/maps/d/viewer?mid=1eHClPp-3rD7-HrdrdgXJTaUKMzg&ll=46.802102750072734%2C24.4550632375001&z=5

49. Sula, C.A., Hackney, S.E., Cunningham, P.: A Survey of Digital Humanities Programs (2017)

50. ViMM: Virtual Multimodal Museum (2017). http://vi-mm.eu/

51. Boochs, F., et al.: Colour and space in cultural heritage: key questions in 3D optical documentation of material culture for conservation, study and preservation. In: Ioannides, M., Magnenat-Thalmann, N., Fink, E., Žarnić, R., Yen, A.-Y., Quak, E. (eds.) EuroMed 2014. LNCS, vol. 8740, pp. 11–24. Springer, Cham (2014). https://doi.org/10.1007/978-3-319-13695-0_2

52. Murphy, M.: Historic Building Information Modelling (HBIM). Innovation in Intelligent Management of Heritage Buildings (i2MHB) – TD Cost Action TD1406 (2017)

Towards a Global Infrastructure for Digital Cultural Heritage

Nadezhda Povroznik[(✉)] [iD]

Perm State University, Ulitsa Bukireva 15, 614990 Perm, Russia
Povroznik.ng@gmail.com

Abstract. The development of global information infrastructure for digital cultural heritage is a key to ensuring the openness and accessibility of objects of such heritage on a global scale, increasing the economic, social and cultural impact of the created resources and services, and more efficiently addressing social priorities. Author shows that documentation systems play an important unifying role in the modern world of information infrastructure for digital cultural heritage. The diversity of information resources requires further study and classification, which is also necessary for more detailed documentation and cataloging of these resources. The development of systems for documenting information resources for digital cultural heritage on a global scale is continuing and has great potential in terms of systematizing data on information resources. This article examines the current state of information infrastructure for digital cultural heritage, identifies primary components and discusses their significance, determining obstacles to the formation of this infrastructure, and tracing the development of the digital cultural heritage infrastructure.

Keywords: E-infrastructure · Digital cultural heritage
Documentation information systems · Information resources and services

1 Introduction

The formation of an information infrastructure for digital cultural heritage is key to ensure the openness and accessibility of objects of digital cultural heritage on a global scale, increasing the economic, social and cultural impact of the created resources and services, and more efficiently addressing social priorities.

According to the UNESCO's Concept of Digital Heritage [1] and the Charter on the Preservation of Digital Heritage [2], the concept of "digital heritage" is based on the notion of "heritage" and refers to "our legacy from the past, what we live with today, and what we pass on to future generations". Cultural heritage includes material objects and intangible things that have cultural, historical, aesthetic, archaeological, scientific, ethnological or anthropological value for groups and individuals transmitted into electronic form, as well as a heritage originally created in the digital form.

Integrating resources for digital cultural heritage and creating an integrated e-infrastructure provides wide opportunities for improving the quality of resource usage in science, education, creative industries, etc. based on the targeted search for the necessary resources in a common user environment. Current challenges are connected

© Springer Nature Switzerland AG 2018
M. Ioannides et al. (Eds.): EuroMed 2018, LNCS 11196, pp. 607–615, 2018.
https://doi.org/10.1007/978-3-030-01762-0_53

not only with the technical and technological side of building a unified infrastructure, but also with overcoming or reducing the dangers around cultural heritage preservation in general, related to political, technogenic, anthropogenic and other factors. In this regard, the pooling of information resources for endangered heritage can be considered an urgent task.

Considering the growing number of information resources of GLAM institutions, projects on the preservation of cultural heritage in digital format, the emergence of diverse resources, and new services for digital cultural heritage, the development of national and international research infrastructures can ensure the development of digital cultural heritage on a global scale. But this requires careful consideration, analysis and study, since the consolidation, systematization and structuring of information resources, as well as the creation of specialized services able to build a single connected space, must all contribute to a global infrastructure for digital cultural heritage. Consideration of the current state of the information infrastructure of the digital cultural heritage requires the allocation of the main types of information resources for cultural heritage on the basis of approaches to their formation, designation and role in the infrastructure, determining trends and challenges for the further systemic digital heritage infrastructure development.

2   Related Work

The study of the infrastructure for digital historical and cultural heritage is connected with the study of the information environments of institutions for storage and memory. Virtual museums, digital libraries and archives, and other resources are discussed and considered from different perspectives, including the methodology of creation, the principles of aggregation, the possibilities of use, and ways to enhance social and cultural impact.

National regulations and strategies for the creation of cultural heritage infrastructures [3] are particularly important for the study of national infrastructures, as they clarify the legal framework and approaches, the principles, the logic of the development of national infrastructures, their structure, purpose and expected results for the economy, culture, science and society.

Research on developing a framework for combining information resources for digital cultural heritage and the process of building digital cultural heritage infrastructures are all relevant for this study. Accordingly, Daniela Fresa discusses the platforms that integrate data of European digital cultural heritage for the formation of a digital infrastructure, showing the importance of cooperation and dialogue between institutions, responsible organizations and stakeholders in this field [4]. In the works of other authors, problems of building digital cultural heritage infrastructures [5], architecture, metadata and interaction of information systems of cultural heritage [6] and other issues have been considered.

This article examines the current state of the information infrastructure for digital historical and cultural heritage, identifies the main components and their significance in the digital infrastructure of the cultural heritage, considers obstacles to the formation of infrastructure, and traces the prospects for the development of the digital cultural heritage infrastructure.

3   Information Resources of Storage and Memory Institutions

Information resources of storage institutions are the basis of the digital infrastructure for cultural heritage. The main types of these resources are virtual museums, electronic archives, libraries and repositories where electronic collections of cultural heritage items from collections of GLAM institutions are presented. The concepts of "electronic archive" and "electronic library" are well established and do not have any significant differences in interpretations, while the term "virtual museum" has a large number of different understandings of the essence of this phenomenon. We understand the term "virtual museum" as the information system, which contains common online collection or several collections of items with metadata, has museum characteristics and allows a researcher to carry out the scientific, educational, exhibition and excursion work in virtual space [7].

The information resources of the storage institutions, and primarily their electronic collections, form the basis of historical and cultural sources for study and use, and also present the virtual world of museums and exhibits in a virtual environment through a whole set of information technologies, including virtual visualization systems. According to the European Group on Museum Statistics (EGMUS), in Europe alone there are about 19,780 museums of different orientations [8], and more than 80% [9] of them have electronic collections with online access or participate in digitization projects. And at the moment it is impossible to estimate even approximately the amount of information resources of storage and memory institutions that are created in the world and provide access to the created electronic collections, because of the under-development of global systems for documenting such resources.

4   National Infrastructures for Digital Cultural Heritage

The development of national information infrastructures for digital cultural heritage is often initiated at the level of the state administration. In various countries, attempts have been made to build national infrastructures for digital cultural heritage, and often such infrastructures are aimed at integrating the information resources of individual institutions-archives (for example, in India [10]), libraries (as in Russia [11]) or museums (as in Scotland [12]).

At the same time, there are projects devoted to the creation of an information infrastructure for digital cultural heritage that unite the resources of GLAM organizations on a national scale. In 2000, for example, the USA adopted a National Digital Information Infrastructure and Preservation Program [13], which laid the foundations of the National Infrastructure for Digital Heritage [14]. Similar national projects are being implemented in Australia [15], the Netherlands [16], New Zealand [17] and in other countries. The achievement of national information infrastructures is the pooling of primary resources, their standardized description and enabling of cross-sectoral research over collections of different storage institutions and national memory.

Some national infrastructures designed for digital cultural heritage are not limited to storage facilities from collections of GLAM-sector organizations, but go beyond them, involving items from smaller collections and community organizations that are often highly personal. Such projects include the TROVE project [18], initiated by the National Library of Australia and developed in cooperation with many institutions of storage and national memory of Australia. Nearly 600 million digital objects (books, images, historic newspapers, maps, music, archival documents etc.) have been published on the TROVE platform, the number of which continues to increase. The strategy for the information resource development is connected with the active involvement of volunteers in the editing of source texts (newspaper publications, books, manuscripts), tagging, and extending the national resource with digital objects from community archives. In addition, an important feature of the TROVE project in comparison with other national projects is the preservation on the platform of the digital web archive of information resources (including the resources of storage organizations and national memory) created since 1996 to the present.

National information infrastructures of digital cultural heritage reflect the level of development of the national policy in the field of digital cultural heritage and the effectiveness of the strategy for the preservation of the cultural heritage as a whole, show the value of cooperation of the national administration, storage institutions, IT industry and academic institutes, solve problems of cataloging, documenting and accessibility of digital cultural heritage sites online, ensure continuous improvement and the infrastructure of the digital cultural heritage, the expansion of their user capabilities and the sustainability of resources over time.

5 International Aggregators

International aggregators of digital cultural heritage sites such as EUROPEANA [19], Google Arts & Culture [20], and the Digital Public Library of America [21], unite electronic collections of selected storage institutions on one platform, as well as national information infrastructures for digital cultural heritage [22].

EUROPEANA is one of the largest of international aggregators of digital cultural heritage in terms of the number of represented organizations and digital objects. The project brings together the resources of the GLAM sector organizations and the national infrastructures of the member countries of the European Union, as well as selected storage and national memory institutions of other countries, including the USA, Russia, Israel, Turkey, and Ukraine. Collections of EUROPEANA [23] include about 60 million exhibits from 3500 organizations. On the EUROPEANA platform, a multilingual interface is implemented, allowing the user to choose one of 27 languages for comfortable use of the resource. Exhibits are dynamically formed in the collections due to an expanded meta-description on topics, chronology, geography, digital format, etc. This approach allows users to search the digital items regardless of the language, country, and origin of the subject, and therefore making the cultural heritage more accessible.

The advantage of such aggregators is wider access to electronic collections of storage and memory institutions from different countries worldwide due to an expanded user base and audience, the implementation of multilingual interfaces, cross-collection search capabilities, high quality digital content, a standardized meta-description of objects, and developed tools and instructions for use in various fields (science, education, enlightenment, studying family history, etc.).

6 Systems and Services for Visualization and Analysis of Sources

Expanding the possibilities for analyzing and visualizing digitized sources requires the development of special tools and services that provide new, broader opportunities for processing source materials. Systems for visualization and analysis of sources have been developed in cooperation with academic research teams and storage institutions. Systems and services of visualization and processing of sources expand the possibilities of using the resources for digital cultural heritage, allow solving specific scientific, research, educational and other tasks.

The architecture of information resources of this type is built on an integrated approach and includes tools that allow performing more complex searches and analytical operations. An important aspect of such systems for visualization and study of cultural heritage are information systems of textual heritage that represent a source (complex of sources) in a multi-layered form, including an image, a recognized text, a semantic publication, often translated into modern language. For example, the portal "MANUSCRIPT. Slavonic written heritage" [24] contains collections of ancient and medieval Slavic and Russian texts, and built-in modules allow the user to view texts, indexes and perform data retrieval, edit and fragment texts, process data for linguistic, paleographic and textual studies, and perform automatic analysis and synthesis of word forms of the Old Russian language, etc.

Resource processing systems and services offer techniques and instructions for the use of digital cultural heritage in specific fields, which increases the involvement of society in the use of resources in the study of the past. Thus, the DocsTeach service [25], developed by the Education Department of the United States National Archives and Records Administration (NARA), allows users to explore primary sources of US history, has a variety of tools for using sources in the educational process, and also offers ways to implement various types of online activities with the involvement of the public.

Endangered and disappearing cultural heritage is particularly fragile. The Convention Concerning the Protection of the World Cultural and Natural Heritage [26] and The World Heritage in Danger [27] by UNESCO define the range of such cultural heritage. Information resources can play a major role in contributing to the visualization of endangered and disappearing cultural heritage. There are systems of virtual reconstruction, created on a wide historical sources basis, such as the virtual reconstruction of the Moscow Strastnoy Monastery in the mid-17th - early 20th centuries [28]. This project of spatial reconstruction includes the restoration of the architectural appearance of the Strastnoy Monastery demolished in 1937 in several time snapshots. Underelying the 3D reconstruction of the monastery and the space of the Strastnaya Square is a large array of archival material on the history and spatial structure of the monastery (drawings, plans, descriptions of the monastery buildings, document management documentation, photographs of the XIX - early XX centuries, engravings, etc.). Reconstruction of threatened or destroyed cultural heritage in the course of conflicts nowadays has a significant social and cultural significance. Such reconstructions, for example, 3D reconstruction of destroyed cultural heritage sites in Syria

[29] are often created mainly in photo and video materials (including photos of travelers) and are designed not only to present monuments online, but also to attract the attention of society to modern threats and challenges.

Systems and services for visualization and processing of sources expand the possibilities of using primary sources and are targeted at particular audiences, offering effective tools for solving social, economic and cultural problems, which increases the impact of digital cultural heritage in specific areas.

7   Catalogs and Systems for Documenting Information Resources for Digital Cultural Heritage

The development of digital heritage information infrastructure is supported not only by the increase in the quantity and quality of the information resources described above, but the development of catalogs and documentation systems.

National information resources represent the cultural heritage of the region as a whole. There are also specialized catalogs and lists devoted to specific types of information resources of digital cultural heritage, for example, to virtual museums. Such a directory is the V-must project (Virtual Museum Transnational Network) [30], which contains a list of significant virtual museums with a developed system of describing information resources, including data on the museums' subjects, the availability of interactive technologies, the probable areas of virtual museum resources and some other parameters.

Documenting and cataloging information resources to create an integrated global environment, can lead to broader cross-cultural interactions with digitized content. Yet there are barriers. Western and Eastern resources are seldom brought together in a single aggregated information space, despite the growing demand for such resources and their value in society. Most resources are not prepared to take into account the needs of this intercultural exchange and provide bilateral user access and experiences. Localization does not have to mean isolation, and the systems for documenting information resources of over the world should allow us to overcome language, search and even cultural boundaries. A global example of cataloging information about museums and galleries as cultural heritage storage facilities is the resource Museum.com [31], which collects information about cultural institutions around the world with the ability to edit information, add descriptions, with links to Web resources.

The Center for Digital Humanities of Perm University, Russia, has developed such a system of documentation – "History-oriented information systems" [32]. In developing the structure of the aggregator a multi-resource approach has been taken, which allows uniting of information resources, oriented towards those related to digital historical and cultural heritage. The meta-description system was developed to document information resources. It includes the main (such as the name of the resource and the web-address, the organization-creator, the authors, the country, the language of the interface and the sources submitted, the year of creation) and additional description parameters (subject, geography, period, sphere of humanitarian knowledge, type of information resource, purpose, target audience, the types of represented cultural heritage objects, the presence of a virtual tour, the availability of ways of interacting with the digital cultural heritage, the presence of a personal user account and other characteristics). At present the platform contains more than 1200 documented information resources and continues to be expanded. The systematization of information about such resources allows the user to filter data while searching and to identify resource groups by common characteristics, enabling targeted search. As such, the creation of this information system dedicated to historically-oriented information resources and cultural heritage, expands the possibilities for finding thematically close information resources, and also to implement various queries based on the description parameters. The expansion and further development of the aggregator aims to make digital cultural heritage materials more accessible, promote a wider and more systematic use of information resources, and ensure involvement of various types cultural heritage information resources in interdisciplinary scientific and educational research.

Thus, the systems for documenting information resources related to digital cultural heritage can be considered as an essential element of a cultural heritage infrastructure, since they provide digital tools and services for organizing information about resources, searching and filtering data.

8 Conclusion

The information infrastructure for digital cultural heritage continues its development toward the formation of an information infrastructure that is global in scale. It is important to note the diversity of information resources for digital cultural heritage, the increase in the quantity and quality of electronic collections that are now freely accessible online, and the recent development of national and international cultural heritage aggregators.

Documentation systems play an important unifying role in the modern world of information infrastructure for digital cultural heritage. The diversity of information resources requires further study and classification, which is also necessary for more detailed documentation and cataloging of these resources. The development of systems for documenting information resources for digital cultural heritage on a global scale is continuing and has great potential in terms of systematizing data on information resources.

The prospect of a global information infrastructure assumes the existence of interrelations between resources, and the search for resources and collections, tools, techniques and instructions for the application of digital cultural heritage in a variety of areas. At the moment, full or partial interoperability between resources cannot be achieved due to technological, technical, or otherwise political and cultural circumstances. The potential for the growth of a such a global information infrastructure as discussed in this paper depends on the further development and improvement of national infrastructures.

The development of infrastructure for digital cultural heritage must take into account the national contexts and expand cross-cultural interactions, and also aim to increase economic, social and cultural impacts. Creation of an integrated, stable and sustainable infrastructure for digital cultural heritage is possible only on the basis of cooperation of key figures on a global scale – national administrations, stakeholders, institutions of GLAM sector, IT companies, and research and academic organizations.

Acknowledgements. The project "Historical information-oriented information systems" was supported by a grant from the Russian Fund for Basic Research and implemented in 2013-2015. Thanks to the staff of the Center for Digital Humanities of Perm State University, the platform continued its development. The author expresses gratitude to the students of the Departments of History and Politics, Philosophy and Sociology and Philological faculty of the Perm State University, who took part in the search for resources for digital cultural heritage, their analysis and expansion of the catalog.

References

1. Concept of Digital Heritage. UNESCO. http://www.unesco.org/new/en/communication-and-information/access-to-knowledge/preservation-of-documentary-heritage/digital-heritage/concept-of-digital-heritage. Accessed 05 Aug 2018
2. Charter on the Preservation of Digital Heritage. UNESCO, 15 October 2003. http://unesdoc.unesco.org/images/0013/001331/133171e.pdf#page=80. Accessed 05 Aug 2018
3. For ex. National Digital Heritage Strategy. Digital Heritage Network (The Netherlands). http://www.den.nl/art/uploads/files/Publicaties/20150608_Nationale_strategie_digitaal_erfgoed_Engels.pdf. Accessed 05 Aug 2018
4. Fresa, D.A.: Data infrastructure for digital cultural heritage: characteristics, requirements, and priority services. Int. J. Hum.Ities Arts Comput. 7(Suppl.), 29–46. (2013). http://www.digitalmeetsculture.net/wp-content/uploads/2012/09/ijhac.2013.0058.pdf. Accessed 05 Aug 2018
5. Benardou, A., Champion, E., Dallas, C., Hughes, L.: Cultural Heritage Infrastructures in Digital Humanities (Digital Research in the Arts and Humanities), pp. 1–190. Routledge, London (2017)
6. Ruthven, I., Chowdhury, G.G. (eds.): Cultural Heritage Information: Access and Management, pp. 1–253. Facet, Cryodon (2015)
7. Povroznik, N.: Typology of virtual museums and their potential for providing information for historical sciences. In: The Proceedings of International Conference "Electronic Imaging & the Visual Arts, EVA-2016", St. Petersburg, 23rd–24th June 2016, pp. 61–65 (2016). http://openbooks.ifmo.ru/ru/file/4148/4148.pdf. Accessed 05 Aug 2018
8. Statistics. Complete Data Table. European Group on Museum Statistic (EGMUS). http://www.egmus.eu/nc/en/statistics/complete_data. Accessed 05 Aug 2018
9. Fresa, A., Promoter, S.: Big data in the digital cultural heritage. In: Chalmers – Initiative Seminar on Big Data, 26 March 2014 (2014). https://www.chalmers.se/en/areas-of-advance/ict/events/Documents/Antonella%20Fresa_Big%20Data%20in%20the%20Digital%20CulturalHeritage.pdf. Accessed 05 Aug 2018
10. National Archives of India. http://www.ndpp.in/digitalarchive/home. Accessed 05 Aug 2018
11. National Information and Library Center LIBNET (Russian Federation). http://www.nilc.ru. Accessed 05 Aug 2018
12. National Museums Scotland. https://www.nms.ac.uk. Accessed 05 Aug 2018
13. National Digital Information Infrastructure and Preservation Program (NDIIPP). http://www.digitalpreservation.gov/about. Accessed 05 Aug 2018
14. Digital Preservation. http://www.digitalpreservation.gov. Accessed 05 Aug 2018
15. Humanities Networked Infrastructure (HuNI). https://huni.net.au. Accessed 05 Aug 2018

16. Netwerk Digitaal Erfgoed (NDE). Digital Heritage Network (DEN). http://www.den.nl. Accessed 05 Aug 2018
17. DIGITALNZ. https://digitalnz.org. Accessed 05 Aug 2018
18. TROVE. https://trove.nla.gov.au. Accessed 05 Aug 2018
19. EUROPEANA. https://www.europeana.eu. Accessed 05 Aug 2018
20. Google Arts & Culture. https://artsandculture.google.com. Accessed 05 Aug 2018
21. Digital Public Library of America (DPLA). https://dp.la. Accessed 05 Aug 2018
22. Internet Culturale. Cataloghi i Collezioni Digitali Delle Biblioteche Italiane. http://www.internetculturale.it/opencms/opencms/it/index.html. Accessed 05 Aug 2018
23. EUROPEANA Collections. https://www.europeana.eu. Accessed 05 Aug 2018
24. Manuscript. Slavonic written heritage. http://mns.udsu.ru. Accessed 05 Aug 2018
25. DocsTeach. National Archives. https://www.docsteach.org. Accessed 05 Aug 2018
26. Convention Concerning the Protection of the World Cultural and Natural Heritage. UNESCO World Heritage Centre. http://whc.unesco.org/en/175. Accessed 05 Aug 2018
27. World Heritage in Danger. UNESCO World Heritage Centre. http://whc.unesco.org/en/158. Accessed 05 Aug 2018
28. The project "Virtual reconstruction of the Moscow Strastnoy Monastery (mid-17th - early 20th centuries): analysis of the evolution of spatial infrastructure based on 3D modeling methods". http://www.hist.msu.ru/Strastnoy. Accessed 05 Aug 2018
29. #NEWPALMYRA. https://www.newpalmyra.org. Accessed 05 Aug 2018
30. Virtual Museum Transnational Network (V-must). http://www.v-must.net. Accessed 05 Aug 2018
31. Museum.com. https://www.museum.com/jb/start. Accessed 05 Aug 2018
32. History-oriented information systems. http://digitalhistory.ru. Accessed 05 Aug 2018

The Role of Heritage Data Science in Digital Heritage

Alejandra Albuerne$^{(\boxtimes)}$ ⓘ, Josep Grau-Bove, and Matija Strlic

Institute for Sustainable Heritage, University College London, London, UK
a.albuerne@ucl.ac.uk

Abstract. The advance of all forms of digital and virtual heritage alongside numerous heritage science and management applications have led to the generation of growing amounts of *heritage data*. This data is increasingly rich, diverse and powerful. To get the most out of heritage data, there is an evident need to effectively understand, manage and exploit it in a way that is sensitive towards its context, responding to its singularities, and that can allow heritage to keep up with global changes regarding expansion of digital technologies and the increasing role of data in decision making and policy development. Through conversations with industry and academia, as well as through their personal research in the field of cultural heritage, the authors have identified a need for enhanced training for data scientists to prepare them for working in the heritage sector. This paper first proposes a definition of the term *heritage data*, so far missing from the literature, and then presents the academic rationale behind the identified need for targeted training in data science for cultural heritage.

Keywords: Heritage data · Data science · Cultural heritage

1 Introduction

The relevance of digital technologies and extent of use of data in today's world is growing at a fast pace. The field of heritage is no exception, having witnessed a vast expansion of digital heritage over the past two decades. The increasing amounts of data being generated give rise to many new possibilities and opportunities, as well as many challenges. There is an evident need to effectively understand, manage and exploit data in the cultural heritage context, not only in order to take advantage of possibilities and manage challenges, but also in order to ensure the heritage sector can keep up with the increasing role of data in decision-making and policy development [1]. This requires data science specific skills which are not part of the traditional skills set of the cultural heritage field.

To what extent are these skills available in the sector is explored in this paper through interrogation of the sector by means of questionnaires and semi-structured interviews, as well as the authors' own professional experience.

The Institute for Sustainable Heritage of University College London (UCL ISH), in collaboration with partners, conducted in 2017 a survey of training provision in heritage science, where 262 active professionals (heritage scientists, curators, conservators and other industry professionals) were requested to provide views on current training

© Springer Nature Switzerland AG 2018
M. Ioannides et al. (Eds.): EuroMed 2018, LNCS 11196, pp. 616–622, 2018.
https://doi.org/10.1007/978-3-030-01762-0_54

offer. This survey was carried out as part of the initiative to set up the European Research Infrastructure for Heritage Science (E-RIHS). Approximately 10% of the questionnaire focused on data science, heritage data analysis and digital training provision.

Between March and May 2018, UCL ISH conducted a series of semi-structured interviews with experts from leading heritage organizations that included The British Library, English Heritage and Historic Environment Scotland in the UK and The Library of Congress in the US, as well as data science experts from the Alan Turing Institute (UK). The interviews focused on the need for data science skills in the field of cultural heritage, addressing aspects such as existing technical challenges, available training and difficulties in recruitment of data scientist to work in heritage institutions.

This evidence is complemented with a desktop review of available university programmes in the UK and in leading European and North-American universities.

A review of this evidence strongly suggests there is a need for targeted training for data scientists to equip them to meet the needs of the heritage sector.

2 Heritage Data

Data science is the set of knowledge and processes that facilitate the creation of data products [2]. It operates with and transforms digital data. The application of data science in the remit of cultural heritage therefore calls for a definition of heritage data. The term heritage data in the remit of cultural heritage first appears in the technical literature in 2006 [3]. It is used to broaden the scope of the existing term archaeological data that had been used in relation to digital applications since the late 20th century, e.g. [4, 5].

Although there is currently no formal definition, heritage data is often used in reference to:

- data generated from the documentation of heritage, be it capture/acquisition, processing/analysis or visualization, e.g. [6, 7];
- ontology of heritage for applications in data management, archiving and web-based dissemination [8, 9].

Maricevic [1] suggests there is at present a notion of heritage data community that is experienced by those involved in the subject, but highlights the gap that exists within the sector in understanding whether there is a common theme of heritage data that can ground this perceived shared sense.

Embracing Maricevic's observation and supported by views expressed by different stakeholders in the heritage sector (see Sects. 1 and 3), we propose defining heritage data as a comprehensive term that leaves out no exceptions and includes both data *as* heritage and data *about* heritage.

2.1 Data *as* Heritage

In their *Charter on the preservation of digital heritage* [10], UNESCO recognises digital contents as heritage that may have both lasting value and significance and must therefore be preserved under the same premises as other forms of cultural heritage for future generations.

The charter refers to a wide range of digital materials that can be identified as heritage, from visual materials, such as moving and still images or graphics, to audio or text. It also makes specific mention to less evident forms of digital objects that may also be considered heritage, including software, web pages or databases. The range of digital materials subject to being identified as heritage is indeed growing.

These digital materials are comprised of digital data and this digital data must therefore also be recognised as heritage.

2.2 Data *About* Heritage

Data related to the documentation, conservation, management and interpretation of heritage constitutes an extensive and increasingly significant body that requires growing amounts of capabilities and resources for its management and exploitation.

This comprehensive definition of heritage data comprises a broad range of data, both quantitative and qualitative, of different origins and for different uses. The commonality lies in the fact that this data exists to create value for the field of cultural heritage. As such, its handling must reflect the values, significance, integrity, ethics, authenticity and other particularities of the heritage sector it belongs to. Alongside this, there is the singular need for longevity that is characteristic of the sector.

Longevity, in terms of digital data, requires reliability and planning at all stages of the data pipeline/cycle: acquisition, analysis - visualization - storage - repurposing - curation and conservation; be it in the form of data standards, archiving and sharing practices, etc. These principles can be relevant for and common to all types of heritage data.

Furthermore, there is a common thread of multidisciplinarity throughout the heritage sector that introduces its own specific challenges, such as bringing together expertise from diverse fields of arts, humanities, social sciences, science and technology.

These commonalities are strong justifications for a holistic definition of *heritage data*. The idea that data science can extract and create new value from data further supports this proposition for a unified theme of *heritage data* and the development of a common set of interrelated skills to support it.

3   A Need for Targeted Training

3.1 Sector Consultations

Consultations conducted by UCL ISH between 2017 and 2018 among the heritage community have yielded findings strongly suggesting that, alongside the need for data science skills, in the cultural heritage sector there is need to enhance the training of data scientists to prepare them for those specific characteristics and challenges of the sector that set it apart from more conventional applications of data science.

As part of the Preparatory Phase project supporting the establishment of the European Research Infrastructure for Heritage Science (www.e-rihs.eu), a stakeholder questionnaire was conducted with 282 respondents from heritage and research institutions. Of the academic courses recently undertaken, only 6% focused on heritage science data analysis, visualization, use and reuse; 3% on digitalization/digital heritage; and 1% on data science. One of the conclusions of the questionnaire was to increase the provision of courses specifically focusing on digital and data skills.

Semi-structured interviews were conducted between March and May 2018 with experts from selected heritage organizations with interest and capabilities in data science (see Sect. 1). The key observations extracted from these interviews are:

- The needs for data science skills are growing in the consulted organizations, as they embrace digital technologies and their collections of heritage data grow. Including data scientists in the work force of heritage organizations is becoming an increasingly regular occurrence.
- Finding data scientists to work successfully in the cultural heritage sector fully embracing its goals, values and ethics is perceived as a challenge by the heritage organizations consulted.
- The need for longevity of most heritage data poses significant challenges as digital technologies advance at a growing pace and the sector attempts to keep up with the changes. This results in specific needs of data migration and recovery that are unique in the remit of data science.
- The lack of heritage data standards is problematic when planning data acquisition, management and curation.
- The experts consulted were unaware of any training currently available that comprehensively addresses the range of data science needs experienced in the sector.

Further to these findings, the recent Arts and Humanities Research Council (UK) report *Heritage And Data: Challenges And Opportunities For The Heritage Sector* [1] identified significant challenges that need to be addressed in heritage data governance.

Outputs on existing training from the E-RHIS survey and from the interviews of sector experts have been complemented with a review of available university programmes in the UK and in leading European and North-American universities. The conclusion is that the diverse skills needed to address the data science challenges of the cultural heritage sector are currently not being taught comprehensively.

The context is important for the work of the data scientists applying their technical skills to cultural heritage. Such data scientists must understand heritage values and how heritage enriches society. The sector is looking for data scientists that have capabilities that go beyond classical technical skills and into skills that are conventionally linked to social sciences or humanities. In particular, these include a critical approach, a consideration of societal issues and strong communication skills that enable them to communicate with multidisciplinary teams and diverse audiences.

Conventional data science masters programmes currently on offer fall short in developing these skills, which are excluded from the programmes' curricula. This has consequences for the heritage sector, which expresses difficulty in finding professionals with these broader sets of skills.

3.2   Addressing the Needs

Heritage Data Diversity

Heritage data is diverse. It encompasses both qualitative and quantitative data generated through many different forms of technology and for very different purposes. Furthermore, there is digitally born data, e.g. through social media and other digital social interaction, which is increasingly collected by heritage institutions and that can offer, among other benefits, exciting opportunities for engaging with the community. This data, together with digitally-born heritage, represents the core of digital collections that require specific curation and conservation approaches. Additionally, there is the need to address the variety of data, both qualitative and quantitative, that is generated around heritage through analysis and measurement, imaging and surveying, or through citizen science and publicly sourced data. This requires a variety of highly technical data science skills.

Furthermore, it is crucial that data scientists working in cultural heritage should have the capacity to be critical about the provenance, quality, accuracy and bias of the data they are managing. With data being collected in growing quantities, the successful interpretation of these large heterogeneous data sets requires expert judgement by professionals with deep knowledge of the heritage domain, beyond data science specific knowledge. This view has been expressed in [1], echoed in interviews of sector experts and is shared by the authors.

Understanding the Heritage Data Pipeline

It is clear that there is a well-established and growing need for heritage researchers and scientists with in-depth understanding of the heritage data pipeline or lifecycle: acquisition - analysis - visualization - storage - repurposing – access - curation and conservation. While there are individual courses available in the UK and the US that address specific aspects of this pipeline, there is currently no Masters programme on offer that addresses the complexities of data acquisition, exploitation, management and conservation in cultural heritage.

There are graduate programmes available that address one or more of the aspects of the heritage data pipeline. Examples include programmes on information science, which generally cover some acquisition and analysis processes, visualization, access, repurposing, etc., the limitation being that the focus is solely in information, leaving many forms of heritage data out. Archaeological programmes frequently address other types of heritage data, such as GIS or 3D scans and models. Heritage science programmes address the acquisition and analysis of heritage conservation data. Digital heritage programmes address multiple aspects of data acquisition and management utilizing state of the art technologies.

All these types of programmes, however, focus only on a fragment of the pipeline or lifecycle of heritage data. Furthermore, they do not attempt to train data scientists: they train other specialisms, be these archaeologists or heritage scientists, who may gain an insight into data science but frequently lack the deep core knowledge and skills that could be applied to diversified problems.

Big Data

The ability to operate with Big Data is also of great importance, as the increasing amounts of data being generated, directly and indirectly as by-products, call for new and innovative strategies for analyzing, managing and preserving data.

Integrating Data Science in the Heritage Interdisciplinary Work

In all the above there is abundant justification for integrating data scientists in the core of the cultural heritage discipline. This research has documented that currently heritage organizations struggle to successfully integrate data science into the core of their work, as they encounter a challenge in meaningfully engaging data scientists in the complexities and multidisciplinarity of heritage challenges, thus facing a disconnect between the objectives of the sector and the contribution of data science. As the role of digital heritage grows in the sector, the need for these skills will also grow.

Targeted training is needed to equip data scientists for becoming integral parts of the heritage sector. Such training should explore the full heritage data pipeline or lifecycle and should equip professionals with specific data science skills such as data visualization, machine learning, data migration, image processing, etc., through direct applications to heritage data and digital heritage in order to provide an understanding of the technical challenges around heritage. As well as technical contents, a deep insight of the context must be provided to include underpinning concepts and challenges such as heritage value and significance, integrity and authenticity, ethics, etc.

This comprehensive training can best prepare data scientists to be fully embedded in the work of heritage organizations from the early days. Without this training, however, the sector is at risk of falling behind in some of the major developments that the scientific community is enabling worldwide. The research carried out to date has further documented that this training is currently unavailable. An effort is required to develop courses and academic programmes that can address this need. Such effort will entail continued collaboration between academia and heritage organizations and practitioners, as well as networks such as E-RIHS, to develop targeted learning objectives and course contents and to think creatively about possible future challenges and opportunities pertinent to heritage data science. UCL ISH is pursuing further research on this subject, continuing their consultations with the heritage community to develop detailed learning objectives for heritage data science with the ultimate objective of strengthening the interdisciplinary heritage sector.

4   Conclusions

Heritage data is defined as a comprehensive term that encompasses both data as heritage and data about heritage, drawing on the commonalities of this data: it is underpinned by heritage values, significance, integrity, ethics and authenticity; it is characterised by a need for longevity; and it is the product or the object of multidisciplinary work.

The needs of the cultural heritage sector for data science training and skills have been explored by means of questionnaires and semi-structured interviews, as well as the authors' own professional experience. These consultations have been complemented with a desktop review of available university programmes in the UK and in leading European and North-American universities.

Findings strongly suggest that there is a need for data science skills that are currently not easy to find in the market and that are not being taught comprehensively. The sector needs data science professional who are familiar with both the specific technical requirements of cultural heritage data and the particularities of the cultural heritage sector.

With the current expansion of heritage data, there is a growing need for professionals with in-depth understanding of the heritage data pipeline or lifecycle in order to exploit, manage and preserve this data and who can exert expert judgment to assess the provenance, quality, accuracy and bias of heritage data. Simultaneously, these experts must understand the heritage sector, its values, principles and ethics and have skills that go beyond classical technical skills and into skills that are conventionally linked to social sciences or humanities, such as critical analysis and communication.

Providing the cultural heritage sector with skilled data scientists that fully embrace its singularities will be crucial for enabling the sector to keep up with global changes regarding expansion of digital technologies and the increasing role of data in decision making and policy development. Continued work is being undertaken at UCL ISH as a collaboration between academia and the professional heritage sector to develop learning objectives and course contents aimed at creating new training opportunities that meet the data science needs identified in the heritage sector.

Acknowledgements. We are grateful to all interviewees and questionnaire respondents for their generous collaboration and to Yujia Luo for her help with Mendeley.

References

1. Harrison, R., Morel, H., Maricevic, M., Penrose, S.: Heritage and Data: Challenges and Opportunities for the Heritage Sector
2. Loukides, M.: What is Data Science? O'Reilly Media, Sebastopol (2011)
3. Meyer, E., Grussenmeyer, P., Perrin, J.P., Durand, A., Drap, P.: Integration of heterogeneous cultural heritage data in a web-based information system: a case study from Vianden Castle, Luxembourg. In: CAA 2006 Proceedings (2006)
4. Reilly, P., Rahtz, S. (eds.): Archaeology in the Information Age: A Global Perspective. One World Archaeology, vol. 21. Routledge, London (1992)
5. Richards, J.D.: Recent trends in computer applications in archaeology. J. Archaeol. Res. **6** (4), 331–382 (1998)
6. Vincent, M.L., López-Menchero Bendicho, V.M., Ioannides, M., Levy, T.E. (eds.): Heritage and Archaeology in the Digital Age: Acquisition, Curation, and Dissemination of Spatial Cultural Heritage Data. QMHSS. Springer, Cham (2017). https://doi.org/10.1007/978-3-319-65370-9
7. Lercari, N., Shiferaw, E., Forte, M., Kopper, R.: Immersive visualization and curation of archaeological heritage data: Çatalhöyük and the Dig@IT App. J. Archaeol. Method Theory **25**(2), 368–392 (2017)
8. http://www.heritagedata.org/blog/vocabularies-provided/
9. Klic, L., Nelson, J.K., Pattuelli, M.C., Provo, A.: Florentine renaissance drawings: a linked catalog for the semantic web. Art Doc. J. Art Libr. Soc. North Am. **37**(1), 33–43 (2018)
10. UNESCO: Charter on the preservation of digital heritage (2003)

Interdisciplinarity of Cultural Heritage Conservation Making and Makers: Through Diversity Towards Compatibility of Approaches

Anna Lobovikov-Katz[1]([⊠]), João Martins[2], Marinos Ioannides[3], Dalik Sojref[4], and Christian Degrigny[5]

[1] Faculty of Architecture and Town Planning,
Technion - Israel Institute of Technology, Technion City, 32000 Haifa, Israel
anna@technion.ac.il
[2] Faculty of Sciences and Technology (UNL) and UNINOVA, Lisbon, Portugal
jf.martins@fct.unl.pt
[3] Department of Electrical Engineering, Computer Engineering and Informatics,
Cyprus University of Technology, Limassol, Cyprus
marinos.ioannides@cut.ac.cy
[4] WTTC, Berlin, Germany
dalik.sojref@wttc.de
[5] Sarl Germolles Palais Ducal en Bourgogne, Mellecey, France
christian.degrigny@gmail.com

Abstract. In conservation of cultural heritage (CCH), experts from diverse areas of knowledge work together, each of them contributing unique expertise. However, in modern dynamic multi- and interdisciplinary collaboration, new contributors often remain conservation outsiders, being deeply submerged in their own research areas with regard to their research methods, their view of hierarchy of aims and values of conservation of cultural heritage, etc. Their understanding of targets of input and outcome of their compartmentalized contribution to specific conservation problems might be incompatible with the principles and criteria of modern CCH, thus affecting productivity of such contribution. This paper focuses on this conflict by examining selected relevant aspects based on the experience of the collaborative interdisciplinary research in conservation of cultural heritage.

Keywords: Interdisciplinarity · Interdisciplinary research
Conservation of cultural heritage (CCH) · Compatibility

1 Introduction - Overview of Problems in Their Context

Modern conservation of cultural heritage (CCH) is a multi- and interdisciplinary field, and it comprises diverse areas of natural sciences, social sciences, humanities, engineering, mathematics, arts and crafts. In order to grasp the magnitude of cross-disciplinary collaboration in this field, one could merely glimpse at the list of areas of expertise of contributors to a single regular research project. They might include

© Springer Nature Switzerland AG 2018
M. Ioannides et al. (Eds.): EuroMed 2018, LNCS 11196, pp. 623–638, 2018.
https://doi.org/10.1007/978-3-030-01762-0_55

chemical engineering, physics, biology, robotics, computer science, material science, mathematics, nanotechnology, history, economics, history of arts, sociology, architecture, archaeology, and others.

To pave the way to adequate solutions, a well-balanced interdisciplinary approach is a must. In its role as the breeding ground for the innovation, interdisciplinarity provides the best framework to set an effective platform for the establishment of win-win partnerships between experts from different fields. Meanwhile, interdisciplinarity has become indispensable to European progress in diverse fields. Once achieved, the true multidisciplinary effort will overcome the fragmentation of this scientific and technological research field and lead to innovative solutions in the field of cultural heritage conservation.

Since the last decades of 20th century many experts from diverse areas of sciences and technology have become "organic" participants of CCH, having developed over time an intrinsic understanding of the philosophy, values and criteria typical of this field. Some of them have experienced professional metamorphoses, e.g. architects became experts in geology, building engineering or computer science (based on actual cases). Such intrinsic interdisciplinarity of experts enriches their understanding of the high level of complexity of CCH, e.g. an archaeologist who is also a conservator understands that his need as the archaeologist - to dig, is in contradiction with the aims of a conservator, who would urge to preserve the historic site *as is* in its geometrical integrity.

However, the dynamism of multidisciplinarity of contemporary research in general, and in CCH in particular, for finding solution to specific problems frequently brings the inclusion of newcomers to each specific field. In the case of a brief or one-time encounter with conservation of cultural heritage, the newly arrived researchers still approach this field by means of specific research "instruments" which are typical of their original research area. This might create an opening for mismatching targets and goals, especially in large collaborative research projects, and, if overlooked at the early stages of research, this might affect the overall productivity of the research.

Interdisciplinary research problems [1] are not something specific to the field of CCH. Many problems outlined in the report of the Institute of Medicine, Academy of Sciences (US) [2], are also common to CCH, e.g. misunderstanding or misinterpretation of terminology, research aims, and others. However, CCH comprises an interdisciplinary exchange of a particularly wide spectrum of areas, which brings a wide range of interdisciplinary compatibility challenges and problems, and the urgency to find solutions. This brief study was motivated by the need to look further into the correlation of selected aspects of the diversity and difference of approaches to CCH among the experts from diverse areas of knowledge involved in conservation either on a permanent or one time basis.

From the authors' experience of interdisciplinary encounters in collaborative research projects in CCH [3, 4], some common tendencies were found. Historically, (CCH) has been based on the humanities-originated aims and values [5–8]. However, the rapid progress in STEM (science, technology, engineering and mathematics) has brought vast application of its results also in CCH, and the inclusion of many non-conservation experts from sciences, engineering and technology in this field. This causes the difference of approaches and interpretations by different experts with regard to many aspects, and especially to the goals of CCH versus technical objectives.

One of the tendencies typical of experts from natural sciences, and especially from information technology, - is the lack of awareness of qualitative characteristics of targeted results, e.g. historic or social values. Another subject which calls for special attention is the dissimilarity of approaches to the issue of authenticity. Definitions and approaches to authenticity have undergone significant changes over the years. While the argument over a comparative value of a tangible conservation object (e.g. historic building) and of its digital counterpart is mostly polarized between the digital and non-digital-associated research communities, the questions related to e.g., authenticity versus justifiable scope of alterations and restorations, vary widely through the entire range of the areas of expertise. In spite of more than a hundred years of a significant development of international documents, in an attempt to reach a universal under-standing in CCH (including the meaning and preservation of authenticity), some diversities of the approaches are still echoing disputes started in the thirties of the 19th century Europe.

Along with recent experience from collaborative research in CCH, this paper summarizes the results of two questionnaires filled in by experts from diverse areas, with diverse levels of involvement with conservation of cultural heritage. The questionnaires were focused on studying their approaches to theoretical issues of conservation of cultural heritage, and to their perception of the results of conservation measures on specific heritage buildings and sites. While our relevant experience and lessons from other EU research projects in cultural heritage contributed to the development of the structure the questionnaires [9, 10], their direction and content were much inspired by the discourses in the framework of the COST Action TD1406 i2MHB (Innovation in Intelligent Management of Heritage Buildings) [11].

2   Difference of Approaches Among the Experts from Different Areas of Science and Technology to Understanding Cultural Built Heritage and Its Conservation

Two questionnaires were aimed to assist us in examining approaches to CCH, with a focus on built heritage, among experts in diverse fields of science, technology, engineering and humanities. Both Questionnaires opened with a theoretical question: What is your vision of major aims of modern conservation of cultural heritage? Beyond this question, and the similarity of questions on professional background of the respondents, each Questionnaire had its own unique focus. The first Questionnaire (Questionnaire 1) was given to a small number of experts in the framework of STSMs (Short-Term Scientific Missions) organized by COST Action TD1406. It aimed to help us with a primary grasping of the problem through qualitative analysis. Questionnaire 1 targeted to study the understanding by different experts of the values of specific heritage buildings and sites and of the conservation measures undertaken there. Though the participants of STSMs were cultural heritage related experts, the scope of this relation varied. A specific focus of the Questionnaire 1 was to compare the interpretations of a set of specific issues on each specific historic site by experts of different scope of association to conservation of cultural heritage. The second Questionnaire (Questionnaire 2) was built basing on the experience of the primarily analysis of Questionnaire 1, and it was focused on studying the approaches to theoretical issue of CCH through the wide range of experts.

2.1 Analysis of Questionnaire 1

Aims and Overview. The main purpose of the survey by Questionnaire 1 was to compare the approaches to the same set of conservation related issues on a specific historic site by experts from diverse areas of expertise, and of different scope of association to conservation of cultural heritage, e.g. experts who stated CCH as their main area of expertise, and by experts who stated their main professional expertise was not conservation. The areas of expertise of the experts involved were as follows: computer science, IT, architecture and conservation of built heritage, theory of conservation, heritage science, art history, archaeology, sociology, while some experts represented more than one area. Eight detailed questionnaires were analyzed with a focus on three Historic Buildings/Sites (HB/S): in Italy (HB/S 1), France (HB/S 2) and Malta (HB/S 3). Each historic site was studied by at least two experts of diverse backgrounds. Of eight respondents three stated that conservation was not their main area of expertise, while two of them stated that it was not their first encounter with conservation of cultural heritage. Questionnaire 1, due to a small number of respondents, was not aimed to provide a representative data. Small number of Questionnaires allowed us to structure it with a significant detail. It was a sort of structured consultation with experts-respondents, aimed to contribute to our more in depth understanding of the issues in question, and to allow us to see what other issues might evolve. Along with qualitative analysis, Questionnaire 1 provided quantitative markers for the comparative analysis of specific aspects, as a further development, based on a previous research [12].

Structure and Analysis of Questionnaire 1. The questionnaire examined the respondents' approach to the following conservation aspects and their interrelationship, with regard to each specific heritage building/site:

- Authenticity
- Geometry
- Materials
- Structure
- The impact of changes induced by historical changes and/or restoration

Questionnaire 1 was composed of twenty questions. The first part of the Questionnaire (Q1, Q3–Q6) was comprised of the questions on professional area of expertise; academic qualifications; whether conservation was the main area of expertise of respondents or not; if not- was it their first acquaintance with this field; what was their major activity (research/practical work/other).

The second part of the Questionnaire (Q7–Q8) was focused on the major data on a specific historic building/site which they studied. Q7 asked about name, location, original construction date. Q8 requested to indicate one or more categories relevant to this historic site, from the following list:

- Historic building/structure
- Group of buildings
- Archaeological site
- Park, garden
- Cultural landscape
- Historic neighborhood/town/village
- Industrial heritage
- Other (please indicate)

Q9–Q16 were designed to provide to the respondents unified tools to express their perception of the relative scope and meaning of the changes undergone by a historic site, their reason, character and visual impact on geometry, material, structure and authenticity.

Q9: Has this historic site undergone significant changes through its history?

Q10: Are the changes most evident on/limited to a specific part of the historic site? What part?

Q11: Are the changes visible on many different parts of the historic site?

Q12: Were some changes caused by restoration/conservation?

Questions 13–14 provided a tool for a qualitative evaluation of a relative visual impact of the changes, through rating scale from 1 (minimal impact) to 5 (maximum impact), in combination with the request to indicate the reason of the changes (please indicate if the changes were mostly the result of *Historic* adaptations to different needs (please mark those "*H*") or/and *Restoration*/conservation (please mark those "*R*"), e.g. high-impact historic change would be marked "*5H*" (Fig. 2).

This rating of visual impact had to be applied to a list of diverse aspects

(a) "Macro" geometry: change built/natural surroundings of the historic site
(b) "Macro" geometry: change of shape of the historic building/site or of its major parts; structure
(c) "Micro" geometry: change of shape of architectural elements, façade details, etc.
(d) Application of new technologies at large scale (the entire site or its main parts)
(e) Application of new technologies limited to minor elements
(f) Application of building materials
(g) Application of decorative materials, art, sculpture
(h) Other

In this way, each line from this list was evaluated ("*H*" and/or "*R*", from 1 to 5), e.g. (e) *Application of new technologies limited to minor elements*: was rated in some cases "*5R*", i.e. restoration of minor elements had a major visual impact on a specific historic building/site. The respondents could also provide detailed data, especially with regard to (d), (e), (f), and (g).

Responses to the only theoretical question of Questionnaire 1 (What is your vision of major aims of modern conservation of cultural heritage?) demonstrated the diversity of approaches. Six main categories were summarized from the open answers to this question, as formulated by the respondents of all eight STSMs. Among the major aims of CCH, as seen by the respondents, the following were stated, some of them expressed by more than one respondent, with regard to each category (Fig. 1):

1. *Values and authenticity*: Preservation of authenticity; Respecting the historical changes; Preservation of historical layers; Values: cultural, social, economic, educational; values of HB and society; (organizing) great source of knowledge; digital understanding

2. *Structure and use*: Preservation of structural elements, the original purpose

3. *HB and environment*: value for its environment; compatibilize urban progress with preservation and protection

4. *Bridging between the new development and the preservation of cultural heritage*: to reach compromise between …; to balance between … (different values; structural stability; the new development and the values…); compatibilize urban progress with preservation and protection; finding a way how to best incorporate new technology

5. *Preventing deterioration*: Preventive conservation; maintenance

6. *Education*: getting the public to recognize HB's true historical value; raising the overall awareness of the importance of the cultural heritage.

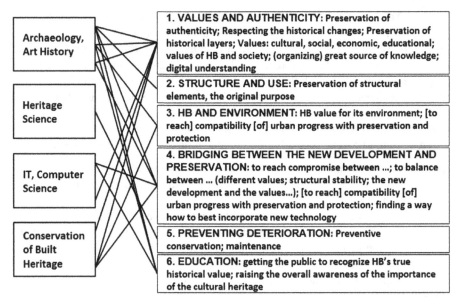

Fig. 1. Vision of major aims of modern conservation of cultural heritage by eight experts from diverse areas of expertise (Archaeology, Art History; Heritage Science; IT, Computer Science; Conservation of Built Heritage), showing their contribution per area to relevant categories and their aspects in CCH © A. Lobovikov-Katz

The selected general conclusions: experts in archaeology and art history, even when conservation was not their main area of expertise, were sometimes more sensitive to minor visual changes, especially with regard to archaeology-related issues, in comparison to conservation experts, e.g. in case of the changes of the interior space, or the use of modern construction for the exposition of earlier historical layers of a building. Archaeologists were more inclined to include "archaeological site" among the categories of built cultural heritage relevant to heritage building/site under their study. Also, the experts in archaeology and art history demonstrated a wider perception of the role of environment, the surroundings of a building, with a tendency to relate not only to a building, but, e.g. a group of building, unlikely the experts in natural sciences, without relevance to the scope of their record in conservation of cultural heritage.

Experts in natural sciences non-surprisingly demonstrated real approach to a subject of study. At the same time, approaches of natural sciences researchers much differ between them, from a rather formalistic one, overlooking some values specific of CCH, to a dedicated sharp analysis of a new to an expert matter. The latter might bring to unexpected results of a value to professional conservation experts.

The diversity of approaches can be exemplified through the analysis of a specific historic site by four experts (HB/S2: the historic site Château de Germolles, Mellecey, France). The historic compound, founded in 13th century, had undergone since then destructions, repairs, alterations, and restoration/conservation of 20th – 21st centuries.

High level of the complexity of this site, which included original parts, evidences of historical contradictions, combination of revolutionary and very subtle restoration interventions, along with evidences of the restoration mistakes of the past, presented an excellent ground for the study of its understanding by different experts. Their

Fig. 2. HB/S2: the historic site Château de Germolles, princely palace and the best-preserved residence of the Dukes of Burgundy, Mellecey, France: from 13th–14th centuries, through reuse, destructions and repairs to restoration/conservation of 20th–21st centuries Photo © A. Lobovikov-Katz

perception of visual impact of the changes undergone by this HB/S, of their origins and of their importance, is exemplified in Table 1.

Table 1. Example of rating of visual impact of diverse types of changes on a historic building/site (HB/S 2) (columns a through g) by four different respondents from diverse areas of expertise (rows 1 to 4). Row 5 (*Verification*) shows correct answers provided by the STSMs host on that specific site (restoration manager, natural science).

Types of changes from the Questionnaire - Q13 - ("H" - Historic adaptations to different needs; "R" - changes caused by Restoration/ conservation):

a) "Macro" geometry: change of surroundings of historic building / site (HB/S)
b) "Macro" geometry: change of shape of HB/S or of its major parts; structure
c) "Micro" geometry: change of shape of architectural elements, façade details
d) Application of new technologies at large scale (entire HB/S or its main parts)
f) Application of new technologies limited to minor elements
f) Application of building materials
g) Application of decorative materials, art, sculpture

	Area of exper-tise	Visual impact of diverse types of changes on HB/S2													
		a		b		c		d		e		f		g	
		H	R	H	R	H	R	H	R	H	R	H	R	H	R
1	Archaeology, Art History	2			4	2/3		2			-2	2	4	4	
2	IT & Computer Science I	2		4			1		1	2			3	-4	
3	IT & Computer Science II	2		2		2			2	3			2	5	
4	Built Heritage Conservation	1			2	3		1	1	3			3		1
5	Verification	2		2		2			1	5			2	5	

Questionnaire 1, as already mentioned, was not intended for quantitative conclusions. At the same time, by use of a simple measuring instrument provided in Q13, combined with other questions' responses, we could observe certain phenomena. First, it seems that it was easy for different experts to grasp changes on a larger scale, e.g. *"Macro" geometry: change of surroundings of historic building/site (HB/S)* (a), or *Application of new technologies at large scale* (entire HB/S or its main parts) (d). Of course, it was important to study the responses in the context of a specific aspects of this specific historic site: in this specific case a major intervention of technology on a large scale was easily visible. At the same time, minor elements like building material, or decorative arts, were also rated in similar way by diverse experts. In other words, the "clearly visible" was easily perceived.

On the other hand, issues that call for a specific knowledge of built heritage and its conservation, were rated in a wider range by different experts, e.g. *"Macro" geometry: change of shape of HB/S or of its major parts; structure* (b). To analyze the latter to the best, a combined understanding of building geometry, material and structure is required. Quite interestingly, with regard to this issue the answers split between the two groups of experts: IT/computer science experts and natural science (*verification*), and those more "humanities-related", i.e. archaeology, art history, architectural/building conservation. With regard to Q14 (*Which changes are significant with regard to building material/ technology/stability:1 (min) to 5 (max)*, of three respondents who answered this question, all pointed out restoration, and not historical changes. The Question provided an option to mark negative impact as "-". Experts in three areas: Archaeology/Art History; IT/Computer Science; Built Heritage Conservation rated the change which they outlined as 4R; -2R; -2R respectively. An expert in Archaeology/Art History pointed out one of the most unique restoration features of that HB/S, while mentioning that it prevents water infiltration, and hence, prevents further destruction of this HB/S.

It is important to mention that both an expert in IT/Computer Science, and in Built Heritage Conservation, pointed the same feature in their response to this Question, and rated it in the same way (−2R). This related to the use of cement in treatment of cracks. Since an expert in IT/Computer Science is a new comer to CCH, this similarity in answer should not be underestimated with regard to interdisciplinary research. Apparently, it occurred as a result of communication on site between the conservation the IT experts. This corresponds to one of our conclusions from this collaborative research projects in CCH: one of the most effective ways to reach the compatibility of results is to bring "digital" and non-conservation experts to the field, and to explain to them problem on-site. From a cross-area point of view, two experts - in Archaeology/Art History and in IT/Computer Science, stated that CH is not their main area of expertise. However, their responses were more immersed in CCH than might have been expected.

With regard to Q17 (*What is your overall impression of the authenticity of the image of this historic site; its parts; its surroundings*), the evaluation (*from 1 (min) to 5 (max)*) was summarized by experts as follow: Archaeology/Art History: "5"; IT/Computer Science I: "4"; IT/Computer Science II: "5"; Built Heritage Conservation: highly valued in description, but not rated in numbers. Two of four experts provided verbal description to the authenticity question. Conservation expert provided a well-reasoned answer, detailing the impact of specific restoration measures and their compatibility. The answer of the IT/Computer Science expert actually focused at the preservation of the historical value and connection, though without using this specific terminology.

Small number of intended respondents allowed for a high-resolution reading into the understanding and perception of a set of specific data by experts from diverse areas of expertise, including those who stated CCH as their main area of expertise (only one of the specific HB/S exemplified here), and those who work in some other area, and this was their first encounter with CCH (e.g. in the framework of a collaborative research project). The analysis of one specific HB/S by diverse experts (in each of three locations) allowed us to understand better their approaches to CCH and brought to the formulation of Questionnaire 2.

2.2   Analysis of Questionnaire 2

Aims of Questionnaire 2. Under COST (European Cooperation in Science and Technology) Action TD1406 i2MHB (Innovation in Intelligent Management of

Heritage Buildings) this anonymous online Questionnaire was aimed to assist us in examining approaches to conservation/preservation of cultural heritage (CH), with a focus on built heritage, among experts in diverse fields of science, technology, engineering and humanities. This corresponded with the objective of this COST Action: *to create a pan-European open network, to promote synergies between Heritage Sciences specialists, industrial stakeholders and research/education players, to achieve a unified common understanding and operation in the Heritage Buildings domain, integrating multidisciplinary expertise, technology and know-how through a novel and independent global framework.* Questionnaire 2 was distributed among the members of the COST Action TD1406 i2MHB, through direct emails sent to leading heritage-related experts, and later made available online on the selected CCH-related platforms. The questionnaire was fully anonymous, and no personal data on the respondents was provided.

Structure of Questionnaire 2. The Questionnaire was composed of 10 questions (including two-rout options following the answer to Q6), asking respondents about

Q1   Professional area of expertise

Q2. Professional or academic qualifications

Q3. What is their major activity: Research/Practical work/Other

Q4. Participation/leading international or major national research/other projects in CCH scholarships (if applicable, number of projects)

Q5. What is their vision of major aims of modern conservation of cultural heritage

Q6. Whether conservation of cultural heritage (CCH) is their main area

   Q7.1   If Q6 answered "No": is the present research/other project their first acquaintance with conservation of cultural heritage

   Q7.2   If Q6 answered "Yes": is their work associated with digital CH or with conservation of tangible/intangible cultural heritage

Q8   Request to rate relative importance, in their opinion, of diverse aspects of modern CCH (from 1 to 10: 10 – most important; 1 – less important)

- Preventive conservation and management
- Preserving authenticity of the shape of heritage building/site
- Preserving historic surroundings of heritage building/site
- Preserving original building materials
- Preserving the artistic value, original works of art
- Preserving social context; contributing to social rehabilitation
- Preserving original type of structure (statically)
- Preserving digital information on a building/site
- Interpretation of a historic building/site and its presentation to general public
- Education for CCH for general public.

Q9   Free comment on any issue, also those not included in the Questionnaire.

Analysis of Questionnaire 2. We have received and analyzed 57 responses. Respondents came from the following main areas:

1. ARCHAEOLOGY, ART HISTORY, architecture, history, other humanities
2. HERITAGE SCIENCE AND TECHNOLOGY incl. air pollution, heritage science, heritage technology
3. STEM (GENERAL) incl. electrical engineering, civil engineering, other
4. IT, COMPUTER SCIENCE, incl. IT, e-Culture, digital tools, Computer science
5. CONSERVATION OF BUILT HERITAGE, incl. building conservation, architectural conservation, conservation theory, urban conservation
6. MANAGEMENT, incl. project management, economics
7. HERITAGE EDUCATION, education, social sciences

Almost equal number of conservation (CE) and non-conservation experts (NCE), significant representation of researchers and practitioners (Fig. 3), and wide range of CCH experience among the respondents were helpful to our research. With regard to the range of the combined number of led and participated international or major national projects in CCH, four groups had been distinguished as indication of the experience of the respondents in CCH (Table 2).

Table 2. Participation/leading international or major national research/other projects in CCH (Groups according to the combined number of participated and led projects per participant)

Group	% of all respondents	Participated & led projects (per respondent)	Led projects (per respondent)
Group I	26%	0–3	0
Group II	28%	4–6	0–5
Group III	21%	7–14	2–8
Group IV	25%	18–62	1–30

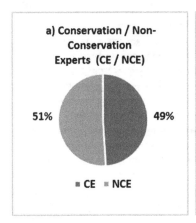
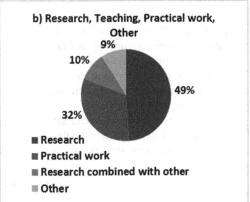

Fig. 3. Scope of the respondents' involvement in conservation of cultural heritage (CCH): (conservation experts (CE) versus non-conservation experts (NCE) (a); their involvement in research and other activities (b).

Correlation between the experience of respondents, their involvement in CCH, (i.e. distinction between conservation experts (CE), and non-conservation experts (NCE) to rating of ten aspects of the contemporary conservation of cultural heritage, as listed in Q8 is visualized in Fig. 4-5. As seen in Fig. 4, there is a common difference between conservation experts (CE) and non-conservation experts (NCE), regardless of their level of participation/leading projects: conservation experts tend to give higher values for all CCH aspects. Surprisingly, there was very little difference between the average values for ten CCH aspect in general (between 8 and 9) between the respondents who had no project leadership and participated very few projects (from 0 to 3,) and those who participated and led the largest number of projects (from 18 to 62 each respondent) (Fig. 5). In general, among the CCH aspects whose importance was perceived with a growing values correspondent to the number of projects, education, preventive conservation, preservation of social context, preservation of artistic values can be mentioned.

Preservation of original building materials and *preservation of the original structure* were seen generally as less important. This might be explained by a relatively limited representation relevant areas of expertise among the respondents, i.e., structural engineering and materials (16% of all respondents).

Preservation of digital information on heritage buildings/sites, with the exception of Group II, has been seen less important through average values in each group. On the one hand, it should be mentioned that only 5% of all respondents' areas of expertise were related directly to IT/computer science. At the same time, we should mention specifically responses to the Q 7.2 of this online Questionnaire, which was accessible only to the conservation experts - CE. Combining these responses with data collected from responses to other questions, 18% of all respondents stated that their work is associated with digital CH or both digital and with conservation of tangible/intangible cultural heritage. Though, as not all the respondents answered clearly to this question, it might be that even more experts are associated with digital CH.

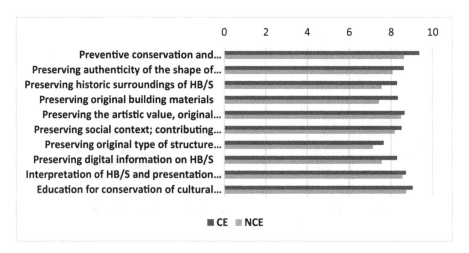

Fig. 4. Rating (from 1 - less important to 10 - most important) relative importance of each of ten CCH aspects of modern conservation of cultural heritage (as listed in Q8): averages of rating by conservation (CE) and non-conservation (NCE) experts © A. Lobovikov-Katz

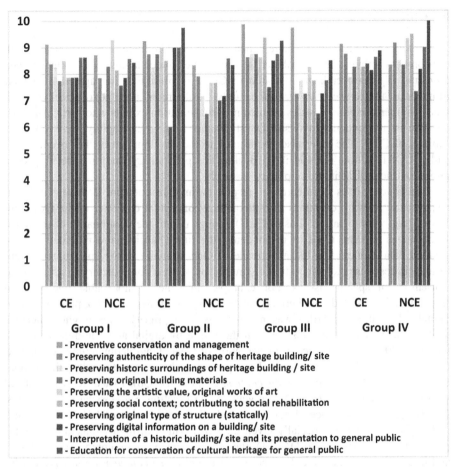

Fig. 5. Rating relative importance (from 1 - less important to 10 - most important) of each of ten CCH aspects of modern conservation of cultural heritage (as listed in Q8): average of rating within each group of respondents with regard to their experience in CCH (Table 2), and to diverse levels of their involvement with CCH - conservation (CE) and non-conservation (NCE) experts © A. Lobovikov-Katz

Nevertheless, the importance of digital heritage is not seen as high priority. Specifically of the Group II, CCH experts, which showed the highest values for the importance of preservation of digital information among all the groups (9 of 10), only one respondent from this group provided a definite answer of association to digital (and also non-digital) CH (which is about 2% of all participants, and about 6% of the respondents from Group II), and none stated IT/computer science as their main area of expertise.

3 Conclusions

Combining an on-site questionnaire which targeted real heritage conservation sites with a theoretical online one, contributed to our deeper understanding of challenges and problems of interdisciplinary research in CCH, flexibility of our approach to their formulation and perspectives for further study. Furthermore, a methodologically guided focus on interdisciplinary issues enabled non-conservation experts who participated the research as respondents to onsite Questionnaire 1, to grasp rapidly some complex subjects of CCH. The latter also contributed to the development of the specific tasks within COST Action TD1406 i2MHB, thus this preliminary study has developed an initial tool helpful in interdisciplinary research.

The general lines of theoretical responses in Questionnaire 2 were similar to responses to relevant questions of a theoretical-conceptual character of the Questionnaire 1 (e.g. with regard to aims of CCH), though due to the dissimilarity of the range of questions and the types of respondents, the first Questionnaire provided a more detailed data. Concluding the experience of Questionnaire 2, the spectrum and tendencies in responses to some questions might be seen as contradictory to an apparent consensus on specific issues. For example, in spite of noticeable relevance of respondents' work to digital heritage (at least 18% of all respondents), preservation of digital information on HB/S was not seen as high priority. This might indicate a tendency of reducing the gaps between the vision by digital and non-digital experts, with regard to the importance of preservation of "real" tangible/intangible heritage, as compared to its digital counterpart. In responses to the request to outline the respondents' *vision of the main aims of the contemporary CCH* (Q8), 14% of responses stated value/s of cultural heritage; 12% - preventive conservation; 8% – social values, needs, society; 10% – importance of education and educational value of CH; 4% - sustainability. But, of course, especially given the participation of highly-ranked experts (as evident from the answers to Q4, Q1), the unique content and combination of themes and ideas was of main value. Free comment to Q9 (*Free comment on any issue, also those not included in the Questionnaire*) invited many interesting responses. Since we cannot bring here as many as we would like, here are only a few of the answers to both questions:

Q8: "I do not like the eclecticism of including modern techniques to preserve ancient buildings, [...] I would prefer to use the same techniques to do restorations"

Q8: "[...] to revive cultural heritage in order to be able to use it in the future. Without the usage it loses its purpose and meaning"

Q9: "I prefer authenticity and integrity of surviving monuments and site, no reconstruction but well executed anastylosis using original elements and supported if necessary with minimal new members from authentic materials, mortars and finishes"

Q9: "It is necessary to balance the investments promoted by the European Community in digital promotion of HB with the investments needed to the preservation and maintenance of the HB. Should we promote beautiful digital images of HB and have in the future only decayed HB?"

Q9: "It's very important to educate not only public but [...] administration on the needed of conservation of heritage".

Questionnaire 1 and Questionnaire 2 provided a multi-layered view of some differences in approaches of conservation experts (CE) and non-conservation experts (NCE) from diverse areas of expertise, with regard to the selected major aspects of modern conservation of cultural heritage. In some responses to Q9 of Questionnaire 2, we have received feedback on the Questionnaire itself, e.g. suggestions to relate in the Questionnaire to "the affect of the cost of conservation within the decision making" in cultural heritage, and to provide information on the types of projects of the respondents (not only their quantity). Three comments supported our efforts, e.g. "Magnificent work"; "The questionnaire is very accurate and will help determine key areas for future research. Excellent work." Further research is needed to continue this preliminary study briefly presented in this paper. A wider research in this area will have the added value of contributing to productivity of the interdisciplinary research in general through the study of relevant challenges of this particular interdisciplinary field - the conservation of cultural heritage.

Acknowledgements. This article is based upon work from COST Action TD1406 i2MHB - Innovation in Intelligent Management of Heritage Buildings, supported by COST (European Cooperation in Science and Technology).

References

1. Tobi, H., Kampen, J.K.: Research design: the methodology for interdisciplinary research framework. Qual. Quant. **52**(3), 1209–1225 (2018)
2. Eisenberg, L., Pellmar, T.C. (eds.): Bridging Disciplines in the Brain, Behavioral, and Clinical Sciences, Institute of Medicine (US) Committee on Building Bridges in the Brain, Behavioral, and Clinical Sciences. National Academies of Sciences, Engineering, Medicine Press, Washington (DC) (2000)
3. Lobovikov-Katz, A., Bueno Benito, G., Marcos Sánchez, V., Martins, J., Sojref, D.: Training schools for conservation of cultural heritage: between expertise, management and education. In: Ioannides, M., et al. (eds.) EuroMed 2016. LNCS, vol. 10058, pp. 880–890. Springer, Cham (2016). https://doi.org/10.1007/978-3-319-48496-9_71
4. Lobovikov-Katz, A.: The virtual and the real: e-learning in interdisciplinary education - the case of cultural heritage. In: The 13th Annual MEITAL National Conference "New Technologies and Their Evaluation in Online Teaching and Learning". Technion – Israel Institute of Technology, Haifa, June 2015 http://meital.iucc.ac.il/conf2015/papers15/A3_3.pdf
5. Jokilehto, J.: A History of Architectural Conservation, Butterworth Heinemann, in association with ICCROM. The Bath Press, Bath (1999)
6. Feilden, B.M.: Conservation of Historic Buildings (3rd edn/ebook) (2001)
7. Harvey, J.: Conservation of Buildings. John Baker, London (1972)
8. Ruskin, J.: The Seven Lamps of Architecture. Bryan Taylor, New York (1894)
9. Lobovikov-Katz, A., Konstanti, A., Labropoulos, K., Moropoulou, A., Cassar, J., De Angelis, R.: The EUROMED 4 project "ELAICH": e-Tools for a teaching environment on EU mediterranean cultural heritage. In: Ioannides, M., Fritsch, D., Leissner, J., Davies, R., Remondino, F., Caffo, R. (eds.) EuroMed 2012. LNCS, vol. 7616, pp. 710–719. Springer, Heidelberg (2012). https://doi.org/10.1007/978-3-642-34234-9_75

10. Hazan, S., Katz, A.L.: The Willing Suspension of Disbelief: The Tangible and the Intangible of Heritage Education in E-Learning and Virtual Museums. In: Ioannides, M., Magnenat-Thalmann, N., Papagiannakis, G. (eds.) Mixed Reality and Gamification for Cultural Heritage, pp. 549–566. Springer, Cham (2017). https://doi.org/10.1007/978-3-319-49607-8_22
11. COST Action TD1406 i2MHB-Innovation in Intelligent Management of Heritage Buildings http://www.cost.eu/COST_Actions/tdp/TD1406? Accessed 12 Aug 2018
12. Lobovikov-Katz, A.: The correlation between the technological and conservation aspects and those of urban appearance in a stone-built environment: an evaluation approach. In: Kourkoulis, S. (ed.) Fracture and Failure of Natural Building Stones – Applications in the Restoration of the Ancient Monuments, Chap. 4.2, pp. 201–213. Springer, Dordrecht (2006). https://doi.org/10.1007/978-1-4020-5077-0_13

Capitalize on the Experience of the ATHENA Project for Cultural Heritage for the Eratosthenes Centre of Excellence for the Benefit of the East Med Region

Diofantos G. Hadjimitsis[1], Kyriacos Themistocleous[1(✉)],
Evagoras Evagorou[1], Silas Michaelides[1], Andreas Christofe[1],
Argyro Nisantzi[1], Kyriacos Neocleous[1], Christiana Papoutsa[1],
Christodoulos Mettas[1], Marios Tzouvaras[1], Eleni Loulli[1],
Georgia Kouta[1], Chris Danezis[1], Rosa Lasaponara[2], Nicola Masini[3],
Daniele Cerra[4], Gunter Schreier[4], and George Papadavid[5]

[1] Department of Civil Engineering and Geomatics,
ERATOSTHENES Research Centre, Cyprus University of Technology,
Saripolou 2-6, Achilleos 1A Building, 3036 Limassol, Cyprus
k.themistocleous@cut.ac.cy
[2] National Research Council, Institute of Methodologies for Environmental
Analysis, C.da S. Loya, 85050 Tito Scalo, Italy
[3] National Research Council, Institute for Archaeological and Monumental
Heritage, C.da S. Loya, 85050 Tito Scalo, Italy
[4] Earth Observation Center (EOC), German Aerospace Center (DLR),
Wessling, 8223 Oberpfaffenhofen, Germany
[5] Agricultural Research Institute (ARI), Pafos District Office, Paphos, Cyprus

Abstract. The "ATHENA" H2020 Twinning project seeks to establish a Center of Excellence in the field of Remote Sensing for Cultural Heritage through the development of an enhanced knowledge base and innovative methods in the areas of Archaeology and Cultural Heritage. This paper presents an overview of the ATHENA twinning project as well a review of the remote sensing in archaeology. The ATHENA stakeholder hub is presented through a WEBGIS platform. The importance of capitalizing on the experience of running the ATHENA project for the benefit of the ERATOSTHENES Centre of Excellence (ECoE) is explained. In recent years, Earth Observation (EO) techniques have been used extensively for archaeological and cultural heritage applications, which makes the ECoE a key player in EO activities in the Eastern Meditteranean region. The different areas that are under the umbrella of the remote sensing in archaeology sector are categorized based on the review findings. Finally, how Earth observation and remote sensing is spread out through research activities in the Eastern Meditteranean region from 1998 to 2018 is presented based on the Scopus engine.

Keywords: Remote sensing · Copernicus · Athena centre for cultural heritage
Excelsior · ECoE

© Springer Nature Switzerland AG 2018
M. Ioannides et al. (Eds.): EuroMed 2018, LNCS 11196, pp. 639–647, 2018.
https://doi.org/10.1007/978-3-030-01762-0_56

1 What Is 'ATHENA'

The "ATHENA" H2020 Twinning project seeks to establish a Center of Excellence (CoE) in the field of Remote Sensing for Cultural Heritage through the development of an enhanced knowledge base, capacity building and innovative methods in the areas of Archaeology and Cultural Heritage (CH). The ATHENA center has been established by twinning the existing Remote Sensing and Geo-environment Research Laboratory/Eratosthenes Research Centre-ERC. at the Cyprus University of Technology (CUT) with counterparts from other Member States of the EU, such as the Institute of Archaeological and Architectural Heritage of the National Research Council of Italy (IBAM-CNR) and the German Aerospace Centre (DLR). The close collaboration between the ATHENA CoE and other experts in the field of Remote Sensing for Cultural Heritage in the EU will form a synergic network that will enhance knowledge transfer and improve capacity building of the existing ERC staff.

The ATHENA project is expected to have direct and indirect social, scientific and economic impacts, through the creation of new jobs, increased research activity and knowledge transfer. The implementation of the project will facilitate future collaborations with experts of the Archaeology and CH sector at a European level, increase the CoE's research capabilities and enhance the research and academic profile of all participants. The location of the ATHENA CoE in Cyprus is especially important, as the region has been inhabited for thousands of years before and there is a wealth of tangible and intangible archaeological and CH remains.

During times of economic instability, national considerations overrule the process of European integration. CH is an integral element of a European set of values and respect for heritage is vital for developing a common European identity. Recently, the CH sector has undergone a number of challenges as a result of the financial crisis that hit Europe, including the decrease of public budgets, urbanization, globalization and technological changes, among others. Within this context, CH professionals are seeking to improve currently used methodologies in order to better understand, protect and valorize the common European past and common identity.

ATHENA seeks to improve and expand collaboration between low performing and leading institutions to use remote sensing technologies to support the CH sector. The ATHENA project was developed based on EU policies and international conventions related to Cultural Heritage protection, management and best practice, including the Europa Nostra policy documents; COM (2014) 477; UNESCO and EU conventions and multilateral treaties related to the protection of CH).

2 Remote Sensing in Archaeology and Cultural Heritage

EO techniques have become an indispensable tool for CH and archaeological investigation. Within the past 20 years, EO techniques have been used for the detection of cultural remains to the documentation, monitoring and preservation as found in the last 20 years. EO techniques are a non-invasive and cost-effective method for accessing data from a large area, especially in the case of archaeolandscapes. Such techniques enable CH experts to gain extremely precise results, thereby facilitating the different phases of heritage management, including survey, mapping, excavation, documentation, monitoring at diverse scales of interest, moving from small artifacts to architectural structures and landscape reconstruction and vizualization. Aerial and satellite data, in-situ data from ground sensors, databases such Geographic Information Systems (GIS) as well as augmented and virtual reality have revolutionized the archaeological and CH sector. For example, it is now possible to integrate satellite and ground archaeological and CH data to reconstruct an ancient environment, including the mapping of past flora and fauna and anthropological aspects.

There are dramatic differences in the cost and capabilities of different EO equipment. The increasing availability of free data and open access software tools can be used with in situ investigations and computer-based analysis, thereby providing new opportunities for the operational exploitation of archaeological results. The impact of EO technologies for archaeology experts [1] as well as end-users, which are currently underexploited, are expected to have a larger diffusion in the cultural heritage access and exploitation in the future, especially in the touristic sector. It is important to highlight the following areas are classified as the most important sectors of the wider area of remote sensing in archaeology research arena: (a) *airborne photography*: UAV [2, 3] and LIDAR [4]; (b) *passive satellite remote sensing* [5]; (c) *active satellite remote sensing*; (d) *ground remote sensing* that includes geophysical survey [6], magnetometry [7] and field spectroscopy [5].

Over the past two decades, the use of space technologies in archaeology and CH has increased for several reasons, including the improved spectral and spatial resolution of satellite sensors, the availability of user-friendly software and the recent trend for archaeologists to study the dynamics of human frequentation in relation to environmental changes. Indeed, EO techniques are very beneficial for archaeological and CH investigations, due to their reduced costs, time and risk associated with excavations and the creation of site strategies that focuses on conservation and preservation. In addition, the multispectral capability of satellite images can also be used to the identify the differences in texture, moisture content, roughness, topography, various types of terrain, vegetation cover, lithological and geological composition and other information used in archaeological studies. For example, crop-marks can be detected by spectral variations in specific channels more sensitive to vegetation (as near infrared) (see Fig. 1) or spectral indices (i.e. mathematical combinations of different spectral channels) as NDVI, SAVI, VI etc. by using multi-spectral images. The thirteen (13) spectral bands (443–2190 nm) and HR imaging capabilities in visible and near-infrared bands at 10 m spatial resolution have been already tested for archaeological prospection and monitoring [8–10].

In addition, local changes in the drainage capability of the soil, which are referred to as damp-marks, can be identified by spectral variations in specific channels more sensitive to moisture or spectral indices (see Fig. 2) as NDVI or difference in moisture in satellite SAR data [2] as in the case of Cosmo Skymed (see Fig. 2) acquired for the archaeological area of Metapontum. As well, shadow marks, which are micro/medium-micro-topographic relief linked to archaeological remains, as artworks, platforms, ditches and shallow remain, can be revealed by changes in colour or texture due to the presence of shadow through the use of spectral data.

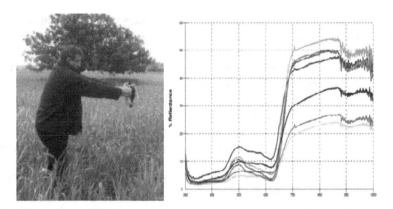

Fig. 1. Field spectroscopy in archaeological sites with typical spectral signatures of buried archaeological crops.

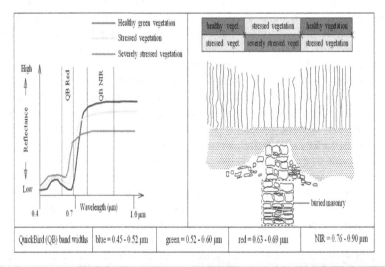

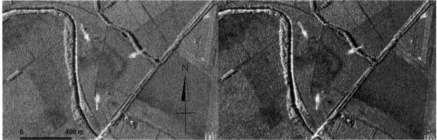

Fig. 2. Up-spectral response by QuickBird imagery of archaeological crop marks-Bottom-Cosmoskymed view of palaeochannels (Damp-marks) in Metapontum archaeological area (additional detail in [2]).

The European Commission Copernicus programme provides new opportunities in the EO sector and supports cultural heritage and cultural heritage monitoring [7]. Indeed, the Copernicus programme uses EO data and services for archaeological remote sensing [7] as highlighted during the Copernicus for Cultural Heritage Workshop (http://workshop.copernicus.eu/cultural-heritage).

The authors provide the following findings regarding a review of research activities using RS and EO techniques in cultural heritage and archaeology, focusing on the east-med region using the Scopus engine as shown in Fig. 3, from 1998 to 2018 [13]. It is important to highlight based on the Scopus results, the active participation of the ERC group in EO, also helped the pillar of cultural heritage which will be one of the pillars of the ECoE.

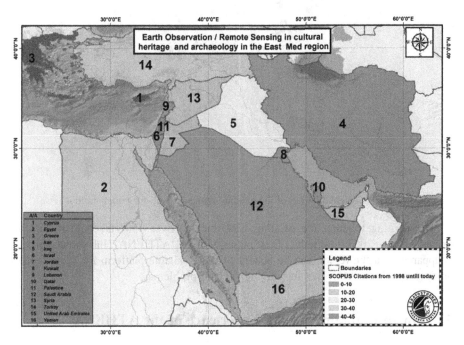

Fig. 3. Research activity in the East-MED region from 1998–2018 using Scopus engine (citations).

3 ATHENA Database: Stakeholder Hub

A relational database has been created to manage the information about the network of Institutions (laboratories, research groups) involved in Remote Sensing and Cultural Heritage. Additionally, information on Projects (including scientific expeditions and scientific missions) focused on EO tools was considered. The current database contains data information concerning **143 institutions** of different states and **14 projects** along with predefined queries to facilitate the search and use of the database (see Fig. 4). Specific queries can be created for specific needs and requests. The information currently offered by the database is a fundamental starting point for the creation of networks and collaborations. It has been conceived as an open updatable tool that will be continuously enriched during and after the project by both project partners and crowd-sourcing. Therefore, a specific web interface will be defined and set in order to enable the updating of the data base, promoting the growth of the network, facilitate contacts and collaborations.

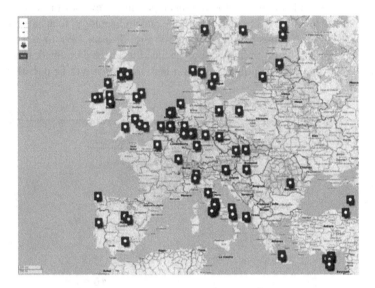

Fig. 4. WebGIS Map of the existing database: hub for collaboration.

By merging together the existing ERC hub of over 450 stakeholders that has expanded since 2007 during the EO activities with the 'ATHENA' Hub shown above, it is apparent that the region can be benefit of this available platform for future collaborations and future activities for solving societal problems.

4   How to Capitalize on the Experience of the ATHENA

One of the main aims of the 'ATHENA' Twinning project [11] after its completion at the end of 2018 is to secure the sustainability of the Centre. This is very challenging since the only source of funding will be competitive funding and services. Indeed, the ATHENA will be one of the pillars of the Eratosthenes Centre of Excellence (ECoE) which will upgraded through the EXCELSIOR H2020 Teaming project (www. excelsior2020.eu) as shown in Fig. 5. The aim of the EXCELSIOR teaming project is to upgrade the existing ERATOSTHENES Research Centre (ERC), established within the Cyprus University of Technology (CUT) into a sustainable, viable and autonomous Centre of Excellence (CoE) for Earth Surveillance and Space-Based Monitoring of the Environment, which will provide the highest quality of related services on the National, European and International levels [12]. The ERATOSTHENES CoE (ECoE), with its extensive expertise and infrastructure, can be a hub for the Earth observation activities in the eastern Mediterranean area due to the key geostrategic position of Cyprus.

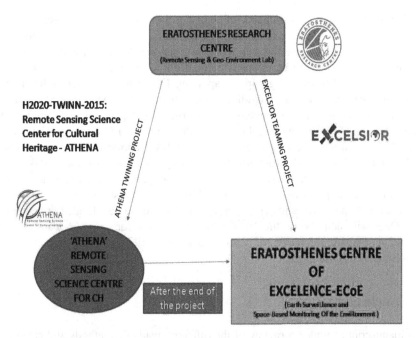

Fig. 5. How to secure sustainability of the 'ATHENA'? Capitalize on the Athena experience at the Eratosthenes Centre of Excellence (www.excelsior2020.eu).

The ERC is already an existing stakeholder hub with over 400 stakeholders from Europe, USA, Asia, Africa. Through ATHENA, this hub has already expanded the potential of the Earth observation area especially in the East Meditteranean Middle East North Africa (EMMENA) region. This hub will benefit society, academia, government and industry. Through the ECoE, EO services in the natural and built environment will be offered including also the cultural heritage. The ERC is a Copernicus Academy member and this assisted the sustainability of the ATHENA cultural heritage pillar within the ECoE. The ERC has already secured some funds through the ATHENA twinning and EXCELSIOR teaming benefits. The knowledge transfer from the twining partners of ATHENA, CNR and DLR to the CUT team (ERC) in the areas of SAR, geophysical surveys has been a great benefit of the ERC.

The ERC is a member of the Copernicus Academy network and has already promoted 'ATHENA' and 'EXCELSIOR' through several stakeholders' meetings, events and workshops. Such activities have already contributed to the Network's goals for providing researchers, scientists and entrepreneurs with the skills required for accessing Copernicus data and information services through a series of trainings and the development of relevant educational material. The Copernicus Academy also works to increase the exchange of ideas and best practices across borders and disciplines while contributing to the development of the use of EO data in general and Copernicus data and information in particular, in various public or private user organizations or industries. through ERC activities by presenting ATHENA and EXCELSIOR, new EO practices in teaching, tools and interactive workshops have been developed.

One of the significant impacts of running the 'ATHENA' project under the umbrella of the ERC 'a pure multi-disciplinary Earth observation group' which have already been capitalized are the following: (a) merging ATHENA and ERC existing stakeholders hubs: this will be an open hub platform for the *regional* and *European* use (b) increase visibility of our group (c) applying EO techniques more efficiently for natural and built environment including cultural heritage (c) social media/networking: promotion of community engagement, fostering an 'open science' environment through the use of digital and social media (d) the use of the EO for the implementation of the *UN Sustainable Development Goals* through the application of satellite remote sensing for real practical problems (d) active participation of local stakeholders (e) securing more funds in the wider area of risk management and environment (natural and built). The implementation of a novel strategic infrastructure unit to monitor natural hazards in Cyprus and eastern-med region through a new funded project named CyCLOPS will help boost the ECoE and the region for monitor, catalogue and understand the natural hazards for any intended application including natural and built environment (e.g., heritage).

5 Conclusions

This manuscript provided a review of the different available methods and categorized within the umbrella of the remote sensing in archaeology. Through 'ATHENA' the existing ERC stakeholder hub has increased and improved for the benefit of the local and the region. One of the aims of the ATHENA Twinning project was to sustain the existing cultural heritage sector within the ERC. Indeed, such goals have been achieved and will be further boosted through the 'EXCELSIOR' H2020 Teaming project in which the existing ERC will be upgraded to a Centre of Excellence-ECoE.

Acknowledgements. The present paper is under the "ATHENA" project H2020-TWINN2015 of European Commission. This project has received funding from the European Union's Horizon 2020 research and innovation programme under grant agreement No 691936 (www.athena2020. eu). The authors also acknowledge the EXCELSIOR (ERATOSTHENES: Excellence Research Centre for Earth Surveillance and Space-Based Monitoring of the Environment) project which is funded by the European Union's Horizon 2020 research and innovation programme, under grant agreement No 7633643: Work programme H2020 under "Spreading Excellence and Widening Participation", call: H2020-WIDESPREAD-04-2017: TeamingPhase1 (Coordination and Support Action) (www.excelsior2020.eu).

References

1. Lasaponara, R., Leucci, G., Masini, N., Persico, R., Scardozzi, G.: Towards an operative use of remote sensing for exploring the past using satellite data: the case study of Hierapolis (Turkey). Remote Sens. Environ. **174**, 148–164 (2016)
2. Chen, F., Lasaponara, R., Masini, N.: An overview of satellite synthetic aperture radar remote sensing in archaeology: from site detection to monitoring. J. Cult. Herit. **23**, 5–11 (2017)

3. Themistocleous, K., Agapiou, A., King, H.M., King, N., Hadjimitsis, D.G.: More than a flight: the extensive contributions of UAV flights to archaeological research – the case study of curium site in Cyprus. In: Ioannides, M., Magnenat-Thalmann, N., Fink, E., Žarnić, R., Yen, A.-Y., Quak, E. (eds.) EuroMed 2014. LNCS, vol. 8740, pp. 396–409. Springer, Cham (2014). https://doi.org/10.1007/978-3-319-13695-0_38

4. Damian, H., et al.: Uncovering archaeological landscapes at Angkor using lidar. Uncovering Archaeol. Landsc. Angkor Using Lidar Proc. Natl. Acad. Sci. U.S.A. **110**(31), 12595–12600 (2013). https://doi.org/10.1073/pnas.1306539110

5. Agapiou, A., Alexakis, D.D., Sarris, A., Hadjimitsis, D.A.: Orthogonal equations of multi-spectral satellite imagery for the identification of un-excavated archaeological sites. Remote Sens. **5**, 6560–6586 (2013)

6. Linford, N.: The application of geophysical methods to archaeological prospection. Rep. Prog. Phys. **69**, 2205–2257 (2006)

7. Neubauer, W.: Magnetische Prospektion in der Archäologie. Verlag der Osterreichis-chenAkademie der Wissenschaften, Wien (2001)

8. Elfadaly, A., Attia, W., Lasaponara, R.: Monitoring the environmental risks around Medinet Habu and Ramesseum Temple at West Luxor, Egypt, Using Remote Sensing and GIS Techniques. J. Archaeol. Method Theory **25**(2), 587–610 (2018)

9. Agapiou, A., Hadjimitsis, D.G., Themistocleous, K., Papadavid, G., Toulios, L.: Detection of archaeological crop marks in Cyprus using vegetation indices from Landsat TM/ETM+ satellite images and field spectroscopy measurements. In: Proceedings of SPIE 7831, Earth Resources and Environmental Remote Sensing/GIS Applications, p. 78310V, 25 October 2010 (2010)

10. Bini, M., et al.: Identification of leveled archeological mounds (Höyük) in the Alluvial Plain of the Ceyhan River (Southern Turkey) by satellite remote-sensing analyses. Remote Sens. **10**, 241 (2018)

11. Hadjimitsis, D., et al.: Establishing a remote sensing science center in Cyprus: first year of activities of ATHENA project. In: 6th International Euro-Mediterranean Conference (EuroMed 2016), 31 October–05 November 2016, Nicosia, Cyprus (2016)

12. Diofantos, G., et al.: Proceedings of SPIE 10428, Earth Resources and Environmental Remote Sensing/GIS Applications VIII, p. 104280F, 5 October 2017 (2013)

13. Lasaponara, R., Masini, N.: Space-based identification of archaeological illegal excavations and a new automatic method for looting feature extraction in desert areas. Surv. Geophys. 1–24 (2018)

On the Pathway to Success:
Becoming a Leading Earth Observation
Centre Through the EXCELSIOR Project

Diofantos G. Hadjimitsis[1], Georgia Kouta[1],
Kyriacos Themistocleous[1(✉)], Silas Michaelides[1],
Kyriacos Neocleous[1], Rodanthi-Elisavet Mamouri[1], Argyro Nisantzi[1],
Christiana Papoutsa[1], Marios Tzouvaras[1], Christodoulos Mettas[1],
Andreas Christofe[1], Evagoras Evagorou[1], Gunter Schreier[2],
Egbert Schwarz[2], Haris Kontoes[3], Ioannis Papoutsis[3],
Albert Ansmann[4], and Giorgos Komodromos[5]

[1] Eratosthenes Research Centre, Remote Sensing and Geo-Environment Lab,
Department of Civil Engineering and Geomatics,
Faculty of Engineering and Technology,
Cyprus University of Technology, Limassol, Cyprus
k.themistocleous@cut.ac.cy
[2] German Aerospace Center, Cologne, Germany
[3] National Observatory of Athens, Athens, Greece
[4] Leibniz Institute for Tropospheric Research, Leipzig, Germany
[5] Department of Electronic Communications, Ministry of Transport,
Communications and Works, Nicosia, Cyprus

Abstract. This paper presents the pathway towards the establishment of the ERATOSTHENES Centre of Excellence (ECoE), through the upgrade of the existing Remote Sensing & Geo-Environment Group - ERATOSTHENES Research Centre (ERC), within the Cyprus University of Technology (CUT). The ECoE aspires to become a sustainable, viable and autonomous Centre of Excellence for Earth Surveillance and Space-Based Monitoring of the Environment. The ECoE will provide the highest quality of related services in the National, European, Eastern Mediterranean and Middle East and Northern Africa areas (EMMENA). Therefore, drawing on the capitalization of experience and knowledge from previous projects and the research areas and international networks of the ERC, this papers highlights the importance of the establishment of the ECoE in the EMMENA area.

Keywords: Centre of Excellence · Remote sensing · Earth Observation
Cyprus · Smart specialization strategy · Environmental monitoring
Cultural heritage · EMMENA

1 Introduction

Earth Observation (EO) technologies are vital for providing reliable up-to-date information to better observe, understand, protect, monitor and predict environmental parameters that regard land, water and air. Such valuable inputs are crucial for more

© Springer Nature Switzerland AG 2018
M. Ioannides et al. (Eds.): EuroMed 2018, LNCS 11196, pp. 648–653, 2018.
https://doi.org/10.1007/978-3-030-01762-0_57

informed decision-making, oriented towards the protection and management of environment and resources. EO includes technological solutions, including satellite observation, navigation and positioning systems. To date, conventional methods are employed for the detection of threats/risks related to pollution events in air, land and water, including the use of physicochemical sampling campaigns and site visits. These techniques are time consuming and require extensive use of manpower and, the same time, create additional environmental issues.

The EXCELSIOR (www.excelsior2020.eu) project envisions the upgrade of the existing ERATOSTHENES Research Centre (ERC) at the Cyprus University of Technology (CUT), into a sustainable, viable and autonomous ERATOSTHENES Centre of Excellence (ECoE) for Earth Surveillance and Space-Based Monitoring of the Environment. The upgrade is addressed through the implementation of a robust plan that will be developed during the current one-year phase of the EXCELSIOR project and will establish the foundations for the development of a competitive and high competence profile to expand the Centre's visibility beyond the national level and develop European, regional and global cooperation. The long-term aim of the upgraded Centre is to create new opportunities for conducting basic and applied research and innovation (R&I) in the areas of the integrated use of remote sensing and space-based techniques for monitoring the environment with applications in several areas, including (but not limited to) the built environment, natural hazards and cultural heritage.

Five partners have united within the EXCELSIOR project with the common vision to upgrade the existing ERC to become a world-class innovation, research and education center, actively contributing to the European Research Area (ERA). These are the Cyprus University of Technology (CUT, acting as the coordinator), the German Aerospace Centre (DLR), the National Observatory of Athens (NOA), the German Leibniz Institute for Tropospheric Research (TROPOS) and the Cyprus Department of Electronic Communications of the Ministry of Transport, Communications and Works (DEC-MTCW).

The existing ERC conducts state-of-the-art research, integrating novel technologies in the areas of Remote Sensing (RS) and space-based EO techniques with the use of Geographic Information Systems (GIS) to develop sustainable and systematic monitoring of areas of interest and the on-time detection of risks. The ultimate goal of the ECoE will be the protection of the environment by providing critical information, through end user products, not only to policy makers but also to other local, national and regional authorities.

The ERC has demonstrated its innovation and dynamics in the field of EO over the past 11 years of its existence and is now focused on upgrading the existing ERC into a Centre of Excellence, which will address the national, European, regional and international needs regarding remote sensing and EO. The upgrade will regard the expansion of this vision to systematic monitoring of environment using EO, space and ground based integrated technologies focusing on natural and built environment (e.g., land, air and water) related applications. The main pillar will be on conducting basic and applied research to bring innovation in the areas of the integrated use of remote sensing and space-based techniques for monitoring the environment. The EXCELSIOR project vision is fully aligned with the Smart Specialisation Strategy (S3Cy) for Cyprus. The

S3Cy has been established by the Government of Cyprus [1], based on priority sectors that have been selected for future sustainable economic growth in Cyprus.

The strong background and individual experience of the ERC in remote sensing and space technologies, combined with the synergies that will be established with the partners of the project, will result in the implementation of a sustainable ECoE, which will address crucial R&I problems of great societal benefit. The research fields of EO and space technology have matured to the point that many challenges lie in the capitalisation on existing knowledge and technologies to enable advances in many diverse application areas stated in the S3Cy, such as health, tourism, agriculture, cultural heritage, transport, blue growth, natural hazards, natural and built environment, etc. The R&I activities of the upgraded ECoE are planned to be directly linked with the thematic areas of the horizontal priorities of Environment and Information & Communication Technologies of S3Cy, through future collaboration with the industry, not only within Cyprus but also with countries in the Eastern Mediterranean, Middle East and North Africa (EMMENA) region.

2 Networking for Research and Innovation

The ERC has built strong and interconnected sustainable network of affiliations with international organizations over the years, thus promoting innovative research, an exchange of expertise and knowledge as well as creating strategic partnerships with the

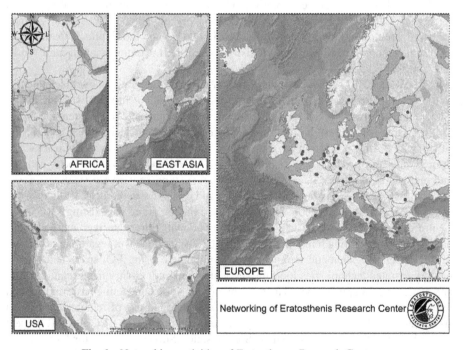

Fig. 1. Networking activities of Eratosthenes Research Centre.

leading scientists in the field of EO and RS. The Centre is a member of several networks including SPIE, EARSeL, EARLINET, ACTRIS, AERONET (NASA), FABSPACE 2.0, GEO-Cradle, ISPRS, NEREUS and CNR and has strong links with organizations such as ESA, DLR, NASA, GEO and Copernicus. The Centre has collaborated with over 300 different research and academic institutions, as well as partners from the private sector and policy makers (see Fig. 1). In 2016, the ERC was accepted as a Copernicus Academy Network Member. As Copernicus Sentinel satellites are observing the Earth from Space, the European Commission is focusing on enabling users to access free data and services. The ERC complies fully with the aim of the Copernicus Academy Network which connects European universities, research institutions, business schools, both private and non-profit organizations, in the Participating Countries of the Programme and beyond. During the past two years, the ERC has contributed to the Network's goals for providing researchers, scientists and entrepreneurs with the skills required for accessing Copernicus data and information services through a series of trainings and the development of relevant educational material.

3   Areas of Expertise of the ERATOSTHENES Research Center

In line with the Copernicus program, which provides products and services on Emergency management, Security, Climate Change as well as Land, Marine and Atmosphere monitoring, the ERC is organised into three main research thematic areas, (Land, Water and Ai) which include all aspects of the natural and built environment. The ERC upgrade will regard the expansion into the ECoE to systematically monitor the environment using EO, and space and in-situ technologies.

The ERC, with its significant experience in the field of Remote Sensing and GIS, has received funding from European, national and industrial sources, including Horizon 2020; FP6, FP7, INTERREG, LIFE+, JPI, MED, ECHO, MARIE-CURIE (ITN), EUREKA, ERASMUS+, Cyprus Research Promotion Foundation (CRPF), etc. Its research is focused in the following thematic areas: Remote Sensing; Cultural Heritage/Archaeology, Geographic Information Systems (GIS), Sustainability, Natural Hazards, Risk assessment, Climate change, Water Resources Management, Atmospheric sciences, Agriculture, Earthquake Engineering, Geology, Urban design, Civil Engineering, Transport Planning/Modelling, Construction Innovation, Life cycle assessment, etc. In the last eleven years, the Centre secured funding for over than 70 projects. These projects are listed and described at www.cyprusremotesensing.com.

The existing ERC has an extensive capacity related to the development of atmospheric correction algorithms for remote sensing data as well in the calibration of remote sensing data using test fields [4–6]. Indeed, this is a beneficial tool for the EMMENA region for the accuracy assessment of all the space-based applications. In the technical report released by Copernicus/ESA 'Copernicus data Quality Control - Technical Note Atmospheric Corrections' [7], four publications on atmospheric corrections by members of ERC [i.e., 8–11] are listed as key references for guidelines.

3.1 The Pillar of Cultural Heritage and Archaeology

Cultural Heritage (CH) constitutes one of the major pillars of the upgraded Centre of Excellence, which will capitalize on the experience of multiple funded projects in the field of CH and Archaeology. The current state-of-the-art in the CH sector of the ERC focuses on the integrated use of field spectroscopy, UAV, geophysical surveys and EO for the detection of archaeological buried remains, risk assessment using space-based techniques, CH protection and surveying. The CH sector is currently running three funded projects: the Twinning ATHENA project (www.athena2020.eu) and two JPI-CH projects, namely, CLIMA (http://www.clima-project.eu) and PROTHEGO (http://www.prothego.eu).

The ATHENA Twinning project aims to establish a Centre of Excellence in the field of Remote Sensing for Cultural Heritage through the development of an enhanced knowledge base and innovative methods in the areas of Archaeology and CH [2]. It focuses on the EU policies and international conventions related to Cultural Heritage protection, management and best practices, such as the Europa Nostra policy documents, the European Commission [3]; UNESCO and EU conventions, and multilateral treaties related to the protection of tangible CH.

4 Expected Impact

The EXCELSIOR project envisions the creation of the ECoE that will conduct basic and applied research in EO and space technologies. The proposed ECoE will utilize its experience in research and innovation in EO and space technologies of the past 11 years in order to create the ECoE. The ECoE aims to develop state-of-the-art integrated applications using space and geo-informatics technologies to monitor the natural and built environment.

One of the most important aspects is to provide economic benefits to individuals and companies in Cyprus and Europe. According to ESA evaluation technical reports, it is noted that significant activities related to EO and space applications are already taking place in Cyprus. The presence of a Centre of Excellence in Cyprus will enhance research and development innovation in the EO sector and will provide new job opportunities for EO experts in Cyprus, Europe and the EMMENA region. The vision of the ECoE is to become a research and innovation hub as well as a entrepreneurial center, since it will include the increased participation of the private sector in research and innovation activities and promote the creation of spin-off companies. The ECoE will be based in Limassol with supportive infrastructure in the coastal municipalities of Cyprus, while its implementation will benefit the EMMENA region.

Acknowledgements. The authors acknowledge the 'EXCELSIOR' (ERATOSTHENES: EXcellence Research Centre for Earth Surveillance and Space-Based Monitoring of the Environment) project. This project has received funding from the European Union's Horizon 2020 research and innovation programme under grant agreement No 7633643 Work programme H2020 under "Spreading Excellence and Widening Participation", call: H2020-WIDESPREAD-04-2017: Teaming Phase 1 (Coordination and Support Action) (www.excelsior2020.eu).

References

1. Government of Cyprus: Smart specialisation strategy for Cyprus (in Greek). http://www. dgepcd.gov.cy/dgepcd/dgepcd.nsf/6966F1D9F8511C00C2257C7D0048701E/$file/S3CY_ FINAL%20corrections%2031032015.pdf. Accessed 26 July 2018
2. Hadjimitsis, D., et al.: Establishing a remote sensing science center in Cyprus: first year of activities of ATHENA project. In: Ioannides, M., et al. (eds.) EuroMed 2016. LNCS, vol. 10059, pp. 275–282. Springer, Cham (2016). https://doi.org/10.1007/978-3-319-48974-2_31
3. European Commission: Communication from the Commission to the European Parliament, the Council, the European Economic and Social Committee and the Committee of the Regions - Towards an integrated approach to cultural heritage for Europe, 477, p. 13. COM (2014). http:// ec.europa.eu/assets/eac/culture/library/publications/2014-heritage-communication_en.pdf. Accessed 26 July 2018
4. Themistocleous, K., Hadjimitsis, D.G.: Development of an image based integrated method for determining and mapping aerosol optical thickness (AOT) over urban areas using the darkest pixel atmospheric correction method, RT equation and GIS: A case study of the Limassol area in Cyprus. J. Photogramm. Remote Sens. **86**, 1–10 (2013)
5. Themistocleous, K., Hadjimitsis, D.G., Retalis, A., Chrysoulakis, N.: Development of a new image based atmospheric correction algorithm for aerosol optical thickness retrieval using the darkest pixel method. J. Appl. Remote Sens. **6**(1), 1–12 (2012)
6. Themistocleous, K., Hadjimitsis, D.G., Retalis, A., Chrysoulakis, N., Michaelides, S.: Precipitation effects on the selection of suitable non-variant targets intended for atmospheric correction of satellite remotely sensed imagery. Atmos. Res. **131**, 73–80 (2012)
7. Vescovi, F.D., Minchella, A.: CSCDA – Coordinated Data-access System (CDS), version 3, Evolutions, Operations and Maintenance Copernicus data Quality Control - Technical Note Atmospheric Corrections. Reference: CDS-TPZ-03-000077-TR, DIL ID: D-067, Issue 2.2, https://spacedata.copernicus.eu/documents/12833/14545/D-067_CQC_T7_TN_07_Atmosp hericCorrections_v2.2.pdf. Accessed 26 July 2018
8. Themistocleous, K., Hadjimitsis, D.G., Retalis, A., Chrysoulakis, N.: The identification of pseudo-invariant targets using ground field spectroscopy measurements intended for the removal of atmospheric effects from satellite imagery: a case study of the Limassol area in Cyprus. Int. J. Remote Sens. **33**(22), 7240–7256 (2012)
9. Hadjimitsis, D.G., Clayton, C.R.I., Hope, V.S.: An assessment of the effectiveness of atmospheric correction algorithms through the remote sensing of some reservoirs. Int. J. Remote Sens. **25**(18), 3651–3674 (2004)
10. Hadjimitsis, D.G.: Aerosol optical thickness (AOT) retrieval over land using satellite image-based algorithm. Air Qual. Atmos. Health **2**(2), 89–97 (2009)
11. Hadjimitsis, D.G., et al.: Atmospheric correction for satellite remotely sensed data intended for agricultural applications: impact on vegetation indices. Nat. Hazards Earth Syst. Sci. **10**, 89–95 (2010)

The Role of Information and Communication Technologies for Enhancing Access to Cultural Content

(The Example of Bulgaria)

Mariela Modeva[✉] [ID]

University of Library Studies and Information Technologies,
Tsarigradsko shosse Bul, 119, 1274 Sofia, Bulgaria
m.modeva@unibit.bg

Abstract. The paper presents the more important highlights of a research on the role of information and communication technologies in expanding access to cultural content in the concrete social context in Bulgaria. The subject now is not studied in a comprehensive way. Separate documents and articles are covered various aspects of the problem. In Bulgaria, there is no comprehensive work devoted to this issue. The author does not claim full comprehensiveness of the subject concerned. Account is taken of the fact that a number of researchers, international and national institutions working on the topic of access to cultural content have been interested in it. Specific accents are made and the current state of the problem in Bulgaria is analyzed. Particular attention is given to the digitization in public cultural institutions of memory - libraries, museums, archives where long term availability of cultural content and its long-term accessibility is provided. Good practices are presented, problems that are more important are outlined, results and conclusions are drawn and recommendations are made for possible solutions to the problems. The results of the study confirmed the hypothesis that information and communication technologies play a key role in preserving cultural values and can foster the expansion of access to cultural content. The conclusions highlight the impact of the digitization of cultural values on the economic growth of Bulgaria by taking into account the education, tourism, research and the involvement of the local industry.

Keywords: Information and communication technologies (ICT)
Long-term availability and access to cultural content

1 Introduction

Long-term availability of cultural content and its long-term accessibility is a central focus of this paper, which aims to clarify the current opportunities for expanding this accessibility through the information and communication technologies (ICT). In the report are introduced, in particular, the opportunities offered by new information technologies to expand access to cultural content. An attempt has been made to reflect the impact of the digitalisation of cultural values on education, tourism and the growth of

© Springer Nature Switzerland AG 2018
M. Ioannides et al. (Eds.): EuroMed 2018, LNCS 11196, pp. 654–663, 2018.
https://doi.org/10.1007/978-3-030-01762-0_58

the local economy. **The study is accomplished with the participation of students from the University of Library Studies and Information Technologies in Sofia, in the period 2016–2018.** We conducted an open source study of programs and projects in the last 10 years (membership of Bulgaria in EU) for the use of ICT in the expansion of access to cultural content in Bulgarian libraries, museums, archives and cultural centers. Official data are available from the National Statistical Institute, the Sociological Agency "Alpha Research" and Eurostat. **The scientific object of the study** is access to cultural content. **The subject of the research** is the role of information and communication technologies in protecting cultural heritage and expanding access to cultural content and its impact to economic growth in Bulgaria.

Hypothesis
Information and communication technologies play a key role in preserving cultural values and can foster the expansion of access to cultural content. The impact of the digitization of cultural values stimulates cultural tourism and its impact on the economic growth of Bulgaria by taking into account the education, research and the involvement of the local industry.

The aim of the research is to select "good practices" for the implementation of information and communication technologies for the purposes of preserving the cultural heritage and ensuring broad access to cultural content. The more important problems are outlined. In this regard, the selected projects presented according to their importance for the Bulgarian society and for the preservation of European cultural values.

The study is based on the current documents and papers of EU providing access to cultural content as European Agenda for Culture. Work Plan for Culture 2015–018[1] and Access to Culture - Policy Analysis, Final Report[2].

2 Methods

The research used common methods of scientific knowledge: theoretical analysis (primary and secondary), synthesis, comparison, summary of more than 100 mainly Internet sources in relation to the study problem; content analysis of international and national program and regulatory documents regulating access to cultural content through the use of information and communication technologies, analysis of statistical data.

Research Limitations. Research investigated programs and projects over the last 10 years. The period coincides with the membership of Bulgaria in the European Union. At that stage there is no analysis of the impact of expanded access to cultural content on consumers.

---

[1] European Agenda for Culture Work Plan for Culture 2015–2018, Final draft report of the Working Group of EU Member States' Experts on promoting access to culture via digital means under the open method of coordination, ver. 16/06/2017.

[2] Access to Culture - Policy Analysis, Final Report, file:///C:/Users/Acer/Desktop/ACCESS/Final_Report_Online_with-Annex.pdf.

Actuality and Significance of the Study. In the modern world, the role of information and communication technologies is growing. Through digitalization and other modern methods, cultural values are long term available and accessible.

In Bulgaria, a number of projects have been launched, which are mostly implemented by public libraries, but the process also starts in archives and museums. However, there is no comprehensive analysis of the role of ICT in expanding access to cultural content and the reasons for the lack of such access in large groups of the country's population.

The significance of the study is determined by the current problems concerning the coordination of the processes of digitization related to the preservation of cultural heritage in the Republic of Bulgaria. The research can be used to support specialized training aimed at enhancing the professional qualification of cultural heritage workers through more efficient use of ICTs and expanding access to cultural content.

Oxfam's annual report reveals that the number of billionaires has increased by one person every two days between March 2016 and March 2017.

According to the report, 3.7 billion people, representing the poorest half of the world, have not increased their wealth before 2017, and 82% of the wealth generated last year has gone to the richest 1% of the global population [3]. In this context, access to cultural content is a central focus of this report, which aims to clarify the possibilities for its expansion.

Culture is a complex and diverse area in which the problems of different sectors relate to the protection of both the tangible and intangible heritage, the state of movable and immovable cultural values and the development of the cultural industries. In the context of a brief study, it is not possible to thoroughly analyze all these dimensions of culture, and in particular the opportunities presented by new information technologies for expanding access to cultural content. There will also be no emphasis on the detailed consideration of the notion of culture. We assume that culture (from Latin culture, coming from colo, colere and meaning education, development, cultivation) is a term with very ambiguous definitions and because of this versatility and multiplicity, it is difficult to define uniformly. Different definitions of culture reflect different understandings or criteria for human activity assessment. Today, the world faces the possibility of being unified in the context of globalization [1]. We accept the treatment of reasoning for culture as an intellectual-creative process that is determined by itself and exists within the framework of the theory of culture.

Statistical Data. At this stage, the statistical data show an unbalanced distribution of resources in the individual settlements of Bulgaria and a correspondingly unfavorable trend regarding the access to cultural content. This is also shown by the data of the National Statistical Institute for 2016 referring to the population aged 25–64, broken down by sex, age, education, employment status and domicile, of which the following are examples [4]:

At this stage, 58.8% of the population did not attend any performances, of which 79.4% were unemployed, 69.9% were economically inactive; 81.2% live in the villages, and 51% in the towns represented evenly by age: 62.1% did not go to the cinema once; 63.6% did not visit any cultural landmarks; 46.9% have not read any books, among them 89.8% have basic and lower education; 52.2% have read less than 5 books, among which the lowest educated group - 69.8%; the percentage of reading newspapers is relatively high - 45.6%; 92.7% don't belong to hobby associations or clubs of interest. According to the very new research, more and more Bulgarians read and buy books, the literature remaining the most popular access to art for the population. This shows a study by Alpha Research, held between May 14 and 20, 2018, on the Day of Bulgarian Education and Slavonic Scripture. Sociologists report that for the past year 66% of people have read at least one book. A new book for their personal library has bought 46% of respondents. Concerts of folk, pop and rock performers are ranked second in popularity as a cultural experience for Bulgarians (47 per cent have visited a similar event). For four years, interest in concerts has increased by about 7%. On the other hand, visitors to opera performances, ballet or other forms of classical music are only 17% a year. One third of people visited a theater in 2017–2018 at least once, and 24% said they were watching a Bulgarian cinema movie. 32% of people say they have visited an exhibition, museum or site with archaeological excavations in the last twelve months. "Alpha Research" explains the interest to cultural heritage with the growing mobility of Bulgarians and the attraction of domestic tourism but also with the ever-diversified offer, genre unification of events in festivals, gradual improvement of the communication by the organizers of cultural events and "the increasing desire of modern man to go beyond everyday life and to seek deeper stances and values in his life." [10]. The percentage of people who have participated in cultural life by participating in amateur dance, theatrical or other artistic groups - only 13%, is quite low.

However, more than half of Bulgarians share satisfaction with the development of cultural activities in their respective cities - 29% say they are very satisfied and 30% - "to a certain extent" satisfied with the opportunities for reaching out to culture. This division is most clearly visible on the line "big city - a small settlement". Highest estimates are received in Sofia, Plovdiv and Rousse, while over 1/3 of the inhabitants of the smaller settlements believe that cultural life is absent [10]. **The general statistical data about all digitalized items in libraries, archives and museums on the national level and the total number of users was not found. It is interesting to compare the mentioned above statistics with the data of Eurostat.** Between 2010 and 2015, the percentage of internet users buying tickets for events increased in all EU Member States except France, reaching an average in the EU of 24% in 2015 compared with 20% five years before. The increase was greatest in Estonia (+26% points) and Sweden (+20% points). Variations by country the percentage of e-shoppers for cultural goods and services varied considerably between EU Member States. In 2015, the number of e-shoppers for the three categories of cultural goods and services was consistently above the EU average in Denmark, Germany, Luxembourg, the Netherlands, Austria, Finland, Sweden and the United Kingdom. The lowest percentages of e-shoppers for the three cultural categories were found in Bulgaria, Greece, Cyprus and Romania. These differences may be due to a preference to shop in person or a lack of trust in the quality of goods or in the security of online payments. The availability of cultural goods online—the variety of the offer and attractive prices—also plays an important role in purchasing choices [5, p. 151]. The trend that emerges based on the abovementioned statistics is that there are clear disparities in the opportunities for a large part of the population to participate in the cultural life of the country. Despite the existence of European programs, the realized projects serve a limited range of participants, in a relatively short period of time and within a predefined budget for the specific project. This does not solve the problem of access to cultural content in the long term, which calls for a completely different approach than the purely project-based one, namely the implementation of sustainable, long-term cultural policies with the participation of cultural institutions themselves, artists and their associations and local communities. It is imperative to include libraries, museums, and cultural centers in common information networks based on developed mechanisms for long-term cooperation.

Special attention needs to be paid to the opportunities for access to culture and cultural content of young people. Moreover, access to culture, in the broad sense of the term, is regulated in a number of international documents, including: Recommendation of the European Parliament and of the Council of the European Union of 18 December 2006 on key competences for lifelong learning; Resolution of the Council of the European Union of 16 November 2007 on a European Agenda for Culture and its strategic objectives; The study on youth access to culture commissioned by the European Commission; The Resolution of the Council of the European Union of 27 November 2009 on a renewed framework for European cooperation in the youth field (2010–2018); The Conclusions of the Council of the European Union of 27 November 2009 on the Promotion of Creative Generation; The Conclusions of the Council of the European Union of 19 November 2010 on the access of young people to culture; The revised European Charter on the Participation of Young People in the Life of Municipalities and Regions adopted by the Congress of Local and Regional Authorities in Europe (X Session, 21 May 2003); Opinion of the International Federation of Librarian Associations and Institutions (IFLA) on open access to information; Report of DG "Culture and Education" of the European Commission "Public and Trade Models for Access in the Digital Age"; The National Youth Strategy 2010–2020, which defines public support for the inclusion of young people in culture and art as the main national target for the development of young people in Bulgaria; The Youth Act, which requires the coordination of youth policies in the field of culture as a basic principle of national youth policy; The Law on Protection and Development of Culture. In this context is also the Appeal of the Bulgarian Association of Culture Workers who address all responsible state institutions and require "facilitating the access of all young people to culture by reducing the related obstacles (financial, linguistic, time and geography), enhancing the role of education and training in the arts within the perspective of lifelong learning and using targeted programs" [6]. In today's information and knowledge society, the outlined picture of a lack of access to culture for a significant part of the population, including a high percentage of young people, is a serious challenge in shaping policies in this area.

European Programs. The funds provided by different programs are significant but not sufficient. The criteria for the following selection is their effectiveness: the eContentplus program (2005–2008), the multiannual Community program for greater accessibility, usability and exploitation of digital content in Europe; ICT Policy Support Program of the Competitiveness and Innovation Framework Program; AthenaPlus - Access to networks providing cultural heritage through Europeana; innovative E-Culture services; BG08 "CULTURAL HERITAGE AND CONTEMPORARY ARTS"; The initiatives "European Capital of Culture", "European Year" (2018 declared a cultural heritage year) and "European Heritage Days"; the program of the National Culture Fund: Cultural Heritage and Cultural Tourism, The funds provided by different programs are significant but not sufficient. with two modules: "Cultural heritage" for preservation and promotion of the intangible cultural heritage of Bulgaria and development of means for improved access to cultural heritage through digital technologies and transmission of cultural content and "Cultural Tourism" for the promotion of Bulgaria's cultural heritage through cultural tourism. An example of "good practice" is the platform for digitization of cultural heritage under the project "Digital Cultural and Historical Heritage of the Municipality of Plovdiv", which supports the "sustainable development of culture as a guarantee for the formation of the value system of the personality and an indicator for achievement of Higher Quality of Life" [7]. As is well known, Plovdiv and Matera are chosen as European Capitals of Culture in 2019, which is another opportunity to present the cultural heritage.

European Projects. The selected below projects show the direct role of Information and Communication Technologies (ICT) for preservation of cultural values and provide better access to cultural heritage (CH). They are example of "good practices" as well. As was mentioned above the criteria for their selection is their importance for the Bulgarian society and for the preservation of European cultural values: *The project of F. M.US.EU.M.* Virtual European Roots Museum with a portal in four languages. On 15 November 2007 a project of the Italian organization EURO INNOVANET under the LLP-Leonardo Da Vinci Program (2007–2010), LLP-LDV/TOI/07/IT/016, was launched. The project is funded by the European Commission and is being implemented in partnership with seven other organizations from Italy, Romania and Bulgaria - Rome Municipality; Research center Centro Ricerche Sociali Soc. Coop. a.r., Rome. Archaeological Museum of Pitilliano; Lucian Blaga University, Sibiu; Banat Museum, Timisoara; Culture Foundation Annymi, Sofia; Regional Historical "Acad. Yordan Ivanov". Association partners from the Bulgarian side are the Regional Museum of History, Rousse and the Archaeological Museum, Veliko Tarnovo. The name of the project is FM.USEU.M (a form of a multimedia system for a European museum), its main purpose is to transfer and systemize the products, and the results achieved and realized during the implementation of the MU.S.EU.M project. European virtual museum with web address www.europeanvirtualmuseum.net, including collections of partner museums, detailed photographed and presented in a three-dimensional model; *The Europeana Project (Europeana - European Digital Library)* and the Bulgarian Libraries. The project has been launched in 2008 at the initiative of the European Commission and aims at facilitating access to digital content stored in the four main types of cultural organizations - libraries, museums, archives and audiovisual archives. The portal helps to find different information, stimulates future digitization initiatives through a single interface (in the native language of each user) enables citizens to find digitized cultural content from established cultural organizations throughout the European Union and to use this content for work, learning and fun. Bulgaria is represented by the National Library and some larger public libraries. The Europeana project is one of the largest European free resource initiatives. For its users, it is a single point of access to millions of books, pictures, films, museum exhibits, and archival documents that are digitized across Europe, and it is an authoritative source of information coming from European cultural and scientific institutions; *Digitization Projects of the National Library "St. St. Cyril and Methodius":* Project Center for Digitization and Storage of Documents and Archives at the National Library (Digital Library), 2006. Financed with targeted funds by the Ministry of Finance and supported by the Ministry of Culture; DAPIS Project (Digital Archives and Documents: Promotion, Study, Preservation), 2007-2009 MES Research Fund; Virtual Library Project - Bulgaria, Stage I; Project Digitization and Preservation of the Writing Wealth of Bulgaria (BG0046), approved for financing under the Financial Mechanism of the European Economic Area (EEA FM); Project Manuscripts and Documentary Monuments from the Bulgarian Lands XII–XVII Century, 2009–2011 MES Research Fund; TELPlus European Library Project 2007; The European Digital Library - NCBM has been a full participant since January 1, 2009 (EC eContentPlus Program); World Digital Library Project - Co-operation agreement and participation contract concluded (mainly provision of digitized rare collections); International Project IMPACT - participation in its second phase [8]; *A joint project of the Central Bank of the Bulgarian Academy of Sciences with the Institute of Literature at the Bulgarian Academy of Sciences and the British Library.* Digitization and presentation in the electronic catalog of the medieval manuscripts and for this purpose a model for describing copies of medieval manuscripts is developed. Digitization of Scientific Heritage Project - 2006 Joint project with the Center for Digitization at the Institute of Mathematics and Informatics - Bulgarian Academy of Sciences. Presentation of the most popular and popular newspapers published in the period 1890–1930; *Academic periodicals project.* Joint project with the Academic Publishing House "Prof. Marin Drinov". The purpose is to make the electronic catalog of the Central Library a portal for access to the electronic versions of the periodicals of the Bulgarian Academy of Sciences. This is the foundation of a project with the LOCKSS Public Library in the United States; *Project Michael:* Multilingual Inventory of Europe's Cultural Heritage [12]. So far, in this site, the section "Social and Human Sciences" contains the resources: Bibliotheca Slavica (UB and Faculty of Slavic Studies at Sofia University St. Kliment Ohridski); Renaissance Art (Archaeological Museum, Plovdiv); Ancient Greek Art (Archaeological Museum, Plovdiv); Multimedia database for authentic musical folklore with over 150 000 records (BAS); Numismatics (Regional Museum of History, Kyustendil); *Project Bibliotheca Slavica.* Since 2002 - today. Open Society Foundation and UNESCO. The project is devoted to the Bulgarian Slavic and University Science. Describes electronically the old, rare and valuable Slavonic books from the University Library "St. Kliment Ohridski ", offers bio-bibliographical information for the lecturers from the Sofia University and the most important Slavonic studies from the 19th and 20th centuries [11]; *"Varna Digital Library"* includes a variety of documents for Varna and the region, owned by the library, as well as materials from other cultural institutes in the city, community centers in the region as well as private collectors. The collection merges digitized documents with metadata - analytical descriptions of artifacts [9].

3 Results

The gathered factuality clearly demonstrates the initiation of a digitization process in a number of public libraries, archives and museums. Progress in libraries is greatest. Numerous European and international programs enable the implementation of projects to fund the preservation of cultural values through digitization and other methods of expanded access to cultural content. A positive sign in political aspect gives the initiative of Pencho Slaveikov Regional Library - Varna and the Europeana Foundation which organized a conference "Vision for European Cultural Heritage 2025", held in the framework of the cultural program of the Bulgarian Presidency of the Council of the European Union on May 28–29, 2018. The conference is a contribution to the European Year of Cultural Heritage and is in line with the key priorities of the Bulgarian presidency in the field of culture [9]. Maria Gabriel stated that the European Commission strategy for digitization of the industry has a budget of 500 million euros and the goal is to develop hubs (in Varna is the first digital innovation hub in Bulgaria) by 2020 in all areas of socio-economic life. After 2020, 90% of jobs will require digital skills. However, 169 million Europeans currently do not meet these requirements. According to European Commission data, more than 17 000 municipalities from the whole European Union have registered for financing projects free public wireless Internet, Bulgaria being one of the first - with more than 200 municipalities registered [13]. **These trends can develop the economy of the regions and give a positive impact to the quality of human resources trough education and training**.

4 Conclusions

Today, there are a number of new opportunities that modern technologies create to ensure the preservation of cultural values on the one hand and to enhance an access to cultural content on the other. First, this is the process of digitization, which has already started successfully for most Bulgarian libraries, archives and museums. **The results of the study confirmed the hypothesis.** What is lacking at this stage is a National Digitization Strategy and a National Center to coordinate the work of all cultural institutions on digitization. In conclusion, we can summarize that the search for opportunities to expand access to cultural content have to be combined with the measures taken against poverty, social exclusion, digital divide and the unbalanced development of the network of cultural institutes throughout the country. Very important is to choose ICT that are suitable for preservation of cultural heritage and to be "user's friendly". **The main problems of digitalization in Bulgaria, which have to be resolved in the near future, are: qualified digitization requires specialized book scanners, as well as applied computer configurations, image processing software, digital content administration software, and a suitable web application for publishing and managing collections on the Internet**. It is also necessary to provide an archival storage of digital objects - servers for permanent archiving. Most of these costs are impossible for the limited budget of the Bulgarian libraries, archives and museums. Another problem is the lack of qualified staff. **The digitization of cultural values facilitates access to cultural content, which can be a motivation for cultural** tourism. **The economic impacts of cultural tourism are extremely important for Bulgaria, its regional planning and economic development. They are seen as "new revenue" and additional investment in arts and culture. The purpose of the development of cultural tourism is to make a dignified heritage a valuable economic resource (Strategic Plan for the Development of Cultural Tourism in Bulgaria, p. 3). Its impact is manifested through sales, profits, tax revenues, income in the cultural sphere, local business development and employment growth in the sector. There is also an increase in local production, as cultural tourism activities are strongly related to other sectors of the economy.** All this helps to keep people in the region, which is a positive indicator of economic growth. **The economic benefits associated with the development of cultural tourism in the destinations are numerous: more visitors mean more revenue in the local economy; development of small business; raising tax revenues; attracting external investors; creating a labor market; contribution to gross domestic product; creating cultural industries; less dependence on seasonality** [2]. According to TripBarometer statistics, there are six trends for 2019, one of which is that the choice of destinations will be determined by the availability of cultural attractions and special offers in the country. 47% of travelers around the world say they have visited a destination because of the culture and people there. According to Eurobarometer data for 2016, 26% of respondents said that culture is the main motive for travel. In Bulgaria, this is claimed by 10% of the tourists, but there are tendencies for increase. **In this context, the recently launched project of the Ministry of Culture for the Digitization of Cultural Values is particularly useful.** The contract is for financial support for the implementation of the project "Digitization of the archive of the immovable cultural objects of world and national significance, construction of a specialized information system, electronic register and public portal" under the procedure "Priority projects in implementation of the Roadmap for implementation of the Strategy for the development of e-government in the Republic of Bulgaria for the period 2016-2020" of the Operational Program" Good Governance". The total value of the project is BGN 2 000 000 (appr. 1 021 294 EURO), with BGN 1 700 000 (appr. 868 100 EURO) provided by the European Social Fund and BGN 300 000 (appr. 153 194 EURO) is the national funding. The implementation of the project's objectives will contribute to the identified needs related to the digitization of the archives of the world wide and national real estate, the introduction of an information system and the provision of services electronically [14]. **The Register is expected to serve not only the needs of the administration but also to serve the needs of education and professional training of specialists in the preservation and socialization of cultural values. An impact assessment and the benefits of this project will be assessed after its completion.**

The author does not claim full comprehensiveness of the subject concerned. **At this stage, there is not enough statistical data on the direct link between the role of ICT in increasing access to cultural content and how it affects growth and the economy taking into account education, tourism, research and the involvement of local industry.** The study will be continued and focused in these issues and can serve to both specialists and researchers, as well as to professionals who want to increase their qualification and level of knowledge in the field of the role of ICT in enhancing access to cultural content and its impact on the development of society and the economy in Bulgaria.

References

1. Erasov, B.: Social Culturology, Sofia (1997)
2. Tylis, K.: Culture as a factor of economic development (2006). http://poieinkaiprattein.org/economy/culture-and-economy/culture-as-a-factor-of-social-andeconomic-development—the-polish-experience-by-karolina-tylus/. Accessed 10 Aug 2018
3. https://www.investor.bg/drugi/338/a/broiat-na-miliarderite-po-sveta-raste-a-s-tova-i-globalnoto-neravenstvo-254255/. 12 Aug 2018
4. http://www.nsi.bg/bg/content/3552/culture. Accessed 15 Mar 2018
5. Culture statistics 2016 edition, Eurostat. file:///F:/ACCESS/KS-04-15-737-EN-N.pdf. Accessed 2 Apr 2018
6. Appeal to participants of the 3rd National Conference "Access of young people to culture" of 12 August 2015, declared by the United Nations International Day of Youth. http://barok.bg/news/562/. Accessed 03 Apr 2018
7. https://www.capital.bg/reklama/2017/12/14/3097371_digitalizaciiata_na_kulturnoto_nasledstvo_lesna_i. Accessed 04 Apr 2018
8. http://www.rodina-bg.org/digitalna-biblioteka. Accessed 23 Apr 2018
9. http://www.chernomore.bg/kultura/2018-05-10/evropeyskoto-kulturno-nasledstvo-obsazhdat-eksperti-vav-varna. Accessed 27 Apr 2018
10. http://alpharesearch.bg/bg/socialni_izsledvania/socialni_publikacii.html. Accessed 22 May 2018
11. www.libsu.uni-sofia.bg/slavica. Accessed 20 Apr 2018
12. http://eprints.nbu.bg/. Accessed 23 Mar 2018
13. https://www.varna24.bg/novini/varna/Mariya-Gabriel-Gordeya-se-che-vuv-Varna-e-purviyat-digitalen-hub-v-Bulgariya-793490. Accessed 28 May 2018
14. http://mc.government.bg/files/4117_OPDU.docx. Accessed 08 Aug 2018

Non Destructive Techniques in Cultural Heritage Conservation

Contribution of e-Documentation to Technical Rescue Works and Conservation of the Mural Painting of the Dome of Blessed Ladislaus' Chapel in St. Anne's Church in Warsaw

Katarzyna Górecka[1(✉)], Ryszard Malarski[2], Piotr Pawłowski[3], and Marek Skłodowski[3]

[1] Faculty of Conservation and Restoration of Art,
Academy of Fine Arts in Warsaw, ul. Wybrzeże Kościuszkowskie 37,
00-379 Warsaw, Poland
katarzyna_gorecka@wp.pl
[2] Faculty of Geodesy and Cartography, Warsaw University of Technology,
Plac Politechniki 1, p. 311, 00-661 Warsaw, Poland
[3] Institute of Fundamental Technological Research,
Polish Academy of Sciences, ul. a. Pawińskiego 5B, 02-106 Warsaw, Poland

Abstract. The paper presents the application of various 3D imagining methods to study the state of the mural painting in the dome of Blessed Ladislaus' Chapel of St. Anne's Church in Warsaw. The temple was built on the embankment of the Vistula river in the XV-th century. The chapel was added to the nave in the XVII-th century. From the beginning this location of the church caused a lot of structural problems. The church stability was disturbed due to digging an underground tunnel nearby in the years 1947–49. The Ladislaus' Chapel, situated close to the tunnel on the side of the escarpment was the most endangered. The current rescue work of the mural painting of the chapel dome required an accurate measurement and inventory of the architectural structure. The dome was measured using various methods: laser scanning and photogrammetry. As a result we obtained 4 models of the chapel dome, which could be combined and compared.

Keywords: Laser scanning · Digital photogrammetry
St. Anne's Church in Warsaw

1 Introduction - Blessed Ladislaus' Chapel of the St. Anne's Church

1.1 Historical Context

St. Anne's Church in Warsaw was founded by Princess Anne of Masovia in 1454 for the Minor Order Friars brought from Cracow. A small gothic building was expanded in the XVI-th century by adding of a huge nave. In 1620 Blessed Ladislaus' Chapel was added to the church building at its north side. The mural decoration of the church and chapel dates from the XVIII-th century. It was accomplished by one of the monks - Walenty

© Springer Nature Switzerland AG 2018
M. Ioannides et al. (Eds.): EuroMed 2018, LNCS 11196, pp. 667–676, 2018.
https://doi.org/10.1007/978-3-030-01762-0_59

Żebrowski. The paintings in the chapel present the life of Blessed Ladislaus of Gielniow. They were created for a special occasion to announce his beatification [1]. The church, one of a few in Warsaw, wasn't heavily destroyed during the II World War.

1.2   The Condition of the Monument and Necessity of Rescue and Conservation Works

The building due to its location has always been exposed to structural problems caused by the subsiding of the Vistula escarpment. In the late 40's during the construction of the WZ (East-West) route running in a tunnel close to the church and over the bridge to the other bank of the Vistula river (Fig. 1), the escarpment slope stability was disturbed. Then the ground around the building was reinforced with piles and the foundation was encircled by a concrete crown.

Fig. 1. The Saint Anne's Church in Warsaw: view from the slope side.

The walls of Blessed Ladislaus' Chapel on the east-west axis cracked several times in the past. The stone base of the lantern was fragmented by serious structural ruptures. Therefore in the early XX-th century, its construction was tied with an iron clamp. In the southern part of the dome at 1/3 of its height, the upper part of the plaster was cracked and detached from the brick support. The chapel walls were repaired several times, hence later putties and retouching are overlapped in many places.

At the beginning of XX-th century the mural paintings of the chapel were renewed by painters who totally repainted the original XVIII-th century composition. After the II World War the over-paintings were removed, but during this operation many parts of the original decoration got lost. In the 80's of the XX-th century, the damaged paintings were restored and missing elements reconstructed. The cohesion of the original plaster and its adhesion to the support diminished. The surface of the painting was very dirty and the colour of the old retouches was changed (Fig. 2).

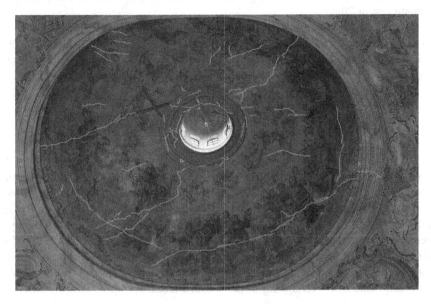

Fig. 2. The Saint Anne's Church in Warsaw: dome of the Blessed Ladislaus' chapel. State before conservation works.

Currently, the condition of the structure is constantly monitored. Comprehensive monitoring of the church itself and the walls retaining the slope includes: determining of the relative slope movement by inclinometer measurements, observations of the level of groundwater using piezometers, inventory of cracks and their changes.

A seasonal displacement of the ground below the foundation of Blessed Ladislaus' Chapel has been noticed. The changes of the width of the plaster cracks were determined by observations of the viewfinders fixed on the chapel wall surface [2].

1.3   The Project of Conservation and Restoration of the XVIII-th Century Painting of the Blessed Ladislaus' Chapel

The main goal of the project is to save the mural painting in the dome of Blessed Ladislaus' Chapel, which is extremely vulnerable to damage caused by seasonal wall structure cracking. Comprehensive conservation and restoration of the XVIII-th century polychrome is included in the scope of work as well. The execution of the project was divided into a few stages. In 2017 mainly technical works were carried out. The walls structure and plaster layers were consolidated, the stone base of the dome lantern was strengthened, old putties and concrete patches were taken out. The painting surface was cleaned from dust and over-paintings. On the lantern vault, an unknown polychrome by Walenty Żebrowski was uncovered from whitewash layers and burnt dust. The works are still in progress. In 2018 the cracks and losses of the plaster layer were filled. During works the researches on technique and technology of the painting were carried out, as well as on their iconographic and religious message [3]. Now we are working on the aesthetical arrangement of the painting decoration. The project will be continued in 2019.

Conservation and restoration works are lead by Katarzyna Górecka Ph.D. and Maria Paruszkiewicz - Pokorna. Eng. Grzegorz Osowicki is responsible for the technical works concerning the structure of the chapel walls and dome. The project is financed by the Polish Ministry of Culture and National Heritage.

2   Methods Applied

2.1   Geodetic Inventory by Using a Laser Scanner

The surface of the chapel dome with a lantern was measured before starting current conservation work in July 2017 using laser scanning. The scan was performed with Z + F IMAGER® 5006 h scanner by the expert team headed by Eng. Ryszard Malarski Ph.D. from the Chair of Geodesy and Cartography, Warsaw University of Technology. The measurement of the dome was made from the highest level of the steel scaffolding, situated at the height of 12 m from the floor level. Due to visibility problems, some fragments of the chapel walls were measured from a lower level of the scaffolding with 70% overlapping of the scanned areas.

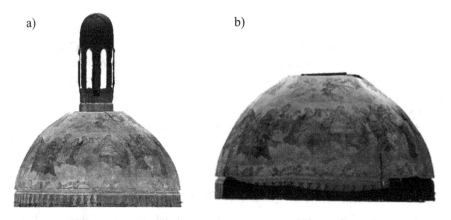

a)   b)

Fig. 3. The point clouds 3D models of the dome of the chapel obtained by terrestrial laser scanning: (a) high-resolution model, (b) decimated point cloud with mapped texture.

Scanner vibrations were damped by pads under the tripod legs. The measurement was made in the "super high" resolution, which provides the distance between the observed points on average of approx. 1.0 mm - depending on the target distance and the angle of incidence of the laser beam. The full resolution point cloud consists of

96 715 492 points (Fig. 3a) which results in a spatial resolution of approx. 194 points per 1 square centimeter. The scans were pre-processed and registered in the Z + F LaserControl software, while the final scans were oriented and aligned in the Astragis ASCAN software. The development of cross-sections and projections was carried out in the CAD environment.

A textured 3D model of the chapel dome based on the scanned data was obtained (c.f. Fig. 3b). The texture was mapped from high-resolution photos onto the decimated, laser scanned point cloud, which was reduced to 2 684 480 points. For each photo, 20 characteristic points were selected and matched to the point cloud. The error of linear and curvilinear distance measurements between points on photos and in the 3D model was kept below 1 mm. The attempt to apply a texture to the point cloud did not bring fully satisfactory results.

2.2 Photogrammetric Measurements Before Conservation Work

To obtain a 3D model of the chapel structures before conservation works a photogrammetric method was also used. The measurements were taken using a camera Canon 5D equipped with a 14 mm focal length lens. The pictures were taken from the scaffolding level in the ambient light (sunlight) and the spatial model of the chapel was calculated in the open-source Regard 3D program [4].

Fig. 4. The point cloud 3D model of the dome of the chapel obtained by photogrammetric measurements before the conservation works.

Ambient lighting used inside a building decreases resolution of fine details in the recorded pictures and therefore limits a number and accuracy of the points forming photogrammetric point clouds. The point cloud calculated on the basis of 106 recorded pictures includes 1 899 406 of registered points (Fig. 4). Taking into account the chapel dome surface area (approx. 50 m^2, calculated by Thomsen formula for surface area of ellipsoid [6]) the average spatial resolution obtained equals 3.8 points per square centimeter. The lower resolution and accuracy as compared with laser scanning results is compensated by the inherent colour information spatially correlated with the points of the cloud. Resulting 3D model of the chapel dome shows some dimensional differences as compared with the model from the laser scan, which is discussed below.

2.3 Photogrammetric Measurements After Conservation Works

Rescue and conservation works of the mural painting in the chapel had a wide range. The appearance of the dome has changed significantly as a result of these works. The following tasks were completed: the stone base of the lantern was reinforced, subsequent cement layers were removed, the original profiles of the lantern beams and the dome cornices were reconstructed, the structure of the chapel walls was consolidated, displaced fragments of the plaster were placed correctly, losses and cracks of the mortar plaster were filled with putties, the surface of the painting was cleaned of dust and over-paintings. For documentation purposes photogrammetric photos after conservation were taken by the company 4K Damian Kwiecień. A new 3D model of the chapel dome was obtained by a photogrammetric method using a camera Canon EOS 5D SR equipped with a 24 mm lens EF F1.4 L USM. Flashing lights Quantuum Quadralite Pulse 800 Pro (temperature of light 5600 K) were used. The 3D model of the chapel dome was generated in the Agisoft Photo Scan Pro 1.3.0 program [5]. The color scale X-Rite Color Checker Classic was applied.

Fig. 5. The point cloud 3D model of the dome of the chapel obtained by photogrammetric measurements after the conservation works.

Average spatial resolution of the obtained point cloud (Fig. 5) is 38 points per square centimeter (19 012 166 spatial points). In the Authors opinion a greater spatial resolution in the case of the second photogrammetric model can be attributed to better lighting conditions resulting in higher quality pictures than in the case of using ambient light only. The model is further compared to those calculated before the conservation work.

3   Results Obtained

3.1   Comparison of Measurements Accuracy

In order to estimate differences between the three geometrical measurements, the resulting point clouds were compared using the CloudCompare open-source software [7]. The decimated laser scanning model was assumed as the reference point cloud for distance measurements. The laser scanning seems to be accurate and not dependent on ambient conditions. The high-resolution model of the dome after the conservation was reduced to 5 208 252 points.

The photogrammetric models were pre-registered by point-pairs picking and then finely aligned using the ICP algorithm. The statistical analysis of the calculated scalar fields shows that 95% of points has the distance to the reference point cloud smaller than 0.036 m in the case of the model of the dome before conservation and 0.0046 m in the case of the model of the dome after conservation. A vertical cross-section of the models presented in Fig. 6, shows that even in the case of lower quality picture sets the obtained geometrical representation is satisfactory. A good correlation between laser scanning and the photogrammetric methods was also visible in the previous project carried out by the Authors, concerning the conservation of a curvilinear painting "Adoration of the Magi" from the Cathedral Church in Namur (Belgium) [8].

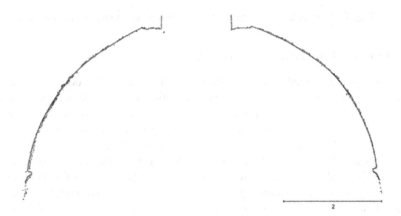

Fig. 6. Comparison of a vertical cross-section of the three point cloud 3D models of the dome of the chapel.

3.2   Measurement of the Architectural Structure

The method of terrestrial laser scanning enabled fast and precise measurement of the object. On the basis of the 3D model, sections and views of the dome of the chapel with a lantern were obtained (Fig. 7). Drawings were made in the CAD environment. The obtained data allowed to determine precisely the length and width of the dome (at the height of the cornice its width is 6.23 m, whereas the length is 7.26 m) and its height is 3.44 m. An asymmetry of the dome has been diagnosed. Its northern part is clearly larger than the south part (of 22 cm) and there is a misalignment of the lantern with respect to the axis of the dome. Establishing the precise size of the object was crucial for the implementation of a new bracing system of the lantern stone base. Based on the measurement, a steel rim was prepared (matching to the perimeter of the lantern drum) and the length of the anchors was estimated.

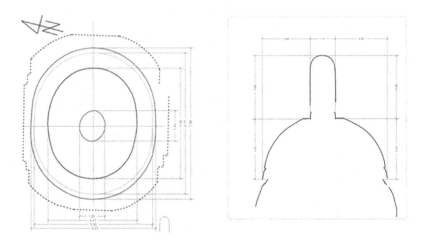

Fig. 7. Horizontal and vertical cross-sections of the dome of the chapel.

3.3   Analysis of the Painting Composition

The photogrammetric method allowed to build a 3D model of the dome with the color texture of the painting decoration before conservation and after cleaning and technical operations (removal of dirt layer and over-paintings). On the basis of the photogrammetric model of the dome, a panoramic unwrapping of the painting composition was made, which facilitated the research on the iconography of the scene (Fig. 8). The high accuracy of the obtained model made it easier to read the attributions of the presented Saints and Blessed. The procession is lead by Blessed Ladislaus of Gielniow to Holy Virgin, presented in the surroundings of the Holy Trinity. The 3D model of the dome's interior is the most complete photographic documentation at this stage of the conservation works. However, manipulating a file of such a high resolution and large size causes some difficulties.

Fig. 8. A panoramic unwrapping of the painting composition.

3.4 Analysis of the Painting Preservation State

The model obtained as a result of the laser scanning was used to analyze the state of preservation of the mural painting of the dome before the actual intervention. On 3D model, detailed cross-sections were made in the places of plaster cracks and old repairs. High accuracy of the model allowed to calculate the depth of plaster cracks and widths and thicknesses of secondary layers (putties). On the model obtained with the photogrammetric method, the range of retouching and reconstructions of the missing parts of the polychrome was evaluated. In the dome only some fragments of the original decoration have survived, as a large part of the mural painting has been reconstructed in the 1980s.

Mapping of the destruction of the painting layers was made on the panoramic photos (Fig. 9). Undoubtedly, in the future this type of mapping directly on the 3D model will be implemented.

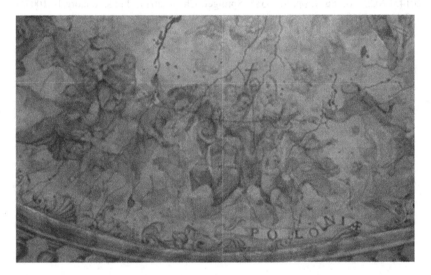

Fig. 9. A mapping of the destruction of the painting layers.

3.5 Monitoring of the Chapel State

The foundation of the chapel is not stable. Seasonal displacements of the slope ground may lead to cracking of the chapel walls and dome in the future. Re-scans of the dome's cup will give the possibility of combining them with previous measurements. In this way, the scanning could be used as a monitoring method supplementary to the geodetic survey of the chapel.

Acknowledgments. Authors wish to express thanks to Maria Pokorna MA in Conservation and Restoration of Art, conducting of the conservation project and to M.Sc.Eng. Grzegorz Osowicki, responsible for the technical works on the church construction. The works presented were supported by the Polish Ministry of Culture and Heritage.

References

1. Kaczmarzyk, D.: Kościół Św. Anny, Warsaw: PWN, pp. 204–221 (1984). (in Polish)
2. Malarski, R., Nagórski, K.: Inventory of cracks and determination of variations of their width in monumental objects, Przegląd Geodezyjny, Nr 5, pp. 39–44 (2013). (in Polish)
3. Górecka, K.: Technical rescue works on the construction of the Saint Anne's church in Warsaw as an opportunity to study the technique, technology and iconography of the XVIII-th century mural paintings. Eur. J. Sci. Theol. **12**(3), 233–242 (2016)
4. Regard3D. http://www.regard3d.org/. Accessed 21 May 2018
5. Agisoft. http://www.agisoft.com/. Accessed 21 May 2018
6. Michon, G.P.: Final Answers. Formulae for Spheroids & Scalene Ellipsoids. http://www.numericana.com/answer/ellipsoid.htm#ellipsoid. Accessed 21 May 2018
7. Cloud Compare. http://www.danielgm.net/cc/
8. Skłodowski, M., Pawłowski, P., Górecka, K.: Geometrical models of old curvilinear paintings. In: Chmielewski, L.J., Kozera, R., Shin, B.-S., Wojciechowski, K. (eds.) ICCVG 2014. LNCS, vol. 8671, pp. 578–585. Springer, Cham (2014). https://doi.org/10.1007/978-3-319-11331-9_69

On the Integration of Digital 2D and 3D Survey Models for the Geometrical Configuration and the Damage Assessment of a Medieval Building in Venice

Antonella Manzo[✉]

Politecnico di Milano, Piazza Leonardo da Vinci, 32, 20133 Milan, Italy
antonella.manzo@polimi.it

Abstract. Nowadays more and more innovative survey techniques allow gathering detailed information about historical buildings, their present conditions, the materials composing them and the structural problems mining their stability. Within this context, the integration of digital 2D and 3D survey models can provide a deeper insight on both the present geometrical configuration and the constructive phases, allowing, at the same time, a detailed damage assessment. More specifically, an overview of the complex geometries, the irregular cross-sections and vertical deviations of the buildings can be achieved by juxtaposing sections taken from the point cloud with orthophotos or images obtained through digital rectification. This method can also be used as a support to visual analyses such as stratigraphic or crack pattern surveys. The present paper discusses the advantages of integrating the modern survey techniques of laser scanning and photogrammetric models through photorealistic images and accurate measurements of the Venetian Byzantine church of Santa Fosca on Torcello Island. This building, indeed, lends itself well to the purpose of this work, due to its peculiar geometrical configuration, the numerous modifications occurred throughout the centuries and the current structural damages.

Keywords: Point cloud survey · 3D photogrammetric models
Stratigraphic analysis · Crack pattern survey · Vertical deviations
Santa Fosca church

1 Introduction

Nowadays the integration of information obtained from plotting results coming from the several digital data acquisition technologies is a very helpful and useful method for the analysis and study of cultural heritage [1, 2]. More in details, in the architectonic field, photogrammetry and topography can give important information about the complex geometries and the constructive techniques of the buildings [3, 4]. Ortophotos obtained through 3D and 2D models as well as 2D images rectification represent the building materials, providing photorealistic textures, used as basis to draw discontinuities and crack patterns on the elevations of the building as well as on the floors and covering systems. On the other hand, the point cloud can help to identify the state of

© Springer Nature Switzerland AG 2018
M. Ioannides et al. (Eds.): EuroMed 2018, LNCS 11196, pp. 677–688, 2018.
https://doi.org/10.1007/978-3-030-01762-0_60

damage of the case study by analyzing the vertical deviations taken from its cross-sections [5]. In fact, as it is well-known, laser scanning outlines the 'skin' of the construction [6] and allows for a very detailed measuring and drawing of the case study: it highlights the irregularities in the geometry, as well as the several deviations and possible settlements of the structure by analysing the slices of the point cloud. The results obtained by means of the integration of the data acquired from both pho-togrammetry and laser scanning are hence more accurate and precise than the tradi-tional investigation techniques.

However, these survey techniques present some disadvantages: (a) the laser scan-ning requires very expensive tools, not accessible to most of the technicians that need to carry out the buildings survey; (b) both point cloud and 3D photogrammetric models are obtained through very time-consuming processes that need complex elaborations. Therefore, in order to avoid wasting time, and to undertake accessible measurements, simpler methods can be chosen depending on the purpose of the analysis.

In view of the above, the present contribution aims at providing an analysis of the geometries, materials and structural problems of Santa Fosca on Torcello Island, an eleventh century church located on the North side of the Venetian Lagoon. In fact, thanks to its very peculiar spatial organization and evident state of damage, this building lends itself well to the purpose of this work. Due to its very uncommon architectural system, indeed, Santa Fosca can be defined as a *unicum*: it is composed of a Greek cross plan with a particularly developed apse and very short West, North and South arms. The intersection of the four arms generates a square central space, delimited at its corners by four masonry pillars and surrounded by eight columns, which support unusual couples of overlapping niches. A wood roof finally covers the central space. By means of this spatial organization, it is possible to achieve the transition from the square at the ground level to the circle at the level of the upper drum. This architectural scheme brought scholars to compare Santa Fosca since the 1800s to a limited group of Middle-Byzantine basilicas built in Greece during the 11th– 12th century: the so-called "churches of the octagonal domed type" [7]. However, unlike Santa Fosca, a masonry dome crowns the central naos of these churches. Probably just for this comparison, the assumption according to which Santa Fosca was originally covered by a dome was mentioned ever more among the scholars, who studied the church in the past [8–11].

The development of 2D and 3D digital models cannot provide an answer to the age-old problem about the dome; however, it can give some hints about its present con-ditions and structural problems.

Firstly, the integration of data obtained from the several survey methods carried out within this contribution can provide a huge number of information related to the geometry of the building. Through the elaboration of a series of images from the 3D photogrammetric and laser scanner models, the proposed approach simplifies the complex perception of the real architecture. Afterwards, the materials, constructive techniques and structural damages are investigated to provide an overall view of the church, its present condition and a deeper knowledge on its most recent history.

2 Combining Point Cloud and 3D Photogrammetry Models for Defining the Geometry

The point cloud used for the analysis of the case study has been acquired by the 3DEG Office (Treviso, Italy) on December 2012 (Fig. 1a). Several scans, afterwards combined together, were produced with a time-of-flight scanner, a Leica ScanStation C10. The acquired data were subsequently processed by means of the CYCLONE software system and imported in Autocad for the analysis of the cross-sections.

Santa Fosca photogrammetric 3D model reconstruction has been carried out instead with Agisoft Photoscan. The 501 photos used for elaborating the model were taken every 3 m at a maximum distance of 3.5 m from the walls. By estimating the camera positions, the program automatically calculated the information for each camera and combined them into a single dense point cloud, whose result is shown in Fig. 1b.

(a)   (b)

Fig. 1. Santa Fosca 3D models: (a) the point cloud of the outside; (b) the photogrammetric model of the inside.

A selection of the slices of the point cloud, combined with the corresponding orthophotos of the photogrammetric model, can provide several cross-sections, showing the masonry pattern as well as the complex inside development of the elevations. As an example, Fig. 2 shows the longitudinal cross-sections in the middle of the central nave (Fig. 2a) and in the middle of the Northern aisle (Fig. 2b). The comparison between the two drawings confirms the very different development of the central space with respect to the lateral ones. In fact, Fig. 2a allows to appreciate the spaciousness of the inside, whereas Fig. 2b highlights the two peculiar couples of hemispherical niches, which, as previously mentioned, allow the transition from the square plan of the ground level to the circular base of the drum.

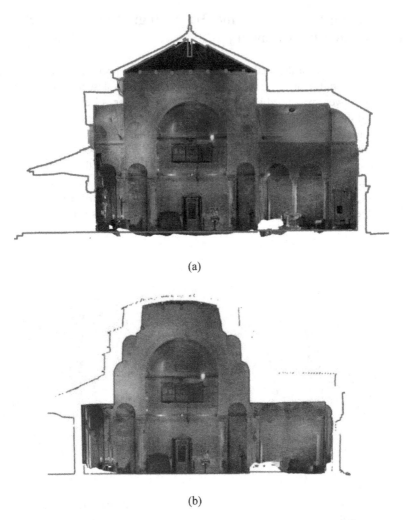

(a)

(b)

Fig. 2. The combination between the slice of the point cloud and the ortophoto for reproducing the Northern inside elevation of Santa Fosca church: (a) the cross-section in the middle of the central nave; (b) the cross-section in the middle of the Northern aisle.

By comparing these two elevations, it is also possible to remark that the drum is vertical in the middle of the church, whereas it is characterised by an irregular development in the proximity of the couples of niches at the corners of the square central space. The irregularities in the geometry of the drum can be further appreciated by inspecting the juxtaposition of the four slices of the point cloud taken at the corners of the square central space in the middle of the aisles and reported in Fig. 3.

It can be here observed that although the builders aimed at the construction of the perfect figure of the circle, this drum has been built in a rather imperfect way.

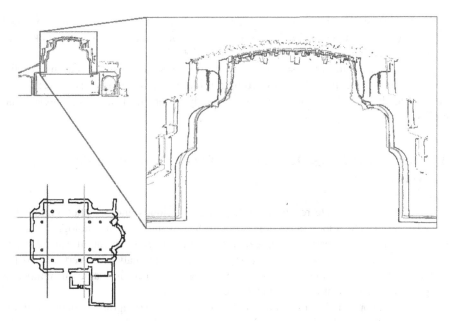

Fig. 3. Juxtaposition of the slices taken in the middle of the aisles

The courses are slightly corbelled, as highlighted by the N-E cross-section of the drum, taken right above the couples of niches (Fig. 4). In fact, at the corners of the central square, the complete realization of the circle is achieved only at the top of the drum and is possible through the presence of the transition elements and the diagonal development of the drum itself. Furthermore, the corresponding orthophoto reveals that different masonry patterns characterise this upper part of the church, composed of

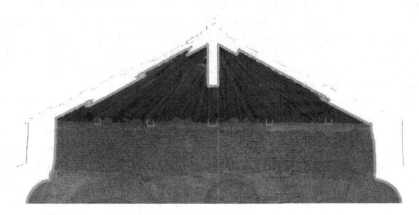

Fig. 4. Detail of the drum looking at the N-E direction: juxtaposition of a diagonal slice with the corresponding ortophoto

portions of reused bricks alternating areas where bricks are very small, the so-called *altinelle*, (not more than 17–18 cm long). The diffusion of these small bricks took place all around the Venetian lagoon until the early 1500s [12].

Unfortunately, the drum stratigraphic analysis was not possible, because of the distance, the lack of light, the repointed mortar hiding the bed mortar. However, it can be noticed that the drum masonry pattern totally differs from the lower arches and niches.

3   The Digital Image Rectification for the Stratigraphic Analysis

Despite the very accurate results provided by point clouds and 3D photogrammetric models, faster and more accessible digital data acquisition technologies can be sometimes more appropriate. As an example, digital image rectification can substitute the elaboration of 3D models in the case of stratigraphic analysis of vertical and flat surfaces. This process, indeed, is not time-consuming, since only a small number of images can be sufficient to cover the entire analysed area.

Such an approach has been chosen to carry out the stratigraphic analysis of the outside elevations under the porch of Santa Fosca church. This analysis was possible, since the pinkish homogeneous plaster covering these elevations was removed during the restoration works carried out in the last years. It was hence possible to appreciate the different stratigraphic sequences and the bed mortars, hence the borders, composing these portions of the walls. On the other hand, it was not possible to carry out the same procedure inside the church since repointing mortar extensively hid the borders of the stratigraphic units and did not allow detecting the stratigraphic sequences and relations.

3.1   The Outside Elevations Under the Porch

All the outside elevations under the porch underwent a digital image rectification by means of the geometrical method of RDF, a software produced by the Venetian University IUAV. As an example, Fig. 5a reports the Western side under the porch resulting from the combination of eight rectified photos. In some cases, the view of the elevations is discontinuous or incomplete, due to scaffolding surrounding the porch during the restoration works.

Figure 5b reports the mapping of the Western elevation under the porch, subsequently undertaken. Four principal stratigraphic units can be recognised: the first two (yellow and orange in the figure) probably belong to medieval construction periods, while the other ones (green and red) result from two interventions of the past century. The same analysis has been carried out for all the elevations under the porch, highlighting that only the Southern side has been completely modified in the last century, whereas on the other walls the most ancient stratigraphic units are still present.

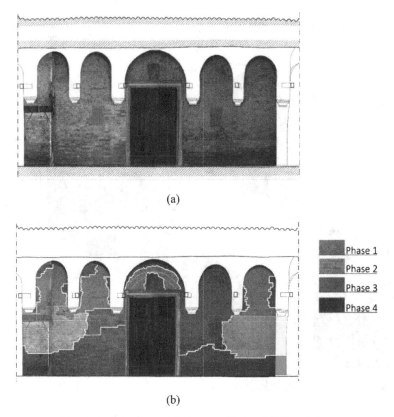

(a)

(b)

Fig. 5. The outer elevation under the porch on the Western side: (a) the result of digital image rectification; (b) the stratigraphic mapping. (Color figure online)

3.2 The Inside Elevations

As already pointed out, it was not possible to carry out a stratigraphic analysis on the inside masonry walls. Some considerations, however, can be put forward through a systematic comparison with the outside masonry pattern and a critical review of the information on the past restorations coming from the available written sources. As an example, the green areas on the Southern and Northern inside elevations in Fig. 6 show the same brick typology present outside and highlighted with the green colour in Fig. 5b. Through the archival documentation, furthermore, it is possible to discover that these portions of the walls were those reconstructed by Domenico Rupolo in the early 1900s, since: (a) the brick dimensions correspond to those described during that intervention; (b) Rupolo extensively demolished and reconstructed the analysed elevations. Additionally, the present condition of both the Northern and Southern façades is compared to a photo of 1910, before Rupolo's intervention, when the Northern wall was seriously damaged. By means of the axonometric view it is possible to notice that crack *a* on the North side, captured in the photo of 1910 and highlighted in green, seems to correspond to discontinuity *a* on the current South elevation.

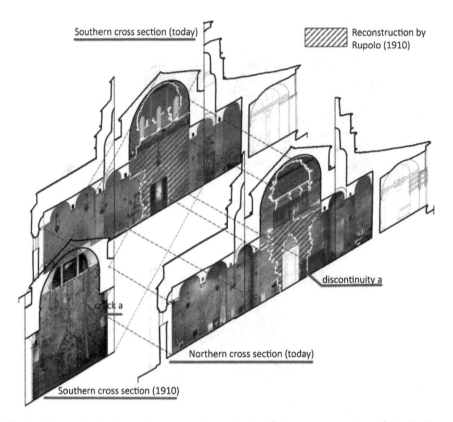

Fig. 6. Comparison between the present discontinuity of the masonry pattern of the Northern side and the crack pattern of the Southern side in 1910.

The digital image rectifications and the photo of 1910, combined with the geometrical survey of the Southern and Northern elevations, allow drawing some remarks about the present and past conditions: it is indeed possible that the mechanism shown in the picture of 1910 was symmetric and involved the Southern façade as well.

4   The Analysis of the State of Damage Through the Integration of the Several Survey Methods

The last step involves the analysis of the structural state of damage of the church: the present crack pattern and the vertical deviations are analysed within this section by integrating the several survey methods, already mentioned in the frame of this work.

On the one hand, for the analysis of the crack pattern the images provided by the digital rectification are combined with the orthophotos of the 3D model. In fact, as already seen, while the former can depict only flat objects, the latter provides also rectified images of the curved portions. In this way, besides the vertical cross sections with the niches and the drum of the central space, previously seen, the projection of the vaults can be elaborated.

The documentation of the vertical deviations is carried out, instead, with the analysis of the cross-sections taken from the point cloud combined with the orthophotos obtained from the 3D photogrammetric model.

4.1   The Crack Pattern Survey

As it can be seen in Figs. 7 and 8, Santa Fosca church shows an evident crack pattern that involves both the intradoses of the vaults and the inside elevations. An outline of such an analysis has been already presented in [13], where some remarks on the most probable causes of damage have been discussed.

In Fig. 7, the crack pattern has been depicted on the geometrical survey integrated with the orthophoto of the intrados of the vaults. Cracks run across the vaults along the crown and along the arches at the keystones, following the usual trend [14]. Some minor fissures develop on the intrados of the Eastern barrel vault from the springers to the crown, closely recalling the typical crack pattern of a masonry dome [15].

The analysis of both the elevations and the vaults plan view points out that the most serious state of damage involves the Western portion (Fig. 8). The discontinuity crossing slantwise the floor on the S-W corner confirms this observation. A differential ground settlement probably mines the stability of this portion.

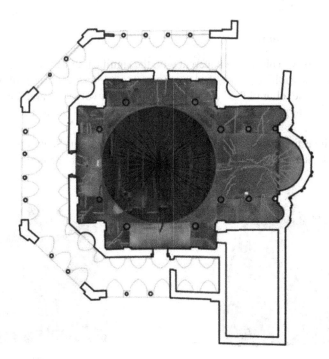

Fig. 7. The orthophoto of the vaults combined with the geometrical survey of Santa Fosca horizontal section

The photo taken in 1910 and shown in Fig. 6 can be recalled, since it shows a fissure that just divides the S-W corner from the rest of the church, confirming hence that even in that period there were probably problems due to ground settlements.

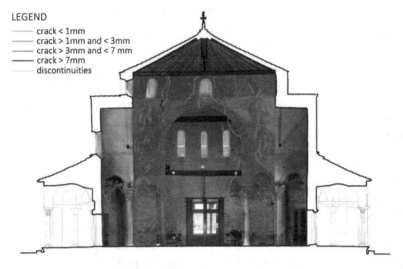

Fig. 8. The orthophoto of the Western elevation combined with the geometrical survey of Santa Fosca horizontal section

4.2   The Out of Plumbs

The fissures observed above are coherent with the significant internal vertical deviation. In Fig. 9, it is possible to notice that the maximum vertical deviation, of about 0.1 m from the ground level until the height of about 3.5 m, involves, again, the S-W corner. In this way, the hypothesis that this portion of the church is subject to ground settlements is confirmed.

Further investigation is required to know the details about Santa Fosca foundation system and hence prove the assumption formulated within this contribution.

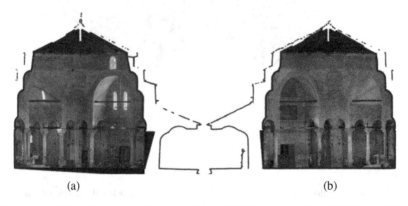

(a)   (b)

Fig. 9. Juxtaposition of point cloud and ortophoto: (a) S-E cross section; (b) N-E cross section.

5 Conclusive Remarks

This framework has shown the advantages of integrating the several modern survey techniques to analyse and study historical buildings. By means of photorealistic images and accurate measurements, it is indeed possible to evaluate dimensions, irregularities, as well as discontinuities in the masonry pattern, aiming at understanding not only the geometry, but also investigating the materials, constructive techniques and structural damages of the case studies.

More specifically, the modern survey technologies have been selected and combined to explain and clarify the complex geometry and to recognise the stratigraphic phases and structural problems of the church of Santa Fosca. In this way, it has been possible to demonstrate that the present building is the result of several complex constructive phases and that currently suffers structural damage probably due to ground settlements.

It is here worth stressing that historical buildings are meant as the first reliable study document to be taken into account, in order to find more information about their present condition and about the past events, too. The several methods shown within this framework are a valid support to reach this goal.

Acknowledgments. The author would like to thank the 3DEG Office for the point cloud and Patriarcato di Venezia for the permission of taking photos of the inside of Santa Fosca church.

References

1. Battini, C., Vecchiattini, R.: Survey and restoration: new ways of interaction. In: The International Archives of the Photogrammetry, Remote Sensing and Spatial Information Sciences, Volume XLII-5/W1, GEOMATICS & RESTORATION – Conservation of Cultural Heritage in the Digital Era, Florence, Italy, 22–24 May 2017, pp. 655–662 (2017)
2. Bevilacqua, M.G., Caroti, G., Piemonte, A., Ruschi, P., Tenchini, L.: 3D survey techniques for the architectural restoration: the case of St. Agata in Pisa. In: The International Archives of the Photogrammetry, Remote Sensing and Spatial Information Sciences, Volume XLII-5/W1, GEOMATICS & RESTORATION – Conservation of Cultural Heritage in the Digital Era, Florence, Italy, 22–24 May 2017, pp. 441–447 (2017)
3. Oreni, D., Fassi, F., Brumana, R., Prandi, F., Tuncer, H.: Laser scanning supports architectural mappings and historical urban view analysis. In: XXI International CIPA Symposium, Athens, Greece, 1–6 October 2007 (2007)
4. Barazzetti, L., Banfi, F., Brumana, R.: Historic BIM in the cloud, in digital heritage progress in cultural heritage: documentation, preservation, and protection. In: 6th International Conference, EuroMed, Proceedings, Part I, Nicosia, Cyprus, 31 October–5 November 2016 (2016)
5. Manzo, A., Chesi, C.: Building techniques and structural damage of historical constructions detected through the point cloud survey. In: Aguilar, R., Torrealva, D., Moreira, S., Pando, M.A., Ramos, L.F. (eds.) Structural Analysis of Historical Constructions. RB, vol. 18, pp. 135–143. Springer, Cham (2019). https://doi.org/10.1007/978-3-319-99441-3_13

6. Vernizzi, C.: Rilievo e "Laser Scanner": dalla nuvola di punti al modello 3D per lo studio delle volte del Duomo di Parma. In: Blasi, C., Coisson, E. (eds.) La Fabbrica del Duomo di Parma. Stabilità, rilievi e modifiche nel tempo, Grafiche Step, Parma (2006)

7. Manzo, A.: Santa Fosca in Torcello and the middle byzantine churches in eastern Greece: preliminary comparison and remarks on common features and differences. Athens J. Hist. **2** (1), 43–58 (2016)

8. Hübsch, H.: Die altchristlichen Kirchen nach den Baudenkmalen und älteren Beschreibungen und der Einfluss des altchristlichen Baustyls auf den Kirchenbau aller späteren Perioden Atlas enthaltend 63 Platten nebst deren Erklärung auf drei Bogen, Karlsruhe (1863)

9. Corroyer, E.: L'Architecture Romane. Société Francaise d'Edition d'Art, Paris (1888)

10. Krautheimer, R.: Early Christian and Byzantine Architecture. Yale University Press (1986)

11. Concina, E.: Santa Fosca di Torcello. In Le chiese di Venezia: l'arte e la storia, Magnus Edizioni, Udine, pp. 120–123 (1995)

12. Piana, M.: Note sulle tecniche murarie dei primi secoli dell'edilizia lagunare. In: Valcanover, F., Wolters, W. (eds.) L'architettura Gotica Veneziana, Atti del Convegno internazionale di Studio Venezia, Venezia, 27 novembre 1996, Istituto Veneto di Scienze Lettere ed Arti, pp. 61–70 (2000)

13. Manzo, A., Chesi, C.: Stability problems of the church of Santa Fosca on Torcello Island. In: Structural Analysis of Historical Constructions (SAHC 2016), Leuven, Belgium, 13–15 September, pp. 1728–1735 (2016)

14. Piccirilli, C.: Consolidamento critico e sue premesse storico-strutturali. Multigrafica Editrice, Roma (1989)

15. Heyman, J.: The Stone Skeleton: Structural Engineering of Masonry Architecture. Cambridge University Press, Cambridge (1995)

A Methodology for the Inspection and Monitoring of the Roof Tiles and Concrete Components of the Sydney Opera House

Gianluca Ranzi[1][(✉)], Osvaldo Vallati[1], and Ian Cashen[2]

[1] The University of Sydney, Sydney, NSW 2006, Australia
gianluca.ranzi@sydney.edu.au
[2] Sydney Opera House Trust, Sydney, NSW 2000, Australia

Abstract. The Sydney Opera House is a world-class performing arts center and is recognized internationally as a modern architectural masterpiece. This paper describes recent work focused at the development of an inspection and monitoring methodology for the roof tiles of the Sydney Opera House that aligns with the current tile tap testing regime. The particularity of the proposed approach relies on its ability to uniquely identify the location of the tile being tap tested within the building geometry and to associate it to the corresponding measurements and condition assessment evaluation. The outcome of this process is presented in a graphical form based on a simple three color ranking scheme that rates the tiles' conditions from good to acceptable and poor. It is expected that such output could be presented in various forms, such as in a BIM model. Within this procedure, the measurements can be stored for future reference and for the evaluation of historical trends. The broader use of this approach is then briefly highlighted by considering other non-destructive testing techniques and an example is presented in the final part of the paper in relation to concrete components.

Keywords: Conservation · Holograms · Non-destructive techniques
Roof tiles · Sydney Opera House

1 Introduction

The Sydney Opera House (SOH) is a masterpiece of late modern architecture and a world-class performing arts center. The building is famous for its innovative use of structural concrete and was included in the World Heritage list in 2007. It is located at Bennelong Point in Sydney and it can be viewed from different parts of the city and the Sydney Harbor. It is regarded as a symbol of the Australian spirit [1] and it is Australia's premier tourist destination. Consistently with Utzon vision [1], it is a lively space of celebration and hosts a wide range of events, including Sydney Vivid shown in Fig. 1.

This paper presents an inspection and monitoring methodology that was developed for the tile tap testing of the roof tiles of the Sydney Opera House within the principles of the building's conservation framework [1, 2]. The particularity of the proposed approach is to complement the current tile tap testing protocols with technologies that

© Springer Nature Switzerland AG 2018
M. Ioannides et al. (Eds.): EuroMed 2018, LNCS 11196, pp. 689–699, 2018.
https://doi.org/10.1007/978-3-030-01762-0_61

identify the location of each tile and associate it to the measurements and to its real-time condition assessment. The post-processing of the data collected during the site testing forms the basis for a monitoring strategy that can produce historic condition assessment trends and that can be available for use and reference to future building managers and inspectors. The outcome of the assessment is presented in a graphical fashion with a simple three color scheme to identify the conditions of the tiles. It is envisaged that such an approach could be integrated within the BIM model of the structure.

The portable equipment required to implement the proposed strategy combines different technologies and includes, among the others, an instrumented hammer developed during a project funded by the Getty Foundation under its 'Keeping It Modern' initiative [4] and a Microsoft HoloLens [5].

In the first part of the paper, a brief overview of the conservation framework of the Sydney Opera House is presented as it underpins the subsequent description of the proposed methodology based on the trials performed on the roof tiles. This approach is particularly useful to manage the complexity of the sails and the large number of roof tiles. To highlight the potential wider applicability of the proposed methodology, the final part of the paper is dedicated to briefly describe its use in combination with other non-destructive techniques relevant to concrete components.

Fig. 1. Sydney Opera House during Vivid Sydney 2018 [6]. (Color figure online)

2   Conservation of the Sydney Opera House

Some of the main documents that provide guidance on the conservation and management of the significant values of the Sydney Opera House are 'Utzon Design Principles' [1] and the 'Conservation Management Plan' (CMP) [2]. The latter document is now at its fourth edition authored by Alan Croker with its previous three editions prepared by Kerr [7, 8]. These guiding documents [1, 2] represent essential references in assisting the conservation of the building while maintaining its prominent function as Australia's foremost performing arts venue.

In the current CMP [2], the entire Sydney Opera House is subdivided into elements and components, in which an element is defined as "a major part or space of the whole building or site" [2] and a component represents a part of an element. With this classification, the exterior part of the roof shells (denoted as "roof shells externally" in the CMP) is regarded as an element and its components, among the others, include the tile lids [2].

The fourth edition of the CMP [2] has introduced two new tables for each element of the structure, i.e. one describing the 'Tolerance for Change' [3] and one specifying 'Opportunities for Change'. The concept of Tolerance for Change represents "a judgement about the role of each of the attributes (form, fabric, function and location) of each component play in supporting the significant value of their respective elements and consequently, how tolerant they are to change without adverse impacts." [2] The tolerance of each component is represented by an integer between 1 and 3, with components ranked as 3 possessing high tolerance for change and those identified by 1 having the least ability for change without adversely impacting the significance of their element. The Opportunities for Change tables provide guidance on further changes that could be explored for a particular component.

Relevant to the scope of this paper, it is recognized that the roof shells and tiles are essential to the significance of the Sydney Opera House. The tolerance of change for the tile lids is ranked as 1 for all four attributes (i.e. least ability for change). The CMP also provides additional considerations on the tile lids in which it recommends to perform "maintenance with replacement only where necessary" and it references a number of its sections for further clarifications. For example, policy 7.3 in Sect. 4.7.2 [2] recommends that the tiles and tile lids should retain their original qualities, while policy 18.2 in Sect. 4.18.1 [2] supports the use of comprehensive monitoring for the structure to inform the maintenance program and to ensure the identification of potential problems. The significance given in the CMP to the tile lids is well depicted by the American architect Louis Kahn when he said that 'the sun did not know how beautiful its light was, until it was reflected off this building' [2]. In this context, the proposed approach intends to provide an additional support and alternative to the current maintenance and monitoring strategies already available for the conservation of the roof tiles.

3   Inspection and Monitoring Methodology

3.1   Introduction

The proposed approach developed for the roof tiles of the Sydney Opera House is presented below. This is then followed, to better highlight the wider applicability of the proposed strategy, by a brief description of its possible use in combination with other non-destructive testing techniques commonly used for concrete components.

3.2   Proposed Site Testing and Monitoring for the Roof Tiles

Inspection of the roof tiles of the Sydney Opera House is carried out at five-year intervals by means of tile tapping tests [9]. This is performed by having technical teams of up-sailors climbing over the sails of the Opera House and tap testing individual tiles.

During the work supported by a Getty Foundation 'Keeping It Modern' grant for the conservation of the Sydney Opera House (during period 2014–2016), the tapping hammer commonly used for these inspections was modified and instrumented to record each tile tap test separately. This was achieved by including a microphone to capture the sound generated during the tap test, a dynamic force sensor to measure the dynamic force applied at the tip of the hammer and an infrared thermometer to evaluate the surface temperature of the tile [4]. This approach was pursued to embrace current testing protocols with the vision of establishing a database of measurements that could be used for the real-time condition assessment of the tiles and to create, over time, historical assessment profiles that could be available to future generations of building managers and inspectors. Some of the key challenges associated with the tile tap testing process consist in correctly relating each site measurement to the location where it is taken within the structure and to effectively post-process measurements for the condition assessment and for the identification of possible situations requiring further attention.

In the case of the Sydney Opera House, its complex geometry and large number of roof tiles (i.e. 1,056,066 tiles) require a bespoke approach for the identification of the location of each tile tap test, for associating it to the recorded measurements and for its condition assessment. For this purpose, different available technologies were considered. Initially, the possibility of installing GPS technology on the instrumented hammer was investigated but was not pursued because the relatively small dimensions of the tiles did not fit within the expected GPS accuracy. Other localization systems that relied on the installation of reference sensors over the building envelope were also evaluated but regarded as too intrusive from a conservation viewpoint because potentially interfering with the form and character of the roof shells as specified, for example, in Policy 7.2 of the CMP [2]. After considering other technologies, it was decided to develop and trial a methodology that relied on the use of the Microsoft HoloLens [5]. This option was regarded as attractive because building upon the current maintenance practice of the Opera House and because having the potential to provide a detailed record of the tile tap testing sessions. With this approach, the outcome of the inspection process is presented visually by classifying the conditions of the tiles with a color ranking scheme that varied between green to depict a tile in good conditions, orange to denote a tile in acceptable conditions and red to distinguish a tile in poor condition. Different algorithms have been implemented and used for the condition assessment of the tiles that made use of both sound and dynamic load measurements. The evaluation criteria was calibrated against the engineering judgment and assessment carried out by an experienced operator. An example of the visual representation that can be produced at the end of this process is presented in Fig. 2 for illustrative purposes. It is envisaged that this type of information could be accessible in various forms, such as within a BIM model of the structure.

The details of the proposed methodology applied to the roof tiles are now outlined in the following.

An overview of the entire portable system required by the proposed approach is shown in Fig. 3 that depicts an operator (and upsailer) before climbing on the sails to carry out the tile tap testing. In particular, the safety helmet has been modified (without affecting the integrity of the helmet for safety purposes) to accommodate adjustable supports for the Microsoft HoloLens. At the time of the initial developments, there was no product of this kind available on the market with the only exception of a helmet developed for military applications [10]. At the beginning of 2018, a new construction site helmet was released [11]. For the purposes of this project, it was preferred to proceed with the bespoke modifications to be applied to the safety helmet already in use by the upsailing inspectors, i.e. a safety helmet for work at height and climbing [12].

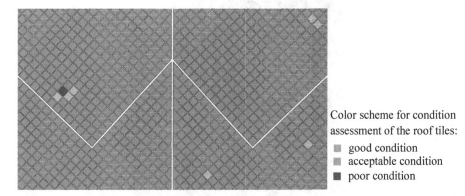

Color scheme for condition assessment of the roof tiles:
good condition
acceptable condition
poor condition

Fig. 2. Outcome of the proposed approach: possible visual representation of the condition assessment of the tiles based on a green-orange-red coloring ranking scheme. (Color figure online)

The modifications were carried out by water jet cutting bespoke plastic components and using readily available supports to enable adjustments of the position of the HoloLens glasses and to accommodate two GoPro cameras on the two sides of the helmet, i.e. one GoPro HERO6 Black and one GoPro HERO5 Session with a dedicated microphone [13]. These were installed on the helmet in a configuration aimed at minimizing the possible unbalance produced by the presence of the additional masses (i.e. HoloLens and cameras) on the helmet. An additional microphone was also installed on the helmet to record the tap test sound. Due to the reflective surface of the tiles and to the exposure to solar radiation, an additional lens was placed over the HoloLens glasses to control the light transmission and enhance visibility of the operator. When exposed to bright light conditions, the operator would not be able to see the hologram or other HoleLens commands without this additional lens and, therefore, would not be in a position to operate and run the application developed for the project. The interactivity between the operator and the HoloLens was programmed in a dedicated application and made use of gestures and of a Microsoft Xbox Wireless Controller [5]. The HoleLens and the instrumented hammer were connected to a small computer placed in the backpack of the operator (Figs. 3 and 4). All operations carried out by the operator were monitored in real-time by the ground team over the internet. An overview of the operator during the proposed testing procedure is depicted in Fig. 4.

The proposed approach requires the preparation of a hologram for each typology of tile lid to be tested and installed on the sails of the Sydney Opera House. An example of a hologram used for this project is presented in Fig. 5 and depicts a typical tile lid located in the higher part of the sails.

Fig. 3. Overview of the upsailing operator equipped with proposed system.

Fig. 4. Operator performing the tap testing of the tiles with the proposed methodology.

At the beginning of the tile tapping session, the operator reaches the testing area of the sails, where he/she selects the hologram of the tile lid to be tested and runs the positioning process of the hologram. This is carried out in a user-friendly manner by taking advantage of image recognition techniques that enable the association of an image attached to the hologram to its printed version attached to the end of a stick available to the operator. In this manner, the operator is able to adjust the position of the tile lid diagram by simply moving the printed image on the stick until the hologram depicting the diagram satisfactory overlaps the real tile lid layout. A moment during this positioning process is outlined in Fig. 6 where the hologram is adjusted to its final position by the operator through slight movements of the image. Once the operator is satisfied with the setup of the hologram, the position of the latter is locked and the operator can start the tile tap testing as, for example, shown in Fig. 7.

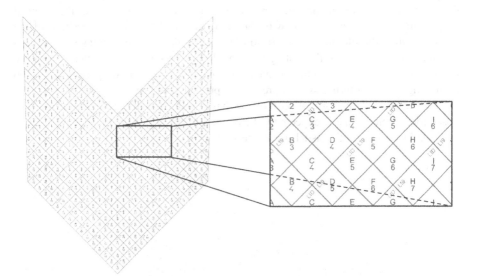

Fig. 5. Example of a hologram of a tile lid.

Fig. 6. Moment during the positioning process of the hologram by moving a stick with a predefined image at its end.

An overview of the testing process is shown in Fig. 8 in which the operator's hand is shown holding the instrumented hammer. The operator's view is complemented by the presence of the hologram in Fig. 8b. With this approach the operator can easily recognize its current position within a tile lid and, in future inspection sessions, it is possible to include additional information within the hologram to assist the work of the operator, for example, by providing a quick overview of the last condition assessment of each tile and its historic assessment profile. During the tile tapping, the condition assessment of each tile is carried out in real-time and made available to the team monitoring the testing session from the ground through the internet. Each tap test is uniquely identified by the time of the hit (i.e. identified through the trigger associated to the dynamic force sensor) and this instant in time is also used to select the relevant frame within the video recorded with the HoloLens to determine the position of the hammer within the tile lid diagram (also in this case making use of image recognition techniques). At the end of the testing session, all post-processed experimental data can be made available to the building manager and maintenance team in a graphical fashion by relying on the coloring system previously presented in Fig. 2.

The initial trials performed on the sails have confirmed the adequacy of the proposed methodology that is expected to be applied in coming years in selected areas of the sails in parallel to the usual tile tap testing regime.

Fig. 7. Operator during the tile tap testing using the proposed approach.

(a) view without hologram (frame taken from one of the GoPro cameras)

(b) view through the operator's HoloLens during the testing of the tiles

Fig. 8. View from operator during tap testing of tiles.

3.3 Combining the Proposed Approach with Other Non-destructive Techniques

The inspection and monitoring approach described in the previous section has also been trialed in combination to non-destructive techniques commonly used for concrete components in a controlled lab environment. In this case, the hologram depicts the typical testing grid that an inspector needs to usually draw on the concrete surface with a marker before testing, therefore enabling savings in time in the setting up of the non-destructive testing session and in the use of the same grid over different testing sessions. Another significant benefit relies on the fact that, by locating the hologram against known reference points of the structure (i.e. known in terms of their location within the structure, for example, by their structural model coordinates), it is possible to associate each non-destructive measurement to its specific location within the entire geometry of the structure being inspected, for example, within the BIM model of the structure if sufficiently detailed.

An example of the proposed approach is shown in Fig. 9 for cover meter measurements. In this case, the position and depth of a measured reinforcing bar (usually

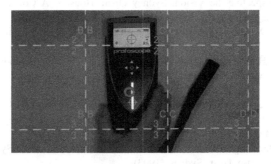

Fig. 9. Use of the proposed approach with the cover meter measurements.

not known before the scanning session) are recorded within the hologram grid that sets the reference geometry. The actual location of the cover meter measurement is identified within the hologram by a cross shown on the cover of the instrument.

4 Conclusions

This paper presented a methodology developed for the inspection and monitoring of the roof tiles of the Sydney Opera House. The proposed procedure builds on the current inspection protocol in place for the roof tiles. Its main advantages include the ability of uniquely locating the tile being tested and the coupling of the location with its measurement and real-time condition assessment. This procedure is achieved by combining the use of an instrumented hammer developed during a project funded by the Getty Foundation through its 'Keeping It Modern' scheme and a Microsoft HoloLens. The approach has been setup so that the outcome of the condition evaluation is presented graphically based on a simple three color ranking scheme in which green, orange and red define the conditions of good, acceptable and poor, respectively. It is envisaged that such a graphical representation can find its way in the BIM model of the structure. The recorded data can also be used for future reference by building managers and inspectors and for the evaluation of historical trends. The wider applicability of this approach has been outlined in the final part of the paper by combining it with non-destructive testing techniques commonly applied to concrete components.

Acknowledgements. The work reported in this paper was supported by the Getty Foundation through its 'Keeping It Modern' initiative [4] and by the Sydney Opera House Trust. The contribution of the first two authors has been partly supported by the Australian Research Council through its Future Fellowship scheme (FT140100130).

References

1. Utzon, J.: Sydney Opera House Utzon Design principles. Sydney Opera House, Sydney (2002)
2. Croker, A.: Respective the Vision: Sydney Opera House – A Conservation Management Plan, 4th edn. Sydney Opera House Trust, Sydney (2017)
3. Burke, S., MacDonald, S.: Creativity and conservation: managing significance at the Sydney Opera House. APT Bull.: J. Preserv. Technol. **45**(2–3), 31–37 (2014)
4. Sydney Opera House webpage on Getty Foundation 'Keeping It Modern' project. https://www.sydneyoperahouse.com/backstage/backstage-articles/getty-foundation.html. Accessed 26 May 2018
5. Microsoft. https://www.microsoft.com/en-au/. Accessed 26 May 2018
6. Sydney Opera House Facebook. https://www.facebook.com/pg/sydneyoperahouse/photos/. Accessed 26 May 2018
7. Kerr, J.S.: Sydney Opera House: A Plan for the Conservation of the Sydney Opera House. Sydney Opera House Trust, Sydney (1993)
8. Kerr, J.S.: Sydney Opera House: A Revised Plan for the Conservation of the Sydney Opera House, 3rd edn. Sydney Opera House, Sydney (2003)

9. Sydney Opera House Trust: Sydney Opera House Annual Report Financial Year 2016–2017, Sydney (2017)
10. Facebook page of LimpidArmor company. https://www.facebook.com/LimpidArmor. Accessed 26 May 2018
11. News release at Trimble. https://www.trimble.com/news/release.aspx?id=012518a. Accessed 26 May 2018
12. Petzl. https://www.petzl.com/INT/en/Professional/Helmets/VERTEX-VENT. Accessed 26 May 2018
13. GoPro. https://shop.gopro.com/APAC/cameras/. Accessed 26 May 2018

Non-invasive Investigation and Documentation in the Bieliński Palace in Otwock Wielki

A. Kaliszewska[1]([⊠]), R. Bieńkowski[1], J. Markiewicz[2], S. Łapiński[3], M. Pilarska[2], and A. Feliks[4]

[1] Department of Modelling and Optimization of Dynamical Systems, System Research Institute, Polish Academy of Sciences, Newelska 6, 01-447 Warsaw, Poland
Agnieszka.Kaliszewska@ibspan.waw.pl
[2] Faculty of Geodesy and Cartography, Institute of Photogrammetry, Remote Sensing and Spatial Information Systems, Warsaw University of Technology, plac Politechniki 1, 00-661 Warsaw, Poland
[3] Faculty of Geodesy and Cartography, Division of Engineering Geodesy and Control Surveying System, Warsaw University of Technology, plac Politechniki 1, 00-661 Warsaw, Poland
[4] Museum of Interiors in Otwock Wielki, National Museum in Warsaw, Zamkowa 49, 05-480 Karczew, Poland

Abstract. The paper presents the ongoing project conducted by an interdisciplinary team at the Bieliński Palace in Otwock Wielki, near Warsaw (Poland). The main aim of the project is to document the architecture and architectural elements with the use of digital methods such as photogrammetry and 3D scanning, as well as investigating the construction phases of the palace, through the analysis of the digital data collected.

The Bieliński Palace is an example of élite architecture of the Baroque period in Poland. Thought the architect responsible for the original plans remains unknown, the plan, the proportions, as well as architectural details find good parallels in the finest buildings of the capital of that time, and show clear inspirations from the western examples of the architecture of the period.

Since the archival data is very scarce, the only way to learn about the history and construction phases of the palace is through a detailed analysis of the building's structure. To this aim we perform a series of analyses of the digital data, such as wall flatness analysis and laser beam refraction intensity. We believe that the careful analysis of the data collected for the purpose of documentation can reveal valuable information that will contribute to our understanding of the building's history.

Keywords: Architecture · Digital data analysis · Photogrammetry TLS

1 Introduction

In this paper we would like to present our ongoing project at the Bieliński Palace in Otwock Wielki (Poland). The investigation is conducted by an interdisciplinary team of scientists from the Systems Research Institute of the Polish Academy of Sciences, the

© Springer Nature Switzerland AG 2018
M. Ioannides et al. (Eds.): EuroMed 2018, LNCS 11196, pp. 700–708, 2018.
https://doi.org/10.1007/978-3-030-01762-0_62

Department of Geodesy and Cartography of the Warsaw Technical University and the National Museum in Warsaw.

1.1   The Palace in Otwock Wielki

The Palace is located on an artificial island in the oxbow of the river Vistula, some 30 km SE of Warsaw. The building is part of a large complex, which includes a park and a grange. For many years it served as the summer residence for the Bieliński noble family (Fig. 1).

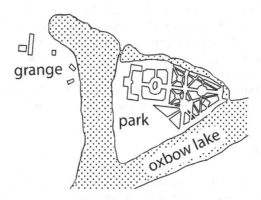

Fig. 1. Simplified plan of the palace complex in Otwock Wielki.

The construction in the palace begun in 1682 and finished by 1689. The palace was commissioned by Kazimierz Ludwik Bieliński. It is not known however who was the architect behind the plans. Architects that are sometimes connected with the plans of the palace are Tylman van Gameren, the baroque architect of king John III Sobieski, Carlo Ceroni and Józef Fontana, all known for their work in Warsaw.

The elements dating back to the 17th century are the main central part with two storeys, and side alcoves and the relief decoration of the exterior of the palace executed in pink stucco (Fig. 2).

Fig. 2. The Bieliński Palace in Otwock Wielki - view from the park.

The palace was remodelled around the year 1757. There is very little information on the duration of the remodelling and if this was a single construction phase or if there have been several phases. In the course of the remodelling the palace gained the actual form. On the right side of the entrance it is likely that an exterior staircase was removed and substituted with an interior one. In addition the plan modifications also included two new towers, as well as two wings and two separate annexes, which housed guest rooms, kitchens and other facilities. These annexes were connected to the main body by narrow galleries at the ground level.

The palace was abandoned for the second half of the 19th and most part of the 20th century, but during the Second World War German forces were stationed at the palace, which added to the progressive degradation of the palace. After the war the whole palace complex became the property of the state and became a summer residence for state officials. During this time various restoration works were done: electrical wiring was installed, new roofing was put in place, several rooms of the basement were cleared and a concrete pavement was constructed in front of the palace. All these works obscured the original tissue of the building. Since 2004 the palace belongs to the National Museum in Warsaw and houses the Museum of Interiors.

2   The Project

The study conducted so far concentrates on two rooms in the East wing of the upper floor. Some initial documentation has also been done in the basement under the main building. These two rooms have been chosen because they preserve mostly the original wall surface, with only minor conservation work (Fig. 3).

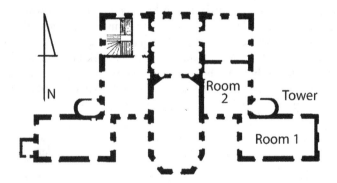

Fig. 3. A schematic plan of the first floor the palace.

The same set of rooms in the West wing have been largely renovated and no original surface remains. The Eastern rooms belong to two construction phases of the palace. Room 1 is located in the wing that was added as a result of the remodelling after 1757, whereas Room 2 belongs to the original part of the palace. Room 2 has direct connection to Room 1 as well as the tower. Hence this area was deemed the perfect location to begin our investigation into the construction phases of the palace. Additionally, the walls of both rooms are entirely decorated with frescoes, which were the second focus of our investigation. The decoration of Room 2 comprises mostly of pastel landscapes with elements of architecture (Fig. 4a), while the main architectural element is a fireplace with a simple stone frame, crowned with antithetic winged stucco sphinxes, carrying on their back a tondo, which once contained a fresco now missing. Room 1 has a different type of decoration, in which the main elements are 9 figurative panels with allegorical scenes (Fig. 4b). Each scene is accompanied by a short Latin sentence within a decorative baroque frame. The additional painted decoration imitates stucco elements around the windows and doors with large gold figures crowning them. The scenes in the panels are executed in monochromatic brownish colours. Preliminary examination of the frescos reviled incised sketches done in wet plaster. The technique of the fresco still needs to be established.

Fig. 4. (a) Fresco decoration of Room 2 and the fireplace, (b) Detail of the decoration in Room 1. (Color figure online)

The goals of the project have been formulated as follows:

1. To establish the sequence of the remodelling on the basis of the examination of the East wing: Was the tower first or the wing with Room 1? Or were they constructed simultaneously? Were the frescoes in Room 1 a part of the original decoration or were they added later?
2. To document the frescoes from Rooms 1 and 2 as well as possible, and to be determine the technique of their execution and the state of preservation [1];
3. To document the basements and to establish the original floor levels;

In the course of the investigation we added another goal, that is to use the recorded data for the analysis, to compare available non-invasive methods and to propose a methodology for working with digital data in the context of documentation and analysis of historic architectural buildings.

Due to the historical nature of the building the projects aims to employ possibly non-invasive analysis to limit the impact on the building degradation.

To this aim the following steps were undertaken:

1. For Rooms 1 and 2 a series of geodetic measurements was carried out in order to establish the ground control points, orthoimages of the rooms were generated, and a TLS point cloud was acquired for both the upper floor rooms as well as the basement;
2. Based on the data gathered the following analysis were conducted: a DSM (digital surface model), the flatness analysis, and the analysis of shaded DSMs.
3. The TLS data was used to analyse the intensity of laser beam reflection.

3   The Investigation

The photos for orthoimages were gathered using three different types of cameras: a Xiaomi action camera, a full frame Canon Mark II and a middle frame Hasselblad 50 and 100 Mpx cameras. Additionally 3D scans were taken with a Z + F 5006h scanner.

Through a series of analyses we were able to establish that action cameras are suitable for generating orthoimages that are sufficient for overall documentations of architectural objects [3]. The middle frame camera proved to be a great source of data for the investigation of architectural details as well as of the incised sketches for the frescoes [4]. The data from the full frame camera were used as reference. The scanner was used in the basement, as photogrammetry proved to be not suitable for rooms with poor light and repetitive wall texture.

The first analysis was the flatness of the wall abutting the tower in Room 1. This method was applied as a part of our investigation into the construction phases of the palace. In order to verify which part was built first, the wing or the tower, we have decided to check the relation between the two. Figure 5 presents the results of a plane being fitted into the point cloud, representing the investigated wall. The colours indicate the deviation of the points from the plane. For this specific wall the deviation between the fitted plane and the point cloud ranges from −0.03 mm to 0.015 mm. This allowed us to map the irregularities of the surface that are not visible to the naked eye. In Fig. 5 we can see changes in the wall surface that we identified as a blocked door and a irregularity in the middle of the wall that could be the result of the tower weight abutting the wall. The same phenomenon seems to happen on the edge of the wall. This might suggest an earlier construction date for the tower than the wing, as the Eastern wing wall was equally affected by the tower and the central, earlier, part of the palace.

The point clouds generated a DSM which is a solid base for analysis, as it reveals the structure of the surface, as the wall flatness analysis does, which otherwise could have gone unnoticed.

We decided to apply shading to the obtained DSMs in order to investigate the incised sketches for the frescoes. On the DSM model we can see the majority of the incisions, which provides the possibility to located them and trace them without the need to perform actual measurements on the fresco (Fig. 6). We hope that by examining those sketches we can learn more about the technique in which the frescoes were executed and about the artist who executed them [2]. We are also looking into the possibility of automatic detection and mapping of such incisions [4].

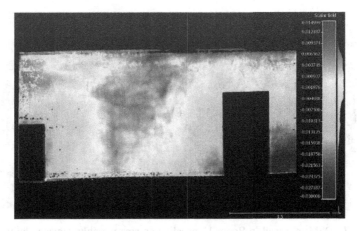

Fig. 5. Wall flatness analysis. The colour denote the distance of the fitted plane from the surface of the wall. The distance ranges from −0.03 to 0.015 mm. (Color figure online)

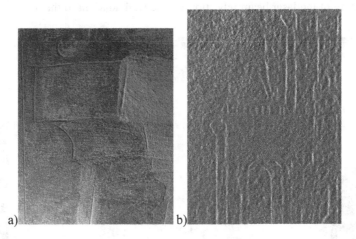

Fig. 6. The preparatory incised sketches for the fresco composition in Room 2: (a) photo (b) visible on the shaded DSM.

Such shaded models can also be used to investigate the surface of the wall. In Fig. 7. We see clear changes in the structure of the fresco, especially in the left-hand upper corner. Our preliminary theory is that they are the result of the wall being exposed to water. We believe that through seasonal monitoring over a period of time and the comparison of the DSMs, we will be able to establish whether this is related to the period of abandonment of the palace of if this an ongoing process, and conservators intervention is required [1].

The data from the laser scanner is not only a source of information about the geometry of the rooms. We investigated the additional dataset referring to the intensity of reflection of the laser beam. This investigation reveals mostly the information about

Fig. 7. DSM of a wall in Room 1, revealing an area possibly damaged by water.

the colours used, as darker colours absorb more light than light colours. Figure 8 shows the intensity of the laser beam reflection for the wall adjacent to the tower in Room 1.

Fig. 8. Intensity of laser beam reflection for a wall in Room 1.

In the area of the middle panel a clear variation of intensity can be seen. The middle section is characterised by a higher beam reflection intensity than the neighbouring areas. The reason for this phenomenon still needs further investigation. This phenomenon may be connected to the fact that the region overlaps with the area of the wall influenced by the construction of the tower (as seen in Fig. 5). The difference of the intensity might be then explained by a change in humidity and/or wall temperature [1], caused by the abutting structure of the tower. This latter aspect shows that the intensity of the laser beam reflection can be used to search for changes in wall construction. It can also be a source of preliminary information before conservation works.

4 Results and Future Work

The conducted analyses have led us to the following preliminary conclusions:

1. The tower and the East wing of the palace were not built at the same time; this observation is corroborated by the wall flatness analysis and the modalities in which the two structures affect one another. Exact chronology of these two structures still remains to be established. The frescos in Room 1 are not part of the original decoration of this room, as evidenced by the blocked door leading to the tower.
2. We were able to assess the general state of the frescoes through the analysis of shaded DSMs and the intensity of the laser beam reflection. We could locate areas that need monitoring and if conservators intervention will be required.
3. The investigation of the relation between the incised fresco sketches and the structure of the surface will help us establish the technique of the frescoes execution without the need for samples. The non-invasive investigations allowed us to obtain information that would have been unavailable with the traditional methods. We strongly believe and hope that these results will help limiting the invasive tests (such as samples or trenches) or in some cases even avoid them.

As for the future works we plan to continue the investigation of the east wing, to further refine the building sequence of the palace.

The second area of interest for the study is the park surrounding the palace, which from old plans seems to have included a pavilion and a small pier for boats on the opposite side of the island from the palace. The planned works will focus on non-invasive methods, such as gravimetry and GPR. A survey of the park area is planned as we have already collected information about chance finds of garden sculptures. If more fragments are located they could provide hints about the style of the garden, of which we have no record. If the non-invasive methods reveal any remains, the last phase of the investigation will be to conduct a small scale excavation to verify the results of the non-invasive tests. The same methods as in the garden, that is gravimetry and GPR, will be employed in the effort to locate the original, exterior staircase.

The initial aim of the project was to document the interiors of the Bieliński Palace in Otwock Wielki using laser scanning and photogrammetry. The use of both these tools is well established in the field of cultural Heritage preservation and documentation. As the work progressed we encountered more and more research questions concerning the construction and chronology of the frescoes and the palace.

Since there are limited excavation possibilities, we decided to tackle the arising questions through the analysis of the already collected digital data. This approach gave promising results as presented above.

The approach is based on the form of documentation that is well established in the field, that is photogrammetry and laser scanning. The advantages of these methods are widely acknowledged amongst researchers. However, the advanced geometrical analysis of data coming from such methods is a relatively new subject. In the case of the investigation in the Bieliński Palace, it turned out to be very helpful in establishing preliminary hypothesis as to the sequence of constructions. And we hope it will allow us a more question-focus approach in the future. Nevertheless, it has to be noted that the analysis themselves provide only partial information about the structure, and in many cases in order to draw solid conclusions, a complete investigation is needed.

References

1. García-Talegón, J., et al.: Assessing pathologies on villamayor stone (Salamanca, Spain) by terrestrial laser scanner intensity data. Int. Arch. Photogramm. Remote Sens. Spat. Inf. Sci. **40** (5/W4), 445–451 (2015). https://doi.org/10.5194/isprsarchives-XL-5-W4-445-2015
2. Mancini, M.F., Salvatore, M.: Surveying illusory architectures painted on vaulted surfaces. In: Ioannides, M., et al. (eds.) EuroMed 2016. LNCS, vol. 10058, pp. 377–386. Springer, Cham (2016). https://doi.org/10.1007/978-3-319-48496-9_30
3. Markiewicz, J., Łapiński, S., Pilarska, M., Bieńkowski, R., Kaliszewska, A.: Investigation into the use of action camera in the documentation of architectural details – the case study. Int. Arch. Photogramm. Remote Sens. Spat. Inf. Sci. **42**(2) (2018). https://doi.org/10.5194/isprs-archives-XLII-2-667-2018
4. Markiewicz, J., Pilarska, M., Łapiński, S., Kaliszewska, A., Bieńkowski, R., Cena, A.: Quality assessment of the use of medium format camera in the investigation of wall paintings. Image-based approach. Measurement. Special Issue, MetroArcheo (2017). https://doi.org/10.1016/j.measurement.2018.07.001. ISSN 0263-2241

Digital Preservation and Record of War Fortifications - A Case Study of Qiong-Lin Defense Tunnel in Taiwan

Wun-Bin Yang[1,2], Yu-Chieh Lin[1], Chin-Fang Cheng[1], and Ya-Ning Yen[1(✉)]

[1] China University of Technology, 56 Sec. 3 ShingLong Rd., Taipei 116, Taiwan
{wunbin,lisa20590151,aabbyy,alexyen}@cute.edu.tw
[2] National Taipei University of Technology, 1, Sec. 3, Zhongxiao E. Rd., Taipei 106, Taiwan

Abstract. The application of digital technology in the preservation of cultural assets is an international common trend. It combines the acquisition and preservation of integrated data which is very practical for the demonstration of various analysis and diversification. In 2017, 19th General Assembly of the International Ruins and Monuments Council Conference held in India states that government have the responsibility to identify, evaluate, record all of heritage sites and raise awareness of their importance. Therefore, digital preservation technology should be made universal in researching digital asset preservation. This project is based on the concept of digitalized conservation technology development. In order to implement the preservation and management of cultural assets, 3D laser scanning and control survey were used to record Taiwan Qiong-Lin civil defense underground tunnel digitally. To achieve the preservation and development of future cultural assets, this project also includes 3D point cloud models for tiled digital topographic map, urban planning, etc.

Keywords: 3D laser scanning · Tunnel · CAD · Digitization
War fortifications

1 Introduction

The preservation of cultural assets technology has evolved from the traditional method to the fast-digital method [6]. Due to the fast-paced nature of technology, the digitized data now has been become more accurate, has better resolution, possessed the combination of integrated data acquisition [7] and preservation technology [1–3]. It is also the main point of our research development.

In 2016, Taiwan Ministry of Culture promoted redevelopment historical scene projects. One of the projects was to bring back the glory of Qiong-Lin Tsai ancestral settlement. Digital resource construction, management, and presentation play an important role on the application of the digital technology on cultural asset and the importance of the national policies implementation. Qiong-Lin settlement (Fig. 1) has a rich traditional architectural characteristic, cultural atmosphere, military monuments,

© Springer Nature Switzerland AG 2018
M. Ioannides et al. (Eds.): EuroMed 2018, LNCS 11196, pp. 709–717, 2018.
https://doi.org/10.1007/978-3-030-01762-0_63

and other resources. In order to fully accomplish Qiong-Lin civil defense underground tunnel (Fig. 2) preservation, this project use 3D laser scanning and control survey to preserve Qiong-Lin civil defense underground tunnel information digitally.

Fig. 1. Qiong-Lin settlement   **Fig. 2.** Qiong-Lin civil defense tunnel main entrance

2   Qiong-Lin Civil Defense Tunnel Overview

Qiong-Lin civil defense tunnel is located in the Qiong-Lin settlement. It was a fortification built by the military and civilian for combat and bombardment defense era Kuomintang and communist party confrontation in 1970. It became an important tourist attraction after the war between Kuomintang and communist party came to end due its special historical background and war atmosphere. Qiong-Lin tunnel serves as the village defense fortification. Its entrance and exit are not only located in the command center office but also connect to the villager house in the settlement so that villager can quickly enter the tunnel for defense in the wartime. At present, only some sections are open for tourist.

In 2012, Qiong-Lin settlement was registered as a cultural heritage site. Although Qiong-Lin underground tunnel is located below the Qiong-Lin settlement, it has not been registered and designated as a cultural asset. Even so it is also count as a preservation site and protected by the Cultural Heritage Preservation Law. Qiong-Lin tunnel condition as shown in Fig. 3.

With great effort, Qiong-Lin civil defense team succeeded in excavating Qiong-Lin tunnel with simple tools in 1968. At the depths of 6 m underground, a well was dug every 20 m, in which, every worker must dig at least 5 m, using crossed picks, tritoothed picks, hoes, spades, dustpans and other tools to dig out the Qiong-Lin Soil Tunnel, which was the longest and largest tunnel in Kinmen [4, 5].

The construction of Qiong-Lin tunnel is mainly based on its ability to withstand artillery bombardments. According to preliminary survey and related historical materials research, the net height of the tunnel is about 2 m, the width is about 1.2 m; in which, the RC wall is 30 cm thick, the top of the tunnel is mainly arch type, however, some parts are flat top, and the wall thickness is up to 50 cm and the tunnel length is 1.413 m [4, 5].

This tunnel has about 12 entrances and exits so that it can connect from the village office to several important facilities, such as bunkers, air-raid shelters, and ancestral halls. A wartime command post is located below the village office.

Tunnel entrance and exit   Liang Yong Bunker appearance   embrasure

Stairs inside Liang Yong Bunker   Main tunnel   Branch tunnel

Fig. 3. Qiong-Lin civil defense tunnel condition

3 Qiong-Lin Civil Defense Tunnel Digitalization and Measurement

The center of Qiong-Lin civil defense tunnel is the command post (called Qiong-Lin office nowadays). Its total length is 1413 m, the height is 2 m. It has 6 m distance above the ground. The tunnel is divided into main and branch tunnel. The main tunnel

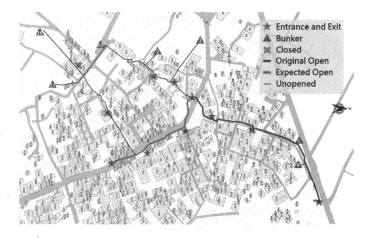

Fig. 4. Qiong-Lin defence tunnel entrance and exit map

is 1.2 km wide and the branch tunnel is 0.8 wide. There are total 7 entrances and exit in the tunnel, 7 Liang Yong Bunker (兩用堡) Constructed with the terrain, Liang-Yong bunker was used for combat and personal refuge. The interior of the bunker was stepped and the lower part was used as a shelter.

There are 4 entrances and exit that lead to the villager house has been closed (Fig. 4). Control survey and 3D laser scanning are performed digitally on entrances exit and Liang Yong Bunker (兩用堡).

3.1   Control Survey

Control survey is a measuring system using horizontal and vertical control (Fig. 5). Known point of horizontal control is measured by using TWD97 coordinate system for Kinmen area assigned by Taiwan Ministry of Interior. Vertical control adopts first class standard coordinates which also assigned by Taiwan Ministry of Interior. It uses full-station theodolite Leica TPS-1025 as control survey instrument.

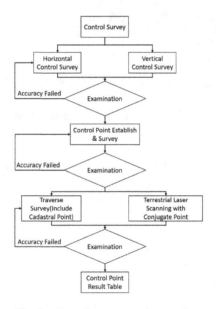

Fig. 5. Control survey work procedure

There are 3 third-class satellite points (WX20, WX26, WX45) and 2 first-class satellite points (KM15, KM17). Known point of horizontal control adopts GPS measurement method and vertical control adopts standard direct measurement method (Fig. 6).

There are four control points (HL01 ~ 04) buried in the survey area. New method of control point use steel pile and steel pile on-site to establish a reference for the tunnel horizontal and vertical control point. New method of control test point also adopts GPS

Fig. 6. Picture of known point measurement procedure

measurement method for horizontal control and standard direct measurement method for vertical control. New method of control point was distributed in Qiong-Lin settlement as shown in Fig. 7.

Fig. 7. New method of control point distribution graph

3.2 Traverse Measurement and Conjugate Point Test

In order to carry out tunnel digital topographic measurement, traverse points were set up at Liang Yong Bunker and tunnel road junction. Angle and distance were measured using total station theodolite instrument. Measurement results were divided into closed least squares adjustment and azimuth coordinate value. Work measurement as shown in Fig. 8.

Fig. 8. Picture of traverse measurement work

In order to provide tunnel 3D laser scanning coordinate transformation and improve the overlay accuracy of tunnel 3D laser scanning, conjugate points were set up at every tunnel entrances and exit. There are at least 4 conjugate points placed in every tunnel entrances and exit. Using traverse point as a reference, center coordinate of each conjugate point test was measured by total station theodolite instrument (Table 1). The test results as shown in Fig. 9.

Table 1. Example of conjugate points.

Point number	N	E	Z	Remarks
A1	2705761.849	186561.540	10.112	A area
A2	2705757.063	186555.917	10.940	A area
A3	2705765.506	186550.133	10.526	A area
A4	2705769.750	186556.051	11.946	A area
D1	2705593.563	186423.749	13.340	D area
D2	2705598.683	186428.324	14.068	D area
D3	2705592.243	186434.051	15.803	D area
D4	2705580.687	186423.004	15.960	D area
….	….	….	….	….

Fig. 9. Picture of conjugate point test

3.3 3D Laser Scanning

FARO Focus3D X 130 is used to perform 3D laser scanning on Qiong-Lin underground tunnel (Fig. 10). The effective scanning distance is over 130 m. High precision mapping was performed and archived digitally. Due to the narrow width of the tunnel, each station scanning is performed within 10 to 20 m.

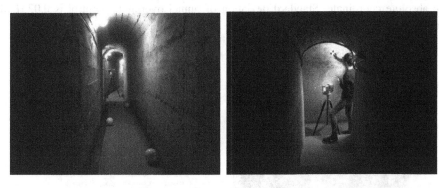

Fig. 10. Picture of tunnel scanning

4 Tunnel Measurement Results

The 3D laser scanner of each station must set up an independent regional coordinate system. In other words, the point cloud data of different scanning station belong to different coordinate system and the scanned coordinate must be converted to a unified

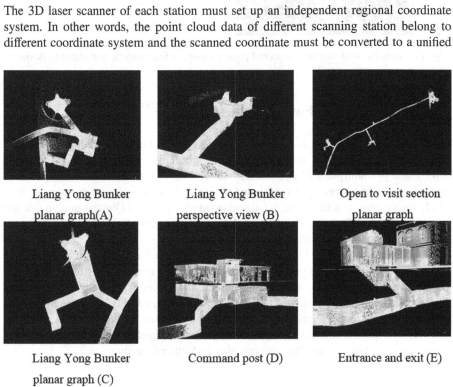

Fig. 11. Point cloud results

coordinate system. Based on the above reason, the location of conjugate point layout is calibrated according to the topographic change planning. The results as shown in Fig. 11.

In order to completely overlay control point and Qiong-Lin point cloud, Integrated coordinate conversion is performed based on FARO laser scanner and total station conjugate point. It can reduce tunnel laser scan. Control point can also be converted to an absolute coordinate. Standard deviation of tunnel overlaying control is 0.0231 M (Fig. 12).

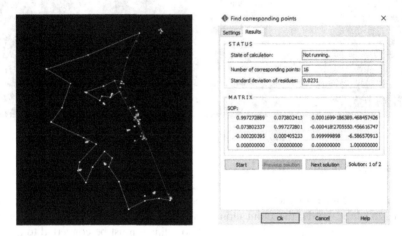

Fig. 12. Traverse total station and control point measurement schematic and standard deviation of tunnel overlaying control

5   Conclusions and Future Suggestions

The geometry of the tunnel is simple, continuous form and only has a little special trait. To fully record Qiong-Lin tunnel cloud point information and reduce the cumulative error made by multiple 3D laser scanner stations, control measurement integration is needed. It also improves the accuracy and efficiency of tunnel measurement procedure. Study results present a complete 3D digital point cloud data of Qiong-Lin civil defense tunnel in Kinmen, Taiwan. Point cloud data can be used to draw tunnel digital topographic map, cadastral drawing map and animation.

The digital data can be used as the basic information for the restoration, reuse and planning of opening to the public for sightseeing of the tunnel. After overlapping the cadastral map with the location of the tunnel, after receiving approval by the land owners, the tunnel will be opened to the public for visit, and thus, enhancing the value of tunnel's reuse and activation. It also gives great benefits for the cadastral survey. It can contribute to the cultural asset preservation and management goal such as improve repairing, recycling, disaster monitoring plan and other contributions.

References

1. Roncat, A., Dublyansky, Y., Spötl, C., Dorninger, P.: Full-3D surveying of caves: a case study of marchenhohle (Austria). In: Proceedings of the International Association for Mathematical Geosciences (IAMG 2011) (2011)
2. Tokovinine, A., Belli, F.E.: From stucco to digital: topometric documentation of Classic Maya facades at Holmul. Digit. Appl. Archaeol. Cult. Herit. **6**, 18–28 (2017)
3. Clini, P., Nespeca, R., Bernetti, A.: All-in-one laser scanning methods for surveying, representing and sharing information on archaeology. Via Flaminia and the Furlo tunnel complex. ISPRS-Int. Arch. Photogramm. Remote Sens. Spatial Inf. Sci. (2), 201–206 (2013)
4. Tsai, S.-G.: A study on adaptive reuse of Kinmen traditional houses—in case of Chyongli'n cluster. National Cheng Kung University (2006)
5. Tsai, Q.: The resplendent Qiong-Ling, Tsai clan association of Kinmen County (2016)
6. Yang, W.-B., Wang, T.-J., Yen, Y.-N.: The application of photogrammetry on digitization and promotion for monuments and temples in Taiwan - taking Chua family ancestral temple as an example. In: Ioannides, M., et al. (eds.) EuroMed 2016. LNCS, vol. 10058, pp. 387–396. Springer, Cham (2016). https://doi.org/10.1007/978-3-319-48496-9_31
7. Yen, Y.N., Weng, K.H., Huang, H.Y.: Study on information management for the conservation of traditional Chinese architectural heritage—3D modelling and metadata representation. In: CIPA 2013 (2013)

Digitizing the Building Site for Restoration Projects: From ALM Technologies to Innovative Material Scenarios

Marco Medici[✉] and Sara Codarin

Department of Architecture, University of Ferrara,
via Ghiara 36, 44121 Ferrara, Italy
{marco.medici, sara.codarin}@unife.it

Abstract. The ongoing synergy between the digitization of the building process and new paradigms related to the production of architectural constructions and building elements, addresses the definition of new scenarios that are worth investigating. The recurring question, indeed, is how the most advanced digital techniques for material production can have a tangible impact on architecture and its morphological languages.

In the field of building design, the chance to turn digital data into matter represents a key point to deal with, in order to demonstrate the possibility to transfer actual benefits from other sectors related to the construction industry. This new technical asset links the digitization of processes with the industrialization of building products.

The present research aims at deepening the opportunity of Additive Layer Manufacturing technologies, alongside the current Building Information Modeling and parametric design methods, to push further the hitherto established decision-making rules and the conventional building site organization, towards a sustainable development.

Keywords: Digitization · Restoration · Additive Layer Manufacturing

1 Digitization Assets Within the Construction Industry

1.1 Introduction

Market variations, socio-economic changes, and new architectural languages have always encouraged the innovation of building processes. Some of these aspects deserve further study, addressed by the new demand of procedural upgrading within the construction industry. Scientific research deals with the experimentation of new design and production methods, which should meet current qualitative standards.

The development of technologies that read digital data and reproduce their spatial characteristics for the production of physical objects [1], encourages the use of new languages requiring technical experimentations and continuous applicability evaluations [2].

For these reasons, the following discussion focuses on the unsolved dichotomy between the industrialization of the production of building components and the

© Springer Nature Switzerland AG 2018
M. Ioannides et al. (Eds.): EuroMed 2018, LNCS 11196, pp. 718–727, 2018.
https://doi.org/10.1007/978-3-030-01762-0_64

digitization of building processes. Therefore, it aims at defining future scenarios in which design chains (process innovation) and production chains (product innovation) can meet.

1.2 Methodological Approach

The construction industry is constantly evolving and often times it struggles to find proper tools in response to the changing needs of the sector.

In the last decades, it has absorbed components of innovation mostly deriving from other segments, such as naval engineering, aeronautics, and serial industrial production. Historically, the industrialization within the building sector has been achieved through the prefabrication of components in response to a market based on new constructions, now showing its limits in the field of intervention on existing buildings, especially on Cultural Heritage, which require a case-by-case approach.

In parallel, a strong shift towards digitization has been outlined, also due to the innovative force brought by the fourth industrial revolution, which focuses on the benefit that digitization and the internet of things (IoT) can introduce.

Nowadays, the digitization of the design and realisation processes represents a need for those professionals who want to work with a common language, reduce uncertainties and increase awareness of design choices.

For these reasons, the efforts through the industrialization and the digitization of the sector are key points that we want to deepen in the following paragraphs, in order to evaluate the positive contribution of innovative development for the preservation and restoration of European Cultural Heritage [3].

2 Industrialization of the Restoration Building Site

Valorization and restoration interventions on buildings of cultural and historical relevance refer to the so-called case-by-case approach. In accordance with its objectives and due to the lack of forecasting guidelines, architects make several decisions directly on-site.

Today, projects on existing buildings are still realized through established techniques used by artisans. However, the artisan techniques are not precisely measurable and controllable through current design tools and they cannot provide a greater control in advance, precision, repeatability, and guaranteed results. Taking as an example the innovations developed in Europe in the 70s, focused on the large-scale construction of new standardized buildings, the most advanced digital technologies allow applying some aspects of the industrialization of building components production for restoration projects. This innovation effort must not be associated with a necessarily serial production, which would be incompatible with the existing constructions. The immediate consequence could be a reduction in costs and a greater reliability over time of the constructive result, especially of non-standardized components that do not allow a precise planning for their realization.

The aspects related to the industrialization in the building industry still refer to the off-site production (i.e. in a protected, safe and under controlled conditions environment) of materials, products and technologies that are subjected to a higher quality supervision. In the traditional building site, on-site industrialisation is yet not evident, even though it could potentially help to increase the perfect execution of unique elements, not realizable through mass production [4].

To confirm this, the possibility to encourage a dialogue between three-dimensional survey and modelling systems with the most advanced Additive Layer Manufacturing machines, outlined by different technological and material alternatives, could play a significant role for further developments.

3   Digitization of the Building Process

3.1   The Role of Representation in the Design Process

Taking into account building renovations, architectural or urban interventions upon existing building stocks, the digital workflow can be described as an inclusive and integrated representation that meets the need of the professionals to communicate with a common language [5]. Since the innovations of production methods are always connected to building processes (from the design to the building site, and to the management), the digital representation is an essential part of the design process that contributes to the final design quality. In particular, if we consider the role of representation for the analysis of existing building stocks, the digital environment acts as an element of comparison with reality, which is intended as a synthesis of spaces, materials and technologies, resulting from complex modification and stratification processes of an urban fabric. In this regard, Maurizio Unali identifies three theoretical-operational spaces of architectural design in relation to representative models introduced by information technology: a representative-instrumental space, a confirmative-creative space, and a media-informative space [6].

A digital model (unlike a physical model) is a mathematical structure elaborated through an ordered system of data and codes, which interfaces through synthetic images that can be translated into practical actions aimed at understanding the different levels of information of the model itself. Furthermore, the possibility to modify the model is set in relation to the different professional skills involved in its elaboration. Indeed, the representation tools for project management constantly develop from the static asset of the design to the dynamism of the model.

3.2   Project Management Through Information Models

It is possible to group the most advanced digital tools (commercially available, intended for the design and management of the functionalities of a building), under the definition of Building Information Modelling (BIM). Although there is not an exhaustive and definitive definition of BIM, the different software are evolving rapidly and their use varies accordingly, even with unconventional approaches.

The adoption of these informative-representative tools allows:

- carrying out transparently the design phases in order to produce conventional graphic works that are correct in terms of representation;

- relating architectural composition, technology, and structure within the whole construction process (BIM 4D), estimation of costs (BIM 5D), certification (BIM 6D), and life-cycle management (BIM 7D + CAFM).

These possibilities allow evaluating in advance and more carefully the sustainability of the works (Fig. 1).

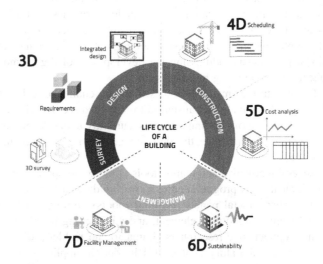

Fig. 1. Diagram of the "size" of the building process that can be managed during the life cycle of a building through the implementation of BIM tools and methods - original graphic reworking. Credits: Marco Medici.

Thanks to the possibilities deriving from the standardization of architectural components, the informative character of the digital model significantly outweighs the geometric aspect. The informative data itself, indeed, acquires the value of design parameter, based on the dimension in which it is interpreted [7].

In this scenario, it is necessary to take into account three fundamental aspects characterizing each model, in accordance with the attributes reference, purpose and cost-effectiveness outlined by Kiviniemi [8]:

- each project field suggests the need to assign different models or a different way to query a model, in order to avoid the redundancy of unnecessary data at a given moment [efficiency];
- it is necessary to define the goal (goals) in advance in order to elaborate a model suitable to achieve the expected results [efficacy];
- the integrated model must include (at least) those parts needed for the desired level of integration in order to produce a profitable result [economy].

4   Bridging the Gap: The Use of ALM

4.1   Large-Scale Automation Tools in Building Constructions

Although BIM methodologies have been developed to meet the requirements for new constructions, the ongoing national research on the theme focuses on how to apply these technologies to a widespread panorama of existing buildings.

Today, the actual implementation of digitization struggles to find a right path, primarily because its character of immateriality causes an incorrect evaluation of the real worth of the phenomenon. This, despite the regulatory effort aimed at identifying new professional profiles and addressing the development of digital models towards possible applications for existing building stocks.

Turning digital data into matter becomes the main challenge to be undertaken in order to find possible benefits to be transferred from related sectors. The most advanced systems for the production of building elements, currently under development, are able to read digital data and reproduce the deriving geometric layout in the real three-dimensional space.

There are several innovative automation tools of the contemporary building site [9], including: mechanical arms programmed to move building materials (brick layering), robotic arms to reshape metal panels (forming robots), milling machines (CNC) to subtract material from a monolithic element, and wire-cutting technologies.

In 2006, the architects and researchers Gramazio and Kohler [10], founders of the Architectural Robotic Laboratory at the ETH in Zurich, applied off-site (but in the future it is expected to be implemented directly on-site) the so-called brick layering technology for the construction of a new building (expansion of the Gantenbein winery). The robotic arm used for the experimentation was able to move and lay one brick at a time inside a prefabricated frame in apparently random positions -functional instead for internal the bioclimatic control in both summer and winter- generating a façade dynamism difficult to achieve by using traditional techniques.

Scientific research has developed methodologies that evaluate carefully the execution accuracy of the technical procedures, the reduction of material waste, and the necessary timing for the installation of building components. For instance, Hadrian robot, one of the most advanced systems, developed by Fastbrick Robotics, is comparable to the work-force of 20 technicians that usually use their manual skills in-situ, with a speed of laying equal to 1000 bricks per hour and the potential to build 150 homes in a year.

Among the building site automation systems, the present study aims at deepening the large-scale Additive Layer Manufacturing, which is a construction technology able to create volumes at any scale, from the design object to the building component [11]. These systems work through the consecutive overlapping (addition) of material layers up to the definition of the expected result, previously digitally modelled (Figs. 2 and 3).

Often times, the term ALM is mistaken for 3D printing, which is instead a subset. The ALM tools that are more responsive to sustainability criteria, in terms of production speed, safety of the production process, costs reduction, limitation of raw materials waste and experimentation with innovative materials, are mainly two: powder-bed deposition (3D printing), and cold extrusion (3D plotting), to be used differently according to design requirements.

Fig. 2. A robotic arm being tested at ETH laboratories in Zurich. This technology is programmed to move and lay building materials off-site. In the future, robotic tools are expected to be used directly in situ. Credits: ETH Zurigo and NCCR Digital Fabrication - Gramazio Kohler Research and Agile & Dexterous Robotics Lab.

Fig. 3. Radiolaria, the first large-scale 3D printed prototype, designed by Shiro Studio and realized with Dshape technology. The volume is made of an insoluble and resistant material similar to stone, which is the result of a mixture of sand, metal oxides and inorganic salt-based binders. Credits: Shiro Studio.

3D printing systems use nozzles to deposit alternating layers of a base material (usually a thin inert, such as sand or gypsum) and an inorganic binder, used to solidify the inert. This technology is able to create free-form monolithic volumes, without geometrical limitations on any axis [12]. A tangible outcome realized, in 2007, through powder-bed deposition can be identified in Radiolaria, the first large-scale prototype resulting from a shared work of the Italian company D-shape and the design firm Shiro Studio [13]. The volume was inspired by the shapes of radiolars, unicellular organisms whose size is between the tenth and one-hundredth of a millimetre. They provide an example of morphological and structural optimization, whose biological principles were systematized through the definition of digital mathematical algorithms. The close observation of nature, in this case, is in complete accordance with ALM construction processes, which consist of the deposition of material only if indispensable, by replicating artificially the typical formation processes of biological elements [14].

3D plotting consists of an extruder programmed to deposit overlapping layers of a viscous mixture (raw soil or concrete) that solidifies rapidly. However, the mechanism can produce a limited range of shapes, as long as every output must be generated following tightly the vertical axis. In this particular case, cold-extrusion systems can create three-dimensional volumes through a "wet" process with a simplification of the building site logistics. Casting formworks, indeed, are no longer required. To make an example, Pylos project, developed at the laboratories of the Institute of Advanced Architecture of Catalonia (IAAC), has led to the realization of raw soil wall modules, designed to support consistent compressive stresses [15]. Depending on the design language to be achieved, the mixtures suitable to be extruded by using a 3D plotter can be based on raw soil (Shamballa Village, Wasproject), plastic polymers (Mataerial, IAAC), or concrete (Yhnova, University of Nantes).

In particular, Additive Layer Manufacturing, in accordance with circular business models aimed at reducing resources consumption and introducing recycled components into new commercial products, encourages the use of construction waste, grinded in controlled percentages inside the mixtures (Fig. 4).

Fig. 4. Experimentation performed at IAAC (Institute for Advanced Architecture of Catalonia) for the realization of building elements made of raw soil through a 3D plotting process. Credits: Sofoklis Giannakopoulos.

4.2 Opportunities to Innovate the Restoration Building Site

The examples so far brought in support of this dissertation have highlighted the need to point future research towards the demonstration that should be declined within the frame of the restoration building site. The relation with the pre-existence requires understanding how ALM technologies can be used to guarantee on the one hand the respect of the existing building and on the other the possibility for the designer to respond coherently to the architectural language.

For this purpose, within the present research, we have analyzed and elaborated different intervention models that allowed us to deduce unresolved technological aspects, as shown in the diagram. First, independently of the additive manufacturing technology used, the limit that the deposit of material takes place on a flat horizontal surface emerges. Working on existing buildings requires instead a greater degree of freedom, in terms of irregular surface and various slopes to which interface the project during construction phases. Possible future evaluations aimed at verifying, in a controlled environment, procedures and methods for the deposit of material on uneven surfaces, could contribute increasing the level of digital documentation of interventions on pre-existing buildings, ensuring the possibility of on-site design adaptation opening possible scenarios of on-site industrialization (Fig. 5).

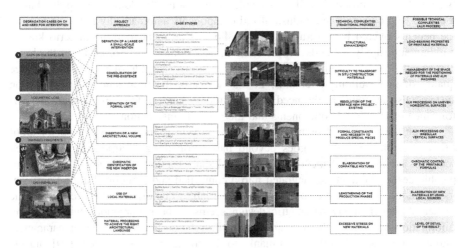

Fig. 5. Synoptic overview of the different intervention models in relation to the technical complexities solved in the traditional project that require a preliminary analysis for the implementation of ALM technologies. Credits: Sara Codarin.

5   Future Development: A New Architectural Language

The definition of new scenarios because of the synergy between the digitization of the building process and new paradigms for the production of building components needs to be widely investigated in the near future, to prevent the technique from prevailing over the critical approach.

The awareness of different aspects such as the most appropriate methodologies of intervention, the proper use of matter, and the suitable tools to create and install it, is a direct consequence of the adopted architectural language, which contributes to go beyond two key concepts that have always characterized building design.

On the one hand, we are witnessing the overcoming of the traditional concept of three-dimensional representation intended as simplification and abstraction of reality. The idea of a digital model of the built environment used to study certain situations is now obsolete. It can no longer be considered simply a physical representation, a simulation, or a software output. According to Rothenberg [16], the human mind has always used the act of modelling as a fundamental process without, however, associating it with an exhaustive representation of reality. This discussion, instead, wants to define the three-dimensional model as a critical result of a creative-interpretive processing, or rather a contribution of knowledge on a building. This process of knowledge enriches our experience, in order to "provide us with more experience of what we could collect, without the mediation of the imaginal, in a relation, let's say, empirical with reality" [17]. The moment we assist to the transfer, directly on the building site, of the material production on a digital basis, the three-dimensional construction model of a building becomes matter itself.

On the other hand, we are observing an update on the concept of standardization, typical of off-site production. If we are able to shorten the "building site supply-chain", the need to produce off-site industrialized components automatically fades, as long as the benefits offered by in-situ production allow us to go beyond the hitherto known building site supply methods. At the same time, the importance of ensuring the high-performance standards introduced in recent years and capable of raising the average quality of new buildings, remains. In this scenario, the proposition of certification systems also responds to the need for a solution regarding the gap between the performance of individual components and their on-site installation.

Given the mentioned premises, it is necessary to introduce the concept of algorithmic design [18], which goes beyond parametric design introducing unexplored scenarios for the management of architectural shapes. From informative data as computable design parameters integrated into a controlled and predefined digital environment, we move on to the elaboration of the variables that drive the project to become matter. Although today parametric design seems to be synonymous with Building Information Modelling, the attempt to turn the relation between different parameters into a shape emerged in the '60 s thanks to the studies of Luigi Moretti [19] and the works of Sergio Musmeci. The exploration of these shapes, achieved without any IT support, can be considered as the precursor of today's algorithmic design that focuses primarily on the definition of the algorithm rule capable of responding as well as possible to the project requirements, once given the input design variables. The elaboration of free-form shapes as a result of this process to explore new languages, in mimesis with natural processes [20], can therefore be implemented immediately thanks to the possibility to translate digital data into matter.

The examples used to support the present discussion, as well as the critical investigation on possible developments, highlight how it is necessary to direct future researches towards this field. In fact, the revolution brought by digitization is configured as the incentive for overcoming the procedures that still depend on traditional methods. They require, indeed, a response that is consistent with current systemic innovations.

References

1. Gershenfeld, N.: How to Make Almost Anything: The Digital Fabrication Revolution. Council on Foreign Relations (2012)
2. Willmann, J., Gramazio, F., Kohler, M., Langenberg, S.: Digital by material. In: Brell-Çokcan, S., Braumann, J. (eds.) Rob | Arch 2012, pp. 12–27. Springer, Vienna (2013). https://doi.org/10.1007/978-3-7091-1465-0_2

3. Maietti, F., Giulio, R.D., Piaia, E., Medici, M., Ferrari, F.: Enhancing heritage fruition through 3D semantic modelling and digital tools: the INCEPTION project. In: IOP Conference Series: Materials Science and Engineering, vol. 364, p. 012089 (2018)
4. Calzolari, M., Codarin, S., Davoli, P.: Innovative technologies for the recovery of the architectural Heritage by 3D printing processes. Presented at the Le nuove frontiere del restauro. Trasferimenti, contaminazioni, ibridazioni, Bressanone, 27 June 2017
5. Medici, M., Modugno, V., Pracucci, A.: How to face the scientific communication today. International challenge and digital technology impact on research outputs dissemination. Firenze University Press (2017)
6. Unali, M.: Qual è il modello di rappresentazione complesso nella rivoluzione informatica. Disegnare idee immagini **38**, 30–39 (2009)
7. Dore, C., Murphy, M.: Semi-automatic generation of as-built BIM facade geometry from laser and image data. J. Inf. Technol. Constr. (ITcon) **19**, 20–46 (2014)
8. Alhava, O., Laine, E., Kiviniemi, A.: Intensive big room process for co-creating value in legacy construction projets. J. Inf. Technol. Constr. **20**, 146–158 (2015)
9. Bock, T., Linner, T.: Site Automation: Automated Robotic On-Site Factories. Cambridge University Press, Cambridge (2016)
10. Wangler, T., et al.: Digital concrete: opportunities and challenges. RILEM Tech. Lett. **1**, 67 (2016)
11. Lipson, H., Kurman, M.: Fabricated: The New World of 3D Printing. Wiley, Hoboken (2013)
12. Kestelier, X.: Design potential for large-scale additive fabrication. Free-form construction. In: Fabricate: Making Digital Architecture, pp. 244–249 (2011)
13. Morgante, A.: Radiolaria pavilion. In: Fabricate: Making Digital Architecture, pp. 234–235 (2011)
14. Menges, A.: Biomimetic design processes in architecture: morphogenetic and evolutionary computational design. Bioinspir. Biomim. **7**, 015003 (2012)
15. Dubor, A., Cabay, E., Chronis, A.: Energy efficient design for 3D printed earth architecture. In: De Rycke, K., et al. (eds.) Humanizing Digital Reality, pp. 383–393. Springer, Singapore (2018). https://doi.org/10.1007/978-981-10-6611-5_33
16. Rothenberg, J.: Ensuring the longevity of digital documents. Sci. Am. **272**(1), 42–47 (1995)
17. Maldonado, T.: Reale e virtuale. Feltrinelli (2005)
18. Tedeschi, A.: AAD, Algorithms-aided design: parametric strategies using Grasshopper. Le Penseur (2014)
19. Mulazzani, M., Bucci, F.: Luigi Moretti: Works and Writings. Princeton Architectural Press, New York (2002)
20. Gershenfeld, N.A.: The Nature of Mathematical Modeling. Cambridge University Pressm, Cambridge (1999)

E-Humanities

Chronologicon Hibernicum: A Probabilistic Chronological Framework for Dating Early Irish Language Developments and Literature

Fangzhe Qiu[1(✉)], David Stifter[1], Bernhard Bauer[1],
Elliott Lash[1], and Tianbo Ji[2]

[1] Maynooth University, Maynooth, Co. Kildare, Ireland
{fangzhe.qiu,david.stifter,bernhard.bauer,
elliott.lash}@mu.ie
[2] Dublin City University, Dublin, Ireland
tianbo.ji2@mail.dcu.ie

Abstract. This paper introduces the ongoing ERC-funded project *Chronologicon Hibernicum*, which studies the diachronic developments of the Irish language between c. 550–950, and aims at refining the absolute chronology of these developments. It presents firstly the project organization, its subject matter and objective, then gives an overview of the potentials and challenges in studying the Early Irish language. The project combines historical linguistic analysis, corpus linguistic methods and Bayesian statistic tools. Finally the paper explains the impact of this project in preserving the Irish cultural heritage and the lessons learned in the first three years.

Keywords: Chronologicon hibernicum · Linguistic dating
Irish cultural heritage

1 Introduction to the Project

1.1 Basic Facts

The research project 'Chronologicon Hibernicum – A Probabilistic Chronological Framework for Dating Early Irish Language Developments and Literature' has received funding through a Consolidator Grant of the European Research Council (ERC) under the European Union's Horizon 2020 research and innovation programme (grant agreement No. 647351). It started in September 2015 and will continue to the end of August 2020. It is hosted in the Department of Early Irish, Maynooth University, Ireland. The project team currently consists of the Principal Investigator (Prof. David Stifter), three full-time postdoctoral researchers (Dr. Bernhard Bauer, Dr. Elliott Lash and Dr. Fangzhe Qiu), two PhD students (Romanas Bulatovas and Lars Nooij) and two research assistants (Ellen Ganly and Tianbo Ji) and will soon welcome an extra staff member.

© Springer Nature Switzerland AG 2018
M. Ioannides et al. (Eds.): EuroMed 2018, LNCS 11196, pp. 731–740, 2018.
https://doi.org/10.1007/978-3-030-01762-0_65

1.2   Subject Matter

The two words *Chronologicon Hibernicum* contain the main aspects of the project in a nutshell. *Chronologicon* is a Greek adjective with the meaning 'pertaining to chronology'. So it is time and the impact that time leaves on language which lies at the heart of this project. *Hibernicum* is the Latin adjective for 'Irish'. The subject matter of *Chronologicon Hibernicum*, or ChronHib in short, is the **diachronic development of the Early Irish language**. Languages change over time, and in all linguistic domains, especially phonology, morphology and syntax, developments of the Irish language are clearly visible in the form of variations through time [1]. In absolute dates, the period studied in the project falls between c. 550 and c. 950 CE, covering what are traditionally termed the Early Old Irish, Old Irish and Early Middle Irish periods.

1.3   Objectives

The project's central objective is **linguistic dating**, i.e. to link the changes in linguistic forms to certain periods of time. On the one side one asks, when was an older form A replace by the newer form B; on the other, at a given point of time T, what is the probability that one finds B instead of A in same context? If these two questions can be answered, then one can predict the age of a text by examining its linguistic profiles.

Traditionally, linguistic dating is done by philological and linguistic analysis of manually curated data. ChronHib aims at revolutionizing the methods used for linguistic dating of Early Irish, by contributing to a chronologically more precise description of the variations in the above-mentioned linguistic domains, and by employing corpus linguistic and advanced statistical methods. It also endeavors to improve, by means of digital humanities techniques, on the availability and reliability of the material basis relevant to the chronology of linguistic developments and of the literature of Early Medieval Ireland.

2   The Early Irish Language: Potentials and Challenges

Since the diachronic development of Early Irish is the subject matter of ChronHib, it is pertinent to give a brief introduction to the Early Irish language and its textual culture.

The Irish language belongs to the Celtic branch of the Indo-European language family, and its closest relatives are Welsh, Breton, Cornish and ancient languages such as Gaulish and Celtiberian. Early Irish refers to the phases of the Irish language before c.1200 CE, including that of Primitive Irish (before c. 550), Old Irish (c. 550–900) and Middle Irish (c. 900–1200). Middle Irish is followed by Early Modern Irish (c. 1200–1700 CE) [2]. Early Irish was mainly spoken in the island of Ireland, but was also used in the Irish colonies in Britain and the Isle of Man. It is the ancestor of modern Irish, Scottish Gaelic and Manx.

Excluding formulaic inscriptions and proper names recorded by Classical authors, the earliest evidence of written Early Irish dates to the 7th century, in Latin script brought to Ireland by Christianity. From the 7th to the 10th century, the written literary tradition was vast in sheer number of texts and variegated in extent and genres. The number of extant texts from this period can be estimated to between eight and nine hundred prose texts of quite diverse length, and this does not even include the extremely rich poetic tradition. The texts include narrative sagas, historical texts (annals, genealogies), pseudo-historical tales, religious writings (homilies, saints' lives, martyrologies), poetry, as well as an extensive learned tradition of law, medicine, grammar and computistics, produced both in Ireland and in the multicultural Irish monasteries on the Continent.

These texts constitute a rich and unique cultural heritage not only of Ireland, but of Western Europe at large. They provide a detailed picture of the social, political and intellectual lives in early medieval Ireland, from the power struggles between kingdoms and diverse theological theories, down to the stories behind local place-names and regulations for bee-keeping. They give an indispensable account of a time when in continental Europe very little of other vernaculars had been rendered into letters, and contemporary records are sparse and obscure. More importantly, they testify to the thriving intellectual activities in Ireland and other parts of Europe, and the close connection between them. Since the majority of these texts are written in Early Irish, the study of Early Irish is quintessential for realizing the full potential of this cultural heritage.

However, Early Irish texts pose many challenges to modern scholars. The first one is the inherent characteristics of Early Irish as a morphologically complex language. Although the inventory of Early Irish inflection is similar to that of Latin or other ancient Indo-European languages, prehistoric phonological changes have rendered the synchronic morphological rules opaque and irregular. For non-specialists, it would be difficult, for instance, to recognize the lexeme *orgaid* '(s)he kills' in *iurtair* 'they will be killed' even with the help of grammars and dictionaries. There are still many gaps and obscurities, even for linguists, in the knowledge of Early Irish, such as the phonological rules that govern the change from *aue* 'grandson' to *ó*, or the reason of occasional omission of the relative particle *-(s)a* in prepositional relative clauses.

The second difficulty lies in the fact that, despite their richness in extent and content, little is known about the historic contexts in which the texts were produced. Almost all of the literature, especially of the early period, has been transmitted anonymously, and for most texts the time and circumstances of composition are unknown. The problem is compounded by transmission. Texts are materialized in the form of manuscripts, yet the absolute majority of medieval Irish texts today exist only in manuscripts made in or after the 12th century, and these texts occasionally underwent substantial revision or modernization on their way through history. Episodes of the famous heroic saga *Táin Bó Cúailnge* ('the Cattle-Raid of Cooley'), may first have been written down in the 8th century and were then joined with other episodes in the 9th century. What we have, however, is a copy from the early 12th century that may well have been partly adapted to the orthography and to the pronunciation of that time. Then we have another completely reworked version, in a very bombastic style, written in the latter part of the 12th century. In a mix like this it is very challenging to disentangle the complex sequence of chronological layers, although most texts are homogenous enough even if they only exist in later copies.

The two challenges, however, can be effectively tackled by fine-tuned linguistic analysis and sufficient linguistic dating. Mining and comparing linguistic data from different periods provide quantifiable measures to the changes in the language, thereby revealing previously unknown or unclear grammatical rules. All of these contribute to our deeper understanding of the nature and development of Early Irish, and help us interpret Early Irish texts more accurately. Meanwhile, close dating of the language makes it possible to identify the period in which a text was written, therefore linking a text to a specific historical setting. Texts can then be put into a precise chronological order, which enables us to trace their transmission and evolution that can reveal a lot about the material and intellectual culture of the time. Linguistic dating elucidates the crucial parameter of time in historical research and therefore is paramount for a better appreciation of the cultural heritage.

3   Methodologies

3.1   Data Collection

Since the Early Irish language is preserved as texts written in medieval manuscripts, these texts provide the data for linguistic dating in ChronHib. They are further categorized as below:

Texts from Contemporary Manuscripts. These are texts written in manuscripts produced before 950. Given the above-mentioned active scribal intervention in the transmission of earlier texts, only texts in manuscripts written before 950 can be trusted as accurately reflecting the linguistic characteristics of Irish in the period under examination. Around 80 texts are known to belong to this category, mostly in manuscripts now kept on the continent [3]. However, the date of the production of the manuscript is not always precisely known, and the relationship between the text and the manuscript sometimes remains obscure. A text on the life of St. Columba was composed by Adomnán of Iona between 688 and 692, and a copy was made by Dorbéine before he died in 713, which is now kept in Schaffhausen, Switzerland [4]. In this case both the manuscript and the text can be closely dated. Milan, Biblioteca Ambrosiana, C 301 inf. contains a copy of the commentary on the Psalms that has been heavily glossed in Irish. This manuscript can be dated to the first quarter of the 9th century, but the glosses seem to have been copied from an earlier source [3].

Texts That Are Non-linguistically Dated but from Later Manuscripts. These are texts that can be dated on non-linguistic grounds to specific periods but are only found in manuscripts produced after 950. A salient example is the 'Law of the Innocents' by Adomnán, the promulgation of which in June, 697 was recorded in the annals [5]. Yet the only copies that survive are from the 15th and the 17th centuries respectively. The poems by Blathmac son of Cú Bretan are found in a single 17th-century manuscript, although the annals report his father's death in 740 [5]. In these cases, scribal modernization has often affected the orthography and to some extent other linguistic features as well, though the rhymes in verses frequently help us restore the original forms. As a result, these texts are of less evidential value to the linguistic profile of Irish between c.550–950 than the first category, but are still invaluable data.

Texts That Cannot Be Dated Non-linguistically. One can generally say that these texts belong to the Early Irish period, even attempt to assign them to specific centuries, judging from their linguistic appearances, but these dates are often impressionistic and too broad for linguistic dating purposes. Nor are these texts found in manuscripts before 950. Consequently, these texts are not used as data for creating diachronic linguistic profiles.

3.2   Pre-processing the Data

Texts from the first and second categories listed in 3.1 constitute the corpus of data used in ChronHib. They are subject to the following pre-processing procedures. Most of the procedures are so far done manually or semi-automatically with search and replace commands, but we are developing fully automatic taggers.

Digitalization. Several digitalized corpora of Early Irish texts have already been published, which can be directly incorporated into the ChronHib database. These include corpora that are already linguistically parsed, such as the *Milan Glosses Database* [6], the *Priscian Glosses Database* [7], and the *Parsed Old and Middle Irish Corpus* [8], as well as a number of text repositories, such as the *Corpus of Electronic Texts* [9] and *Thesaurus Linguae Hibernicae* [10]. Other target texts have either been edited in the two-volume *Thesaurus Palaeohibernicus* [11], or have been published in individual critical editions, such as the Patrician texts in the Book of Armagh [12], or the *Vita Sancti Columbae* [4]. These edited texts are OCR-ed into digital format, and are proofread against the manuscript images.

Tokenization. Texts are broken down into sentences or glosses, and further into individual tokens consisting of minimally analyzable lexical units called 'morphs'. For example, the verbal complex *arnacha·toirsitis* 'so that they might not take her' [6] (48d27) is tokenized into *ar* 'so that', *nach* 'that not', *a* 'her', *to* (preverb), *r* (augment) and *toirsitis* 'they might take' respectively. To date the ChronHib corpus consists of 111,272 tagged tokens from 69 dated texts, and is still expanding.

Lemmatization, POS- and Morphological Tagging. Each token is assigned a lemma (the citation form of a lexeme), and given tags on its part-of-speech (POS) and morphological information according to a unified tagset, as exemplified in Table 1. Other information, such as etymology, mutation or onomastic compounds, is also annotated when applicable.

Variation-Tagging. A table has been created that lists 326 linguistic variations that we have currently identified to have occurred in the Irish language during the period c. 550–950. These include phonological, orthographical, morphological, syntactical and lexical variations. Each variation is given an ID (e.g. PH030) and a description stating the possible values of the variable (e.g. 'pretonic /e/ becomes /a/'). For each variable, the linguistic condition is defined (e.g. in the pretonic position in PH030), the values are usually binary (e.g. /e/ vs. /a/ in PH030), and sometimes the chronological order of the values is known (e.g. /e/ is earlier than /a/ in PH030).

Every token in the corpus is then tagged as to: (1) which variation could have possibly happened in the linguistic condition provided by the token, and (2) which

Table 1. Examples of lemmatization and POS-tagging in the *ChronHib* corpus.

Morph	Lemma	POS	Classification	Gender	Meaning	Morphological analysis
ar	*ara 1*	conjunction			so that, in order that	
nach	*nád 1*	particle	relative		that not	
a	*3sg.fem. inf.pron.*	pronoun	infixed		her	Class C
to	*do·*	particle	preverb			
r	*ro 1*	particle	augment		perfective or potential aspect	
·toirsitis	*do·fich*	verb	S1		to take, to attack	aug.3pl.past.subj.

value of the variable does the token show. One of the binary values of the variable, normally the earlier one if chronological order is known, is tagged **No,** while the other value **Yes.** Unclear instances are tagged **Maybe.** Table 2 offers some examples:

Table 2. Examples of variation-tagging in the *ChronHib* corpus.

Morph	Var.ID	Var.Description	Value
Achid	OR005	use <ai> instead of earlier <i> to represent the schwa in the unstressed syllable CəC'	**No**
das	MO072	use of new infixed pronoun forms instead of old ones	**Yes**
Feradach	PH029	posttonic, non-final short vowels are reduced to schwa	**Maybe**

3.3   Data Analysis

Synchronic Linguistic Profiles. By means of the close tagging described in Sect. 3.2, qualitative linguistic information can be transformed into a quantitative one. We can produce a numerical account of the linguistic variations of a text that has been dated by non-linguistic criteria. Since such a text represents the linguistic reality of a certain period, we can use the account of variations as a synchronic linguistic profile of that period. For instance, Table 3 shows the number of tags for a few phonological variations in the Schaffhausen copy of *Vita Sancti Columbae* (688x713), which tells us that at the end of the 7th century, while some changes (e.g. PH010 and PH025) have not yet started to happen in Irish (given that the innovative form tagged by **Yes** does not occur at all, the percentage of **Yes** being 0%), other changes have already begun (e.g. PH008) or have reached completion (e.g. PH028) (given that the older form tagged by **No** does not occur at all, the percentage of **Yes** being 100%).

When texts from different periods are tagged for linguistic variations, we have individual synchronic profiles of the Irish language from these periods. It has to be

Table 3. Examples of variations in *Vita Sancti Columbae*

ID	n (tokens)	No	Yes	Maybe	Yes percentage in all tokens
PH006	16	15	1	0	6.25%
PH008	212	147	41	24	19.34%
PH010	13	13	0	0	0.00%
PH013	145	136	1	8	0.69%
PH015	25	24	1	0	4.00%
PH025	30	30	0	0	0.00%
PH028	17	0	17	0	100.00%

remembered that these profiles are not continuous or exhaustive: they constitute random samples of a constantly changing language during c. 550–950.

Statistical Analysis. Because language changes are by nature probabilistic and cumulative rather than categorical and abrupt, the linguistic profiles are expressed by frequencies, both of the values of variations, and of the appearance or absence of certain forms and structures. Moreover, the periods that can be profiled are neither continuous nor evenly distributed. Therefore statistical methods must be employed, especially Bayesian statistics, which allows to make statements about prior knowledge in the light of newer information, i.e. 'degrees of belief' about propositions whose truth or falsity is uncertain can enter the equation [13, 14].

Synchronic profiles are combined to form a diachronic linguistic profile that consists of three major variables: date, variation and the number of tags. The statistical analysis will serialize the numbers of tags per variation according to the dates, and run multi-variable regression to create an absolute chronology of linguistic changes in Irish, which will inform us of the probabilities of certain linguistic features at any given temporal point within the investigated period. The detailed statistical methods are to be developed later in the project.

Testing of the Absolute Chronology. A small portion (about 10%) of tokens from dated texts will not join the statistical analysis. They are reserved as control data for testing the accuracy of the absolute chronology. These will be profiled separately, and their profiles will be mapped onto the absolute chronology to calculate their possible dates. If the predicted date matches the actual date (margin of error allowed), then the absolute chronology is valid; if not, the new data from the control group will be used to improve the calculation.

3.4 Application to Undated Texts

If proven sufficiently accurate, the absolute chronology framework can then be used to predict the date of a hitherto undated Irish text. An undated text undergoes the preprocessing as specified in Sect. 3.2, and a synchronic linguistic profile is created for it. The profile is then subject to multi-variable statistic tests to calculate the probability of its date by comparing it to the profiles of texts of known dates and to the absolute chronology. The result will be the confidence interval (or credible interval in Bayesian statistics) of the date of the text, interpreted as a range of years with corresponding probability. We will try to achieve a balance between the precision of date and the confidence level. The text can thus be quantitatively linguistically dated. Again, the actual statistical methods for this step remain to be developed at a later stage of the project.

4   Technology

The digitalization of data employs OCR scanning and translation of TEI and HTML files into .csv and .xlsx formats. We use Python scripts to tokenize Early Irish texts, and the tokens are then imported into a database developed on the FileMaker™ software for lemmatization and tagging.

Data processed on FileMaker™ are then exported, by the help of Python scripts, to a server-based database built upon MySQL. MySQL is the most popular free open-source relational database management system. Users can manage MySQL with MySQL Workbench – a unified visual tool for database developers which provides data modeling, SQL development, and comprehensive administration tools for server configuration, user administration, backup, and much more.

The project website uses HTML5 and Flask. On the frontend, we use a free Bootstrap website template as our index page, in which HTML, CSS and JavaScript (including pure JavaScript, jQuery and Ajax) are introduced. The backend is Flask, a Python website micro-framework based on Werkzeug and Jinja 2.

For the server side, the website and database are deployed on Maynooth University's Apache Server in which we can automatically back up our data and rollback if error occurs.

5   Impact and Expected Outcomes

The ChronHib database will soon be online for open access [15]. It is by far the largest linguistically annotated digital corpus of Early Irish texts. It serves as an electronic archive, which can be freely browsed and searched by anyone interested in early medieval history, literature, scribal practice or any other related fields. As an intensively annotated linguistic corpus, it also appeals not only to researchers of Early Irish, but also to linguists further afield as data for comparative or general linguistic studies.

This annotated corpus will also be the basis of an automatic tagger program for Early Irish texts. Trained by existing data and equipped with machine-learning techniques, this tagger will be able to annotate Early Irish texts (morphological, POS or syntactic) with a high accuracy.

In the process of building the corpus, we have established various standards and ontologies in collecting, annotating and analyzing data of Early Irish. The tagset developed by the project, for instance, is at present the most efficient and comprehensive for Early Irish. Our method of variation tagging is innovative, not only in the discipline of Early Irish, but also in diachronic linguistics at large. These formal expressions and methodologies are valuable assets and will benefit future researches.

The absolute chronology of linguistic developments in Early Irish and the statistical models will be the most important outcome of this project. Many new insights will be gained into the Early Irish language, which is a crucial component of the Irish culture heritage. The language is also the key to understanding the intellectual history and the textual culture in the Irish cultural sphere. ChronHib will create an authoritative reference point for linguistic dating, which will assign trustworthy dates to texts of medieval Ireland, thereby unravelling the complex intertextuality of Irish literature. Because Early Irish is beset with all the typical problems of Natural Language Processing on a historical language, such as small size of corpus, unstandardized spelling, morphological complexity and imbalance of registers, the statistical models developed for Early Irish will greatly advance the toolkit for processing other historical languages as well. These outcomes will be presented in the form of scholarly articles and books.

6   Lessons Learned

The lack of a sufficiently precise standard for the linguistic analysis of Old Irish has been a major delaying factor. There is no uniform system of tagging in the standard dictionary of Old Irish, nor in existing printed and digital editions. As a consequence, data cannot simply be imported from pre-existing collections. Likewise, the pre-existing databases based on Filemaker™, on which we built our initial corpus, tagged Early Irish texts slightly differently as they had been designed specifically for individual texts. We only realized after a while that the structures and tagsets of these databases do not suit the diversity and tagging needs of our corpus. In addition to this, since we used individually installed Filemaker™, the annotation practices varied from one member to another. It has taken us a very long time afterwards to harmonize all previous works into a uniformed format. Looking back, we should have established our standard structure and tagset and built the server-based database at the very beginning to avoid wasting time in harmonizing them at a later stage.

A related problem consists in the fact that the textual editions that our corpus is based on turned out to be less reliable philologically than we had assumed initially. The alternatives to cope with this problem are, either to simply accept errors into the analysis of our corpora, or to use the opportunity of corpus-building to improve the texts philologically, which, however, slows down the tagging process.

Acknowledgements. This paper is written as part of the research project *Chronologicon Hibernicum*, which has received funding from the European Research Council (ERC) under the European Union's Horizon 2020 research and innovation programme (Grant agreement No. 647351).

References

1. Stifter, D.: Towards the linguistic dating of early Irish law texts. In: Ahlqvist, A., O'Neill, P. (eds.) Medieval Irish Law: Text and Context, pp. 163–208. The University of Sydney, Sydney (2013)
2. McCone, K.: Towards a relative chronology of ancient and medieval Celtic sound changes. Maynooth University, Maynooth (1996)

3. Bronner, D.: Verzeichnis altirischer Quellen. Philipps Universität Marburg, Marburg (2013)
4. Anderson, A.O., Anderson, M.O. (eds.): Adomnan's Life of Columba. Thomas Nelson & Sons, London (1961)
5. Mac Airt, S., Mac Niocaill, G. (eds.): The Annals of Ulster (to A.D. 1131). Dublin Institute for Advanced Studies, Dublin (1983)
6. Griffith, A., Stifter, D.: Dictionary of the Old Irish glosses in the Milan MS Ambr. C301 inf. http://www.univie.ac.at/indogermanistik/milan_glosses.htm. Accessed 13 Aug 2018
7. Bauer, B.: The online database of the Old Irish Priscian glosses. http://www.univie.ac.at/indogermanistik/priscian/. Accessed 13 Aug 2018
8. Lash, E.: The Parsed Old and Middle-Irish Corpus. https://www.dias.ie/celt/celt-publications-2/celt-the-parsed-old-and-middle-irish-corpus-pomic/. Accessed 13 Aug 2018
9. Corpus of Electronic Texts. https://celt.ucc.ie//index.html. Accessed 13 Aug 2018
10. Thesaurus Linguae Hibernicae. http://www.ucd.ie/tlh/. Accessed 13 Aug 2018
11. Stokes, W., Strachan, J. (eds.): Thesaurus Palaeohibernicus. Dublin Institute for Advanced Studies, Dublin (1987)
12. Bieler, L.: The Patrician Texts in the Book of Armagh. Dublin Institute for Advanced Studies, Dublin (1979)
13. Bayes, T.: An essay towards solving a problem in the doctrine of chances. Philos. Trans. Roy. Soc. London **53**, 370–418 (1763)
14. Malakoff, D.: Bayes offers a 'new' way to make sense of numbers. Science **286**, 1460–1464 (1999)
15. ChronHib. http://chronhib.maynoothuniversity.ie. Accessed 13 Aug 2018

Ancient Asian Character Recognition for Literature Preservation and Understanding

Lin Meng[1]([⊠]) [iD], C. V. Aravinda[2] [iD], K. R. Uday Kumar Reddy[2],
Tomonori Izumi[1], and Katsuhiro Yamazaki[1]

[1] Department of Electronic and Computer Engineering, Ritsumeikan University,
Kusatsu, Shiga 525-8577, Japan
`menglin@fc.ritsumei.ac.jp`, {`t-izumi,yamazaki`}`@se.ritsumei.ac.jp`
[2] Department of Computer Science and Engineering,
N.M.A.M. Institute of Technology, Nitte, Karkala 574110, Karnataka, India
{`aravinda.cv,krudaykumar`}`@nitte.edu.in`

Abstract. This paper introduces a project for automatically recognizing ancient Asian characters by image processing and deep learning with the aim of preserving Asian culture. The ancient characters examined include Chinese and Indian characters, which are the most mysterious, wildly used, and historic in the ancient world, and also feature multiply types. The automatic recognition method consists of preprocessing and recognition processing. The preprocessing includes character segmentation and noise reduction, and the recognition processing has a conventional recognition and deep learning. The conventional recognition method consists of feature extraction and similarity calculation or classification, and data augmentation is a key part of the deep learning. Experimental results show that deep learning achieves a better recognition accuracy than conventional image processing. Our aim is to preserve ancient literature by digitizing it and clarifying the characters and how they change throughout history by means of accurate character recognition. We also hope to help people discover new knowledge from ancient literature.

Keywords: Ancient Asian character recognition
Character segmentation · Noise reduction · Deep learning
Ancient literature preservation · Ancient literature discovery

1 Introduction

China and India are two of world's most mysterious countries, what with their vast territory, long history, and rich cultural heritage. The two countries have influences and continue to influence the surrounding countries and each other

---

Supported by Japan Society for the Promotion of Science(JSPS) (26870713).

M. Ioannides et al. (Eds.): EuroMed 2018, LNCS 11196, pp. 741–751, 2018.
https://doi.org/10.1007/978-3-030-01762-0_66

not only in terms of culture but also politics, economics, etc. over a long period of time. For understanding and analyzing these various influences, researchers should be able to read and understand the relevant ancient literature. Automatic character recognition is becoming crucial here due to the huge amount of ancient literature involved. However, automatic recognition for ancient Asian characters is a difficult task, for the following reasons.

1. The characters are Multi-type, and also include un-uniformed types. Moreover, some of the characters are not used currently, causing significant problems when it comes to identifying the era and finding scholars in the relevant field.
2. Much of the literature is recoded on special materials such as bone, shell, stone, as paper was only invented around 2,000 years ago. Such documents are currently preserved in the form of rubbings, which will almost certainly lead to recognition problems in the future due to the aging process.
3. Huge collections of ancient literatures are not be organized make the problem more challenging. The aging process will also result in more difficulties with recognition and organization.

This project aims to recognize ancient Asian characters (Chinese and Indian characters) automatically by means of image processing and deep learning in order to preserve and understand the ancient literatures and assist with organizing Asian culture and history.

The automatic recognition method for ancient Asian characters consists of preprocessing and recognition processing. The preprocessing includes character segmentation, noise reduction, and normalization, and the recognition processing includes conventional recognition method and deep learning. The conventional recognition method consists of feature extraction and similarity calculation or classification, and data augmentation is a key part of the deep learning method.

We have previously done research on ancient character recognition. In this paper, we introduces current work and discusses how to improve the recognition method. We also briefly discuss future work.

In Sect. 2 of this paper, we focus on the recognition of Chinese characters, and in Sect. 3, we discuss Indian characters. We lists recognition results and discuss future work in Sect. 4. We conclude the paper with a brief summary and mention of future work in Sect. 5.

2   Recognition of Chinese Characters

2.1   Overview of Chinese Characters

Chinese characters have a long history, which widespread use in China, Japan, Singapore and surrounding countries (over roughly half of the Asia). And the Chinese characters are still be used in some special fields in other countries.

Ancient Chinese characters comprise multiple types including oracle bone inscriptions (OBIs), Zhuan-type, Li-type, Xing-type, Cao-type and Kai-type.

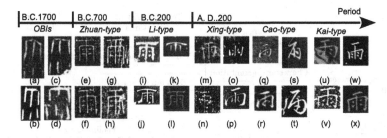

Fig. 1. Example of Chinese characters.

Figure 1 shows examples of each of these types depicting four ways of writing the character for "Rain", as taken from [1,2].

Oracle bone inscriptions (OBIs), one of the oldest character types, were inscribed on cattle bone or turtle shells about 3000 years ago and were discovered in 1899. However, only few studies have described them. The Zhuan-type was used during from B.C 700 to B. C 200, and Li-type is evaluated from Zhuan-type used from B.C 200. The Kai-type, Xing-type and Cao-type evolved from Li-type and have been used from A. D. 200 onward. The Kai-type is an uniform, and the Xing-type and Cao-type are speed-writing type. Because these character types evolved over a long period of time, they have numerous variations, and that greatly increases the difficult of recognition.

Moreover, the aging process has caused these characters to become less legible. For example, the characters in Fig. 1(d) and (u) are broken, and lots of noise exists in the ones in Fig. 1(g) and (h). Figure 2 shows recognition methods of our project, including conventional recognition method (a) which is based on image processing theory and deep learning which is base on machine learning (b).

2.2   Conventional Recognition Method

Figure 2(a) shows the conventional recognition method, which first constructs a multi-type character database, and then compares the features of the original target character with the templates in the database by calculating the similarity calculation. It then uses the similarity for decision result.

Some of the character types do not exist, so these template database are constructed by specialists. For example, the OBIs database is constructed by a College Letters professor at Ritsumeikan university [8].

For the character segmentation, we use a Gaussian filter, elliptic Gaussian filter and Gabor filter to enhance the character regions and extract the characters. The experimental results show that elliptic Gaussian filter is most effective for region extraction in OBIs [10].

As for the noise reduction, because of aging, big and small noises exist on the character images. We use Gaussian filtering blurring and binarization to reduce the smaller noises. Analyzing using a histogram revealed Gaussian filtering results divided into two peaks, so the Otsu method was used to determine

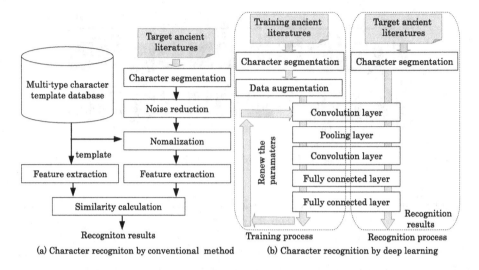

Fig. 2. Characters recognition methods.

the threshold for binarization. However, the bigger noises remain. To reduce the bigger noises, we use labeling method that last scans the binarized image and counts the pixel numbers of each connected object. We use a histogram method to detect big changes in the histogram of objects for detecting the threshold. If an object's pixel number is less than a threshold the object is treated for noise reduction. In this way, we are able to successfully reduce the bigger noises and the characters become more clear.

For normalization, due to the sizes difference between the characters and the templates, we used affine transformation to change the labeling result space into the template space. For feature extraction, we used the Hilditch Thinning algorithm to extract the skeletons of characters and used Hough transform along with clustering to extract the line points of characters and templates. For similarity calculation, we used two methods in our experimentations: template matching using normalized correlation coefficient [3] and distance calculation of the feature point lines between templates and a target image [4–7].

2.3 Deep Learning

Figure 2(b) shows the deep learning method for character recognition which consists of training and recognition processing. Deep learning consists of several convolution layers, pooling layers, and fully connected layers. Convolution layers have parameters (kernel) that are learned so that these filters are adjusted automatically to extract the most useful feature for the recognition at hand without any pre-selection of feature. Pooling layers are used to compress the results of previous convolution layers. Fully connected layers have full connections to all activations in the previous layers for judgement of the recognition results.

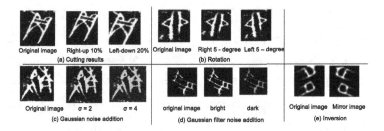

Fig. 3. Data augmentation.

In the training processing, parameters are determined by training a large amount of data [15,16]. However, some characters do not have a large number of images. The data should therefore be augmented before training. The data augmentation includes rotation, inversion, brightness changing, Gaussian noise addition and cutting. The data augmentation results are shown in Fig. 3. Rotation, which is training for characters that are oblique, consists of rotation from $\pm 5°$ to $\pm 30°$ by increments of $\pm 5°$. Inversion is training for mirror characters. Brightness changing is training for aging in documents that are not clear. Gaussian noise addition is training for aging when noise exists, where σ changes from 2 to 5. Cutting is training for the miss-segmentation characters, cutting the image four sides with 95, 90, 85, 80%. Hence, every image is augmented with 16 kinds cutting, 4 kinds Gaussian noise addition, 12 kinds rotations, 2 kinds inversion and 2 kinds brightness changing, which generates 3,072 new images.

For the recognition, we use AlexNet [15] and GoogLeNet [16] to select the optimum network for character recognition. GoogLeNet has 38 layers and Dropout is tuned for reducing over-fitting in the character recognition.

3   Recognition in Indian Characters

3.1   Overview of Indian Characters

High accuracy OCR systems are reported for English with excellent performance in presence of printing variations and document degradation. For Indian and many other oriental languages, OCR systems are not yet able to successfully recognize printed document images of varying scripts, quality, size, style and font. compared to European languages, Indian languages pose many additional challenges. Some of them are (i) Large number of vowels, consonants, and conjuncts, (ii) Most scripts spread over several zones, (iii) inflectional in nature and having complex character grapheme, (iv) lack of statistical analysis of most popular fonts and/or databases, (v) lack of standard test databases (ground truth data) of the Indian languages, Also issues like, (i) lack of standard representation for the fonts and encoding, (ii) lack of support from operating system, browsers and keyboard, and (iii) lack of language processing routines, add to the complexity of the design and implementation of a document image retrieval system [12–14].

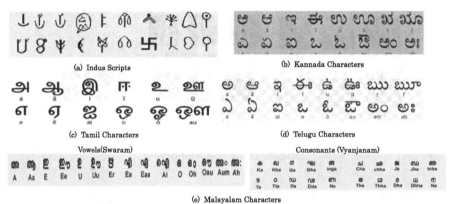

(a) Indus Scripts

(b) Kannada Characters

(c) Tamil Characters

(d) Telugu Characters

Vowels(Swaram)   Consonants (Vyanjanam)

(e) Malayalam Characters

Fig. 4. Indian characters.

There are several kinds south Indian language. A parts of these languages are shown in Fig. 4.

Indus Script (Fig. 4(a)) Indus script survived in the period of 2500–3000 BC. Earlier than Brahmi or Indic Script. Indic scripts are descended from the Brahmi script. Classifying historical document manually is cumbersome. One of the serious problems is identifying era and finding scholars in the field of epigraphy.

Kannada Script (Fig. 4(b)) is one of the real Dravidian dialects of southern India and one of the soonest dialects confirm epigraphically in India and talked by around 50 million individuals in the Indian conditions of Karnataka. The script has 49 characters in its Alpha syllabary and is phonemic. The Kannada character set is practically indistinguishable to that of other Indian dialects. The characters are characterized into three classifications: swaras (vowels), vyanjanas (consonants) and yogavaahas (part vowel, part consonants).

Tamil Scirpt (Fig. 4(c)) is a Dravidian dialect talked prevalently by Tamils in India and Sri Lanka, of speakers in numerous other nations. It is the official dialect of the Indian condition of Tamil Nadu, furthermore has official status in Sri Lanka and Singapore and having more than 7 million speakers. Tamil is one of the real dialects of the world. The Tamil script has 12 vowels, 18 consonants and five grantha letters. The script, be that as it may, is syllabic and not alphabetic. The complete script, in this way, comprises of the 31 letters in their autonomous structure, and an extra 216 combatant letters speaking to each conceivable mix of a vowel and a consonant.

Telugu Script (Fig. 4(d)), another Dravidian dialect talked by around 5 million individuals in the southern Indian condition of Andhra Pradesh and neighbouring states, furthermore in Bahrain, Fiji, Malaysia, Mauritius, Singapore and the UAE. Telugu is a syllabic dialect. Like most dialects of India, each image in

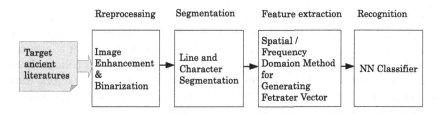

Fig. 5. Indian character recognition method.

Telugu script speaks to a complete syllable. Authoritatively, there are 18 vowels, 36 consonants, and three double images. Of these, 13 vowels, 35.

Malayalam Script (Fig. 4(e)) is the dialect talked prevalently in the condition of Kerala, in southern India. It is one of the 23 official dialects of India, talked by around 37 million individuals. The dialect has a place with the group of Dravidian dialects. Both the dialect and its written work framework are firmly identified with Tamil; in any case, Malayalam has a script of its own. Malayalam dialect script comprises of 51 letters counting 16 vowels and 37 consonants. The prior style of composing is currently substituted with another style and this new script decreases the distinctive letters for typeset from 900 to under 90.

3.2   Indian Character Recognition

The system is intended to isolate each character from an input image containing handwritten Kannada text, recognize the character band also print its corresponding Unicode onto a text file which can be edited and saved for future use. The Fig. 5 shows the flow of various stages in the system. This system mainly breaks down the recognition process into four fundamental sequential stages:

- Pre-processing
- Segmentation
- Feature extraction and Classification
  - Hu's Invariant Moments
  - Zernike Moments
  - Zonal Features
  - Fourier-Wavelet Co-efficients

Segmentation is one of the most important phases of HCR system. The process of segmentation contains 2 stages which are the Line Segmentation, character segmentation. In *line Segmentation*, the lines of a text block are detected by scanning the input image horizontally. Frequency of black pixels in each row is counted in order to construct the row histogram. When frequency of black pixels in a row is zero it denotes a boundary between two white pixels consecutive lines. That is, the lines of a text block are segmented by finding the valleys of the projection profile computed by a row-wise sum of black pixel values. In

Character segmentation each line obtained from the line segmentation is taken as input. In each line, a character is detected by vertically scanning the line image. Frequency of black pixels in each column is counted in order to construct the column histogram. When frequency of black pixel in each column is zero it denotes a boundary between two white pixel consecutive characters. Hence characters of a line are segmented by finding the valleys of the projection profile computed by column wise sum of black pixel values.

Feature extraction is a crucial step for character recognition, and most research has been devoted to finding measures that concisely represent a pattern and at the same time contain enough information to ensure reliable recognition. Feature Extraction using Spatial Domain Methods Spatial domain method is based on the image bitmap such as projection of the image function onto different lines, moments of the image and dividing the image into different zones.

NN Classifier (nearest-neighbour classifier) is a method for large-scale. The training phase of the algorithm consists only of storing the feature vectors and class labels of the training samples. In the actual classification phase, the same features as before are computed for the test samples. Distances from the new vector to all stored vectors are computed. Then Classification and recognition is achieved on the basis of similarity measurement. An Artificial Neural Network (ANN) is a computational model widely used in pattern recognition. It has been used extensively both for the recognition of non-Indian as well as Indian characters. Recognition of handwritten characters is a very complex problem. Feed forward back propagation network is used for subsequent recognition and classification of image.

4   Discussion

For the recognition of Chinese characters of OBIs, we found that template matching achieved an 87% recognition rate in the experiment using 22 normalized OBIs and that the template matching was weakly at the character is oblique [3]. The distance calculation method of using the extracted line points achieved a 90% recognition rate [6].

The deep learning method achieved a 92.0% recognition rate by data augmentation, which is far beyond the recognition without data augmentation which is only 39.2%. Moreover, it achieved a 94.4% recognition rate after changing the dropout [9]. In terms of the rubbing image of the multi-type Chinese characters recognition, we achieved a 96% recognition by GoogLenet which is better than the Alexnet, which was 94% [11]. Table 1 lists the recognition rate of Indian

Table 1. Character recognition rate (%)

	Vowels	Consonants	Consonant conjunct	Votaksharas
Printed	85–90	80–82	75–78	80
Handwritten	75–80	70	65–68	60–63

characters by the proposed method (conventional image processing method). It is divided into printed type and handwritten type to correspond with the two types of ancient literature that exist. The results show that the recognition rates are less than 90% [17–19].

Overall, we found that deep learning achieves a good result for the recognition of Chinese characters, although the deep learning still has a few challenges to overcome with the recognition of Indian characters. We also found that data augmentation is an important process in the recognition of all characters. These results will be useful for the construction of a recognition platform that can recognize Chinese and Indian character in the same system and translate each other. Moreover, they hold the key to not only understanding ancient literature but also utilizing the discovery of the relationship between these ancient literatures and the various countries of Asia.

On the application, this project aims to recognize several kinds of ancient Asian characters. The proposed system will help people who are interesting in ancient Asian literature, but he/she may be not a specialist and cannot understand all the characters. The users can upload the literature images which contain the non-understood characters, and the system will translate it into understandable characters. Furthermore, the system will help researchers in different fields to use the literature. In this case, when people have non-understood characters, they may upload the images and request for the corresponding characters.

The system aims to cover the major ancient Asian character recognition. It may be the first attempt and there are few similar researches exists. It may help researchers understanding the ancient Asian characters. However, we did not open the project to public yet and the application cannot be used for researchers at this moment. It is one of our future work to open the application to common users. Furthermore, It is hard to collect the dataset, and calculate time is complexity while training the data sets in the case of using deep learning.

5 Conclusion

This project aims to recognize ancient Asian characters automatically by image processing and deep learning for preservation the Asian culture. The ancient characters examined are Chinese multi-type characters and Indian characters, which are the most mysterious and wildly used in the ancient world. Experimental results demonstrate that deep learning achieves a better accuracy than conventional methods. In the future, we will adapt deep learning for recognizing Indian characters, and translate this characters into modern language. Our long-term goal is to preserve ancient literature though digital means and understanding of the evaluation of these characters along with the changing times. We also hope to help people discover rich new knowledge from ancient literature by understanding the characters.

References

1. Pu, M.Z., Xie, H.Y.: Shanghai Bo Wu Guan Cang Jia Gu Wen Zi. Shanghai Bo Wu Guan (2009)
2. Rubbing characters Database (Kyoto University). http://coe21.zinbun.kyoto-u.ac.jp/djvuchar. Accessed 8 Aug 2018
3. Meng, L., Fujikawa, Y., Ochiai, A., Izumi, T., Yamazaki, K.: Recognition of oracular bone inscriptions using template matching. Int. J. Comput. Theory Eng. **8**(1), 53–57 (2016). (in Japanese)
4. Meng, L., Izumi, T., Oyanagi, S.: Recognition of oracular bone inscriptions by clustering and matching on the hough space. J. Inst. Image Electron. Eng. Jpn. **44**(4), 627–636 (2015). (in Japanese)
5. Meng, L.: Recognition of oracle bone inscriptions by extracting line features on image processing. In: Proceedings of the 6th International Conference on Pattern Recognition Applications and Methods (ICPRAM 2017), pp. 606–611 (2017)
6. Meng, L.: Two-stage recognition for oracle bone inscriptions. In: Battiato, S., Gallo, G., Schettini, R., Stanco, F. (eds.) ICIAP 2017. LNCS, vol. 10485, pp. 672–682. Springer, Cham (2017). https://doi.org/10.1007/978-3-319-68548-9_61
7. Meng, L.: Recognition of Oracle Bone Inscriptions Using Image Processing, 1st edn. HOKUTO PRINT, Kyoto (2016). (in Japanese)
8. Ochiai, A.: Oracle Bone Inscriptions Database. http://koukotsu.sakura.ne.jp/top.html. Accessed 8 Aug 2018
9. Kamitoku, N., Meng, L., Yamazaki, K.: Recognition of oracle bone inscriptions using deep learning. In: The 80th National Convention of Information Processing Society of Japan, 2S-07 (2018). (in Japanese)
10. Watanabe, S., Meng, L., Izumi, T.: Methods to extract character regions of oracle bone inscriptions. In: The 248th Technical Report of the Institute of Image Electronics Engineers of Japan (2018). (in Japanese)
11. Kishi, M., Nabeya, M., Nogami, K., Meng, L., Yamazaki, K.: Multi-typeface recognition of rubbing using deep learning and creation of spatiotemporal database. In: The 80th National Convention of Information Processing Society of Japan, 2S-08 (2018). (in Japanese)
12. Aravinda, C.V., Prakash, H.N.: A review on various HandWritten cursive characters segmentation techniques. In: 2nd International Conference on Applied and Theoretical Computing and Communication Technology (iCATccT), pp. 647–651 (2016)
13. Aravinda, C.V., Prakash, H.N.: A review recognition for south india languages using statistical feature extraction and distance classifier. Int. J. Nat. Lang. Comput. (IJNLC) **5**(4), 37–48 (2016)
14. Aravinda, C.V., Prakash, H.N.: Template matching method for Kannada Handwriten recognition based on correlation analysis. In: 2014 International Conference on Contemporary Computing and Informatics (IC3I), pp. 857–861 (2014)
15. Krizhevsky, A., Sutskever, I., Hinton, G.E.: ImageNet classification with deep convolutional neural networks. In: Advances in Neural Information Processing Systems 25 (NIPS 2012) (2012)
16. Szegedy, C., et al.: Going deeper with convolutions. In : 2015 IEEE Conference on Computer Vision and Pattern Recognition (CVPR 2015) (2015)
17. Aravinda, C.V., Prakash, H.N.: A machine editable format for Kannada handwritten character recognition using a dissect and connect technique. IJETAE **4**, 1–5 (2014)

18. Aravinda, C.V., Prakash, H.N., Lavanya, S.: Kannada handwritten character recognition using multi feature extraction technique. Int. J. Sci. Res. (IJSR) **3**(10), 911–916 (2014)
19. Aravinda, C.V., Prakash, H.N.: Template matching method for kannada handwritten recognition based on correlation analysis. In: 2014 International Conference on Contemporary Computing and Informatics (IC3I) (2014)

Preservation and Management of Greek Dialectal Data

Eleni Galiotou[1(✉)], Nikitas Karanikolas[1], and Angela Ralli[2]

[1] University of West Attica, University Campus 1, Ag. Spyridonos 28,
122 43 Aigaleo, Athens, Greece
{egali,nnk}@uniwa.gr
[2] University of Patras, University Campus, 265 04 Rio, Patras, Greece
ralli@upatras.gr

Abstract. Greek dialects of Asia Minor are considered as ideal case studies on the elucidation of the evolution of the Greek language as well on different phenomena of language contact, due to their longtime contact with the Turkish language and their relative isolation from the other Greek dialects. In fact, the dialects in question constitute a rich cultural and language heritage in threat of extinction. Therefore, there is an urgent need of describing and preserving this invaluable heritage. In this paper, an innovative system of archiving and management of digitized written and oral data from three Greek dialects of Asia Minor (Pontic, Cappadocian, Aivaliot) is presented. The system also contains a search and retrieve component which enables: (a) a combined search at different levels of linguistic representation, (b) combined search in both written and oral data and (c) access to metadata.

Keywords: Greek dialects · Corpora · Preservation · Digitization
Multimedia databases · Computational dialectology

1 Introduction

The availability of dialectal corpora on electronic media and the development of computational tools is of major importance for the sustainability and awareness of dialects which constitute an invaluable cultural heritage. Moreover, the use of specialized software contributes in a decisive way to the study of language change and dialect contact. To this end, several attempts are reported such as the voice language map of Japanese dialects [14], the Linguistic Atlas of Middle and South Atlantic States (LAMSAS) [11], the Scottish Corpus of Text and Speech (SCOTS) [1], and the Corpus of contemporary Catalan (COD) [15]. Software tools have also been developed such as the set of Natural Language Processing tools for the processing of Swiss German oral dialectal data [13] or the DynaSAND (Dynamic Syntactic Atlas of Dutch Dialects), an on-line tool for the processing of Dutch syntactic variation [3] which is enriched and enhanced with a web service interface to the DynaSAND corpus, so that the data from the corpus can be used for other applications as well. The AMiGre[1] project constitutes

---

[1] http://amigre.upatras.gr/.

© Springer Nature Switzerland AG 2018
M. Ioannides et al. (Eds.): EuroMed 2018, LNCS 11196, pp. 752–761, 2018.
https://doi.org/10.1007/978-3-030-01762-0_67

the first attempt at an overall comparative study of Greek dialects of Asia Minor. Moreover, it constitutes the first attempt in Greece to combine Theoretical Linguistics and Information Technology in order to present both raw and processed material in the digital space with the use of innovative software [4]. The project resulted in the scientific presentation of Greek dialectal data to the academia under the form of a multimedia corpus, an electronic tri-dialectal dictionary[2] [6] and a number of publications. In this paper, we describe the system of archiving and managing oral and written dialectal data, the nucleus of which is a multimedia database which enables the parallel display of raw and processed data as well as the coding of a large number of metadata. In Sect. 2 below, the compilation of the digitized written and oral corpora is presented. The system of archiving and processing oral and written dialectal data is described in Sect. 3. Next, the data entry and management subsystem and the search and retrieve subsystem are described in Sects. 4 and 5 respectively. Finally, conclusions are drawn and reference to future work is made in Sect. 6.

2 Digitized Oral and Written Corpora

2.1 Written Data

The compilation of the digitized written corpus was performed in 4 stages [10]:

Collection and Cataloguing: Initially, a bibliographic record of primary and secondary sources was created. Primary sources include narrations, tales, legends, songs, folklore descriptions, descriptions of facts. Secondary sources include linguistic studies, grammatical descriptions, dictionaries, glossaries etc. A bibliographic database containing more than 1250 bibliographic references was created. The largest part of the sources concern the Pontic dialect, while the representation of Aivaliot is limited. Obviously, this imbalance appears in the digitized dialectal corpus as well.

Digitization: Then a digitized corpus of 2,000,000 words was built based on specific selection criteria: The selected texts were published before 1940 due to the intellectual properties constraint. Nevertheless, the value of the digitized corpus was not reduced since, primary sources before 1922, that is before the relocation of populations in the Greek state, are of utmost importance in the study of Asia Minor dialects. Moreover, texts published after 1940 were also included in the corpus, such as those of the Center for Asia Minor Studies, after written permission of the owners. The digitized material contains mainly prose texts. Songs or poems were not included in the corpus since, on the one hand, they display linguistic phenomena directly related to verse and, on the other hand, information on their origin is incomplete. A representative sample of manuscripts was also included in the corpus based on their oldness and the type of text they preserve. The selected texts belong to rare or personal collections and well-known important handbooks for the study of the dialects in question. The digitization was

---

[2] The tri-dialectal dictionary consisting of 7,500 dialectal lemmas of Pontic, Aivaliot and Cappadocian is already available to researchers, upon request and the permission of the director of the project, Prof. Angela Ralli (http://lepokam.philology.upatras.gr).

performed with the use of a portable scanner so as to assure the quantity and the quality of the images and avoid the deterioration of the quality of the texts. The resulting digital images were further processed in order to assure a uniform appearance in the final digitized corpus.

Transcription: Texts containing 200,000 words were selected from the digitized corpus and transcribed without use of and Optical Character Recognition (OCR) or Hand-written Text Recognition (HCR) software. An OCR software would face difficulties in recognizing the polytonic system and the hand-written texts. Moreover, training a HTR software would be time-prohibitive due to the wide disparities of the digitized material (many various handwritings, special symbols, paper or ink qualities). Texts were transcribed using the Greek alphabet and the established historical spelling, while dialectal particularities on the morphological/phonological level were rendered with the use of capital Greek letters and a few Latin ones only in the case of phonological annotations by the editors or the authors. This particular transcription system was developed by the AMiGre research group and it is based on the SAMPA phonetic alphabet [16] which was adapted to the data and the aims of the project. This uniform transcription system enables searching all kinds of linguistic phenomena in the digitized corpus containing texts from all three dialects. Pontic and Cappadocian are represented by approx. 95,000 words, while Aivaliot is represented by approx. 10,000 words. This imbalance is due to the fact that written sources of Aivaliot are limited in number and extent. Therefore, a large number of oral Aivaliot sources were also digitized, in order for the sample to become representative of all three dialects. The hardest problem in the transcription process was the non-standard writing of dialects due to the strong tendency of researchers to follow a personalized transcription system, in particular with respect to phonological particularities which could not be transcribed with the established transcription system of Standard Modern Greek (SMG). Therefore, texts containing a large number of unclear elements were not transcribed. The phonological mapping of symbols is presented in the Table 1 below.

Annotation: A part of the digitized corpus containing 50,000 words was annotated. The annotated corpus does not contain texts in the Aivaliot dialect due to the lack of written documents in this language. Therefore, the distribution of words in the annotated corpus is 25,000 Pontic and 25,000 Cappadocian words. The annotation was performed in .xls files from which data were imported in the multimedia database. The linguistic annotation was performed at the phonological and morphological levels, while information concerning loan words and archaisms was also added. As far as phonology is concerned, annotation was performed on a unit (vowel, consonant) or syllable level. In order to annotate a phonological phenomenon, reference is made to the earliest known antecedent of the dialect. In most cases, reference goes back to Medieval Greek, while, sometimes, Hellenistic Koine is considered as the earliest known antecedent As far as Morphology is concerned, annotation is performed at the word level emphasizing information on inflection and derivation.

At this level of morphological annotation, synchronic information is provided for a complete description of the dialects and therefore, the historical aspect imposed by phonological information is missing. Note that, the full phonological and

Table 1. Transcription system

International phonetic alphabet	Original source symbols	AMiGre
æ	Ä	A
œ, ø	Ö	O
ɯ	I	I
ə	ə	E
y	Ü	Y
b, d, g	b, d, g	b, d, g ή μπ, ντ, γκ, γγ
mb, nd, ng	μb, vd, vg	μb, vd, vg
q	Q	q
ʎ	λ´, λ̂	Λ
ɲ	ν´	N
ʃ	σ´, σ̂, χ´, χ̂	Σ
ʒ	ζ´, ζ̂	Z
tʃ	τσ´, τσ̂	τΣ
dʒ	dζ´, ντζ̂	dZ
c	κ´, κ̂	K
ç	χ´, χ̂	X
j	γ´, γ̂	Γ
ɟ	γκ´, γκ̂	G
pʰ tʰ kʰ	', p t k	πh, τh, κh

morphological annotation faced significant difficulties due to the lack of a systematic study and basic resources of the dialects such as dictionaries and grammars.

2.2 Oral Data

As for oral resources, the multimedia database contains: digitized recordings of native speakers, spelling transcription and translation of about 1/3 of the recorded conversations, morphological annotation of inflection, derivation and compounding, as well as phonological annotation of intonational phrases, words, syllables and phonemes [12]. The oral corpus contains about 180 h of recorded raw data which were granted the written permission of the informants. Field researchers were native speakers of the dialect under investigation, capable of applying ethnographic methods of data collection and recording everyday conversations. The transcription and the translation of conversations in Pontic and Cappadocian was performed by field researchers, while conversations in Aivaliot were transcribed and translated by native speakers of the Lesbian dialect which is very close to Aivaliot. The spelling transcription was performed with the use of the Praat[3] software. Then, in the transcribed and translated recordings, turn-takings of each speaker, intonational phrases, words, syllables and phonemes were identified. Metadata concerning the dialect, the informants and the

---

[3] http://www.praat.org.

communicative situation were also collected. More specifically, as for the dialect, information about its name, its place of origin, the informant, and the place of recording is provided. As for the informants, the provided information concerns the gender, the educational level, their origin, the status of the origin group at the place of recording, their neighborhood and everyday relationships. Moreover, as for the communicative situation, information is provided on the number of participants in the recording, their social relationship, as well as the kind of the recording (formal or friendly conversation, interview, questionnaire etc.).

2.3   The Asia Minor Archive

The above-mentioned corpora, together with the tri-dialectal dictionary, constitute the Asia Minor Archive, which is stored at the server of the Laboratory of Modern Greek Dialects (LMGD) of the University of Patras[4], the personnel of which assures its long-term maintenance and preservation. All processed written and oral data, together with those of the rest of raw oral material are accessible only to the researchers of LMGD, through a specific application. It is worth mentioning that the corpora were processed by using ELAN[5] for multimodal annotation and phonetically analyzed with the use of Praat resulting in the representation of vowels, diphthongs, consonants and consonant clusters appearing on different layers (tiers). One more tier was added, that of morphological representation, consisting of word internal morphological segmentation, constituent recognition and categorization. Segments and consonants were transcribed with the IPA[6] symbols, while morphological words and syllables with the use of the SAMPA alphabet as adapted to the needs of our project. An advanced software tool such as Labb-CAT[7] which provides the user with the possibility to store audio or video recordings, text transcripts and other annotations should be able to deal with the variety of linguistic information and annotation types. Yet, the system in question could not deal with our basic requirements, that is, (a) annotations at different linguistic levels, and (b) combined search at both the oral and written corpora. Consequently, we opted for the design and implementation of a software which would be tailored to our needs [7, 8]. The system is described below:

3   A System of Archiving and Processing Dialectal Data

3.1   Data Representation

Annotations on written documents are performed at 3 levels: text, page, word. Oral documents comprise recordings of one speaker or a small group of speakers. For each speaker a turn taking corresponds to an intonational phrase and is composed of morphological words. Morphological words are composed of syllables which, in turn, are

---

[4] http://lmgd.philology.upatras.gr.

[5] http://tla.mpi.nl/tools/tla-tools/elan/.

[6] http://www.langsci.ucl.ac.uk/ipa/ipachart.html.

[7] http://onzeminer.sourceforge.net/.

composed of phonemes. Therefore, oral documents are annotated at more than 3 levels. The structures of oral and written documents were unified into one general structure which incorporates the following correspondences: The *Dialogue (Outer)* level represents a dialogue between speakers in oral documents. The Document level represents a speaker or a written document. The *Part* level corresponds to a speaker's utterance or a page of a written document. The *Word* level corresponds to morphological words in both types of documents while, the *Inner* level corresponds to syllables, phonemes etc. in oral documents. The hierarchical general documents structure is depicted in Fig. 1. Dialectal data are of particular interest as for their representation and management on electronic media due to the variety of forms and types of files included in the archiving and management system. As to oral documents, the system keeps: digital recordings (.wav files), initial annotations in TextGrid files (Praat output files) and computationally editable annotations for all supported levels. As for written documents, the system keeps: digitized original pages (.jpg files), transcriptions of original texts (text files) and computationally editable annotations for all supported levels. Our system also provides the possibility to add syntactic or semantic information in the future if necessary [5]. The computationally editable elements are stored in three databases: (a) The "Struct" database: a set of tables that implement the abstract hierarchical structure of both oral and written documents. (b) The EAV database of annotations: Since it was not possible to initially define all the entities and their attributes, we used an EAV (Entity-Attribute-Value) schema [2] which was extended in order to support free and predefined sets of values (vocabularies), multiple attribute values and property display dependencies. (c) The Inner database: it also implements an EAV schema and stores word segments and corresponding annotations.

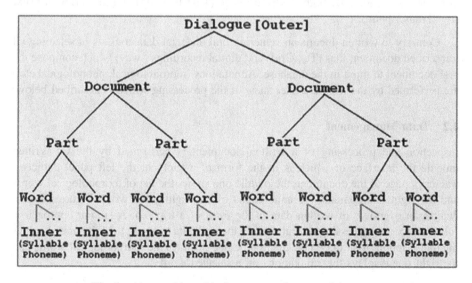

Fig. 1. Abstract hierarchical structure of a general document

3.2   Application Overview

Our system comprises two basic modules, G. Written and G. Oral for the management of written and oral documents respectively [5]. Both subsystems were designed and implemented as a triptych (Part-Word-Annotations) and they invoke a number of web-like applications which comprise:

- A phonological tagger for both oral and written documents.
- A morphological tagger for both oral and written documents.
- A syntactic tagger which assigns syntactic information on a sequence of words.
- A semantic tagger which assigns semantic information on a sequence of words

Note that only the first two taggers were used for the purpose of the AMiGre project. The applications also comprise a preview of image resources, transcription and annotation and a module for storing and updating metadata. The entry of written data is a step-by-step (page-by-page) process, while oral documents are massively introduced in the system. Finally, the *"Search and Retrieve"* subsystem invokes all the web-like applications for a combined search in both oral and written data.

4   Data Entry and Management Subsystem

4.1   Data Entry

The step-by-step entry process of written documents is summarized as:

(a) create a blank document
(b) enter written document page by page
(c) for each page, enter both digitized image (Text Imaging) and transcription (Text Transcription).

Contrary to written documents, entering oral dialectal data consists of selecting all transcribed document files (TextGrid) and digital recordings (.wav) which compose the oral document to input in the database. Annotations (morphological, phonological etc.) are performed by the user at a later stage of the processing which is described below.

4.2   Data Management

Inspection and processing of a written document is performed by the G. Written module the interface of which is in the form of a triptych; the left panel depicts a transcript page of the document, the middle one shows the list of morphological words and the right one contains the annotations of the highlighted word. Figure 2 below depicts an overview of written data in the form of a triptych. A similar approach is followed for the processing of oral data. In the oral data triptych, the left panel displays the transcription of an utterance, the middle one displays the morphological words and the right one displays the annotations on a selected word.

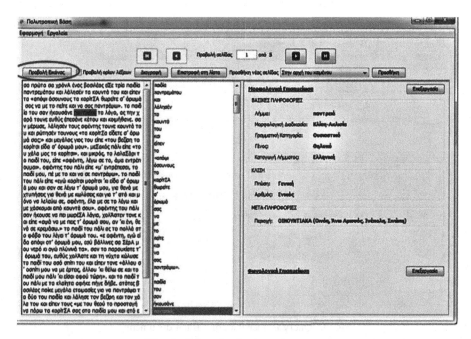

Fig. 2. Triptych of written documents

5   The Search and Retrieve Subsystem

Our search and retrieve subsystem is designed as to meet the following requirements: (a) Intuitive usage. (b) Multiple annotation values [9]. (c) Value and distance constraints for each search criterion. (d) Conjunction of research criteria (e) Focus on a specific level such as Document, Part, Word, Inner. (f) Retrieval requirements for data aggregations and artifacts – on the fly created data. Table 2 below depicts the structure of a query:

Table 2.   Structure of a search query

Word/Token/Phenomenon			Location					
<Value>	{Between, And, Or, Exact}	<Value>	<EAV subschema> (annotations/ meta-information)	<Attribute>	<Part distances>	<Word distances>	<Interval_no distances>

In Fig. 3 below, a query on written documents is depicted. It specifies a query in the metadata field for the author Richard Dawkins of documents published in 19...

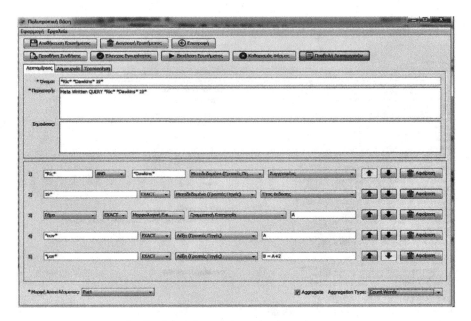

Fig. 3. Query in metadata of written documents

6   Conclusions

In this paper, we have presented the design and development of a system of compilation and management of written and oral data from three Greek dialects of Asia Minor. The system is installed on the server of the LMGD and presently accessible only to the scientific personnel of the Laboratory. The nucleus of the system is a multimedia database which allows for a parallel display of raw and processed data as well as the coding of a large number of metadata. The system requirements were generalized so as to avoid restriction to specific dialects or specific linguistic phenomena. Therefore, we claim that it can be used for the preservation and management of different languages and dialects since it can be adapted to the needs of new research outcomes. Future work includes further development of software tools for the measurement of the phonetic and syntactic distances between the three dialects.

Acknowledgements. This research was co-financed by the European Union (European Social Fund–ESF) and Greek national funds through the Operational Program "Education and Life-long Learning" of the National Strategic Reference framework (NSRF) - Research Funding Program: "THALIS. Investing in knowledge society" through the European Social Fund. We wish to thank our colleagues: Konstantinos Athanasakos, Athanassios Karasimos, Maria Koliopoulou, George Koronakis, Nikolaos Koutsoukos, Io Manolessou, Theodoros Markopoulos, Nikolaos Pantelidis, Dimitris Papazachariou.

References

1. Anderson, J., Beavan, D., Kay, C.: SCOTS: scottish corpus of texts and speech. In: Beal, J. C., Corrigan, K.P., Moisl, H.L. (eds.) Creating and Digitizing Language Corpora, vol. 1, pp. 17–34. Palgrave Macmillan UK, London (2007). https://doi.org/10.1057/9780230223936_2

2. Anhøj, J.: Generic design of web-based clinical databases. J. Med. Internet Res. (4) (2003). https://www.jmir.org/2003/4/e27/]

3. Barbiers, S., et al.: Dynamic Syntactic Atlas of the Dutch dialects (DynaSAND). Meertens Institute, Amsterdam (2006). http://www.meertens.knaw.nl/sand/

4. Galiotou, E., et al.: Asia minor greek: towards a computational processing. Procedia – Soc. Behav. Sci. **147**, 458–466 (2014). Special issue: Proc. IC-ININFO 2013

5. Karanikolas, N., Galiotou, E., Athanasakos, K., Koronakis, G.: A multimodal system of archiving and processing and management of written and oral language and dialect resources (in Greek). In: Ralli, A. (ed.) THALIS Project: "Pontus, Cappadocia, Aivali: in search of Asia Minor Greek" (in Greek), University of Patras, pp. 69–98 (2015)

6. Karanikolas, N.N., Galiotou, E., Xydopoulos, G.J., Ralli, A., Athanasakos, K., Koronakis, G.: Structuring a multimedia tri-dialectal dictionary. In: Habernal, I., Matoušek, V. (eds.) TSD 2013. LNCS (LNAI), vol. 8082, pp. 509–518. Springer, Heidelberg (2013). https://doi.org/10.1007/978-3-642-40585-3_64

7. Karanikolas, N., Galiotou, E., Papazachariou, D., Athanasakos, K., Koronakis, G., Ralli, A.: Towards a computational processing of oral dialectal data. In: Proceedings of the 19th PCI 2015, Athens, 1–3 October 2015, pp. 337–341. ACM Press (2015)

8. Karanikolas, N.N., Galiotou, E., Ralli, A.: Towards a unified exploitation of electronic dialectal corpora: problems and perspectives. In: Sojka, P., Horák, A., Kopeček, I., Pala, K. (eds.) TSD 2014. LNCS (LNAI), vol. 8655, pp. 257–266. Springer, Cham (2014). https://doi.org/10.1007/978-3-319-10816-2_32

9. Karanikolas, N., Skourlas, C.: Personal digital libraries: a self-archiving approach. Libr. Rev. **63**(6/7), 436–451 (2014)

10. Koliopoulou, M., Manolessou, I., Markopoulos, Th., Pantelidis, N.: A digitized corpus for three Asia Minor dialects (in Greek). In: Ralli, A. (ed.) THALIS Project: "Pontus, Cappadocia, Aivali: in search of Asia Minor Greek" (in Greek), University of Patras, pp. 43–54 (2015)

11. Nerbonne, J., Kleiweg, P.: Lexical distance in LAMSAS. Comput. Humanit. **37**(3), 339–357 (2003)

12. Papazachariou, D., Karasimos, A.: Organization and coding of oral resources in an innovative multimodal database: the case of the AMiGre corpus (in Greek). In: Ralli, A. (ed.) THALIS Project: "Pontus, Cappadocia, Aivali: in search of Asia Minor Greek" (in Greek), University of Patras, pp. 55–68 (2015)

13. Scherrer, Y.: Natural language processing for swiss German dialects. In: The 55th Annual Conference of the Int. Linguistic Association, New Paltz, NY (USA) (2010)

14. Ubul, A., Kake, H., Sakoguchi, Y., Kishie, S.: Research on oral map in regional dialect using Google map. Int. J. Comput. Tech. **2**(2), 31–35 (2015)

15. Valls, E., Nerbonne, J., Prokić, J., Wieling, M., Clua, E., Lloret, M.-R.: Applying levenshtein distance to catalan dialects. A brief comparison of two dialectometric approaches. Verba **39**, 35–61 (2012)

16. Wells, J.C.: SAMPA computer readable phonetic alphabet. In: Gibbon, D., Moore, R., Winski, R. (ed.) Handbook of Standards and Resources for Spoken Language Systems. Mouton de Gruyter, Berlin & New York (1997)

Unlocking Potential Knowledge Hidden in Rubbing:
Multi-style Character Recognition Using Deep Learning and Spatiotemporal Rubbing Database Creation

Lin Meng[(✉)] [iD], Masahiro Kishi, Kana Nogami, Michiko Nabeya, and Katsuhiro Yamazaki

Department of Electronic and Computer Engineering, Ritsumeikan University, Kusatsu, Shiga 525-8577, Japan
menglin@fc.ritsumei.ac.jp, yamazaki@se.ritsumei.ac.jp

Abstract. Rubbings are among the oldest ancient literatures and potentially contain a lot of knowledge waiting to be unlocked. Constructing a rubbing database has therefore become an important research topic in terms of discovering and clarifying the potential knowledge. However, current rubbing databases are very simply, and there is no process in place for discovering the potential knowledge discovery. Moreover, the rubbing characters need to be recognized manually because there are so many different character styles and because the rubbings are in various stages of damage due to the aging process, and this takes an enormous amount of time and effort. In this work, our aim is to construct a spatiotemporal rubbing database based on multi-style Chinese character recognition using deep learning, that visualizes the spatiotemporal information in the form of a keyword of rubbing images on a map. The idea is that the potential knowledge unlocked by the keyword will help with research on historical information organization, climatic variation, disaster prediction and response, and more.

Keywords: Discovering potential knowledge · Rubbing
Multi-style rubbing-character recognition
Spatiotemporal rubbing database

1 Introduction

Before the invention of paper roughly 2,000 years ago, people inscribed characters on animal bone, turtle shell, stone, and metal as a means of recording ancient literature. Additionally, in China, Japan, and other cultures, people and governments kept up the habit of recording important information on stone for another 2,000 years or so after paper was invented.

Supported by Japan Society for the Promotion of Science(JSPS) (18K18337).

M. Ioannides et al. (Eds.): EuroMed 2018, LNCS 11196, pp. 762–771, 2018.
https://doi.org/10.1007/978-3-030-01762-0_68

With the invention of paper, people began using rubbings of the earlier bone, shell, and stone records in order to make copies of the ancient literature and spread the culture. A rubbing is a reproduction of the texture of a surface created by placing a piece of paper over the inscription and then rubbing the paper with ink or pencil. Rubbings of Chinese characters are widely seen across China, Japan, and various areas surrounding China. The styles include oracle bone inscriptions (OBIs), Zhuan-style, Li-style, Xing-style, Cao-style, and Kai-style. OBIs and Zhuan-style are no longer in use, so very few people today can actually read them, while Cao-style and Xing-style contain lots of variations, making them difficult to understand. Hence, the recognition of multi-style rubbing characters is very difficult. It is extremely difficult to organize these ancient literatures. Most of them were recorded in the form of rubbings, and the information they contain has not been properly classified yet. Creating a database to help uncover the potential knowledge is thus very important and will help us get a better understanding of the politics, economics, disasters, etc. of the past.

In this project, our aim is to recognize multi-style characters in rubbings from China and Japan by means of deep learning and to create a spatiotemporal rubbing database to assist in the discovery of potential knowledge contained in the rubbings. Character recognition includes data set generation and augmentation, training, tuning, and recognition. In creating this database, we collect information on the archaeological site (found location) and the described time and then decide on a keyword for each rubbing. Then, we determine the appearance frequency of the keyword for every location. Displaying the appearance frequency of the keyword on a map sorted by time helps us achieve an accurate visualization of the keyword and pave the way for discovery of potential knowledge.

The contributions of this project are shown as follows: At first, the project focuses on rubbing character recognition using deep learning which is widely used in image recognition. In addition, the most important contribution of recognition is that a rubbing image fitted noise reduction method and data augmentation are proposed by analyzing the rubbing images and mis-recognition and improving the recognition rate. Secondly, the most important contribution of this paper is creating a spatiotemporal rubbing database for unlocking the potential knowledge hidden in the rubbing. In the authors' opinion, no paper introduces the creation of spatiotemporal rubbing database for unlocking the potential knowledge. The paper not only proposes a recognition method, but also provides a tool for some of research fields which want to get new information from history. For example, Natural disaster researchers may input the keywords of natural disaster to the database, then the natural disaster location and time will be displayed spatiotemporally for helping researchers to analyze the disaster. The second example is that the economist may input the important economic index keywords of rice price to spatiotemporally display the rice price which helps to analyze the history of economy.

Section 2 describes the current research related to rubbing. Section 3 goes over the research flow of our project. Section 4 shows the recognition and experimental results. Section 5 discusses the creation of the spatiotemporal rubbing database and visualization of keywords for discovering potential knowledge. Section 6 concludes the paper with a brief summary and mention of future work.

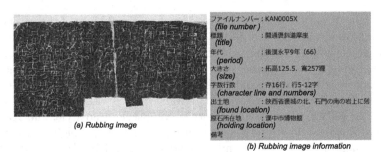

Fig. 1. Example of rubbing image.

2   Current Research Related to Rubbing

There have been several studies by researchers around the world relating to the organization of rubbings.

The Historiographical Institute, University of Tokyo constructed a database called Ink Rubbing Copy of Inscriptions that lists 2,400 rubbing images and information on each, including rubbing image size, found location, and the first collector. The images can be expanded for easier reading and analysis [1]. The National Central Library of Taiwan constructed a database named Rare Books & Special Collections (Rubbing) that has 13,634 rubbing images belonging to 7,093 types of objects. The database can be searched by title and author of the rubbing, and it displays the found location, time, and an image of the rubbing [2]. The Institute of History and Philology, Academia Sinica of Taiwan constructed a database that holds 21,556 OBI rubbing images, 13,717 gold and bronze rubbing images, and 8,000 stone rubbing images. The database lists the size, title, and an image of the rubbing [3].

These databases store only the image, title, and a partial translation into modern characters. The most complete database is the Rubbing Characters Database created by the Institute for Research in Humanities, Kyoto University, with government funding from the 21st Century Center Of Excellence Program (COE JSPS). This database includes 5,000 rubbings from China's Han period (starting in 206 B.C.) to Qing period (finishing in 1912 A.D.). The database segments the characters from rubbing images and has generated 1.8 million rubbing characters that are searchable online. The database also includes the whole image of each rubbing and its related information (found location, period, etc.) [4].

All of these databases are generated by hand, which takes a lot of time and memory. For example, the segmentation of characters from rubbing images in the Rubbing Characters Database takes a long time [5]. Another problem is that the rich information of these databases contain seems doomed to stagnate, as there is no active analysis or discovery being performed.

The goal of this research is to segment articles and characters from rubbing images directly and automatically, recognize the characters automatically by

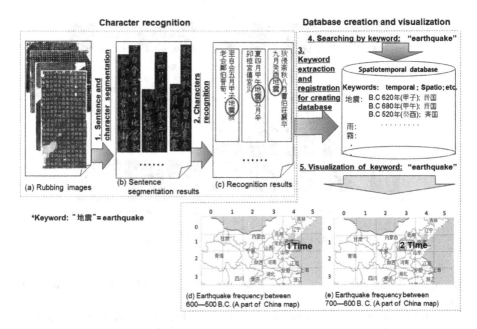

Fig. 2. Overview of project.

deep learning, and extract keywords from rubbing image and list the found location and time for the creation of a spatiotemporal rubbing database. Ultimately, we hope that visualizing the spatiotemporal information of the keywords on a map will spearhead the discovery of ancient knowledge, thus facilitating research on historical information organization, climatic variation, disaster prediction and response, and more.

3 Overview of Our Project

In this project, we use rubbing images from Kyoto University's Rubbing Characters Database. An example of a rubbing image and its information (scripted directly from [4]) is shown in Fig. 1. As shown in Fig. 1(a), the characters are not clear and some are even broken, making them difficult to recognize directly. Hence, character recognition is a significant challenge in our project. Figure 1(b) shows the information on rubbing title, period, size, found location, and holding location, as translated into English which are written in a mark of (). The file numbers were assigned by the database creator at Kyoto University, and we use them in our database too [8].

Figure 2 shows the overview of our project, consisting of multi-style character recognition, spatiotemporal database creation, and visualization.

In multi-style character recognition, we use image processing to segment the sentences and characters from the rubbing image and then use image processing and deep learning to recognize the characters [11]. Figure 2(a) shows some

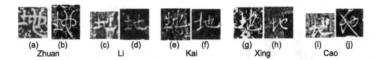

(a)   (b)   (c)   (d)   (e)   (f)   (g)   (h)   (i)   (j)
    Zhuan   Li   Kai   Xing   Cao

Fig. 3. Multi-style character of "earth".

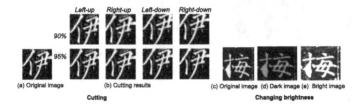

Fig. 4. Parts of data augmentation results.

examples of rubbing images, (b) is a part of the segmentation results, and (c) is recognition results.

In terms of the spatiotemporal database creation and visualization, the keywords are decided and then the information of each keyword is extracted and registered into the database. This information is spatio (when the characters were scribed), temporal (where the object was found), etc. In Fig. 2, "earthquake" is the designated keyword, and for easy understanding we mark the earthquake keywords by cycle. Visualization of the keyword is done after registering all of the keyword information in the database. It can be referenced to determine how many times the keyword appears in every area. In Fig. 2(d) and (e), we can see that there are one or two times a big earthquake struck between 700–500 B.C. in Shandong and in Hebai (indicated by squares) by visualizing the "earthquake" keyword in the spatiotemporal database.

In fact, a huge earthquake occurred in this area in 1976, and several hundred thousand people died. We do not know whether there is any relationship between these earthquakes, as this is outside the scope of our work. However, we do believe this database is an effective means of organizing data relating to history and disasters, which may help with predicting disasters in the future.

4   Character Recognition Using Deep Learning

4.1   Dataset Generation and Augmentation

Deep learning is a popular and effective technique for image recognition. In this project, we use AlexNet [6] and GoogLeNet [7] for obtaining the results and select the better Network from AlexNet and GoogLeNet for future character recognition. AlexNet [6] consists of eight layers, including five convolution layers for extracting the feature, and three fully connected layers for judging the recognition results. GoogLeNet is a complex network model and consists of 22 layers.

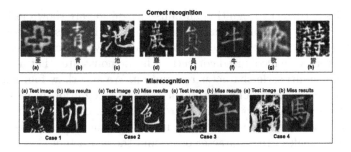

Fig. 5. Example of mis-recognition.

It is used to assess its quality in the context of object detection and classification. One of the important contributions is that inception module is designed for realizing dimensionality reduction.

A large dataset should ideally be generated for training in deep learning. Here, the characters styles are divided into Zhuan, Li, Kan, Xing, and Cao, as shown in Fig. 3. However, there are many variations, and some characters have broken due to aging, which makes the recognition more difficult. For the initial experiment, we collected 105,781 character images of 100 different kinds. Five hundred clear images are used for teaching data, so every kind of character has five styles. We used 103,281 images for training and 2,000 images for testing, which were taken at random from the Rubbing Character Database.

However, 105,781 character images are not enough for training. To achieve a higher accuracy, data augmentation is an effective method for augmenting training data. We analyzed the rubbing characters and found that sometimes segmented characters are not in the center of image, and sometimes the brightness is different. Therefore, we propose data augmentation that includes Changing Brightness and Cutting for increasing the training dataset. Changing Brightness is for training character images that have different brightness due to aging. In this process, brightness is changed to 70% and 200%. Cutting is for training mis-segmented images where the character is not in the center of the image. Cutting is used to cut the area of an image into four sides (95, 90, 85, 80%). Every image is augmented with 17 kinds Cutting and 3 kinds Changing Brightness, which generates 51 new images. The data augmentation results are shown in Fig. 4.

4.2   Recognition

For the recognition, we use AlexNet [6], to select the better Network from the two networks for character recognition. One hundred kinds of characters for a total of 105,781 character images were used for the experiments. The experimental environment is Intel®Xeon CPU Ef-1620 v4 (8 cores); GPU GTX1080Ti (3584 cores) x 4; memory: 64 GB; frame: Caffe tool; epoch: 30. The results of the experiment are listed in Table 1. GoogLeNet achieved a 96% recognition accuracy, which is 2% higher than AlexNet.

Examples of correct recognition and mis-recognition are shown in Fig. 5. The correct recognition examples include images with (b) big noise, (c) some broken characters, (d) (h) complex characters, and (g) not very clear characters. Even so, these characters were recognized correctly. This demonstrates that deep learning is effective for multi-style character recognition. We also show four examples of mis-recognition in Fig. 5. The reason for the mis-recognition in case 1 is that there are parts of a different character around the test characters. In case 2, the variation of Cao-style was not included in the training data. In cases 3 and 4, there is a big break in the character or around the characters.

For correcting the mis-recognition in case 1, we use a labeling method to get rid of the noise surrounding the test characters. First, we use Gaussian filtering with blurring and binarization for reducing the smaller noises. The threshold is set using the Otsu method [9]. Then we use the labeling to calculate the size and the center of gravity of every component. If the center of gravity is near the four sides of the image and the size is smaller, we get rid of the component as noise [10]. By this noise reduction, we improved the accuracy in GoogLenet by 1%. Adding the variation of Cao-style into the training data would fix the mis-recognition in case 2. Cases 3 and 4 are more complex, and solving them will be the focus of a future work.

5   Spatiotemporal Rubbing Database Creation and Visualization

5.1   Database Creation

Figure 6 shows the spatiotemporal rubbing database creation. The database consists of Fig. 6(b) Rubbing administration table (RAT) and (c) Keyword administration table (KAT). In RAT, basic information of rubbing is recorded when a new description is found and is created as a rubbing image. As Fig. 6(b) shows that the information includes the Period (the dynasty of article was described), the File number decided by discoverer in order, the Title decided by history experts, the Date (the described data, if it is known), and the Article folder which keeps the rubbing images and the recognition results. KAT keeps the file number of rubbing images where the keyword appears. It is hard to collect the rubbing images. Currently we use the rubbing images of [4] which has 2400 rubbings for the experimentation. In addition, half of the rubbing images of [4] does not give us enough information about each rubbing. For example, some of them do not give founded location and some of them does not give us the

Table 1. Character recognition rate (%)

Network	Training time	Recognition rate
Alexnet	9 h 34 m	94
GoogLenet	28 h	96

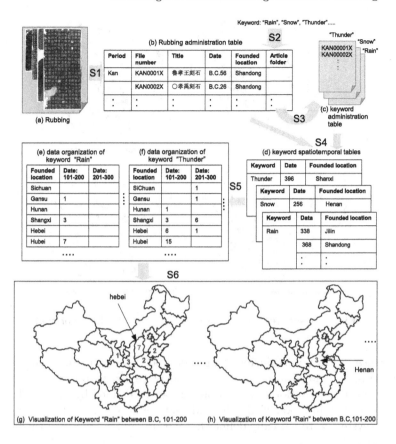

Fig. 6. Spatiotemporal rubbing database creation.

described data. Without these information, the database cannot implement its functions. Hence, Google and Baidu search engines were used to obtain these data by us to complete the database. Furthermore, some of the rubbing images are not segmented and readable easily like Fig. 1(a). The segmentation is one of the complexity of this project which should be improved in the future.

The detailed database creation flow is shown Fig. 6 in from Step 1 (S1) to Step 6 (S6). In Step 1, a rubbing administration table is created by registering the information of a rubbing after the sentence of the rubbing image is recognized. The rubbing administration table stores the period, rubbing file number, rubbing file title, found location, and folder address of the rubbing article. In Step 2, the keyword is defined. In Step 3, we search for the keyword from among all the rubbing articles and record all of the rubbing file numbers in which the keyword appears. In Step 4, we created the keyword spatiotemporal tables. Every keyword has one table, which includes the date and found location of the keywords for keeping the spatio and temporal information. In Step 5, the data are organized on the basis of the keywords to show the frequency of appearance in every area during the decided period. Step 6 shows and visualizes the frequency of

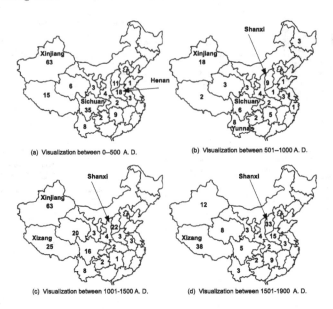

(a) Visualization between 0–500 A. D.

(b) Visualization between 501–1000 A. D.

(c) Visualization between 1001-1500 A. D.

(d) Visualization between 1501-1900 A. D.

Fig. 7. Visual results of keyword "Rain" (Color figure online)

appearance in every area during the decided period on a map. In this way, the changing of a keyword in terms of time and place can be observed on a China map. As for the definition of a keyword, it can be defined by a user who wants to know the potential knowledge behind that keyword. In the future we aim to have the system automatically define the keyword and discovery of the potential knowledge.

5.2   Discussion on Visualization

Currently, the spatiotemporal rubbing database we created contains only the keywords "Rain", "Rabbit", "Swallow", "House", "Haze", "Deer", "Grass", "Bird", "Rice", "Fog", and "Thunder" for visualization.

Figure 7 shows the visualization results of keyword "Rain" by dividing 500 years on a map of China. Higher appearance frequency is indicated by red. As shown, there were people residing in the middle of China (Changjiang river and Huanghe river) who recorded some information about rain. At first glance, this information seems to be self-explanatory. However, as this is the initial level of experimentation, we feel that collaborating with researchers from different backgrounds (history, sociology, etc.) would enable us to determine additional keywords for clarifying potential knowledge as a next step.

6   Conclusion

Rubbings are among the oldest ancient literatures in the world and potentially contain a lot of knowledge waiting to be unlocked. In this project, we aim to recognize multi-style characters in rubbing images and create a spatiotemporal rubbing database for discovering potential knowledge in these rubbings. We generated a dataset and augmented it by cutting and changing the brightness of rubbing images. Experimental results showed that GoogLeNet achieved a 96% recognition accuracy, which is better than AlexNet. When we added noise reduction, we improved the accuracy by about 1%. The information in the spatiotemporal rubbing database includes the archaeological site (found location) and described time. We decided on keywords and collected the appearance frequency of each keyword in different places. Displaying this appearance frequency on a map ordered by timeframe helps us to effectively visualize the keywords and discover potential knowledge. At present, our visualization requires some tweaking in order to generate more excitement when it comes to knowledge discovery. Hence, adding more keywords and performing additional experiments will be our future work. Furthermore, adding more rubbing images to expand the database is another important future work.

References

1. Database of the Ink Rubbing Copy of Inscriptions, Historiographical Institute The University of Tokyo. http://wwwap.hi.u-tokyo.ac.jp/ships/shipscontroller-e. Accessed 8 Aug 2018
2. Rare Books & Special Collections (Rubbing), National Central Library. http://rarebook.ncl.edu.tw/gold/introduce/index.htm. Accessed 8 Aug 2018
3. IHP Digital Archives Online, Institute of History and Philology, Academia Sinica. http://ihparchive.ihp.sinica.edu.tw/ihpkmc/ihpkm?@@0.17550824359630524. Accessed 8 Aug 2018
4. Rubbing characters Database, Kyoto University. http://coe21.zinbun.kyoto-u.ac.jp/djvuchar. Accessed 8 Aug 2018
5. Yasuoka, K.: Character database of digital rubbings: its progress and problems. In: IPSJ SIG Technical Report, vol. 2013-CH97, no. 11, pp. 1–6 (2013). (in Japanese)
6. Krizhevsky, A., Sutskever, I., Hinton, G.E.: ImageNet classification with deep convolutional neural networks. In: Advances in Neural Information Processing Systems 25 (NIPS 2012) (2012)
7. Szegedy, C., et al.: Going deeper with convolutions. In: 2015 IEEE Conference on Computer Vision and Pattern Recognition (CVPR 2015) (2015)
8. Kishi, M., Nabeya, M., Nogami, K., Meng, L., Yamazaki, K.: Multi-type recognition of rubbing using deep learning and creation of spatiotemporal database. In: the 80th National Convention of Information Processing Society of Japan, 2S-08 (2018). (in Japanese)
9. Meng, L.: Two-stage recognition for oracle bone inscriptions. In: Battiato, S., Gallo, G., Schettini, R., Stanco, F. (eds.) ICIAP 2017. LNCS, vol. 10485, pp. 672–682. Springer, Cham (2017). https://doi.org/10.1007/978-3-319-68548-9_61
10. He, L.F., Chao, Y.Y., Suzuki, K.: A run-based two-scan labeling algorithm. IEEE Tras. Image Process. **17**(5), 749–756 (2008)
11. Watanabe, S., Meng, L., Izumi, T.: Methods to extract character regions of oracle bone inscriptions. In: The 248th technical report of the Institute of Image Electronics Engineers of Japan (2018). (in Japanese)

Author Index

Printed in the United States
By Bookmasters